D1367138

# ELECTRONIC LEARNING COMMUNITIES
## Issues and Practices

# ELECTRONIC LEARNING COMMUNITIES
# Issues and Practices

*Senior Editor*

## Sorel Reisman, PhD
**California State University, Fullerton**

*Associate Editors*

## John G. Flores, PhD
**United States Distance Learning Association**

## Denzil Edge, PhD
*The Learning House*

80 Mason Street
Greenwich, Connecticut 06830

**Library of Congress Cataloging-in-Publication Data**

Electronic learning communities : issues and practices / senior editor, Sorel Reisman ; associate editors, John G. Flores and Denzil Edge.
 p. cm.
Includes bibliographical references.
 ISBN 1-931576-96-3 (pbk.) – ISBN 1-931576-97-1 (hardcover)
 1. Distance education–Computer-assisted instruction. 2. Educational technology. I. Reisman, Sorel. II. Flores, John G. III. Edge, Denzil.
 LC5803.C65E54 2003
 371.3'58–dc21

2003000183

Printed in the United States of America

# CONTENTS

# CONTRIBUTORS

| | |
|---|---|
| *James Benjamin* | University of Toledo |
| *Catherine S. Bolek* | University of Maryland—Eastern Shore |
| *David Brigham* | Excelsior College |
| *John G. Bryan* | University of Cincinnati |
| *Sally Dresdow* | University of Wisconsin—Green Bay |
| *Denzil Edge* | The Learning House |
| *Sharon Edge* | University of Louisville |
| *Mark Evans* | California State University—Bakersfield |
| *Barbara Fennema* | Ohio SchoolNet |
| *John G. Flores* | United States Distance Learning Association |
| *Ronald G. Forsythe* | University of Maryland—Eastern Shore |
| *Robert Gail* | University of Phoenix |
| *Chiara Gratton-Lavoie* | California State University—Fullerton |
| *Xiaoxing Han* | Athens Technical College |
| *Lisa Holstrom* | University of Cincinnati |
| *Maggie McVay Lynch* | Portland State University |
| *Sally Mavor* | Escola Superior da Educação de Leiria, Portugal |
| *Matthew E. Mooney* | University of Arizona |
| *William Peirce* | Prince George's Community College |
| *Don Plunkett* | City University of New York |
| *Sorel Reisman* | California State University—Fullerton |

| | |
|---|---|
| *Penelope Walters Swenson* | California State University—Bakersfield |
| *Denise Stanley* | California State University—Fullerton |
| *Beverly Trayner* | School of Business Sciences Setúbal, Portugal |

PREFACE

# ELECTRONIC LEARNING COMMUNITIES
## Issues and Practices

### Sorel Reisman

## INTRODUCTION

My first experience with an electronic learning community was in 1964. As part of a sophomore-level calculus class, I and sixty other electrical engineering students were introduced to the programming language Kingston FORTRAN II, and our first assignment was to write (keypunch) a computer program to solve a differential equation using the Runge-Kutta method (Compare that with first assignments today that require students to write a program to add a series of numbers!) Our computing facility was an IBM 1620/1710 located in a 30' x 30' air-conditioned room packed with pushing and shoving undergraduates from all the other engineering departments. Each of us was trying to get our stack of cards into the card reader, hoping that the line printer wouldn't jam while the compile and execute phases attempted to run to completion. Since few of those batch jobs ever ran through successfully, most of us were exposed to computer language unlike any other ever documented by computer manufacturers!

Electronic Learning Communities—Issues and Practices, pages ix–xvii.
Copyright © 2003 by Information Age Publishing, Inc.
All rights of reproduction in any form reserved.
ISBN: 1-931576-96-3 (pbk.), 1-931576-97-1 (hardcover)

But we were a community. We all had a shared set of objectives. Clearly we were in a learning mode. You might even say we shared a common vocabulary. And (although I didn't realize it until I read some of the chapters in this book) since electronic computing had brought us together, we were an *electronic learning community.*

Much has changed in the ensuing decades. Today we think about electronic learning communities as Internet- or Web-enabled or -supplemented instruction in which there is some degree of ongoing involvement/participation between and among an instructor and students. Through a great deal of trial and error and through many phases of instructional technology development, this concept of the electronic learning community has evolved from the kind of scenario described above, to today.

Electronic learning is not new. And while many may be surprised to hear it, multimedia-enhanced electronic learning is also not new. From the mid 1960s until the late 1970s, computer-based electronic learning (known as computer assisted instruction (CAI) or computer based training (CBT) was a mode of instructional delivery in which a learner accessed mainframe computer-based lesson material (courseware) developed and programmed by one or more instructional designers and computer programmers. My own first experience with CAI was at General Electric in 1967 where I used an ASR-33 teletype with a 10 character/second printer connected to a timeshared GE host computer to interact with text-based courseware from which I attempted to learn Dartmouth BASIC. This model of CAI was widely adopted as CBT and used successfully for training in industry until the 1980s. During those years, the field of instructional technology evolved and matured because it was essential that corporate instructional developers produce cost-effective methodologies to justify the return on the investment in training.

During the mid 1960s through to the late 1980s another aspect of electronic teaching/learning that evolved was the enhancement of CAI/CBT with "multimedia." Today, multimedia means CD-ROMS, DVDs, or Java applets, but from an instructional technology standpoint, it is not the medium that is the message. Instead it is the audio and video information that enhances the instruction, regardless of its source. In the 1960s and early 1970s, multimedia-enhanced electronic instruction was explored by IBM with its IBM 1500 system, by Mitre Corporation with its TICCIT system, and by Control Data Corporation with its PLATO System. Except for PLATO, the other two systems functionally operated as standalone workstations for individual learners, delivering audio and video integrated with CAI courseware.

PLATO was different. PLATO workstations were connected to a network of CDC mainframes, allowing each workstation to communicate with other connected workstations. Interestingly, despite the networking, almost all of PLATO's instructional use was based on the CAI model of the single learner interacting with standalone, workstation-based courseware. Interaction with other online users was relegated to non-instructional applications, the most popular being (what else?) the highly interactive game, Snoopy and the Red Baron.

To play, a user on a PLATO workstation would challenge anyone else on the network; when another (anonymous) user rose to the challenge, both user workstations would synchronously display two stick-figure airplanes, one as Snoopy, under control of one user-workstation, and the other the Red Baron under control of the other workstation. Each would then proceed to chase the other around the screen, attempting to "shoot down" his opponent. Incredible as it sounds, this was actually fun. In fact, while on a fact-finding visit to the Champagne/Urbana campus of the University of Illinois, the showcase of PLATO, I became so involved in a deadly virtual dual, that I missed my homeward-bound plane connection.

With the appearance of personal computers (Apple, Atari, and Commodore) in the late 1970s and their "legitimization" for business with the IBM PC in 1981/82, instructional developers began transforming their mainframe-based instructional design methodologies to be able to develop PC-based courseware. At the same time, based on those early multimedia systems mentioned above, PC application programmers, using optical laser discs, began to develop multimedia function for PC courseware. For about 10 years instructional technology was focused on standalone PCs that delivered courseware enhanced by multimedia effects controlled or generated by increasingly faster microprocessors together with CD-ROMs. During that time, CBT continued to be a viable industrial training mode, but still, although enhanced with multimedia, a standalone instructional activity in which a learner interacted alone, with courseware.

In the late 1980s with the "consumerization" of personal computers and later the introduction of the Internet, electronic virtual communities began to take root with MUDs (Multi-User Dungeon/Domain/Dimension) and MOOs (Object Oriented or Multi-User Object Oriented systems). With the subsequent introduction of Web browsers in 1993, such communities became ubiquitous on the World Wide Web (WWW). Always eager to improve themselves and their methodologies, educators saw the community-building aspect of the WWW as an opportunity to address the isolation problem that individual students using CBT courseware experienced. Students learning at a distance, whether their instruction was totally workstation-based or based on correspondence courses delivered via traditional mail, were said by critics to be receiving a lesser quality of instruction because of the absence or poor quality of communication with peers and/ or instructors. By integrating principles of Web-based electronic communities together with some of the practices of multimedia CAI/CBT, principles of the British Open University, instructional television, and traditional classroom instruction, new forms and formats of instruction became possible. And as they say, "The rest is history!"

Brief as this history is, the steady growth of electronic learning communities has been and continues to be remarkable. The research firm Eduventures, Inc., in a report from Syllabus online news (10/4/2002 News http://www.syllabus.com/news.asp) released a study on distance learning showing that the market for fully online degree programs is growing at an annual rate of 40%. In 2001/2002 more than 350,000 students were enrolled in fully online degree-granting programs, generating $1.75B in tuition. And a recent report from brandon-hall.com (cited in the September, 2002 issue of T.H.E. Journal, p. 12) stated, "US spending on online training is expected to skyrocket during the next eight years," from less than $10B in 2002 to projected spending of more than $210B in 2010!

## THIS BOOK

We first conceived of this book at a meeting of the publications board of the United States Distance Learning Association (USDLA) in Washington, DC in 1999. At that time we recognized that because methodologies and circumstances related to computer-based learning at a distance were changing so quickly, there was a real need by practitioners and academics for a reference/text that focused on best practices in this field. At that time the economy was in overdrive, and industry and universities were excited about anything that was Internet-related, and one of those things was electronic communities.

In the last three years we have witnessed the collapse of dotcom companies and have come to understand that the notion of electronic communities can be best realized from within a particular application environment in which "community members" share common values, objectives, and goals. For example, the IEEE Computer Society, one the foremost professional and academic computer associations in the world is focusing on reengineering its "conventional" Web presence into an electronic community of shared resources for its membership (www.computer.org). Another example is MERLOT (Multimedia Educational Resource for Learning and Online Teaching—see www.merlot.org). MERLOT originated as a repository of discipline-specific online teaching/learning objects, but it is currently undergoing significant changes including the addition of electronic communities such as Teaching Well Online (MERLOT TWO). With these kinds of initiatives taking place throughout the world of the Web, it became clear that any book that focused on education at a distance had to be from a perspective of electronic communities.

So in many ways, we have come full circle since my first electronic learning community experience of almost 40 years ago. Now, for an unforgettable learning experience, as then, instructors and students learning at a distance must function together as a community. They must all have a shared set of learning objectives and they must actively participate in the instruction. Of course for effective communication all must have a common vocabulary. And the catalyst among them all is electronic computing. Without any argument then, the theme of this book, driven by distance education (DE), distance learning (DL), or e-learning has to be—*electronic learning communities.*

## CHAPTER ORGANIZATION AND OUTLINES

This book has 14 chapters. Each is a single repository of expertise and guidance for researchers and practitioners. Alternatively, the 14 chapters lend themselves to a semester-long graduate course focusing on instructional technology issues and practices. The chapters contain timeless information, and singly or in groups represent the most compelling topics in this field, topics essential for researchers, practitioners (instructors and administrators), or graduate students facing the challenges of working with electronic learning communities.

### Chapter 1—Interactive Online Educational Experiences: E-volution of Graded Projects (Benjamin)

Distance learning has come a long way since the days of correspondence courses communicated via "snail mail." Benjamin describes the "technological" changes that have taken place over the decades to bring us Internet-based distance learning. He then leads the reader through a discourse on alternative distance learning models, concluding that, "A fully developed conceptualization of distance education must incorporate the concepts of context, feedback, pervasive noise, nonverbal as well as verbal messages, teachers and students as both originators and receivers of messages that incorporate the totality of the people involved in the educational process." The chapter continues with a description of the evolution of five types of activities from the traditional classroom to the online classroom, and finally and appropriately concludes the chapter and this book with prognostications of the future of technology and instruction.

### Chapter 2—Hybrid Courses as Learning Communities (Swenson and Evans)

Despite the grand visions of many of the promoters of distance education, the reality is that when instructors undertake to use the Web in their classrooms, they typically do not immediately abandon their traditional classroom sessions. Instead they use the Web to supplement or enhance their teaching, thereby creating something that has come to be called "hybrid courses." In Chapter 2, Swenson and Evans explore a variety of practical models of hybrid courses that also employ online strategies. They approach DE from the practical perspective utilized by most DE instructors, one that recognizes that completely online courses are not always possible, or even desirable. Their observation that, "Courses that now are exclusively online will migrate to being hybrids" is very interesting and even very controversial since it flies in the face of the direction that many proponents of DE wish to go, away from hybrids to totally online. However, the authors' experience and descriptions of hybrid courses is broader than our conventional ones and in many ways extend the practicality of hybrid offerings beyond traditional considerations.

### Chapter 3—Building Electronic Communities for Distance Learners: Beyond the Course Level (Brigham)

Most of the distance learning efforts in higher education today, whether hybrid or fully online, were initiated by individual instructors motivated by technology alone or by a real vision of how they could improve student learning. When such courses are successful, other instructors begin to experiment, and before long their institutions find themselves needing to address issues alien to traditional academic learning environments. In Brigham's chapter, as in Holstrom's and Bryan's (Chapter 5), the institutional programmatic needs of electronic communities are addressed. With the examples of Excelsior College, the Empire State College Community and Human Services Program, and the University of Texas TeleCampus Law and Order Website, Brigham provides detailed guidelines on issues that must be considered at an institutional level in the planning and development of Web-based electronic learning communities beyond the course level. The chapter concludes with a description of five trends of emerging technologies essential for the development of electronic communities.

### Chapter 4—Faculty-Librarian Collaboration in Online Course Development (Edge)

A little-appreciated resource that institutions can and should utilize in the development of infrastructures for the institutional programmatic support of distance education is the library. Edge introduces us to some serious concerns and issues regarding the important, yet minimally recognized role that libraries can play. Issues described in this chapter range from the strategic (e.g. the responsibility of higher education to produce information-literate graduates), to the more tactical (e.g. the role that libraries can play in providing 24/7 support for distance education classes). In her role at the University of Louisville, Edge has developed and presents a model of library services utilization for institutions of higher education to emulate when they plan broad scale distance education programs.

### Chapter 5—A Different Practice: Spanning the Digital Divide Through Distance Learning (Holstrom and Bryan)

There is much debate and controversy regarding the appropriateness of distance learning for every kind of learner. Holstrom's and Bryan's chapter illustrates how distance education can transform the lives of the widest spectrum of society by focusing on the "low tech side of the digital divide." They describe their experiences and successes in developing an online version of their Early Childhood Learning Community for preschool Head Start Teachers at the University of Cincinnati, and how in planning that program, a significant effort was made to understand the demographics of that "low tech side." However, it soon becomes clear while reading this chapter, that the issues and their solutions are relevant to any institutional programs in which online learning communities are to be initiated.

### *Chapter 6—Preparing Faculty Members to Teach in the E-learning Environment (Fennema)*

Fennema discusses distance learning in the context of the rest of the demographic spectrum. In this chapter she contends that "e-learning" is a phenomenon of the *information age*, an age and environment in which learning can take place anywhere, anytime, and among any groups of people in the world. She explains that new knowledge, skills, and institutionally supported learning management systems are necessary to be successful in this new age. This is because so many learners in this demographic are becoming increasingly socially and technically prepared to participate in e-learning. The chapter illustrates how a well-designed training program, utilizing a state-of-the-art learning management system (LMS), can be employed to train instructors to meet the needs of information age learners.

### *Chapter 7—Grow Your Own: Course Management the Way You Want It (Mooney)*

Mooney presents an interesting contrarian's viewpoint to Fenema's insofar as the kind of LMS necessary for a successful implementation of a distance learning program. Mooney contends that it is not always necessary to implement institution-wide programs that, for example, imply the licensing of an enterprise-wide LMS such as Blackboard or WebCT. Instead, he describes a rationale and approach for developing home grown systems and processes that more than adequately meet programmatic and not just single course needs. The decisions made by his institution, while being specifically related to the design and development of their local LMS, are quite relevant to any institution that deploys an LMS.

### *Chapter 8—Strategies for Teaching Thinking and Promoting Intellectual Development in Online Classes (Peirce)*

Peirce is very clear about the kinds of instructional strategies that should be used to teach higher order thinking in completely online courses. He refutes naysayers who claim that distance education cannot be successful in this pursuit, by summarizing with extensive references, research that demonstrates that higher order thinking can be taught effectively in online classes. The chapter presents detailed strategies, including interesting examples that can be used to 1) engage students thoughtfully in course content, 2) teach disciplinary thinking, 3) promote critical consciousness, and 4) promote intellectual development.

*Chapter 9—Online Learning as an Improvement? The Case of Economic Principles (Gratton-Lavoie and Stanley)*

Although Peirce provides significant positive evidence regarding the effectiveness of DE to teach critical thinking, it is not always easy for individual instructors to replicate research findings in their own teaching environments. Since real instructional settings bear no resemblance to experimental ones, it is often impossible to control factors that affect treatments that we wish to measure. The study described here by Gratton-Lavoie and Stanley illustrates the complexity of assessing student learning outcomes, especially when comparing online and traditional instruction in introductory courses. Their findings concerning students in introductory economics courses are unsettling since they directly contradict other similar studies in their discipline. Another reason to be concerned about their findings is that many public debates, rightly or wrongly look to DE as a way to reduce the cost of traditional instruction for the projected increased enrollments higher education is expecting in the next few years. Because most of those students will initially enroll in courses such as the one described in this chapter, perhaps researchers should study more practical issues related to this demographic and address, from an institutional programmatic standpoint, the problems described by these researcher/instructors.

*Chapter 10—Developing an Effective Online Orientation Course to Prepare Students for Success in a Web-Based Learning Environment (McVay Lynch)*

McVay Lynch's chapter describes how one institution, faced with a policy conflict that required the school to deal with outcomes such as those described by Gratton-Lavoie and Stanley, undertook a proactive program to deal with their problem. Their solution, following a thorough review of the literature, was "the creation and implementation of a student orientation course that would provide a significant impact on the problem." This chapter describes the development of this course, and how it was implemented (adapted and upgraded) to meet a variety of the university's administrative and academic needs. The phenomenal success of the course, in terms of the difficulties encountered prior to its introduction, the effects on faculty retention and recruitment, and the subsequent positive learning outcomes, suggests that in some environments administrative mandates are necessary to move an institution forward into the information age.

### Chapter 11—Course Management as a Pedagogical Imperative (Han, Dresdow, Gail, and Plunkett)

Han et al. lament that there has been considerable research done regarding how instructors might manage their own online courses, but there is not a large body of documented knowledge and experience regarding the role that administrations must play to help instructors optimize their online teaching/learning responsibilities. The authors distinguish between *course management* and *program management*. The former is as what instructors must do to administer an online course and the latter is the responsibility of corporate or administrative management, depending on whether the courses/programs are offered by an institution of higher education or a for-profit entity. This chapter provides significant guidance for instructors who must manage all the electronic communications necessary for successful online teaching. It also provides detailed instances of the kinds of issues that comprise program management, and illustrates these through policies and practices utilized by five different institutions that offer online instruction.

### Chapter 12—Exclusion in International Online Learning Communities (Mavor and Traynor)

Distance learning is said to offer the advantages of anytime and anyplace delivery of instruction. In some cases these advantages can turn into disadvantages, especially if some of the concerns expressed by Mavor and Traynor are not addressed. In this chapter the authors examine in detail, the description of support materials and courseware developed outside of Portugal, intended for use within that country. Such materials, as they illustrate, are not always as they appear. Often, words, phrases, and even fonts, whether intentionally crafted or not, can affect the utility of the material in international instructional environments. Through the comments of students who participated in such a course, they conclude: "Given the diversity of learning backgrounds and discourses in an international course, it is imperative that considerable care be taken to avoid misrepresentation of the values and practices of the course." This is especially true if the course-based instructional strategies rely on electronic communities in which participants are of diverse nationalities and/or are communicating from different geographic locations. They supplement their conclusions with a list of features desirable in online software that can be used to address these needs.

*Chapter 13—Yours, Theirs, Mine: Just Who Owns Those Distance Courses? (Bryan)*

A topic leading the headlines of so many 21st Century business, trade, and academic publications concerns the ownership of digital media. Scholars and lawyers are addressing these issues in so many venues, in the entertainment industry (where concerns relate to movies, music, videos, games, etc.), in the medical industry (where concerns revolve around the use of digitized medical records and patient privacy), and of course in our own environment of teaching and learning (where the concern is about who owns and controls instructional material). Bryan's chapter on intellectual property offers a perspective on the history of one of the most contentious issues related to distance learning. Considering the complexity of the topic, both from a legal perspective as well as from a personal or moral one, this chapter provides us with a clear sense of the issues as well as one institution's policies for dealing with them.

*Chapter 14—Writing Winning Distance Education Teaching and Learning Grants (Bolek and Forsythe)*

The world is awash with fears and doubts about the future. If there is any certainty at all, it is that there will be less money available for social programs, including those related to teaching and learning at all levels of education. If ever there was a "handy dandy" guide for soliciting funds for DE projects, it is this chapter by Bolek and Forsythe. The chapter contains 1) an extraordinary guide to funding sources, 2) a how-to guide for preparing fund seeking proposals, 3) a lengthy list of reasons that proposals may be rejected, and 4) a detailed (and successfully funded) proposal that can serve as a template for fund-seekers. The fortunate few who seem to have sufficient resources to address their DE needs in the short term, should mentally bookmark this chapter for the inevitable day when the information here be invaluable.

## ACKNOWLEDGMENT

No book preface can be complete without the author's acknowledgement of those who provided support during the lengthy period it takes to complete such a project. And this book is no different. First I'd like to express my gratitude to the chapter authors without whom, of course, this book would simply not exist. I must acknowledge the cooperation and willingness of all the authors who willingly and without (much) coercion maintained communication with me during the lengthy period in which revisions and e-mails flowed back and forth across the country and even across oceans. I truly do appreciate all their work and cooperation.

Next I would like to thank my friends and co-editors Denny and John for their support and advice from the first time we discussed (over martinis) the need for this book, to the next time we discussed (over martinis), the progress of the book, until we congratulated ourselves (over martinis), on its completion. Without them, no reader would have access to this incredibly vast resource of timeless information on electronic learning communities.

Finally, I would like to thank my wife Gail who has suffered with and because of me through the interminable months, days, and hours that I worked with the authors, my co-editors, reviewers, and colleagues in both academia and industry while we brought this baby to fruition. She just can't wait for me to start working on the next one!

CHAPTER 1

# INTERACTIVE ONLINE EDUCATIONAL EXPERIENCES
# E-volution of Graded Projects

### James Benjamin

As online learning has expanded and evolved, there have been growing demands to improve online educational experiences to take full advantage of the new media. This chapter investigates the twin forces shaping the evolution of distance learning: the development of technology, especially the Internet, with its corollary consideration of communication systems and the shift from instructor-centered to learner-centered instruction in higher education with its concomitant emphasis on interactive communication. As learning technologies have evolved, so too have our instructional practices. The chapter also discusses the issues and recommendations for evolving traditional classroom experiences into projects requiring interactive media. Specifically, the chapter examines five specific types of interactive classroom experience: 1) the evolution of traditional papers into hypertext and hypermedia papers, 2) the progression from oral presentations to student created Web presentations, 3) the transformation of library assignments into structured Internet searches called WebQuests, 4) the development of journal assignments into online journals or "blogs," and 5) the unique opportunities of online discussions as a new form of group discussion. Finally, the chapter

Electronic Learning Communities—Issues and Practices, pages 1–26.
Copyright © 2003 by Information Age Publishing, Inc.
All rights of reproduction in any form reserved.
ISBN: 1-931576-96-3 (pbk.), 1-931576-97-1 (hardcover)

identifies six forces that are likely to shape the future of distance education activities.

**KEYWORDS:**  distance learning technology, communication in distance learning, distance learning activities, hypertext, WebQuests, blogs, online discussions, Web presentations, future of distance learning activities

## INTRODUCTION AND OBJECTIVES

Instruction in distance learning and instruction in the traditional classroom bear a symbiotic relationship. The traditional classroom, of course, provided the basis for the development of distance learning instruction. Changes in distance learning have shaped the evolution of instruction in the traditional classroom. It has been the implicit goal of distance learning to emulate the traditional classroom. The last years of the 20th Century witnessed revolutionary changes in distance learning in the form of explosive growth and rapid development of technology. This chapter discusses the issues and recommendations for evolving traditional classroom experiences into projects requiring interactive media.

The chapter's objectives are to provide background on the problems of making full use of the potential of interactive media. We specifically focus on two correlative forces that shaped the evolution of distance learning: 1) the development of technology, especially the Internet, with its complementary consideration of communication systems, and 2) the shift from instructor-centered to learner-centered instruction in higher education with its concomitant emphasis on interactive communication. Another objective is to present specific recommendations for developing and evaluating each of five types of interactive online experiences. We examine how written papers have evolved into hypertext and hypermedia assignments, how public presentations have developed Web presentations, how library assignments have transformed into Internet search assignments, how journal assignments have become online journal or blog assignments, and how small group discussions have evolved into online discussions. Our final objective is to explore the future of interactive media in the digital classroom. We note six predictions about the future of interactive media in the digital classroom.

## PROBLEMS MAKING FULL USE OF THE POTENTIAL OF INTERACTIVE MEDIA

There is no doubt that the United States is involved in revolutionary changes brought about by the burgeoning growth of distance education.

According to a study by the National Center for Education Statistics, "all but nine percent of both public 2- and 4-year institutions either offered or planned to offer distance education courses in the next three years" and "total enrollment in distance education courses across all postsecondary degree-granting institutions approximately doubled from 1995 to 1997-98, from 754,000 to 1.6 million" (2000, pp. ii-iii).

This revolution is being shaped by two correlative forces: development of digital distance learning technology, especially the Internet with its associated consideration of communication systems, and the shift from instructor-centered to learner-centered approaches to education with its related emphasis on interactive communication. Improvements in distance learning technology have shaped the nature of courses and have influenced how students and faculty communicate. The shift from instructor-centered education to learner-centered instruction has made interactive communication in distance education courses imperative.

## Development of Distance Learning Technology

Distance learning has evolved from correspondence courses to Internet courses. But Internet courses are not merely correspondence courses on the Web. Instead, the development of distance learning technology has allowed contemporary distance learning courses to make use of sophisticated digital communication systems that go far beyond the limitations of a print correspondence course.

### Print Media

The impetus for distance education was the compelling need to provide education in remote locations. Thus, correspondence courses developed because it was difficult for learners to attend classes in the same locale as the instructor. One of the earliest forms of a correspondence course was the rhetorical instruction provided by the *Rhetorica ad Herrenium,* written around 86 BCE and sometimes attributed to Cicero. This epistolary form of distance education evolved from the need to provide training in the vital art of rhetoric. In the ancient world, the ability to compose and deliver effective arguments was essential to civic life. Greek and Roman educators emphasized the study of rhetoric because success in ancient societies was based on the ability to convince other people in the courts, in political settings, and even in social gatherings. Because citizens in legal disputes were expected to plead their own cases, the ability to use rhetoric effectively was crucial if justice were to prevail. Because citizens were expected to participate in their governments, the skill of using rhetoric was necessary if government were to follow the best course of action. In short, rhetoric flourished for very practical purposes, and so it is to be expected that instruction in rhetoric would extend to students at remote sites who were not able to study in person with a rhetorician. For additional information, see Teresa Morgan's *Literate Education in the Hellenistic and Roman Worlds* (1998) and Henri I Marrou's *History of Education in Antiquity* (1964).

Correspondence courses, in more contemporary terms, flourished for a very similar reason: there was a need for instruction to be delivered to remote audiences who could not meet regularly with an instructor in the same place and at the same time. Anna Ticknor, for example, has been cited as establishing The Society to Encourage Studies at Home in 1873 "for the purposes of educational opportunities for women of all classes in the society"; the society reportedly served more than 10,000 students over the 24 years of its existence (Nasseh, 1997).

### Broadcast Media

With newer communication technologies such as radio and television came new opportunities to reach remote students. While radio instruction is popular in developing nations (Tilson, 1994), instruction by radio in the United States failed to garner much interest (Watkins & Wright, 1991). In the United States, instructional television eclipsed instructional radio due in part to its capacity for visual as well as audio communication, but also because there was private funding from the Ford Foundation and from government sponsored programs such as the 1962 Educational Television Facilities Act, the 1967 act establishing Corporation for Public Broadcasting, and the 1972 FCC ruling requiring cable systems to offer an educational channel (Moore & Kearsley, 1996, pp. 27-29). In recent years the role of television in distance education has evolved from broadcast to interactive videoconferencing by compressed video signals. The traditional classroom served as the basis for distance learning instruction. Courses have sought to replicate, insofar as possible, the educational experience available in the traditional, face-to-face classroom. Television, in its myriad forms, from broadcast to cable to videocassette, became the most popular medium because it "so closely approximates the appearance of face-to-face instruction, which many teachers and students prefer" (Verduin & Clark, 1991, p. 74).

### Interactive Media

In addition to the media of print, radio and television, distance learning adapted still newer forms of communication technology, the computer. The computer became a new educational medium just as it became an indispensable tool in business and entertainment. The earliest forms of computer instruction provided drill and tutorials but failed to reach wide adoption because of the complexity and costs required to develop more sophisticated instructional applications. There have been tremendous strides in this form of instruction due in part to corporations' willingness to invest in equipment and design teams that were able to focus on specific training projects (Horton, 2000, pp. 8-9). Distance learning too, sought to employ the computer as a tool. For example, course material delivered on CD-ROM permitted students to experience a high technology form of correspondence course that went beyond the drill and tutorials of early computerized instruction.

For a more complete discussion of the development of computer based learning, see S. Reisman & W. Carr (1991) "Perspectives on Multimedia Systems in Education."

The most recent technology to be adapted for distance education is the Internet, a technology that is largely responsible for the explosive growth in distance learning. The Department of Education's National Center for Education Statistics (2000) reported that the meteoric growth in distance learning is largely attributed to the popularity of the Internet as a distance learning technology (p. 54).

Internet courses have been met with some skepticism. Concerns range from the limits of bandwidth and student access to technology (Kouki & Wright, 1999, pp. 110-111) to concerns about the quality of instruction possible through a medium that does not allow personal contact between student and teacher (National Education Association, 2000, pp. 41-49). The genuine limitations of student access and available bandwidth are being gradually resolved by lower costs for computer equipment and Internet services and by the ubiquity of publicly available computers connected to the Internet. Concerns about the quality of instruction are being addressed by the establishment of standards for effective online instruction and by the development of interactive communicative technology in Internet courses.

## Distance Learning Technology and Communication

Within the field of distance learning there is a growing recognition that effective instruction is based on effective communication (Berge, 1997; Moore, 1994; Rossman, 1999; Sherry, Billig & Tavalin, 2000). It is important, then, to examine the dimensions of communication inherent in each of the distance learning formats.

### Print Media

Correspondence courses relied primarily on print media. The instructor used print materials for instruction, and assignments were turned in as a written document that, in turn, was critiqued and returned to the student in written form. Print has many advantages as an instructional medium. Both students and faculty are familiar with the technology; it is relatively inexpensive; it is easily indexed, and the information can be readily retrieved. As an informational medium, print is effective at presenting factual communication and is graphically rich. Disadvantages of the print medium in distance education is that it is relatively static, that it requires more involvement on the part of the reader, and that print is not particularly effective at communicating action and emotion. Print is also less spontaneous and less effective at expressing social relationships (Crystal, 1995; Biber, 1991). Furthermore, there is significantly delayed feedback in the interaction between participants in the communication process. Delayed feedback, the extreme of asynchronicity, seriously affects the "flow" of the communication and may lead to perceptions of information flowing too slowly compared to the communication flow in a more familiar face-to-face instructional setting.

This does not mean that correspondence courses are not effective. Summarizing a wide variety of research articles, Robert E. Freeman noted,

> The more recent studies, which are in general more rigorous, reach much the same conclusions as do the bulk of the studies—that correspondence methods achieve similar, if not superior, cognitive results when compared with conventional methods of teaching (cited in Welch 1993, p. 6).

In a study of correspondence courses by Laverenz (1979), students were found to be satisfied with the communication in their courses. It is accurate to note, however, that the exclusive reliance on print, and the delays caused by postal services do affect the nature of communication in a correspondence course. It is also likely that if these studies were replicated in this new age of e-mails and instant messaging, there would be less satisfaction with correspondence courses conducted via the postal service.

### Broadcast Media

The nature and effect of communication in broadcast media such as radio and television have been extensively studied (Lowery & DeFleur 1995; Perry, 2002). As distance learning instructional technologies, these broadcast media have the advantage of being dynamic, immediate, and familiar to contemporary learners. They more closely approximate the traditional classroom because they employ extensive use of oral communication and, in the case of television, also offer visual information and stimulation. The disadvantages of broadcast media include the one-way nature of the communication, the special equipment needed for developing the media, the difficulty of making changes in adapting to the specific needs and interests of the individual learners, and the lack of learner-learner interaction (Moore & Kearsley, 1996, p. 96; Belanger & Jordan, 2000, pp. 78-81).

### Interactive Media

Newer generations of radio and television distance learning technology, in the form of audio conferencing and videoconferencing, overcome some of the problems of broadcast radio and television as instructional media by allowing interactive dialogue and the establishment of a more personal relationship among the participants. As D. R. Garrison concluded,

> Physical distance of the student does not necessitate a cognitive and affective separation from the teacher. With a communication technology such as audio teleconferencing, it would appear that a sense of common purpose and mutual exploration of worthwhile educational goals can be established and maintained at a distance (1990, p. 23).

These media allow more communicative interaction which, in turn, improves attitudes, performance on tests, and can be linked to retention in courses (Baath, 1982; Kwiatek, 1982-83). Surprisingly, one study showed little or no impact of interaction on student attitudes and satisfaction, although the author contends that a methodological factor may have accounted for this result (Beare, 1989).

There remain, however, disadvantages to audio and videoconferencing as distance learning communication systems. The technology involved in these formats is expensive since, in addition to the high cost of equipment that must be at each sending/receiving point in the communication network, there are also potentially expensive line charges. The technology is limited primarily to point-to-point communication because the costs for bridging significantly raise the per minute line charge. Furthermore, there are inherent technical problems that limit the number of points possible in the network and the utility of the mechanism for the comparatively higher student-teacher ratios of a traditional classroom (Kouki & Wright, 1999, pp. 34-64). Finally, considerable time and effort must be expended to train faculty to make effective use of these technologies (Gehlauf, Shatz, & Frye, 1991), and additional development must be put into careful instructional design (Price & Repman, 1994).

The invention of Internet connectivity has transformed computer based instruction because it has added a communication system that not only provides a media rich system for delivering information, but also adds communication conferencing components. The importance of adding both synchronous and asynchronous communication capabilities should not be ignored. Moore, Winograd and Lange make the point explicitly:

> The increased capabilities of Internet and Web-based distance learning are why the number of institutions offering Internet courses that utilize online asynchronous communication increased by 38% over the past three years, while the number of institutions offering pre-recorded video and two-way videoconferencing, what were at one time considered the preeminent forms of distance learning, remained essentially the same (2001, p. 1.4).

While the Internet as a technology for distance learning instruction is a relatively recent development, there is a large and rapidly growing body of literature about computer mediated communication (Wood & Smith,

2001). The primary advantage of using the Internet as a distance learning technology is that it can employ a wide variety of media formats including print, graphics, animation, voice and video. Another advantage is that there are tools available that can allow synchronous as well as asynchronous communication between students and instructors, between individual students, and among individuals and groups of individuals involved in the course.

Websites can be designed to run simulations, to run surveys, to offer and even score quizzes, and to provide a dynamic database so that the grade entries for a given student are always available to that student. Students can access databases of information from college libraries, and they can tap myriad sources of information including the Library of Congress with its multimedia resources. Papers and other assignments can be posted to the Internet for review by the professor alone or for review by other students for peer comments and suggestions. Information and links can be updated easily and immediately, making the classroom infinitely adaptable to circumstances and to the specific needs of a given group of students. Work can be repeated and drills can be conducted without disrupting the learning of other class members. In short, the Internet offers many instructional features that are not available in the traditional classroom.

There are also disadvantages to Internet based distance learning instruction. Technical barriers include Internet network demands that can create denial of service or slow service at peak traffic times, platform incompatibilities among the participants in the distance learning environment, lack of learner familiarity with how the technology works, techniques related to overcoming problems when they are encountered, and insufficient bandwidth for digitally dense educational materials such as video, high density graphics, and simulations. The Internet, despite significant improvements, remains unstable. Its reliability still needs to be improved. It is likely that continued improvements in software, hardware and infrastructure will eventually make the Internet as stable and reliable as the telephone.

Additional disadvantages include the need to devote time and resources to instructional design and development that takes advantage of the educational possibilities of the Internet, and the need to devote training and support to both instructors and students in using the new technologies (Simonson, et al., 2000, pp. 186-187). There is also a danger that the fascination with the technology will obscure educational objectives.

In short, Internet based distance education is not suitable to all subjects, to all professors, nor to all students. Some subjects do not lend themselves readily or at all to total Internet instruction. For example, an interpersonal communication course requiring a live face-to-face interview to be observed and assessed in the traditional classroom could not be replicated using the Internet as the exclusive communication system. Even assuming that the parties could use Web cameras and microphones, the experience of spontaneous interpersonal communication with its full range of verbal and nonverbal messages is curtailed by the interposition of the Internet media.

Some professors are not suited to distance teaching through the Internet. Some are skeptical about the technology and its effectiveness in delivering the depth, rigor and interactivity possible in the traditional classroom. Some professors are unwilling to devote the time and effort needed to design and develop an Internet course given other competing demands on their time, such as the need to conduct research. Others are concerned about the legal constraints of copyright and intellectual property. Some are uncomfortable with a transition from lecture to other forms of content delivery; some are reluctant to forego the social dimensions of teaching that come about only through live, face-to-face interaction with students.

Finally, Internet based instruction is not suitable for all students. Some students, especially undergraduate students, are not accustomed to organizational and time management demands of Internet learning. Some students, like some professors, are technophobic or find the additional time and effort needed to learn to use the learning technology to be prohibitive. Some students, like some faculty, require the personal communicative contact involved in mentoring to be successful (Bothon, 1998; Palloff & Pratt, 2001, pp. 112-113 and 145ff).

### *Summary*

Distance education technology has evolved from print, through electronic broadcast media, to interactive Internet platforms. Some skeptics have suggested that distance learning has come full circle, returning to digital correspondence courses (Russell, 1999; Schutte, 1996; Phipps & Merisotis, 1999). Internet courses using computer technologies, far from being high tech correspondence courses, can offer the greatest possibility of providing certain educational experiences that are equal to, and in some ways even more effective than, traditional classroom settings. But if the goal of matching or even improving the learning environment of a traditional classroom is to be achieved, the instructional practices must evolve in order to take the fullest advantage of the possibilities of the "virtual classroom."

## Learner Centered Models

The second force shaping the changes in distance education is the shift from instructor-centered to learner-centered approaches to education with its concomitant emphasis on interactive communication. This force can best be understood by examining the relationship between models of distance education and models of communication.

### Fundamental Distance Learning Models

Models of distance learning education abound. One such model is distance learning as independent study. Charles Wedemeyer (1971) is widely credited with laying the foundations for distance education theory by describing distance education as independent study. He wrote that:

> . . . independent study consists of various forms of teaching-learning in which teachers and learners carry out their essential tasks and responsibilities apart from one another, communicating in a variety of ways for the purpose of freeing internal learners from inappropriate class pacings or patterns, of providing external learners with opportunities to continue learning in their own environments, and of developing in all learners the capacity to carry on self-directed learning (1971, p. 550).

Simonson, et al. (2000, p 29) suggested that Wedemeyer's independent study model consists of the elements of teacher—mode (i.e. communication system)—learner(s)—content. Thus, the model of distance learning incorporates teachers and learners engaged in mutual pursuit of educational goals though some type of communication system.

But what of the shift from teacher-centric to learner-centered experiences? Moore (1972) acknowledged the influence of Wedemeyer's model in his advocacy of the element of the "autonomous learner." In Moore's view, the nature of distance education compels us to recognize the paradigmatic shift from instructor-determined to learner-determined educational experiences. As he indicated in a 1994 editorial,

> In the years since I first wrote about learner autonomy, we have experienced a telecommunications revolution . . . . These technologies give us the ability to link instructors with groups of learners, as well as with individuals, and to link individual learners into virtual groups. Distance educators still face the important challenge of engaging with individual students in ways that build on and develop personal learning autonomy (1994, p. 2).

Clearly the model advanced in this view suggests that the instructional communication places an emphasis on the teacher's constructing the communication in such a way that the students undertake the responsibility for understanding, interpreting, and accepting, rejecting, or integrating the content of the course. The goal of the distance educator, then, is not to communicate by only presenting information, but to apply the principles of effective communication by inviting distance education students to participate with the instructor in a learning endeavor. The Wedemeyer-Moore model explicitly acknowledges the importance of placing the distance learner at the center of consideration.

Interestingly, this model, with its focus on the learner, parallels the contemporary development of rhetorical communication theory. While early rhetorical theory focused on developing rationale in order to advise rhetors about the most effective means to influence their audiences, contemporary rhetorical theorists suggest that the objective is for the rhetor to adapt the message to the nature of the receiver and to invite the receiver to share the rhetor's point of view. As rhetoricians Chaim Perelman and L. Olbrechts-Tyteca wrote about rhetoric, "There is only one rule in this matter, adaptation of the speech to the audience, whatever its nature" (1969, p. 25).

### *Inclusive Distance Learning Model*

Another conceptualization of distance education of particular interest is the Wagner-Maxwell (1986) model that integrates precepts of learning theories, instructional theories, instructional design, and instructional delivery. As described in Wagner's revision (1994, p. 11), this model of distance education involves synthesizing research from four arenas:

1. learning and learning theories (e.g., behaviorism) "that empirically define and describe human learned capabilities;"
2. instructional theories (e.g., Keller's Attention, Relevance, Confidence, Satisfaction theory) "that prescribe interventions to improve learning and performance;"
3. instructional design (assessment, design, and evaluation) that "tailors learning and performance prescriptions to fit situational contingencies," and;
4. instructional delivery (e.g., product and process concerns related to instructional technology) that "deals with the media and methods of transmitting information and instruction."

Wagner's model seeks to incorporate the proven aspects of all of these dimensions of a distance learning course to accommodate interaction.

### *Communication Based Models*

When a communication model is described in the literature on distance learning, it is usually based on a transmission model originally developed by Claude E. Shannon and Warren Weaver in 1949. Compare the Shannon Weaver model in Figure 1 with the model of communication in Figure 2 that Simonson, et al. (2000, p. 71) generated for their recent book on distance education.

Over the years, communication theorists have extensively revised the Shannon Weaver model to reflect a more developed view of human communication. More contemporary conceptualizations view communication as transactions among sources and receivers rather than the transmission

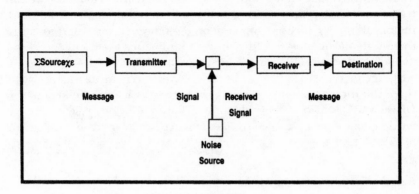

FIGURE 1
The Shannon Weaver Communication Model

of sources to receivers. Contemporary communication research views communication as an interaction in which sources are both senders of messages and receivers of feedback from receivers. Receivers are viewed as both recipients of the sender's messages and as sources of their own messages directed to the source. Furthermore, noise is seen as potentially pervading the entire communication process rather than being viewed merely as something that distorts messages as they pass through the channel. Messages are recognized as nonverbal as well as verbal. Finally, the context of

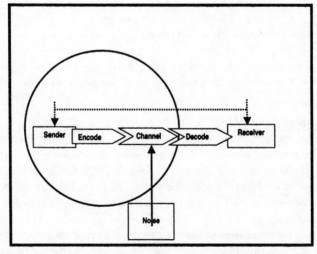

FIGURE 2
The Simonson, et al. Communication Model (2001)

the communication process is seen to influence the communication process. A contemporary communication more closely resembles Figure 3.

This more fully developed model of communication reflects contemporary understanding of the nature of human communication which, as we have seen, characterizes a more fully developed model of distance education. A fully developed conceptualization of distance education must incorporate the concepts of context, feedback, pervasive noise, nonverbal as well as verbal messages, and teachers and students as both originators and receivers of messages that incorporate the totality of the people involved in the educational process.

Distance learning models that incorporate the interactive communication elements must acknowledge fully the nature of instructors and students as participants in the instructional communication process (Palloff & Pratt, 1999, pp. 21-45). Such a model would also recognize the impact that the channels of communication have on the instructional process (Hillman, Willis, & Gunawardena, 1994). Both instructors and students would be skilled in the ability to construct meaningful, well-ordered and clearly expressed messages that accomplish the intended purposes, to employ good practices of prompt, unambiguous feedback, and to be sensitive to the feedback provided by the other participants in the communication. They would also be aware of the impact of physical, psychological, and

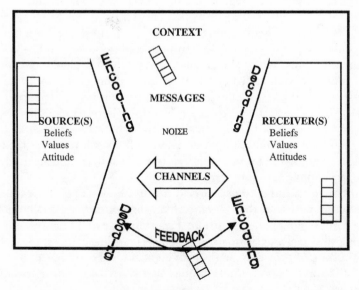

FIGURE 3
A Transactional Communication Model (after Benjamin, 1997)

semantic noises that may interfere with the proper reception and interpretation of messages, and they would be sensitive to the influence of contextual constraints and opportunities.

Every event in the distance education arena is potentially a communicative event. Therefore instructors should seek to employ effective instructional communication, not only in the transmission of information through such forms as online lectures and readings, but they should also seek to apply those principles of interactive communication to the activities that we ask our students to undertake in pursuit of the objectives of the course.

Donald C. Bryant, another rhetorician, explained that the function of rhetoric is to adjust people to ideas and ideas to people (Byrant, 1953). Effective distance learning instruction recognizes this function in the virtual classroom. To be learner-centered is not to pander to the whims of students as some have suggested (Stoll, 1999, p. 13), but to demonstrate rhetorical sensitivity to the nature of the learners in an attempt to adjust content to learners and learners to content by taking full advantage of the principles of the kind of effective interactive communication outlined above.

## FIVE TYPES OF INTERACTIVE ONLINE EXPERIENCES

"To be effective, distance teaching materials should ensure that students undertake frequent and regular activities over and above reading, watching, or listening" (Perraton, 1998, p. 127). This precept in Hilary Perraton's essay, "A Theory for Distance Education" is essential in understanding the role of activities in both traditional and online courses. Textbooks and instructional manuals urge faculty to engage their students through experiential, individual, and group activities that provide learners with an enriched classroom experience. In some cases, these experiences are formalized in separate "laboratory" sections; in other cases, the experiences are incorporated into activities within the classroom setting. In a basic communication class, for example, students will read the textbook, watch video clips, and listen to lectures, but they will also engage in dyadic, group, and public speaking activities.

If distance learning courses are to substitute effectively for traditional classroom experience, then distance learning courses, especially Internet courses, must adapt the classroom experiential experiences to the new teaching and learning formats. If distance learning courses are to fulfill their promise of providing an enriched educational experience, they must take full advantage of the possibilities that distance learning technology permits.

In the following pages we will explore the evolution of five types of activities, from the traditional classroom to the online classroom. These activities are:

1.  the transformation of the term paper to hypertext papers,
2.  the evolution of public presentations to Web presentations,
3.  the transfiguration of library research assignments into WebQuests,
4.  the alteration of journal assignments into blogs, and
5.  the evolution of class discussions into online discussions.

## Hypertext and Hypermedia Papers

One of the most venerable assignments in the traditional classroom is the written report. The term paper or short report is an activity adopted in a wide variety of courses. Students are assigned to conduct independent research and to submit a formal report on their findings. Papers may be informative, seeking to report on independent research findings or to synthesize the findings of others, or persuasive, seeking to argue a specific point of view on a controversial topic. The rubric for the term paper typically includes specifications of length, format, and mechanics of the paper, and often includes an indication of which style guide to employ in references and citations. The rubric for term papers also references the expectations about the content and structure of the paper, and may include specific expectations about organizational form or topics to be covered by the report.

The advent of the Internet and computer based publishing has introduced the concepts of hypertext and hypermedia. Hypertext allows the writer to link text to other pieces of information, either in other documents or in other parts of the same document, so a reference to a term may be linked to a callout that defines the term, or to another section of the report that details that term. Hypermedia allow links and displays of other media, so an icon of a microphone may be linked to a sound file to illustrate the pronunciation of a word or phrase. With hypertext and hypermedia papers, students are encouraged to go beyond the traditional, linear written report. Students writing hypermedia pages can easily include visual amplification of images, charts and graphs in their print reports. Going beyond the printed report, students can also include audio and video material in the form of prerecorded audio or video files to illustrate or amplify their points. In hypertext papers they can also link segments of their reports to other pages or to online material. In short, student papers can become as media-rich as the professor's presentations.

The rubrics for these reports must be modified from the traditional term paper. For example, page or word counts may not be appropriate indicators for hypermedia or hypertext papers. Instead, the rubric must include assessments of the adequacy, clarity, relevance, and functionality of the hypermedia and hypertext links to enhance the information in the report.

## Creating Web Presentations

Another common assignment in the traditional classroom is the oral presentation. Students are often expected to do class presentations reporting on an assigned topic. These assignments, like the written report, call upon the student to present material in an organized and lively manner. The assignments may include a requirement to use presentation aids such as overheads, models, or computer generated slides. They also often involve a requirement to answer questions from the audience. The rubrics for oral presentations, such as a term paper, focus on content, form and mechanics. They usually include elements of development and organization, auditory and visual delivery, and assessment of the supporting materials used in the presentation. Mechanical aspects such as grammar and time limits may also be incorporated in the rubric for an oral presentation.

In distance learning, live presentations may be prohibited by the limited equipment available to students and by the bandwidth available for transmitting visual and auditory presentations. However, such reports can be produced in the form of a narrated slideshow converted to a Web presentation. In a narrated slide show, students can record audio background for the slides they have created. The file can be submitted either in its native format, or can be readily converted to HTML. To emulate the question and answer period, students can log onto a chatroom or onto a synchronous audio connection such as Microsoft's NetMeeting.

The rubric for a Web presentation can utilize all of the criteria for evaluating a classroom presentation except for those pertaining to visual delivery, such as eye contact and gestures.

## WebQuests

Written or oral reports are often preceded by a unit on library research. A traditional classroom activity that seeks to apply this training is the library treasure hunt or scavenger hunt. In this activity, students using library resources, either singly or in small groups, are given a set of questions to answer based on the metaphor of a hunt. To avoid the pitfall of looking for random, trivial answers, the hunt can be focused on questions relevant to the course topic. The rubric for this activity usually involves scores for the most correct answers in a limited period of time, and may involve turning in a photocopy of one or more of the findings.

Developed in 1995 by Bernie Dodge and Tom March, the WebQuest is a modernization of the traditional library treasure hunt. WebQuests make use of currently available sources related to the student's ability to search effectively for specific information relevant to the course. The WebQuest is defined as "an inquiry-oriented activity in which most or all of the information used by learners is drawn from the Web. WebQuests are designed to use learners' time well, to focus on using information rather than looking for it, and to support learners' thinking at the levels of analysis, synthesis and evaluation" (Dodge, 2001). As described in Dodge's "Some Thoughts About WebQuests," there are six crucial elements in a WebQuest assignment:

> WebQuests of either short or long duration are deliberately designed to make the best use of a learner's time. There is questionable educational benefit in having learners surfing the net without a clear task in mind, and most schools must ration student connect time severely. To achieve that efficiency and clarity of purpose, WebQuests should contain at least the following parts:
>
> 1. An *introduction* that sets the stage and provides some background information.
>
> 2. A *task* that is doable and interesting.
>
> 3. A set of *information sources* needed to complete the task. Many (though not necessarily all) of the resources are embedded in the WebQuest document itself as anchors pointing to information on the World Wide Web. Information sources might include Web documents, experts available via e-mail or realtime conferencing, searchable databases on the net, and books and other documents physically available in the learner's setting. Because pointers to resources are included, the learner is not left to wander through Webspace completely adrift.
>
> 4. A description of the *process* the learners should go through in accomplishing the task. The process should be broken out into clearly described steps.
>
> 5. Some *guidance* on how to organize the information acquired. This can take the form of guiding questions, or directions to complete organizational frameworks such as timelines, concept maps, or cause-and-effect diagrams. . . .
>
> 6. A *conclusion* that brings closure to the quest, reminds the learners about what they've learned, and perhaps encourages them to extend the experience into other domains (Dodge, 1995).

Extensive information and links to examples are included in the WebQuest page maintained at http://Webquest.sdsu.edu/Webquest.html.

## Blogs

A fourth type of activity commonly used in traditional classrooms is the journal assignment. Here students are asked to keep a written record of observations, thoughts, insights, analyses, etc. For example, students may be asked to keep a record of the nonverbal norms that they encounter in a week. The journals are collected and reviewed by the professor. The rubric for journals usually includes the mechanics of writing (correct spelling, grammar, etc.) as well as the quality of the entries (appropriate to the assigned task, the ability to apply the course material to real life observations and reflections, etc.).

The blog is a relatively new concept. Blog is short for Web log and consists of an online journal that may be frequently accessed and updated chronologically. Many blogs are more like diaries than journals; that is, they are unstructured recordings of emotions and reactions rather than focused descriptions and reflections. However, the idea of the blog as an online journal is being adapted by many professors who have traditionally used journal assignments. Furthermore, because the blog is a Web document, students can take advantage of the media-rich possibilities of the Web. For example, field recordings can be made and included in the blog entry. Students can upload video examples of observations, and respond through audio entries or a more traditional written record.

While this digital version of the journal assignment can be used as a private communication between the student and professor, most blog assignments take advantage of the public nature of the Web to encourage other students to learn from the observations of others. The rubric for the blog is similar to that of the journal assignment. Students are assessed both on the mechanics and substance of their blog entries. Because the blog is a Web document, there may be additional assessments of the hypertext and hypermedia included in the blog pages.

## Online Discussions

Group discussions have also been a staple type of activity in the traditional classroom. Typically, the class is divided into small groups and assigned to answer a question or series of questions designed by the professor. Group discussion may focus on gathering and reporting information or on problem solving. Group assignments may be short term or may extend over several class periods. For example, students might be assigned to develop a solution to the parking problem on campus by following the standard problem-solving agenda of defining the problem, generating criteria for solutions, brainstorming possible solutions, evaluating the solutions, and selecting the optimal solution.

While most group discussion assignments are conducted in class, meetings are sometimes required out of class. Out of class meetings are frequently problematical for students in traditional classes because of the difficulties of widely differing schedules and competing demands on group members' time. The rubrics for classroom discussions usually include both the quantity and quality of participation in the discussion, undertaking leadership roles in the discussion, and the final outcome of the discussion.

Group discussion assignments in distance learning formats consist of two types: threaded (asynchronous) discussion and realtime (synchronous), or chatroom discussion. In the threaded discussion, students are asked to participate by posting to a common site. Contributions can be linked, or threaded to specific topics, or to other postings. For example, students may be asked to post comments on a case study or to debate an issue by responding to the positions taken by other students. Moore, Winograd and Lange (2001) note that:

> . . . most instructors I have worked with have had real qualms over the prospect of giving up face-to-face discussions that can be so powerful in the traditional classroom. And yet, over and over again, these same instructors express astonishment and happiness over the quality and quantity of discussion that occurs asynchronously in their online classroom through the threads (p. 11.19).

Chatroom discussions are often less successful in distance learning classes, primarily because it is difficult to find a common time that all students can meet in the chatroom, a problem compounded if the students are in different time zones. Furthermore, the chatroom involves spontaneous communication and therefore does not allow the time available for thought and reflection that is afforded to the asynchronous, threaded discussion entry. Nevertheless, the chatroom can provide an opportunity for students and faculty to interact in realtime, similar (although not identical to) the face-to-face classroom assignment. Furthermore, chatrooms have the advantage of eliminating commute time, but have the disadvantage of relying upon an unstable medium that might drop them from participation or may cause delays in logging into the chatroom.

The rubric for online discussion usually includes quality issues like the classroom discussion (demonstration of critical thinking and clear communication in the contributions) and quantity matters (frequency and responsiveness of the contributions within the assigned timeframes). The standards for assessment might be more stringent for threaded discussions than for realtime chats given the qualitative differences inherent in the two forms of discussion.

## Summary

In summary, we have noted a need to make distance learning courses more engaging for students. We outlined the evolution of five common types of assignments, from the traditional classroom to the online class site. We noted that written reports have evolved into hypertext and hypermedia papers; that classroom presentations have developed into Web-based presentations; that library assignments have been transformed into WebQuests; that journal assignments have evolved into blogs; and that group assignments have become online discussions. In the next section we examine the future of interactive media in the distance learning classroom.

## THE FUTURE OF INTERACTIVE MEDIA IN THE DIGITAL CLASSROOM

Prognosticating is always a dangerous enterprise, and there is a temptation to be meekly correct rather than boldly wrong. If one could really predict the future with any accuracy, there would be no need for casinos, or for Wall Street for that matter. Nevertheless, it is important to try to determine the forces that will shape student learning in the future so that we can proactively respond to the trends that will shape the future of distance learning. The following represents six estimations of future direction of the evolution we have been describing.

First, the continued penetration of computers into student households combined with increasing computer power and declining costs of computer peripherals will significantly influence the use of multimedia in educational activities. Many universities now require students to purchase personal computers, and all universities make computers available for their students. Computers with fast processors, sound cards, CD-ROM drives, and high capacity removable storage are now standard. High speed Internet connections are becoming more widely available in homes, and those with limited bandwidth can achieve acceptable levels of service through streaming media.

These forces will create a demand for more (and better) integration of multimedia material in courses, but will also make student activities more sophisticated. For example, rather than reading a description of a case study, students will be able to interact with the case by observing audio/visual simulations of the case and even discovering the impact of "what if" interventions they might devise on the outcome of the case. Current SMIL (synchronized multimedia integration language) technology will become common, and continued improvement of digital multimedia technology will make the creation of simultaneous multimedia presentations feasible for both faculty and students. Increasing familiarity with multimedia computing will allow students to compose sophisticated reports and projects that incorporate multimedia elements and interactivity for their audiences.

Another prediction is that textbook publishers will continue to redefine the nature of textbooks and ancillaries. The publishing industry has also been affected by the technological and pedagogical influences described in this chapter. Textbooks and course supplements have begun to incorporate distance learning technology. Textbooks now incorporate references to Internet links, are frequently accompanied by CD-ROMs, and some are entirely CD-ROM experiences usually accompanied by links to an Internet Website. Ancillaries now include online activities, digital media archives, and specialized references to teaching online. Publishers are developing and maintaining Websites to supplement their list of titles. Some publishers are developing distance learning "cartridges" of materials that can be readily adapted to popular distance learning platforms such as WebCT and Blackboard.

Textbook authors and publishers will continue to develop ever more sophisticated textbooks and ancillaries that will allow students to test their knowledge of the material and to apply the concepts they have learned to problems designed specifically for the textbook material.

Third, the advent of Internet 2 (and 3) and high speed modem connections will make it possible for distance learning courses to provide teleconferencing to individual students. It will also make complex simulations and remote control of laboratory activities feasible. As access to wide bandwidth increases and the Internet becomes more robust, limitations of the current technology in video and audio conferencing will be resolved. We can expect that the relatively primitive forms of videoconferencing currently available to faculty and students will evolve into sophisticated communication systems as bandwidth via Internet 2 becomes more available to colleges and universities.

We can expect the price of communication technology, currently affordable only by major corporations, to continue to fall, making it affordable for individual students to purchase for their distance learning classes. We can expect that the programming necessary not only for videoconferencing but for full scale computer peer conferencing to evolve. Faculty and students will have affordable access to sophisticated whiteboards, computer resource sharing, and multipoint interaction. This will provide new opportunities for faculty and students to collaborate in activities designed to achieve the educational objectives of the courses.

Fourth, centralized development of course materials by publishers and consortia of educational personnel will allow instruction to be individualized to allow more tutoring of distance learning students within the context of courses. Currently, most courses are developed and taught individually, and most learning activities are solitary enterprises. But many courses for distance learning are being designed by teams of instructional designers, media artists, and faculty; these courses are being facilitated by faculty and teaching assistants. With professional quality interactive teaching materials widely available from publishers, the selection, organization, and management skills of the instructor and teaching assistants become more important. Furthermore, as mentioned above, textbook publishers are developing the content for entire courses to be taught by faculty who select the specific textbooks for use in courses. This allows for greater standardization of course material and higher quality of media design than would be possible by a single faculty member. It also allows faculty to devote more time to the individualization and adaptation to the specific students that is necessary for effective instruction. We can expect that as course materials become more readily available, individual faculty will have class time freed to do individualized tutoring and interaction with students. We can also anticipate that faculty teaching multi-section courses, and even educational institutions, may form consortia to share resources needed to develop very sophisticated course content.

There are at least two threats in this prediction. First there is the threat that publishers and consortia will discourage competition, and courses will become so standardized and routine that we no longer have a wide range of ideas and approaches to select for our courses and our students. We could find a two tier system emerging, with course content developed only at larger institutions and implemented in tutorials at smaller institutions. Secondly, there is the danger that course development will become so costly and time-consuming that new ideas for courses and new courses will be restricted. Without the ability to incorporate new ideas into existing courses, content becomes stultified. Without the ability to develop materials for new courses, higher education will be ossified, unable to readily adapt to changes in fields of study and to incorporate new knowledge uncovered by research.

Fifth, wireless capabilities will make accessing e-mail and research databases possible anywhere and any time. This will put greater emphasis on the need for time management and knowledge management in distance learning endeavors. Experience in teaching Internet courses rapidly leads to the conclusion that "anywhere and anytime" can too readily become "everywhere and all the time." Both faculty and students must learn new strategies for time management. We cannot expect faculty to be instantly available whenever a student requires assistance. Faculty need to set boundaries and priorities for their instructional time. They need to establish but limit online office hours. By the same token, students accustomed to the immediacy of Internet access must learn to manage their study time effectively, given the limited time available with instructors but the unlimited and immediate availability of the prepackaged course material. Students too, must learn skills to manage learning and study time independent of the traditional habits of structured class and study times.

Like time management, students and faculty need to adopt new techniques of knowledge management. Faculty must cope with keeping current in fields that now have a plethora of material including more journals, more books, online journals, and publication of up-to-the-minute research on Websites. With this explosion of information, professors face the danger of information overload in which everything becomes a top priority creating an inability to filter out the cascading cacophony of information. Students also experience the stress of having to juggle not one field, but dozens of fields in their general education, major and minor fields of instruction. Students must learn to manage the flood of information that rushes to them each time they enter their virtual classrooms. Competing demands to master increasingly complex subjects, and to acquire increasingly sophisticated skills requires them to discern what is valuable from what is popular, what will serve them in the long term versus what they need to succeed in the short term of the specific courses, and what they need to adapt to the future demands of their lives and careers.

Finally, the role of the traditional classroom will change as the distance learning technologies and techniques shape higher education. Computer and Web-assisted instruction is a rapidly growing byproduct of distance learning. Web and computer assisted materials can free the traditional classroom for more individualized instruction that focuses on the strengths provided in the face-to-face interactions between instructors and students and among students, while other interactions can be shifted to out-of-class time. For example, traditional lecture, drills and mastery testing can be done online, leaving class time for individual consultations and attention to the specific educational needs of the students in a class. Out of class group activities can be conducted asynchronously or at times mutually convenient to the group members without the necessity of getting to and meeting in a specific location. The traditional classroom can also adapt distance learning technology to those student populations that cannot access the regular classroom due to disability or distance constraints.

Distance learning technology can allow guest lecturers to be recruited from outside the immediate geographic area and can eliminate the time and expense of travel to the classroom, yet retain the full impact of interaction possible in face-to-face interactions. Access to grading and interactive tests that provide guidance and feedback on specific items will help students identify the specific areas they need to study further. Using the tracking features of Websites, faculty can take note of student progress outside of the classroom and can provide more guidance about the specific dimensions of the course. Using the instant accumulation of findings from online questionnaires, faculty can receive formative feedback on the course for their specific class and can adapt to suggestions students make during the course. In short, the traditional classroom of the future will be a hybrid, taking advantage of the advantages of distance learning and the advances in distance learning technology.

## FOR FURTHER THOUGHT AND STUDY

Arnold, C. C., & Bowers, J. W. (1984). *Handbook of rhetorical and communication theory.* Boston: Allyn and Bacon.

Crystal, D. (2001). *Language and the Internet.* Cambridge: Cambridge University Press.

Moore, M. G., & Cozine, G. T. (2000). *Web-based communications, the Internet, and distance education.* University Park, PA: American Center for the Study of Distance Education.

Watkins, L. B., & Wright, J. S. (1991). *The Foundations of American Distance Education: A Century of Collegiate Correspondence Study.* Dubuque, IA: Kendall/Hunt Publishing Company.

## REFERENCES

Baath, J. (1982). Experimental research on computer assisted distance education. In Distance Education: A World Perspective. Athabasca University/International Council for Correspondence Education.

Beare, P. L. (1989). The comparative effectiveness of videotape, audiotape, and telelecture in delivering continuing teacher education. *The American Journal of Distance Education, 3* (2), 57-66.

Belanger, F., & Jordan, D. H. (2000). *Evaluation and implementation of distance learning: Technologies, tools and techniques.* London: Idea Group.

Benjamin, J. (1997). *Principles, elements, and types of persuasion.* Fort Worth: Harcourt Brace.

Berge, Z. L. (1997). Group computer conferencing: Summary of characteristics and implications for future research. In E. D. Wagner & M.A. Koble (Eds.), *Distance education symposium 3: Course design,* (pp. 42-57). University Park, PA: The Pennsylvania State University.

Biber, D. (1991). *Variation across speech and writing.* Cambridge: Cambridge University Press.

Bothun, G. D. (1998). Distance education: Effective learning or content-free credits. *Cause/Effect, 21* (2), 28-31. [On-line] Available: http://www.educause.edu/asp/doclib/abstract.asp?ID=CEM9827

Bryant, D. C. (1953). Rhetoric: Its functions and its scope. *The Quarterly Journal of Speech 39,* 401-424..

Crystal, D. (1995) *The Cambridge encyclopedia of the English language.* Cambridge: Cambridge University Press.

Dodge, B. (1995). Some thoughts about Webquests. Online. Available: http://edWeb.sdsu.edu/courses/edtec596/about_Webquests.html.

Dodge, B. (2001). Webquest page site overview. Online. Available: http://Webquest.sdsu.edu/overview.htm

Garrison, D. R. (1990). An analysis and evaluation of audio teleconferencing to facilitate education at a distance. *The American Journal of Distance Education, 4* (3), 13-24.

Gehlauf, D. N., Shatz, M. A., & Frye, T. W. (1991). Faculty perceptions of interactive television instructional strategies: Implications for training. *The American Journal of Distance Education, 5* (3), 20-28.

Hillman, D. C. A., Willis, D. J., & Gunawardena, C. N. (1994). Learner-interface interaction in distance education: An extension of contemporary models and strategies for practitioners. *The American Journal of Distance Education, 8* (2), 30-42.

Horton, W. (2000). *Designing Web-based training.* New York: John Wiley.

Kouki, R., & Wright, D. (1999). *Telelearning via the Internet.* London: Idea Group Publishing.

Kwiatek, K. K. (1982-83). New ideas in the workplace: Learning from interactive television. *Journal of Educational Technology Systems, 11* (2), 117-129.

Laverenz, T. R. (1979). *Student perceptions of instructional quality of correspondence study curses: Report of nine school comparative study.* Lexington,, KY: University of Kentucky.

Lowery, S. A., & DeFleur, M. L. (1995). *Milestones in mass communication research: media effects.* 3$^{rd}$ edition. White Plains, NY: Longman Publishers.

Marrou, H. I. (1964). *A history of education in antiquity,* trans. George Lamb. New York: The New American Library.

Moore, G. S., Winograd, K., & Lange, D. (2001). *You can teach online: Building a creative learning environment.* New York: McGraw-Hill.

Moore, M. G. (1972). Learner autonomy: the second dimension of independent learning. *Convergence, 5* (2), 76-88.

Moore, M. G. (1989). Three types of interaction. *The American Journal of Distance Education, 3* (2), 1-6.

Moore, M. G. (1994). Autonomy and interdependence. *The American Journal of Distance Education, 8* (2), 1-5.

Moore, M. G., & Kearsley, G. (1996). *Distance education: A systems view.* Belmont, CA: Wadsworth.

Morgan, T. J. (1998). *Literate education in the Hellenistic and Roman worlds.* New York: Cambridge University Press.

Nasseh, B. (1997). A Brief History of Distance Education. Online. Available: http://www.bsu.edu/classes/nasseh/study/research.html.

National Center for Education Statistics, (2000). *The condition of education 2000: Distance learning in postsecondary education.* [On-line]. Available: http://nces.ed.gov/pubs2000/coe2000/section5/indicator53.html

National Education Association. (2000). *A survey of traditional and distance learning higher education members.* Washington, DC: National Education Association.

Palloff, R. M., & Pratt, K. (1999). *Building learning communities in cyberspace: Effective strategies for the online classroom.* San Francisco: Jossey-Bass.

Palloff, R. M.,& Pratt, K. (2001) *Lessons from the cyberspace classroom: The realities of online teaching.* San Francisco: Jossey-Bass.

Perelman, C.,& Olbrechts-Tyteca, L. (1969). *The new rhetoric: A Treatise on argumentation,* trans. John Wilkinson and Purcell Weaver. Notre Dame, IN: Notre Dame University Press.

Perraton, H. (1988). A theory for distance education. In D. Stewart, D. Keegan, & B. Holmberg (Eds.). *Distance education: International perspectives.* New York: Routledge.

Perry, D. K. (2002). *Theory and research in mass communication: contexts and consequences.* Mahwah, NJ: Lawrence Erlbaum Associates.

Phipps, R. & Merisotis, J. (1999). *What's the difference?* Washington, D. C.: Institute for Higher Education Policy.

Price, R., & Repman, J. (1994). Instructional design for college-level courses using interactive television. *DEOSNEWS, 4* (5) [On-line] Available: http://www.ed.psu.edu/acsde/deos/deosnews/deosnews4_5.asp

Reisman, S. & Carr, W. (1991). Perspectives on multimedia systems in education. *IBM Systems Journal, 30* (3), 280 - 295.

Rossman, M. H. (1999). Successful online teaching using an asynchronous learner discussion forum. *Journal of Asynchronous Learning Networks, 3* (2). [On-line]. Available: http://www.aln.org/alnWeb/journal/Vol3_issue2/Rossman.htm

Russell, T. (1999). *The no significant distance phenomenon.* Chapel Hill, NC: Office of Instructional Telecommunications, North Carolina State University.

Schutte, J. (1996). Virtual teaching in higher education. [On-line]. Available: http://www.csun.edu/sociology/virexp.htm

Shannon, C. E.,& Weaver, W. *The mathematical theory of communication.* Urbana: University of Illinois Press, 1949.

Sherry, L., Billig, S., & Tavalin, F. (2000). Good online conversation: Building on research to inform practice. *Journal of Interactive Learning Research, 11* (1), 85-127.

Simonson, M., Smaldino, S. Albright, M.,& Zvacek, S. (2000). *Teaching and learning at a distance.* Columbus, OH: Merrill.

Stoll, C. (1999). *High tech heretic: Why computers don't belong in the classroom and other reflections by a computer contrarian.* New York: Doubleday.

Tilson, T. (1994). Instructional Radio. *International encyclopedia of education.* London: Pergamon.

U. S. Department of Education, National Center for Education Statistics, (December, 1999). *Distance education at post secondary education institution: 1997-1998.* NCES 2000-13, by Laurie Lewis, Kyle Snow, Elizabeth Farris, Douglas Levin. Bernie Greene, project officer. Washington, DC: U. S. Department of Education.

Verduin, J. R.,& Clark, T. A. (1991). *Distance education: The foundations of effective practice.* San Francisco: Jossey-Bass.

Wagner, E. D. (1994). In support of a functional definition of interaction. *The American Journal of Distance Education, 8* (2), 6-29.

Wagner, E. D., & Maxwell, K. (1986). Developers by design. *Performance and Instruction, 25* (8), 11-15.

Watkins, L. B., & Wright, J. S. (1991). *The foundations of American distance education: A century of collegiate correspondence study.* Dubuque, IA: Kendall/Hunt Publishing Company.

Wedemeyer, C. (1971). Independent study. In L. C. Deighton (Ed.). *The encyclopedia of education, 4.* New York: Macmillan.

Welch, S. R. (Ed.) (1993). The effectiveness of the home study method. *National Home Study Council Occasional Paper Number 9.* [On-line]. Available: http://www.detc.org/downloads/4DaEffectiveness_44F.pdf

Wood, A. F. & Smith, M. J. (2001) *Online communication: Linking technology, identity, and culture.* Mahwah, NJ: Lawrence Erlbaum Associates.

## CHAPTER 2

# HYBRID COURSES AS LEARNING COMMUNITIES

## Penelope Walters Swenson and Mark Evans

With institutions and instructors seeking the benefits of online instruction combined with a high level of personal contact, hybrid courses are increasing. Students and faculty are embracing new models of teaching and learning. Hybrid or blended models are being incorporated into the range of courses offered by colleges and universities within the United States and internationally. This chapter follows the development of hybrid courses from two starting points: courses that are exclusively face-to-face and courses that are exclusively online. Instructors in both groups will find opportunities to increase both student learning and satisfaction by considering hybrid modifications.

Within the chapter a variety of hybrid course types are explored. Most common is the hybrid that blends face-to-face instruction with online discussions and projects. Another hybrid blends online instruction and discussion with an internship, while yet another combines instruction developed by the university instructor with professional development from a commercial or agency source. Streaming video, video or telephone conferencing and other technologies are being used to enhance the level of person-to-person contact even over great distances. Hybrid courses, at their best, emphasize quality instruction and human contact.

Best practices and developments in hybrid courses are considered in this chapter. Issues of intellectual property, accreditation, technology and peda-

Electronic Learning Communities—Issues and Practices, pages 27–71.
ISBN: 1-931576-96-3 (pbk.), 1-931576-97-1 (hardcover)

gogical support for both instructors and students, and course quality are discussed. The best qualities of hybrid courses are listed as are problems with such courses. The chapter makes recommendations for planning effective hybrid courses and looks at the changing roles for instructors within those courses. In many hybrid courses, asynchronous discussion is critical to student learning. Quality indicators for asynchronous courses are considered. The chapter looks at the current research on hybrid courses and concludes with a list of questions that may be answered by designing and implementing effective hybrid courses.

**KEYWORDS:**  asynchronous discussion, hybrid, intellectual property, best practice, community of learners, learning management systems (LMS), virtual field experience, reflective thinking, learning object, accreditation, rubric, and blended

## AN OVERVIEW OF ISSUES

"Hybrid," in the context of technology-based instruction, is the term most frequently used to describe courses that combine online practices together with other instructional tools or models. More recently, hybrid has come to mean distance learning instruction that uses a variety of media, usually in terms of "multimedia." Some hybrid or "blended" courses (Troha, 2002) use commercial Web-based materials together with instructor developed materials in online or face-to-face settings. Another variation combines existing online professional development courses, university expertise, and/or course offerings. New hybrids are being launched all the time, as new instructional configurations and new technologies emerge. In this chapter a hybrid course is defined as a course with substantial online elements plus other models and media such as instructional television (ITV), CD-ROMs, video, and video- and/or tele-conferencing.

While some might consider any combination of such configurations to mean a course is a hybrid, there are some essential elements necessary for a hybrid course to be viable. Hybrid courses are more than just the use of a traditional text with the remaining aspects being online. For example (in this chapter), an independent study model of one or two students using e-mail and telephone contact with the instructor is not a hybrid course. Hybrid courses must have at least *several* participating students and an instructor. While this chapter only focuses on instruction in higher education, hybrid courses also are available in K-12 and in industry.

Quality hybrid courses that include online components require the use of technology together with a high level of engagement, activities, participation, and active involvement of the students and the instructor. Clearly, the nature of instruction, whether traditional or online is evolving, and successful hybrid courses must take advantage of this evolution (see Figure 1).

In the context of this changing environment, students today are not steeped in tradition about the infallibility of instructors; they look for interesting, engaging, and timely courses. Recently, a student characterized a course as "...interesting, hard, and worth it." Today, instructors must be more than information suppliers. Students already have many ways to access information. They want instructors who are guides. They also seek classes offered in places and at times that fit their lifestyles. Students are canny and concerned consumers. Generally, they are media savvy and many expect to use technologies such as e-mail and the World Wide Web in their classes.

These expectations, stemming mainly from the ubiquity of easy-to-use technology, are changing how instructors deal with information. Instructors who begin their attempts to deploy instructional technology with only the use of e-mail as a communication tool, then move on to develop course supportive Websites, will likely soon attempt to use asynchronous classroom discussions. The availability of Learning Management Systems (LMS) such as Blackboard and WebCT can help to expedite these kinds of transitions. The road to hybrid courses using an LMS can begin with a few modest steps. LMSs allow instructors to start by experimentation, easily enabling them to create hybrid instructional environments, often initially for simple distribution of classroom materials, and later for the purpose of increasing student reflection on those course materials, eventually to foster broader student engagement through more complex classroom interactions than are typical in a traditional instructional setting.

| Yesterday | Today |
|---|---|
| Instructor as lecturer | Instructor as guide and facilitator |
| Education as an individual effort | Education as both an individual and group effort |
| Professor centered | Learner centered |
| Student passive | Student active |
| Assessment by traditional testing | Imbedded performance-based assessment |
| Grading on the curve | Grading by meeting standards |
| Professor and books major sources of information | Wide range of educational media including print, Web, video |
| Professor knowledgeable in all or most areas | All are learners in some areas of the course |
| Professor publishes in hard to access journals | Professor may post research on Web and publish in available online journals |
| Learning is centered in the university during posted hours | Learning is anytime, anywhere |
| Course changes little from year to year | Courses updated on basis of research, current information |
| All learners in same place | Learners may be anywhere |

FIGURE 1
Yesterday and Today in Classrooms and Online

However, as useful and motivating as the use of LMSs might be in the classroom, moving to an online environment, even a hybrid one, can increase concerns about such issues as accountability and quality from school curriculum committees, administrators, and accrediting agencies. While a face-to-face course can be monitored by a dean or by peers, online and hybrid courses oftentimes seem invisible or unseen by those who are not part of the teaching/learning experience. Texts may not be in the bookstore, or not even be assigned in such courses. Course hours may not be shown in the catalog, or there may appear to be too few scheduled class sessions. Course materials may be used that are not produced by the instructor, yet the name of the university is on the course. Legal issues such as intellectual property rights are concerns with hybrid courses, particularly when multiple individuals, institutions or entities are involved in their development and delivery. Since hybrid course development seldom is funded, intellectual property issues may not be resolved before a course is in use. Both legal and quality issues must be addressed and resolved before courses are developed or collaborations begun.

Another concern is one of course quality. Commercial vendors of professional development courses often seek university collaborations to acquire legitimization of their courses and programs under the university's name. Some vendors have high quality programs and maintain and upgrade them on a consistent basis. Other vendors may initially have excellent materials, but the quality may slip as finances shrink. University partners can assure oversight and mechanisms for moving out of hybrid collaboration should the quality provided by a vendor decrease.

Within a university, quality is a complex issue. In academia, although this is not yet the norm, a solution to the quality issue might be accreditation, and once granted, could provide an assurance of quality. It is well-recognized that hybrid courses (which oftentimes evolve into fully online courses) must begin at least equal in quality to their face-to-face equivalents. They must be subject to the same review processes as other courses. Research, like that of Poindexter, Heck, and Ferrarini (2000) is beginning to suggest that hybrid courses can be at least as effective as traditional courses, but substantial research is still not available.

Best practices, however, are starting to be documented. So far, we know that hybrids, like their more evolved fully online successor courses, must be high quality, interactive, and engaging. They must not be independent study sessions driven by text readings and answers to questions e-mailed to the instructor. Students need preparation for taking hybrid courses. They need to know how to work the technology and conduct research. In order to develop an effective community of learners in a hybrid course, it is essential that the course objectives explicitly state the value of teamwork, reflection, and supportive discussion.

The other essential ingredient in hybrid (and fully online) courses is the matching of appropriate tools to pedagogical activities. All too often, a fascination with technology can take the instructor's focus off pedagogy and the need to serve students. Technology is not central to hybrid courses; students are. Sometimes the most effective tool for a course is a formal lecture; other times attending a field trip to attend a play may be. Sometimes the most effective tool is an asynchronous discussion. Still another activity may call for a hotlist that provides active links to Internet sites, whether in the context of independent study or perhaps a collaborative research project. Effective instructors understand the objectives of their courses, learning theory, and the potential impact of a variety of tools and technologies on student learning outcomes. According to Willis (2002) "...those who think the Web is the ultimate solution to all instructional problems should review the research literature of the 50s stating the same thing...about the overhead projector" (p. 327).

## MOVING TOWARD A HYBRID

Instructors who use a smart classroom (i.e., a classroom with an Internet-connected computer attached to an overhead projector) may find themselves showing students Websites that relate to the course. Students may be seen furiously copying the URLs for Websites into their notes so they may refer to them later. Often the instructor notes this and begins to write the URLs on the whiteboard. This may lead to his distributing a list. As the list becomes longer and longer, the instructor determines that he will save paper and create a linked list on his Website to which he can refer students who wish to review the links. These links become numerous and essential to the course material. Many are so well done that the instructor begins to use them as if they were text materials, giving assignments to be completed outside class. He starts posting outlines for each upcoming lecture. Soon the instructor is assigning group projects based on the Website content. He begins looking for ways to have these groups communicate at times other than the lab period or after class. He checks with his colleagues, some of whom may be using discussion boards or other technologies.

Moving from a conventional classroom to a fully online program may not be the goal of many users of distance learning tools. As mentioned above, Learning Management Systems such as Blackboard and WebCT increasingly are used to supplement traditional courses. The range of options, from posting course syllabi to using threaded discussions is becoming an increasingly appealing way to supplement conventional courses. Instructors who have no intention of abandoning face-to-face courses are finding these options useful. Within LMSs, instructors have a large compliment of tools and options available. Poindexter, Heck, and Ferrarini (2000) found uses of the Web "...can be grouped into three general categories: communication supplements, course management aids, and course content supplements" (p. 2), with course content supplements seeming to be the most popular, usually through the use of faculty Websites. The California State University, Bakersfield is typical of campuses where instructors are encouraged, but not required to have such Websites. Over half of the instructors have sites designed to provide students with materials that traditionally are handouts.

A random review of instructional homepages at California State University, Bakersfield, one of 23 regional campuses in the California State University System, and at the California University of Pennsylvania, one of 14 regional universities in the Pennsylvania State System of Higher Education, reveals many similarities in hybrid course instructional strategies. For example, an English instructor supplements her face-to-face course with writing and study guides, suggested sites, course syllabi, a dictionary of terms, and recommended readings. Several instructors from subject areas including psychology, engineering, biology, and foreign languages post syllabi, readings, and course-related links. Multiple instructors in the areas of business and public administration have links to problems, simulations, and statistical tutorials, in addition to extensive reading lists, assignments, and even homework answers. At least one instructor, also from business, posts PowerPoint presentations for review.

Course management support on the Websites includes syllabi, assignments, and even grades on password-protected sites. Schedules and calendars also are common. Some instructors use the online testing functions of LMSs to supplement projects and for class testing. A few Websites provide discussion access through threaded discussions, but communication supplements are most commonly supported through LMSs, not faculty Websites.

Because LMSs are versatile, many instructors migrate the materials they have had on personal course Websites to a supplement within an LMS such as WebCT or Blackboard. LMSs are more secure and materials that copyright holders might not allow on a public Website often may be used within a password-protected course. In the example below, the instructor develops an online presence first using a personal course Website, and then migrating to the university's LMS.

Marta is a fine presenter. Students enjoy her courses. She likes the excitement and dynamism of teaching. She provides a wealth of information. Calling herself a neo-constructivist, she strives to have students bring in their own experiences within the discipline, and combining them with additional information and the experiences of others, develops new and/or increased student understanding. Her classes are filled with activities, discussion, short lecture, presentations, and group work. Class periods are conducted once or twice weekly, with sessions of at least two hours. Despite the long class periods, Marta's students remain engaged.

With the availability of the Web, Marta began developing a Website containing course syllabi, hotlists, assignment sheets, calendars, frequently asked questions, and announcements. She started using the student e-mail system to alert students to changes and notices regarding class. A service to which she subscribed offered the monthly professional updates in Adobe PDF files that she could post for her students on the Web instead of photocopying the multi-page master for each. The service, however, required that the files be password-protected. Marta consulted with the university Web services, and they suggested posting most of what she had been doing plus the monthly professional materials. It sounded like a bit of a hassle, yet it would be much better than trying to copy all that material for each class. She soon became a LMS user.

At a workshop in the Teaching and Learning Center about the LMS, a colleague extolled the virtues of threaded discussions. She agreed to try a question each week and use the threaded discussion. Students who seldom spoke in class became engaged in the online discussion. Marta also looked forward to the discussions. They were different from the in-class discussions, and offered new opportunities for students to engage each other and the concepts of the course.

Now Marta is using the LMS as a significant supplement. She even uses the LMS for students to submit papers, and take tests. She is contemplating using the grading module. Two of her best students, Lori and Javier, talk to her individually at class Wednesday night. Lori's mother is seriously ill. She will miss the next two weeks of class. Javier's supervisor is requiring him to work Wednesday evenings for the next month. More classes will be missed. Then she discovers that several other students will miss next week also. She decides to accommodate the several students by posting materials, assignments, and a full class session online for next week. She maintains that she will meet live with the students who can attend, yet those who must miss will have class too.

The alternative online section works. Marta develops online ways for Lori and Javier to keep up, and she begins thinking about a different sort of hybrid course. She wonders if she could be as effective using some weekly lessons online, alternating with face-to-face teaching.

Marta is moving from supplements online to significant portions of the course online.

Where is the tipping point from doing supplements to face-to-face instruction and actually going to a hybrid course? The process generally follows a pattern:

1. initial use of technology tools including presentation software by the instructor;
2. e-mail becomes a major tool for communication;

3. resources, including syllabi, assignments, and hotlists, posted online; and
4. asynchronous discussions online.

When a substantial portion of the course discussion or other activity is online, the course is a hybrid.

## A VARIETY OF HYBRIDS

Many hybrid courses have 30-75% of the course online with the remainder offered face-to-face. Reasons for this are both pedagogical and practical. For example, often universities serve distant communities requiring students to travel to a central meeting place, remote from the main campus, for their classes. In such circumstances the instructor too must travel from home or from the university to the distant meeting place to present the course, often in the evening or on weekends, then return home. Students enjoy the contact and the opportunity to take credit courses from a regional university. Their alternative has been weekend courses at the distant campus or e-mail/correspondence classes. The logistics for these courses are complex and expensive for the university. A more practical solution is to require some classroom time—perhaps 3 weekends—at the university (or distant center) and some online instruction.

Whether the course is statistics, sociology, English, history, criminal justice, or geology, distant courses offered in a three weekend face-to-face format often lack the opportunity for students to ponder, practice, and reflect. A few course meetings in person with the remaining sessions online provides students with the opportunity to meet the instructor and interact with their peers in a face-to-face manner, allowing them to "get to know" each other better. Interacting and presenting online is somewhat uncomfortable for some initially, yet most students learn to appreciate the strengths of both face-to-face and online.

In some cases, such hybrid instructional strategies are essential. Some disciplines require reflective thinking as part of the course of study. Groups working together using asynchronous communication to focus on reflective thinking can be more effective than independent study in traditional learning environments. Through examining groups of similar students in the same course, working in a face-to-face environment, or using threaded discussions, Hawkes and Romiszowski found that "...computer-mediated discourse achieves a higher overall reflective level than reflections generated by teachers in face-to-face discourse" (2001).

This improved involvement may relate to several factors. Within a conventional discussion, even with 25 students, only a few actually participate. Others students will appear to be involved and seem to agree or support points, but they often say little or nothing. Many classrooms are not set up for effective discussion, so the exchange becomes instructor to student and back to the instructor, then from instructor to another student, rather than student to student with some instructor guidance, when needed. When classrooms or discussion groups have an individual or two who dominate the conversation, others are denied an opportunity to contribute. Asynchronous discussions change the focus from one or two to many. All have the opportunity and obligation to contribute, particularly if participation is graded. Sometimes students must reflect on the experience to see how a community of learners develops.

Jamie, a student in the online section of a hybrid course complained toward the end of the class that contact in a face-to-face setting was much more profound. Jamie added that much was learned and the discussions were very valuable in the online setting however. Jamie said, "I learn more about people in the face-to-face classes."

The instructor wrote Jamie, "I know where you work from your introduction, and about your ideas and your commitments from your postings." She went on to name several examples. Then she continued, "I do not know several things that I would if we were together in a classroom though." Jamie quickly replied to that e-mail wondering what those unknowns were. The instructor replied, "I do not know your age, gender, race, hair color, and other such details. Considering that we were concerned with ideas, principles, and ways to make plans work, those details just do not seem to be as important as your ideas and commitments."

Jamie's next response was not as quick. "I need to consider this more. I wonder if I would have revealed so much about how I think and what is important if we had been face-to-face. Actually. I learned a lot about my colleagues. Important things."

Through threaded discussions, power roles can be changed. Even in courses where students have face-to-face sessions, the online discussions assume a more egalitarian tone with increased participation.

Jamie, from the example above, was part of a class that had 10 total instructional sessions plus a final exam. For 12 of the students, the course was delivered with four face-to-face sessions and six online sessions. Jamie and two others were not among the 12 because they lived too far from the campus to be able to participate frequently in the face-to-face sessions; their participation was completely online.

Instructor Johnson agrees to teach a course to practicing school administrators at a remote center 120 miles from campus. In the past, such courses have been conducted with three Friday night and all day Saturday combinations with the instructor staying overnight. Twelve students are enrolled with three more distant students asking to take the course by independent study. Johnson considers her options.

Ten hours on each of the three weekends seems like a tight schedule for developing reflective thinking and reading materials. Doing assignments that spiral one from another is nearly impossible with only a week between session one and session two, then another week between sessions two and three. A plan develops. Meet with the 12 on four evenings. Hold the other six meetings online. Provide online sessions for the distant three students at the four meetings through the quarter, one each at the beginning and the end with two in the middle.

The face-to-face meetings are successful. The 12 students come prepared. Their six online sessions reflect preparation and a high level of motivation. Not unusual for practicing school administrators, there are time conflicts, and during the three sessions of the face-to-face meetings at least one student is absent. Absent students are directed to join the online group for the week. Familiar with their colleagues and the format, they do so willingly.

The distant students are motivated, but their involvement is spotty. They are accustomed to a more independent type of program where the individual works only with the instructor, answering questions and e-mailing responses. When required to become involved with colleagues, there is hesitation. It is a change and this change requires engagement. Also, the weeks with only three online sessions are more difficult for the three students than those with the additional 12 online.

After about three weeks, some of the "hybrid 12" begin entering discussions during the sessions which are not required for them. Johnson asks one if he is seeking extra credit. "No, I just wondered what they were talking about and had to put in my two cents worth." While participation was not consistent, several of the 12 did bounce into discussions making contributions from their reading, experience, and even the face-to-face session.

Johnson is impressed favorably with how well the mix works for students, but she sees she is preparing for a class within a class and that it is very taxing and time consuming. She tries to structure the plan for the face-to-face session to serve as the online component too. That saves her time, yet she still must post the unit, set up discussions, and monitor the discussion area throughout the week.

While there was an addition of time to Johnson's schedule, she did achieve the goals of producing increased access for students throughout the service area and improving the quality of the distance programs for both the clustered and the scattered students.

In late 1999, the Teachers College at Columbia University designed a common discussion and collaboration area for students from an online class with 22 students, and a face-to-face class with 11 students. Syllabi, assignments, and online discussion were common to both groups. Both groups received the same information and material. Online students were able to attend face-to-face sessions, but this was not an often-used option. When project time came, many of the groups were comprised of both online and face-to-face students. They grouped themselves based on what they deemed were critical issues. The hybrid format was successful in merging the two groups (Mouza, Kaplan, & Espinet, 2000).

Even with a primarily online course, one or two face-to-face sessions are desirable. Often the first week of an online course is filled with stress for the student new to online learning. A face-to-face session with an hour or two in a computer lab will allay the concerns. During that session, students should login on the LMS and begin one assignment, preferably an introduction or enjoyable activity. They should be told to reply to one or two colleagues' e-mails and discussion threads. Moving around, an instructor can gain insights into possible problems and help students with a personal touch. Offering additional help over the telephone later usually is not needed, but very welcome when students are having difficulty.

Josin Sethi is furious. His class is on WebCT and he cannot get on. The student help desk is not helpful. The student support staffer just suggests that WebCT is difficult and tells Josin to talk with the instructor, Dr. Ortega. Josin resorts to calling the instructor at 10:00 PM. She is not home. Her husband says to check the schedule that notes she is out of state at a conference. Josin resorts to e-mail. His words are angry. He is computer literate and things are just not working. He wants an A in the course and this is affecting his efforts. He notes that the instructor should have introduced the students to the program and not made them carve out success for themselves.

Dr. Ortega is presenting at a conference across the country. She reads Josin's e-mail about the time she expects he is finishing his work day. She calls his school number and tells the secretary she needs to speak with Mr. Sethi. Soon Josin is on the telephone. He still is angry. Dr. Ortega tries to calm him and suggests that he get on the course Website. She walks him through the process of getting online and into the assignments and discussion area. He tries the discussion once and is successful. He does it again. Another success. Dr. Ortega compliments his skills and offers encouragement.

Josin's anger born of frustration has turned. "Thanks. I did not expect you would call from Virginia. I thought I was stuck until you returned to campus. You did not have to call me."

Dr. Ortega smiles in her Virginia hotel room. "Josin, I want you to be successful. Thanks for letting me know there was a problem. And, Josin, next time I will not have the first meeting of a hybrid course online. See you in the online discussions and in our classroom session soon."

Telephone help to solve a problem can save a student. Josin was ready to complain loud and long about learning to use technology. He was considering dropping the course. He was angry with the instructor. A 15 minute call saved the situation. The instructor also established that she too was learning. Human contact and intervention is important to students. For a hybrid course, the contact should be strategically placed. An initial session in the computer room would clearly have established a better tone for the course.

Many distance learning programs that seem completely online initially include a face-to-face component. For some programs it is an intense day or even week on campus. One graduate program is online most weeks, but requires a monthly campus session. Faculty members who have taught numerous online courses say that early face-to-face sessions improve the course experience. Additionally, if project presentation is part of the course, a capstone session at the end is desirable (Willis, 2002). Does this make the program a hybrid? If there is extensive use of the face-to-face component, probably. There are many variations within hybrid models.

## Teacher Education Field Experience by Videoconference

Hybrid instruction, as mentioned in the introduction to this chapter, can take many forms, including the blending of videoconferencing with face-to-face or asynchronous discussion. For example, teacher education programs usually include a field experience that can be examined in the context and definition of hybrid classes. Each student goes to a classroom and observes the teacher-class processes, often using a list that guides what he or she is required to see. Upon returning to the university, students discuss their individual experiences and the instructor seeks to generalize about classrooms and highlight certain situations and practices. Because the experiences are so diverse, it is difficult to have students reflect on what they observed and arrive at meaningful conclusions that will assist them as they move toward student teaching (Rosen & Bloom, 2002).

To make the diverse field experiences into shared experiences and structured reflection, Rosen and Bloom (2002) developed a virtual field experience, delivered by satellite or ISDN videoconference systems. Teacher education students meeting in a variety of locations can participate in a shared learning experience. The live videoconference can be rebroadcast with a different group of student participants, possibly students whose employment allows only evening sessions. The videoconferences follow a specified format. First, there is a segment of teaching done by a cooperating teacher at his or her own site. Second is an opportunity for the elementary school children in the observed classroom to ask questions of the observers. Third is the time for teacher education students to ask questions of the children. Steps four and five involve questions back and forth between teacher education students and the cooperating teacher who just taught the segment. These steps are completed online (Rosen & Bloom, 2002).

Rosen and Bloom suggest that holding face-to-face sessions both before and after each videoconference enhances the experience. They stress that this reinforces student reflection and provides them with the opportunity to build upon experiences of the other student teachers. Using this video-conference system, they are able to introduce students in their teacher education programs to teachers and teaching circumstances in a variety of grade levels, economic situations, and social settings. Students share their experience with other pre-service teachers. They may even revisit segments to see how a particular teacher used a teaching technique. Discussions may continue asynchronously with students and their instructor on aspects of the shared classroom observation experience as the instructor seeks to assist students in reflecting and linking practice with theory.

Desktop videoconferencing does not require satellite studios and specialized classrooms. This technology, which is becoming increasingly affordable and reliable, uses familiar equipment in computer lab settings, thus making the opportunity more and more available to students at all levels of education.

## CD/Web Hybrids

Large multimedia files are difficult for learners at home, without high speed network connections, to download. Such files, containing charts, video clips, graphs, hypermedia, etc. can enrich learning at a distance. They also can help distance learning reach adults with a variety of learning styles. Diaz (1999) suggests that creating a media-rich Website and putting it on CD-ROM enables students to move back and forth from Web to CD media. Bandwidth-intense activities, such as short lectures, demonstrations, interactive learning experiences, and intense graphics, would be accessed from the CD-ROM. Asynchronous discussions, chatrooms, testing, updated reading lists, and similar, more text-based activities would be accessed from the Web. For the student, file download time is eliminated as is potential frustration from not having the right programs to display PowerPoint or video files. When students spend less time on technology and more time on learning, they can become more successful learners (Diaz, 1999). However, if instructors need to update their materials frequently, the use of CD-ROMs becomes problematic. Changing and updating content on CD-ROMs requires significant effort and is not without added expense; yet CD-ROMs remain a good interim solution to the problems of low bandwidth.

## Streaming Media Rather than CD-ROMs and Videoconferencing

Streaming media (audio alone, and/or audio plus video) is an option for enriching distance learning courses. Instructors can lecture on-campus, and remote students can listen to the lecture through realtime streaming media. As well, the streamed media can be captured and streamed at a later time, or placed on a Website for access at the convenience of the student. Media capture for delayed streaming allows for post production editing, thus enabling editors to improve the quality of the production and also reducing the size of the file. Distance students with high bandwidth connectivity appreciate hearing and seeing the instructor and student colleagues as part of their overall learning experience. But while bandwidth is decreasing as an issue, in many rural areas of the country, many are still limited to low bandwidth dial-up connections thereby making the reception of steaming media, especially video, less than ideal.

## Online Skills Training and Face-To-Face Practice

Often a gap exists between the skills and procedures taught in the classroom and the actual use of the skills. As pre-professional programs combine the teaching of skills with internships or practica, Web-based support can provide an effective means to enhance the entire program and reduce that gap. Certain skills may be needed before starting an internship. For example, in an internship in the lab of a co-generation plant, the plant management may require certain safety tests and rules reviews. Clearly, this can be easily accomplished via the Web. After the intern reports to the facility, she can participate in ongoing discussions (with her classmates, instructor, or plant management) online tied to the university curriculum. Through the Web she can be exposed to current research, best practices in co-generation worldwide, and be reflecting on what she is doing in her intern position.

David Garcia is an intern school administrator. (An intern, supported jointly by the university and a school district, is permitted to be employed while completing coursework to qualify for the regular credential.) Serving as the Dean of Students in a large suburban high school, he constantly is dealing with questions of law and human resources, in addition to needing to exercise wisdom and common sense. Having been a teacher for seven years, David thought the transition would be easy. Now he has many questions and while he has a good relationship with the principal (his position mentor), he knows he cannot get a half hour of time daily from the principal to respond to his questions. When David signed up as an intern, he knew there would be meetings at the university. Instead of weekly face-to-face meetings, however, the university faculty member set up occasional on-campus meetings and an ongoing, asynchronous discussion within the campus' LMS.

David is in a group with nine other interns. He is required to go online at least three times a week to check in and participate. Tonight, with his list of questions in hand, he logs on. Marka, another intern dean, has posted a question about suspension conferences. That is one of his questions too. David enters the discussion. Checking his watch, he reluctantly logs off, vowing to check the discussion early in the morning before work. When David logs on at 5:45 AM, he sees a brief message with a URL from his instructor, Professor McCallum. He clicks on the URL. It is an article by a principal about parents in denial and suspension conferences—exactly what he needs. He also reads a post from Tran, an assistant principal in a middle school who just had an experience with a student suspension involving a deceptive student and a parent who was convinced her daughter was a victim, not an actor. David reads the article and Trans' post, then replies, adding some additional thoughts and questions in the discussion.

These kinds of hybrid instructional environments are used in professional programs to prepare and train a professionals such as school administrators, nurses, managers, hospitality industry managers, teachers, and engineers, for academic and continuing education credits. A just-in-time orientation such as the one described above can add valuable resources when the intern needs them. The intern has support from the day position mentor as well as his or her university instructor and university colleagues. Another variation on this approach is employed in areas with scattered populations of students where multiple programs collaborate in an online manner. This is particularly effective in programs that operate with a common set of standards and training/teaching objectives.

## Competency-Based Choices

Some competency-based courses allow students to progress at their own rate through sets of required competencies, testing out of some and moving on to the next ones. Adapting this instructional strategy to a Web-based model is relatively easy if, for example, the competencies are demonstrated in a text format, as responses in words—sometimes through labeling a diagram, through describing the steps of a process, relating an appropriate dialog, or even short answers to questions. Students receive course content via the Web. They take practice tests on the Web. Their unit completion test is given in a more secure setting, perhaps in a proctored session. Within this system, there is minimal contact with the instructor and none with other students.

Another approach to this competency-based choice concept is to provide a range of activities, face-to-face, video, and online, that will satisfy and/or present specific course competency requirements. Many university general education programs allow students to demonstrate their mastery of and/or proficiency in a subject matter in a variety of student-selectable ways. For example, if the proficiency is in Health and Nutrition, the choices may include one or more of:

1.   active participation in a weekly fitness group.
2.   an individual fitness program with testing at beginning and end.
3.   an online nutrition project.
4.   an online fitness program based on a fitness diagram.

Students can select the option that most fits their interests, needs, and time options. While all these represent hybrid courses as defined at the beginning of this chapter, item #3 and #4 represent examples of technology-based hybrid courses.

## Learning Group with Choices

At Triton College, a community college near Chicago, the Interdisciplinary Studies Department (ISD) was trying to solve a series of problems including increasing student performance and satisfaction. Students could take certain classes online or face-to-face. Those online tended to feel as if they were not part of the College and online classes had a lower completion rate. But the face-to-face classes also had problems. Students who missed classes and dropped courses cited reasons like work schedules and personal life issues as conflicting with their study obligations (Wager & Salzman, 2001).

Wager and Salzman found that a bright spot in the Triton ISD program was the University Center, a community wherein general education core courses were taught in a highly coordinated setting with combined assignments, teaming, and other activities that built a sense of engagement. Consequently, students in the University Center had a significantly higher probability of completing courses, and faculty wanted to emulate this community feeling by building it into the online groups. They sought ways to integrate both the face-to-face students and the online students, creating a common community (p. 2).

The ISD adopted a LMS and determined that three classes would form the core of the program of study. Students were enrolled into a single course section in a ratio of one online student to two face-to-face students. Students selected online or face-to-face based on their own predictions of how they would take most courses, but they were not required to stay in one format or the other. Instructors worked together, supporting the students and assisting in developing a greater sense of belonging for the students. According to Wager and Salzman, "There were two primary goals in planning all three classes: To create online courses that linked to each other, and to create a structure that allowed on-campus and online students the flexibility of moving back and forth between the two modes of delivery" (p. 2).

Administrative problems within the Triton ISD program were overcome or set aside, and students easily moved between the online and face-to-face modes. Sometimes an online student came to campus for a face-to-face session just to make sure he understood, or because the topic was particularly exciting. In another case, a face-to-face student participated online for a week because of child-care problems. Dialogue among instructors encouraged a higher level of dialogue among students (Wager & Salzman, 2001). The initiative suggests that many options are available and the demarcation between face-to-face and online can be flexible, giving students choices while holding them accountable.

## Collaboration with Dotcoms and Other Non-Accredited Programs

An online course offered collaboratively by a university together with a commercial or agency partner is an example of another hybrid model. Both the university and the partner bring expertise and credibility to the venture. Commercially developed course materials frequently include; streaming video, CD-ROM materials with simulations and other graphics intense applications, synchronous and asynchronous discussions, white boards, illustrations, e-mail communications, videoconferencing, reference materials with extensive and contemporary hyperlinks, animations, specialized work environments, and customized tools designed specially for the course.

Many commercial and other non-university organizations offer professional training and development programs for teachers, nurses, engineers, corporate management, etc. Some of these organizations developed and marketed online programs long before most universities seriously entered this field. Several organizations have been aggressive in promoting their products to universities as an easy way for the university to become involved with online instruction. Most of these vendors offer high quality instructional/training materials as a result of their intensive market research that considers market demands, new legislation, best practices, and assessment results from their own experiences as well as the experience of others. However, some vendors offer material of questionable or variable quality. A collaborative group of states involved in distance education, the Western Cooperative for Educational Telecommunications, raised this concern in their *Best Practices* document:

> Although important elements of a program may be supplied by consortial partners or outsourced to other organizations, including contractors who may not be accredited, the responsibility for performance remains with the institution awarding the degree or certificate. It is the institution in which the student is enrolled, not its suppliers or partners that has a contract with the student. Therefore, the criteria for selecting consortial partners, and the means to monitor and evaluate their work, are important aspects of the program plan. In considering consortial agreements, attention to issues such as assuring that enhancing service to students is a primary consideration and that incentives do not compromise the integrity of the institution or of the educational program. Consideration is also given to the effect of administrative arrangements and cost-sharing on an institution's decision-making regarding curriculum (WICHE, n.d.).

While high quality professional development programs are being offered online by both commercial and non-commercial entities, the interests of the student must outweigh other advantages, including the potential for bringing in additional funding. University partnerships can be formed that are advantageous to students. The advantages may include: increased variety of courses, useful and timely course content, practical and professional material, communication with in-course colleagues from distant geographic locations, and a high degree of access convenience. Professional development, however, is not university coursework.

Converting professional development courses to university coursework and assuring its quality take a significant effort. Where the provider is well known and the course outlines and materials are readily available, the process is easier. Since all aspects of the professional development course become part of the university curriculum, it is necessary to obtain those materials, syllabi, and access to any rubrics, processes, or other assessment instruments. Of course if the university does not provide an instructor for these courses, it must ensure that the qualifications of the trainer meet the university's qualifications.

Supplemental course materials too must be at a standard similar to what would be developed or used if the course were developed by the university. Course syllabi must reflect course rigor and have objectives of standards like those of courses with a strong activity base. Special attention must be paid to the level of student/student and student/instructor involvement. Several questions need to be asked to ensure that such courses meet the standards of the university:

- Are students highly engaged over a period of time?
- Is reflective thinking stimulated?
- Are there online discussions and required numbers of posts?

- Is the course rigorous?
- Who monitors the posts and at what level?
- What types of projects or other products are required?
- What are the safeguards to assure quality control of presentations?
- Does a qualified guide or instructor lead the course or is it self-directed?
- Do students come to the program seeking credits without the expectation of effort?
- How does the university monitor this process and assure consistent high quality?
- Are there barriers that prevent university oversight?

The assessment procedures applied to student participation and projects is an issue of great importance. Unfortunately, professional development seminars and courses sometimes emphasize enrollment over engagement and/or learning outcomes. It is possible to reduce these kinds of risks by carefully selecting the course instructors. Usually, professional development course presenters/instructors are highly qualified and can be hired as adjuncts by the university, making these courses more closely associated with the university than they might otherwise be. Sometimes these courses can be overseen by presenters who are employed by the company and not the university, while the instruction takes place with some level of university review and oversight before credit is conferred. Responsibility for grading in these circumstances must be worked out, but the university remains responsible for course integrity. Yet another option is for the university to assign an instructor to do oversight, including a review of projects and participation, then require additional work, such as a literature review or a significant paper, of a credit-seeking student. In that situation, the instructor assures quality and assigns the grade.

Leslie enrolls in a course that offers graduate units through her regional university. She needs three units to move to a new level on the teacher salary schedule. The course is an interactive collaborative effort between the university and a Web-based company that provides professional development. She is attracted by the course, "Developing Thematic Units Using Web-based Resources," and the three units. Anticipating an easy "A," Leslie is amazed when she receives an e-mail from Instructor Sayeed. Dr. Sayeed describes the process for securing credit. It includes participating in the discussions and completing the project within the course, led by an employee of the Web-based company. Sayeed attaches a rubric. He notes that he will check to assure that Leslie has performed at the highest level. After completing those requirements, Dr. Sayeed notes that Leslie will complete a paper with several references on the topic which he will grade using another attached rubric. Leslie's thoughts of an easy "A" vanish. "At least it is online so I can do it at home," she says.

Credit seeking students may enroll in such programs for one of two reasons. An incentive for some is that in many careers, continuing education units or professional development programs granting university units are desirable for salary increments. Others may be degree-seeking students seeking undergraduate or graduate credit. Continuing education units are of less concern to the university since they have no status toward a degree and often have a numbering system making the lower status obvious. Units counting toward a degree must be attached to courses with high credibility and integrity.

Many excellent professional development courses have well developed and maintained Websites with resources, outlines, readings, discussion areas, libraries, and week-by-week plans that can be accepted as they are, or modified. Within such structures, a university instructor is the instructor of record and is in complete control of the course. The instructor takes advantage of already-developed learning tools and teaching resources. He makes the assignments, establishes the ground rules, sets the standards, and grades the performances.

> Luis sees an interesting course listed in the Spring schedule. He checks into the course further, discovering it is online and on the site maintained by a professional development company in his field of study. He finds that an instructor, Dr. Sharp, will be leading the full course. As he begins the course, he sees the instructor is using the high quality materials provided by the company for their own private and costly training. Dr. Sharp adds his own materials and style to the course, and the arrangement fits the university schedule. Luis is pleased that he can have the best training available in his interest area and work with a favorite instructor.

Partnering with a commercial organization or agency can have advantages for the university. Small departments, for example, can increase the options available to students. Expensive course development work is completed and continually upgraded by the organization. Instructors have access to state-of-the art tools for teaching. Other advantages include reaching students in areas not currently served, maximizing university resources, and securing no-cost professional development for instructors. While some commercial ventures promote these partnerships as ways to make money, this cannot be a reason to develop a partnership. Service to students and maintaining institutional quality and integrity must be the guiding principles in considering such potential partnerships.

University governance bodies have processes for approving courses and matters impacting instruction. Contracts with commercial organizations and agencies also must be subject to review and approval by university officers. Partnerships with commercial organizations merit special scrutiny. The values enumerated by the Council of Regional Accrediting Commissions (2000) regarding online and face-to-face programs provide a standard regarding instructional issues. Questions of intellectual property rights, provision for student services, administration and management, and fiscal arrangements must also be considered.

When partnered courses become part of the university catalog and essential for programs, planning for possible partnership dissolution must occur too. Technology ventures are commonly short-lived. Frequently, agency staffs change or have funding problems due to grants expiring or funding cutbacks. Dependence on a technology vendor or agency without having an "exit plan" places students and their degrees at risk. Every adopted course should have an option that could replace the collaborative course. In some cases, it would be a change from offering the course through the media rich environment of the technology vendor to a more Spartan, but stable offering of the same course elsewhere within the university. The options should be clear to university planners from the outset.

## Course Packs, Web-Sites, and Support from Textbook Vendors

In the last few years, textbook publishers and LMS vendors have entered into collaborations in order to offer richer learning materials for students. They are providing Websites, "pre-assembled course content," materials to supplement face-to-face courses, and materials for "robust, interactive and educationally rich online" courses to instructors who adopt specific texts. Often the texts are sold with electronic keys to allow students to access the sites if the instructor selects the online course option.

> Instructor Drabecki has been teaching for 20 years at State. Never considered an innovator by his colleagues, Drabecki has established a pattern of being current. Web resources intrigue him, but gathering enough current resources to enrich his course is overwhelming. There is no tech specialist assigned to the history department, so that is not an option for Dr. Drabecki. The sales representative for the text he uses comes by. Mike shows Dr. Drabecki the 8th edition of the text. It comes with a Web supplement. Mike calls up the Web and shows Dr. Drabecki how easy it is to access. There even is a CD with interactive maps, video, and a simulation. A full day training session, with a catered lunch, will be offered next week. Dr. Drabecki checks his calendar. He agrees to attend. "How much more will this cost?" Mike replies that it is included with the new texts which cost $12 more than the earlier edition. He notes for purchasers of a used text, there will be an added fee of $12. "You said everything is easy and updated frequently, so I suppose this could be a good way to get my courses into the 21st Century."

LMS vendors such as WebCT and Blackboard offer a range of learning objects. Some courses have been developed and purchased by the vendor for general use by instructors at subscribing campuses. These courses include materials that may be incorporated as a supplement or as an online class. While some of the materials are correlated with a particular text, others are generic and are available without additional cost. The level of adoption or adaptation ranges from a full adoption of a pre-developed course with the instructor just contributing in the discussion areas, to adaptation of materials and accepting pieces and parts into a course developed by the instructor. In the latter case, the pieces of the course become learning objects.

## Instructional Television and Online

Blending instructional television (ITV) with online offers students multiple ways to learn and gives instructors added teaching options. Lectures, demonstrations, performances, video field trips, live discussions with class members in the studio and remotely, and expert panels can be offered live in the ITV period. Reflective discussions and accessing print resources are part of the online time.

For the student who wants a connection to faces and voices, the ITV segment can provide visual contact with the instructor. Pictures and short videos of class members may be introduced. Students who are near the campus studio have the opportunity to attend one or more sessions in a face-to-face mode. Videotapes of sessions are made available to students unable to receive the signal or who miss a session.

Jason and Reina, instructors at a regional comprehensive university, discovered that their students, who worked at regular day jobs, saved one night per week for courses. Generally the instructors, who each offered a required course in the Masters program, would block their courses back-to-back to assure the one evening model. Students both appreciated the one night plan and cursed it. The evening was long. Each course was three credits, meaning the classes last nearly six hours.

Reina is offered an opportunity to teach her class using ITV. She calls Jason. Together they plan. Tuesday night, from 4:30 PM to 7:30 PM, is the time slot available. They develop a sketch of their plan. Reina is scheduled for ITV on the odd Tuesdays. Jason has the even Tuesdays. During the opposite weeks from the ITV session, the class sessions are online. Assignments for ITV weeks also are online. Examinations, discussions, charts, hotlists, and more are online. At 8:00 PM on the first night, Jason and Reina are in the computer lab to assist students in accessing the LMS. It is not a required meeting although all students are required to be online by the first meeting or attend the session. Additionally, students who wish to attend in the ITV class are welcomed and invited.

The arrangement established by Jason and Reina makes highly efficient use of the ITV classroom/studio. Working students are advantaged in time and flexibility. Face-to-face contact is possible and encouraged, but not required. Students who must miss a class session can tape it or check out a tape from the university. Asynchronous discussions and online assignments encourage a high level of participation. Both Jason and Reina require student presentations for which several options are available. Some presentations can be taped and presented via ITV, while others can be done in PowerPoint, converted, then posted to the course site. Yet others can be presented live via ITV. Both instructors make certain that class sessions are varied and course quality is maintained.

## Conference Calls and Learning Management Systems (LMS)

Competitive telephone rates combined with improved technology make conference calls easier than in the past. To provide students with synchronous voice communication, some courses add a weekly conference call for which students have a toll-free number and call-in code. They call in and are part of a live discussion. The notes of the discussion are placed on the course Website to assist in maintaining continuity. While students comment that they would like to see each other face-to-face, the calls plus pictures posted on the Website provide what most believe to be a good substitute. As students hear voices during the weekly conversations, some remember them and the printed messages assume those voices. During the conference calls, immediate concerns can be addressed in addition to the presentation of content with structured discussions.

Bettina works on rotating shifts. She wants to complete her degree. Online seemed to be a great way, but now she has doubts. The isolation she feels at work combined with the difficulty of relating to people online is undermining Bettina's confidence in being able to complete the program. She likes the online discussions. The readings are stimulating, but the lack of contact is too much. When she sees the hybrid course description combining online with a weekly conference call, Bettina decides to try it. She arranges to take lunch at the times the conference call is scheduled.

Dr. Piers posts photos of class members on the class Website along with their introductions. Bettina prints them. She has them on the table when they talk on the conference call. "You know, this feels like a real class," she announces one night during the call. Dr. Piers notices Bettina and several others are chatting in the Lounge area of the discussions in addition to completing the assigned posts and responses.

Connectedness is important to students. One student in a hybrid course titled a post, "Hey, is anybody out there?" She needed reassurance about a technology issue. She needed the connection to colleagues and the instructor.

### Broadcasts Plus Online, Face-To-face, or Other Contacts

Public Broadcasting and the Department of Defense (DOD) are both involved in distance learning, often with a hybrid addition. Some of the DOD courses count for transferable lower division college credit. The PBS/Adult Learning Service coordinates their offerings with hundreds of universities across the United States and Canada. Several specialized and regional agencies or university collaboratives are combining efforts to present materials via broadcast, supported by additional distance learning media.

Hybrid potentials abound but the issues of quality and integrity loom large. It is incumbent upon both the university as a whole and instructors to fully research feasible options. The reputation of the instructor, department, and the university itself depend on offering quality programs that produce acceptable learning outcomes. Accreditation agencies apply the same high standards to hybrids and online courses as they do to face-to-face courses. All programs must measure up.

## QUALITY, LEGAL, AND SUPPORT ISSUES WITH HYBRID COURSES

### Accreditation

Major concerns have been raised about the quality of all online instruction, including hybrid courses. Concerns regarding quality of higher education courses presented entirely or partially on the Web or through other distance learning media have been raised by instructors, accrediting agencies, potential employers, students, and many others. What constitutes quality? How can academic integrity be maintained? How can students be served as well as or better than the traditional on campus classroom model?

The Council of Regional Accrediting Commissions (2000) acted together to allay concerns by setting standards for online, and, by extension, partially online programs. Program integrity is a major issue. Their statement speaks to several areas. Distance education should involve a learning community, in creating, offering, and evaluating programs.

Learning should be interactive. Programs and courses should be substantive and have academic integrity. Student needs must be met and resources must be provided in distance courses. Colleges and universities are responsible for programs offered under their logo. Institutions are responsible for assessment, quality control, and program improvement. Additionally, the colleges and universities are required to participate in accreditation (C-RAC, 2000).

The Best Practices document developed by the Western Cooperative for Educational Telecommunications suggests further implications in the areas of the institution, curriculum and instruction, faculty and student support, and assessment and evaluation. Each of the five components has sub-categories and questions to assist in a review of the specifics (WICHE, n.d.). The questions apply well to hybrid courses in addition to all online programs.

## Support for Students and Instructors

While online programs may secure grant funding to help establish the courses and infrastructure, hybrid programs tend to grow out of traditional, face-to-face courses. Because of this development mode, seldom are hybrids funded. Important support questions remain, some of which are introduced in the WICHE document. Is there institutional support for the LMS or for other special media being used? What training for faculty is available? What are the hours of a help desk for faculty and for students? Are student/graduate assistants available to assist the faculty member with design if there is not other institutional support? Will institutional upgrades be maintained unobtrusively and backups be made routinely? Does the institution support and encourage technology innovation? Does the support include funding for specific projects? What are the institutional implications if the instructor uses free online services for posting of materials, asynchronous discussions, online chat, sharing of projects, and posting of links?

> Luz teaches a lower division course that is popular with students. Recently, she was frustrated by the difficulty of getting anything posted through university services. She was told she could have an asynchronous discussion with password access placed on her Website, but, after she requested it, she waited a few days and became frustrated when it was still unavailable. She told her colleague Martine who suggested a commercial free service that had many of the features of the university LMS, but, he noted that it was very simple to access. She went to the site. Luz did not like the advertisements that popped up and resided in banners that changed frequently, but she did like the simplicity of access. She posted her materials and discussion topics. Then she talked with her students at the next face-to-face session so they would under-

stand what they would be required to do. She entered all of their e-mail addresses and the students were enrolled.

Finally, the discussions are going very well. Students complain about the pop-up advertisements, but, Luz decides that both the ease of posting and the excellence of student participation are worth these inconveniences. A few others have difficulty getting on the site; when they call the university help desk, no assistance is available for the unsupported site. Luz must help students herself. Eventually all are online. By week 10 of the semester, she has the routine down. Students are engaged. Materials are available. Even the forgetful student cannot lose his or her syllabus or assignment sheet.

One afternoon, at the end of class, a young woman stands near the door. She wants to talk. "I have been in your class and I tried to do everything you asked."

Luz nods. The student is nervous. "Come up to my office. We can talk there."

"My father says I cannot go on that site any longer." The student is the first in her family to attend college. She was even the first to complete high school. Her parents are laborers who both respect and fear education. They are sacrificing for her to attend the university.

Luz encourages the student to be more specific. "I have been getting these." She hands Luz a few sheets of paper. They are graphic, sexually-oriented mailings sent to the student's e-mail address.

"Your father relates these to the course?"

"We never received anything like this until I went to that Website. He is sure there is a connection. I thought about it a lot. Maybe there is. I did accidentally click on one of the pop-up ads. I think it was after that these things started coming into our computer."

After the student leaves, with the situation unresolved, Luz calls a consultant at Web Services, explaining the situation and seeking some ideas for blocking the e-mails and pop-ups. "Bad deal," begins the consultant. "There is nothing we can do. Not even the new pop-up software works that well, and, besides, it would need to be purchased by each student for his or her computer. You know the university does not want us using those sites for just that reason. I'd take the site down right away. I'd also suggest to the students that they change their e-mail addresses."

Luz goes over to Martine's office and explains the situation. "I'm torn. The process works so well. I am in control. At least I was until this happened. Students like the discussions. But I find myself out there alone. And at least one father had banned the site. I know it is not the site, but he sees it that way."

Luz figured it correctly. Her university is not supporting anything they do not have on-site. She is alone. She starts asking questions like those listed above. She finds her campus had a small center called the IISC, the Instructional

Improvement and Support Center. She calls. They have a seminar for Blackboard, the campus LMS, starting next week. She enrolls.

Support is an important issue for students and instructors. Some universities have 24/7 support while others have support only during the weekdays. Support questions include:

- Where do students get help?
- How do instructors get help?
- What type of support is offered?
- What is the timeline for securing support?
- What security is afforded?
- Are courses set up and populated for the instructor?
- Can students be added or deleted manually?
- Is the server adequate?

On many campuses, a center for improving teaching has as one of its duties to assist instructors with moving into increased technology use. Often there is a faculty member on special assignment who understands the issues relating to instructors, university policies on technology, and Web services. That individual can assist the instructor in securing training on the LMS, information on student assistants or other help, and, possibly funding to aid in the development of a new or enhanced course. Often the connection between technology services and the academic programs side is fraught with territorial issues. Knowing both what Web services are available and how to access them are critical elements in developing a quality hybrid course with a Web component.

## Intellectual Property Rights Issues

Developing a hybrid course utilizing technology-mediated instruction often is a team effort. Who owns the course and the course materials? Is it the faculty member who was the creative impetus for the course and who made all the critical decisions regarding instructional objectives and content? Or is it the university that invested heavily in servers, course management software, broadcast studios, digitizing equipment, a broadband infrastructure supporting remote sites, and accompanying support staff? And, what is "ownership," anyway? Institutions and their faculty both have a vital stake in the answers to these questions, as the following case illustrates:

Dr. Washington taught at State for three years. State is a regional university in a small city surrounded by sparsely populated areas. Dr. Washington developed a very popular hybrid course melding one face-to-face meeting and video case studies with online content and activities. The course satisfies a state requirement in reading for elementary teachers. The hybrid delivery system has enabled State's School of Education to comprehensively serve its entire region for the first time. Dr. Washington has made presentations at professional meetings and is developing a national reputation as someone who can creatively marshal instructional technologies to enhance access across far-flung service regions. He is leaving State for Coastal University and plans to take the reading course with him. In fact, Coastal recruited Dr. Washington, in part, because of this course. However, State has 125 new credential applicants from remote areas as a result of this distance education effort. They will not be able to enroll in the credential program if it cannot be delivered through hybrid courses. State insists it owns the course because of its large investment in the multimedia/online support infrastructure that Dr. Washington utilized to develop the course while serving as its employee.

Copyright protection is vested with the creator of a protectable work upon its creation, whether or not the work is registered with the US Copyright Office. The copyright provides its owner with rights to publicly display the work, distribute it, make reproductions of it, and make derivative works that incorporate elements of the original copyrighted work. Yet, the work-for-hire doctrine stipulates that the employer is the owner when an employee within the scope of employment creates the work. Although the courts have held in specific cases that the faculty is the creator of the work and copyright holder, the decisions are context-specific. Generally, there still is considerable uncertainty regarding copyright ownership in academe, especially for hybrid course materials resulting from team efforts where the university has taken specific actions in support of the work. Fortunately, uncertainty need not be a major impediment to innovation. If the law is unclear regarding ownership by default, the parties can enter into an agreement that specifies ownership. The specification can consist of blanket joint ownership of all rights (not recommended) or a more careful allocation of each right (Consortium for Educational Technology for University Systems, 1997).

Perhaps even more important than the ability to clarify ownership rights that are uncertain in statute and case law, specific individual rights can be unbundled and transferred or shared with other parties, either exclusively or nonexclusively (i.e., public display, distribution, reproduction, use in derivative works). This is the critical path for achieving the purpose of creating intellectual property rights as set forth in the US Constitution: to further the general welfare by promoting progress in science and the useful arts. Although there are potential conflicts of interest between faculty and university when a third party is brought in to sell course materials developed through their team effort, this pales in importance compared to their shared interest in acquiring and disseminating knowledge.

In the above case, if it is assumed Dr. Washington holds the copyright for the reading methods course, he has the right to teach the course at Coastal, to update it, to be identified as author of the course materials he developed, and to let colleagues at Coastal use the materials. Dr. Washington's interests are not undermined if he signs an agreement with State that allows it to continue using the course materials to meet needs in its service region. If State holds the copyright, its interests are not harmed by an agreement that grants Dr. Washington the right to use the course materials at Coastal, and to update and modify them as needed. If it is unclear who the legal creator is, an agreement still can be signed sharing and allocating rights of the work so as to meet the principal need of each party. An outcome serving the general welfare can be achieved, regardless of who initially holds the property rights.

Campuses can develop a memo of understanding (MOU) to provide course development assistance and, perhaps, a stipend to faculty for developing course materials that further its goal of enhancing access. The extraordinary support as well as language in the MOU ensure the university it will be able to continue using the materials to meet student needs when the course developer does not teach the course. Faculty needs are met through an acknowledgment of authorship and rights to use and alter the work under a subsequent employer.

Many faculty members have created course materials without extra support that subsequently became essential elements of the university's program to reach remote students with access problems. Program continuity can be threatened when this occurs and the faculty member's teaching assignment subsequently changes. Satisfactory resolutions are possible, especially when common interests in creating and disseminating knowledge are acknowledged. In one case, the course developer considered the course to be a departmental offering and simply allowed his colleague to duplicate his Website as a starting point for the evolving hybrid course. In another case, the course developer was hesitant to turn over the Website without some compensation. However, he accepted a modest royalty equivalent to what other instructors received as course development stipends in return for allowing his colleague to use the Website as his starting point. It is a wise investment for a university to provide some course development support in return for a signed agreement granting it the right to use the technology-mediated course materials when needed for program continuity.

## STRENGTHS AND WEAKNESSES OF HYBRID FACE-TO-FACE AND ONLINE COURSES

Most of the strengths discussed herein focus on the face-to-face and online model that is somewhere on the 60-40 or 40-60 split. There is material that may be best taught face-to-face while other material is most effectively taught online. Knowing which is most effective where, recently has become an area of research.

Parker and Gemino (2001) compared a face-to-face course and a Web-based course (asynchronous learning network or ALN) by the same instructor, using the same text, and covering the same material and reported three major findings. First, the overall final exam scores showed no significant differences. Second, students in the Web-based course had significantly higher scores than their face-to-face colleagues on the conceptual section of the final exam. Third, the online students had significantly lower scores than their face-to-face colleagues on the technique section of the final exam. Parker and Gemino conclude, "… courses that contain largely conceptual material may offer excellent opportunities for ALN, while courses focusing on technique may be best provided in a traditional place-based environment" (pp. 72-73).

Hybrid courses offer instructors the opportunity to select the best modes for delivering instruction and then use them. They also allow adapting schedules to meet the needs of the instructor and/or students.

Rich wants to present a paper at a fall conference. His heaviest teaching load also is in the fall. Making his schedule more complex is the fact that several of his students each fall are varsity football players who must travel. The schedule for the conference often coincides with a major trip his football players take. Deciding this year will be different, Rich enrolls in LMS training. His syllabus and schedule reflect that he will have several assignments and activities online. He tells the students this schedule will allow him to present at a conference and the football players to stay up with the class by working online while away. Several laugh. Rich has been using Webpages and online class notes for two years. With the help of a student assistant, he designs two weeks of class plus two introductory lessons and places them, plus some quizzes, on the LMS. He decides to meet twice in the computer lab and try the introductory lessons with his class. His student assistant helps him orient the students. They take one quiz and work on part of a lesson. Rick is amazed. Even those unsure at the beginning of the class period seem to be doing fine by the end. He asks very targeted questions at the end of the course during the evaluation period to see how the students feel about their online sessions compared with face-to-face sessions only. He is pleased with the results. The athletes especially appreciate the online segment during big game week. Rick's presentation goes well too.

Hybrid courses allow learners with a variety of options that may assist them to excel. Reflection is encouraged in the asynchronous discussions. Projects can be started face-to-face and continued online. Presentations can be developed in many formats, and offered online or face-to-face. Materials are available online and easily accessed. Pre-tests and tests can be taken online and feedback can be immediate.

Students who feel intimidated with an entirely online course may find hybrids to be very comfortable. Communication is more direct and immediate. E-mail announcements keep the course on track. When one or two students have a question, the instructor responds, and then sends the response to all. Poindexter, Heck, and Ferrarini (2000) found that established online office hours are used more than conventional office hours (p. 7). Communication is broadened between and among students and between students and the instructor in this hybrid model.

## Best Qualities of Hybrid Courses

Students and instructors have been evaluating hybrids, particularly those combining face-to-face with online modes. Positive comments (in random importance) about this type of hybrid include:

- Course materials are available all the time.
- They are more student-centered than lecture.
- Available online tools include white-boards, graphs, charts, hotlists, grade packages, discussions, and chat.
- Students enter asynchronous discussions at times convenient to them.
- Driving time may be decreased.
- Links to outside readings are provided.
- Pre-tests on the Web help prepare for the mid-term and final.
- Presentations use a variety of media.
- Multiple adult learning styles are accommodated.
- Discussions online are stimulating and engaging, involving more than just a few.
- Students do not fall behind as easily in hybrids as in all online.
- Communities can be developed that support learning more than just in class.
- It is easier to get into a group and work on a project.

## Problems with hybrid courses

On the other hand, as with most things, there can be some drawbacks or difficulties:

- Institutional support for the LMS may only be available during limited hours.
- Instructors frequently are not well trained to use the LMS.

- Incomplete grades are more difficult to make up if asynchronous discussions and group projects are part of the course.
- Students may lack technology skills needed to navigate the LMS.
- Students postpone completing assignments online and fall behind even to the point of needing a grade of "incomplete."
- Students need additional instruction and practice using and evaluating Websites for research.
- Within some LMSs, it is difficult to update materials after uploading them.
- Enrolling students who register late creates logistical problems.
- Students and instructors both complain about the time needed to participate in asynchronous discussions because so much is added from day to day.
- It is easy to duplicate activities to the point that it becomes like teaching two separate courses.

With courses that have substantial collaborative online components, incompletes are difficult. Most universities offer a semester or two to finish the incomplete. For the instructor, a dilemma is created. How can the online environment be recreated for an individual student? It is best for the student to participate in a learning community. If the course is not offered each semester, there is a need to create a simulated online section for the incomplete. This raises both an issue of quality and an issue of law for the student and instructor. Students must have a way to clear incompletes. Archiving dialogues and other online materials can be helpful and used to simulate the online environment. The best solution is not to have incompletes, yet that is not within the control of the instructor or, even, the student.

## Planning for effective hybrid courses

As with any effective course, extensive planning is necessary to deliver a hybrid course. The use of face-to-face and technology-based modes requires attention to greater detail, scheduling and coordination than for a totally online or traditional course. To assure the best possible hybrid course, questions like these must be addressed:

- What are the goals and objectives of the course?
- Who is the audience?
- What are the specific needs of the students who will take this course?
- What are the resources?
- How can the resources be best arranged to meet the needs of the students?

- Are the requirements of the course consistent with the hybrid elements being used?
- What training is available to the instructor?
- What level of support will the instructor have to make the technology work?
- Is the system reliable for off-site students and faculty using equipment ranging from T-1 to 56 KB modems?
- How will academic needs like dealing with incompletes be handled?
- When students have difficulty with the technology, who do they call?
- Are there any course modules, assessments, and rubrics that cannot be developed in advance of the course start?

Time is a major issue in planning and carrying out effective online or hybrid courses. Palloff and Pratt (1999) calculated the time involved in both face-to-face teaching and online teaching. Their chart (Figure 2) is reproduced with an additional column representing a hybrid course that is equally divided between face-to-face and online.

Both students and instructors note the time commitment. One instructor received the following message in an e-mail from a graduate student:

| Instructor Activity | Face-to-Face Class | Online Class | Hybrid Class |
|---|---|---|---|
| Preparation | 2 hours per week to: Review assigned reading Review lecture materials Review and prepare in-class activities | 2 hours per week to: Review assigned reading Prepare discussion questions and "lecture" material in the form of a paragraph or two | 2 to 2.5 hours per week to: Review assigned reading Review lecture materials for face-to-face and/or prepare online discussion questions. Review and prepare in-class activities. |
| Class time | 2.5 hours per week of assigned class time | 2 hours *daily* to: Read student posts Respond to student posts | 1.5 hours per week of assigned class time 1 hour *daily* to: Read posts Respond to posts |
| Follow-up | 2 to 3 hours per week for: Individual contact with students Reading student assignments | 2 to 3 hours per week for: Individual contact with students via e-mail and phone Reading student assignments | 2 to 3 hours per week for: Individual contact with students in person or by e-mail and phone Reading assignments |
| Totals for the week | 6.5 to 7.5 hours per week | 18 to 19 hours per week | 10.5 to 12 hours per week |

*Note:*   Columns one through three adapted from Palloff and Pratt (1999, p. 50).

FIGURE 2
Time Comparisons for Three Models During a One Week Period

Dr. S.,

Turn that _____ WebCT off. I hate it. I've completed the final and find myself
going back into the discussions and commenting further. I am addicted. Do
you know of a 12 step program? I have never done anything like this online
and I loved it.

Lavinia

## Changing Roles for the Instructor in Hybrid Courses

Students complain about the increased workload in online and hybrid
courses, and instructors too react to those added hours. Both groups, however, generally respond very positively to taking or teaching another hybrid
course. Roles change and learning occurs.

An instructor moves from role to role while leading a face-to-face
course. One day she may be a lecturer, another a discussion leader, yet
another a supporter of student presenters. With the face-to-face and online
hybrid course the instructor assumes new roles. She moves deeper into
how students learn, and develops new assessment strategies. She finds new
ways to guide without depending on her physical presence. She manages
elements in a far more detailed fashion than entering a classroom and
teaching. She copes with technical changes and student nervousness about
the medium. Learning to be responsive when necessary and quiet when
that is the right choice; she is an active electronic learning community
builder and an excellent communicator. In both settings, the hybrid
instructor is a cheerleader, a support, and a guide.

The classroom format places the instructor in the center. Even when she
encourages discussion among class members, they tend to look to her for
approval and support. Quality hybrid courses necessitate a more fluid
arrangement regarding support. Hallmarks for hybrids using asynchronous discussion underscore varied relationships and the need for interaction between and among elements. No longer can class discussion be
teacher to student and back to teacher.

## Best Instructor Practices in Hybrid Courses

The instructor seeking to be effective in a hybrid course:

* Establishes himself as a guide, facilitator, and planner;
* Organizes the course with a schedule for all elements;

- Provides training for students in the use of the LMS and for doing Web-based research;
- Offers clear expectations regarding postings, participation, assignments, reading, including consideration of time to be spent and/or products to be created;
- Designs engaging activities, especially those online;
- Involves himself, but does not dominate;
- Provides frequent feedback using online replies, private e-mail, meetings with students, or calls;
- Gives students rubrics and other tools for self-evaluation and assessment;
- Adjusts or changes the course to take advantage of the media;
- Establishes what will be online and what will be in other media;
- Emphasizes interaction and participation;
- Encourages mentoring and support among students;
- Varies discussion questions to require depth or breadth;
- Requires research and readings to be cited in some responses;
- Develops and nurtures the electronic learning community;
- Sets the course pace;
- Tries special features and online postings before students use them;
- Establishes collaborations that mirror real world applications;
- Provides periodic summaries of face-to-face classes and online discussions;
- Conducts ongoing assessment of the course;
- Compares the quality of the hybrid course with the on-campus course during and after the course.

While seeking to provide the best possible course, the instructor also establishes time limits for himself. He cannot teach every hour of every day. Setting limits does not sacrifice quality. As the student in the e-mail mentioned earlier said, "It is addicting." Such limits also discourage over-commenting. Instructors in hybrid courses appreciate how the hybrid often can accommodate students. An effective instructor accepts that he or she cannot adjust for every student in every situation.

## Indicators of Quality in a Hybrid Course Using Asynchronous Discussion

### *Students are Part of a Community*
Many face-to-face courses have avoided the issue of developing a class community. In some, the only community that develops is the one before and after the lecture. Lecture courses promote one-way dissemination of

information. Asynchronous discussions should promote the development of a learning community with a high level of student engagement.

### Responsibilities are Shared

The students encourage and support the development of ideas and the use of civility. Students take responsibility to extend the learning done in the face-to-face sessions into the online sessions. Leadership in a discussion may come from a range of reasons including being the first to post, a recent experience with what is being discussed, an insight from the readings, a reflection connecting multiple sources, or access to additional resources. Unlike a face-to-face discussion, leadership is not the province of the frequent talker. Participants learn to question and suggest without being negative.

### Discussions Focus on Issues Central to the Essence of the Course

Questions for discussion are well conceived and planned. Questions vary in depth and breadth. They relate directly to the expected outcomes for the course. Students can see the importance of the questions and their relevance.

### Discussions are Purposeful

Students and the instructor keep the discussion moving toward deeper understanding of the subject or objective. Social discussion can take place in a "lounge" area of the discussion board established for that purpose. While the development of community is important, the community must be a learning community (Palloff & Pratt, 1999).

### Discussions Relate Directly to Lectures, Class Activities, Projects, and Readings

In well-developed courses, whether online or face-to-face, all instructional elements relate to the desired outcomes. Resources are shared between and among students. Citations supporting responses are required when appropriate. With hybrid or online courses, integration is particularly important. For students, following asynchronous discussions is time consuming. They are concerned that the time is well spent.

### Interaction is Primarily Student-to-Student and It Becomes Increasingly Collaborative

Students build on the responses of others. They share ideas. They develop synthesis. They ask each other questions. They confirm, compliment, and encourage. They develop consensus without discouraging other possibilities. The instructor remains in the background, seen, but not dominating. From time to time, the instructor will enter in to encourage or draw the discussion back to the central issues, but, if the discussion questions are well cast and the resources relevant, as the community develops, the instructor's need to guide decreases.

### Social Learning Can and Does Occur within these Discussions

Asynchronous discussions can be as caring and humane as face-to-face discussions. Within the learning community, asynchronous discussion enhances the opportunities for all students to participate and learn. Collaboration, understanding, and even social skills can be improved within these discussions.

At the end of the final face-to-face session, Bret approaches Dr. Jacobs. Bret is in his mid-forties. He has one professional degree and is seeking another in a different field. "Thanks for the class Dr. J. It really has had an effect on me. I learned a lot." Dr. Jacobs smiles. She has heard these thankyous before, often from students who imagine they could be on the bubble between an "A" and a "B."

Bret continues, "You know, the online part of the class really had an effect." Dr. Jacobs is more interested now. "If I had learned 10 years ago what I have learned online in those discussions, I might still be married."

Dr. Jacobs is puzzled. "Bret, I don't understand. We were talking about administrative problems and issues. What did you learn?"

"You know when you talk, the words just don't hang there in front of you, but online they do. See, when I say something, people react. I think what I said was mostly moderate and reasonable and the person reacting is the unreasonable one."

"OK." Dr. Jacobs is completely engaged.

"When I quickly type a response to a question or someone else's post, my words hang there. When people react, I see what they are reacting to. My words, especially early in the class, looked like I thought I knew everything and anyone who did not agree was wrong. It is good to go back and look, even days later. Did you notice how I was becoming more moderate? Even in our face-to-face sessions? Some of the comments from others really got me thinking and reflecting."

Dr. Jacobs agrees. "That will help you with leading others. But how does that relate to what you said earlier?"

Bret laughs. "She said I was too overbearing and always thought I was right. I saw in my conversation that I have that tendency and I'm working on it now."

Dr. Jacobs muses as she tells a colleague about the event. "One of our objectives in that course was to improve leadership and collaboration skills. Bret showed me how that can work online. I went back and looked at the discussions more carefully. The community came together. They learned. Bret learned."

Dr. Jacobs established a learning community in which students were supported and encouraged as learners. The course objectives were embedded in every discussion. Students assumed responsibility for supporting, encouraging, and teaching each other. Bret became part of the community, and he became a collaborator and contributor. He modified his abrasive edges and sought ways to engage in polite, meaningful conversation about issues. The high quality asynchronous discussion was effective for Bret and his colleagues. In other courses, shy students have become more outgoing after interacting online (Palloff & Pratt, 1999). The point of developing hybrid courses is to use the best tools to accomplish increased student learning.

## A CASE IN THE NOT-SO-DISTANT FUTURE

Recently, the daughter of one of the authors was married. The new son-in-law wanted his parents in Eastern Europe to see the reception and to participate. This young man bought an inexpensive Web-camera, and using a common dial-up connection, broadcast both text and visuals to dozens of relatives and friends in Europe and other areas of the world. Pictures on the Web the next day would not communicate the same level of human contact that visuals and text brought in realtime. While the situation of these parents is different from class participants, the desire for human contact was present and it was satisfied by inexpensive technology.

Currently, individual students can use the same technology to present to their class colleagues. Software to do such presentations is free or inexpensive. The cameras are reasonably priced. But what is coming? Individual student presentations to the group are good, yet not all students are sophisticated enough with loading and preparing that they can all be equally successful. The varieties of cameras, computers, and software are nearly endless and Web support at universities cannot provide enough assistance. Tomorrow will be different.

Marcus Tovar and three of his colleagues at the engineering unit on a remote U.S. Air Force facility enrolled in a graduate course on composite materials and stress testing offered by State University. Fifteen other engineers across the United States also have enrolled. The instructor is an expert in the field and he is in contact with Bert Rutan and other leaders in developing and using composite materials in aircraft. The course description notes that Rutan will be one of the discussion leaders and presenters. Marc and his colleagues wonder how that will be possible in the online course, but they are anxious to see it happen.

A week before the course begins, a package comes to Marc. He opens it. There is a small camera unit including a microphone and activation buttons, a CD-ROM, a short document titled "Quick Set-Up," and a course manual. Marc reads that the conference sessions can be done either individually or in clusters. In his written introduction, Dr. Marsdale mentions that there are three areas where multiple students work together. Dr. Marsdale suggests the clusters might start together and see how that works for them. He also suggests that everyone set up the equipment and software on their home computers.

On the CD-ROM are numerous items. First is the software for the camera unit and the interactive conferencing. Modified drafting and simulation testing software is also on the CD-ROM. The software loads without difficulty and almost immediately Marc is testing everything. It works. He calls his colleagues. Their experience is the same. Their units are working. They can do an internal test and try a short session with each other as the group. Dr. Marsdale suggested they try sending charts and simulation results. They do and find all is functional. The biggest problem the group encounters is slowing down conversation so that they are polite to each other.

Class begins with introductions. Marc was anticipating the two minute introductions so he prepared a short movie about himself and his projects. He posted it before class started as did most of the others. His is, he surmises, the best movie however. Marc and his two colleagues clip names and other data with pictures, and place the material in a class file. Marc wants to remember the individuals and thinks this will help him within the class and for future networking.

Dr. Marsdale asks the class about difficulties getting set up. Jessica reports she had an initial problem. "Working at 2:30 AM, I thought no one would be at the help desk. I was surprised. In 20 minutes I was up and running." Marsdale smiles.

"We tried to anticipate difficulties. I'll be checking with you through the course and even after about your experiences. But now, let's get into the schedule." Dr. Marsdale says the video meetings will be weekly at this particular time, but that students collaborating on a project can set additional video meetings as needed. He indicates the asynchronous discussions will be ongoing as will the active simulations and posting of animated drawings. His expectations are clear.

"There will be three guests during the semester. The first will be Burt Rutan. I know you are familiar with his work. Some of you may even fly a LongEZ kit plane. Burt will present a lecture with footage of some of his latest designs. It will begin at 7 PM next Monday. At 8:15 he will be available for your questions. For the next week, Burt will be on the asynchronous discussion board posting questions and answering yours. Please note there will be simulations and drawings assigned through the week too. Remember, this is a five unit course."

Marc and his two colleagues meet at his house for the Rutan lecture. They enjoy the stimulation of the small group. It works well. The individuals seem pleased with their involvement. By the third week, a community is developing. Marc finds three others in the class who share his interests. The group project looms on the horizon. Marc suggests the four of them get together in a video meeting to discuss project possibilities. They agree and set a time.

At lunch, Marc and his two local colleagues are discussing the differences between the early online courses and this one. Davida says, "Even if you guys were not here, I would feel like I am part of a class. The other online courses were good. They helped me complete my degree and that was critical. This one is giving me new knowledge and I feel like a person."

Support and use of effective tools must characterize the development of hybrid courses today and in the future. Technology should not impede the progress of students, but rather, enhance their learning. Tomorrow's hybrids will be user-friendly and well focused on student learning and success.

## CONCLUSIONS

Hybrid courses offer additional, effective tools to instructors. Lecture-only courses are becoming less prevalent as technology options increase and instructors become increasingly familiar with those technologies. Many universities and colleges are requiring students to take at least one online course during their program, so even campus-based students are gaining online skills. These campus-based students miss the face-to-face contact, yet they appreciate many aspects of the online courses, including the flexibility of their time. Instructors are questioning the need to meet face-to-face two or three times weekly when online sessions are highly effective. Hybrid courses are meeting these newly discovered concerns.

Universities, through their centers for teaching, are offering professional development to faculty members seeking to expand and enhance skills. Increasingly, technology skills are among the professional development opportunities. Spaces in the technology seminars are filling and additional sections are being proposed. Projects like MERLOT (www.MERLOT.ORG) offer instructors learning objects and other technology-based materials to enhance courses. Blackboard, WebCT, and other LMS developers offering sessions at conferences find their workshops filled. Instructors vie to have smart classrooms, laptops, high speed connections, access to ITV studios, and other means to develop enhanced classes. Many of these enhanced classes become hybrid courses.

Hybrid courses, in the research that has been conducted, are successful. The Research Initiative for Teaching Effectiveness at the University of Central Florida found that a "…comparison of success and withdrawal rates in courses with varying Web presence reveals that classes featuring both face-to-face and Web components achieve higher success rates than those that are fully online or face-to-face" (Dziuban & Moskal, n.d., p. 2).

Part of the reported successes may relate to instructors' using Web components with which they are comfortable and familiar. While universities and colleges have promoted and, in some cases, required, instructors to teach online, hybrid courses most often grow out of an instructor's sense of efficacy. Hybrid courses respond to questions such as:

- How can I provide the student who needs it, an opportunity to see the demonstration again and again?
- What can I do to assure all students are involved in the discussion, and not just the same few?
- How do I accommodate the students who are far from campus, and minimize their travel?
- What can we do to reach disabled students more effectively?
- How do I create a situation where a far distant student can take a course with on-campus students?
- How do I create cadres of students in remote pockets of population within our large service region?
- How do I personalize assignments and still get everyone participating?
- What means can I use to connect practice and field work to theory?
- How do I create a community of learners?
- What helps students become reflective learners?
- How do I take advantage of the Web enhancements offered by the publisher of my text?
- Why am I recreating the professional development done so well on the Web by that vendor?
- How do I get away from the read-the-chapter-and-answer-the-questions type of independent study?
- How can I make my instructional television course more interactive?
- What modes of teaching will reach the greatest numbers of students in my classes?

Establishing a learning community is central to the success of online courses and is highly important in hybrid courses that use asynchronous discussion widely. Developing community is fragile without some face-to-face contact (Palloff & Pratt, 1999). Hybrids may offer face-to-face or other forms of seemingly more personal interaction, including video-conferencing, during those critical periods of creating the learning community.

Hybrid courses can meld practice and theory in a wide variety of ways. One is through bringing in guest discussion leaders from the profession or field and having them participate in synchronous and/or asynchronous discussions for a week. Another is using the videoconference to view professional activities, combined with either a face-to-face course or one that is in a LMS. Looking at practice and participating in reflective discussions extends learning and offers a range of perspectives. Hybrid courses, however, change the teaching and learning equation. They are more centered on the student.

Faculty members are accustomed to being in control. Staying in the center of asynchronous discussions is difficult if all students are participating. Allowing and encouraging them to become a learning community is crucial to the success of the course. The solution for the instructor is to encourage students to respond to each other. Occasionally, the instructor joins in, but does not seek to dominate. The asynchronous discussion is not and cannot be a mirror of the face-to-face or synchronous discussion. It is a new and different mode of communicating and learning. "Without a legacy of tradition to overcome, faculty are more likely to experiment with new techniques" (Poindexter, Heck & Ferrarini, 2000, p. 2). The online aspect of a hybrid course can become consuming and student expectations may change in unanticipated ways. There are substantial adjustments for instructors and for students.

In a hybrid Summer session course both instructor and students find they will have times where they are traveling. Several students will miss a week, but the hybrid nature of the course was designed to accommodate those trips. Instructor Baher writes her students, sending the message to all by e-mail, "I will not be online for two days due to driving from Ohio to Arizona. I've read your posts this morning and will be back on Friday morning. Any problems, try your colleagues or the help desk." Two students express concerns in the Questions area. Other students offer suggestions. One student notes that the instructor should not be able to take two days off. Another reminds her that a traditional course would not meet every day. Friday comes and Instructor Baher is back online. She is glad it was only two days. There are 120 new posts in the asynchronous discussion from the 20 students enrolled. Instructor Baher must read them all.

Hybrid courses take more time than standard, face-to-face courses. Posting, reading, encouraging takes time. Adopting pieces from commercial sources, i.e. LMS vendors, textbook publishers, and professional development vendors with an online presence eliminates some of the initial work of establishing a course. Adopting commercial materials also may limit the instructor from pursuing areas he or she would explore in another format. During the semester or quarter, regardless of the preparation, the instructor spends intensive time checking on many online components.

Hybrid courses will continue to flourish as instructors tip from Web-enhanced courses to having a substantial portion of their courses online or using other technologies that do not require students to be together in a classroom. Some of the innovations that will contribute further to these developments include:

- Inexpensive videoconferencing that will work even with 56 KB modems and inexpensive cameras;
- Internet2 with its promise of high-bandwidth and new applications;
- Intuitive applications for students and instructors that include student portfolios, assessments, etc.;
- Course portals allowing for instant updates and simple uploads;
- Web-based student services;
- Library and research portals with embedded teaching modules to assist students, particularly those at a distance from the library, in learning to conduct research;
- Toolboxes for instructors and students that assist with developing and posting presentations and modules;
- Seamless LMSs;
- Handheld computing devices to make online available almost anywhere.

Courses that now are exclusively online will migrate to being hybrids as these and other technology tools for communication and support are refined or developed. The experience we have had with online courses underscores the profound need for community and for human experience. Exclusively online can and will work for many students, yet the human need for personal engagement remains. The desire for face-to-face or similar personal contact is high in evaluations of online courses. Distance learning needs personal touches. Hybrid courses tread a middle path. Their increasing use is caused, in part, by this need for the human touch, whether through conference calls, face-to-face, videoconferencing, or increased telephone contact by the instructor. Hybrid course growth suggests there need not be a gulf between online and face-to-face models, but a healthy exchange and fluidity of movement between the two, enriching teaching practice and benefiting students.

## REFERENCES

Brown, D. G. (Ed.) (2000). *Teaching with technology: Seventy-five instructors from eight universities tell their stories.* Bolton, MA: Anker Publishing.

Cakici, K. (2001). Distance education and what is coming next? *Information Technology & Teacher Education Annual: Proceedings of SITE 2001.* 153-54.

Chute, A. G., Thompson, M. M., & Hancock, B. W. (1999). *The McGraw-Hill Handbook of Distance Learning.* New York: McGraw-Hill.

Consortium for Educational Technology for University Systems (CETUS). (1997). Ownership of new works at the university: unbundling of rights and the pursuit of higher learning. Retrieved July 10, 2002, from *http://www.cetus.org/ownership.pdf*

Council of Regional Accrediting Commissions (2000). *Statement of commitment by the regional accrediting commissions for the evaluation of electronically offered degree and certificate programs.* Retrieved June 24, 2002, from *http://www.wiche.edu/telecom/Accrediting%20-%20Commitment.pdf*

Diaz, D. P. (1999). CD/web hybrids: Delivering multimedia to the online learner. *Journal of Educational Multimedia and Hypermedia, 8(1), 89-98.* Retrieved June 22, 2002, from http://home.earthlink.net/~davidpdiaz/LTS/html_docs/cdhybrid.htm

Dziuban, C. & Moskal, P. (n.d.). *Distributed learning program impact evaluation.* Retrieved June 29, 2002, from http://www.tltgroup.org/resources/F_Eval_Cases/UCF_DistribLearn.htm

Hawkes, M., & Romiszowski, A. (2001). Examining the reflective outcomes of asynchronous computer-mediated communication on inservice teacher development. *Journal of Technology and Teacher Education, 9(2),* 285-308.

Kumari, D. S. (2001, September). Connecting graduate students to virtual guests through asynchronous discussions—analysis of an experience. *Journal of Asynchronous Learning Networks, 5(2).* Retrieved June 24, 2002, from http://www.aln.org/alnweb/journal/jaln-vol5issue2v2.htm

Leh, A. S. C. (2002). What did we learn in the six hybrid courses? *Information Technology & Teacher Education Annual: Proceedings of SITE 2002.* 854-858.

Morrow, D. (2002). An examination of types of learner interactivity in an online professional development course. *Information Technology & Teacher Education Annual: Proceedings of SITE 2002,* 871-875.

Mouza, C., Kaplan, D., & Espinet, I. (2000). *A web-based model for online collaboration between distance learning and campus students.* WebNet 2000 World Conference on the WWW and Internet Proceedings. San Antonio, TX. (ERIC Document Reproduction Service No. ED488758).

Palloff, R. M., & Pratt, K. (1999). *Building learning communities in cyberspace: Effective strategies for the online classroom.* San Francisco: Jossey-Bass Publishers.

Parker, D. & Gemino, A. (2001, September). Inside online learning: Comparing conceptual and technique learning performance in place-based and aln formats. *Journal of Asynchronous Learning Networks, 5(2).* Retrieved June 24, 2002, from http://www.aln.org/alnweb/journal/jaln-vol5issue2v2.htm

Poindexter, S. E., Heck, B. S., & Ferrarini, T. H. (2000). Hybrid courses: Determining the effectiveness of using the internet. *TechEd 2000 Proceedings.* (ERIC Document Reproduction Service No. ED456801).

Rosen, D., & Bloom, A. (2002). Structuring distance education programs to enhance preservice teacher preparation. *Information Technology & Teacher Education Annual: Proceedings of SITE 2002,* 297-298.

Troha, F. J., (2002, May). Bulletproof instructional design: A model for blended learning. *USDLA Journal. 16(5).* Retrieved June 24, 2002, from http://www.usdla.org/html/journal/MAY02_Issue/article03.html.

Wagner, J., & Salzman, A. (2001). *Removing the boxes: Using webct to reduce differences between on-line and on-campus classes.* Paper presented at the WebCT 3rd Annual

User Conference. Retrieved June 23, 2002, from http://booboo.webct.com/2001/papers/Wagner.pdf.

Western Cooperative for Educational Telecommunications (n.d.). *Best practices for electronically offered degree and certificate programs.* Retrieved June 24, 2002, from http://www.wiche.edu/telecom/Accrediting%20-%20Practices.pdf.

Willis, B. (2002). The guiding assumptions of successful distance education programs. *Information Technology & Teacher Education Annual: Proceedings of SITE 2002.* 326-329.

CHAPTER 3

# BUILDING ELECTRONIC COMMUNITIES FOR DISTANCE LEARNERS
## Beyond the Course Level

**David Brigham**

Colleges and universities tend to organize electronic communities of distance learners around individual courses rather than around programs. This chapter encourages administrators of distance learning programs to create electronic communities of distance learners that extend beyond the course level. By organizing institutional resources around degree programs or schools, administrators can foster a sense of community among distance learners, faculty, and staff. This sense of community can enrich students' educational experiences and facilitate progress toward degree completion. The author identifies key issues and challenges administrators must address as they design, develop, and implement electronic communities for distance learners. The chapter includes four examples of colleges and universities that are addressing these issues and challenges today. These examples include two electronic communities developed at Excelsior College, one at Empire State College, and one at the University of Texas Austin and Arlington. The author identifies future trends and opportunities of emerging technologies and discusses the implications of creating electronic communities beyond the course level. He also identifies research opportunities.

Electronic Learning Communities—Issues and Practices, pages 73–134.
Copyright © 2003 by Information Age Publishing, Inc.
All rights of reproduction in any form reserved.
ISBN: 1-931576-96-3 (pbk.), 1-931576-97-1 (hardcover)

**KEYWORDS:**   electronic communities, online communities, distance learning, support services, distance learners

Creating a sense of community among distance learners separated by barriers of time and distance poses challenges for colleges and universities with distance learning programs. Unlike students enrolled in traditional campus-based educational programs, distance students do not experience face-to-face interaction with their instructors, classmates, and others associated with the campus. Nor do distance learners experience many aspects of campus-based study such as visiting a campus bookstore, attending college social functions and educational events, or attending college sporting events. Viewed in this way, the challenges of creating a sense of community among distance learners seem daunting. However, as student access to the Internet becomes the norm (Nesler, 2001) and as distance learning programs expand, these challenges become more manageable, if not achievable.

Crucial to a discussion of community building in distance education is a consideration of what constitutes an electronic community within the context of distance learning programs established by institutions of higher education. Are electronic communities of distance learners different from the countless numbers of electronic communities that have sprouted in the wide-open spaces of the Internet every day for the last decade (Rheingold, 1993)? These groups typically form around shared interests. What are the shared interests of distance learners? What should be the organizing factor around which to build an electronic community—a course, a program, a department, a school, or an institution? How should administrators responsible for overseeing distance learning programs define community for their distance learners?

For the most part, colleges and universities have organized and continue to organize electronic communities of distance learners around individual courses rather than around programs, departments, or schools. At the course level, the primary focus is on creating electronic environments that help students acquire subject matter knowledge and skills. These environments are commonly referred to as *learning communities*. Resources are available (Palloff & Pratt, 2001) that encourage instructors to use a variety of techniques to create learning communities within online courses. In addition, learning management systems such as Blackboard or WebCT include built-in Web-based tools such as discussion boards, chatrooms, and class directories that enable instructors to fashion learning communities tailored to each course and the unique needs of students who enroll in that course.

From an educational perspective attempting to establish a learning community in an online course is a laudable goal. Students and instructors are able to enrich each other's learning through collaboration and interaction for the life of the course. However, for the most part, when the course ends, so does the community. Even though a few relationships established among learners may continue privately after the course is over, for all intents and purposes most relationships among students end as soon as the learning community is disbanded. When students enroll in their next course, the process begins again, presumably with a new instructor and a new set of classmates.

Since establishing an ongoing sense of community among distance learners is not likely to happen at the course level, administrators need to explore alternative approaches to organizing electronic communities. These approaches should enable distance learners to form long-term relationships with fellow students, faculty, and staff and permit them to continue to reap the benefits of membership in an academic community long after they have completed their programs. The purpose of this chapter is to encourage distance educators to consider building electronic communities by organizing institutional resources around programs, departments, or schools and to discuss the issues they may face should they decide to venture down this road.

## Chapter Objectives

This chapter has the following objectives:

1. To introduce and provide examples of electronic communities of distance students at the school and program levels.
2. To identify issues and challenges in designing and developing an electronic community for distance students.
3. To show how colleges and universities are addressing these issues and challenges.
4. To identify future trends and opportunities of emerging technologies.
5. To discuss the implications of creating an electronic community beyond the course level, and to identify research opportunities.

## Approach

The five sections of this chapter follow the order of the chapter objectives. The chapter begins with a brief look at two electronic communities of distance in a college setting, one at the school level and the other at the program level. I have used these examples (and others) throughout the chapter to inform issues, discuss problems and solutions, and to suggest guidelines for practitioners and future researchers. The issues I have identified in this chapter emerge, in part, from my experiences designing, developing, implementing, and evaluating Excelsior College's Electronic Peer Network. Therefore these issues are firmly grounded in practice. I have also included examples of electronic communities from Empire State College and the University of Texas TeleCampus.

## Electronic Communities at the School and Program Levels

The Excelsior College Electronic Peer Network [http://gl.excelsior.edu] was instituted by Excelsior College [http://www.excelsior.edu] in 1998 to provide Excelsior College undergraduates with a means to interact academically and socially as they advance towards educational, career, and personal goals. The Electronic Peer Network (EPN) is an illustration of an electronic community organized on the school level. In February 2002 Excelsior College established the Masters in Liberal Studies (MLS) Electronic Peer Network [http://gl.excelsior.edu/MLS], an electronic community organized on the program level. (Public access to the EPN and MSL/EPN Websites is limited as many areas are password protected.)

A brief description of the institutional context that gave rise to the EPN and MLS/EPN is necessary to understand the features and components included in them. Excelsior College (formerly Regents College) is a regionally accredited, private, nontraditional institution designed for working adults who choose to complete their college degrees in a self-paced, portable manner. The College has an administrative staff of 250 with headquarters in Albany, New York. Excelsior College has no campus or classrooms. With an enrollment of about 18,000 students Excelsior College awards degrees in 32 programs at the associate and baccalaureate levels in business, liberal arts, nursing, and technology, and at the masters level in liberal studies and nursing.

The College serves students at the undergraduate level through the assessment of prior learning, academic advising, learning support services, educational brokering of courses, and credit-by-examination. Undergraduate students earn credits toward their degrees in many ways but primarily by taking Excelsior College examinations, transferring credits from regionally accredited institutions, or using faculty-evaluated collegiate training programs from business, industry, and the United States military. Although the College does not offer its own courses at the undergraduate level, it provides a full range of courses at the graduate level for the Masters in Liberal Studies and Master of Science in Nursing programs.

Residing in 50 states and several countries, Excelsior College students have not historically had convenient access to fellow students for academic and emotional support, nor have they had opportunities to engage in collaborative learning. In fact, prior to the establishment of the EPN, many students completed their degree programs without ever having had contact with another Excelsior College student. Data from student surveys conducted by the College suggested consistently that students felt isolated, and to facilitate progress in their programs they wanted to interact with other students. (Brigham,1998). However, attempts by the College to form learning networks by distributing paper directories containing contact information (phone and postal mailing addresses) failed to link more than a few hundred students. Attempts in the early 1990s to link students with an electronic bulletin board also failed to establish the level of participation sought by the College. However, the advent of the World Wide Web and its subsequent growth provided an opportunity for the College to link students successfully.

The first version of the EPN opened in May 1998 with 31 students. Since then the EPN has grown steadily to a community of over 9,000 distance students. The current EPN is organized around the schools of business, liberal arts, nursing, and technology, each with its own homepage,

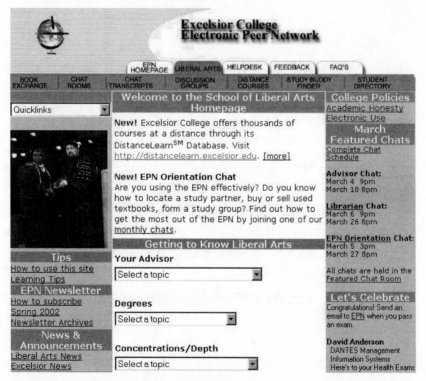

FIGURE 1
The Electronic Peer Network Homepage for the Excelsior College
School of Liberal Arts

customized to meet student and program needs. Figure 1 provides a view of the EPN homepage for the Excelsior College School of Liberal Arts as it appeared in March 2002.

Excelsior College liberal arts students access the Liberal Arts homepage through the main EPN homepage [http://gl.excelsior.edu] by clicking on the Liberal Arts tab. They enter their username and password and arrive at the Liberal Arts homepage (see Figure 1) where they can select from an array of resources. By clicking on the toolbar links at the top of this page,

FIGURE 2
The Electronic Peer Network Homepage for the
Master in Liberal Arts Program

students can access the book exchange to buy used books from other students (or sell their own), participate in synchronous chats (facilitated and unfacilitated), and join asynchronous discussion groups (academically or socially oriented). From the toolbar links they may also access thousands of distance courses from regionally accredited institutions, form a study group (via *STUDY BUDDY FINDER*), or obtain information from the student directory. In addition, students can access an array of links providing program and career information, learning tips, or post a note celebrating a recent achievement (see *Let's Celebrate* in the right column of the page). Section 2 of this chapter provides more details on the EPN features.

The Excelsior College Masters in Liberal Studies (MLS) EPN Homepage (see Figure 2) incorporates most of the features of the EPN, but these features are organized at the program level rather than the school level. One of the differences in the MLS/EPN homepage is the presence of a Bulletin Board and a Lotus LearningSpace tab on the tool bar near the top of the page. The Bulletin Board button links to an informal asynchronous discussion area, and the LearningSpace tab links to MLS online courses. (LearningSpace is the learning management system used by Excelsior for Web courses.) Students taking Web courses participate in course level online communities designed for each course. Thus, online course environments are integrated into a broader electronic community organizational structure. In addition to these differences between the EPN and MLS/EPN homepages, the area below the welcome area contains program information organized by the three program tiers of the MLS program, and an additional area established to make students aware of professional organizations related to Liberal Studies.

The Excelsior College EPN and MLS/EPN Websites provide illustrations of electronic communities organized on a broader level than the course level. However, it is the interaction among students and the relationships they establish within these Websites that define a community.

Palloff and Pratt (1999, p. 32) associate the following outcomes with the presence of an online community:

- Active interaction involving both course content and personal communication.
- Collaborative learning evidenced by comments directed primarily student to student rather than student to instructor.
- Socially constructed meaning evidenced by agreement or questioning, with the intent to achieve agreement on issues of meaning.
- Sharing of resources among students.
- Expressions of support and encouragement exchanged between students, as well as willingness to critically evaluate the work of others.

Palloff's and Pratt's outcomes are intended as indicators of community established within an online course environment. Nevertheless, these indicators are also useful at the program level or higher, although the focus changes. Within a course the focus is on organizing a learning community around a specific, well-defined subject area. On a program or school level, the focus broadens well beyond a particular course as students share resources associated with several courses within a degree program or several degree programs within a school.

Student messages posted on the EPN in discussion groups, chatrooms, book exchange, and *STUDY BUDDY FINDER* provide a wealth of evidence that the outcomes identified by Palloff and Pratt are being achieved. However, a broader framework (see Figure 3) that subsumes Palloff's and Pratt's outcomes better align with the purposes of the EPN. This framework includes four types of linked outcomes: academic interaction, social interaction, information sharing, and resource sharing. But even this broad framework does not capture fully the essence of the EPN community since interactions among students invariably involve a mixture of these four elements. The best way to capture the sense of community generated by the EPN is by including student comments speaking directly to this topic.

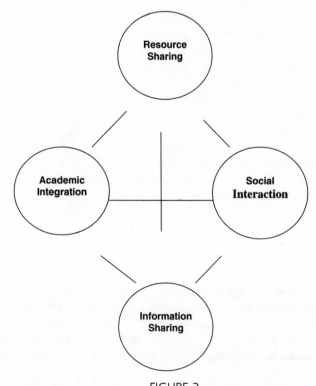

FIGURE 3
Outcomes Framework for the Excelsior College Electronic Peer Network

***Student One:***

As an Excelsior College BSN student who joined the college almost two years ago, I've been extremely blessed to now have the EPN to utilize for peer student communication. Most students like myself are used to a classroom setting in which to learn; joining Excelsior made the learning and self-discipline much more structured. Prior to having the EPN, there were times where I felt very alone, had questions or anxiety I needed answered or released, but had really no peer access. Now with the EPN, I log on several times during the day, communicate with other nursing students about studying, upcoming tests, give moral support, and relieve many of the normal college stressors.

Another big asset the EPN has brought to myself is a way to meet other students like myself, who are striving to achieve goals while maintaining busy jobs and lives. Many of my college colleagues call or e-mail me and we discuss and support each other and give advice on exams and clinical tests, and we also support each other when we have personal downfalls or stressors in our lives.

Student One's comments suggest the existence of most of the outcomes Palloff and Pratt associate with the presence of an online community, particularly the last regarding "expressions of support and encouragement exchanged between students." Student One says that he "felt very alone" and experienced "anxiety" and indicated that he communicates with other students to receive "support." His comments also suggest his behavior provides evidence of Palloff's and Pratt's "active interaction" and "collaborative learning" outcomes. Student One's comments also fall into three of the outcomes areas identified in the Outcomes Framework for the Electronic Peer Network (see Figure 3), namely academic interaction, social interaction, and information sharing.

The comments of Student Two also reflect Palloff's and Pratt's outcomes. Student Two made these comments as student speaker at Excelsior College's commencement exercises in 2000. Her comments are extracted from her prepared speech to her fellow graduates.

***Student Two:***

One of the most significant challenges to earning a degree through our virtual university is our isolation from each other. We are taking the same tough courses that other students take in their university classrooms, and prepare for in their study groups, but we are doing it on our own. But through the Electronic Peer Network on the Regents Website we've found a way to overcome this sense of being disconnected. Through the EPN I found support from all of you when I needed you. When I was studying for one particularly difficult exam, I sent an e-mail to virtually everyone listed as having an interest in that area. I got lots of great responses, which helped me focus my studies, understand where I was lacking, and get questions answered when there was no one else to ask. I also passed this advice on to others who needed assistance, and heard back that it was helpful to them as well. Sometimes, the help I needed was available on the message boards—from finding a particular course, to finding a desperately needed textbook; my fellow students provided great advice on the EPN. Even at a distance, we created a valuable community.

In this virtual community I've met many remarkable students. These new friends include Holger from Germany, who had to put off his studies for a year when he was called up to serve in Kosovo. I met Beth from North Carolina, who has found a management job after serving as a clerk throughout her career, because she did not have a degree, even though she was in the position of teaching her supervisors their own jobs. I've spoken to Diana from right here in Albany, who recently got her dream job and her diploma almost simultaneously. I also corresponded with Susan who is going on to study for an MBA this fall, while living and working in Dubai. And although I live in California, I swapped textbooks with Ken in Florida, who works nights at the Orlando airport and studies days to finish his program as quickly as possible.

Student Two's comments suggest active interaction and collaboration of an academic and personal nature among students from around the globe. Her comments indicate that the relationships she was able to establish were more than casual as she refers to her fellow students as "new friends" and provides details of important personal aspects of their lives. Her comments also indicate that EPN students are learning, in part, by collaborating with each other (beyond the context of a course), sharing resources and information, and providing mutual support and encouragement. Like Student One, Student Two acknowledges feelings of isolation associated with distance learning and attributes the EPN with providing a means to overcome these feelings.

To fully appreciate the significance of Student Three's comments (below), the context in which they were made must be explained. The EPN has a discussion group called "Don't Drop Out." Students contemplating dropping out of their program post messages in this area, presumably as a plea for help from their peers. When students see a post in this discussion area, they respond quickly with encouraging comments and offers of help. Student Three's words of encouragement were written in response to a student who had posted a plea for help in "Don't Drop Out." However, Student Three's comments take on an additional dimension because a year earlier she had written a similar plea for help herself when she was planning to drop out of her program. Exchanges of motivational support of the type illustrated by Student Three (and other EPN members) have implications for the design of interventions to promote course and program completion of distance learners.

*Student Three:*

> Regents students are very special people. You see, we are individuals who
> don't give up. We continue, and continue, and continue. We are doing it the
> hard way. The Regents Nursing Program is extremely tough. You absolutely
> can't fake your way through this one and when you finally complete your
> studies, you will not only feel extremely proud, but you will definitely "know
> your stuff." You will be ready to take charge and the medical establishment
> really highly recognizes the Regents graduate for we are self-starters, motiva-
> tors, know how to get things done in a timely manner, very disciplined, and
> make the best charge nurse. Hey, my first nursing job after completing my
> ASN, I was hired as Nurse Supervisor over a Geriatric Psych Unit and skill
> hall. I felt more than prepared to take on the tasks. It's difficult but the
> Regents training helped me. It will help you. Anything worth having always
> takes time, effort, and determination. So don't give up. Try, try, again.
> Remember, you too can do it. Good luck to you!

A closer look at Student Three's language suggests that she (and presumably others) are developing an identity as "Regents students." Student
Three identifies what she perceives as shared values or attributes of
Regents students. These include persistence ("we are individuals who don't
give up"), initiative ("we are self-starters"), task oriented ("get things done
in a timely manner"), disciplined, and professionally competent. Student
Three's comments also indicate pride in being affiliated with her college
("the medical establishment really recognizes the Regent graduate"). Even
though it is highly unlikely that Student Three has had any face-to-face
contact with another Regents College (except briefly during her clinical
examination), she apparently is able to identify with her fellow students
and her college. In short, her comments suggest that she has formed an
attachment to her electronic community and the College.

The Excelsior College EPN and MLS/EPN constitute two examples of
electronic communities organized beyond the course level. I have
included these examples for purposes of illustration. I am not suggesting
they be viewed as models to be imitated. (Additional examples of electronic communities at the program level appear in the next two sections of
this chapter.) Nor do I wish to imply that colleges and universities should
abandon or decrease their efforts to provide dynamic learning communities within courses. On the contrary, distance learners need to experience
electronic environments that foster a sense of belonging and connection
to each other and to the college on as many levels as possible.

I have provided a snapshot of two electronic communities established
for distance learners, and I have indicated how students use and value
them. However, many issues and challenges have to be addressed to design
and build supportive online environments. The next section of this chapter addresses these issues and challenges.

## ISSUES AND CHALLENGES

Designing, developing, implementing, and maintaining an electronic community of distance learners requires substantial time, energy, resources, and institutional commitment. This process requires distance learning program administrators to make choices, often with insufficient information, and at times to move the project forward with insufficient resources. Program administrators are likely to become immersed quickly in the project and at a greater level of detail than they had planned, from needs assessment through implementation and ongoing maintenance (Brigham, 1998). Moreover, many issues and problems that surface along the way carry the potential for delaying or derailing the project. By being aware of these issues ahead of time, administrators should be better prepared to address them.

The purpose of this section is to identify and discuss key issues associated with developing electronic communities of distance learners, particularly adults, at the program level or higher. This section begins with a discussion of three key macro-level issues: community definition, program selection, and project management. The choices administrators make regarding these front-end decisions have significant implications for the short and long-term success of the community. The remainder of this section discusses the many issues (e.g., identity vs. anonymity of community members) that administrators must face during the design and development phases of the community. Decisions regarding these issues will influence heavily the character and activity of the community.

### Macro-level Issues and Challenges: Community Definition

Identifying distance learners with a compelling need for academic and social support is a key issue. The level of interaction and participation in the electronic community (and therefore the success or failure of that community) will depend, in part, on how this community is defined. Therefore, it is imperative that administrators carefully identify the needs of various populations of distance learners to ensure that participation in an electronic community will met their needs.

Other factors being equal, the more compelling the student need for support, the greater the likelihood of building a successful electronic community. At the program level, administrators can look at preliminary indicators that suggest a compelling need for interaction among students, faculty, and staff. Programs that have capstone examinations or professional certification examinations may be good candidates because high-stakes examinations generate a high level of anxiety for adult learners studying at a distance. Sharing examination preparation materials, trading study tips, and participating in examination study groups are activities that can help alleviate pre-examination anxiety. In addition, interaction with advisors, faculty, staff, and students who have passed the examination further contributes to anxiety reduction and builds student confidence.

Interactions on Excelsior College's Electronic Peer Network provide evidence that high stakes examinations can be fertile ground for growing an electronic community. A review of the level of interaction of various groups of students on Excelsior College's EPN indicates that nursing students preparing for the Clinical Performance Examination in Nursing (CPNE) have historically been the most active students on the EPN. The CPNE is a two-day examination that takes place in a hospital setting so that nursing professionals can assess student knowledge and skills as they care for real patients. The financial costs to students who prepare for and take the CPNE may involve two to three thousand dollars spent on workshops, examination fees, and travel expenses. From a student perspective, preparing for and taking the CPNE is an expensive proposition. Moreover, the consequences of failing the CPNE go beyond the loss of time and resources invested in preparation since students must pass the CPNE to obtain their associates degree. These factors make the CPNE a high stakes examination. It is not surprising that students preparing for this examination seek support from others. They attend more EPN chat sessions, post more discussion group questions, use more EPN features (such as *STUDY BUDDY FINDER*), and visit more HTML pages than any other group of students on the EPN (M. Gabrielsen, personal communication, March 29, 2002).

Other indicators that may suggest a compelling student need for support include programs that have high dropout rates or decreasing enrollments, programs with many and varied avenues to degree completion, and programs that have internships or fieldwork components. Indicators of compelling need such as these suggest a starting point when considering programs likely to benefit most from the establishment of an electronic community. However, only a thorough needs assessment involving major stakeholders of candidate programs will produce an appropriate statement of student needs.

When identifying distance learners most likely to benefit from participating in an electronic community, it is also important to take into account the potential size and scope of that community. Other factors being equal, more interaction will occur in a community with more members than with fewer. In fact, certain activities or features of electronic communities such as open, unscheduled chatrooms may require a critical mass to function well. For example, an ongoing problem experienced by students using the Excelsior College EPN is that students often fail to find someone present in the open chatrooms when they login. EPN chat transcripts indicate students frequently miss each other by minutes. Having a greater number of

EPN members would increase the likelihood of students meeting each other in the chatrooms. The issue of scope comes into play when deciding how broadly to define a community. In general, the more broadly an electronic community is defined (e.g., at the school rather than the program level), the less likely students are to have similar academic interests and needs. Although Website organization can, in part, help to bring students with common interests together (e.g., providing homepages for each program), the problem of providing resources to support each program mushrooms. On the other hand, defining a program more broadly provides a potentially greater number of participants in the community thereby increasing the chances for interaction. The goal is to create a balance between size and scope.

## Macro-level Issues and Challenges: Program Selection

Selecting a program or programs around which to build an electronic community is a key issue that involves more than a consideration of student need. While compelling student need is a necessary condition for success, it is not sufficient to ensure success. Several additional conditions must be present to design, develop, and implement an electronic community in a higher education setting. The degree to which these conditions are present should play a key role in selecting a participating program.

The professional literature provides insight and guidance in identifying the conditions that promote program improvement in higher education. Robert Diamond (1998) identifies two factors that determine whether a project should be undertaken: "The project must meet the academic priorities established for the institution, and there should be good reasons to believe it will succeed" (p. 31). The distance learning administrator should obtain documentation and verification from the department dean or equivalent administrator that shows how well building an electronic community of distance learners aligns with institutional and departmental goals. Without strong alignment it is unlikely that the project will receive the resources and commitment necessary to carry out and sustain it. The technological character of electronic communities and the current emphasis of colleges and universities to maximize technology, particularly the Internet, to deliver and support instructional programs make this alignment more probable than in the past.

Diamond (1989, pp.37-38) suggests that educators use the following questions to guide them through the project selection process:

1. Is the project needed?
2. Is the academic area stable?
3. What is the potential for success?

4. Does the agency have the necessary resources available?
5. Are there political factors that should be considered?

Just as undertaking a thorough needs assessment involving data collection from program stakeholders is an essential input into the project selection process, so is determining the stability of the program under consideration. If the program is in danger of discontinuation, the establishment and continuation of an electronic community would be at risk. In general, programs in a state of flux (e.g., experiencing key personnel changes) or in decline should be avoided until stability is achieved, and the outlook for long-term growth is assured.

Determining the potential for the success of an educational project involves several factors, particularly the level of commitment of the dean, faculty, and staff who will be involved with the design, development, implementation, and ongoing support of the electronic community. Department staff must understand the commitment they will be asked to make in terms of time, resources, and energy during all phases of the project, including its continuation and expansion. Determining the commitment level of technical staff within or outside of the academic department is also necessary. The program-selection decision must take into account political factors. What is the priority level of this project within the department and at higher administrative levels? If the project runs into trouble and requires more resources, is someone available at a high enough level and with enough power to smooth the way to project completion?

In selecting a program or programs around which to build an electronic community, distance learning administrators should consider factors that may affect the potential for diffusion to other programs or schools within the college. Establishing and maintaining an electronic community on a program level is likely to be experienced as an innovation by program and department staff. By being aware of the key principles of the diffusion of innovations, the administrator can try to enhance the prospects for diffusion to other programs throughout the institution.

Based on extensive research, Everett Rogers (1971) has identified five characteristics of innovation that explain the rate at which innovations are adopted: relative advantage, compatibility, complexity, trialability, and observability (pp.15-16). Within the context of program selection, the most relevant is observability. Rogers defines observability as "the degree to which the results of an innovation are visible to others," and explains that "the easier it is for individuals to see the results of an innovation, the more likely they are to adopt" (p.16). It follows that the distance learning administrator should try to situate the electronic community in an environment where it will be highly visible to the rest of the institution. This may mean building the electronic community around a program that regularly receives recognition for excellence within and outside the college. The more positive recognition the program receives, the more the electronic community will receive. However, visibility carries with it a risk. If the electronic community fails to realize its potential, that failure will also be highly visible and will make it more difficult to implement a revised version elsewhere once problem areas have been addressed.

After reviewing and weighing the factors and conditions associated with successful project development, the distance learning administrator must select the program around which to develop the electronic community. If a candidate program cannot be found that satisfies these selection criteria, the project should not go forward. However, once these criteria have been met, planning the project can begin in earnest.

## Macro-level Issues and Challenges: Project Management

Designing, developing, and implementing an electronic community of distance learners is a complex project requiring a coordinated effort of a team of professionals working together with a common, clear purpose over an extended period of time. The distance learning administrator bears the primary responsibility for organizing the project on a macro level and seeing that it is carried out efficiently and effectively. For all intents and purposes, this person is the project leader.

The professional literature contains many detailed models (Diamond, 1989; Greer, 1992; Gustafson & Branch, 1997; Piskurich, 2000) for managing projects involving educational technology. While these detailed models have been developed for a variety of purposes and settings, they share common elements that provide guidance to project leaders. These include planning, designing, developing, implementing, and evaluating a project.

### Planning the Project

The project leader and the key administrator of the program selected to participate in the project need to meet regularly to plan the project. They must establish ownership of the project and clarify their roles in the decision-making process. They must also prepare a document that defines clearly and concisely the purpose, scope, goals, and objectives of the project. They must talk to key players, particularly the chief administrator in charge of technology, to identify and coordinate resources for the project, and to faculty and staff who are opinion leaders. Rogers' (1983) work on the diffusion of innovations suggests that opinion leaders help to facilitate change. These preliminary discussions should produce a tentative project schedule, a project budget, a list of project team members with roles and responsibilities defined, and an agenda for the project kickoff meeting.

The kickoff meeting is a crucial meeting that will set the tone for the rest of the project. The goal of this meeting is to provide project participants with a clear understanding of the purpose, goals, objectives, and scope of the project, team member roles and responsibilities, and a project schedule. The meeting also gives participants a chance to provide feedback on the current project plan and to make suggestions for improving it. Participants should leave the meeting with a clear sense of how the project will unfold as well as a definition of their roles in the project. The meeting should also generate a sense of excitement about the next phase of the project.

### Designing the Project

The project team must prepare a detailed set of design specifications that will serve as a blueprint for the development of the Website and resources necessary to support it. These specifications should be firmly based on the assessment of student needs. During the design phase of the project, useful guiding questions are: What do students want to be able to do and when do they want to be able to do it? The answers to these questions will determine Website features and content. Of course, in addition to student needs, program administrators, faculty, and staff needs must be included.

In the early stages of the design process, it is important to aim high so that ideas are not excluded at the outset that may have been achievable if they had been included. Diamond (1989) suggests that the first attempts at creating a design should be to design for the ideal; that is, to create an ideal program without being limited by existing resources or practicalities. Arriving at an ideal design may take several meetings, as this process is creative (requiring time for incubation and reflection) and iterative. After the ideal design has been completed, if necessary, it can be adjusted to fit reality. If some features cannot be included in the current design, they should be reserved for consideration in the future when conditions may change (e.g., better technology) so that they become feasible.

As work progresses on the design, it will become increasing detailed and the project manager will need to face several issues such as access, privacy, security, and technology. The technical members of the team will continually lay out an array of options to the project manager and ask for guidance. In many cases, the project manager will need to consult with the project leader, program administrator, and other key players before proceeding. (These issues are discussed later in this section of the chapter.)

### Developing the Project

The development phase begins when the design specifications have been completed. The Web developer on the team will set up a test environment accessible by project team members. This phase of the project can be quite labor-intensive for the project team and leader as the Web developer offers various Website designs and requests feedback from graphics, color selection, and layout. Project managers and leaders often underestimate the amount of involvement they will have to devote to approving various aspects of the design and development of the Website. However, if the project leader's involvement is minimized, costly re-work may have to be done if changes are needed later. One technique that is used to avoid or minimize reworking is rapid prototyping. Rapid prototyping involves taking one piece of a design and developing it completely with all the features of the finished product, and then field-testing it with end-users (Piskurich, 2000). Developers tweak this piece, field-test it again and continue this cycle until it has been perfected. These features are incorporated into the development of the rest of the design. The development of navigation buttons on Web pages lends itself to this approach since once the buttons have been tested, they can be made into templates that apply to all or most of the pages of a Website.

Extensive field-testing of the Website with internal staff and student volunteers is vital before making the site available to students in general. Field-testing should include testing all processes associated with the Website including registration and password support, and backup systems. In addition, users with varying levels of online experience and users with different types of modems, browsers, and computer configurations should test each feature. This type of testing will help to minimize problems when the Website opens. During the later stages of development, testing should be done on the actual server that will be used when the URL is given out to students.

### Implementing the Project

After field-testing of the Website has been completed and the project team is satisfied that everything is in place and working properly, the project leader can give approval to go live. It is especially important that all staff associated with maintaining the Website as well as backup personnel be available during the first week of operation to monitor Website performance and to give help to students using the site.

## Design and Development Issues and Challenges

During the design and development stages of creating an electronic community, the project administrator, in conjunction with the program administrator, will face many issues that will influence heavily the character of the community and its development. These issues typically surface during consultations with technical staff who want to know how to set security parameters and configure the software for the Website. For example, technical staff may ask if students should be able to create their own username, whether usernames or e-mail addresses should appear when students post messages, whether students should be able to edit and delete their own messages, setup their own discussion categories, or have access to view other students' directory information. To technical staff the answers to these questions become design specifications necessary to move the project forward. To project and program administrators, however, answering these questions (and a dizzying array of similar questions throughout the design and development process), involves coming rapidly to grips with fundamental issues that have implications for all prospective community members.

### Identity vs. Anonymity

One of the most basic issues that project administrators must address before the registration component of the Website can be built is whether community members will have their real identities revealed to others using the Website. Answering this question involves deciding whether students registering for the Website will have the ability to create fictional usernames instead of using their real names. Discussion and chat software automatically display student usernames on messages posted in chat and discussion areas. Therefore, students who create fictional usernames when they register are able to keep their real names from being displayed on messages they post. The decision an administrator makes on this issue can affect the types of messages posted and the tone of the discussion because people act differently under conditions of anonymity than they do when their identify is known.

When users are allowed to create their own usernames, they are likely to behave in a much less inhibited away. Donath (1999) found this to be true in his analysis of the relationship between anonymity and computer behavior in Usenet groups. Coates (1998) thinks about this issue as a tradeoff in which conditions of anonymity lead, in part, to "greater safety" and "more freedom," while conditions of identity lead to "commitment" and a "greater likelihood that people will be truthful with each other" (p. 5). Axelrod (1984) identifies the ability of people to be able to identify each other as one of three conditions necessary for cooperation. However, in spite of an expressed preference towards having people declare their identify in electronic environments, Coates (1998) describes a case in which a member of an electronic community used another community member's e-mail address to discover the location of their residence and to make "uninvited visits" (p. 5). After this incident, Coates said he instituted a system that allowed members to use fictitious usernames and e-mail addresses on the condition that members use them consistently.

### Privacy and Security

The level of privacy and security provided to community members is another important issue that project and program administrators must address. It is useful to think about two types of privacy and security. One involves protecting community members from the world external to the electronic community, while the other involves protecting community members within the community environment.

Colleges and university are legally obligated to maintain information about students in a safe, secure environment and must follow strict guidelines and regulations designed to protect students' rights to privacy. These include guidelines established by the American Association of Collegiate Registrars and Admissions Officers (AACRAO) and the Association of Records Managers and Administrators (ARMA), and regulations included in the Family Educational Rights and Privacy Act (FERPA). While these guidelines and regulations were developed before the advent of the Web, they apply equally to Web environments. Project administrators must ensure that the electronic community they are building enjoys the same level of security (i.e., encryption, firewalls, redundancy) as other Websites at the college. In addition, administrators should look for opportunities to communicate the level of security built into the Website. This information can help to reassure students who are reluctant to give out information such as social security numbers over the Web as a part of the registration process. In fact, even with this assurance provided, some students may still refuse to register online. For example, students must use their social security numbers and birth dates to join the EPN. Since the establishment of the EPN in 1998 two students have asked to be registered manually to avoid "putting their social security on the Web." One wonders how many prospective EPN members may not have joined because of this requirement.

Deciding what information to request from students when they join the electronic community and how much of that information will be displayed to other community members is another issue that project and program administrators must address. On one hand, a certain amount of basic information such as students' names and e-mail addresses may seem reasonable to request from students at the time of registration. On the other hand, how much more information may be collected (and for what purposes) without violating student expectations for privacy, particularly if this information is displayed in a student directory accessible by others? In addition, program administrators will quickly realize that there is an opportunity to ask questions at the time of registration that may enhance the value of the Website to community members.

### Rules, Policies, and Procedures

Establishing rules, policies, and procedures for a new electronic community poses a challenge for project and program administrators. Administrators must ensure that the rules and policies they develop are aligned with current institutional practice and that the procedures provide a useful operational framework for the community. Three key areas deserve special attention: the permission statement, an academic honesty policy state-ment, and an electronic use policy.

The *permission statement* is a means for an institution to address issues of privacy and confidentiality. It should state clearly what information will be collected during the registration process and who will have access to it. The permission statement should also state who will have access to student mes-sages posted on the Website and for what purposes. If information posted on the Website will be used for institutional research, this should also be included in the permission statement. After reading the statement, students should be given a chance to accept the statement, not to accept it, and/or to ask for more information from the institution. Because of the legal impli-cations associated with the use of student information, legal council should approve the permission statement before it is implemented.

An institution's *academic honesty policy* is another area deserving special attention. Given the ease with which students can share information on the Web and the expectation of Web users to share information freely, it is cru-cial that administrators make students aware of the institution's academic honesty policy, particularly as the policy relates to electronic environments. It is important that students be required to agree to abide by the academic honesty policy as part of the registration process. Administrators should review the most recent version of their institution's academic honesty pol-icy to see if it specifically mentions cheating by electronic means. If it does not, the policy should be revised and updated.

An institution's *electronic use policy* is another key policy that administra-tors should review or develop and incorporate into the registration pro-cess. An electronic use policy communicates the institution's position on using the Internet as a learning resource, and provides a framework for guiding, and ultimately for monitoring student behavior while online. An electronic use policy should define clearly appropriate and inappropriate online behavior for students and specify the consequences that will result when students violate the policy. Little should be left to students' imagina-tions regarding what they are and are not allowed to do on the institution's Website.

If an institution does not have an electronic use policy, the program administrator may find it expedient to prepare one specifically for the new electronic community so that it can be used as a basis for developing one for the whole institution. In fact, Excelsior College used this approach. The College developed a specific policy for the EPN and then modified and expanded it to apply to all online activities in which students might be engaged at the institution.

### Monitoring and Evaluating the Website

Moore (1999) argues that an effective monitoring and evaluation system is necessary for a successful distance education program. Although

Moore's comments were intended to refer primarily to the instructional and course management aspects of distance learning programs, they also apply to electronic communities where an effective monitoring and evaluation system is necessary for success. The challenge posed to program administrators is to identify which aspects of the electronic community will be monitored, by whom, when, and how often. They must also decide what will be done with the information generated by monitoring.

One of the purposes of monitoring an electronic community is to ensure that community members comply with the academic honesty and electronic use policies. Violations of the academic honesty policy must be discovered quickly and addressed immediately. Procedures should be in place so that staff monitoring the Website can also bring borderline violations to the attention of the appropriate program administrator so that borderline violations do not develop into full-blown violations. Similar procedures should exist to monitor student compliance with the electronic use policy so that appropriate staff can intervene when problems are discovered. Since each message must be read by a staff member, this type of monitoring can be labor-intensive, depending on the number of daily student posts to the Website.

Another purpose of monitoring Website messages is to ensure that students who request assistance receive it in a timely manner. For example, students may request help locating resources or help using a feature of the Website. Staff monitoring the Website throughout the day can provide this assistance, or they can contact appropriate staff who can provide assistance. This type of monitoring leads to Website improvements. For example, the EPN book exchange resulted from staff reports of an increasing number of messages appearing on discussion boards from students seeking books from other students. Similarly when students began using the discussion area to look for other students with whom to study, the EPN *STUDY BUDDY FINDER* was created. Website monitoring provided the impetus for both of these popular Website features. (These features will be examined more closely in the next section of this chapter.)

Program administrators should also develop a system for monitoring student access to the Website and to each page within the Website. Web statistics software packages are available that provide an abundance of detailed information about the number of pages accessed, when they were accessed, and for how long. However, the challenge is to sort selectively through this detail, organize and interpret the results, and convert this information into Website improvements. Ultimately, program administrators must design a monitoring system that will effectively combine the results obtained by monitoring Webpage use with the observations of staff who monitor posted messages.

Although Website monitoring will provide much useful information that can result in Website improvements, it does not provide direct feedback from students. Program administrators must develop a way to obtain feedback from students on the usefulness of Website features and features they would like to see created. Monthly online surveys and feedback boxes strategically located on the Website may become part of the feedback system. Another approach is to arrange appointments with students who are able to login to the Website while on the telephone with staff, and have the students report their thoughts while accessing various Website features. Although labor-intensive, this approach can yield valuable information about how students perceive and use the Website.

### Staffing

Administrators often underestimate the number of staff required to operate and support an electronic community and the amount of time they must commit to their tasks. Depending on the purpose, size, and scope of the electronic community, existing staff may not be able or, in some cases, willing to perform the functions necessary to support the new community. It may be difficult for the distance learning administrators to obtain support from staff in other parts of the institution. Staff may view the time they spend supporting the electronic community as time spent in addition to their existing job responsibilities rather than as another way to perform their jobs.

While institutional context dictates the number and type of staff required to maintain an electronic community, certain generic functions are required to operate and maintain a viable community of distance learners. These functions include providing leadership and oversight, administering Website content and activities, facilitating chat and discussion groups, developing Webpage content, editing and maintaining Webpages, monitoring the Website, providing high-level technical support, and providing password learning support. The project leader should work with the program administrator to set up a staffing structure that will enable these functions to be performed reliably and continuously. The ways in which these functions are staffed will depend on the staff available, their skills, and the availability of training.

The leadership and oversight function is crucial to the short- and long-term success of the project. Someone must take ownership and responsibility for ensuring that political support for the electronic community is strong, so that it continues to be funded, particularly when new programs come under scrutiny in tight budget years. The administrator with this responsibility must promote the community to the key decision-makers within the college by regular updates and reports of success. This administrator must also have a clear vision for the community and continually make that vision become a reality by working with staff to set short- and long-term goals, to measure progress toward those goals, and to make mid-course corrections to respond to changing student needs.

Just as someone must accept ownership and responsibility for the electronic community, someone must also take responsibility for administering Website content and activities. This person plays a key role in deciding what content is posted on the Website, when it is posted, where, and what content is archived. This content includes informational Webpages, the number and type of discussion groups created, and links to resources within and outside of the college. The Website administrator actively communicates with community members to assess and address student needs, and to facilitate interaction among members. This person works closely with program faculty and staff to assess their needs and to coordinate their activities on the Website. In addition, the Website administrator continually monitors the flow of communication on the Website and directs community members to requested resources. The decisions of the Website administrator should be driven by a student-centered focus that helps students meet their needs for academic and social interaction, and their need for information and resources.

Synchronous chats and asynchronous discussion groups are likely to be a part of an electronic community. While many of these may be unfacilitated, some are likely to require faculty or staff facilitators. Depending on student needs, a dozen or more facilitators may be required to staff these chats on a regular basis throughout the year. Supervision, scheduling, and training are all aspects of implementing a system of facilitated chats. In addition, finding staff to facilitate chats in the evenings when adult distance learners are available to chat can be a problem for staff who are accustomed to working nine-to-five.

Developing content for Webpages can also place significant demands on faculty and staff time. Faculty and staff typically supply three basic types of content for a Website: content from existing publications (print or electronic), content from existing publications that needs to be modified, and new content. Providing content from existing publications may involve minimal updating and editing and therefore requires little time. However, modifying content from existing publications, particularly if that content was not written specifically for the Web, can take significant amounts of time, as will producing new content. For example, developing the career resources section of the EPN took hundreds of hours to develop, even though a base of content existed on which to build.

Content submitted by faculty and staff for posting on the Website is not likely to arrive as nicely formatted HTML documents. Someone must convert this content (usually received as word-processed documents) into HTML documents that conform to the standards of the Website. This is job of a Web editor who must also maintain the existing pages of the Website. This person manages all of the documents on the Website, e.g., by assigning logical file names, deleting old information, checking and repairing links, and trouble shooting any page display problems manifested by various Web browsers. Although it is advisable to have one person ultimately responsible for editing Webpages, it is sometimes possible to parcel out some of these tasks to others. For example, on the EPN, two administrative assistants from different departments edit their programs' weekly and monthly schedules of events.

Monitoring the content posted on the Website is a task that can involve many people. In fact, the more people monitoring the Website the more likely inappropriate content or unanswered student messages will be spotted and referred to appropriate staff for action. For example, specific staff can be assigned to check student posts in specific discussion groups or in specific chatrooms. Staff need to be trained on what to look for and what to do if they find something inappropriate, or a problem that needs attention. To a certain extent, the content administrator and Web editor will be monitoring the site continuously; nevertheless, it should not be left up to them to spot problem issues.

Given the many technical problems that can occur on a Website and the high level of technical expertise required to address them, skilled technical staff, at the applications engineer level should be designated to support the Website. Technical staff should be available to respond to Website development needs including, but not be limited to, setting up new interactive databases and selecting, installing, and maintaining software and hardware. It is important that a portion of technical staff time be earmarked for supporting the electronic community. This responsibility should be written into the job descriptions of technical staff.

Providing timely password support is another function necessary for a successful Website. No matter how user-friendly the registration system, the need for someone to supply forgotten or nonfunctioning usernames and passwords remains. This person should also be able to update community members' directory information upon the request of the student. Ideally, this support should be available when students need it most. For adult distance learners this is likely to be during the evenings and on weekends; however, this may not be possible because of staffing limitations. In addition, a clear standard should be made available to students regarding the turnaround time for messages requesting password support. (EPN members are comfortable with a response time of one business day.)

Provision of learning support can take many forms. On one hand it could mean requesting faculty or staff to answer student questions about subject matter by entering a response in a discussion group. On the other, it might mean arranging a facilitated chat with the college librarian to help students locate and select appropriate resources for their research projects. Providing learning support could also mean creating a new set of online resources such as Web links organized around a particular topic, or arranging tutorial help for students. The circle of faculty and staff that may need to provide help to community members could become quite broad and touch many departments and staff support units throughout the institution.

## Commercialization

The increasing presence of the commercial world in educational environments is another issue administrators may face. While administrators may wish to keep the commercial world outside the educational environment, it may intrude nonetheless. Advertisements for commercial vendors may appear in signature files attached to student messages posted on discussion boards. Or students may embed advertisements for their own businesses within signature files or messages. Administrators will have to decide the level of commercialization permitted in the community and make it clear to students in the electronic use policy. It is far more difficult to limit or eradicate commercialization after it becomes a problem than to prevent it from occurring in the first place.

The issue of Website commercialization comes quickly to the forefront for institutions that accept a Web portal company's services in exchange for permission to advertise products and services to community members. (These companies may offer a licensing option that is free of advertising, but at a substantial price.) Portal companies provide technology that enables colleges to enhance their Websites so that students have convenient online access to college services. Through the college's "portal" Website students are given the ability to register for courses, use the library, check their accounts, or participate in discussion groups or chats. Permission to advertise typically includes the right to place banner ads and other forms of advertising on the Website. It also permits companies to send advertisements directly to students via e-mail.

Some educators have voiced opposition to what they see as the commercialization or commoditization of student learning, while others do not seem to be concerned. At Appalachian State University, Clark (2001) describes his experiences with a well-known portal company, Campus Pipeline. He observes that Appalachian students are "essentially defined as a target demographic" (p.145). He wonders why other institutions that use Campus Pipeline fail to complain about the proliferation of "advertisements and targeted e-mail messages" (p. 146). Administrators contemplating enlisting the aid of portal companies should consider the effects of commercialization of their Websites in light of the technological benefits gained.

## Control and Participation

Establishing an electronic community gives rise to the issue of who will control the Website after it has been implemented. To some extent the decision-making structure (or a variation) that was used to create and develop the Website may be used to maintain and guide its future development. Who will decide what program content is appropriate for posting on the Website and in what form (e.g., PDF files or HTML)? Who will decide whether a student posting violates the academic honesty policy? What areas of the Website should receive priority in terms of development? How will staffing performance problems be addressed? A clear decision-making structure needs to be established to address these types of questions effectively and efficiently.

It is reasonable to assume that an important goal of the institution in establishing an electronic community is to have distance learners actively participate in the community by posting messages and sharing resources with one another. However, the potential also exists for community members to play a role in the policies and procedures under which the community operates and to influence the future development of the Website. Should students have input into the electronic use policy that governs their behavior on the Website or is this the purview of the institution? Should a student advisory board be established to make recommendations regarding issues affecting the electronic community? Should a student union-style government be set up with elected officers? If so, does the institution have the resources to supervise and manage this activity? Or is student participation in the electronic community to be limited to interactions among community members and providing feedback on services to the Website administrator? The way an administrator answers these questions will determine, in part, the character of the Website, and perhaps the level of interactivity.

### Costs

Ensuring that the electronic community continues to be funded is of crucial importance to the survival of the community. Although one of the macro-level criteria for selecting a program around which to build an electronic community is ability of the department to provide resources necessary to sustain the community, program funding and priorities can change rapidly. Therefore someone needs to monitor, protect, and project funding for the electronic community to ensure that adequate funding has been provided for present operations and future development. Some costs, such as the need for new hardware, software, and consultants, are easier to identify than others. Other costs, such as the time spent by staff to maintain and support the community, are not as apparent. To obtain an accurate picture of the cost of an electronic community, these costs should be calculated, including percentages of salaries, benefits, and overhead. However, from a pragmatic, political perspective administrators may decide not to include these costs in their calculations unless doing so is the practice of the institution. Otherwise, it would be difficult to compare fairly the cost of the electronic community with other programs competing for the same funds.

Part of the stewardship role is to continually be on the lookout for ways to reduce direct costs to the department or school by leveraging existing institutional resources. For example, instead of spending tens of thousands of dollars to purchase a new Web server on which to install the software running the electronic community, use existing server space. Instead of hiring part-time staff, find internal staff willing to take on these tasks. Administrators should also be continually applying for grants to fund further development of the community. Finally, there are also situations when outsourcing some or all aspects of the community may be advisable.

### Promotion

Regardless of how well an electronic community is designed or how potentially useful it is for distance learners, it must be promoted to draw students to the Website. Program administrators should develop and implement short- and long-term promotion strategies so that community membership grows and is sustained indefinitely. These strategies may include inserting announcements inside program materials, attaching signature files automatically to e-mail messages, announcements on appropriate Websites, holding virtual open houses, mailing students promotional flyers, and sending e-mail announcements to students enrolled in the program. It is also important to promote the electronic community to faculty and staff. This can be done by giving face-to-face presentations, e-mailing Website announcements and links, and inviting faculty and staff to participate in or host chats. Sharing complimentary messages from students, and advertising community events are also effective promotional techniques.

This section has provided an overview and discussion of many key issues and challenges administrators of distance learning programs can expect to face when designing, developing, implementing, and maintaining an electronic community of distance learners. To the uninitiated, the number and complexity of the issues involved may seem daunting. However, the way in which these issues play out depends on the institutional context. Some administrators may find that their institution has policies and procedures in place that already address many of these issues, while others will find they have to create new policies and procedures. In any case, by giving attention to these issues before attempting to establish an electronic community, administrators should increase their chances of success.

## SOLUTIONS AND RECOMMENDATIONS IN DEALING WITH THE ISSUES

The purpose of this section is to show how colleges and universities are addressing the issues and challenges associated with designing, developing, and implementing electronic communities of distance learners. Since only a few institutions seem to be building communities beyond the course level, this section provides a detailed examination of the Excelsior College

Electronic Peer Network (EPN). The EPN has existed for nearly four years and has become an integral part of the College. In addition, this section provides examples of more recent efforts to build electronic communities at the program level, for graduate students in the Masters of Liberal Studies program at Excelsior College, students enrolled in the Community and Human Services Program at Empire State College, and students enrolled in the Bachelor's Completion in Criminology and Criminal Justice Online Program at the University of Texas Telecampus.

## The Excelsior College Electronic Peer Network

The following case study is based on my experiences as head of the Office of Learning Services at Excelsior College where I was intimately involved with the conception, design, development, and implementation of the Excelsior College Electronic Peer Network (EPN). Although I have tried to achieve a measure of objectivity in describing the development of this electronic community, the following first-person account inevitably reflects my unique perspective and biases. (Note that the general institutional context and the rationale for creating the EPN are located at the beginning of this chapter.)

### Community Definition

As the head of the Office of Learning Services, deciding which students to include in the electronic community was not an issue. My job at the College was to provide support services for all students. Therefore, the EPN would include all students who wished to belong. This decision had far-reaching implications on the design, development, and implementation of the Website.

### Program Selection

Since the EPN was to include all schools, and presumably all degree programs of the College, deciding which program among competing programs to include in the EPN was also not an issue. However, if the EPN were to succeed, it was important to ensure that the project goals were aligned with the mission and strategic priorities of the College, and that the project addressed a compelling student need. Moreover, it was critical that the project receive the resources necessary for successful completion, implementation, and ongoing maintenance.

Creating the EPN did, in fact, appear to align well with the College's mission and strategic initiatives at the time. According to the mission statement contained in its strategic plan (Regents College, 1997), the College exists to "advance the learning of students, primarily adults, who choose to pursue their education in a flexible, self paced manner" (p.4). The mission statement also indicates that the College accomplishes its mission, in part, by "offering high-quality innovative educational opportunities at a distance to all." The strategic plan contained 10 strategic initiatives designed to advance the College toward achieving its mission. Strategic initiatives particularly relevant to the development of the EPN include "building a learning infrastructure" and "maximizing the use of technology" (p.11).

Demonstrating to decision-makers the need to establish a communication network that would link Excelsior College students was not difficult. In fact, the College had established the position of Learning Network Coordinator in my office to address these needs (Brigham, 1998). However, this position was eliminated when it became apparent that the College did not have an effective method of building and delivering this network. But when the College became an Internet node in 1997, and Internet use began to increase rapidly, the means to address student needs to communicate appeared to be at hand.

Despite the alignment of the EPN, the College's strategic plans, and student needs, it was not clear to me that the College was willing and able to provide the necessary resources. The College had become an Internet node relatively late and was struggling to catch up with other institutions. The Excelsior College Office of Information and Technology (OITS) had a long queue of important projects that had been deferred while the Internet node was being established. Fearing that the EPN would languish in queue for months, if not years, I looked for a way to bring visibility, funding and political support to the project. Obtaining a grant seemed to offer a viable solution.

Fortunately, the National Center on Adult Learning (NCAL) was requesting proposals for practitioner-based research. I prepared a proposal which, if approved, would provide the College with a $5,000 grant (the maximum offered) to develop the EPN, with the understanding that the College would contribute an additional $12,500. Although I was encouraged by the substantial support my proposal received from the vice-president for academic affairs, I had difficulty obtaining the signature from our chief financial officer. He understood, and quite correctly, that if this project were implemented successfully, it could have significant, long-term cost implications. However, since I had brought the proposal to him for his signature one hour before the proposal deadline, a decision had to be made quickly. Ten minutes before the deadline for submitting the proposal, he relented, signed the proposal, and faxed it in. The proposal was accepted and the EPN (which eventually proved to cost the College over 10 times the amount estimated in the proposal) was born.

Despite the initial reluctance of the financial officer to fund the EPN proposal, once the project began, funding was forthcoming and sustained. The project also received strong support at the executive staff level at the College. The vice-president for academic affairs saw the EPN as an innovative and effective way to carry out the College's mission to serve distance learners. Whenever an opportunity presented itself, she promoted the development of the EPN to faculty and staff. It was also apparent that the president of the College also supported the EPN, for on several occasions he referred to the development of the EPN as an example of how the College uses technology to help adult learners achieve educational goals. Consequently, political support appeared to be available at the highest levels of the institution. At this stage the EPN appeared to satisfy Diamond's (1998) conditions for program improvement: the project was aligned with the academic priorities of the institution, and there were several reasons to believe that it would succeed.

### Planning the EPN

The process used to plan the EPN is best characterized as informal and relatively unstructured. As the recipient of the NCAL grant I became the de facto project leader and project manager. It was my responsibility to ensure that Excelsior College carry out the goals, conditions, and timetable specified in the grant agreement. However, at the time I failed to recognize the importance of assembling a formal project team, holding a kickoff meeting, and getting key staff on board from the outset. Instead, I met with key administrators and staff of the College on what I perceived to be a need-to-know basis to share my vision for the EPN and to obtain staff support and input. As a result of this approach, staff tended to view the development of the EPN as a project of the Office of Learning Services rather than a project in which they had an important role. Many staff seemed uncertain of the implications that the project had for them. In fact, given the innovative nature of the project, no one, including myself, knew how the project would impact staff. In hindsight, while this approach may have enabled the project to move forward in the early stages, it ultimately may have created obstacles that could have been avoided had staff been brought on board earlier.

### Designing the EPN

One of the disadvantages in preparing a set of design specifications for an innovative project such as the EPN is that there are no models available to follow or templates to modify. Therefore it was not possible to benefit from the experience of others who had gone before. On the other hand, not having models available enabled me to follow Diamond's (1989) approach and think in the ideal. Unencumbered by reality, I tried to take a student perspective and identified those things students might do or find on a Website that would help them advance in their degree programs. These included several types of interaction with peers, faculty, and staff, and the ability to obtain needed information, resources, and services. From this list, I formed basic EPN components such as a book exchange and a student directory. However, translating these components into technological solutions was another matter. I found myself facing many Web-based technologies with which I had only a casual familiarity, and trying to decide which technology was most appropriate for the purposes I had intended. I asked the Office of Technology and Information Services (OITS) for help.

Taking on the EPN project proved to be extremely taxing on OITS's resources as that office typically plans work months or years in advance. Adding a substantial project such as the EPN to their work plan with little advance notice strained their capacity. (Had OITS been involved much earlier in the project planning process, the design phase would almost certainly have gone more smoothly.) Nevertheless, the head of OITS set up a technical design team consisting of internal and external technical specialists to work with me. After several weeks of meetings, we produced a set of specifications detailed enough to proceed. Once the specifications had reached an appropriate level of detail, we were more accurately able to identify development costs and a production schedule.

### Developing the EPN

Developing the EPN was and remains an ongoing process. The first version of the EPN was launched in May 1998 and the second version was launched in January 2001. Between these versions, design and development and revision was ongoing as we discovered what did and did not work well for our students, faculty, and staff.

The primary EPN components identified in development of the first version of the EPN included the following: a registration system, a student directory database, chatrooms, threaded discussion groups, a book exchange database, and Webpages. These components were to be developed on a Lotus platform using a Lotus Domino Server. Lotus was selected by OITS as a platform so that the College could leverage its existing Lotus products and in-house knowledge and skills. This decision had consequences for the choices of software available for use on the EPN. (The EPN continues to use a Lotus platform today.)

The registration component was the most difficult piece of the EPN to develop because a secure environment had to be created that would link to our student information system. Users registering for the EPN must enter their social security number and date of birth. This information is encrypted and verified against the student information system database before the registration is completed. OITS retained the services of an outside consultant to work with internal staff to develop this registration system. OITS also used an outside consultant to design the graphics for the EPN homepage. All other EPN components were designed and implemented in-house. However, even when a consultant was used, the process was labor-intensive for internal staff. Staff had to work closely with the consultant to communicate needs and to ensure software and hardware compatibility with existing computer systems. In addition, staff had to field-test and approve the consultant's work.

When it became apparent that the development of the EPN was going to take nearly 10 months, I established a listserv so that students would not have to wait for the EPN to be completed before they could begin communicating. A small number of students from all four schools within the College joined the listserv and began discussing a wide range of topics. However, an increasing proportion of nursing students (who represented about 60% of the College's enrollments) began to join the listserv. Soon these students dominated listserv discussions with nursing-specific content that was of little interest to students in other schools. At the request of students enrolled in schools other than nursing, I created an additional listserv. This listserv was established so that students in business, liberal arts, and technology and engineering would not receive messages intended for nursing students. Although a few students chose to join both listservs, most did not.

The two listservs proved to be a valuable means of assessing student needs. These listservs provided the opportunity to analyze the content of posted messages to obtain student feedback about components and content planned for the EPN Website. Throughout the listserv phase of the EPN, the nursing students were the most active, particularly those who were preparing for the high stakes Clinical Performance Nursing Examination (CPNE). These students appeared to have a particularly compelling need to interact and to access resources related to the CPNE.

The first version of the EPN (see Figure 4) homepage reflected the way I had defined the community, i.e., at the institutional level. A single homepage organized resources for all four schools and 32 programs. I had thought of the EPN as a sort of virtual student union in which students from all programs would interact, much as they do face-to-face on campuses across the country. I had assumed that students would be interested in interacting with students from other programs and schools. However, over time it became apparent that students were more interested in interacting with students enrolled in their own schools and degree programs than with others. The exception to this was that students from all programs wanted access to all students to buy or sell books in common subject areas such as English composition. Another problem with the way the first version of the EPN was structured was that students did not like having to be exposed to discussion groups, program announcements, and other resources that were intended for students in other programs. To these students the unwanted information and resources became visual clutter or noise on the Website. It became clear that students wanted a Website organized around their school or program, not the institution as a whole. These changes would be implemented in the second version of the EPN.

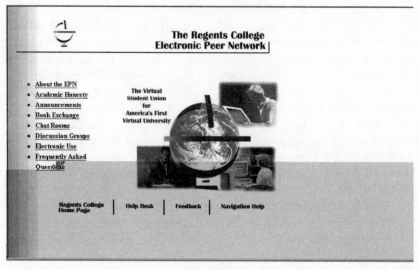

FIGURE 4
The First Version of the Excelsior College EPN Homepage

### Implementing the EPN

In May 1998, after extensive student and staff field-testing, the first version of the EPN was ready. I posted an announcement on the two listservs, giving the date the Website would open and the date that the listservs would close. However, students on the nursing listserv requested that their listserv be kept open. They cited the friendships they had formed on the listserv and the fear of not being able to sustain them in threaded discussion groups on the new Website. Some said that the listserv was a more convenient way to interact with other students. Listserv messages arrive in student mailboxes, and students can easily respond to them or delete them. Others felt they might not be able to navigate the new Website. I agreed to extend the listserv for one month so that listserv members would have time to learn how to use the EPN Website. In addition, to facilitate the transition of these students to the Website environment, I created a threaded discussion group with the same name as the nursing listserv. Nevertheless, for whatever reason, the fears expressed by some of these students may have been borne out, as that discussion group did not achieve the level of interactivity of the listserv it had replaced. (To this day, Learning Services staff continue to debate whether listservs should become integrated into the EPN.)

The second version of the EPN was implemented in January 2001. Shortly after the first version had been implemented, the Office of Learning Services hired a full-time EPN director to administer the EPN. The

EPN director was able to devote full time to developing the EPN around student needs and interests. As a result of input from students, we redefined the EPN community as consisting of four distinct communities, one for each school in the College. This narrower definition of community led us to organize and customize resources specific to each school, and to each program within a particular school while allowing resources used by everyone to be shared among students from all schools. Thus, resources such as the book exchange database, chatrooms, the student directory, and *STUDY BUDDY FINDER* appear on each homepage and can be assessed easily by all. This revised structure of the EPN resulted in each school's having what amounted to its own homepage. However, for a number of reasons, it made sense to have students access their school's homepage through a common EPN home or gateway page (see Figure 5).

FIGURE 5
Excelsior College EPN Homepage

The EPN homepage has several functions, some of which are apparent, and some are not. The EPN homepage provides a common reference point that helps to communicate to students that they belong to a community larger than their individual school. As EPN members, students have access (should they desire to use it) to EPN members in each school. The EPN homepage also enables EPN members to click on the toolbar tab identifying their school so that they can go to their school's homepage where they will find school-specific resources. In addition, since the EPN homepage is not password protected, students who have forgotten their username or password or who have other technical difficulties accessing the EPN can get help by e-mailing the EPN help desk. Newly enrolled students can use the EPN homepage to obtain an overview of the EPN by clicking *About This Site* and then a link to join the EPN. Visitors can also access this overview and view sample resources such as the *Career Resources* and *Photo Gallery.*

The School of Nursing Homepage (see Figure 6) provides an example of how the EPN school homepages are customized to meet the needs of students, faculty, and staff for each school. Table 1 summarizes the key features that are available on this page.

### Identity vs. Anonymity

Whether to allow students to select fictitious usernames so that they could hide their identifies has never been an issue for EPN administrators. Students who join the EPN are requested to provide their first name and last name on the registration form. They are told that the first letter of the first name they enter and the last name that they enter will form their username. They may, in fact, enter a fictitious name. Nothing has been built into the system to prevent them from doing so. However, a student rarely chooses to enter a fictitious name (although there have been a few humorous examples). Students voluntarily use their real names presumably because they are mature adults and they realize the contact information they provide during registration will be used to form a student directory. If they want to be contacted by other students (ostensibly a primary reason students join the EPN), the information they provide must be correct.

When the registration form was designed in 1997, the option of requiring students to use their real first name and last name was not discussed. However, now that I am sensitized to this issue, even though using fictitious names has not been a problem on the EPN, I would favor a system that automatically forms student usernames from the first and last names listed on the student information system. This would ensure that students' identities are made known to other EPN members and prevent the problem our technical support staff encounter occasionally when students enter nicknames, middle initials, and misspellings of their name.

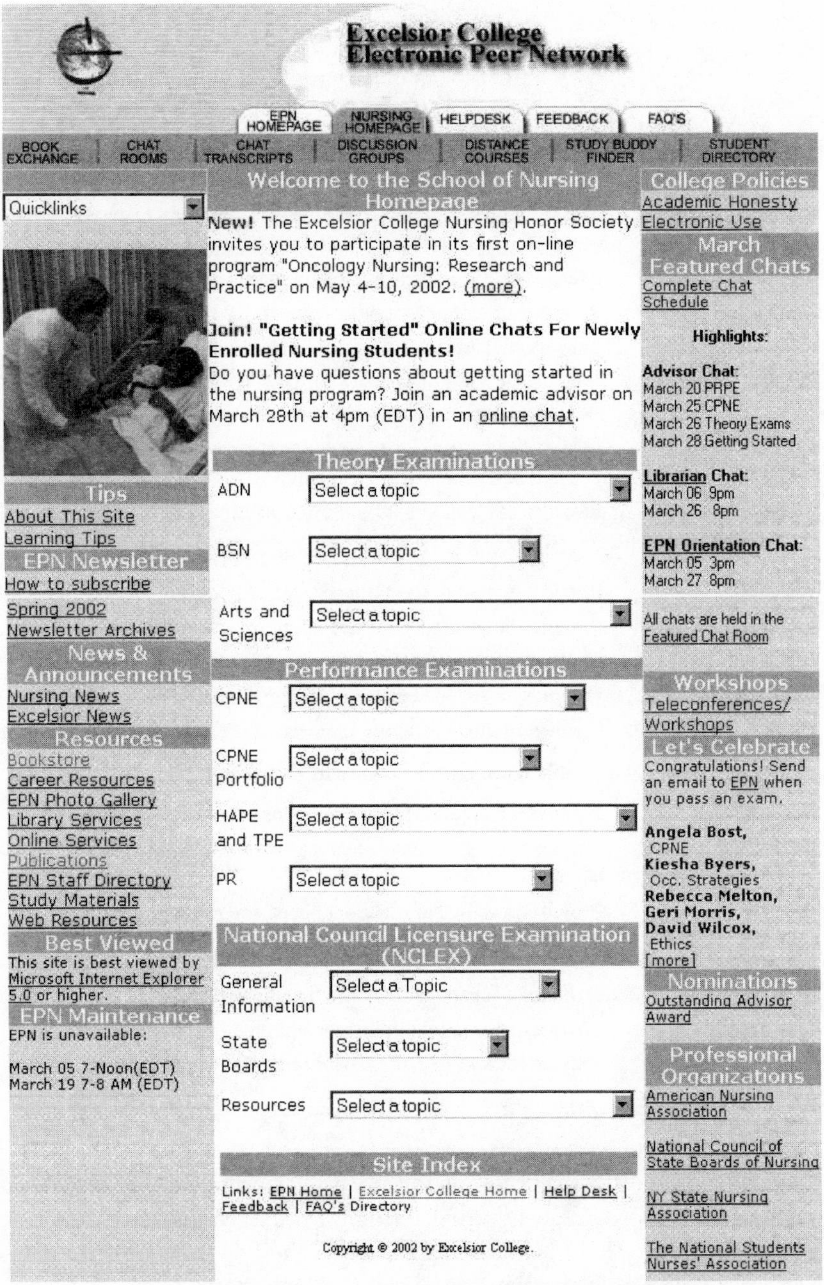

FIGURE 6
Excelsior College School of Nursing EPN Homepage

TABLE 1
Key Features and Functions of the Excelsior College
School of Nursing EPN Homepage

| Key Feature | Function |
|---|---|
| **Accessible from tool bar at top of page** | |
| Book exchange | Enables students to buy and sell their used study materials |
| chatroom | Enables students to participate in facilitated chats lead by Excelsior College faculty, staff, or guests, and in informal chats |
| Chat transcript | Provides a record of facilitated and unfacilitated chats |
| Discussion group | Enables students to join asynchronous, threaded discussions |
| Distance course | Provides access to DistanceLearn (http://distancelearn.excelsior.edu) a searchable database of distance courses |
| STUDY BUDDY FINDER | Enables students to locate study partner |
| Student directory | Provides contact and program information of EPN members |
| **Accessible from left column of homepage** | |
| Bookstore | Provides access to the College's online bookstore |
| Career resources | Provides links to an extensive array of career resources |
| EPN photo gallery | Contains photos of EPN staff, advisors, and commencement |
| Library services | Provides access to Excelsior College Virtual Library |
| Online services | Enables students to access their records (e.g., transcripts) |
| **Accessible from center column of homepage** | |
| Welcome area | Provides an area for posting announcements and news |
| Theory and performance examinations | Provides strategies and resources for exam preparation |
| NCLEX | Provides resources for national licensure exam preparation |
| **Accessible from right column of homepage** | |
| Featured Chats | Provides a schedule of about 20 facilitated chats per month |
| Let's Celebrate | Provides an area for public recognition of student achievements |
| Professional Organizations | Provides access to professional organizations in nursing |

Aside from the practical reasons for requiring students to use their real names as their usernames when registering for the EPN, there are issues of values. Part of the shared values articulated in the Excelsior College Electronic Use Policy indicates that students will interact with others "in a positive, cooperative, supportive manner" and "treat fellow students, staff, and faculty with mutual respect." Moreover, students must agree to another clause in this document—that they will not "post messages or chat under an alias or maintain multiple usernames for electronic sessions without authorization." Using fictitious usernames appears to violate the spirit (if not the letter) of the electronic use policy that all students must accept as a condition of their EPN membership.

### Privacy and Security

Students joining the EPN register in a safe, secure electronic environment. In collecting and displaying EPN student directory information, the College follows the guidelines established by the American Association of Collegiate Registrars and Admissions Officers (AACRAO), the Association of Records Managers and Administrators (ARMA), and regulations included in the Family Educational Rights and Privacy Act (FERPA). The director of student records at the College has reviewed and approved the EPN registration system to ensure compliance.

Students joining the EPN must enter their social security number and date of birth on an authorization screen. This information is required to ensure that students are enrolled at the College or that they are alumni. This information is encrypted (128 bit encryption) and sent for authentication to a server that uses strong encryption. Once authenticated, students continue through the registration process. Student must complete the following required fields on the registration form: first and last names, e-mail address, name of degree program, city of residence, state or province, and country. However, this information is not verified and could be fictitious (as explained earlier). Students must also indicate their degree program. In addition to this required information, students may voluntarily provide more detailed directory information such as street addresses and telephone numbers.

Information collected during registration automatically becomes part of a searchable student directory made available to EPN members by an icon on the school homepages. Students search the directory to find contact information about EPN members, to locate students who live in their geographic area, or to find others in their degree program. Until January 2001, students registering for the EPN were asked to identify at least one subject area or topic they were willing to be contacted about by other students. These topics include traditional academic subjects and others that promote independent learning such as time management. This information allowed students to search the directory to find others to help them with a particular subject or topic area. However, this information becomes dated quickly so that students who were willing to help someone with a certain topic when they had registered, found they were being contacted months or years later for help. (*STUDY BUDDY FINDER* replaced this function.)

While the registration process offers administrators an opportunity to collect information from students, administrators must be judicious in the type and number of questions they ask. In general students are willing to provide information about themselves if it is done in a password-protected environment with the understanding that other students will use this information for contact purposes. However, students may be reluctant to answer questions that they perceive as unnecessary or as threatening their privacy. This situation occurred when the EPN was first established. As part of the registration process, anyone registering for the EPN had to answer 10 questions designed to identify those who were "at risk" and those who were "not at risk" of completing their degrees. The intent was to track participation patterns of both groups of students and design interventions to support students at risk. The questions required students to indicate details about their past academic records including the number of college credits they had earned, when they had earned their last credits, their GPA upon admittance to Excelsior College, and whether they had any "F" or "D" grades on their transcripts. While the registration form explained that this information was being collected for research purposes and would be treated confidentially, many students questioned why they were being asked these kinds of questions. Eventually, we discontinued the questions.

### Rules, Policies, and Procedures

When students register for the EPN, they must indicate that they will accept the rules, policies, and procedures expressed in the permission statement, academic honesty policy, and the electronic use policy. If they choose not to accept them, their registration will not be processed. These students may contact appropriate staff to discuss concerns or questions.

A permission statement allows the College to make information about students available to others as specified in the statement. Following is the current EPN permission statement. This statement was developed with the advice and review of legal counsel.

> Excelsior College has my permission to make available to other registered members of the Excelsior College Electronic Peer Network (EPN) any information I provide for the Student Directory. I understand that this information will include my name, e-mail address, name of degree program, city of residence, state or province, country and any additional information I choose to enter into the student directory.
>
> I also give my permission for Excelsior College staff and others who have obtained permission from the Dean of Learning Services to have access to this information and messages or responses to messages I post in any area of the EPN for maintenance, support, or educational purposes.
>
> In addition, Excelsior College may use information obtained from this Website for institutional research. However, this data will be treated in a manner which will protect my privacy. I understand that my social security number and date of birth are used to verify my identity as an Excelsior College student and will not be made available to a third party.

After prospective EPN members are presented with the permission statement, they are given the opportunity to read the College's academic honesty policy [http://gl.excelsior.edu/epn2/ec_open.nsf/pages/acad_hon.htm]. The College had to revise its pre-EPN academic honesty policy when a student posted a message in an EPN discussion group inviting students who had taken an Excelsior College examination to come to her Website and post any information they could remember about examination questions. Before this incident, Excelsior College's academic honesty policy did not contain language relevant to electronic environments. However, the current policy contains the following paragraph as part of its definition of academic dishonesty. Bold-faced font appears on the Website version to emphasize that this policy applies in electronic environments.

> Academic dishonesty includes: altering or misusing documents; impersonating, misrepresenting or knowingly providing false information as to one's identity; cheating on examinations; plagiarism; **attempting to gain advance information of examination questions from any source, or collaborating with others for that purpose; and sharing information about examination questions or content via electronic discussion groups or in any other way, by a student who has taken an examination** (Excelsior College, 1998).

The last policy that students registering for the EPN must accept is the College's electronic use policy (Excelsior College, 2001). This document [http://gl.excelsior.edu/epn2/ec_open.nsf/pages/e_use.htm] originally began as policy written specifically for EPN members, but eventually evolved into a college-wide policy that is used in all electronic environments in which students participate. This policy communicates the College's support for students using the Internet to facilitate learning, and specifies appropriate and inappropriate online behavior and the consequences for students who choose to engage in inappropriate behavior.

The electronic use policy is important, in part, because it expresses the shared values of members of the College, particularly in the section that lists those things that students agree to do,—such as interacting with others "in a positive, cooperative, supportive manner and display respect for the privacy and rights of others." EPN members must also agree to "treat fellow students, staff, and faculty with mutual respect and understanding." This language sets the tone and framework for interactions that occur on the EPN. The electronic use policy is useful for students and administrators because it lists 12 specific behaviors that are considered inappropriate by the College. While some of these behaviors may seem obvious, others (e.g., installing links to Excelsior College Websites on personal Websites) are not. Putting this information in an electronic use policy provides guidelines for students who are not sure what is considered inappropriate. Specifying these behaviors in a policy document also provides administrators with a justification to intervene when an EPN member violates or is in danger of violating the electronic use policy.

### Monitoring and Evaluating the Website

Learning Services staff systematically monitor all student messages posted on the EPN. Monitoring activities include reading messages posted in discussion groups, chatrooms, on the book exchange, and on the *STUDY BUDDY FINDER*. Staff monitor EPN messages to ensure that students are adhering to the academic honesty and electronic use policies, and that messages requesting assistance receive a reply. In addition, staff monitor student messages to assist students who encounter technical difficulties, to check Webpages for broken links, and for other types of technical problems. The EPN director also prepares monthly summaries of Web statistics that show the relative level of use of various areas of the Website.

At an institution that administers over 40,000 examinations per year across the United States, monitoring student online activity for messages that might compromise the integrity of an examination is an important activity. However, during the three and a half years of the EPN's existence, only one student has been found to have violated the academic honesty policy. This student was suspended from the College. College staff discovered two other students maintained personal Websites that disclosed inappropriate information about Excelsior College examinations. However, students operating these Websites complied readily with requests to remove this information. In each case, staff contacted these students within hours after the violations were discovered. The College has also had a few instances when students appeared to join the EPN to vent their perceived grievances against the College. In these cases, the EPN director deleted the messages and contacted the offending students to explain that such posts violated the electronic use policy. In all but one case the students apologized for their behavior and ceased inappropriate messages. One student continued to send inappropriate messages and was denied further access to the EPN. Overall, monitoring the EPN has provided evidence that virtually all students appear to be complying with the academic honesty and electronic use policies while on the Website.

Students posting messages on the EPN sometimes request assistance from faculty or staff rather than from peers, or they might post an urgent message requiring an immediate response. In these cases, the EPN director dispatches these messages to the appropriate faculty or staff who post a response on the EPN so that other students can benefit from their comments. The EPN director maintains a list of faculty and staff with expertise in various content areas. Students typically receive responses to their questions by the next business day.

The EPN maintains two mailboxes that are monitored each business day, and occasionally on evenings and weekends. One mailbox receives messages requesting technical assistance (usually password support). The other mailbox receives comments or questions about all other aspects of the EPN. Faculty and staff also use this mailbox to communicate with the EPN director.

Website statistics software monitors Website pages and databases continuously and provides an abundance of general and specific information about student activity on the Website. The EPN director generates and examines Website statistics on a regular basis to obtain specific information that she can use to improve services for students. For example, Website statistics indicate that most EPN members access the Website between 8:00 PM and 10:00 PM (EST) on weekdays, and that many also access it from 2:00 PM and 4:00 PM (EST). Therefore she tries to schedule facilitated chats during these times so that more students can attend. By compiling monthly summaries, the EPN director can track the level of Website activity over time to establish usage level benchmarks and trends. This information can be displayed for the Website as a whole, or to some extent by school. (Usage levels of databases that are shared by all students such as the book exchange cannot be separated by school.) For example, statistics show that nursing students and liberal arts students are the most active students on the Website. These statistics suggest that while the Website may be addressing the needs of nursing and liberal arts students, it may not be addressing fully the needs of business and technology students.

While Website statistics provide useful information regarding student activity on the Website, direct feedback from students is essential. The EPN has feedback boxes strategically placed on the Website to encourage students to provide feedback on their experience using various features of the Website and to provide ideas for new features. In addition, the EPN director regularly sends online surveys to students to determine how well the EPN is meeting their needs. These surveys sometimes go to a broad sampling of EPN members or, more often than not, they target specific groups of students such as all students who have posted a message on the *STUDY BUDDY FINDER*. Surveys that target specific groups of students have proven to be more effective in capturing information that can be used to improve the EPN. The EPN director triangulates information obtained from surveys with information obtained from Website statistics and comments from the feedback boxes.

### Staffing

Keeping the EPN operating and responsive to changing student and program needs involves a number of staff, some of whom have all or parts of their jobs dedicated to EPN activities, and many others who do not. Given the range of information and resources created or re-purposed for the EPN, it is difficult to give an accurate picture of EPN staffing. At the risk of over-simplifying the staffing structure, I tend to think about EPN staff as falling into two groups: those who have all or part of their jobs dedicated to EPN activities, and those who do not. Table 2 lists staff by position, their EPN function, the hours per week devoted to EPN activities, and the school or administrative office in which they work. In addition to these, other staff at the College, particularly OITS staff, are also called upon to troubleshoot problems or assist with other projects.

Although nurse educators, advisors, and others who work outside of the Office of Learning Services currently participate willingly and ably in EPN activities today, this was not always the case. During the first year of the EPN, staff tended to view interacting with students on the EPN as an additional duty that was being required of them instead of as another avenue to communicate with their students. It took several meetings over several weeks to gain their support. Only recently have staff begun to come up

TABLE 2
EPN Staff Time Dedicated to EPN Activities

| Position | EPN Function | Hours/ week | School or Unit |
|---|---|---|---|
| **EPN Staff with time officially dedicated to the EPN** | | | |
| **EPN Director** | Directs daily operations Administers content Develops all services | 37.5 | Learning Services |
| **Learning Services Administrative Assistant** | Provides password support Monitors transcripts and registrations Assists with Web editing | 9 | Learning Services |
| **Dean of Learning Services** | Provides political support and overall leadership | 5 | Learning Services |
| **Applications Engineer** | Provides all specialized technical Website development and support | 19 | Office of Information Technology Services |
| **EPN Staff without time officially dedicated to the EPN** | | | |
| **Nurse Educators** | Monitor discussion groups, facilitate chats | 5 | School of Nursing |
| **Advisors** | Facilitate chats | 4 | All schools |
| **Librarian** | Facilitate chats | 1 | Johns Hopkins librarian |
| **Examination Administrator** | Monitor discussion group | 1 | Assessment Unit |
| **Dean of Learning Services** | Monitor discussion groups | 1 | Learning Services |
| **Advisor** | Develop career resources | 2 | School of Liberal Arts |

with new ways to use the EPN to provide services and resources to students. In fact, there is some pressure to make the EPN automatically available to all students as the main student Website for the College. However, if and when this happens, a new staffing structure and additional resources may be needed to implement this idea.

### Costs

At $130,000, EPN startup costs substantially exceeded the $17,500 specified in the original grant proposal. Major cost categories included computer hardware, software, consulting fees, and personnel, all of which accounted for two-thirds of the total startup costs. (Personnel costs include salaries, fringe benefits, and overhead.) Annual operating expenses currently run between $200,000 and $250,000 with personnel costs constituting over 90% of total costs. The EPN appears to be on solid ground in terms of continued funding for the foreseeable future. Learning Services has a separate budget to fund its EPN activities and the application engineer position dedicated to the EPN on a half-time basis appears to be secure.

### Promotion

The development of the EPN occurred when use of the Internet to deliver educational services was considered new and innovative. I appeared on National Public Radio with the president of our College to discuss the EPN, and the vice-president for academic affairs appeared on a local television broadcast for the same purpose. Our staff and faculty shared this high level of interest in the EPN. Consequently, my promotional efforts to the schools within the College were much easier than they might have otherwise been. Aided by the active commitment of the vice-president of academic affairs, I took every opportunity to share with College staff the plans for the EPN. I kept them updated via e-mail as the EPN reached development milestones. I wanted to bring as much visibility as possible to this project so that the College would be more likely to continue to fund it. The support of the advising staff was also required for long-term success as advisors give students guidance on educational resources. Therefore we asked advisors to serve as EPN field-testers. We wanted them to become familiar with the EPN so they could enthusiastically recommend it to students.

Promotion of the EPN to students was and remains essential since it depends on a continual supply of new student members to grow and prosper. Promotional efforts include placing announcements on the College's Websites, in student enrollment kits, in College catalogs, in study materials, and in other publications widely distributed to students. In addition, staff attach information about the EPN to their signature files and mention the EPN when conversing with students. EPN members who travel to Albany to participate in commencement ceremonies are given carnations to wear on their graduation robes and an opportunity to have free digital photos with family members.

### Lessons Learned

Following are 10 lessons that I have learned from my experiences designing, developing, and implementing the EPN. Some of these affirm the steps I had taken, while others point to things I underestimated or overlooked:

1. *Secure and cultivate political support from the highest levels.*
   Political support from key administrators kept the EPN project high on the Office of Information Technology Service's priority list during the development stage. This support has also led to continued funding.

2. *The visible part of the EPN on the Website represents the tip of an iceberg.*
   The amount of resources, time, and energy required to develop and maintain an electronic community on this scale is far greater than I could have imagined. Far more staff are involved supporting the EPN than I had anticipated, and that number continues to grow.

3. *Working with technology consultants is a labor-intensive process.*
   Before this project I had little idea of the amount of detail that consultants require to develop a Website capable of supporting a community of distance learners. This held true for both internal and external consultants.

4. *Hold a formal project kickoff meeting and establish a formal project team.*
   Failing to hold a formal project kickoff meeting denied staff the opportunity to gain an understanding of the purpose, goals, and objectives of the project, and to have input into them. Failing to establish a formal project team put the burden for carrying the project forward on my shoulders and prevented the project from benefiting from the synergy of a group.

5. *Operating a successful EPN requires active and continuous management.*
   One person such as the EPN director must be responsible for managing the daily operation of the Website. This person facilitates student interaction on the Website, coordinates the participation of faculty and staff in Website activities, and ensures that the Website meets everyone's needs.

6. *Identify groups within groups and separate them.*
   Although maintaining a few shared databases or discussion groups is advisable, in general students prefer to have resources grouped according to school or program.

7. *Select statistical software as the Website structure is being defined.*
   The types of reports a Website monitoring software package produces depends, in part, on the structure of the Website it is monitoring. When designing the structure of the Website, the Web designer should consider the capabilities of the statistical software that will be used to monitor the Website and the types of reports that will be most useful to the Website administrator.

8. *Systematically promote the Website to prospective students, enrolled students, faculty, and staff.*
   As efforts to promote the EPN increase, the numbers of new EPN registrations also increase. These efforts also encourage prospective students to enroll in the College, and faculty and staff to support the EPN.

9. *Belonging to an electronic community such as the EPN can make the difference between distance learners' completing their programs or dropping out.*
   Several EPN members have attributed their success in completing their degree programs to the academic and emotional support they received from other EPN members.

10. *The establishment of an EPN can serve as a change agent for a college.*
    The EPN has impacted the College in many ways, particularly in the areas of technology and staffing. It has also changed the way staff interact with students.

## The Excelsior College Masters of Arts in Liberal Studies Electronic Peer Network

The Excelsior College Masters in Liberal Studies Electronic Peer Network (MLS/EPN) is an electronic community organized at the program level. Following is a brief account of its design, development, and implementation.

The MLS program began in October 1998 as Excelsior College's first graduate program. This program is delivered at a distance and consists of a combination of online courses and independent study. About 90 students are currently enrolled in the program. Three Excelsior College staff administer the MLS program, primarily from their offices in Albany, New York: a program director, a graduate student advisor, and a program administrative assistant.

The MLS/EPN [http://gl.excelsior.edu/epn2/mls_open.nsf/pages/mlshome.htm ] was created at the request of the MLS program director. He indicated that the existing College Website and the Web course environment were not meeting the needs of MLS students. After preliminary reviews of student and program needs, Learning Services agreed to work with the MLS program director and his staff to create a customized version of the existing EPN. To the extent possible, the MLS/EPN (Figure 2) would use the existing EPN framework. This approach would save time and resources while also addressing student needs.

The project team included the EPN director, the MLS program director, and an applications engineer. The EPN director served as the project manager, and for all intents and purposes, she became the project leader, although she consulted periodically with the Dean of Learning Services. The MLS director made decisions about what content and features to include on the Website. This project team drew on additional resources from the Office of Information Technology Services (OITS) as needed, but did not find it necessary to employ the services of outside consultants. Political support for creating the new Website was strong as the dean of Liberal Arts gave her approval as did the vice-president for academic affairs. The design and development (including field-testing with MLS staff, faculty, and students) required about three and one-half months. Staff took various amounts of time from their schedules to work on this project.

One of the differences between the MLS/EPN and the EPN Websites is that the MLS/EPN has a Lotus LearningSpace button on the tool bar. LearningSpace is the commercial name for the learning management system used to deliver the MLS Web courses. Another difference is that MLS students do not register online to join the MLS/EPN. Instead, when they enroll in the MLS program, they are e-mailed a username formed from their first and last names, and a password that enables them to access all the College's Websites. Unlike EPN members, MLS/EPN members cannot use fictitious usernames. In addition, since these students do not register via the Web, they do not have to provide their social security number or date of birth. Privacy and security issues are therefore minimized for these students. At this time, MLS students are also e-mailed the academic honesty policy and the electronic use policy. The e-mail explains that accessing any of the College's password-protected Web services signifies that they have accepted these two policies.

Learning Services staff perform most, but not all the functions necessary to keep the Website operational. The EPN director manages the day-to-day operations such as updating and monitoring the Website, and the Learning Services administrative assistant provides password support. The same OITS applications engineer that supports the EPN also supports the MLS/EPN. In addition, the two Websites share the same Website monitoring software package. It was successfully reconfigured to monitor the MLS/EPN separately. While it is too early to determine how successful this Website will be in building community, the early signs are that it too will be successful.

## The Empire State College Community and Human Services Program

Empire State College is developing an electronic community at the program level for students enrolled in its Community and Human Services Program. Empire State College [http://www.esc.edu] is a regionally accredited, nonresidential college serving adults through flexible, individualized approaches to learning. The College has its administrative headquarters in Saratoga Springs, New York and is a member of the State University of New York system of universities and colleges.

The Office of Educational Technology received a grant to develop new courses in Community and Human Services (CHS), business, and information technology that would allow students in these areas of study to complete their degrees online. Another goal of the grant was to create an electronic community that would increase student success in completing the CHS program. Program administrators identified CHS students as having greater need for support than business students. While many business students had jobs that required them to work online, and had already demonstrated their ability to succeed, CHS students were expected to be less comfortable taking their degrees online. This was borne out at the start of the program when CHS students expressed many concerns about their educational media. In addition, the nature of CHS as a helping profession seemed compatible with the support afforded by an electronic community.

The project was initiated by the Office of Educational Technology and developed with a group of CHS faculty from throughout the college. The College's Center for Learning and Technology provided technical support for the project. The project team met monthly and used Lotus Notes databases to exchange information during the design and development phases.

The CHS program uses a cohort approach to establish learning communities at the course level and then expands these communities to the program level so that interaction occurs among cohorts. About 20 students have entered the program in four cohorts of four to eight people (March, 2001; May, 2001; September, 2001; and January, 2002). Students begin the program by taking two online courses in degree planning provided through the College's Center for Distance Learning. They work in special sections of both courses that are focused on their area of study and are supported by a faculty member, an advisor, an instructional designer, and a researcher. Faculty encourage students to communicate through each course's roundtable section.

The CHS students also make use of a new degree-planning tool, developed by the College for this program, which enables them to share and review their degree plans online. This tool helps them apply somewhat abstract degree guidelines to their own prior learning and academic goals. As their academic programs become concrete, the students are able to see what others have done and to encourage one another in their goals. During the first course, students are unaware that there are Center for Distance Learning students in other sections of the course. In the second course, CHS students participate in their own discussion groups but can see the contributions of other students.

After students complete the educational planning courses, the roundtable discussion databases are transferred to a special password-protected Website where students can communicate with students from other cohorts. This Website has been designed specifically for CHS students. Resources available on this Website include access to a CHS advisor's description of upcoming CHS courses, and selected learning resources. The discussion groups associated with this Website are asynchronous. However, the College has provided students with lists of student Internet messaging IDs and e-mail addresses to facilitate synchronous communication. (A student has also set up a Yahoo chatroom for her classmates.) The Website also includes a "Meet Your Colleagues" page displaying a montage of CHS student photos that further enhances a sense of community among students. A small team administers and maintains the Website. This team consists of the faculty and staff who support educational planning.

Another community building strategy of the program is a residency. Since Empire State College degree programs are highly individualized, program administrators provided an opportunity for students to meet face-to-face to help the student cohorts to merge into a single group and better identify with their program. The residency also gave faculty and staff an opportunity to receive detailed feedback from the students.

A final element of the project is the development of a series of one-credit seminars that are intended to provide students with another opportunity to interact with one another over a number of semesters, and to help them develop a sense of membership in a disciplinary community beyond the course level (E. Gould, personal communication, March 29, 2002).

## University of Texas TeleCampus Law and Order Website

The University of Texas TeleCampus Austin and Arlington are developing the Law and Order Website [http://distance.uta.edu/Telecampus/CCJO/homepage.html], a program-wide electronic community supporting students enrolled in the University's Bachelor's Completion in Criminology and Criminal Justice Online Program (CCJO). The CCJO program prepares students for professional careers and advancement opportunities in criminal justice or related fields and is designed for students who have already completed their first two years of undergraduate courses. Students completing the program earn a Bachelor of Arts from UT Arlington or UT Permian Basin. Or they may earn a Bachelor of Science degree from UT

Brownsville. UT Dallas also contributes coursework for the program. The CCJO program is fully online and does not require any onsite visits.

Funded by the UT TeleCampus [http://www.TeleCampus.utsystem.edu/], the Law and Order Website is being developed at UT Arlington by the Center for Distance Education [http://www.uta.edu/uta/distance.html]. The goal is to enrich and deepen students' education through online resources, activities, and events. Project administrators recognize that people working in criminology and criminal justice (e.g., policemen) tend to consider themselves part of a community of law enforcement professionals. They seek to transfer students' existing sense of community to an online environment. The start of the new CCJO in Spring 2002 presented an opportunity to open the Law and Order Website. About 125 students and faculty from participating UT campuses make up this community.

Resources currently available to students via the Law and Order Website homepage include links to newsletters, guest lectures, a discussion board, and program-related information and resources. The newsletter will be published each semester, and students and faculty are invited to submit articles. The Spring 2002 issue of the newsletter is available for downloading from the Website as a PDF file. In the Spring and Fall, Law and Order will host a guest lecturer from the field of criminology and criminal justice. Guest lectures will be available to the students to watch at any time via the Website. In addition, project administrators will encourage guest lecturers to be available to answer students' questions on the discussion board for a week or two after a lecture. Students access the discussion board from the portal page of Prometheus (the UT TeleCampus course platform) where they are encouraged to participate in threaded discussions about program, academic, and career issues. Program-related information and resources on the Website include links to a digital library, faculty biographies, and professional associations.

Several features of the Law and Order Website are either under development or planned for the future. Access to the UT Arlington's Center for Criminal Justice Research and Training is currently under development. The Center was established in 1977. Its main purpose has been to provide assistance to criminal justice agencies, governmental institutions, and citizen groups concerned with the administration and operation of the criminal justice system. Planned for the future are articles of interest to students, an electronic honor society, "e-mentors," an alumni association, and a student congress. Project administrators encourage students, faculty, and staff to submit ideas for improving and expanding the Website.

The project was developed by focusing on providing online versions of elements of collaboration and shared experience thought to foster community among students. The development team included the associate director of UT Arlington's Center for Distance Education, the Center's instructional designer charged with developing courses for the CCJO program, and a UT Arlington criminology and criminal justice graduate student. Development work began in August 2001 and culminated with the launch of the Website in January 2002. This development team is also responsible for the daily monitoring and maintenance of the Website.

Students register for CCJO courses through the UT TeleCampus and agree to abide by university policies (e.g., the academic honesty policy). Once the students have registered for a course, the UT TeleCampus sends the names of CCJO students to UT Arlington's Center for Distance Education where the instructional designer adds their names to the discussion board. This area of the Website is password-protected. Student anonymity is not an issue as students use their real names on the discussion boards.

The CCJO program and the Law and Order Website are promoted on a Webpage at the UT TeleCampus Website. Upon enrollment in the CCJO program, each student receives a welcome packet, the Law and Order newsletter, a mouse pad, a t-shirt, and other promotional items. Students also receive a welcome e-mail with directions for accessing the Law and Order Website; they are encouraged to take advantages of the resources it offers. While many students and faculty are new to online learning, early signs of success are positive. For example, program administrators report that participation in a contest to select the community's name was impressive. Project administrators expect the Law and Order Website to continue to grow and evolve (M. Gantz, personal communication, March 29, 2002).

## FUTURE TRENDS AND OPPORTUNITIES OF EMERGING TECHNOLOGIES

In one form or another distance learning has been around for centuries, but primarily as a print-based enterprise. As new technologies emerged during the 20th Century, they provided distance educators with opportunities to deliver education in new and exciting ways. Key technologies that have influenced the development of distance learning include the telephone, radio, film, and television (in its many forms). In fact, these technologies gave rise to several large-scale distance learning institutions such as the British Open University in the 1970's. However, distance learning in the United States continued to remain out of the educational mainstream until the World Wide Web began to be used in the 1990's by colleges and universities to deliver courses and degree programs.

It is interesting to note that even though many US colleges and universities had for years used the Internet to deliver courses by computer conferencing, listservs, and e-mail, it wasn't until the World Wide Web came into existence that US distance learning programs began to flourish. This phenomenon may, in part, be because Web courses can incorporate all prior useful technologies including electronic text, graphics, audio, and video. Combined with a delivery system increasingly accessible to students and prospective students, from home, work, and school, Web courses become a powerful force in education. On a program level or higher, Web-based technologies also provide colleges and universities the opportunity to enrich and deepen students' educational experiences by establishing and cultivating electronic communities of distance learners. This section identifies five trends of emerging technologies with respect to the development of electronic communities.

## Trend 1: Hosted Portal Services

While portal technology is just beginning to make its presence felt in higher education, it is becoming widely used by businesses hoping to capture their share of customers on the Web. According to Menkart (2001), portal technology has grown rapidly in the corporate world over the last two years and will continue to grow for the foreseeable future. Menkart suggests that business portals must have technology that provides "content, community, and commerce." He describes three approaches that businesses use to implement portals. One is for the business (or an integrator for the business) to piece together a Website out of existing Internet technologies. However, this approach is difficult and expensive because several hardware and software components have to be integrated, maintained, and continuously updated. Another approach is to purchase what Menkart calls "shrink-wrapped software" that minimizes some of the compatibility issues but still is expensive for the business to maintain. The third approach is to use hosted services so that the Website is run and managed by an outside company on their servers using their infrastructure. The business using this service uses a browser to select the interactive functions, look and feel, and content that will appear on their Website.

The use of portal technology in higher education appears to be following a similar path. Colleges and universities are experimenting with portal providers that integrate Internet technologies installed on the institutions' servers. However, this type of portal technology tends to require a high level of maintenance. Thus, if properly priced, the hosted services approach may become an attractive alternative. Once a college or university adapts a hosted portal solution on a campus-wide basis, the possibilities for establishing electronic communities at the program level and beyond seem limitless.

## Trend 2: High-speed Access

Over the next few years increasing numbers of adults will enjoy high-speed access to the Internet until high-speed access eventually becomes the norm. While there will continue to be access problems in rural and remote areas unable to benefit from DSL, cable, or other forms of high-speed access, many of these users will be able to have high-speed access from work or public places such as a local library. At some point, colleges and universities will be able to design their Websites with the assumption that students have high-speed access. This approach will enable administrators of electronic community Websites to incorporate bandwidth-intensive technologies such as digital video and videoconferencing into their Websites. For example, many of the facilitated chats that are now delivered in a text-based chatroom might be done in real-time via two-way videoconferencing, and archived for asynchronous access. Or Website administrators might facilitate student use of desktop videoconferencing or other technologies that allow students to participate in study or support groups with peers or mentors. High-speed access brings significant opportunities to enhance electronic community Websites in ways that were not possible before.

## Trend 3: Customization and Personalization

Technologies that permit users to customize their Websites will become increasingly common on college and university Websites. Customization permits users to select options that they want to appear on their homepage for their Website (e.g., selecting certain cities to appear on a weather.com homepage). Administrators of electronic communities may have the option of incorporating this technology into their Websites, or, perhaps the electronic community itself will become one of the options from which students choose from within the context of the larger institutional Website. Either way, from a community building perspective, the effects of customization may not necessarily contribute to students' sense of community as they could choose a very narrow range of options and isolate themselves from others.

Personalization of Websites has the potential for a much greater impact than customization. Personalization refers to the ability of a Website to actively present information based on information stored in the database. In the commercial world, visitors to a Website might be asked to register. Information entered at the time of registration may cause certain types of advertising to be displayed when the visitor returns. Another approach is for Website software to monitor customer purchases and save this information in a database to suggest future purchases. Those who have purchased products from Amazon.com are familiar with this approach. Personalization technology provides colleges and universities with the ability to send students e-mails based on information in the student information system. For example, students who have been identified by their records as high risk could be sent e-mails informing them of services such as writing centers or counseling centers that might assist them. Personalization could also be built into electronic communities so that students who have joined a particular special interest group might receive a suggestion to join a related group. Of course there are many issues of privacy that colleges and universities would have to sort out if they decide to use personalization techniques.

## Trend 4: Instant Messaging

Instant messaging (IM) is a technology that is gaining popularity with the general public and with business. In fact, a Gartner report has predicted that by 2005 more messages will be sent by IM worldwide than by e-mail (Kirsner, 2002a, 2002b). People who have IM messaging installed on their personal computer see a window open on their screen when they start up their computer and connect to the Internet. This window contains a buddy list or contact list of people who are online at that moment. By clicking on a name and entering a message in the window, people on the list can communicate in real-time. Most instant messaging software also allows users to create their own chatrooms, exchange Web links, share images or photos, play sounds, and exchange files. They also permit users to talk to each other via their personal computer instead of using a telephone. Major instant messenger applications include AOL's AIM, Mirablis's ICQ, MSN Explorer, and Yahoo! Messenger. Each product uses its own proprietary protocol for communication. However, Internet Engineering Task Force [http://www.ietf.org/html.charters/impp-charter.html] is developing a standard protocol for instant messaging. Interoperability standards should address this problem. In fact, Odigo already enables users of its messaging software to chat with AIM, MSN Messenger, ICQ, and Yahoo Messenger users (although AOL blocks Odigo messages).

Internet messaging has, for the most part, remained outside of higher education environments. However, as interoperability among applications is attained and security improved, administrators of electronic communities will evaluate IM for potential use. At the least, IM applications lend themselves to real-time sessions with staff who could help students navigate the electronic community, provide real-time password support, or provide learning support. Students might also find IM to be a useful tool for studying with a partner or providing emotional support. In addition, the ability to send images and to hear each other's voices could help to personalize relationships. Administrators of electronic communities would do well to monitor developments in Internet messaging for possible use.

## Trend 5: Communications Convergence

Continued advances in communications convergence or application integration will provide an opportunity for members of an electronic community to communicate in increasingly convenient ways. Products are currently available (e.g., OZ ICS) that allow users to connect instantly to each other by computer, phone, pager, or mobile phone through a point-and-click contact menu. For example, users who log into the system view their contact list of others who are also online at that moment and the device (e.g., PDA or phone) they are using. Then they can initiate a conversation with one or more members of the group and use all the features associated with instant messaging. In addition, they can check their e-mail, download files, or view Webpages as needed. As standards are being developed for presence services and wireless application protocol (WAP), we can expect more and better integration of electronic communication devices to continue. As distance learners begin to adopt these technologies in their business and personal lives, administrators of electronic communities will need to assess member needs and investigate the possibility (and advisability) of incorporating this emerging technology into their communities.

## IMPLICATIONS AND RESEARCH OPPORTUNITIES

Creating electronic communities for distance learners at the program level and beyond has several implications to institutions that provide them. The continuing maintenance of electronic communities also provides several opportunities for research. The purpose of this section of this chapter is to discuss these implications and to identify research opportunities.

## Implications

The implications of creating electronic communities of distance learners becomes clearer by examining the broader societal context in which they are being created. Today, powerful, external environmental factors are forcing colleges and universities to change the way that they carry out their missions. These forces include a steady growth in the number of adults returning to higher education in the US and abroad (Maehl, 2000; UNESCO, 1998), and the need of adults to continue working and living at home while earning their degrees. With the advent of the World Wide Web as a course delivery system, colleges and universities are under pressure to convert campus-based degree programs to online delivery so that adults can study from home. In addition, student expectations for fast, economical, personal, and courteous service place additional pressures on colleges and universities. Furthermore, regional accrediting agencies (Middle States Commission on Higher Education, 2002a, 2002b) and others (Phipps, 2000; Southern Regional Education Board, 1998) concerned with educational quality are specifying standards and benchmarks that require institutions delivering programs electronically to provide a full array of student services to support these programs.

Best practice documents identify several student support services that must be provided by an institution engaged in distance learning. These support services include but are not limited to online access to the library, academic advising, the bookstore, course registration, financial aid, course and college orientation, and tutoring. One best practice document (Middle States Commission on Higher Education, 2002a) explicitly recommends that institutions provide a "sense of community" for distance learners:

> The institution recognizes that a sense of community is important to the success of many students, and that an ongoing, long-term relationship is beneficial to both student and institution. The design and administration of the program takes this factor into account as appropriate, through such actions as encouraging study groups, providing student directories (with the permission of those listed), including off-campus students in institutional publications and events, including these students in definitions of the academic community through such mechanisms as student government representation, invitations to campus events including graduation ceremonies, and similar strategies of inclusion (p. 12).

One of the questions included in this document for determining if an institution is meeting this standard is, "Do representative students feel that they are part of a community, or that they are entirely on their own?" (p.12). Implementing this standard has several resource implications for institutions.

Creating an electronic community of distance learners and converting student support services to online delivery is a process that requires a significant amount of resources (Brigham, 2001). Institutions must be willing to budget for appropriate staff, training, and technology to support the change. They must also take steps to change an academic culture accustomed to interacting with students via written correspondence, telephone, and face-to-face, to one that interacts with students electronically. Depending on the existing organizational structure, this conversion may also require new, flatter organizational structures that can respond rapidly to students' changing needs. Perhaps one of the most difficult aspects of this transition to online support services is meeting student expectations for fast, efficient service and to have these services available during evenings and on weekends (preferably 24/7). Adult students expect to have a response to an e-mail or message posted on a discussion board within hours.

A less obvious implication of building an electronic community around a program is the community's potential to increase student enrollments in that program. With the proliferation of online programs, prospective students are able to comparison shop for programs that best meet their needs. Cost, college reputation, program length, transfer credit policy, student-centeredness, and other factors influence their enrollment decision. Just as traditional students visit campuses as part of the process of the college selection process, distance learners visit college Websites to determine if a program is right for them. Programs that offer membership in an electronic community would give that program a competitive edge over programs that do not. In fact, as electronic communities become more common at the program level, distance learners may come to expect them, and eschew programs that do not offer them.

Another implication of organizing electronic communities around distance programs is their potential effect on the expectations of on-campus students. Just as students who live on-campus frequently register for online courses, if given the chance they are likely to join electronic communities too. Program administrators will need to decide whether to limit membership in the electronic community to distance learners or also to allow on-campus students to participate. However, even if on-campus students are not allowed to participate, will it be long before they ask for electronic communities of their own?

## Research Opportunities

Few colleges and universities have implemented electronic communities for distance learners beyond the course level. And those that have are in their early stages of development. Therefore, until more electronic communities are formed, there will be few communities available on which to conduct research. Depending on the purpose of the research, a wide range of research methodologies could conceivably be used to investigate electronic communities. However, two approaches seem to be particularly appropriate: social network analysis and case study research.

Social network analysis recognizes that when people are linked together by computers and they form relationships, a social network is formed. According to Garton, Haythornthwaite, & Wellman (1997):

> Social network analysts seek to describe networks of relations as fully as possible, tease out the prominent patterns in such networks, trace the flow of information (and other resources) through them, and discover what effects these relations and networks have on people and organizations (p.3).

The social network approach provides a set of concepts and vocabulary for describing a social network that reveals the dynamics and roles of network members within the whole network. Even though this approach would take some time to learn for those who are unfamiliar with it, the effort invested in learning to apply social network analysis to an electronic community should produce ample rewards in understanding.

A case study approach might also be an effective research strategy. A strength of the case study approach is that it allows researchers to investigate a phenomenon within a real-life context by using multiple sources and types of evidence (Yin, 1994). Since the contexts in which electronic communities are implemented are likely to vary from one institution to another, it is important to take context into account when undertaking research. The case study is a good vehicle for doing this because a case study can include a detailed, real-life description of the object of the case study.

Following are four areas and several sample questions that might be useful to consider when conducting research on electronic communities beyond the course level.

### Recruitment of Prospective Students

- Does the presence of an electronic community supporting a degree program play a role in prospective students' decision to enroll in that program? If so, how big a factor is it?
- What features of an electronic community do prospective students find most/least appealing?
- What level of exposure to an electronic community do prospective students need to experience before forming an opinion about the value of an electronic community for them? (e.g. Do they need to participate in a sample chat?)
- What are the characteristics of students who are highly motivated by the prospect of joining an electronic community?

### Student Participation Patterns

- What components or features of an electronic community facility do members use most/least and value most/least highly?
- What are the characteristics of students who are the most and least active electronic community members?
- What are the participation patterns of students identified as "at risk" and "not at risk?"
- What do the network of relations and the flow of information look like among community members?

### Outcomes

- What are the effects of membership in an electronic community on learner satisfaction, program achievement level, and program completion?

- How does the level of participation in an electronic community affect learner satisfaction, learner achievement level, and program completion?
- How do learner satisfaction, program achievement level, and program completion levels of members of an electronic community compare with those who are not members?
- What are the effects of membership in an electronic community on the likelihood for graduates of the program to join an alumni association?
- What are the effects of membership in an electronic community on the level of giving of alumni?

### *Institutional Impacts*

- How does the presence of an electronic community affect the number and quality of relationships established among faculty and staff and members of the electronic community?
- What unanticipated outcomes on the department, school, or institution have occurred as a result of establishing an electronic community?
- What has been the impact on institutional resources of creating an electronic community?

## CONCLUSION

This chapter has encouraged administrators of distance learning programs to look beyond the course level when seeking to build a lasting sense of community among distance learners, faculty, and staff. Successfully designing, developing, and implementing electronic communities at the program level or higher requires effective administrative leadership, careful planning, technological support, and committed faculty and staff. The difficulty of finding appropriate examples to include in this chapter suggests that colleges and universities have yet to recognize the potential of electronic communities to attract prospective students, to facilitate the progress of enrolled students, and to maintain relationships with alumni. However, this situation is likely to change in the near future.

With few exceptions the development of online courses has outpaced the development of the online services required to support them. When colleges and universities began to deliver courses online, accrediting agencies and others questioned whether distance learners were being supported as well as students taking courses on campus. Institutions of higher education responded, in part, by making online courses more interactive (e.g., by adding discussion groups, chatrooms) and by making resources such as campus libraries accessible to distance learners. More recently, colleges and universities are focusing on delivering whole degree programs to distance learners. As administrators become more aware of the value distance learners place on having access to program level electronic communities, they will be more likely to create them. Eventually electronic communities organized at the program level will become standard practice as institutions rise to meet the ever-increasing expectations of distance learners.

## REFERENCES

Axelrood (1984). *The evolution of cooperation.* New York: Basic Books.

Brigham, D.E. (2001). Converting student support services to online delivery. *International Review of Research in Open and Distance Learning.* 1(2), [http://www.irrodl.org/content/v1.2/regents.html].

Brigham, D.E. (1998). An electronic peer network for adult learners. Saratoga, NY: Empire State College, National Center on Adult Learning.

Diamond, R. M. (1989). *Designing and improving courses and curricula in higher education.* San Francisco: Jossey-Bass.

Donath, J. S. (1999). Identify and deception in the virtual community. In M. A. Smith & P. Kollock (Eds.), *Communities in Cyberspace.* (pp. 29-59). London: Routledge.

Clark, N. (2001). Education, communication, and consuption: Piping in the academic community. In C. Werry & M. Mowbray (Eds.), *Online Communities.* (pp. 129-151). Upper Saddle River, NY: Prentice Hall.

Coate, J. (1998). Cyberspace innkeeping: Building online community. Retrieved Feburary 28, 2002 from [http://www.sfgate.com/~tex/innkeeping].

Excelsior College (1998). *Academic honesty policy.* [http://gl.excelsior.edu/epn2/ec_open.nsf/pages/acad_hon.htm].

Excelsior College (2001). *Electronic use policy.* [http://gl.excelsior.edu/epn2/ec_open.nsf/pages/e_use.htm].

Garton, L., Haythornthwaite, C., & Wellman, B. (1997). Studying online social networks. *Journal of Computer-Mediated Communication.* 3(1) 1-30.

Greer, (1992). *ID Project Management Tools and Techniques for Instructional Designers and Developers.* Englewood Cliffs, NJ: Educational Technology Publications.

Gustafson, K. L. & Branch, R. M. (1997). *Survey of instructional development models* (3rd ed.). Syracuse, NY: ERIC Clearinghouse on Information & Technology, Syracuse University.

Kirsner, S. (2002a, April). Customer Friendly IM. [Electronic Version]. *Darwin Magazine.* Retrieved April 5, 2002 from [http://www.darwinmag.com/read/040102/ecosystem.html].

Kirsner, S. (2002b, February). IM is here. RU prepared? [Electronic Version]. *Darwin Magazine.* Retrieved April 5, 2002 from [http://www.darwinmag.com/read/020102/ecosystem.html].

Maehl, W. H. (2000). *Lifelong learning at its best.* San Francisco: Jossey-Bass, Inc.

Menkart, J. (2001). Internet portal technology remains hot market for 2002. Unisys World, 22, 19.

Middle States Commission on Higher Education (2002a). Best Practices for Electronically Offered Degree and Certificate Programs. Washington, D.C.: Middle States Commission on Higher Education.

Middle States Commission on Higher Education (2002b). Characteristics of Excellence in Higher Education. Washington, D.C.: Middle States Commission on Higher Education.

Moore, M. G. (1999). Monitoring and evaluation. *The American Journal of Distance Education*, 13(2), 1-3.

Nesler, M. S. (2001). *2000 computer behavior survey*. Albany, NY: Excelsior College, Office of Institutional Research.

Palloff, R. M., & Pratt, K. (1999). *Building learning communities in cyberspace*. San Francisco: Jossey-Bass.

Palloff, R. M., & Pratt, K. (2001). *Lessons from the cyberspace classroom: The realities of online teaching.*. San Francisco: Jossey-Bass.

Piskurich, G. M. (2000). *Rapid instructional design*. San Franciso: Jossey-Bass Pfeiffer.

Regents College (1997). *Strategic long-range plan for Regents College*. Unpublished manuscript, Regents College at, Albany, NY.

Rheingold, H. (1993). *The virtual community: Homesteading on the electronic frontier*. Reading, MA: Addison-Wesley.

Rogers, E. M. (1983). *Diffusion of innovations*. (3rd ed.). New York: The Free Press.

Southern Regional Education Board, (1998). *Principles of good practice*. Retrieved April 9, 2002. [http://www.electroniccampus.org/student/srecinfo/publications/pr inciples.asp].

UNESCO (1998). *World declaration on higher education for the twenty-first century: Vision and action*. Retrieved April 4, 2002: [http://www.unesco.org/education/educprog/wche/declaration_eng.ht m].

Werry, C. & Mowbray, M. (Eds.). (2001). *Online communities*. Upper Saddle River, NJ: Prentice Hall.

Yin, R.K. (1994). *Case study research*. (2nd ed.) Thousand Oaks, CA: SAGE Publications.

CHAPTER 4

# FACULTY-LIBRARIAN COLLABORATION IN ONLINE COURSE DEVELOPMENT

**Sharon M. Edge**

On-campus library resources are an expected and integral part of the learning environment. Global learners who enroll in distance education (DE) courses should presume to receive the same access to this fundamental educational resource as do on-campus learners. Experienced and knowledgeable librarians can become a vital link in the provision of distance learning library services (DLLS) to DE faculty and learners alike. The practice of faculty collaboration with librarians can result in the development and deployment of information-rich, scholarly online courses. DLLS librarians can focus attention on the benefits of utilizing copyrighted electronic journal articles from databases, which college and university libraries purchase annually, as an adjunct to Web resources. The Association of College and Research Libraries' *Guidelines for Distance Learning Library Services* (2000), the reference point for this chapter, illustrated the pitfalls of relying solely on information content freely accessible on the Web for course enrichment. Issues related to identification of copyright-compliant electronic journal articles, compilation of electronic reading lists of journal articles, and remote access to and use of electronic library databases are discussed. To demonstrate the benefits of utilizing existing library services in DE course delivery, the services offered by DLLS at the University of Louisville are presented.

Electronic Learning Communities—Issues and Practices, pages 135–185.
Copyright © 2003 by Information Age Publishing, Inc.
All rights of reproduction in any form reserved.
ISBN: 1-931576-96-3 (pbk.), 1-931576-97-1 (hardcover)

**KEYWORDS:** accreditation, collaboration, competencies, fluency, information, librarian, library, literacy, distance education, distance learning, online learning.

## INTRODUCTION

Raish (2000) pointed out that most distance education (DE) proposals routinely ignore the importance of libraries, even though online education programs need access to a first-class library and qualified librarians. In a review of articles on the topic, Beagle (2000) concluded that "only a few mention issues related to library access or resource integration [and that] only a small number of courseware evaluations posted on academic Web-sites include criteria related to libraries" (p. 367). Beagle also noted several articles that point to greater library involvement in online learning and a more "active role [for librarians] in technical, pedagogical, and instructional support decisions concerning Web-based learning environments" (p. 367).

O'Leary (2000) maintained that the growth of DE provides opportunities for libraries to extend and leverage their role by providing an array of remotely delivered services. According to Pace (2001), distance learning library service (DLLS) providers are developing some of the most sophisticated services and marketing strategies in university library systems and are influencing the services that are offered to all library users. In many institutions, the library becomes the closest thing to 24/7 service available for DE learners. For example, at the University of Louisville (U of L), library personnel monitor e-mail and phone inquiries from DE learners approximately 18 hours per day.

Troll (2001) investigated the changing role of libraries and questioned the impact that the growing interest in online courses and DE are having on library use. She challenged libraries to consider a number of environmental factors, including changes in the literate habits of Web use versus library use, changes in learners and curricula, changes in the technological infrastructure, and the availability of information resources and services provided by entities external to the library.

This chapter demonstrates that DE programs need librarians and library resources and services primarily to meet the institutional goals of producing educated citizens for the Information Age and to fulfill accreditation expectations for DE programs. The chapter also confirms that collaboration between librarians and teaching faculty results in the design of information-rich curricula that foster technological, media, and information fluency. Clearly, collaboration results in a greater return for faculty and learners on the institutional investment in electronic databases of library resources.

## ISSUES, CONTROVERSIES, AND PROBLEMS

Issues and controversies inherent in the use of information resources have increased in direct proportion to the development of DE programs. Examples include: the lack of concern for the library in the initial phase of course development; the consequences of relying on the Web instead of articles from scholarly journals for research data; the reliance on fee-based library service providers that duplicate resources that are freely available from libraries; and the role that faculty play in fostering information, technology, and media fluency in their learners.

### Understanding Our Student Population

The American Council on Education reported 10 years of longitudinal research on the nature of the higher education student population (as cited in Choy, 2002). The report indicated that "about three-quarters of all four-year college learners now earn a paycheck, and about one-quarter of them work full-time [and that] just over one third of those who graduated were still repaying student loans of about $150 per month 4 years after they graduated" (as cited in Choy, pp. 5-6). It comes as no surprise that education is expensive. As the costs of a college education rises, studies, such as the report from the National Center for Public Policy and Higher Education, encourage combating the trend (as cited in Hebel, 2002).

Preparing learners to become responsible citizens has different meanings to different groups. To two librarians at Georgia State University (GSU) it means teaching learners to be aware of the structure and impact of information and information technology on their lives and the importance of critically thinking about the information they use to make everyday decisions (Burtle & Sugarman, 2002). They concluded:

> Teaching faculty recognized that GSU librarians are, in fact, faculty members who can make valuable contributions to the university's educational mission. Since we attended faculty meetings with teaching faculty and participated in discussions about student learning, teaching techniques, successes, and problems, teaching faculty have come to recognize librarians as equal partners in the teaching mission of the university (p. 279).

### Understanding the Information Age

Halal (1992) stated, "One of the primary reasons that the United States is in economic decline is that an outmoded education system has left most

American youngsters functionally ill-equipped to cope with a high-tech society" (p. 15). Schools must provide learners with opportunities to function successfully in an information-rich environment so that they will not be overwhelmed by such an environment when they enter the workplace. Schools must provide opportunities for learners to work in teams on solving problems that require the application of information. Schools must provide opportunities for learners to develop their information-seeking skills via non-print media and electronic information and education networks they will be using as adults. When K-12 schools fail to provide learners with educational opportunities that enhance these information skills, learners enter college without them. Higher education institutions then become responsible for developing these information skills in their learners.

Most higher education goals and objectives convey aspirations that are often difficult to translate into practical benefit. One of the changes brought by the Information Age is the ability to access global information and share that information with individuals around the world. One of the goals of higher education in a democratic society has always been to promote critical thinking as a habit of mind so that one can develop the skills necessary for civic engagement. The currency of the new information economy has become knowledge, which increases productivity. It is a commodity dependent upon the ability to find, evaluate, and use information.

## What Does Becoming Educated Mean?

Most higher education institutions have goals that include preparing learners to become responsible citizens as an outcome of their college or university education. Burniske (2000) addressed the idea of what it means to be educated and the difficulty of determining when someone has acquired the critical literacy that describes a liberally educated or learned person by noting that "unfortunately, competence with one form of literacy does not guarantee fluency with another." He proposed a taxonomy of literacy that includes media literacy. Media literacy was further defined by and the Alliance for a Media Literate America (AMLA, 2002). Most importantly, Burniske maintained that "we must adopt a holistic approach, establishing a 'literacy-across-the curriculum' program similar to writing-across-the curriculum initiatives."

Learning can be fun, but it is not always easy. A faculty member at Duke University, one of the best-regarded private institutions of higher education in the United States, lamented that intellectual life is optional for learners at his institution (Rojstaczer, 2001). He pointed out that administrators are interested in increasing enrollment and that most learners prefer colleges where they feel comfortable rather than intellectually intense.

He observed that his institution "principally provides social and economic credentials for its learners [while they] only go through the motions academically and remain intellectually disengaged." Rojstaczer maintained that only about 20 colleges and universities in the United States, mostly elite liberal arts colleges, have managed to hold the high ground and achieve the high level of intellectual commitment and ambience that Duke craves.

The Associated Colleges of the South (ACS, 2001) sponsors an information fluency initiative that seems to be having a significant impact on integration fluency into the curriculum of liberal arts colleges. Davidson College (2001) is an example of a highly selective liberal arts college in North Carolina that instituted faculty-librarian collaborative partnerships to ensure the integration of information fluency into the curriculum. At Davidson College, several professors who have been awarded ACS-funded information grants have collaborated with information technologists and librarians to integrate information competencies into their biology, psychology, and English courses (see ACS Website). In addition to retaining faculty members who are collectively raising classroom standards and challenging their learners, liberal arts colleges expect to graduate learners who are effective, critical thinkers fluent in the use of information to solve problems.

In 1999, the National Research Council (NRC) published a report on becoming fluent with information technology. The definition of information fluency stresses the intellectual capabilities of problem solving, including the ability to define and clarify a problem, understand the advantages and disadvantages of apparent solutions to problems, cope with unexpected consequences, and quickly upgrade skills to adapt to a changing environment. The chair of the committee that produced the NRC report pointed out that all learners need to be able to engage in algorithmic thinking, which includes logical reasoning and the ability to manage complexity (F. Olsen, 2000).

Technological advances in computers and telecommunications have changed our definitions of literacy and our ways of preparing literate individuals (Brevik, 1991; Drucker, 1993; J. K. Olsen, 1992; Tuman, 1992; Varlejs, 1991). Citizenship in a technological society requires new kinds of literacy skills, namely, information literacy skills. Ridgeway (1990) commented:

> Information-literate persons must be able to recognize when information is needed and have the ability to locate, evaluate and use effectively the needed information . . . . Information-literate people are those who have learned how to learn. They know how to learn because they know how knowledge is organized, how to find information, and how to use information in a way that others can learn from them (p. 645).

The views of these early proponents of information literacy were instrumental in this author's (1992) decision to collaborate with teaching faculty to incorporate information skills into the first DE courses offered at U of L.

The tradition and commitment of U of L's distance learning library services (DLLS) to instilling information competency skills in learners were enhanced with the hiring of a Dean of University Libraries noted for her work in information literacy. She immediately established a library liaison program that promoted faculty-librarian collaboration on the incorporation of information skills into the university curriculum (Rader, 2001). U of L's Website http://www.louisville.edu/infoliteracy/infolitoutcomes. htm] includes the university's (2001) working document on the integration and promotion of information literacy through class assignments.

## Web Versus Library Databases

Hordes of learners who are unaware of the library resources at their educational institutions and who do not want to pay for fee-based information services have flocked to the Web. In May of 2002, the Council on Library and Information Resources (CLIR) released the preliminary findings of a survey (in press) designed to determine how the Web affects the work of learners and scholars and the consequences that its use will have on campus libraries. The full results of the study were to be published in the Summer of 2002 (Greenstein & Healy, 2002).

How do people find what they are looking for on the Web? Silicon Valley.com reported on a study designed to determine if the same foraging theories that describe how animals behave while seeking prey can predict how people ferret out information on the Internet ("Scents and Sensibilities," 2001). Although some professors and librarians lament the fact that today's learners are not information literate, others believe that they are very efficient at locating only the information that they must have in order to meet their professors' expectations. MacAdam (2000) proposed a new set of assumptions regarding the information-seeking habits of today's college students and commented that "the single most important step academic librarians can take right now is to help faculty find ways to develop curriculum bridges from the natural critical nature of students to the formal contextual judgments they must make in any specific subject discipline" (p. 87). Some studies have indicated that high school learners use the Web intelligently, that learners are not just using Websites (Jenkins, 2002), and that learners plagiarize less often than previously thought (Kellogg, 2002).

The Online Computer Library Center (OCLC, 2002) commissioned a national year-long blind research study of 1,050 college students who used the Web. The study concluded:

College and university students look to campus libraries and library websites [sic] for their information needs and value access to accurate, up-to-date information with easily identifiable authors. They are aware of the shortcomings of information available from the web [*sic*] and of their needs for assistance in finding information in electronic or paper formats.

In spite of the aforementioned encouraging studies, the citation of Websites for scholarly research remains problematic because the uniform resource locators (URLs) often become inaccessible over time. In a longitudinal study, Germain (2000) examined the accessibility of 64 URLs cited in 31 academic journal articles and found an increasing decline in their availability. This phenomenon is commonly referred to as link-rot. Since Germain's study, other researchers (Davis, 2002; Davis & Cohen, 2001; Koehler, 2002) have examined Webpage change and persistence and the effect of the Web on citation behavior.

Kiernan (2002) reported on research from two professors at the University of Nebraska who measured the impact of link-rot on online education and found that it is similar to the decay of radioactive substances. Kiernan noted that the study illustrates the extent of a practical problem of offering courses online: the need for someone to periodically check on an online course's links and remove or update any that have expired. He pointed out that "academic departments often do not budget for such maintenance costs or consider in tenure-and-promotion evaluations how much time such maintenance takes." Libraries at academic institutions license hundreds or thousands of scholarly online research journals that cost hundreds of thousands of dollars and make them available for remote access. Citing more scholarly research material from online journals instead of Websites that may disappear from online courses would be a more effective use of institutions' electronic and faculty resources.

Faculty developing online courses often attempt to combat the link-rot phenomenon by copying URLs for journal articles from online databases into courses without realizing that URLs for articles in most databases are dynamic rather than static. A link for a journal article that is simply copied from a database and inserted into a course will eventually become inactive when the URL changes. DE faculty can work with librarians to develop electronic readings lists (i.e. electronic course packs) that can be placed on eReserve to solve this problem.

## What is eReserve?

*eReserve* is a system for creating collections of electronic readings lists with citations in a standard bibliographic format (e.g., APA) that link to the full-text of journal articles considered as required reading for a course.

These articles are accessible by DE learners with library usernames and passwords at no additional charge. At U of L, library usernames and passwords are issued to learners and faculty in DE programs for which a collaborative arrangement has been established between the academic unit and DLLS. The electronic reading lists prepared for eReserve (i.e., electronic course packs) can be accessed from a link within a professor's course.

After a faculty member provides a list of the articles needed for an electronic reading list, DLLS personnel search for the articles in the online databases. The articles that can be found in electronic format are then assembled into collections of electronic reading lists. Citations for articles that are not available in electronic format are also included, along with a link to the journal article request form. Upon receipt of the form, with the copyright box checked, DLLS personnel obtain a copy of the article and either send it directly to the DE learner in PDF format or post it on a password-protected Website for the learner to download.

Libraries use proprietary software to create durable links that stabilize the URLs for subsequent use. More recently, options for use of persistent and durable links by faculty have been provided by library database aggregators, such as EBSCO HOST and ProQuest. However, most faculty either do not have the technical expertise or do not want to become involved in the level of detail required to create persistent or durable links. They find that asking DLLS personnel to create an electronic readings page (i.e., an eReserve page) for their DE courses is a much simpler alternative.

### *Fee-Based Library Service Providers Versus Library Databases*

It is understandable that as textbook prices rise, learners search for less expensive information alternatives (E. Carlson, 2002; Wagner, 2001). A few learners may buy only the textbooks that are absolutely necessary and may choose to use library resources when otherwise possible. Other learners appear to have fallen prey to aggressively marketed, fee-based services that offer them the same resources that can be obtained for free from libraries (Casey, 2002; Rinear, 2002).

At U of L, DLLS personnel have been assembling collections of electronic journal articles (i.e., eReserve) for faculty teaching in DE programs since the Summer of 1998. DLLS staff no longer scan printed material for eReserve. Instead, they assist faculty with the location of relevant material from the electronic databases licensed by U of L's Library System, of which DLLS is an administrative unit, with an emphasis on the ProQuest databases as the easiest ones to use for the assembly of eReserve.

The resources offered by commercial services are fewer in number and more selective than the resources available from most libraries. Librarians and professors are concerned about the presentation of biased points of views due to the information filtering that results from using a more selective collection of resources. Libraries are committed to freedom of inquiry based on access to diverse opinions and opposing views from world literature.

## Faculty Expectations: Can Just Anyone Teach?

The question of teaching credentials in higher education was a topic of discussion in the *Chronicle of Higher Education's* Ms. Mentor column (Toth, 2000). However, good credentials do not necessarily ensure good teaching. To determine the characteristics of a good teacher, David Shribman (2001) traveled all over North American for a year talking with people about their most memorable teachers. Arnone (2002) reported on interviews with some "favorite" professors who stand out in alumni memories. He concluded that "creativity and a personal touch are two common traits of favorite professors." He also cited a past president of the Education Commission of the States as noting, "What makes such professors special . . . . is their ability to connect emotionally with students." Arnone also commented that although many of these professors refuse to give up face-to-face interaction, "they do use technology in the classroom .... Most of these professors view distance education positively and believe that online courses can provide just as much opportunity for personal interaction as traditional ones."

Several individuals have addressed the competencies needed by faculty delivering DE courses (Hakim, 2002; Rockwell, Schauer, Fritz, & Marx, 2000) and the topic of competencies of distance educators rises periodically in the DEOS-L online mailing list provided by the American Center for the Study of Distance Education at the Pennsylvania State University (as cited in Saba, 2002).

Faculty are key to the successful use of library resources by learners. It is important that faculty become aware of the library resources and services that are available not only for DE learners but also for themselves. Instructors must become informationally competent. Librarians are eager to share the possibilities for equitable library service for DE learners with faculty so that they can exercise their important role in enhancing the research skills of their learners.

The barriers that learners encounter when accessing library resources and services remotely for DE courses are compounded by the barriers that faculty members developing the courses encounter. First, a desire to integrate information resources into the curriculum must either emanate from the professor or be instilled in the professor by university administrators and/or librarians. DE faculty need to become proficient in the necessary skills to use DE library services before those services are made available to DE learners in their courses. When DE faculty recognize the value of using scholarly resources in their courses, they will be able to instill in their learners the importance of using scholarly library resources. (See Appendix A for a list of benefits that DLLS provides to DE faculty.) If barriers to the faculty integration of scholarly information resources into the curriculum are not eliminated, learners will never encounter the opportunity to meet the institution's desired educational outcome, namely, graduates with the ability to locate, evaluate, and use information effectively as lifelong learners in the workplace and the community. This author has reviewed the literature on the challenges faced by faculty in developing DE courses and a discussion of the barriers to the integration of information resources into the curriculum (Edge & Edge, 2000). The author now directs the reader to examples of best practice sites for DE and information literacy.

## BEST PRACTICES

Regional accrediting agency expectations and programmatic/discipline accreditation expectations provide a framework for best practices. ACRL's (2000) *Guidelines for Distance Learning Library Services* serve as the foundation for the definition of DLLS. Stanley Fish, Dean of the College of Liberal Arts and Sciences at the University of Illinois at Chicago, attempted to answer the question, "What are best practices?" After providing an irreverent analysis of the use of the best practice concept in higher education, Fish (2002) observed that "[the concept of] 'Best Practices' is itself a practice, an industry focused on itself and equipped with its own internal machinery, including a version of the Academy Awards that allows practitioners to recognized and honor one another publicly." Fish attacked three pieties that often accompany best practices rhetoric:

a.   always prioritize,
b.   pick your battles, and
c.   keep your eye on the big picture.

He stated that these concepts are based on the idea that administrative energy and influence are finite, must be either hoarded lest they run out, or saved for the big things. Fish's "devil in the details" recommendation is that administrators must "sweat the details." He maintained that if the pressure to do things right does not emanate from the administrator's office, it will not emanate from anywhere.

The Council for Higher Education Accreditation (CHEA, 2001) maintains a distance learning and accreditation review section in the Good Practices Database on its Website [http://www.chea.org/good-practices/index.cfm]. The Sloan-C Quality Education Online Website also includes an Effective Practices Sharing section [http://www.sloan-c.org/effective-practices/login.htm]. Nearly every virtual university has established principles of good practice such as those developed by the Western Interstate

Commission for Higher Education (WICHE, 1999). Various professional associations, such as the American Association for Higher Education Assessment Forum (AAHE, 1996), have also established principles of good practice for assessing student learning. In the Information Age, many professional groups stress the importance of learners being able to think algorithmically by being fluent with information technology (Phillips, 1999). In addition to being computer literate, learners are now also expected to become information literate (ACRL, 2000).

Tom Kirk (2002) leads the ACRL Best Practices Initiative on Information Literacy [http://www.ala.org/acrl/nili/criteria.html]. In April 2002, he was interviewed by the TLT Group for a Webcast [http://www.tlt-group.org/calendar/interviewarchives2001.htm] which presented a definition of information literacy and discussed the use of the term *information literacy* versus *computer literacy, information fluency,* or a number of other terms applied to programs for helping learners learn how to use information resources. The Webcast also addressed the roles of academic departments, faculty, professional development staff, and librarians in developing responsible programs for helping learners use information resources.

ACRL's (2000) guidelines provided the following definition of DLLS:

> *Distance learning library services* [DLLS] refers to those library services in support of college, university, or other post-secondary [*sic*] courses and programs offered away from a main campus, or in the absence of a traditional campus, and regardless of where credit is given. These courses may be taught in traditional or non-traditional [*sic*] formats or media, may or may not require physical facilities, and may or may not involve live interaction of teachers and learners. The phrase is inclusive of courses in all post-secondary programs designated as extension, extended, off-campus, extended campus, distance, distributed, open, flexible, franchising, virtual, synchronous, or asynchronous.

The origins and revisions of the guidelines are available on the ACRL (2000) Website [http://www.ala.org/acrl/guides/distlrng.html]. One noteworthy aspect is the diversity and extent of support among consortia and representatives of professional and accrediting associations who provided information on their own efforts to ensure excellence of library services for postsecondary DE programs. Among the groups responding are the Canadian Association of College and University Libraries of the Canadian Library Association, College Librarians and Media Specialists (CLAMS), the Commission on Colleges of the Northwest Association of Schools and Colleges (NASC), the Consortium for Educational Technology for University Systems (CETUS), the Interinstitutional Library Council (ILC) of the Oregon State System of Higher Education (OSSHE), Libraries and the Western Governors University Conference, the Southern Association of Colleges and Schools (SACS), and WICHE. (See ARCL's Website for detailed descriptions of each organization.)

The DLLS guidelines were established by ACRL, a division of the American Library Association (ALA), in 2000. The introductory paragraph of this standards document declared:

> Library resources and services in institutions of higher education must meet the needs of all their faculty, learners, and academic support staff, wherever these individuals are located, whether on a main campus, off campus, in distance education or extended campus programs, or in the absence of a campus at all; in courses taken for credit or non-credit; in continuing education programs; in courses attended in person or by means of electronic transmission; or any other means of distance education (ACRL, 2000). The "Guidelines" delineate the elements necessary to achieving these ends. The "Guidelines" are intended to serve as a gateway to adherence to the ACRL Standards in the appropriate areas and in accordance with the size and type of originating institution.

According to ACRL's (2000) guidelines:

> Library services offered to the distance learning community should be designed to meet effectively a wide range of informational, bibliographic, and user needs. The exact combination of central and site staffing [for DLLS] will differ from institution to institution. The following library services, though not necessarily exhaustive, are essential:

> - Reference assistance;
> - Computer-based bibliographic and informational services;
> - Reliable, rapid, secure access to institutional and other networks, including the Internet;
> - Consultation services;
> - Program of library user instruction designed to instill independent and effective information literacy skills while specifically meeting the learner-support needs of the distance learning community;
> - Assistance with and instruction in the use of non-print media and equipment;
> - Reciprocal or contractual borrowing, or interlibrary loan services using broadest application of fair use of copyrighted materials;
> - Prompt document delivery such as a courier system and/or electronic transmission;
> - Access to reserve materials in accordance with copyright fair use policies;
> - Adequate service hours for optimum access by users;
> - Promotion of library services to the distance learning community, including documented and updated policies, regulations, and procedures for systematic development, and management of information resources.

## Best Practices for DLLS

In the spirit of ACRL's (2000) guidelines, creative and insightful ideas were put forth at the Distance Learning Services Discussion Group session held during the American Library Association Midwinter Meeting (2002) as being representative of good DE library practices for providing instruction on the use of library resources through a variety of methods: providing electronic reserves, producing customized Webpages with links to resources, offering toll-free telephone numbers, using templates for class Webpages, saving long reference e-mail messages for future use, and producing a Frequently-Asked Questions Webpage. These ideas were consistent with this author's lists of good DE library practices for learners. (See Appendices B, C, and D.)

## DISTANCE LEARNING LIBRARY SERVICES AT U OF L

Effective DE programs require the development and utilization of collaborative partnerships. DLLS was initiated at U of L in 1992, nearly a decade prior to the ACRL *Guidelines for Distance Learning Library Services* that were finalized in December 2000. This collaborative partnership between faculty and DLLS personnel at U of L contributed to the success of the DE program in the Department of Special Education and served as a model for the development of a university-wide model for effective library instructional and support services for DE. DLLS has designed and provided a decade of services for DE learners at U of L during a period of immense growth in distance and online learning (1992-2002).

### Overview of DLLS at U of L

DLLS [2002; http://www.louisville.edu/library/distance] staff serve approximately 20 different U of L DE and international graduate degree programs in business, education, engineering, and social work. U of L faculty offer courses via satellite television, interactive videoconferencing, online via the Web, and on-site in various locations around the world. Most learners in the United States access their courses and the U of L libraries from their homes or offices. The chief off-campus locations are Fort Knox, Athens, Greece, Cairo, Egypt, Hong Kong, Singapore, and Panama. A major accomplishment of DLLS during the Summer and Fall of 2001 was the successful implementation of library service for three new Army online programs: Human Resource Education, Public Administration, and Justice Administration.

DLLS personnel are responsible for ensuring equitable remote access to library resources and services for U of L DE learners and professors, regardless of their location and time zone. During the 2001-2002 fiscal year, DLLS staff provided library services to 3,756 course enrollments in

209 different U of L DE and international program courses. The library faculty administrator of DLLS is responsible for the following duties, plus any unanticipated ones that require attention:

- Leading and coordinating library programs and services that support DE courses in U of L programs designated as DE for accreditation reviews.
- Assisting with information resources and services sections of DE accreditation projects as requested by U of L academic units.
- Providing data to the Dean of University Libraries for use with university administration and academic units to determine methods of sharing costs of library services with DE programs.
- Arranging for the transfer of funds from U of L academic units for library services provided for DE programs.
- Reporting U of L student and faculty use of DLLS resources and services to U of L's Institute for International Development and to coordinators of other university DE programs served by DLLS.
- Planning and implementing library services for emerging DE programs.

The DLLS library faculty administrator (the author of this chapter) serves as library liaison for currently supported and emerging U of L DE programs. She also serves on the U of L Library System's Information Literacy Team. The DLLS Faculty Administrator and the DLLS Program Coordinator conduct instructional sessions (e.g., face-to-face, via television, or via the Web) for U of L learners enrolled in DE programs. Both individuals also develop and revise instructional content about library resources and services for U of L DE programs.

The DLLS professional/administrative Program Coordinator is primarily responsible for the following duties, along with any others that may be assigned:

- Providing technical support for DLLS.
- Maintaining the electronic course reserve system for DE learners and faculty.
- Administering document delivery services for DE learners and faculty.

As part of her technical support duties, the DLLS Program Coordinator maintains the library Web portals for approximately 20 DE programs. In 2001, she worked closely with the U of L Library System's Webmaster on the implementation of a new, improved proxy server that facilitated better access to electronic library databases by members of the U of L DE community outside of the louisville.edu domain. In collaboration with Office of Libraries Technology personnel, the DLLS Program Coordinator also updated the method of generating and compiling statistics on the number of instances in which DE learners enter library databases to perform research.

DLLS personnel meet the instructional needs of DE faculty members by sharing information about electronic full-text articles in library databases and by encouraging the integration of these electronic library resources into their online courses via the DLLS eReserve system. In the process of creating electronic reading lists of journal articles, DLLS personnel also exercise vigilance in regard to the U of L Library System's database licensing and copyright compliance obligations. Faculty members send bibliographies of items that they consider required reading for their learners to the DLLS Program Coordinator. After DLLS personnel research the citations to determine their availability in electronic format, durable links to the items are prepared, and the articles are integrated into the faculty member's online course. Upon entry of a DLLS library user ID and password, learners can gain access to journal articles specified by the professor as required readings.

Learners can ask library personnel to deliver journal articles to their homes or workplaces via fax or as e-mail attachments. Books are delivered to the learners' homes via first-class mail. In January 1995, the Ekstrom Library installed a digital micro-printer to enable the conversion of microfiche and microfilm resources into digital format for transmission via fax or computer so that DE learners could gain remote access to the huge microfiche and microfilm collections housed in U of L's libraries. In addition to delivering materials from its own collection, U of L's libraries also provide access via interlibrary loan to material held in other libraries, and utilize various commercial document delivery services and the Internet to deliver material via fax and electronically. In 2001, DLLS personnel retrieved from the U of L Library System's stacks collections, and from other sources outside the university, approximately 1,600 journal articles and other items that were not immediately available in electronic format from library research databases. These items were delivered via e-mail, fax, and first-class mail to U of L DE learners who needed them for course assignments and independent research.

For independent research, learners enrolled in DE courses at U of L can consult with library personnel by e-mail, fax, or phone and can use their computers to search remote databases to identify library materials relevant to their research topics. DLLS records indicate that DE learners entered library databases well over 10,000 times in 2001. From online databases, learners can read, download, or print the full text of articles directly into their personal computers.

Most importantly, DLLS at U of L is committed to an information literacy program designed to enhance the ability of DE learners to use appropriate technologies to retrieve information needed for independent study and research on a self-service basis. DLLS personnel schedule themselves to work several evening and weekend shifts so that DE learners in different time zones can receive prompt, personal responses to their e-mail and phone inquires. They willingly adjust their schedules on short notice to troubleshoot and provide solutions to problems when the need arises. DLLS is committed to enhancing the technological and information competencies of DE learners and faculty. Through the instructional activities and individual assistance that DLLS personnel provide via phone and e-mail for approximately 18 hours each day, they contribute to the computer and information fluency of U of L DE learners and faculty.

## Origin of DLLS at U of L

The original library support for DE projects at U of L was a spontaneous, collaborative effort that developed as the result of a long-standing librarian-teaching faculty relationship between a faculty member in the Department of Special Education and another professor serving as Head of Document Access and Delivery Services. During the Spring of 1992, the Office of the Provost and the Office of Information Technology at U of L announced a Technology Incentive Grant Program. The Special Education faculty member proposed the development of a live, interactive DE course offered for academic credit via satellite and cable television with learners participating via phone and/or computer from their home or workplace. The goal was to develop DE courses that would be of equal or superior quality to the same courses offered on campus. Many of the DE learners were not expected to be near a major popular center with a library capable of meeting their graduate level research needs. In accordance with her philosophy that library research is an essential component of quality education, the librarian developed a companion proposal designed to provide library services for U of L's Department of Special Education's DE program. Rather than relying on reciprocal borrowing arrangements with other libraries to meet the needs of U of L's DE learners, the librarian proposed offering research support directly from the university library via electronic means. Both proposals were funded, and U of L's first, interactive DE course was offered in the Spring of 1993 with a full complement of electronic library services.

In the early days of U of L's Department of Special Education's DE program, standards were developed for the purposes of coordination and cooperation. The success of the DE program was enhanced by the support of numerous units on the U of L campus. This wider support system provided immediate ownership for the program because the entire campus contributed to the success of the program. The standards set for program development and support stated that:

- Courses would be developed by U of L's Director of Distance Learning and the faculty member.
- Courses would have a producer/director assigned from Television Services (if course delivery were to be via interactive television) or a Webmaster from Information Technology (if the course were to be Web-based).
- Courses would have full library support equivalent to that provided for on-campus learners.
- Printed materials developed by the faculty member would be produced by Information Technology Services.
- Guidelines, course syllabus, and program information would be provided via a DE Webpage.
- Printed materials and books for the course would be sold and shipped by the university bookstore by next-day air to the student.
- Enrollment assistance would be provided by U of L's Advising Center in the School of Education, Admissions Office, and the Registrar's Office.
- Financial support would be provided through a tuition recovery system.

Since 1994, U of L's Department of Special Education DE program has won three awards from the United States Distance Learning Association (USDLA). The library component of U of L's School of Education's premier DE program has been a contributing factor to the recognition of its excellence. Effective collaboration between DLLS personnel involved in the original incentive grant project and the School of Education's instructional faculty established the faculty-librarian collaborative model for DE at U of L. This has resulted in the integration of the library's document delivery and reference services and information competency instruction into the professors' DE courses. "One-stop shopping" on the professors' home pages now enables DE learners to access learning resources in a manner that is equivalent or superior to that offered to learners in similar on-campus programs.

U of L's DLLS has a 10-year partnership with faculty in providing a full range of library services to learners enrolled in credit courses and degree programs offered via DE. It is important to release DE learners from being prisoners of time and to assist them in their race to acquire the print or electronic material needed to meet their immediate course-related information and research needs. In the process of using a system that integrates library access mechanisms into the professors' home pages, learners will begin to view library services and information competencies as an integral part of the lifelong learning process.

According to York (1993), "The technologies that have expanded the delivery of distance education [DE] courses and the technologies for providing library resources are converging in ways that argue the need for strong, on-going partnerships between library and distance education programs . . . . The technologies revolutionizing the delivery of distance education [DE] courses also are revolutionizing library services. The concept of the 'library without walls' is the logical complement to the 'classroom without walls'" (p. 1). U of L's program of library support for DE was firmly grounded in York's work and on the principles espoused in ACRL's (1990) *Guidelines for Extended Campus Library Services.* York wrote:

> Library service is considered as an integral aspect of the student's educational experience rather than merely as a "support" system. Learning depends not only on classroom instruction and dialogue but also on the student's ability to seek out and critically analyze information. Library services are not just another support service; they are a necessary component of any educational experience and an integral part of a lifelong learning process. As distance education [DE] degree programs continue to grow and are influenced by technology, planning is essential to meet the information needs of learners enrolled in these programs (p. 1).

The faculty-librarian collaborators at U of L were convinced that the parent institution receiving tuition payment should bear the responsibility of providing support for its DE programs rather than expect other libraries in learners' home communities to assume this responsibility, especially when materials might not be readily available in community libraries. This belief was reinforced by the declaration in ACRL's (1990) guidelines that "the parent institution is responsible for providing support which addresses the information needs of its extended campus programs. This support should provide library service[s] to the extended campus community equivalent with that provided to the on-campus community." These guidelines were the precursor to ACRL's (2000) guidelines.

The U of L faculty/librarian collaborators also believed that because DE learners pay the same tuition as on-campus learners, they are entitled to the same high level of library services. York (1993; p. 1) commented that "one of the challenges to distance learning programs is to foster library and information literacy among off-campus learners and to provide library resources that will allow them equivalent access to materials and services as their on-campus counterparts." (Appendix E shows a comparison of on-campus and DE library services at U of L; see also Appendix I).

One of the key components of U of L's program of library support for DE was the integration of library services into the structure of each course via the professor's home page and course-related print materials. A strong belief in the value of information competencies as a necessary component of any educational experience and an integral element of lifelong learning was balanced against the concerns of professors about protecting their valuable class time for discipline-specific course content.

The faculty-librarian collaborators in this project were mindful of the implications of the (1994) report of the National Commission on Time and Learning. Learners enrolled in colleges and universities today lead busy lives, they need quick and accurate access to information. According to the report of the National Center for Education Statistics (NCES, 2002), nearly 75% of undergraduate learners are considered "non-traditional" and approximately half of the nontraditional learners were independent, indicating that they had already entered the workforce. The workplace is becoming increasingly information based, so educators must help learners acquire the information competencies they need to function in this environment.

As mentioned previously, the collaborative intent of these faculty-librarian companion research proposals at U of L was to provide "one-stop shopping" for learners, who must, of necessity, communicate with their professors. For many learners, communication with professors via the Web was a new experience in that they had not previously accessed either their professors or library services remotely. The collaborators believed that information competencies are acquired and that one must be able to crawl before one can walk. Therefore, the U of L system was designed to enable learners to access library services using the same access mechanism to contact their professors.

This integrated approach enables professors to focus valuable class time on discipline-specific course content without having to allocate separate time for instruction in information competency skills. Learners learn how to access library services by following the links on a professor's home page linked to the DLLS Webpages. As learners become more familiar with the use of information resources specified by professors, they are introduced to the broader world of independent research in online library databases.

Some of the principles incorporated into U of L's Library Support for DE program are:

- centralization of access,
- immediacy of access,
- rapid turnaround time for remote delivery, and
- empowerment of learners to access information and to perform their own research on a self-service basis.

In the process of using a system that integrates library access mechanisms into DE courses, learners can begin to view library services and information fluency as an integral part of the lifelong learning process.

Three sets of services that embody the aforementioned principles are offered to U of L DE learners and faculty:

a. document delivery,
b. reference services, and
c. information competency instruction.

## Document Delivery

The DLLS document delivery goal is to make specifically identified library materials available to learners in the shortest possible time. The program is designed to enable DE learners to retrieve the full text of material online when possible. If full-text material is not available online on a self-service basis, DLLS staff obtain the material from any place in the world and deliver it to learners in their homes or workplaces. The document delivery service includes:

- remote access by DE learners to required readings placed on course reserve by DE professors (provided electronically on a self-service basis for items available in full-text, scanned into machine-readable form, or delivered upon request via fax or mail for items not available in electronic format);
- remote access by DE learners, via the Web (using a proxy server), to the full complement of library resources available for independent research to on-campus learners;
- retrieval of books from U of L's libraries' stacks, including check out and delivery of books to homes or workplaces of DE learners and faculty;
- retrieval and photocopying of journal articles in U of L's libraries, and delivery of the articles to DE learners and faculty;
- retrieval of material in micro-format held in U of L's libraries, including digitizing of micro-format text for delivery to DE learners and faculty;
- retrieval from other libraries via the Online Computer Library Center's (OCLC) electronic interlibrary loan system, of books not held in U of L's libraries, for delivery directly to the homes and workplaces of DE learners and faculty; and
- retrieval for DE learners and faculty of journal articles not held at U of L, via the Internet, using the Ariel proprietary document delivery system.

Initially, journal articles were delivered electronically to DE learners using the Ariel document delivery system. More recently, articles are converted to PDF format and are either e-mailed or posted on password-protected pages for retrieval by the learners and faculty using Adobe Acrobat. Document delivery procedures are carefully reviewed by the University Library's Scholarly Communications Librarian ("Endowed Chair," 2002) to ensure compliance with copyright guidelines.

Request forms for document delivery are available electronically on the Web via DE professors' home pages. Request forms include notice of copyright compliance and a checkbox indicating willingness to pay additional charges over the amount subsidized by the libraries.

Because U of L's DE learners are encouraged to obtain their citations from the world of literature at-large using the databases provided, access to the university's online catalog Minerva, is not emphasized. DE learners are not expected to determine ownership of items by the libraries of the home institution before submitting requests, because library personnel are committed to delivering the material, even it is not physically present on campus.

DE learners are informed that their library requests should be submitted well in advance of any deadlines because not all requested items will be immediately available. They are told that although some material can be obtained within a few days, it may take two or three weeks to obtain material, depending on the source. Requests are processed in the order received. No rush charges are levied because all DE requests are considered as "rush" in order to achieve equity of access. Items are delivered by e-mail (preferably), fax, or, upon request, first-class mail taken directly to a US post office rather than being processed through the campus mail courier service. Commercial express mail delivery is used at the end of the semester and in other exceptional cases. Faculty couriers have occasionally been used to deliver books to DE learners in international programs.

### Reference

The reference goal of DLLS is to enable DE learners at remote locations to identify resources on a topic of their choice. Reference services provided for DE learners and faculty include 1) provision of access to online library databases for literature searches, and 2) availability of a reference librarian for consultation via a DLLS toll-free number.

A *Librarian Assistance* section is included on the DLLS home page. One link associated with the *Librarian Assistance* page provides the option of sending a question directly to the DLLS e-mail service account. DLLS personnel monitor this account throughout the week, even when no one is in the office. The DLLS faculty administrator is on-call most evenings and weekends. If she is not available, or if the question is outside of a discipline in which she feels comfortable, the question is referred to the general reference department or to a reference librarian subject specialist.

### Information Competency Instruction

Learning depends not only on classroom instruction and dialogue but also on the ability to find, evaluate, and analyze information. The ultimate goal of U of L's DLLS is to enhance learners' ability to retrieve information needed for their course work, as well as for lifelong learning, on a self-service basis. During the initial proposal project in 1992, a printed handout of approximately 20 pages was inserted into each professor's course notebook, which is purchased by all learners. The handout provided step-by-step instructions, including illustrations of computer screen captures, on how to connect to and use the professor's home page to gain access to library services needed for that particular course. A toll-free phone number and telephone assistance were provided to learners having difficulty connecting and to those who, after gaining access, still needed assistance navigating the course Webpages. Today, most library instruction is available online or via the telephone.

For the initial project, library personnel, in conjunction with instructional television personnel, developed a short video that focused in jargon-free language on ways to identify books and journal articles on a topic and how to get specifically identified books or journal articles. The video quickly became out of date as technology changed. Now, librarians participate in televised instruction via satellite and compressed video. For courses in U of L's School of Education, librarians have taped video segments in advance and have participated in live televised classes, interacting with learners via the phone. In other education courses and in the Kent School of Social Work master's programs offered via compressed video, librarians have provided live televised instruction via videoconferencing links, and they have responded to questions from learners at the linked remote sites.

DLLS personnel also conduct on-site library instruction for various DE programs. Every year during the late Summer, DLLS personnel hold instructional sessions for cohort groups in U of L's Department of Special Education's Virtual Impairment Teacher Preparation Program and for new learners entering the Kent doctoral program in Social Work. DLLS personnel also attend departmental social functions in the DE programs they service. Occasionally, opportunities for direct instruction to international learners occur. When administrative personnel from U of L's international master's programs in Athens, Cairo, Panama, and Singapore come to campus for graduation, on-site DLLS instructional sessions are held so they can learn how to assist DE learners at their respective locations. During the Summer of 2002 when a new German MBA program was instituted, an entire cohort of German learners arrived on campus and was invited to participate in a DLLS instructional session as part of the orientation to this new DE program.

Any time a new DE program emerges, DLLS personnel seek opportunities to attend a faculty meeting in the academic department planning the program, for the purpose of presenting an overview of library services available for DE learners. DE faculty are invited to the DLLS offices for follow-up sessions to determine any unique journal or library database needs and to learn more about the process of creating electronic reading lists pages for their courses.

Instructions are embedded in the DLLS Webpages at points where experience has shown that the most DE learners have questions (e.g., how to use the Acrobat Reader). However, the most useful instruction for learners continues to be offered on a one-on-one basis.

After verification of enrollment, DLLS personnel send instructions to DE learners to apply for a library username and password. Instructions are also sent to the professors of the DE courses. When library usernames and passwords are e-mailed to learners, they are accompanied by attachments that explain how to navigate DLLS Webpages to search library databases and how to submit requests for items that are not available in full-text format in the databases. When learners request items that are, indeed, available in full-text in the databases, DLLS personnel reply with instructions that explain how to find the items immediately online in full text on a self-service basis.

The *Librarian Assistance* section of the DLLS Webpages includes links to tutorials on how to use the most popular library full-text databases as well as information about how to use search engines more effectively to find scholarly research material on the Internet. The *Library Assistance* section also includes links to online reference resources (e.g., dictionaries and encyclopedias) and to resources that aid in citing print and electronic material in standard formats such those required by the American Psychological Association (APA). Citations on the reading lists for DE professors are posted in the scholarly format preferred by the professors. The *Librarian Assistance* section also includes a form for requesting verification of an incomplete or incorrect citation for a book or article.

U of L's DLLS personnel strive to teach DE learners how to find the material they need in the most effective and efficient manner at any time of the day or night on a self-service basis. The intent is not only to meet immediate, course-related needs but also to instill in DE learners and faculty the belief that information fluency is a necessary component of any educational experience and an integral element of lifelong learning.

## Resources for DLLS

### *Technology*

The librarians initially recommended the use of two databases that would cover most of the titles available in North America: the Library of Congress database and the FirstSearch World Cat database containing records of nearly 50 million items cataloged by the approximately 41,000 member libraries of OCLC. The university's own online catalog was not emphasized to DE learners because the philosophy was to obtain material needed by DE learners regardless of the location of the material or the learners and the belief that no student's research should be constrained by the holdings of a particular library.

Subsequently, OCLC FirstSearch database was provided primarily because of access to the full-text of journal articles available in its FastDoc database. When FirstSearch was implemented as a text-based system, it was perceived as having an interface that could be used by users with little online search experience or no Web access. Originally, FirstSearch was utilized on a per-search basis, however, during the Fall of 1996, FirstSearch access to a selected set of databases was obtained on a subscription basis through a statewide consortium agreement. When library database vendors (e.g., ProQuest and EBSCO HOST) placed an emphasis on full-text format, the number of journals articles available online exploded. As of June 2002, DE learners at U of L had access to more than 15,000 full-text electronic journals.

eReserve was tested as an alternative for required readings during the Summer of 1997 by utilizing materials already available electronically in full text. In this model, the DE professor located articles of interest and e-mailed them to the DLLS Program Coordinator who linked the articles to the professor's home page under the "Selected Journal Articles for Your Research" section. For copyright compliance, learners were required to enter a user ID and password to ensure access only by learners officially registered for the course. Now, DLLS accepts lists of articles needed by DE professors for a reading lists page, and searches to determine their availability in full-text format. Durable links are created for those items for which full-text versions can be found. Items not available in full-text format are listed on the readings page with instructions on how to request copies of the item for electronic, fax, or first-class mail delivery.

For delivery of research material not already available in electronic format, DLLS personnel produce copies of materials held locally in U of L's libraries. They use a regular photocopy machine, a scan/fax/copier, and a digital micro-printer. The latter two pieces of equipment can fax the digitized document to the user without having to print a paper copy for faxing. For access to material not held locally, the Ingenta (formerly UnCover) document delivery service is used as the first choice of commercial vendors because of the ability to fax the document with a 24-hour turnaround time. Material unavailable through Ingenta is requested via the OCLC Interlibrary Loan service, with requested delivery via the Internet using the Ariel document transmission system. With the advent of a new university e-mail system, it became possible to attach documents received via Ariel to e-mail for electronic delivery to DE learners. Now, electronic copies of journal articles are produced in PDF format and are either sent to DE learners via e-mail or are posted for retrieval in PDF format in a password-protected section of the DLLS Webpages.

## Staffing

Originally, there was no separately funded unit or program of library support for DE at U of L. The Library Support for DE program was initiated as a collaborative, self-supporting project staffed overtime in Document Access and Delivery Services. Staff overtime and student assistance wages were recovered from the instructional programs they supported. Librarian time was considered as extended professional development and collaborative activity undertaken with no additional compensation. The librarian who initiated the project in the Fall of 1992 continued the job responsibilities she had before becoming involved with DE, and none of the librarian time spent in direct information instruction to DE learners was charged back to the DE programs served.

In April of 1998, because of the growth in DE programs at U of L and the U of L Library System's Information Literacy program, the Dean of University Libraries reallocated funds to establish and maintain separate offices for DLLS operations. As of the Summer of 2002, DLLS at U of L was staffed by one full-time faculty librarian, one full-time professional administrative program coordinator, and approximately 50 student assistant hours per week.

### Fees Charged to Learners

In the interest of providing equitable service to DE learners, the same policies regarding fees for library services for learners on campus are applied. For on-campus users, U of L's libraries pay the first $25 of the cost of obtaining material not held in the university's collections. DE learners are asked to indicate on the request form any portion of the cost over $25 that they will pay for an item. DE learners are notified of and, upon approval, billed for any charges above $25. The $25 library subsidy is not charged back to the academic unit offering the DE program because it is a service offered to all university learners.

Traditionally, academic units administering DE programs at U of L have responded positively to the DLLS expectation of cost sharing for library services provided to their programs. Their contribution of $30 per course enrollment does not provide full cost recovery for the library. It barely covers the cost of one interlibrary loan per student for each student in the course during the entire semester. On February 25, 2002, nearly a decade after DLLS for DE learners was initiated at U of L, Board of Trustees implemented a policy on tuition assessment and revenue allocation for DE courses. The first item under the split of tuition revenue was related to the U of L Library System. The policy stated, "[DLLS] will receive $30 per student per course subsequent to a report each semester on services provided to distance education learners." This Board action formalized the traditional academic unit cost-sharing policy for library services for DE programs. The policy is consistent with the statements regarding finances in the Resources section of the ACRL's (2000) *Guidelines for Distance Learning Library Services*. Although the U of L Library System continues to subsidize the major portion of the cost of library services for DE programs, the academic unit's cost sharing is important. The cost sharing helps support one of the most expensive services offered by DLLS, and it raises the academic units' awareness of the importance of library services and information competencies in DE programs.

## Evaluation and Assessment

Many higher education accrediting agencies have begun to address the issue of adequacy of library support for academic degree and certificate programs offered electronically via DE. The SACS Commission on Colleges is U of L's regional accreditation agency. The SACS *Criteria for Accreditation* (1998) included a specific section (5.1.7) on Library/Learning Resources for Distance Learning Activities. Long (1997) tendered some specific questions to determine whether an institution is in compliance with the SACS criteria for providing library and other learning resources for distance learning programs. Goodson (2001) provided excerpts of key passages from SACS and other regional accrediting associations regarding library services for DE. Administrators and faculty engaged in DE program planning need to be mindful of these accreditation expectations. U of L's DLLS has been called upon on several occasions to provide demonstrations of library services for DE programs for visiting accreditation teams from SACS.

SACS (1998) stated that "the library and other learning resources must be evaluated regularly and systematically to ensure that they are meeting the needs of their users and are supporting the programs and purpose of the institution" (section 5.1.7). For each semester since the Spring of 1993, all learners enrolled in DE courses at U of L have been surveyed by library personnel regarding the adequacy of library services for their DE courses. The survey has remained essentially the same for nearly a decade except for the addition of questions related to enhancement of library services. A retrospective analysis of usage data and user feedback regarding the services provided, in comparison with the costs involved, should garner some interesting conclusions. The results of such an analysis are beyond the scope of this chapter, but they could prove useful in attempting to define and measure the library's effect on educational outcomes, particularly in regard to information competencies gained as a result of library services for DE.

Library personnel must become familiar with the program needs for DE initiatives early in the faculty-administrative planning process to allow time to plan and budget appropriately for library support for programs that will meet accreditation criteria. The Dean of University Libraries has taken steps to insure that library representatives continue to be involved in planning efforts by other academic units for DE programs in any format. At U of L, new DE initiatives and the instructional faculty coordinators assigned to them are communicated by the Provost's Office to DLLS, and library personnel request invitations to give presentations of available resources and services to the faculty coordinators of DE programs. Through U of L's Library Liaison Program, librarians who serve as liaisons to the academic units also stress the availability of DLLS and the role that librarians can plan in the accreditation of emerging DE programs.

## Role of Librarians in Achieving Institutional Outcomes

The AAHE (2001) Assessment Conference held in Denver highlighted the focus on assessment activities in institutions of higher education. The plenary address discussed the Diverse Democracy Project, a major project that "sought to identify desired higher education outcomes for a diverse society and explored institutional goals that prepare learners for a diverse democracy." Lakos (2001) observed that universities and colleges are feeling pressured, especially from accreditation bodies, to deliver assessable learning outcomes. Lakos concluded that "although assessment in institutions of higher education is becoming a necessity, it is not yet well integrated into the organizational culture [and that] external accreditation bodies still drive institutional assessment." At the 2002 Assessment Conference held in Boston, librarians were expected to continue showcasing the libraries' commitment to learning outcomes and the contributions the profession can make to learning outcomes assessment.

After providing a brief history of accreditation, Dalrymple (2001) defined accreditation as the external validation of an internal quality assurance process. Dalrymple also provided evidence that librarians have become increasingly committed to evaluation and outcomes assessment in their own profession. With the advent of issues associated with the accreditation of DE programs, the librarian's role in accreditation reviews has become even stronger.

Librarians need to be aware that information literacy is only one aspect of a wide range of information skills that learners need in the Information Age. DE learners and other learners need to achieve information fluency that incorporates the technological skills to access electronic information resources. They also need media fluency that empowers them to be critical thinkers and creative producers of an increasingly wide range of messages using image, language, and sound. Familiarity with professional guidelines for DLLS, information literacy, information fluency, and media literacy will help to focus library instruction efforts.

Librarians also need to exercise collaboration skills with administrators and faculty who are planning DE programs, and they must become aware of what DE faculty members indicate they need for themselves and for their learners. Butler (1998) provided an example of what faculty have to say about DE and library support in faculty focus groups organized by the

University of Minnesota Libraries. The chief faculty concern was a desire to minimize the difference between what an on-campus learner can do/ access and what an off-campus learner could do/access in regard to library resources and services. Faculty recognized the advantage of "one-stop shopping" and acknowledged that connecting library services to DE programs would lend more credibility to DE as an effective teaching strategy.

Finally, librarians need to achieve an awareness of future trends and opportunities of emerging technologies. Some of the first uses of emerging technologies (e.g., proxy servers for remote access to library databases) have been implemented in order to extend library services to DE programs. Coffman (2001) and Marshall (2002) reported on the use of virtual reference services in DE. Issues related to the use of DE technologies for teaching information competencies at a distance have been presented by Dewald, Scholz-Crane, Booth, and Levin (2000) and Getty, Burd, Burns, and Piele (2000).

## Consumer Awareness Questions

Learners who have gained some experience with a DE course that has effectively integrated information resources and services into the course content, may, in the future, have built-in expectations that will cause them to ask questions about library support for their future DE courses (see Appendix F for a list of such questions). Faculty members who have gained some experience with a DE course that has effectively integrated information resources and services into the course content, may, in the future, have built-in expectations that will cause them to ask questions about library support for their future DE courses (see Appendix G for a list of such questions). Even though an organization may have in place a long-range plan that addresses the integration of information resources and services into the DE curriculum, certain questions are bound to arise and present themselves as problems to be addressed by administrators (see Appendix H for a list of such questions).

## FUTURE TRENDS, EMERGING TECHNOLOGIES, AND RESEARCH

- The (2000) Academic Library Trends and Statistics (as cited in Thompson, 2002) focused on library services for DE via a two-part survey. The first part included demographics and details of how academic libraries administer their DE programs; the second part provided data on reference, materials, and library instruction for DE learners. Thompson summarized the results of the survey by noting that "the results support the notion that [DE] is becoming an important part of higher education and that increasingly there will be technical and budgetary implications for academic libraries."

- On June 3, 2002, the Library of Congress and OCLC developed QuestionPoint, a new subscription-based online reference service that evolved from the Collaborative Digital Reference Service (CDRS) pilot project. Users of libraries who subscribe to the service can submit questions at any time of the day or night through their library's Website. Questions not answered online from the users' own library are forwarded to participating libraries around the world at no charge to the learners, if their library has subscribed to the QuestionPoint service (S. Carlson, 2002). Issues related to digital reference services were addressed at the Distance Learning Services (DLS) Discussion Group session held during the American Library Association 2002 Midwinter Meeting. A report on the issues discussed is provided in the Spring 2002 DLS Newsletter .

- Ideally, learners should not have to pay for information they can obtain free from their libraries. However, either because of their professors' lack of awareness of library resources and services or because of aggressive marketing by commercial vendors, learners are being led into the information marketplace. Hughes (2000) presented an overview of some of the major issues associated with the entry of commercial information services into higher education. She touched on some of the implications of fee-based services for libraries and the challenges they present to librarians seeking to preserve the common good in a competitive market.

- At the 2002 American Library Association Conference in Atlanta, the Co-Anchor of CNN Student News moderated a session sponsored by DLS. This panel of knowledge experts and information executives debated the topics of plagiarism, duplication of resources, marketing of library services, and information competency. Bringing learners, librarians, and commercial information providers such as Authority Finder [http://www.authorityfinder.com] and Questia [http://www.questia.com] together in forums should lead to a greater understanding of the issues that will help librarians and vendors determine their places in the new competitive information environment and enable learners to make informed choices about their information options.

## Impact of ACRL's Guidelines

- Caspers, Fritts, and Gover (2001) have studied the usefulness of ACRL's guidelines since their inception in 1990 and revision in 2000.

The Ad Hoc Committee on Distance Education within the American Library Association' Reference and User Services Association (RUSA)/Business Reference and Services Section (BRASS) has completed a study that explores the impact of ACRL's (2000) guidelines on providing services to business DE learners .

- Librarians at North Carolina (NC) State University have documented a plan for integrating information competencies into engineering programs at the curriculum level at NC State. Illene Rockman is the Manager of the Information Competence Initiative for the 23 campuses of the California State University System. When researching the use of information competencies in the disciplines for her own research, she sought contributions from discipline-based faculty who were actively engaged in collaborative partners with library faculty (personal communication, February 27, 2002). Librarians live among the world's scholarly literature. Because academic librarians are often reviewed by the same criteria for promotion and tenure as their faculty colleagues, they are also frequent contributors to the published literature. Teaching faculty can expect that library faculty will be willing participants in studies of information competencies within a particular discipline. For example, Buxbaum (in press) highlighted issues and trends in faculty-librarian collaboration on the development of DLLS for business students. Thomas (2000) analyzed the information-seeking behavior of graduate students in social work.
- ACRL's Distance Learning Section Research Committee undertook an international survey to determine key research topics. The results of this survey were reported by Slade (2000), who commented:

  > Academic librarians who support distance learning programs appear to be unanimous in their view that the number one research priority in this area is collaboration with faculty to integrate library and electronic resources into Web-based distance learning courses. This topic emerged with the highest number of votes (42) and the highest overall ranking in the survey.

- In an effort to address the topic, ACRL's Education and Behavioral Sciences Section (EBSS) Committee held a program at the 2002 ALA conference in Atlanta. Wilson (2000) emphasized that success today demands collaboration, and Basefsky (2000) maintained that information training for administrators pays dividends for the library. Lippincott (2002) demonstrated how librarians, learners, and faculty are creating learning communities and creating opportunities for an expanded teaching and learning role for academic librarians.
- Potential opportunities for collaborative excellence in the incorporation of information incorporation skills into the curriculum are present in every institution. Frank, Beasley, and Kroll (2001) pointed out some of these activities by stating, "Although a significant num-

ber of academic libraries have some role in the learning community within their institutions, the results of these initiatives have not been generally reported in the literature." It is important that the work being done on many campuses by librarians, to integrate information competencies into the general curriculum, be presented in the literature and in non-librarian-specific general higher education conferences such as AAHE and DE professional conferences such as those of USDLA, the Sloan International Conferences on Asynchronous Learning Networks (ALN), and the MERLOT International Conferences. The general higher education community needs to hear what librarians can bring to the table and how they can become partners in general education, in the various disciplines, and in online learning endeavors.

## CONCLUSION

This final review of some points that reiterate the importance of faculty-librarian collaboration on the integration of information resources and services into the DE curriculum reminds the reader that the incorporation of scholarly content into DE courses is essential for the development of technological, informational, and media fluency in DE learners.

Faculty collaboration with librarians can result in the development and deployment of information-rich, scholarly online courses. Through the specific services that librarians provide to DE learners, librarians can become a vital part of the learners' learning community. When librarians are integrally involved in online course development, they can provide supporting data for evaluation and accreditation of DE programs. The following points, which reiterate the importance of faculty-librarian collaboration on the integration of information resources and services into the distance education curriculum, should be considered when planning a DE program:

- University libraries that offer DLLS provide a service that can assist academic units to meet accreditation guidelines for DE programs.
- Librarians should be involved in the early stages of planning DE programs.
- Librarians may be called upon to provide demonstrations of library services to DE accreditation visits.
- According to the guidelines of regional accrediting agencies, DE learners are entitled to have access to library resources and services that are equivalent to those provided to on-campus learners.
- A state-supported virtual library is not equivalent to discipline-specific college and university library resources and services.

- Learning management system resources and libraries are not equivalent to college and university library resources and services.
- Commercial products such as XanEdu (a ProQuest product available via the Blackboard Resource Center) are not equivalent to university library resources and services. XanEdu CoursePacks, although made available at no charge to faculty, result in DE learners having to pay for journal articles for which the university has already paid a license fee—articles that could be made available to them at no charge via the DLLS reading lists (eReserve) function.
- All scholarly resources are not freely available on the Web.
- Disappearance of cited Web resources is an increasing problem.
- Faculty who teach online are, in general, not familiar with the scholarly resources available to them as a result of university licensing fees for scholarly electronic databases for incorporation in their online instruction.
- Faculty-librarian collaboration is needed to understand faculty instructional needs and to enhance faculty skills in identifying relevant scholarly resources for incorporation in their instruction.

Outcome statements, such as the following from the U of L (2001) document *Integration of Information Literacy at U of L*, should be kept in mind when planning DE programs:

Learners graduating from U of L will understand that research is a process that takes time, that it is not necessarily linear, and that to be informed and engaged citizens, they need to be prepared to apply the information skills they learn here in all aspects of their lives.

Professors in DE programs need the same information skills that are desirable in their learners. Faculty-librarian collaboration is essential for the incorporation of scholarly content in DE instruction and for the development of technological, informational, and media fluency in DE learners.

## REFERENCES

Abdullah, M. H. (2000). Media Literacy. *ERIC Digest*, D152. Bloomington, IN: ERIC Clearinghouse on Reading English and Communication. (ERIC Document Reproduction No. ED442147). Retrieved June 5, 2002, from http://www.ed.gov/databases/ERIC_Digests/ed442147.html.

Alliance for a Media Literate America (2002). Retrieved June 5, 2002, from http://www.amlainfo.org.

American Association for Higher Education (1996). *Assessment forum*. Retrieved June 5, 2002, from http://www.aahe.org/principl.htm.

Arnone, M. (2002). Many learners' favorite professors shun distance education [Electronic version]. *Chronicle of Higher Education, 48*(35), 1-7.

Associated Colleges of the South (2001). Toward information fluency in the liberal arts. *Report from the Information Fluency Task Force.* Retrieved June 7, 2002, from http://www.colleges.org/if/IF_Gudielines.doc.

Association of College and Research libraries (1990). Guidelines for extended campus library services. College & Research Libraries News, *51*(4), 353-355.

Association of College and Research Libraries (2000). *Guidelines for distance learning library services.* Retrieved June 6, 2002, from http://www.ala.org/acrl/guides/distlrng.html.

Basefsky, S. (2000). The other client. *College & Research Library News, 61*(2), 100-101.

Beagle, D. (2000). Web-based learning environments: Do libraries matter? *College & Research Libraries, 61*(4), 367-379.

Brevik, P. S. (1991). Literacy in an information society. *Educational Leadership, 49*(1), 87.

Burniske, R. W. (2000). Literacy in the cyber age. *Ubiquity.* Retrieved June 5, 2002, from http://www.acm.org/ubiquity/book/r_burniske_2.html.

Burtle, L. G., & Sugarman, T. S. (2002). The citizen in the information age. *College & Research Libraries News, 63*(4), 276-279.

Butler, J. (1998). What faculty say about distance learning and library support. *Faculty Focus Groups Report.* Retrieved June 5, 2002, from http://www.lib.umn.edu/dist/testing/dlfocus.phtml.

Buxbaum, S (Ed.). (in press). Library services for business students in distance education: Issues and trends [Special issue]. *Journal of Business and Finance Librarianship.*

Carlson, E. (2002). Learners burned by book prices. *Daily Illini online.* Retrieved June 5, 2002, from http://www.dailyillini.com/jan02/jan22/news/stories/news_story01.shtml.

Carlson, S. (2002). *New service allows the public to pose reference questions without visiting the library.* Retrieved June 5, 2002, from http://chronicle.com/free/2002-05/2002053101t.htm.

Casey, A. M. (2002). Competitors or models? A word from the chair. *DLS Newsletter, 11*(2), 1. Retrieved June 5, 2002, from http://caspian.switchinc.org/~distlearn/news.

Caspers, J., Fritts, J., & Gover, H. (2001). Beyond the rhetoric: A study of the impact of the ACRL guidelines for distance learning services. *Journal of Library Administration, 31*(3/4), 127-148.

Choy, S. (2002). Access and persistence: Findings from ten years of longitudinal research on learners. *Washington, DC: American Council on Education. Center for Policy Analysis.* Retrieved June 30, 2002, from http://www.acenet.edu/bookstore/pdf/2002_access&persistence.pdf.

Coffman, S. (2000). Distance education and virtual reference: Where are we headed? *Computers in Libraries, 21*(4), 20-25. Retrieved September 10, 2001, from EBSCO Academic Search Elite database.

Coonin, B., Diamond, W., Friedman, C. R., Hankel, M., Spurling, L., & Oppenheim, M. (2001). Serving business distance education learners. *Reference & User Services Quarterly, 41*(2), 144-158.

Council for Higher Education Accreditation (2001) *Good practices database.* Retrieved June 6, 2002, from http://www.chea.org/good-practices/index.cfm.

Council on Library and Information Resources (in press). *Dimensions and use of the scholarly information environment.* Washington, DC: Author.

Dalrymple, P. W. (2001). Understanding accreditation: The librarian's role in educational evaluation. *Libraries and the Academy, 1*(1), 23-32.

Davis, P. M. (2002). The effect of the Web on undergraduate citation behavior: A 2000 update. *College & Research Libraries, 63*(1), 53-60.

Davis, P. M., & Cohen, S. A. (2001). The effect of the Web on undergraduate citation behavior 1996-1999. *Journal of the American Society for Information Science and Technology, 52*(4), 309-314.

Davidson College (2001). Information fluency lunches. *Davidson Library Columns,* 1-5.

Dermody, M., & Dew, S. (2002). DLS discussion group, New Orleans ALA midwinter meetings. *DLS Newsletter, 11*(2), 2. Retrieved June 5, 2002, from http://caspian.switchinc.org/~distlearn/news/.

DLLS (2002). *Office of distance learning library services: University of Louisville.* Retrieved June 5, 2002, from http://www.louisville.edu/library/distance.

Drucker, P. (1993). *The post industrial society.* New York: HarperBusiness.

Dewald, N., Scholz-Crane, A., Booth, A., & Levine, C. (2000). Information literacy at a distance: Instructional design issues. *Journal of Academic Librarianship, 26*(1), 33-44.

Edge, S., & Edge, D. (2000). Integration of information resources into distance learning programs. *Ed at a Distance, 14*(7), 3-17.

Endowed chair to be copyright resource for U of L (2002). Retrieved June 7, 2002, from http://newsbreak.louisville.edu/020405/buttler.html.

Fish, S. (2002). Keep your eye on the small picture [Electronic version]. *Chronicle of Higher Education, 48*(21), 1-3. Retrieved June 6, 2002, from http://chronicle.com/jobs/2002-02/2002020101c.htm.

Frank, D. G., Beasley, S., & Kroll, S. (2001). Opportunities for collaborative excellence: What learning communities offer [Electronic version]. *College & Research Libraries News, 62*(10), 1008-11. Retrieved June 28, 2002, from http://www.ala.org/acrl/franketal.html.

Germain, C. A. (2000). URLs: Uniform resource locators or unreliable resource locators? *College & Reserach Libraries, 61*(4), 359-365.

Getty, N. K., Burd, B., Burns, S. K., & Piele, L. (2000). Using courseware to deliver library instruction via the Web: Four examples. *Reference Services Review, 28*(4), 349-360.

Goodson, C. F. (2001). *Providing library services for distance education learners.* New York: Neal-Schuman.

Greenstein, D., & Healy, L. (2002, May/June). National survey documents effects of Internet use on libraries. *CLIR Issues, xx*(27), 1-4. Retrieved June 5, 2002, from http://www.clir.org/pubs/issues/issues27.html.

Hakim, M.A. (2002). Navigating the Web of discourse on the scholarship of teaching and learning: An annotated Webliography [Electronic version]. *College & Research Libraries News, 63*(7), 502-505. Retrieved June 30, 2002, from http://www.ala.org/acrl/resjuly02.html.

Halal, W. E. (1992). Information technology revolution. *Futurist, 26*(4), 10-15.

Hebel, S. (2002). Report urges disciplined spending by states to make college more affordable [Electronic version]. *Chronicle of Higher Education.* Retrieved June 5, 2002, from http://chronicle.com/daily/2002-05/200205021n.htm.

Huges, C. A. (2002). Information services for higher education: A new competitive space. *D-Lib Magazine, 6*(12), 1-8. Retrieved June 5, 2002, from http://www.chronicle.com/daily/2002-05/200005021n.htm.

Jenkins, P. (2002). They're not just using Websites: A citation study of 116 student papers. *College & Research Libraries News, 63*(3), 164-165.

Kellogg, A. (2002). *Learners plagiarize less than many think, a new study finds* [Electronic version]. Retrieved June 5, 2002, from http://www.chronicle.com/free/2002/02/2002020101t.htm.

Kiernan, V. (2002). Nebraska researchers measure the extent of 'link rot' in distance education [Electronic version]. *Chronicle of Higher Education.* Retrieved June 5, 2002, from http://chronicle.com/free/2002/04/2002041001u.htm.

Kirk, T. (2002). *Best practices in information literacy* [Webcast]. Retrieved June 5, 2002, from http://www.tltgroup.org/calendar/interviewarchives2001.htm.

Koehler, W. C., Jr. (2002). Web page change and persistence—a four-year longitudinal study. *Journal of the American Society for Information Science and Technology, 53*(2), 162-171.

Lakos, A. (2001). From expectation to results: What are we finding, and how are we improving? *ARL Bimonthly Report, 218.* Retrieved June 5, 2002, from http://www.arl.org/newsltr/218/lakos.htmlm

Lippincott, J. K. (2002). Developing collaborative relationships. *College & Research Library News, 63*(3), 190-193.

Long, S. (1997). *Using SACS criteria for evaluating distance learning programs.* Paper presented at the Visions of the Future: Distance Learning for the 21st Century conference, Lubbock, TX.

MacAdam, B. (2000). From the other side of the river: Re-conceptualizing the educational mission of libraries. *College & Undergraduate Libraries, 6*(2), 77-93.

Marshall, J. (2002). Distance education, electronic reference and library service. *DLS Newsletter, 11*(2), 3. Retrieved June 7, 2002, from http://caspian.switch-inc.org/~distlearn/news/.

McCollum, K. (1998). High-school learners use the web intelligently for research, survey finds [Electronic version]. *Chronicle of Higher Education.* Retrieved June 5, 2002, from http://chronicle.com/daily/98/11/98112501t.htm.

National Center for Education Statistics (NCES) (2002). *The condition of education 2002.* Washington, DC: Author. Retrieved June 7, 2002, from http://nces.ed.gov/programs/coe/.

National Commission on Time and Learning. (1994). *Prisoners of time.* Washington, DC: Author.

National Research Council. (1999). *Being fluent with information technology.* Retrieved June 6, 2002, from http://www.nap.edu/books/030906399X/html/.

Nerz, H. F., & Weiner, S. T. (2001). *Information competencies: A strategic approach.* Paper presented at the 2001 American Society for Engineering Education (ASEE) annual conference & exposition, San Diego, CA. Retrieved June 5, 2002, from http://www.asee.org/conferences/annual2001/bestpapers.cfm.

O'Leary, M. (2000). Distance learning and libraries. *Online, 24*(4), 94-96. Retrieved June 5, 2002, from EBSCO Academic Search Premier database.

Olsen, F. (2000). Computer scientist says all learners should learn to think algorithmically [Electronic version]. *Chronicle of Higher Education.* Retrieved June 5, 2002, from http://chronicle.com/free/2000-03/2000032201t.htm.

Olsen, J. K. (1992). The electronic library and literacy. *New Directions for Higher Education, 78*(91), 91.

Online Computer Library Center (2002). *How academic librarians can influence students Web-based information choices.* OCLC White Paper on the Information Habits of College Students. Retrieved July 15, 2002, from http://www2.oclc.org/oclc/pdf/printondemand/informationhabits.pdf.

Pace, A. K. (2001). Coming full circle: Distance learning service: It's closer than you think. *Computers in Libraries, 21*(4), 49-51. Retrieved June 5, 2002, from ProQuest Direct database.

Phillips, D. (1999). *Teaching computer literacy* [Audio file]. National Public Radio (NPR) Morning Edition, November 11, 1999. Retrieved June 5, 2002, from http://www.npr.org/archives/.

Rader, H. (2001). A new academic library model: Partnerships for learning and teaching at the University of Louisville. *College & Research Libraries News, 62*(4).

Raish, M. (2000). What about the library? [Electronic version]. *Ubiquity.* Retrieved June 5, 2002 from http://www.acm.org/ubiquity/views/m_raish_1.html.

Ridgeway, T. (1990). Information literacy: An introductory reading list. *College & Research Library News, 51*(7), 645-648.

Rinear, K. (2002). Commercial library services: Promise and peril for academic libraries. *Distance Education Report, 6*(6), 8.

Rockwell, K., Schauer, J., Fritz, S. M., & Marx, D. B. (2000). Faculty education, assistance and support needed to deliver education via distance. *Online Journal of Distance Learning Administration, 3*(2), Retrieved June 5, 2002, from http://www.westga.edu/~distance/rockwell32.html.

Rojstaczer, S. (2001). When intellectual life is optional for learners [Electronic version]. *Chronicle of Higher Education, 47*(2), B5. Retrieved June 5, 2002, from http://www.chronicle.com/free/v47/i32/32b00501.htm.

Saba, F. (2002). *Competencies of distance educators?* Message posted to DEOS-L mailing list. Retrieved June 5, 2002, from http://www.ed.psu.edu/acsde/deos/deos-l/deosl.asp.

Scents and sensibilities. (2001). *Economist, 359*(8219), 1-3. Retrieved June 5, 2002, from EBSCO Business Source Premier database.

Shribman, D. M. (2001). *I remember my teacher: 365 reminiscences of the teachers who changed our lives.* Kansas City, MO: Andrews McMeel.

Slade, A. L. (2000). *Research on library services for distance learning: What are the priorities?* Retrieved June 7, 2002, from http://gateway3.uvic.ca/dls/rescom.htm.

Sloan-C Quality Education Online. Effective Practices Sharing. Retrieved June 28, 2002, from *http://www.sloan-c.org/effectivepractices/login.htm*

Southern Association of Colleges and Schools (1998). *Criteria for accreditation: Section 5.1.7: Library/learning resources for distance learning activities.* Atlanta, GA: Author. Retrieved June 7, 2002, from http://www.sacscoc.org/commpub.asp.

Thompson, H. (2002). The library's role in distance education: Survey results from ACRL's 2000 Academic Library Trends and Statistics. *College & Research Libraries News, 63*(5), 338-340. Retrieved June 5, 2002, from http://caspian.switchinc.org/~distlearn/news/.

Thomas, J. E. (2000). Never enough: Graduate student use of journals—citation analysis of social work theses. *Behavioral & Social Sciences Librarian, 19*(1), 1-16.

Toth, E. (2000). Can just anyone teach? [Electronic version]. *Chronicle of Higher Education.* Retrieved June 6, 2002, from http://www.chronicle.com/jobs/2000-07/200072101c.htm.

Troll, D. A. (2001). How and why are libraries changing? [Draft white paper]. Washington, DC: Digital Library Federation. Retrieved June 30, 2002, from http://www.diglib.org/use/whitepaper.htm.

Tuman, M. C. (1992). *Word perfect: Literacy in the computer age.* Pittsburgh: University of Pittsburgh Press.

University of Louisville (2000). Principle 10 in Appendix 12: Recommended guiding principles for distance education. *University of Louisville Report of the Task Force on Distance Education.* Retrieved June 6, 2002, from http://distance.louisville.edu/index2.html.

University of Louisville (2001). *Integration of information literacy at U of L: Working document of the University Libraries Information literacy team.* Retrieved June 6, 2002, from http://www.louisville.edu/infoliteracy/infolitoutcomes.htm.

Varlejs, J. (1991). *Information literacy: Learning how to learn.* Jefferson, NC: McFarland.

Wagner, J. (2001). Learners search for alternatives as textbook prices rise [Electronic version]. *Daily Illini online.* Retrieved June 5, 2002, from http://www.dailyillini.com/aug01/aug30/news/stories/news_story05.shtml.

Western Interstate Commission for Higher Education (1999). *Principles of good practice for electronically offered academic degree and certificate programs.* Bolder, CO. Retrieved June 7, 2002, from http://www.wiche.edu/telecom/projects/balancing/principles.htm.

Williams, P. (2000). Making informed decisions about staffing and training: Roles and competencies for distance education programs in higher education. *Online Journal of Distance Learning Administration, 3*(2). Retrieved June 5, 2002, from http://www.westga.edu/~distance/williams32.html.

Wilson, B. (2000). The Lone Ranger is dead. *College & Research Libraries, 61*(8), 698-701.

York, V. (1993). *A guide for planning library integration into distance education programs.* Boulder, CO: WICHE.

## APPENDIX A: BENEFITS OF DLLS TO DE FACULTY

By using DLLS resources and services, faculty will be able to:

1. Demonstrate a contribution to the mission of the institution and its goals of producing informed citizens who are fluent in the use of information, technological, and media literacies.
2. Demonstrate fiscal responsibility and combat the high cost of education by not expecting DE learners to buy resources that are freely available from online library databases.
3. Collaborate in advance with librarians to ensure that resources relevant to courses are readily available and to identify and incorporate licensed full-text electronic articles in course content.

4. Expect the best of DE learners because they will be able to meet research expectations.
5. Eliminate the frustrations that DE learners may experience when looking for articles that are not immediately available.
6. Collaborate with librarians to be aware of recent, licensed database subscriptions.
7. Extend the broadest possible range of resources to learners rather than a limited subset of materials available from commercial providers (e.g., Blackboard, XanEdu).
8. Collaborate with librarians for assistance generating an electronic reading list (sometimes referred to as eReserve). Librarians will search to determine whether desired material is available in electronic format and licensed for use via a link from within the course.
9. Have librarians format required readings in the preferred bibliographic citation format (e.g., APA) so that learners become accustomed to seeing items cited properly.
10. Have librarians provide links to online citation assistance.
11. Have librarians provide forms for learners to use when requesting material not immediately available online in full text in electronic databases.
12. Encourage learners to not use only the items owned or licensed by the institution or from one particular commercial vendor (e.g., XanEdu, Blackboard "library").
13. Have learners who do not have to search the online catalog of the institution's library before requesting material that is not immediately available in the electronic databases to which they have access. DLLS personnel can determine whether the item is owned locally; if not, they can request the item for elsewhere for delivery to the student.
14. Ask librarians to assist in determining the legality of using copyrighted material in course content and in obtaining copyright permission when needed.
15. Ask librarians to assist with managing and formatting bibliographic citations for teaching and research projects.
16. Ask librarians to provide recommendations for promotion and tenure files and awards, and to serve as joint authors for publications and presentations.

## APPENDIX B: BEST LIBRARY PRACTICES FOR STUDENTS

Following are a series of statements that students should be able to express after information resources and library resources have been successfully integrated into DE courses:

1. I don't have to go to a bookstore or copy shop and pay for items that professors require me to read.
2. I don't have to worry about whether the library is open when I'm off work or with family on evenings and weekends.
3. I don't have to pay for a campus parking permit.
4. I don't have to figure out the library's organizational structure (e.g., the difference between reference and reserve) to locate the required readings.
5. I don't have to locate journal volumes on shelves to find the specific articles I need. Electronic journals are always available.
6. I don't have to spend time photocopying journal articles.
7. I don't need to search for library personnel to help me in the evenings and weekends.
8. I don't have to figure out how to cite the journal articles I've been requested to read.
9. I don't have to go to another Web address to get to the library. Library links embedded in my DE course.
10. I don't have to add to the paper and clutter in my life because the material I need is available online.

Following are a series of statements that demonstrate the benefits of DLLS to DE learners' research efforts:

1. I don't have to spend time figuring out how to search the library catalog to determine whether the library owns an item I need.
2. I don't have to waste time going to the library building only to discover that the item I thought would be there is not on the shelves and can't be found.
3. I don't have to submit a request to library personnel to ask them to get the item for me via interlibrary loan or document delivery.
4. I don't need to return to the library to pick up items that have been ordered for me because I can get them sent to me via e-mail.
5. I don't have to rely on someone else's terms rather than the words I want to use for searching library databases.
6. I don't have to rely on a selected set of databases from one vendor that may not include the journals my professor wants me to use in my research.
7. I don't have to waste time figuring out which library databases contain the actual articles in full-text electronic format and which don't.
8. I don't have to call or visit the library during the hours it is open or when a librarian is on duty to get help from a librarian.
9. I don't have to call a separate Information Technology (IT) help desk to get assistance with computer problems related to library use.
10. I don't have to wait for articles to arrive via mail or fax.

11. I don't have to figure out by myself how to receive articles via e-mail or what to do if I'm using a free e-mail account that won't accept large files.
12. I don't have to worry about using my own money to buy from document delivery suppliers items not immediately available online.
13. I don't have to worry that something I cited from the Web will disappear before my professor provides a grade.
14. I don't have to pay extra money for database access.
15. I can use my course password for database access.

## APPENDIX C: BEST LIBRARY PRACTICES FOR FACULTY

Faculty who have had a positive experience with library services for their DE courses should be able to express the following statements:

1. I don't have to worry about the barriers my learners might encounter when doing library research.
2. I don't have to limit my learners to research material that is available only in full-text format in library databases.
3. I don't have to worry about whether or not I'm complying with copyright when I use journal articles in my course content.
4. I don't have to worry about whether bibliographic citations for research material are in the correct style.
5. I don't have to search to determine which electronic databases include the journals that have articles I would like for my learners to read.
6. I don't have to get copies of articles assembled into a paper course pack.
7. My learners don't have to pay extra (beyond the cost of any textbooks) for course packs.
8. The content of my course is information rich with scholarly articles from research databases rather than from links to Web sources that may disappear.
9. I don't have to answer my learners' computer or technical questions because library personnel monitor e-mail accounts on evenings and weekends to respond to their questions.
10. I can access library resources when off campus.
11. I can ask library personnel to come to my office to explain new databases.
12. I can ask a colleague or librarian for help because understanding librarians are eager to explain library resources and their use in my DE course.
13. I can browse the most recent issues of journals online.

14. I can easily retrieve articles from library databases and use library database plagiarism detection tools.
15. I don't have to go to the library or use a graduate assistant's time to retrieve information resources for use in course development.

To ameliorate the efforts between DLLS and DE faculty, the following guidelines are offered for consideration:

1. At least 6 months before your DE course is to be offered, contact the Office of the University Librarian at your institution to determine the individual who is responsible for library services to DE learners. Distinguish among the different types of individuals who work in libraries. Recognize that many, if not most, of the individuals at public service desks in libraries are student assistants who may not be familiar with the library's DE operations for off-campus learners.
2. Ask either the university librarian or the person in charge of DLLS whether the administrator responsible for your DE degree program has made the necessary advanced fiscal arrangements with the institution's library administration for funding of library services for your course.
3. If your course is eligible for DLLS, establish a rapport with the library personnel charged with providing those services. Although most librarians will make office calls and will demonstrate their services remotely, you would benefit from making a personal visit to the library.
4. Provide a copy of your course syllabus or a list of the bibliographic citations from your syllabus to the appropriate library personnel to determine the availability of full-text formats of the items in electronic format.
5. Designate the items that you want to be posted as required reading lists (also known as eReserve). Understand that if you wish to use any items for which the library does not already have a license that enables posting on eReserve, you will need to request copyright clearance. Fair use allows for the spontaneous posting of items on eReserve for one semester only. Copyright clearance is required for posting items on eReserve during subsequent offerings of the course. Copyright clearance takes time, so if you intend to use the item again, request clearance during the first semester the item is posted.
6. Search a general purpose full-text database (e.g., ProQuest Direct) to determine whether recent articles on your topic are available. The contents of electronic databases change based on journal publisher/vendor aggregator agreements; the interfaces for searching databases also change. If you are not comfortable searching data-

bases, ask the librarian for assistance, or provide a list of relevant topics that will enable the librarian to do a preliminary search to identify more current literature for your course content.

7. Be aware that databases contain options for searching in foreign languages. Ask library personnel to demonstrate these optional search interfaces if your DE learners speak another language.

8. Insert a link to the DLLS Webpage in your course.

9. Recognize that your DE learners will not be able to access library databases from off campus without a username and password.

10. Obtain a library username and password yourself, and try accessing the databases from off campus using an e-mail account other than your university e-mail account. DE learners usually use their own e-mail accounts (e.g., AOL).

11. If the library offers a tutorial or skills test that shows learners how to use databases and/or request items that are not immediately available, avail yourself of it. Determine whether you want to use it to orient your learners to DLLS for their course or whether you want to give them course participation credit for completing it. Library personnel can provide a list of the names of the learners who successfully complete the tutorial or skills test.

## APPENDIX D: BEST LIBRARY PRACTICES FOR ADMINISTRATORS

The administrator of U of L's DLLS has served on a number of the university's DE and study groups. The most recent of these groups included a set of Recommended Guiding Principles for Distance Education as Appendix 12 of U of L's (2000) *Distance Education Task Force Report*. These principles were adapted from the American Council on Education's (1996) report, *Guiding Principles for Distance Education in a Learning Society*, and from the Western Cooperative for Educational Telecommunications report, *Principles of Good Practice for Electronically Offered Academic Degree and Certificate Programs*.

1. U of L's DE Principle 10 in Appendix 12 of the aforementioned report stated: DE also requires the integration of library services to support instruction.

2. Participants in DE and international programs approved through the Office of the University Provost are entitled to library resources and services equivalent to those provided for students and faculty in the traditional U of L campus setting.

3. Responsibility for provision of DLLS should be specifically assigned and separately funded so as not to compete with library resources and services available to on-campus faculty, staff, and students.

4. Advance planning and collaboration of teaching faculty with DLLS is required to ensure that appropriate library/learning resources are integrated into course instruction in DE and international programs and that copyright issues are addressed.

5. The ability to locate, evaluate, and use information is a desired educational outcome for all members of the U of L community.

6. DE and international programs faculty should become proficient in the technology skills required for use of DLLS before those services are made available to DE learners in their courses.

7. Data on use of library resources and services for independent research in DE and international programs should be collected and made available for unit assessments and accreditation reviews.

## DLLS-Administrator Collaboration

It behooves university administrators to be in the vanguard of promoting DLLS for DE courses. Following are suggestions to facilitate this outcome:

1. Hold university administrators, faculty, and staff accountable for achieving learning outcomes consistent with the university's mission, particularly those related to becoming informed citizens.

2. Be willing to learn the differences among virtual libraries, digital libraries, electronic full-text databases, and DLLS.

3. Foster an organizational climate of trust and motivation. Don't micromanage or assume the worst of people.

4. Foster innovation.

5. Identify the individual in the institution who can serve as a resource for the legalities of access to licensed databases and fair use of copyrighted material in an instructional environment (e.g., Scholarly Communications Librarian).

6. Promote faculty-librarian collaboration to foster use of expensive resources and incorporation of information resources into the curriculum. Don't assume all faculty know the difference between proprietary information that the university has a license to access and information that is feely available on the Web.

7. Insist that IT and library personnel collaborate effectively to enable remote access to licensed databases.

8. Recognize that DE requires library services for new users above and beyond those available for on-campus students, and be willing to allocate a portion of new revenue streams from DE learner tuition to library resources and services.

9. Ensure a separate funding stream for library services to DE learners to avoid potential on-campus political issues.

10. Include librarians in planning for consortium approaches to DE. When engaging in consortium agreements, be mindful of the adequacy of library collections, including those of virtual libraries; the limitations of database licenses to authorized users of respective institutions; and the arrangements for retrieval and delivery, preferably electronically, of library material not already available in electronic format.

11. Recognize that most university faculty are not trained in pedagogy. Provide opportunities for faculty to enhance their instructional and information-use skills.

12. Foster faculty-librarian collaboration. Librarians are held to the same criteria for promotion in rank and tenure as faculty at most institutions. Librarians have a set of professional competencies that they are expected to meet, and they teach, too. They are in a position to observe and note differences in the instructional competencies and effectiveness of the teaching faculty in the various disciplines either directly or through their students who use the library.

13. Involve librarians at the beginning of the establishment of a DE program. Advance notice is required for evaluating the adequacy of discipline-specific electronic full-text journals in the library collection and for developing library services for the program. Librarians may have participated in previous evaluations of DE programs for accreditation. Regardless, they have a perspective on how previous programs have dealt with roadblocks, and they can maintain data and provide documentation for the accreditation process.

## APPENDIX E: COMPARISON OF ON-CAMPUS AND DE LIBRARY SERVICES AT U OF L

| *Library Services* | *Available to On-Campus Learners from U of L On-Campus Libraries* | *Provided to DE Learners by U of L DLLS* |
|---|---|---|
| **ACCESS** | | |
| **Authentication of Enrollment in U of L Distance Education Programs** | N/A | Yes |
| **Remote Access to Databases** | | |
| U of L-licensed databases | Yes | Yes |
| KYVL databases | Yes | Yes |
| | | |
| **SEARCHING BY LIBRARY STAFF** | | |
| **Searching for Items Not Found Immediately Online by DE Learners** | | |
| to determine whether available in electronic format from U of L & KYVL databases | No | Yes |
| to determine whether available in non-electronic format in U of L campus libraries | No | Yes |
| to determine whether available from sources external to U of L | Yes | Yes |
| | | |
| **RETRIEVAL BY LIBRARY STAFF** | | |
| **Library Staff Retrieval of Items Not Available in Electronic Databases** | | |
| from U of L libraries | No | Yes |
| from other libraries not at U of L | Yes | Yes |
| from commercial document delivery vendors | Yes | Yes |
| | | |
| **COPYING BY LIBRARY STAFF** | | |
| **Library Staff Copying of Items from Print Format** | No | Yes |
| **Library Staff Digitizing of Text from MicroFormat and Print Format** | No | Yes |
| | | |
| **DELIVERY BY LIBRARY STAFF** | | |
| **Library Staff Delivery of Item To Homes and/or Workplaces** via | No | Yes |
| E-mail | No | Yes |
| Fax | No | Yes |
| US Postal Service | No | Yes |
| Express Mail Services | No | Yes |

| Library Services | Available to On-Campus Learners from U of L On-Campus Libraries | Provided to DE Learners by U of L DLLS |
|---|---|---|
| **DELIVERY BY LIBRARY STAFF** | | |
| KYVL Courier | N/A | Yes |
| Faculty Courier to International Sites | N/A | Yes |
| | | |
| **ELECTRONIC COURSE RESERVE** | | |
| **eReserve (including monitoring of license/ copyright compliance)** | | |
| processing of electronic journal articles for course reserve | No | Yes |
| processing (including scanning) of non-electronic material for course reserve | Yes | No |
| collaboration on integration of eReserve material into online course content | No | Yes |
| | | |
| **LIBRARY INSTRUCTION** | | |
| **Instructional Content** | | |
| in electronic database usage | Yes | Yes |
| in information literacy | Yes | Yes |
| in technical aspects of using Distance Learning Library Services | No | Yes |
| **Instructional Delivery Method** | | |
| live in library collaborative learning center and classroom | Yes | Yes |
| live video via satellite TV broadcast and interactive videoconferencing (KTLN) | No | Yes |
| previously prepared multimedia (voice/audio) modules delivered via the web | No | Yes |
| Web tutorials | Yes | Yes |
| Webpages (text instructions only) | Yes | Yes |
| individual librarian consultation/explanation of search techniques | Yes | Yes |
| | | |
| **REFERENCE** | | |
| regular | Yes | Yes |
| extended | No | Yes |

## APPENDIX F: CONSUMER QUESTIONS
## THAT DE LEARNERS MIGHT ASK

1. Does the library convert a request for an item not immediately available into an interlibrary loan?
2. Does the library cover the cost of retrieving, photocopying, and delivering articles?
3. Is there a limit on the number of items I can request per semester or a maximum dollar amount that the library will spend to send articles to me that are not immediately available online?
4. Are online help sheets on library databases provided?
5. Does the library maintain a DE eReserve for items that my professor requires me to read?
6. Can I choose or change my library username and password?
7. Can I get books delivered directly to my home?
8. Are book deliveries made via first class mail or priority delivery?
9. Are library personnel available at a toll-free phone number, and do they monitor e-mail on evenings and weekends?
10. Is a librarian rather than a student assistant available to answer my questions in the evenings and on weekends?
11. Do library personnel scan articles for inclusion in DE courses?
12. Do library personnel insert electronic articles in course content?

## APPENDIX G: CONSUMER QUESTIONS THAT
## FACULTY MIGHT ASK

1. How can I get DE learners to use the library if I don't use it myself?
2. Does the library have a separate unit that deals with my DE learners' needs?
3. Does the library provide online guides or tutorials to library databases/vendor gateways?
4. Will library personnel accept lists of items that I want my learners to read and tell me which ones are available in full text?
5. Do library personnel prepare electronic reading lists that will eliminate the need for learners to purchase a course pack?
6. Will library personnel help my learners learn to perform independent research?
7. Will library personnel provide a link to the library for insertion in my online course?
8. How can I determine which journals are best to publish in so that my article will be available online and in a respected scholarly journal?

9. Can library personnel explain the difference between the limited information resources available from my learning management system vendor and the more extensive information resources available from the library?

10. Will library personnel provide data on the use of the library by my learners?

11. Does the library provide a separate Web portal for my program or course, or do learners have to search among library Webpages for different departments?

12. Does the library charge my department for the library services it provides to my learners?

13. Is library use by faculty included in the student enrollment charge?

14. Are learners charged on a per use basis or by course enrollment?

15. Does the library subsidize the cost of articles provided to learners?

16. How can learners obtain items not included in databases?

17. Does the library support individual DE courses as well as DE degree programs?

18. Why don't libraries scan book chapters and articles for me to include in my online course?

19. What if I want my learners to use online databases that the library doesn't own?

## APPENDIX H: CONSUMER QUESTIONS THAT ADMINISTRATORS MIGHT ASK

1. Why can't we just expect the library to serve DE learners like they do other learners?

2. On-campus learners already have off-campus access to library databases through a proxy server. Why can't DE learners get access to library databases the same way?

3. If DE learners have off-campus access to library databases, why do they need anything else?

4. Why can't we just reimburse the library on a per use basis rather than provide financial support for every student in the class?

5. Why does material need to be requested from elsewhere? Why can't learners use only what the library already owns?

6. We already spend $1M a year for library databases. Why can't learners use those?

7. We have a state-funded virtual library. Why can't learners use that?

8. Why can't learners use their local public libraries?

9. Why can't the regular departments in the university libraries serve DE learners?

10. How will we know whether DE learners are using the services provided?
11. Why can't librarians provide the services the learners need without involving faculty?
12. What proof can the library offer that learners are using the library and are satisfied with the service?
13. Why can't learners use the same username and password for their online course and the library?
14. Why isn't the library included within the learning management system adequate for learners?
15. Why do librarians need to know about the content that professors include in their online courses?
16. Faculty already know how to use the Web. Why do faculty need to collaborate with librarians?
17. Why aren't libraries as easy to use as the Web?
18. How much does it cost annually for the libraries to operate a service for DE learners?
19. Why are some DE degree programs more expensive than others to serve?
20. How can we determine the quality of an online course?
21. How can I increase the chances that our institution's DE degree programs will be accredited?
22. Why do library personnel build separate learning portals for each academic program?
23. Do the library and the administrative unit responsible for helping faculty develop online courses have a good working relationship?
24. How is the enrollment of DE learners authenticated? Library access can be granted only to currently enrolled learners and faculty. Who is responsible for providing enrollment records to the library?
25. How much does the library charge for photocopying journal articles?
26. How much does the library charge for arranging an interlibrary loan?
27. Why can't we just pass the cost of library services on to the learners?
28. How do we measure superior academic skills, specifically lifelong learning skills?

## APPENDIX I: COMPARISON OF ON-CAMPUS AND DE LIBRARY SERVICES AT U OF L

1. On-campus learners self-authenticate for electronic database access by e-mail activation of their Athena computer account. Athena accounts are generated from computerized enrollment updates.

On-campus learners present themselves with a picture ID at a U of L campus computer user center to make password changes to their Athena accounts.

2. DLLS authenticates off-campus DE learners based on enrollment lists obtained from the Registrar's Office or from academic units while registration is in process.

3. Databases licensed by U of L are more discipline-specific than those licensed by KYVL.

4. KYVL databases are incorporated along with the databases licensed by U of L in the U of L Library System's Research Center Webpage.

5. Library staff do assist on-campus learners with verification of holdings but do not generally accept and screen batches of requests for items from on-campus learners.

6. On-campus learners are expected to retrieve physical material from campus libraries on a self-service basis. DLLS staff retrieve physical material from campus libraries for DE learners.

7. On-campus learners are expected to determine on a self-service basis that material is not immediately available on campus before submitting an interlibrary loan request for it. DLLS does not require DE learners to submit interlibrary loan requests (i.e., pre-screen requests for local holdings). DLLS does the screening.

8. DLLS utilizes document delivery vendors more intensely than interlibrary loan to decrease delivery time for DE learners. Delivery of books between libraries usually is accomplished via a slower "Library Rate" or courier.

9. On-campus learners are expected to do their own copying; DLLS staff copy material for DE learners.

10. On-campus learners are expected to view and print material from micro-format on a self-service basis. DLLS digitizes material from micro-format (and print) for electronic delivery to DE learners.

11. On-campus learners who request items via interlibrary loan are generally expected to pick them up in person from the Hold Shelf in the Ekstrom Library. Although photocopies obtained via interlibrary loan can be delivered to campus offices, all books obtained from other libraries must be picked up in person.

12. DLLS staff deliver requested items to the homes or workplaces of U of L DE learners, preferably via e-mail. First-class or priority mail is used when e-mail or fax is not possible. Express mail services are used occasionally on weekends and usually at the end of semester. International deliveries that cannot be accomplished via e-mail are arranged on a case-by-case basis.

13. DLLS focuses on processing of electronic journal articles for course reserve that can be accessed by DE learners using their DLLS username and password.

14. eReserve for on-campus learners consists primarily of print material scanned into electronic format with access via an Athena username and password.
15. DLLS collaborate with DE faculty on the integration of electronic journal articles processed for eReserve into DE course content.
16. DLLS explain technical (e.g., TIFF multi-page graphics readers, PDF files, etc.) as well as library issues.
17. Library instruction for on-campus learners is usually delivered in a live classroom format. DLLS staff participate actively in video and online delivery of library instructional content.
18. On-campus learners can consult with a librarian until 8:00 PM Sunday through Thursday evenings and until 6:00 PM Friday and Saturday evenings, except for holidays.
19. DLLS serves learners in multiple time zones and offers toll-free 800 access (within the United States) for DE learners. Call forwarding to a DLLS librarian or staff person is available from 7:00 AM through midnight daily, including most holiday periods. DLLS e-mail is monitored continuously (except between the hours of midnight and 7:00 AM), and reference assistance for DE learners is available on a similar schedule.

CHAPTER 5

# A DIFFERENT PRACTICE
## Spanning the Digital Divide Through Distance Learning

**Lisa Holstrom and John G. Bryan**

This case study focuses on the Early Childhood Learning Community, an atypical workforce development initiative that uses distance learning to advance the education and careers of early childhood teachers, a population typically on the low-tech side of the digital divide to which distance programs have only begun to reach out. As a byproduct of the distance program, this population is also spanning the digital divide, acquiring skills and an appreciation for the opportunities presented by technology. The new skills of this population have profoundly affected the teachers themselves, but they also benefit the teachers' own students. The case study describes the many special considerations required to address the program's curricular, instructional, support, marketing, and financial planning issues. It also describes the surprises, successes, and failures of this ambitious program's first two years.

**KEYWORDS:** course development, digital divide, early childhood learning community (ECLC), financial feasibility, Head Start, literacy, marketing, needs assessment, support services

Electronic Learning Communities—Issues and Practices, pages 187–238.
Copyright © 2003 by Information Age Publishing, Inc.
All rights of reproduction in any form reserved.
ISBN: 1-931576-96-3 (pbk.), 1-931576-97-1 (hardcover)

## DIMENSIONS OF THE DIGITAL DIVIDE

From a student essay written for a preparatory English composition course:

> My personal feelings about my enrollment in the Early Childhood Learning Community (ECLC) Program are simply that this program introduced me to my strengths and weaknesses. My weakness is that I get really upset when I approach difficult situations regarding my courses. When I was enrolled in the Eastern Shore Community College and working on my obtaining my CDA (Child Development Associate, a basic professional credential that precedes the associate's degree), this was a piece of cake compared to the ECLC Program. I now understand that I am at the University level, which is basically a higher learning institution. Hard work and attention to detail is a must.
>
> My strengths regarding my enrollment in the ECLC Program, is my ability to adapt and re-direct myself by not placing unrealistic goals, and to not be afraid to ask my instructors for help and perspective. I will often times solicit guidance from my peers as well. The most important strength of all is my ability to now apply Early Childhood Theories into practice in my classroom, and the ability to extend this knowledge to my children's parents. This is a great feeling! The ECLC Program has taught me how to concentrate and to become an Early Childhood Professional. Now, when I announce that I am a Lead Teacher I can perform just as the title states.
>
> I had not been to school for 20 years or more. When I started with ECLC Program, I did not know how I would be able to keep up with the younger students just out of high school. I had no prior computer skills, and my grammar skills were poor. All I had was the will and determination to learn and to apply myself if I were given a chance.
>
> I can proudly say that I have been in the ECLC Program for two years now, and I have learned how to work on a computer to include connecting to and surfing the Web. I have increased my grammatical and writing skills, I can communicate better orally, and now my agency Program Coordinator has asked me to deliver training during our agency's 2002 Pre-service Training.
>
> Hard work and dedication does pay off. I am proof. I thank the ECLC Program for all of my travels to gain success in working with children and their families.                              —[Rochelle, a pseudonym for a real student][1]

Rochelle typifies the population that lives on the low-tech side of the digital divide. She is low-income, is African-American, was a high-school graduate but with low literacy for an adult, had little computer access, and had no computer skills. Employed as a Head Start teacher working with pre-school children, she had little use for an e-mail address, and little concept of what the Internet is or offers. Rochelle works 40 hours a week and comes home to significant family responsibilities, leaving little time for attending workshops or classes to acquire new skills. Now add to that profile a further complication in Rochelle's life. In 1998, Congress mandated that 50% of a Head Start center's teachers have at least an associate's degree by 2003. The State of Ohio, where Rochelle lives, has mandated that 100% of State-funded Head Start teachers have at least an associate's degree by 2008. To keep her job, Rochelle would have to get a college degree—doing so without changing any of her life circumstances. Distance education offered her few options, even if she had initially been aware of its possibilities.

Distance education can do more than efficiently and conveniently enhance the educational opportunities of technosavvy populations living on the high-tech side of the digital divide. Distance education can transform lives. For Rochelle, e-learning has opened new revelations about her abilities and her possibilities. To a great extent, she can self-assess her performance and identify both her strengths and her weaknesses. Distance education can be powerful, empowering, and self-actualizing, building a bridge across the digital divide to span not only technology deficits but also educational, social, economic, and career-opportunity deficits.

This chapter addresses challenges and opportunities that educators in e-learning environments must consider as they leave the now-comfortable position of using distance learning to address the high-tech side of the divide, and use technologies to approach a more challenging population. When we succeed in matching the appropriate technology to the needs of this new audience, the people in that audience will find their lives changed. We hope that more academic administrators and directors of distance courses, training, and degrees will consider marketing to populations on the low-tech side of the divide. In the discussions that follow, we use the distance education program in which Rochelle is enrolled to explore critical issues, possible solutions, and examples of best practices.

## The Low-Tech Side of the Divide

Spanning the divide is neither easy nor cheap. Doing so requires a reassessment of assumptions about both delivery systems and students. It requires institutional commitment. It requires more support systems, more daily maintenance, quick adaptability to changing circumstances, a different marketing strategy, and considerable understanding of and faith in the people on the other side of the divide.

In some respects, Rochelle resembles other adults enrolled in distance learning programs. Her age, her need, and her desire for additional education match the concentration of distance learners. In most other respects, though, her demographic profile differs from most distance learners in the United States who are typically white, are middle-income, have careers in progress, already have significant college credit if not at least one degree, are pursuing technologically oriented programs of study, own computers, have Internet connections at home, and have better-than-average computer literacy. Accordingly, higher education has directed this first generation of Internet-based distance learning programs to the high-tech side of the digital divide where the technology constitutes a great aid rather than an impediment to learning.

### Census 2000

In a special study published in September 2001, "Home Computers and Internet Use in the United States: August 2000," the US Census Bureau and the US Department of Commerce reported that more than half of US households have computers, with 42% having Internet access. For married adults with combined incomes over $75,000, the percentage jumps to almost 90% with home computers and Internet access. Almost every child now in every income level has access to a computer at school; this marks a significant improvement over the previous census report.

The report also indicated that computer access and usage for low-income adults is a different story. Among family households with incomes less than $25,000, only 28% had a computer and 19% had Internet access. Although community technology centers have made advancements in local computer access, most of the adults in these households still have little access to computers. Beyond access is the issue of incentive: many low-income adults have little incentive to acquire new technology skills unless required to do so by their jobs. Rochelle fits this profile.

### Access, Outreach, and the Divide

Institutions of higher education that identify access and outreach as part of their mission should concern themselves with this adult population, its lack of computer skills, and its lack of readiness for an increasingly technological society. They should also concern themselves with future generations of citizens whose parents and teachers are on that side of the divide. The future expectations for use of technology will be even greater for today's children. Unlike Rochelle, most adults on her side of the digital divide have no federal mandate that offers such clear options: learn, or lose your job. Rochelle has a built-in incentive; where is the incentive for her neighbors and friends?

While most distance learning programs target that portion of the population that already possesses computer access and skills, the interest in and demand for distance programs is growing well beyond that population. A recent poll sponsored by the KnowledgeWorks Foundation found that 73% of Ohioans want college-level distance learning opportunities expanded and investment increased. And Ohio has many community colleges and state schools that are accessible to most students. In states where higher education institutions are more removed from rural populations, that percentage may be much higher.

### Challenge and Opportunity

Therein lie both a challenge and an opportunity: the challenge is to meet the demand from a population that lacks access and skills. The opportunity is to narrow the digital divide by meeting that demand. On our small scale at the University of Cincinnati, we have found that appropriate and relevant distance education provides an opportunity and motivation for people on the low-tech side of the divide to acquire computer skills and to establish a long-term interest in furthering their engagement with technology.

## Digital Differences

As the data from the Census 2000 show, low-income adults still have little access to computers, few computer skills, and little incentive to use technology. Damarin (2000) points out that perhaps a more reasonable description of the technology deficit that exists is "digital differences." The problem, she reasons, goes beyond "the haves" and "the have-nots." Where do you locate someone with a 286 computer? An old dot matrix printer? How do you account for the gender differences in usage among users? For those of us in education, the problem of digital differences is not a gap between two distinct levels of Internet/computer access, but a multidimensional continuum in which students and their high-tech equipment vary in a multitude of ways.

This framework is useful for several reasons, foremost of which is that it shows us as educators that we need not build a bridge, an all-or-nothing effort to help students find the opposite side. The bridge metaphor implies that if we build it, they will come. If we give students hardware and software, they'll find themselves on the hi-tech side of the divide and contribute to new statistics in the next census.

We need to realize that enabling small steps, rather than a giant leap, empowers students to advance of their own volition. Students don't have to come to our courses completely computer literate; we can build their new technology skills into our courses. Through our inherent power and responsibility as educators, we can create a motivation and incentive, a reason for students to incorporate technology into their daily lives.

Conceptualizing digital differences among students also liberates us as educators to offer distance education courses to those students who we previously assumed were the "have nots." Many of us were hesitant to offer our courses online for fear we were alienating our older non-traditional students who didn't have the computer skills to excel in an online course. In many cases, these students benefit greatly from the convenience and flexibility of these courses, but there is little supply and little demand. Certainly, the lack of demand is a function of the lack of marketing to populations who aren't reached through usual Internet channels. New marketing strategies or old traditional strategies need to be launched and supported to create the necessary demand.

Various studies have shown that new technology skills, like the acquisition of many new skills, leads to a student's increased self-esteem and self-efficacy (e.g. Eastin & LaRose, 2000; Lee, 2000). Distance education provides students with direct experience, "long-term acquisition of skill sets reinforced over time" (Eastin & LaRose, 2000). Creating courses for all students becomes not only a revenue-stream, for those of us that need to worry about such things, but it also creates a moral imperative.

Damarin (2000) declares that the issue revolves around equity.

> ...as educators increase the use of technology for teaching and learning, they must attend to principles for making digital content maximally accessible. Sometimes, this means choosing implementations which are not state-of-the-art from the high-tech perspective. ... Accommodation to diverse students with multiple platforms must take precedence over the desire to use only the most powerful tools when equity is a major consideration (p.21).

Few distance education programs are geared toward low-income level adults, and even fewer are recorded in the technology literature. Gould and Anderson (2000) used interactive multimedia to deliver nutrition education to low-income persons. Berkshire and Smith (2000) reported on their findings using high-touch, high-tech distance learning with native Alaskan learners. Lee (2000) implemented a cybercounseling program to bring counseling services to low-income adults. These examples are further evidence that course work and other services can be successful if the student population is aware of the program, and the technology is appropriate for the market and the content being delivered.

## A DIFFERENT PRACTICE:
## THE EARLY CHILDHOOD LEARNING COMMUNITY

Rochelle is enrolled in the Early Childhood Learning Community (ECLC), an associate degree program in early childhood care and education. University College, which operates ECLC, is a two-year college on the main campus of the University of Cincinnati (UC). The college first offered an Early Childhood degree in 1970. Since then, the on-campus program has enjoyed considerable success and now enrolls about 150 majors, most of them women and many of them well beyond traditional college age. The federal mandate mentioned above, included in the Head Start Reauthorization of 1998, led us to begin exploring the creation of a distance version of the program in 1999. In Spring 2000, we offered the distance program's first course, relying on integrated satellite-broadcast video and Internet-based interactivity. By Spring 2002, we had created and deployed 23 of the program's 27 courses. ECLC now enrolls some 300 students from Virginia to California, in Singapore and Venezuela. Our links to and collaboration with the National Head Start Association and Head Start Quality Improvement Centers throughout the country have assisted us in extending the program nationwide. Despite the program's origins in the Head Start mandate, word of the program has spread beyond that community, and we enroll as many students from proprietary early childhood centers as we do from Head Start centers.

The program includes course work for a complete associate's degree, including English, math, sociology, philosophy, and psychology, as well as early childhood content courses. Each course consists of about 20 hours of pre-recorded coursework on video, which may resemble traditional lectures or may more closely resemble a television talk show, depending on the instructor's intentions. The videos are produced by a professional video production company, RISE Learning Solutions, also located in Cincinnati and already heavily involved in the production of training videos for the early childhood community. Unlike many pre-recorded video courses, ECLC's productions use commercial-quality equipment, multiple cameras, professional technical crews (even a make-up artist), and a professional production studio and editing facilities. Each course video is broadcast by an EchoStar satellite and is simultaneously streamed over the Internet—though we know of no viewers who rely on the streaming video—indicative of the students' greater comfort with lower level technologies and of their lack of access to fast Internet connections. Students may also lease the videos on VHS tape or CD-ROMs.

Students' regular interactions with each other and with instructors occur through the Internet and the Blackboard learning management system licensed by the university. Existing university faculty taped the lectures and often served as the instructors for the online portions of the course.

Although part of a large research university, University College is an open-admissions "teaching college" with faculty whose primary interest and work assignments are to help less prepared students succeed in acquiring knowledge and career-oriented skills and in becoming life-long learners. As an open-admissions college, we concentrate on helping our students meet the particular challenges they face, ranging from academic deficits (60% require developmental courses upon admission) to learning disabilities. We use extensive entrance placement testing to route students into appropriately targeted courses, and we use extensive support services—such as tutoring—to promote student persistence and success.

For most of our history we have focused these efforts to benefit our own community, the diverse urban youth of Cincinnati. Now ECLC extends this mission to a new virtual community, geographically dispersed but sharing the common challenges and potential of our on-campus student population. ECLC's creation of technology-rich, responsive, student-centered learning opportunities ensure the success of non-traditional teachers in both urban and rural settings, of all racial and ethnic origins, throughout the world. Most students in the program have little or no access to college because of locale, or work and family obligations.

## A MODEL FOR BUILDING A DISTANCE PROGRAM THAT EMPOWERS

Lee (2000) offers us a useful model for building a program anchored in technology and directed toward low-income users. He suggests a four-step process: assess, partner, train, and affect policy. While these processes are vital to creating any successful program, they are crucial when delivering content to low-income students. Less than careful *assessment* of student needs could lead to using technology that is inaccessible or irrelevant to students' lives. In order for technology to be empowering for its users, it must be built upon a foundation that meets students' needs. It also must be flexible enough to grow as students develop more complex technological skills. Equally important, *partnering* allows a program to include stakeholders in the development and delivery of the training. Partnering can also extend the reach of marketing efforts and have a direct impact on the financial feasibility, especially when partners are able to support the program's start-up costs. Partners such as community and professional organizations can bring with them a wealth of knowledge about the target population that is equally valuable.

In Lee's model, *Train/Educate* refers to the process of program delivery. And while providing educational opportunities is the primary goal of e-learning programs, Lee adds *Affect Policy* as another objective in building a program. Particularly when low-income students are involved, affecting policy concerning issues of access and skill building is crucial. Many program administrators may find that partnering with politicians and other policy-makers at the local, regional and national level facilitates the program-building process. This is because policy-makers now see themselves as stakeholders in the program and have a vested interest in watching the program grow and succeed.

We would expand this model to include two additional important steps: marketing and assessing financial feasibility. Letting students know that a program is available and accessible is just as vital to overcome barriers as needs assessment and partnering. Equally important is assessing financial feasibility. Such an assessment not only helps build a business plan, it helps shape the program.

And the model is recursive. Needs assessment is an on-going process and new findings are incorporated into the resultant curriculum and into partnerships that are formed. Our model, then, would look like Figure 1.

Needs assessment is key to the entire planning and delivery process; it is the foundation upon which pedagogy and appropriate technology depend. Distance programs often fail due to overestimation of students' skills, inappropriate use of technology, or the lack of a comprehensive marketing plan. Careful needs analysis can alleviate these expensive errors.

## ASSESSING NEEDS

Building a successful distance education program must begin with an accurate assessment of students' needs. In this section, we will discuss the process of assessment and various needs that may be common to many low-income learners. The case study of the Early Childhood Learning Community, coupled with examples from other programs, will demonstrate how appropriate technology evolves from students' needs. We have found that the needs include English literacy, computer access and literacy, relevant content, and a comprehensive support infrastructure.

Our research into the skills of childcare providers led us to talk to leaders in their organizations at the national, state, and local levels. We worked with current teachers, retired teachers, and other interested stakeholders

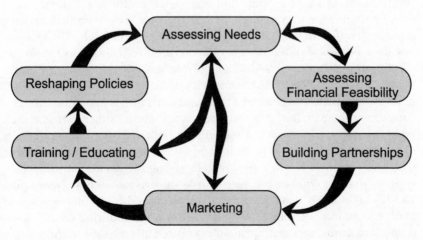

FIGURE 1
A Model of Program Development for Distance Learning

as we designed our program. Our existing on-campus program in early childhood care and education, which enrolls about 150 students, also made us familiar with the profile of childcare providers, not just through student contact but through our faculty's own work experience in the field, their participation in professional societies and advisory boards, through collaborations with Head Start grantees, and through the university's operation of a progressive childcare and Head Start center on campus. We understood the educational, social, cultural, racial, and economic backgrounds of childcare workers, and we understood the full range of their educational needs—often better than they understood it themselves.

## Assessing Students Through Placement

Placement of students at course levels suitable to their preparedness encourages student persistence and success, both on campus and at a distance. For distance students, the technology both helps and hinders placement issues. It helps in that some academic deficiencies can be overcome through simple technological solutions. For example, a student's ability to repeatedly play recorded video class sessions can overcome certain learning disabilities that are less easily accommodated in the traditional classroom. The result is that a student may not need to be placed at a course level as low as would be necessary otherwise. But the circumstances of our distance program also hinders placement. Our ECLC offerings are not as varied or as finely tuned as our on-campus courses are to different preparedness levels. For example, on campus, we offer six levels of freshman composition. ECLC offers only four levels—largely for two reasons: 1) the development costs are very high, and 2) the number of enrolled students remains insufficient to financially justify six placement levels. The technology does not erase differences in preparedness, of course, and so we do administer placement tests—though currently we still use hard-copy instruments that are mailed to each student's supervisor. (The copyright holder of one of our principal placement tests will not allow us to digitize the company's instrument.) Tests are proctored by a student's supervisor who then returns completed tests with a signed statement verifying the authenticity of the work. Students may place into an intensive developmental course if their preparedness is below freshman-level English. Section enrollment is kept low in these courses; the instructor-to-student ratio is never more than 1-to-12. Likewise, a math placement test is offered and a developmental math course has been implemented. Care was taken during course development to assure that math principles covered are relevant to the student population. For example, many problems revolve around inventory of supplies in the early childhood classroom.

## English Literacy

For those of us toward the fortunate end of the digital continuum, the phrase "computer-mediated" has positive connotations, suggesting enhancement, increased accessibility, and even fun and excitement. But for students at the opposite end of the continuum, the phrase suggests impediments to be overcome. It can often mean that the content which is "computer-mediated" is outside the student's reach, either literally or figuratively. It can also mean that a student's reading and writing skills will be challenged.

A study published by The Children's Partnership (2000) found "the vast majority of information on the Net is written for an audience that reads at an average or advanced literacy level. Yet, 44 million American adults, roughly 22% do not have the reading and writing skills necessary for functioning in every day life" (p. 8). Compound that issue with the 32 million Americans who do not speak English as a first language and we realize that a significant part of the US population is excluded from the majority of the Internet's content. If distance education programs are constructed in the same manner, students are removed from critical resources and content.

In an on-campus classroom or in videoconferencing, face-to-face contact often enables an instructor to look beyond a student's literacy to assess that person's understanding of essential concepts. (We are using the term *literacy* to refer to both reading and writing proficiency.) Oral communication and body cues may say what his or her writing cannot. Oral communication may also help an instructor reach a student whose reading comprehension is weak.

## If Everything Depended on Your Writing

Without face-to-face contact, as in many distance-education courses, student interaction and assessment depend almost entirely on written communication; students' academic performance depends on how well they can express themselves in writing. They may have learned the skills or concepts, but they must also be able to demonstrate that learning through their writing. In many distance courses, this dependency on written communication holds true not only for English and other writing-intensive courses, but for all courses and for many related activities, such as online academic advising. From ECLC's earliest days, though, we understood how significant that dependency would be for our student population. Many adult students rarely write full sentences and paragraphs in the typical work day; instead, they jot notes and lists, often compressed to fit on a Post-It note. So when an adult whose last student experience is years in the past submits a written assignment for the first time in college, it often consists of written fragments of knowledge, not complex arrangements of introductions, topic sentences, supporting elaboration, and citations of authoritative sources.

Like many distance learners, ECLC students must write essays and analyses, explain their math solutions, post to discussion boards, occasionally chat in realtime, and generally express in writing every question, idea, understanding, misunderstanding, and rationale. To the instructor, an ECLC student is his or her writing. For ECLC students with recent academic experience, this issue is no more significant than it is for on-campus students. The majority of our students are older with high school preparation that has been forgotten, ignored, or poorly taught. Imagine yourself, for a moment, being assessed entirely on your writing, stripped of your physical being, the nuances of your voice, the facial expressions. How daunting is that? And think of those colleagues, if not of yourself, who seem to be possessed by a different, often rash personality when dashing off e-mail. Would they wish to be sized up by nothing more than their written expressions?

So, our students face a genuine problem that threatens their academic persistence and job security. Their academic success in early childhood education relies on their written communication, and their academic English preparation has typically been weak. To address this significant problem—one that, admittedly, exceeded our expectations, we have sought funding from various agencies to help support student literacy. As of March 2002, we have succeeded in receiving external support for literacy enhancement. Those funds have supported an online English tutor for each distance course, regardless of content. In other words, each student has access to a tutor in every course, whether it is an English course, an English literature course, or an early childhood course. Tutors are available both synchronously and asynchronously, to answer the quick question during chatroom office hours. For example, a typical question to the synchronous tutor would be, "Does this sentence make sense?" or, "Should I say 'data is' or 'data are' in this sentence?" Asynchronous tutors review an entire paper and make suggestions within 24-48 hours. Many students depend on the accessibility and reliability of tutoring assistance.

The funds also support a literacy specialist to work with faculty in designing assignments to parallel the students' evolving literacy skills. Ideally, this would mean starting the quarter with assignments that allow students to build upon their literacy skills, either with a self-introduction on a discussion board, or a one-paragraph summary of the video lecture. While some instructors have been reluctant to "cater to" or "be easy on" students in this manner, others have had great success in ramping up assignments during the quarter. Rochelle's essay at the beginning of this chapter is a poignant example of the self-discovery that often accompanies the new skills and new self-esteem.

Our specialist also identified differences in literacy issues between native and non-native speakers of English. We work with a large migrant population whose first language is Spanish. Many instructors could not discern differences in style or grammar between students for whom English is a first language and those for whom English is a second language; consequently they approached all students with the same instruction. Our specialist pointed out the patterns that tend to appear in written communications of non-native speakers of English so instructors could tailor their instruction and suggestions to meet those students' needs.

Among the specialist's other duties is to work with faculty on issues of tone in e-mail and postings, a concern heightened by the fact that students' only understanding of their instructors' personality came from e-mail and postings. And probably as important, the specialist has trained the faculty who don't teach English to refrain from trying to teach English, a tendency that often does more harm than good.

Finally, to promote the effectiveness of written communication for distance students, we strongly advise them to enroll in English composition courses from their first term in the program and to continue the sequence of composition courses concurrently with their early-childhood content courses. To that end, our faculty have decided to offer placement testing via regular mail, paper and pencil; tests are mailed to each student's supervisor. They are proctored by a student's supervisor who then returns completed tests with a signed statement verifying the authenticity of the work. Preparatory Composition is designed for students who place at that developmental level in our placement testing, or who opt not to take the placement tests. This course, as well as the entire English sequence, utilizes relevant writing exercises and readings. For example, the assignments in English 103 center around the types of writings that teachers do on-the-job: letters to parents, intervention plans, and reflective essays about their own practice.

## Informing Our Technology Decisions

Our research also shaped our decision to deliver most of our content through video rather than a text-based course. During the initial production, we were anxious about our choice; video production was *very* expensive and each of the 27 courses would contain 20 hours of video. Instructors spent grueling two-week periods putting their entire ten-week courses on tape in a studio where the "meter was always running." Some instructors questioned the expense and work when a text-based course appeared "so easy." A few administrators—generally those unfamiliar with our student population—questioned our insistence on using such "out-of-date" technology for delivering content, and they would later question our use of satellite broadcasts instead of streaming video.

In 1999, we spoke with conviction about the necessity of video for content and of delivery media that didn't require fast Internet connections. In hindsight, we were more right than we could have imagined. Students report that they often watch a lecture multiple times. Non-native speakers of English are able to discuss the lectures in their native language and then return to the lectures in English for confirmation. Students appreciate seeing an instructor looking into the camera and saying, "This is important. Please write this down." This group of students also enjoys putting a human face to the instruction while taking advantage of the flexibility and convenience of video. For this population of non-traditional working women, delivering content through video was the right choice.

## Computer Access and Literacy

Little access to technology and the subsequent lack of skills to manipulate it are the biggest challenges facing both the low-income distance learner and the institution that wants to deliver the instruction via computer. The statistics from Census 2000 are very telling: only 1 in 4 households earning less than $25,000 per year has a computer, and fewer than 1 in 5 has Internet access.

Our greatest challenge has consisted of helping students ascend steep learning curves in manipulating the technology of distance education—while also overcoming the usual risks for attrition that face non-traditional and other first-time college students. Lectures on video are accessible and familiar technology, and they continue to provide efficient and effective content delivery. But we are also committed to building an electronic community of learners that simulates the classroom environment. That requires ECLC students to have Internet skills, e-mail addresses, and the ability to send and receive e-mail, to attach files to e-mail, and to navigate Blackboard. Once students have acquired these basic skills and mastered them through sustained practice, we introduce more sophisticated skills, such as uploading and downloading files and converting file types.

Student surveys show that two-thirds of our students have never owned an e-mail address before enrolling in ECLC, or they have used one sporadically. While many had computer access in the workplace, they had no incentive to acquire computer skills. The federal mandate provided a catalyst for their acquiring further education, and distance education became their reason to acquire computer skills! To accommodate that sudden demand for technology assistance, our ECLC support staff became experts in the variety of e-mail addresses and accounts and clients available, in identifying systems that do and don't allow attachments, in steering students toward appropriate Internet browser versions, and in guiding students to download and install Adobe Systems' Acrobat Reader. Most of this occurs by telephone as we ease the students into the technology. The person casually passing the open door of our office is likely to hear half of a phone conversation: "When the arrow changes to a hand, that means you can click there." And while our central university tech help-desk also assists ECLC students, our students prefer the familiar names, voices, and rapport of our ECLC staff; they have come to rely on us and to see us as their one stop for everything from financial aid counseling to resolving satellite reception problems.

A student's computer literacy, or skills in using the technology, can enhance or impede the student's written communication. In many cases, writing a two-page paper was a difficult endeavor, but typing the paper was a major impediment and headache. Keyboarding skills were minimal. For those few occasions where participation in a chatroom was encouraged, students with slow typing skills were at a disadvantage. Discussion board postings allowed students to reflect and collect their thoughts while typing at their leisure. Practice has improved many students' keyboarding skills, but typing papers and postings still tends to be a very time-consuming chore for some.

As pointed out earlier by Damarin (2000), talking about computer access can oversimplify a complicated issue. We found out early in the program that while some students did have computer access, the equipment was slow and inadequate for the high-tech shows that tempted us. Our solution was to broadcast the videotaped lectures via satellite rather than utilize the state-of-the-art technology of streaming video. More than a few university administrators questioned our decisions, pointing out the accessibility and cost-effectiveness of streaming video versus the $1000 per hour cost of satellite broadcast.

## Informing Our Content Delivery Choices

Our challenge then was to devise a delivery method that met students' needs and was cost effective. This section describes our decision-making process.

Again, student needs drove our decision. Satellite broadcast brought the lectures to the students in their workplaces and their homes. The small 18" satellite dishes that we used are readily available for minimal cost. Although other educational programming is broadcast over subscription channels which carry additional fees, our broadcast channel is available to students at no additional charge. Streamed video was certainly a considered option because it was cost effective and no special computer software is needed to watch it. Most students use dial-up modems, however, and downloading even complex graphics is difficult, if not impossible. Also, we could not ignore the bills that students incur when their phone is tied up for long periods of time or when their ISP charges by the minute.

To address our need to deliver content cost-effectively, we researched various channels and shopped for the best rate. For our initial broadcasts we were charged $1000 per hour, which we understood to be standard for the industry. After two years of experience and additional contacts with channel proprietors, we have been able to negotiate a rate of one-third our original cost. We were also able to leverage the number of hours per week we need to broadcast; during the academic year we deliver between 16 and 20 hours of videotaped lectures for 8-10 different courses. Many students still depend upon this delivery medium. We also began leasing our lectures on VHS tapes for students who could not afford the satellite dish equipment or did not have access to the broadcasts. For example, the satellite coverage does not reach students in other countries, Alaska, Hawaii, and some areas of the US where mountains and canyons obstruct line of sight to the satellite. We also enroll a group of students who move from state to state with migrant workers, and they needed a portable system for viewing the class lectures.

Although we are very concerned about our students on the low-tech side of the digital divide, we also recognize that some students with more technology skills do enroll, and others learn quickly and are ready for higher-tech challenges. To meet their needs, we recently began providing students the course videos on CD-ROM. For now, VHS tapes and satellite broadcast will continue to be available for those students who prefer those formats. (In many cases, students' computers are too outdated to play a video CD and retain the high production value of the videos; audio and video tracks are jerky and difficult to follow.) For other students, CD-ROMs are a more convenient way to access the course lectures. Distribution of the digitally recorded media will also offer other significant advantages. They are easier to replay, and they offer opportunities for indexing and better organization of recorded material. The recorded video can be combined with supplementary text material, and live links to the Internet can be inserted. And for our operation, CD-ROMs are much easier than VHS tapes to store and mail.

Our students report that they use computers in their workplaces, at the homes of relatives, at the homes of co-workers and peers, and in their own homes. Many students are very interested, however, in owning their own computer, but the complicated nature of ordering one is often intimidating. Expense is also a factor. To address this need, we are completing negotiations of a partnership with Hewlett-Packard and Sehi Corporation to bring heavily discounted computer technology to those students who want it. Because a computer is considered an education-related expense for the distance learner, ECLC students may use surplus financial aid toward its purchase. Like other organizations that leverage their collective strength to benefit individual members or employees, we had enough participants to interest computer manufacturers. And our initial announcement of this opportunity to our distance students elicited a very strong response, indicating more clearly than any other aspect of the program that this population has been empowered to move themselves along the digital continuum. In other words, our students already have technology access sufficient to meet their basic educational needs, but their engagement with the technology has now grown to the level that they are committing their personal resources to improve that access. That's very telling.

Now, 90% of our students report that they use a computer regularly, in addition to the time they spend doing course work. They are using computers and the Internet for lesson plan ideas, to solve behavioral and other classroom problems, to research issues, and to search for best practices. Seventy-four percent of our students talk with a positive attitude to their own students about computers. They include computers in the pretend centers and other areas of the classroom, and they label the computer's parts just like they label other classroom items. One teacher shared the following story:

> The Internet has played a vital role in my classroom teaching. I will give you an example: I had a mother of a child in my classroom that was told by a medical professional that her child had a brain disorder; well the medical professional gave her no resources or anything about this certain disorder and she was very concerned, but too shy to ask the doctor questions. I took her to a computer at my center and showed her how to search for information about this certain disorder. She had never touched a computer before and thanked me for helping her to better understand what her son was going through. I felt this way when she had research to back her, she would be bold to ask questions. I would of never been able to help her like that if it wasn't for the Internet and having information at the click of a mouse. Matter of fact, the same mother saved her income tax money and bought a computer and is now getting her own Internet access in her home. Helping this mother, in turn, helped the child in my classroom.
>
> —[Donna, a pseudonym for a real student]

We continue to be pleasantly surprised by the impact of new technology skills on student learners and on the people within their realms of influence.

## Comprehensive Support Services

As many experienced college educators know, students' first-year experiences often a make or break their academic futures and forever alter their decisions regarding and attitudes towards college, jobs, and careers. Recognizing the importance of positive initial experiences, many funders are now dedicating financial resources to help and support first-year students as they become acclimated to college life. More significantly, most of American higher education has now abandoned the bankrupt notion that the freshman year is intended to weed out students who "just aren't college material."

From our earliest conversations about the program's design in Summer 1999, we realized that our intended students were not likely to have the computer skills or access that students in many distance programs enjoy, and that they would require intensive support systems. Those realizations led to our heavy reliance on video and on the multiple modes of delivering video. It also led us to develop significant support services to assist a student population that would need more hand-holding than most traditional students, and would need it without ever stepping onto our campus.

## Support for the Technology

Recognizing that many students were acclimating to a technology culture concurrent with their adjustment to a college culture, we wrote and produced an "Orientation to Distance Learning" video that is mailed to students upon our receipt of their program applications. The 34-minute video includes interviews with faculty about the importance and rigor of college course work, a visual orientation to the Blackboard course management system, a set of frequently asked (and answered) student questions, and video introductions to the staff in our main office. This video is in its second edition, as the first edition had more of a marketing focus and did not include enough programmatic details to truly orient students to a different way of learning. As we began experimenting with CD-ROMs, this was the first video that we piloted because its size was very manageable in a CD-ROM format. The orientation then did double-duty, as we sent it out to students as a CD-ROM trial and as an orientation to let students test the video CD on their equipment before ordering course lectures in this new format.

The on-campus technology help-desks are essential in the student support we offer. The consultants are available on evenings and weekends, when most of our students are working on their computers. Specific assistance with Blackboard is available as is help with Microsoft Office, e-mail, Internet, and general hardware questions.

Also, early in the program we realized that students needed to learn minimal technology skills prior to beginning their course work. Three hours before an assignment is due is not the proper time to learn how to send e-mails with attachments, or learn to use the "digital drop box" in Blackboard. Students' academic performances were contingent upon how well they could negotiate through Blackboard. This obvious need led us to develop a free practice course which students complete before beginning the program. It is a self-guided, interactive tutorial, which culminates in a self-assessment of one's new skills. Our office is notified via Blackboard when a student has completed the mini-course, and subsequently they are registered for their "real" courses. Student feedback has been tremendously favorable, with many sending us e-mails of appreciation, using their newly developed skills, of course!

## Literacy Support

The literacy support services mentioned earlier have also been an important development in our array of student services. Anticipating and responding to students' needs led us to offer this additional level of tutoring and support at no cost to the student.

## Advising

Our administration has dedicated the services of several advisors strictly to assist our distance students. Since over 60% of our students are transfers, advisors review faxed copies of transcripts to allow students to preview their advanced standing before actually enrolling in the program. The official advanced standing is processed after matriculation, similar to our on-campus students' review. The preview allows students to make informed decisions about switching schools, most often in the middle of their program. In addition, advisors help with registration information, communicate with students about programmatic issues, and even counsel personal problems. Much of this advising is accomplished via phone or fax. As students advance through the program and improve their technological and writing skills, e-mail becomes the primary advising medium.

## Assessment of Student Learning

Testing policies and procedures of distance programs are often met with skepticism from faculty and students alike. Authenticating a student's work, especially the work of a distance learner, can be a troublesome issue for instructors. As explained earlier, our placement tests are proctored by a student's supervisor who then returns completed tests with a signed statement verifying the authenticity of the work. These are the only tests, however, that are proctored. In fact, very few courses assess student learning through written tests.

Our faculty strongly advocate teaching preschool children using a constructivist model to knowledge acquisition, and they model this approach through their own college courses. Therefore, assessment of student learning occurs primarily through written reflective essays, summary statements, and self-evaluations, as well as postings to the discussion board. This service to students does not completely alleviate the instructors' worries about authenticity; on-campus and online instructors must always be alert to the possibility of plagiarism and cheating. At the least, this method of written assessment minimizes the opportunities for test-sharing and collaborative submissions.

## Student Feedback as a Key to Providing Good Support

Our early research revealed, for those of us not already familiar with typical characteristics of early childhood educators, that these adult students relish opportunities to provide feedback, anecdotes, and criticism about their experiences, from dealing with higher education to dealing with parents. Student satisfaction and course evaluation instruments help us assess various aspects of our student services. In response to student suggestions, practice courses have been re-designed, orientations intensified, and literacy services developed. Last year we held an on-campus open house at the request of several students. Although most students could not travel to visit us, a group of students did visit and enjoyed seeing our physical campus and offices, touring the video production studios, and being treated to lunch.

Distance learners, particularly low-income students who are at higher risk for attrition, need multiple levels of support from every corner of their lives. Our support team begins with our office staff, extends to other university units, and continues to the student's workplace. We also found that the burden was on us to press for the adaptation of existing support systems to the needs of our students. Together, our program's custom services and the adapted elements of existing university support systems comprise a comprehensive system of student support and service.

We became student advocates on a campus that had not adapted its extensive systems to the needs of students at a distance. We worked beyond our own areas of direct responsibility to make admission, financial-aid, credit-evaluation, registration, and book-ordering systems adapt to meet these invisible students' needs. On a campus that knew how to serve 33,000 flesh-and-blood students, many systems *assumed* the physical presence of all students: financial-aid personnel required students to sign a promissory note in person; textbooks were shelved on the bookstore's main floor with little readiness for the logistics of phone orders and book shipping; CD-ROMs with discounted software had to be picked up in person; some computer systems required in-person visits to a basement office for password changes; and so on.

We began meeting regularly with other university departments to discuss potential problems and ways in which our office could help other units help our students. Prior to our meetings, many accommodations of our students' needs were ad hoc rather than systemic. For example, initially the campus bookstore manager responded to an ECLC student's book order by pulling the necessary books from the shelves on the main floor and returning to her office to box and ship them. Such an approach—though appreciated for its reflection of an accommodating attitude—was clearly impractical for the hundreds of orders that would be coming. Not only would the bookstore find itself losing money on such transactions, the response time would be unacceptable to students. In fact, in the first three terms of the program, students often received books after the term began and dissatisfaction with bookstore service was high. (We should note here that one of the characteristics of this student population is their tendency to procrastinate in applying for admission to the program and in registering for classes. Unlike the traditional high school senior who applies in December or January for the following autumn, these students typically apply on the day they register for their first class, which is often the first day of classes in a term. Such patterns of late application and registration confound planning and logistics.)

We learned about the inadequacy of the bookstore's approach through student feedback, which led us to begin working with bookstore personnel. Soon they recognized that our students would never visit campus—unlike students in some of the university's hybrid distance/on-campus courses—and that their approach would have to adapt. They reorganized their process and began storing books in the manager's office. They added personnel during quarterly periods when ordering activity is highest. Books now arrive early and on-time, and students are very satisfied with the improved service. As a part of our support team, bookstore staff now provide an important level of student support—and not just in delivering books. More recently they have assumed responsibility for filling software media orders and for shipping and handling course videotapes and CD-ROMs leased by students.

Through student feedback we learned that in addition to support systems, other UC systems required adaptation to the distance market. For example, the university had instituted a student health insurance fee for all students. The fee was applied by default to student bills unless students signed a waiver indicating that they had private health insurance. The revenues from this fee supported both the operations of the on-campus student clinic and health insurance for students needing treatment. Getting students across the country to sign and return the waiver became just another logistical problem. More troubling—and this was the element that elicited the most strident response from students—was a policy that would require payment of the fee (more than $200 per term) by students who had neither private insurance nor the opportunity to ever use the services we offered on campus. Beyond the policy change needed to exempt our students from this fee were the software coding changes needed to exempt our students from the default billing. With the university's student information and billing system backlogged with coding change requests, we negotiated an expedient with the student clinic. We simply sent them a list of all our students, and they manually exempted the students from the fee.

Responding to other student requests, we devised a vehicle for offering college credit for life experience, a process that must be carefully designed and used if the credit is to have credibility and if the institution is to retain its accreditation. This large research university did not yield easily to students' claims that their life experience was worthy of college credit. And perhaps understandably, faculty felt that college credit carried an understanding that a student's learning was assessed during the credit attainment process. Students often express an interest in having higher education validate their experience in the field, but our research had not prepared us for the urgency of our students' demand. In response to their requests, we devised a strategy that satisfied both students and faculty, focusing on educational outcomes rather than educational processes. We designed tests for several key content courses to assess whether students had acquired and could demonstrate the knowledge covered in the courses. Successful demonstration of the acquired knowledge would yield credit without course enrollment. Failure on the test would yield no credit, and the student would have to take the course to earn the credit.

Finally, because our team orientation extends to the student's workplace, we have a series of courses and practicum experiences that allow co-workers to mentor and support one another. We were concerned from the outset that a student may be the sole student at any given workplace and we wanted to head off any feelings of isolation. It was important that this student's co-workers and supervisors realize the opportunities that exist for professional growth and how their co-worker was taking advantage of them through distance education. Involving other staff members in our support team has encouraged mentoring and support in the workplace, and that alleviates any feelings of isolation.

## FINANCIAL FEASIBILITY

While we have focused on a model of developing a distance program that matches technology, support systems, and marketing to a population on the low-tech side of the digital divide, among the program's most significant challenges was the assessment of financial feasibility, the development of a business plan that would earn the university's backing, and the use of all that information to adjust the design of the program.

Because the university was entering the distance learning market at a relatively late stage (when compared with more aggressive competitors), we had chosen to select a niche market that would not already be in play but that would have a compelling reason for accepting our promotional appeals. For those reasons, we identified the early childhood education market as especially appropriate, but that market also presented particular problems: as described in detail above, the students would require special technology and course production approaches, an intensive marketing effort, expensive course distribution systems, and additional support services—all of which meant higher than normal development and operating costs.

## Program Costs: Special Technology

As explained elsewhere in this chapter, the students targeted by the program lived on the low-tech side of the digital divide, and we assumed from the beginning that we would have to exert special efforts in helping them overcome the technological barriers. Any instructional solution that relied exclusively on text-based online courses would likely fail. These students were not ready for communication that seemed impersonal, unstructured, and unfamiliar. We needed a more familiar technology that would ease the transition. So, that most fundamental—and most expensive—decision led us to use pre-recorded video as the core of each course. Pre-recording video that would be replayed for several terms, if not for several years, enabled us to focus the faculty on planning each recording session and on approaching each session as a "performance" instead of as just another lecture. However, we had all viewed "telecourses" that should have embarrassed both the faculty and the institutions that created and distributed them: poor lighting, fresh-from-the-tomb faces, static images, fixed points of view, voices-in-a-barrel audio; those were the hallmarks of higher education by video. And those characteristics stood in contrast not only to the flesh-and-blood presence of the traditional classroom, but also to the dynamic, highly produced, breathlessly engaging video of everyday television. We had to do better.

With the expert guidance of RISE Learning Solutions, a video production company that specializes in early childhood education and training, we developed a plan for production, in a professional television studio, of the courses' video. Each course's recording entailed use of three or four broadcast-quality cameras, direct-to-tape recording, direct-input computer video, Chyron graphics generation, professional lighting and sound, professional make-up, a custom set, and a full professional crew, including camera operators, a lighting engineer, a sound engineer, a director, and a producer—in addition to the faculty member and "studio students," the students and staff we hired to sit in on the taping sessions to ask questions as real students would. In addition to such technical services, a RISE producer worked with our faculty to help them understand the nature of the medium, its differences from a live classroom presentation, and the kind of approaches that work well on tape. The RISE producer also worked to help convert the faculty's PowerPoint slides to a format that worked well within the medium. (For example, some colors that work well on a computer monitor don't work well when converted to a television signal.) The cost of all that production was about $66,000 per course, each consisting of about 20 hours of video. (Some courses cost slightly more, some slightly less, depending on many variables such as licensing fees for incorporation of professional video segments in our tapes, and shifting the emphasis of a few courses away from video.) That cost does not include "talent"; that is, the cost of faculty/course development or faculty time during taping. For 27 courses, that average rate accrues a start-up cost of $1.8M for this one program! That was before accounting for marketing, distribution, instruction, royalties, and overhead.

## Program Costs: Marketing

Another section of this chapter describes our marketing strategies and efforts, but clearly a major cost of launching, growing, and sustaining the program has been its marketing, including labor, travel, design and printing of promotional materials, print advertising, purchase of mailing lists, postage, toll-free telephone lines, conference presentations and exhibitions, and overhead. We also found that effective marketing relied on far more human contact than we had anticipated. Indeed, direct mail appeals and advertising drew few quick enrollments. Instead, most prospective students required long phone conversations and follow-up. And retaining students once enrolled required an ongoing promotional effort to encourage the students, to remove bureaucratic barriers, to remind them of logistical requirements, and to help them adjust to an alien set of expectations.

Some marketing efforts required minimal expenditures. We entered co-marketing agreements with other organizations in the field of early childhood education, provided they were not directly competing with us. In such arrangements our partners agreed to insert our promotional materials in their mailings and publications. We also used the opportunities of conferences and conventions to present information on the program. While the travel costs associated with such presentations were accounted for as marketing, in many cases our faculty or staff would have been attending even if the distance program did not exist.

Our initial business plan, composed in September 1999, estimated that we would spend about $158,000 per year for the program's first five years. By March 2000, when we offered the first course, our revised business plan reduced the annual marketing budget to about $87,000. Actual expenditures have approximated that later budget plan. Presumably, our lower-than-projected marketing costs have also resulted in lower-than-projected enrollments, but frankly, the logistical issues that required a year to resolve would have been very unforgiving of enrollments at the projected levels. We recognized that as we launched the program's first academic term and resisted the temptation to market what we could not have successfully delivered on a more ambitious scale.

## Program Costs: Distribution

Because our business plan anticipated rapid early growth of enrollments, because we anticipated that most of our student base would consist of Head Start teachers, because hundreds of Head Start centers already have digital satellite receivers in order to receive programming from the National Head Start Association's HeadsUp! Network, and because we wished to avoid undertaking labor-intensive handling and shipping of videotapes, we based distribution on a digital broadcast model in which distribution costs are fixed and unaffected by enrollment fluctuations or rapid growth. We chose EchoStar's Dish Network because it already carried HeadsUp! Network. Students who already had access to satellite reception would pay nothing to receive the broadcast since it would appear on a channel in the "free and clear." This approach received some debate internally since we knew that the programming could be captured and recorded by anyone, including competing colleges, despite the clear copyright notifications. We decided, however, that most of the value of the programming lay in the credit that we would attach to it by enrolling students.

In Fall 1999, we projected a cost of $750 per hour of broadcast time plus $75 per hour for backhaul (transmission of the signal from Cincinnati to the center where EchoStar feeds the signal up to the satellite for broadcast across North America). With about 20 hours of broadcast time per course, each course per term would cost us $16,500. Under such a model, we obviously would have to enroll large numbers of students to cover our costs. By the time we actually began broadcasting in March 2000, EchoStar's rate had dropped to $500 per hour for broadcast with the same backhaul charges. (These educational rates are much lower than commercial rates.) Later in the year, though, the rate jumped to $1,000 per hour. With early enrollments not measuring up to projections, we began seeking alternatives, and found a state-subsidized educational broadcaster that was interested in carrying our content, also used the same satellite, and initially would broadcast for us at only $85 per hour, including backhaul. They also simultaneously streamed the video through their Website, although we know of few of our students whose Internet connections permit acceptable-quality streaming video. After several months, however, they increased rates, and we are now paying $350 per hour.

These volatile rates were a function of broadcast demand, the number of hours we needed to uplink to the EchoStar satellite, and the shopping we did for the best rate. Initially, we paid a substantial per hour charge because we had few hours to broadcast and as the "new kids on the block" were not in a position to negotiate a better rate. As our broadcasted hours per week climbed, we were able to shop around and search for a better alternative. Our search led us to a state-subsidized educational broadcaster that allowed us to broadcast at an introductory charge of only $85 per hour. This remarkable savings from the previously incurred $1000 per hour allowed us to further diversify our offerings. Because we are not located in the state that subsidized the educational channel, the broadcasters eventually raised their rates to the current $350 per hour charge.

Over the last two years, enrollments have risen to levels that may make satellite broadcasting financially sustainable. However, our experience now shows that in the interest of high-quality student services, we have distributed increasing numbers of course videos by mailing tapes directly to students. We had never intended to do so, but several circumstances made that necessary. When we shifted to the lower-cost broadcast provider, the regularity of broadcasting suffered. Broadcasts sometimes started late or were pre-empted without notice, and though the provider willingly rebroadcast the missed courses, students relying on programmed VCRs often weren't aware of a problem until the rebroadcast had occurred. We felt an obligation in such cases to send videotapes to students. The cost of VHS tape duplication varies greatly among vendors, but we currently pay $3.25 per one-hour tape.

Recently, we began moving from VHS tapes to CD-ROMs. Our surveys of students found that virtually all had CD-ROM or DVD drives in their computers. The conversion from VHS to CD-ROM costs us $30 per one-hour tape, and each duplicated CD-ROM costs us from $1.50 to $1.75, depending on quantity ordered. More significantly, the storage, handling, mailing, and durability of CD-ROMs is much better than VHS tapes. During the current transition, we intend to offer students the option of leasing either the videotapes or buying the CD-ROMs. Leased tapes would be handled and shipped by the university bookstore along with the course textbooks, which students order online. Eventually, we intend to eliminate both the satellite broadcasts and VHS tapes and use CD-ROMs and streaming video exclusively.

## Program Costs: Instruction

Our instructional model—two-thirds video and one-third Internet inter-action—incurred heavy production costs, as described above, but the instructional costs associated with that model were quite reasonable. We divided the instructional elements into three parts:

1. course development,
2. videotaping, and
3. online instruction.

Paraphrased from the memorandum of understanding that we had with the faculty, the duties consisted of:

### Course Development

Those activities necessary to ready the course for video and audio recording and for placement on the ECLC Website. It consisted of the preparation of lectures, notes, PowerPoint slides, bibliographies of reading materials, exercises, assignments, quizzes, examinations, and other ancillary materials. Course development also included collaboration and coordination with administrators of the program and with the video production company.

### Course Videotaping

Rendering of the video portion of the course on videotape or other fixed audio-visual medium, as well as the performance of all activities necessary for that process. Course videotaping included conversion of notes, lectures, PowerPoint slides, and other information in formats suitable for recording and broadcast of the course materials; the review of profession-ally published or recorded materials for possible inclusion in the course; and the performance of lectures and discussions for recording by the video production company. Course videotaping also included those activities necessary to ensure that the video content of the course was rendered in an aesthetically professional manner; such activities included the timely provision of materials to the production company, a timely presence in the recording studio, wearing of make-up as applied by the production company, and the wearing of appropriate attire.

### Course Support and Assessment

Those activities necessary to promote, support, and assess learning by students enrolled in the course, contemporaneous with the offering of the course. Such activities included coordination of interactive course compo-nents with the contemporaneous course broadcasts; online group and one-to-one, synchronous and asynchronous discussion of lectures and readings; explanation of concepts and materials presented in the course broadcasts; guidance of students in their preparation for quizzes, exams, and assignments; administering and grading of quizzes, exams, and assignments; direction of students to other academic and programmatic resources; calculation and assignment of final course grades; and coordination of the course logistics with UC.

Course development and course videotaping were conceived as one-time events (for the life of a course) that could be broadcast repeatedly for several years. Course support and assessment—or "online instruction" as we more commonly call it—occurred during every 10-week term that the course would be offered. We initially paid a lower rate for each section of "course support and assessment" because we conceived of the video content as the "center" of each course. However, in this model of instruction we have been unable to convince the faculty charged with "course support and assessment" that the video content—not their work with students online—is the "center" of the course. They treat the video as ancillary material because they are so acculturated to the traditional model of individual student engagement. The result was the faculty's devoting more time and energy to online instruction than intended, leading to complaints about the compensation associated with those efforts, and ultimately to an increase in the compensation rate. Ultimately, while a departure from the design model, the attention and intensity of instruction given to individual students undoubtedly yield better student learning, retention, and success.

### Course Redevelopment

Another activity that we envisioned is "course redevelopment." That is the review, reassessment, and other activities necessary to bring an existing course's content and appearance up-to-date. Such redevelopment could apply to the video, interactive material, or both portions of the course, and could include videotaping new material as well as development of quizzes, exams, PowerPoint slides, assignments, readings, and other ancillary materials. Redevelopment ordinarily would not replace all parts of the original course; if the entire course is to be replaced, such duty should be considered "course development."

We originally expected each course to be "redeveloped" after three years of use. Although we are not yet three years beyond the first course's development, we anticipate that the cycle will likely be longer for general-education courses than for the specialty courses in early childhood education.

The compensation faculty received for these instructional elements consists of the following, exclusive of fringe benefits (which add 30% to the labor costs):

| Course development | $2,300 |
|---|---|
| Course videotaping | $2,300 |
| Course support and assessment | $1,500 |
| Course redevelopment | $1,500 |

The original business plan had envisioned that the latter two activities would be compensated at a rate of about $1,150 instead of $1,500.

We also plan to compensate on-site mentors who assist groups of students with local computer problems, lead group discussions, and serve as "cooperating teachers" during the students' student teaching. However, in this case, the compensation will take the form of a one-credit scholarship used for a mentoring course required for cooperating teachers.

## Program Costs: Royalties

Elsewhere in this chapter we discuss details of the intellectual property issues associated with the program. [Editor's note: See Chapter 13, "Yours, Theirs, Mine: Just Who Owns Those Distance Courses?"] Important to resolving those issues was the creation of royalties for long-term use of videotaped course content. We wished to compensate those faculty whose work continued to generate revenues for the university through student tuition even though those faculty had already been paid for development and production of the video content. We believed not only in the fairness of such an arrangement, but also predicted that the guarantee of royalties would provide an incentive to faculty to create high-quality courses whose content was more enduring. A poorly conceived and produced course would be more likely to be redeveloped or entirely replaced sooner rather than later.

We also wanted the developers to be satisfied with their compensation and not to feel exploited by the university's ownership and continuing use of the materials. Like many professions and trades historically "threatened" by new technologies, faculty often see the recording and mass distribution of their work as an attempt to reduce dependence on them or even to eliminate them—despite plentiful evidence that the provision of textbooks, CD-ROMs, PowerPoint files, transparencies, and other faculty-produced materials has displaced no faculty jobs.

On the other hand, we did not want to establish a royalty structure that constituted a "commission on enrollments" (tying royalty amounts to the number of students enrolled) since the instructional variable most closely linked to that number would be the "course support and assessment"—the online instruction that included communicating with and assessing the performance of individual students. Producing and broadcasting the video content bore no relationship to the numbers of students enrolled—at least, not beyond the assumption that we were dealing with a mass audience.

The terms of our agreements with course developers now provide for a royalty payment of $500 for each academic term in which a course developed by that faculty member is offered, regardless of the number of students enrolled or the number of sections offered. The royalty will continue indefinitely, even if the recipient leaves the university's employment. Faculty have found these terms satisfactory, and other distance programs on campus are considering adoption of the model for their own programs.

## Program Costs: Overhead

Anyone who has developed project or program budgets for an organization that includes more than a handful of people understands the powerful effect of overhead on costs. Someone must pay for the general overhead: space, furnishings, equipment, software, utilities, supplies, printing, housekeeping, grounds-keeping, security, maintenance, communications, postage, and parking. Someone must also pay the administrative overhead: directors, marketers, clerical workers, technicians, advisors, registrars, bookkeepers, and billing/collection agents. Even heavy reliance on telecommuters working in their homes does not escape overhead. On every human being employed in the enterprise there is labor overhead: medical and dental coverage, disability and life insurance, social security, pension and 401k/403b contributions, vacation, and sick leave.

General and administrative overhead may add 50% or more to the direct costs of the program. In our case, some overhead items—such as the services of the registrar, admissions and financial-aid offices, and IT help-desk—did not separately burden the program because those offices and services already existed and the additional burden of this program was small in the context of a university with 33,000 students. Overhead items directly attributable to the creation of the program and not previously existing have become program costs: mostly labor and some equipment, software, supplies, printing, communications, and postage. In the current fiscal year we expect such overhead to amount to only about 28% of total program expenditures.

Labor overhead may add 25% or more of direct labor costs to program costs. In our case we must pay 30% of direct labor costs into a university benefits pool. In the case of administrative staff those costs will vary only as salaries and staff growth occurs. In the case of faculty, the costs are directly connected to enrollments, program growth, and the frequency of course rotations among the academic terms. All of the forms of faculty compensation described above—including royalty payments—incur the required

30% contribution to the benefits pool. So, when we pay $2,300 to a course developer, we must pay an additional $690 to the university's benefits pool. Each $500 royalty payment actually costs the program $650.

## Program Revenues: Tuition

### *Enrollments*
Our business plan for the program rather successfully anticipated the much higher costs of targeting a population that required all the additional program features described above. The difficulty, though, was in projecting market demand. We were far less successful in that pursuit.

The earliest estimates of student demand for the program made several assumptions:

- Our target market would consist of Head Start teachers, about 110,000 people nationwide.
- A small percentage of Head Start teachers already possess a college degree.
- In order to preserve their job security, a large percentage of Head Start teachers nationwide would seek an associate's degree by 2003 (the federal mandate's deadline for 50% of each grantee's teaching staff to have the degree).
- A majority of those seeking an associate degree would do so in the field of early childhood education.
- A majority of those seeking such a degree would not have ready access to an accredited early childhood degree program.
- Professional development funds provided by Head Start would pay a significant portion of the tuition for coursework.
- Marketing to this population would require some direct-mail and conference contacts but would rely primarily on telephone contact, a more personal and reassuring method of getting reticent people to accept the dual risks of college and of distance media.

Several of these assumptions have proven valid, but some had flaws, of which the most significant was the assumption that a majority of Head Start teachers would feel compelled to seek a degree. That tenure-track faculty endure a six- or seven-year probationary period in order to earn virtual lifetime job security may have skewed our assumptions about the importance of and compulsion toward job security. Head Start teachers by contrast, often have long histories of job changes, mostly at low wages with few or no benefits and no job security. And at the time the program was launching in 1999, the American economy was at the climax of the longest expansion in its history. Some economists were describing a new economy in which, like a rocket escaping earth's gravity, we had finally slipped the surly bonds of the business cycle. Pizza shops were offering $500 signing bonuses to hire delivery people. The shortage of certified teachers nationwide had encouraged some states to wrest exclusive control of certification away from higher education and vest local boards of education with that power. That was not an environment in which we should have assumed that a Head Start teacher would invest the years, energy, money, time-away-from-family, and anxiety necessary to secure a job paying $7.50 an hour.

For many people on the low-tech side of the digital divide, long-range aspirations have little opportunity to displace the fulfillment of immediate needs. Learning new technologies, investing in education that offers only distant rewards, or doing other things that many of us value and recognize as being in our self-interests can be complicated by the lack of awareness of the value of technology skills.

Of course, two years have changed our economic climate, and our recent surges in enrollments may be partly attributable to that change. From Winter to Spring terms of the current academic year, our enrollment increased almost 60%. We think that this growth also reflects the momentum of the program, the exponential effects of word-of-mouth marketing, and some shifts in our marketing strategy.

The federal mandate, we can see in retrospect, was aimed more at Head Start grantees than at Head Start teachers. That is, by threatening grantees with the loss of their grants, Congress has given grantees a powerful incentive to find locally effective means of moving their teachers toward higher education. Our marketing to Head Start centers has intensified, and most of our students have come to us through the encouragement of center directors.

### Setting Tuition Rates

In the distance-learning marketplace, tuitions vary widely and an institution's distance rates may not match tuition rates for the same on-campus courses. A survey of community colleges in all 50 states found that "there is no difference between the tuition rate charged for distance education and the rate charged for on-campus courses for in-state students" in 31 states. The remaining 19 states reported a difference or a policy of leaving those decisions to local institutions. In many states, tuition and fees for distance students exceed those for on-campus students (Education Commission of the States, 2000).

In establishing this new distance program, we considered several factors in setting the tuition rate. No doubt the most compelling was our need to cover operating costs and recover our start-up costs—preferably over a period of five or six years, though we now believe we won't achieve that recovery rate. Early in our explorations of the distance marketplace we discussed collaboration with one corporate/community-college partnership that was directly competing with our program. However, we found their academic standards and pedagogical approach entirely incompatible with our own. And while their tuition was also about 85% less than our own, giving us some fear of their ability to undercut us in the marketplace, we also failed to see how their program could survive, and indeed, we understand it will soon fold. Many enterprises that require heavy start-up costs benefit from collaborations that share the initial capitalization, and that has been the ostensible purpose of organizations such as the American Distance Education Consortium. Collaborations also help reduce price competition if they result in greater uniformity of pricing, a practice that would be described as "price-fixing" if we were private, for-profit entities. From a marketing perspective, though, such collaboration makes little sense. It breaks down brand differentiation and blurs the institution's position in the marketplace, making it just another timid participant in a timid venture.

In setting tuition, we also wanted to approximate on-campus rates, thereby affirming the sense that our educational services and credentials had some definable value, apart from what the market and our costs dictated.

Finally, in setting tuition, we wished to approximate what we thought the market would bear. Without geographic boundaries, however, bureaucratically-determined tuition policies make little sense as resident/non-resident and the public/private distinctions blur and sometimes become irrelevant. Instead, the free market determines the quick and the dead. This shift has brought an array of market issues new to higher education. Institutions must assess their position, not only in relation to traditional rivals (often long defined by geography or category), but in relation to an entirely new set of rivals and within a market of students who may or may not resemble an institution's on-campus population. How will this new market value:

- the brand of the institution?
- its credits' portability?
- its degrees' credibility?
- the convenience of its services?
- the credentials of its faculty?
- its pricing?
- its academic support systems?
- the effectiveness of its instruction?

In short, the proliferation of choices in this marketplace is forcing institutions to compete on terms that may not be in play within their usual geography and categories.

For both Ohio and out-of-state residents, our tuition rate for the period from Spring 1999 through Spring 2002 remained constant at $132 per credit hour (on the quarter system), reflecting our sensitivity to the disappointing demand in the program's first year. When we set the rate, it exceeded the $123 on-campus rate. Today it is lower than the on-campus rate of $138 which includes prorated general, campus-life, and technology fees. For students who receive professional development funds from Head Start or from their private employers, the price is a bargain. With enrollments climbing rapidly—and with this and virtually every other public American university and state government struggling with budget deficits—we have decided to raise tuition for Fall 2002 to match the on-campus rate of $152 per credit hour, an increase of 15% for the program. Informal surveys suggest that current students will not abandon the program over such a sudden increase; indeed, many of them have told us that our rates compare quite well with other providers. However, the effect of the higher rate on prospective new students may never be absolutely discernable.

## Program Revenues: State Subsidy

Ohio has fallen in relation to other states' support for higher education, now 38th in spending per $1,000 of personal income of the state's population, and 35th (Hart, 2002) or 41st (Kirwin, 2001) in per capita spending (depending on sources), while achieving the distinction of ranking first among all states in growth of spending on prison construction (Reynolds, 2001). (During the last two decades of the 20th century, Ohio's spending on prisons grew by 491% while spending on higher education grew 80%.) So, while the state has not yet decided whether to pay enrollment-based state subsidies on students enrolled in distance programs (it currently pays only for Ohio residents enrolled in state-supported colleges), the issue may be virtually irrelevant for all but the largest programs. State subsidy was not even considered in development of our business plan.

## Program Revenues: Student Fees

An institution with little experience in off-site education may forget that students who never come to campus will likely object to fees that support computer labs, student activities, and construction of other facilities such as recreation centers and student unions. Many universities levy special fees to support services or facilities of special interest to students, separating those costs from tuition, thereby often gaining student support, guaranteeing that the funds will be used only for designated purposes, and complicating comparisons of the cost of attending different institutions. Charging distance students for on-campus services and facilities may help pay the bills, but it may make the program uncompetitive and may engender ill will among students. "Universities that have considered the issue have come up with a variety of responses. Some have erased traditional fees for online students, only to begin charging them technology fees that cost as much or more. Other institutions waive some fees for online students, but keep others" (Carnevale, 2001). UC sensibly permitted us to offer our program's distance students a flat per-credit tuition rate with no additional fees attached. While we therefore receive none of those revenues for the program, we are also more competitive with other distance programs nationwide—an especially important factor in recruiting a student population that is more than typically price sensitive.

## Program Revenues: Grant Funds

Because the program fulfills several public policy goals, we have succeeded in winning grant funds from governments and foundations for aspects of the program, from infusing the curriculum with an emphasis on literacy to providing online tutoring to course development. To date, we have received about $250,000 in grant funds.

## Summary of Financial Feasibility

In Spring 2002, enrollments were only about 10% of what we had projected in the earliest drafts of our business plan—though later revisions cut those projections to more realistic levels. The disparity between projected and actual enrollments yielded a similar disparity in program revenues, but only somewhat lower program costs. Because so much of the development cost occurred in the production of video, cost savings related to enrollments are occurring only in course support and assessment and in administrative support services.

With enrollment at about 400, the program's current revenues exceed current operating costs (exclusive of the costs of producing the final three courses in the program), but not amortized start-up costs. Assuming that enrollments continue to grow and assuming that we can defer course redevelopment a little longer than originally planned, that margin will grow, enabling us to offset the heavy start-up costs (see Figure 2). Clearly, the size and financial resources of this large university enabled us to undertake this project without needing immediate "profitability." This program's heavy reliance on video technology, therefore, would probably not be a workable model for smaller institutions or companies—but let us emphasize that we

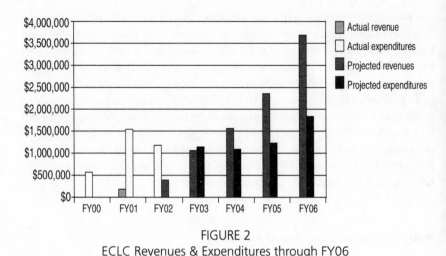

FIGURE 2
ECLC Revenues & Expenditures through FY06

remain convinced that the program's marketing and learning objectives would be entirely unreachable without that reliance on video.

## BUILDING PARTNERSHIPS

Facilitating the development and provision of student services and appropriate technology typically requires building and cultivating partnerships—especially when serving people who require extensive support systems and who enjoy few resources. Having identified student needs and gaps in the institution's ability to fulfill those needs, the program may well need to seek partners who can fill those gaps.

Perhaps the most obvious prospective partners are those organizations that have a vested interest in seeing the particular target population of students enroll and succeed. An employer that hopes to upgrade its employees' education and is willing to fund some or all of the cost of that education has an incentive to partner. In our case, Head Start center directors and Head Start grantees often go to extraordinary lengths to facilitate our access and service to their employees.

Similarly, advocacy groups for students within the target market often see partnering with higher education as advancing their own objectives. One of our best partners in ECLC has been the National Head Start Association. Another has been the Head Start Bureau, the federal agency that awards Head Start grants nationwide and that is charged with promoting compliance with Congress's mandate for Head Start teachers.

Professional organizations within the target market make good partnership candidates (Post & Lubeck, 2000; Becker, 1999). In some cases, they
can lend their infrastructure and systems in assessing student needs, marketing to and serving students, and helping to extend the program's reach
within the market. Our faculty were already active in their field's professional societies, and that helped us forge relationships that promoted our
visibility in the field.

Private businesses are likely partners (Lynn, 2001; Roach, 2001). Typically less bureaucratic than universities, corporations can often shift their
priorities more quickly, hire (as well as lay off) personnel with less notice,
and adjust their policies to respond to immediate imperatives. Private partners can fill logistical and service needs without necessarily diluting the
brand or market position of the institution. For example, to launch our
marketing efforts quickly, our video production partner (a non-profit educational corporation) was able to lend us a well-qualified former teacher to
contact Head Start centers by telephone. The same company was also
instrumental in helping us find competitive satellite broadcast vendors,
and in helping us network with organizations active in our target market.

Other colleges and universities often fail to surface as potential partners
because they are usually seen as competitors, not as collaborators. (Partnering with natural competitors can present problems, as touched on
below in the discussion of marketing.) Recent funding efforts by FIPSE
and others have emphasized partnering among institutions, forcing many
universities to broaden their definition of a "partner." If the institutions
have complementary rather than competitive programs, and if shared
finances can be worked out, collaborating with other colleges makes more
efficient use of resources, extends each institution's catalog of offerings
and student services, helps reduce each college's individual risk, and provides more robust capitalization.

An institution as decentralized as ours also offers opportunities for productive partnerships. Certainly, our relationships with on-campus units
such as the bookstore have evolved into partnerships. Because the bookstore is an auxiliary operation that receives no subsidy from the university,
accommodating our program's and students' needs is just good business.

## MARKETING

### If You Build It, They May Not Come

Probably the most overlooked aspect of distance education is reaching
the target population, or marketing. Institutions of higher education have
only recently begun to market themselves in the way the private corpora-

tions have been promoting their products and services. It could be argued that many universities are still not reaching their populations with their mission and message.

Several faculty members recently confessed to us that they know nothing about marketing; however, when asked who was responsible for student recruitment, they acknowledged that they play a role in ensuring that classroom seats are full. That willingness to see a faculty role in marketing is not common in our experience. Some faculty assume that if they provide high-quality instruction, students will show up to enroll. Some faculty and academic administrators believe that their institution's admissions offices hold all responsibility for recruiting students. Any small program in a large university understands the folly of that attitude. Admissions offices are often consumed with student recruitment to the institution at large, and can do very little to address the needs of specific populations or niche markets. They often focus on a certain geographical region where alumni are concentrated. Or, they center their efforts where their statistics indicate a greater number of potential students in proportion to the recruiting investment. Marketing of the small program, especially one delivered via distance education, may never surface in the marketing priorities of the university. In other words, the distance education program will likely have to market itself and recruit its own students.

## Targeting, the Key to Good Marketing

Targeting a specific market within a larger population takes more focus and a more certain understanding of the target market. This section describes the multi-faceted approach needed to effectively market an educational program. Reaching the target market takes repetition, an obvious presence in a variety of venues, and allocated funds to support these efforts. An example from an academic publishing house may help readers to understand the comprehensive and cohesive efforts needed.

### Direct Mail

The publisher identifies target faculty by purchasing mailing lists from list vendors who do nothing but compile and sell such lists. Or the publisher may have identified the faculty through previous buying habits and professional affiliations. Next, the publisher sends advertisements by mail. The mailing tries to grab the target audience's attention through any of several strategies. The mailing typically lists the features and benefits of the offered products, hoping to appeal to the reader's self-interest. Finally, it identifies how the reader may receive more information or place an order.

### Advertising

The publisher places a display ad in a journal. The ad may graphically resemble the direct-mail piece, promoting recall of the company and its product. Just as important as the ad, though, is its placement. Spending heavily to place the ad in a mass-circulation magazine like *Time* magazine would be a poor investment because it would reach far more people outside the product's target market than those inside it.

### Professional Conferences

The publisher may display in an exhibition booth at an academic conference devoted to the relevant discipline. The publisher will staff the booth with personnel ready to answer questions and take orders. These personal interactions are important to the marketing process because they establish contact with a knowledgeable representative of that company in a setting that often provides more time and focus for discussion. The exhibition booth also provides the prospective buyer with an opportunity to page through the latest edition, and provides the publisher a face-to-face opportunity to address concerns and assess unmet needs.

Professional conferences may also provide an even better opportunity: If the publisher's authors are on the program, the credibility of the publications grows—even if the authors say absolutely nothing about their books during conference sessions devoted to academic matters.

### Follow-Up Contact

Exhibition booth prizes do more than attract people to the booth. The information gathered identifies prospects for follow-up contact, a visit or phone call from the publisher's regional representative to the faculty member's office.

### Cultivating the Converts

Just as retaining current students should be easier and cheaper than recruiting new students, so developing "repeat business" should be easier and cheaper than selling to new markets. In the publishing industry, that issue is more complicated than in many other businesses because the publishing brand and services generally mean far less to the target market than do the reputation and quality of the books' authors. Thus, publishers often focus on "value-added" elements, such as ancillary teaching materials that directly benefit the market. Responsiveness to faculty queries and rapid delivery of products also engenders good will. Most importantly, the publisher's anticipation of future needs gives the faculty member fewer reasons to shop around for alternatives.

Can a distance education program approach marketing with a similar strategy? Well, we have. And although our enrollments are less than anticipated, we attribute that more to flawed planning than to flawed marketing.

### ECLC's Marketing Program

As the model discussed earlier emphasized, successful marketing is built upon successfully assessing the needs of the target student population, the target market. Will new legislative or economic imperatives mandate changes in the skills and education required for their jobs? Are job categories being phased out, forcing people to acquire new skills? Is an industry moving to higher standards for entry credentials? What career ladders are available to these students? Does an industry provide professional development funding that would promote further education for students? What barriers impede the students' pursuing an on-campus program? How will new technology knowledge benefit their careers? Their personal lives?

Developing a marketing strategy also requires a thorough understanding of the organizations, unions, and professional groups that represent potential students; the trade journals in their job areas; the local, state, and regional and national meetings and conventions that attract them. If the budget allows, investigating sources of demographic information (such as government offices and radio and television stations) may provide helpful insights into patterns of the target market.

Like the textbook publisher, a distance education program will market through multiple media to ensure maximum visibility. Marketing materials will emphasize student benefits and distinctive characteristics of this program. Application or enrollment instructions will be convenient and accessible through technology that is appropriate to the targeted students.

If all of this research and information seems overwhelming, it is often because we are trained as educators; we are not marketing professionals with MBAs. Although the following description of the marketing of the ECLC program did not involve the use of a third-party business partner, many distance education programs are turning to third parties for their expertise and extensive reach to perform those marketing duties that faculty and academic administrators don't feel qualified or have time to do. These companies are generally successful, but often charge 30%-70% of the generated tuition as their fee. Many programs feel that is a small price relative to the cost of the institutional infrastructure that would be needed to generate a similar number of students.

ECLC's marketing efforts began in June 1999, even before we were fully committed to launching the program. The initial element was a 15-minute video profiling the first cohort of Head Start teachers to graduate from our on-campus program. This professionally produced video offered inspirational interviews (a number of viewers have described it as a "tear-jerker") with the graduates and their families, all focusing on the surprise of academic success at a stage in their lives when they had assumed they would never get a college degree. Later, we would re-edit the video for marketing purposes.

The marketing program continued modestly in Fall 1999 with the creation of a direct mail brochure announcing the creation of the program.

Relying on lists of Head Start centers in Ohio, we mailed the brochure, not to elicit applications, but to stimulate interest and inquiries.

By the beginning of 2000, we created a successor direct-mail package that included a new brochure and a marketing video. This second brochure was mailed beyond Ohio to all states where we knew legislators had funded the installation of satellite dishes at childcare providers or had passed stricter educational standards for Head Start teachers. That included about 2,200 centers in six states. When recipients of the second brochure called to inquire, we followed up by sending the marketing video, a seven-minute piece that relied heavily on recorded testimonials from people prominent in the Head Start community.

About the same time, we were developing, "Orientation to Distance Learning," a 35-minute video that served two purposes. In addition to conveying information about academic survival skills and basic use of the technologies, the video ended up marketing the program as it attempted to reassure the audience that they could indeed succeed in the program.

We observed other vendors at conferences and quickly ordered colorful table covers and give-always such as highlighters and key chains. We began a schedule of exhibiting at national and regional conferences to promote our program and awareness of distance education opportunities. Luring participants to our booth with door prizes and free pens, we continue to use this avenue to recruit new students. Increasingly, these exhibits have also facilitated meeting with current students.

From those conference exhibits we bring home names and phone numbers of prospective students and then follow up with calls in a week or two. The follow-up is important to reinforce the conference contact. After all, when just about anyone returns to work after a few days away, all the best intentions to pursue the new ideas gained at a conference tend to get crushed by the work that accumulated during the absence. Follow-up calls also help with people who have responded to our mailings by e-mail or by calling our toll-free phone number.

Although it is expensive, we have advertised in several national magazines that target childcare providers. This outlay has increased our national visibility and our credibility within the target market. Purchasing ad space in journals published by our partners has also strengthened our ties and demonstrated our respect for and value of their organizations.

Our direct-mail publications have brought good results. Brief, often humorous flyers seem to stimulate the best responses while long, informational letters or brochures overwhelm recipients and get ignored. Mailing lists can be purchased from companies that specialize in direct-response marketing, but professional organizations and state agencies often allow their non-profit partners to use their mailing lists if they perceive congruence of their interests with the program's interests. We have been fortunate that the National Head Start Association and the HeadsUp! Network have included our marketing materials in many of their regular member mailings.

Finally, a major element in our marketing program is our cultivation of our current students. Beyond our efforts to support their needs, we work at keeping our administrative office in touch with the students instead of simply handing them off to faculty. We track their "presence" in our courses and contact them if they disappear. We send them e-mail reminders about impending events such as registration for the next term. Collectively, these efforts both promote the program and student persistence and success in the program.

## TRAINING/EDUCATING

### A Custom Curriculum

In general, the program consists of 27 three-credit courses, including a practicum that requires supervision of student teaching, one of our current design challenges. Those courses include the general-education core: composition, English, math, psychology, sociology, and philosophy. While many distance programs choose to focus on major courses and assume that students will pick up general education requirements at local colleges, our understanding of this student population recognized that few of them would be able to do that and that most would likely fail to complete and receive the degree if we left general education to the students' own ingenuity. Not only did we doubt their access to such coursework, we doubted that they would be able to sustain their self-discipline and interest in pursuing such ostensibly irrelevant courses. By controlling the entire curriculum, we shaped a general education core that reflected student interests and that mirrored the content of the major content courses. For example, the literature course is devoted to reflections of childhood in American fiction and poetry, a subject of interest to early childhood educators. Faculty teaching other courses whose material could not be so narrowly focused used anecdotes and illustrations that would resonate with this particular student population.

### Exploiting the Video Medium

The choice of video did more than provide an accessible technology; it provided opportunities for exploiting the medium. In this regard, many of our faculty greatly exceeded our expectations. Recognizing that their on-camera efforts would be repeated term after term for at least three years, the faculty planned and orchestrated their on-camera time in ways they probably never would have for the traditional classroom. They developed demonstrations, invited guest experts, and prepared workbooks to help students follow the video. They thought through the pacing of on-camera presentations to ensure that their coverage of material went as intended. (We should note that keeping video production costs down required us to use direct-to-tape recording, meaning that each hour of video was done in a single take and no post-production editing could be assumed to be possible. Only gross mistakes were later edited out.) Initially, we advised faculty that they should think of their on-camera courses as an opportunity to give that special, once-in-a-term lecture that rises above others in its cogency, momentum, and chemistry with the students. They did just that.

A few, especially those who fare well with traditional lecture formats, used the medium to continue that pedagogy. We provided "studio students," that is, employees and students hired to play the parts of students on-camera, asking questions and responding to the lecturer's questions. But most faculty also recognized that the medium presented opportunities beyond the "special lecture." Indeed, they obviously devoted much thought to reconceiving the classroom experience. One pair of faculty ran their literature course like a TV talk show—with humor, banter between the two instructors, and guest appearances by other faculty. Another faculty member, struggling to transform a developmental writing class into a format that worked on video, chose to work with two students on camera, each taking turns writing and editing on a laptop whose video output could be fed directly onto the videotape. In most of these cases, the faculty began the process of designing their courses for video with strong doubts that the medium could work for them and their students. Without exception, they ended the experience as converts.

## Exploiting the Online Medium

Our use of Blackboard differed little from what goes on in hundreds of other online courses at scores of other institutions—with one exception. Because our students typically enter our curriculum with years between themselves and their last academic writing, and with weak writing skills, our faculty have found ways of using Blackboard to "ramp up" the students' academic writing. In the first few terms of the program, those faculty who quickly assigned a three- or four-page paper to be submitted early in a course were stunned at what they received. Many of the students had no sense of how to write a paper, of even how to write a grammatical sentence. (Other parts of this chapter discuss literacy issues in some detail, and the few student quotes in this chapter show that while our students have made progress, their writing continues to need work.) Soon, the faculty developed techniques of building literacy by requiring that students make multiple weekly entries on the course discussion board. As the students became accustomed to conducting their discussions online, their writing became more fluent, more confident. And as other students responded to discussion-board postings, the writers' feedback loop was closed, often alerting them when they had expressed themselves unclearly or differently than intended.

## Academic Outcomes

The effects of all our efforts to support the intertwined academic and technological needs of our distance students have surpassed our expectations. Over the last two years, student retention within a single term has risen from 50% to 83%, exceeding national averages for distance programs. More students are finishing the quarter with a grade of C or better and continuing to enroll the following quarter. About 20 students each quarter make the dean's list. Much of our early attrition, in fact, was attributable to problems with technology, including a home-grown and very buggy precursor to Blackboard. And some attrition was attributable to the lack of the support services described above. Periodic anonymous surveys of ECLC students show high satisfaction with the program—although we occasionally have students unhappy with grades or with the tone of a faculty member's e-mails and postings. Through the surveys, students identified these strengths:

- ability to tape classes for review,
- new technology knowledge,
- meeting and interacting with other students,
- helpful instructors and staff, and
- relevant courses.

These problems were also identified:

- billing process, registration blocks, and complications of centers' paying bill, and
- technology: computer goes down, network is down.

That they do not identify other sources of technology problems, such as inability to communicate with faculty or frustration at not knowing the technology, is significant—though, admittedly, the survey was conducted with the use of Blackboard and so requires some proficiency to participate.

In fact, the wish list expressed by survey respondents asked for nothing connected with technology, except access to more distance learning:
Other issues:

- Would like financial aid to be applied toward book purchases.
- Would like more scholarship opportunities.
- Social work degree is needed.
- More online tutors would be welcome.
- A published student directory would be interesting.
- Over 50% would like to pursue a bachelor's degree with licensure; they are willing to do the necessary placements.

## Behavioral Effects

Most importantly with regard to effects on closing the digital divide, our students reported they use computers more than is required for their course work. Before becoming actively involved in distance education, 66% of our students reported that they did not use e-mail at all, or only very sporadically. Now, 90% use a computer regularly for enjoyment, for additional classroom resources, and to help and mentor the parents of the children they serve. They also report that they are using the Internet to research and solve problems and issues encountered in their classrooms.

## Cultural Effects

As anticipated when Congress mandated more education for Head Start teachers, benefits to the teachers "trickle down" to the children they teach and care for. Seventy-six percent of ECLC students claim that they have a positive attitude toward computers and that they share that attitude with their own students. Toddlers and young children are learning that computers and the skills to use them are important life skills. As these children grown up, they will likely have the motivation and confidence to pursue access to technology, even if their economic circumstances impede their progress. And as they develop those skills, their economic circumstances are likely to improve, finally helping to close entirely the digital divide within their communities.

Despite being thrown into a college culture and a technology culture, these teachers have been resilient and dedicated. Their discussion boards are full of encouraging comments to one another, peers that they've never met face-to-face. "Veterans" of our distance program spontaneously mentor the "rookies" with advice on inexpensive Internet connections, technology support, and other insights. Whether across the country or across the city, ECLC students strive to promote their peers' success. It's not uncommon for our office to get a phone call in which we hear something like this: "Hi, this is Odessa, and I'm at Maxine's house, and we're trying to send an e-mail with an attachment. Can you help?" They share their houses, computers, experiences, and even their e-mail addresses (a practice we discourage).

One student summarizes her experiences with typical enthusiasm:

> I love this way of learning. Because I am a Family Childcare Provider the technology allows me to work at home as well as attend college. Last quarter was my first experience but, it certainly will not be my last. I don't intend to ever step foot on another college campus again. I have shouted the benefits of this program all over the state. Welcome to the new millennium!
> —[Devlyn, a pseudonym for a real student]

## AFFECTING POLICY

Throughout this chapter we have alluded to numerous policy shifts resulting from the newly discovered needs of the ECLC program. Some additional shifts deserve special attention, especially those related to institutional policy assumptions, academic administration, and intellectual property.

### Institutional Policy Assumptions

In describing support services, we have discussed the difficulty of adapting a large and often bureaucratic institution to a different set of assumptions regarding the needs and presence of students. The outcomes of that process, however, have been profound and extend beyond our program to other programs, both on campus and at a distance. One example should suffice: Above we described the problematic student health insurance fee. The fee of more than $200 could not benefit our students, but initially, unless they filled out and mailed in forms claiming that they had private health insurance, they were billed by default. As we worked with various university offices to solve the problem, the discussion widened as did the circle of people involved in the discussion. Eventually, the university abandoned its longstanding practice of using the fee to support the student clinic, deciding that students at a distance constituted only one population that was being unfairly targeted by the fee. The university's Board of Trustees approved the change in 2001.

## Academic Administration

The University of Cincinnati's academic organization resembles that of most American universities. In simplified form, the line of authority—excluding non-academic units—looks like the arrangement of units in Figure 3. In such an arrangement, administrators organize, deliver, and support the curriculum designed and taught by faculty, although aspects of the curriculum require approval of both a dean and higher levels of university administration. The organization reflects a division of labor in academic units that assumes greater efficiency and effectiveness when specialists' duties are constrained by their specialties. It also reflects the assumption that all students can pretty much be served by the same people.

By contrast, the organization shown in Figure 4 reflects a scheme in which a variety of offices and officers work to shape curricula and services specifically for distance students. As with almost any change in academic administration, establishing a special office for ECLC met some resistance. However, after two years of fine-tuning our operations, appropriate relationships have been established and as a result, students are receiving very effective service.

Our special office consists of an Administrative Director, an Academic Director, and two staff personnel dedicated to student support services. Duties of the Administrative Director include budget management, program planning, oversight of student services, marketing, and management of strategic alliances and partnerships. The Academic Director works directly with faculty and academic aspects of the program, including resolving student concerns with instruction, faculty development and training, recruiting and hiring instructors, and assuring the program's alignment with our on-campus program, state standards, and national standards.

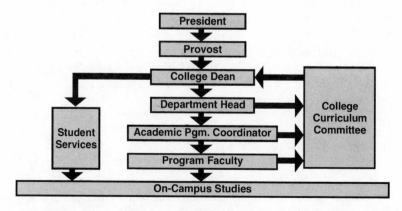

FIGURE 3
Traditional Academic Administration for On-Compus Programs

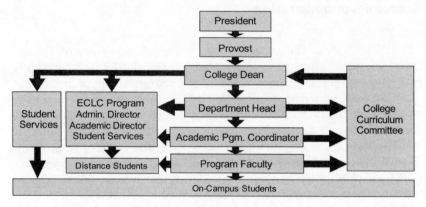

FIGURE 4
Academic Administration Reorganized to Support Distance Program

Our student support personnel not only interact regularly with new and continuing students, but they also interact with other university units such as financial aid and admissions offices. The entire group works as a team to implement a model of continuous program improvement. Staff and student suggestions are often incorporated into the services offered and are constantly evaluated to measure their effectiveness.

## CONCLUSION

Delivering any distance program is challenging, but delivering one across the digital divide has required ingenuity, adaptable technologies, resourceful and dedicated faculty and staff, supportive partners, a ready market, institutional commitment and flexibility, and significant capital. It has also required careful attention to all the elements of the model described in this chapter. Although only two years old, the Early Childhood Learning Community is succeeding because those various resources and approaches are coming together. Right now, it's a different approach to distance education, but we hope that others will soon follow.

## NOTES

1.   Students quoted in this chapter are enrolled in a developmental English course that is preparing them for freshman level English. Their quotations have been reprinted without corrections to original syntax or grammar. The authors believe this decision will allow readers to better understand the students' needs as

discussed in this chapter while getting a personal glimpse into how students are empowered.

## REFERENCES

Abramson, T. (2002). Improved communication through online discussion. Proceedings of 13th International Conference for Society for Information Technology & Teacher Education, March 18-23, 2002, Nashville, Tennessee.

Adkins, M. (2002). Assessing the readiness of distance learning students. Proceedings of 13th International Conference for Society for Information Technology & Teacher Education, March 18-23, 2002, Nashville, Tennessee.

Arnone, M. (2002). Historically black colleges grapple with online education. *The Chronicle of Higher Education*, April 5, 2002. Retrieved April 5, 2002, from www.chronicle.com/infotech.

Becker, J. (1999). Cyberspace regionalization project: Simultaneously bridging the digital and racial divide. Paper presented at the Secretary's Conference on Educational Technology, 1999: *Evaluating the Effectiveness of Technology*, Washington, DC.

Berge, Z. (1998). Barriers to online teaching in post-secondary institutions: Can policy changes fix it? *Online Journal of Distance Learning Administration*, 1 (2), Summer. Retrieved January 7, 2002, from http://www.westga.edu/~distance/Berge12.html.

Berge, Z., & Muilenburg, L. (2000). Barriers to distance education as perceived by managers and administrators: Results of a survey. In Melanie Clay (Ed.), *Distance Learning Administration Annual 2000*.

Berkshire, S. & Smith, G. (2000). Bridging the great divide: Connecting Alaska native learners and leaders via "high-touch—high tech" distance learning. *National Association of African American Studies and National Association of Hispanic & Latino Studies: 2000 Monograph Series*.

Bishop, A.P. (2000). Communities for the new century. *Journal of Adolescent & Adult Literacy, 43* (5), 472-78.

Carnevale, D. (2001). Should distance students pay for campus-based services? Chronicle of Higher Education, September 14, 2001. Retrieved March 19, 2002, from http://chronicle.com/free/v48/i03/03a03501.htm.

Care, W.D. (2000). Women in distance education: Overcoming barriers to learning. *New Horizons in Adult Education 14* (2) 4-12. Retrieved November 15, 2001 from http://www.nova.edu/~aed/horizons/vol14n2.html#WOMEN%20IN%20DISTANCE%20EDUCATION:%20OVERCOMING%20BARRIERS.

Carvin, A. (2000). More than just access: Fitting literacy and content into the digital divide equation. *Educause Review, 35* (6), 38-47.

Children's Partnership (2000). Online content for low-Income and underserved Americans: The digital divide's new frontier. http://www.childrenspartnership.org/pub/low_income/index.html.

Damarin, S.K. (2000). The 'digital divide' vs. digital differences: Principles for equitable use of technology in education. *Educational Technology, 40* (4), 17-22.

Demirbilek, M. & Cilesiz, S. (2002). A review of impediments to distance education. Proceedings of 13th International Conference for Society for Information Technology & Teacher Education, March 18-23, 2002, Nashville, Tennessee.

Eastin, M. & LaRose, R. (2000). Internet self-efficacy and the psychology of the digital divide. *Journal of Computer-Mediated Communication, 6* (1). Retrieved Nov. 15, 2001 http://www.asc.usc.org/jcmc/vol6/issue1/eatin.html.

Education Commission of the States (2000). *State funding for community colleges: A 50-State survey,* November 2000. Retrieved April 15, 2002, from http:// www.communitycollegepolicy.org/pdf/CC%20Finance%20Survey .pdf.

Foster, J.J. (2002). Why some African American youth's selves are driving the digital divide. Proceedings of 13th International Conference for Society for Information Technology & Teacher Education, March 18-23, 2002, Nashville, Tennessee.

Galusha, J.M. (1997). Barriers to learning in distance education. *Interpersonal Computing and Technology: An Electronic Journal for the 21st Century, 5* (3-4), 6-14. Retrieved Nov. 15, 2001, from http://jan.ucc.nau.edu/~ipct-j/1997/n4/ galusha.html.

Hart, B. (2002). Support slipping for state universities. *Arizona Republic,* February 17, 2002. Retrieved February 18, 2002, from www.azcentral.com/news/specials/universities/universities.html.

Hausman, R.M. & Hausman, K.K. (1999). Use of selected available technology to provide relatively inexpensive distance learning courses along the Texas/Mexico "Border Corridor." Paper presented at the American Council on Rural Special Education Conference, Albuquerque, NM.

Holstrom, L.A. & Bryan, J.G. (2002). Using distance education to narrow the digital divide. Paper presented at the Ohio Learning Network Conference, Columbus, OH.

Kirwin, B. (2001). Remarks to the Board of Trustees. Speech presented to the Ohio State University Board of Trustees, June 1, 2001. Retrieved from http://president.ohio-state.edu/speeches/trustees_6-1-01.html.

Knezek, G. & Christensen, R. (2002). Influence of home access on attitudes, skills, and level of use for teachers and students in technology integrating classrooms. Proceedings of 13th International Conference for Society for Information Technology & Teacher Education, March 18-23, 2002, Nashville, Tennessee.

Lee, C.C. (2000). Cybercounseling and empowerment: Bridging the digital divide. ERIC Clearinghouse on Counseling and Student Services. Retrieved Nov. 15, 2001, from http://www.ericcass.uncg.edu.

Litton, E.F. Bridging the digital divide: A school's success story. Proceedings of 13th International Conference for Society for Information Technology & Teacher Education, March 18-23, 2002, Nashville, Tennessee.

Lloyd, A. (2000). Pedagogy vs. competition in higher education distance learning. *Educational Technology and Society, 3* (2), 23-34.

Loftus, M. (2001). But what's it like? *US News and World Report,* Oct. 15, 2001, 56-57.

Lonergan, J.M. (2000). Internet access and content for urban schools and communities. Retrieved Nov. 15, 2001 from http://ericir.syr.edu/plWeb-cgi/obtain.pl.

Lynn, B. (2001). Getting into the education business. *American Way,* 11.01.01, 78-85.

Machtmes, K. & Asher, J.W. (2000). A meta-analysis of the effectiveness of tele-course in distance education. *The American Journal of Distance Education, 14* (1), ***

Menlove, R. & Lignugaris-Kraft, B. University and school district partners go the distance to "grow" special education teachers in rural communities. Proceedings of Growing Partnerships for Rural Special Education, San Diego, CA.

Neighborhood Networks (1999). Engaging education: Integrating work, technology, and learning for adults. Retrieved Dec. 2, 2001, from http://www.hud.gov/nnw/resourcesforcenters/nnwguide015.pdf

Perez, S. & Foshay, R. (2002). Adding up the distance: Can developmental studies work in a distance learning environment? *THE Journal, 29* (8), 16-24.

Post, J. & Lubeck, S. (2000). Head Start-university collaborations: Widening the circle. *Childhood Education, 76* (5), 277-82.

Prestera, G.E. & Moller, L.A. (2001). Organizational alignment supporting distance education in post-secondary institutions. *Online Journal of Distance Learning Administration, 4* (4). Retrieved January 7, 2002, from http://www.westga.edu/~distance/ojdla/winter44/prestera44.html.

Puma, M.J., Chaplin, D.D., & Pape, A.D. (2001) E-rate and the Digital Divide: A preliminary analysis from the integrated studies of education technology. Retrieved Nov. 15, 2001 from www.urban.org/education/erate.html.

Reynolds, R. & Beiser, V. (2001). Prison spending growing six times faster than higher education spending. *MotherJones.com.* Retrieved March 18, 2002, from www.motherjones.com/about_us/pressroom/prisons_release.html.

Roach, R. (2001). AOL Time Warner playing a part in bridging the technology gap. *Black Issues in Higher Education,* March 15.

Scalese, E.R. (2002). Distance education: Can the institute affect persistence? International Conference for Society for Information Technology & Teacher Education, March 18-23, 2002, Nashville, Tennessee.

Singleton, S. & Mast, L. (2000). How does the empty glass fill? A modern philosophy of the digital divide. *Educause Review, 35* (6), 29-36.

Thompson, M. (1998). Distance learners in higher education. In Chere Campbell Gibson, ed., *Distance Learners in Higher Education: Institutional Responses for Quality Outcomes.* Madison, WI: Atwood Publishing, 10-18.

Towell, E. & Neeley, L. (1999). Internet courses, mature learners: Two undervalued market segments. *New Horizons in Adult Education, 14* (2), 13-19 Retrieved November 15, 2001 from http://www.nova.edu/~aed/horizons/vol14n2.html#WOMEN%20IN%20                                     DIS-TANCE%20EDUCATION:%20OVERCOMING%20BARRIERS.

Treviranus, J. & Coombs, N. (2000). Bridging the digital divide in higher education. Paper presented at EDUCAUSE 2000, Nashville, TN.

US Census Bureau (2001). Home computers and Internet use in the United States: August 2000. Retrieved Oct. 17, 2001 from http://www.census.gov/prod/2001pubs/p23-207.pdf.

Vaughn, C. (2000). Reaching out: A starter kit for adult education distance learning programs. Retrieved Nov. 3, 2001, from http://www.vcu.edu/aelWeb/reaching.pdf.

Wallace, L. (1996). Changes in the demographics and motivations of distance education students. *Journal of Distance Education, XI* (1).

Whitworth, J.M. (1999). Reaching out to the teachers in Appalachia via distance education. Eric document ED443658.

Willis, B. (2002). The guiding assumptions of successful distance education programs. International Conference for Society for Information Technology & Teacher Education, March 18-23, 2002, Nashville, Tennessee.

## CHAPTER 6

# PREPARING FACULTY MEMBERS TO TEACH IN THE E-LEARNING ENVIRONMENT

**Barbara Fennema**

This chapter presents a pedagogical and epistemological endorsement for providing e-learning opportunities in higher education, support for the use of a Learning Management System (LMS), and the services that the LMS should provide to the user, the most essential being the training of the faculty members who are expected to use it. The chapter emphasizes the need for multi-faceted training of faculty members who are expected to create and/or teach courses using an LMS. This chapter concludes with deductions about the success of training faculty members from an epistemological standpoint, the success of using the specific LMS described herein, and suggestions for further research in this area.

**KEYWORDS:** faculty training, faculty development, e-learning, distance education, learning management system, LMS, courseware

## INTRODUCTION

The objectives of this chapter are:

- evaluate the need for an e-learning environment in higher education,

Electronic Learning Communities—Issues and Practices, pages 239–269.
Copyright © 2003 by Information Age Publishing, Inc.
All rights of reproduction in any form reserved.
ISBN: 1-931576-96-3 (pbk.), 1-931576-97-1 (hardcover)

- discuss the issues facing the institution and specifically, the faculty member who is expected to create an e-learning course,
- analyze one LMS platform,
- analyze the services of one LMS provider,
- determine the need to train faculty to create and teach in an e-learning environment,
- review of a case study about the success of training faculty members at one institution of higher education, and to
- present conclusions about the success of training faculty members for creating courses and teaching in an e-learning environment.

The author defines e-learning as the appropriate use of technology to create a rich, robust, interactive, communicative, relevant learning experience within either the traditional face-to-face classroom or the distance-learning classroom. Distance learning is seen as a subset of e-learning. The focus of this chapter is on the application of e-learning in the distance learning classroom, even though the author defines the term e-learning in a much broader sense.

## THE NEED

### The Information Age

According to the article by Roueche and Roueche (2001), *Pursuing the Best Thinking in the Information Age*, the period of time in which we are currently living can be identified as an "Information Age" because "the ability to process, store, and exchange information and knowledge now forms the core of ... production," and an "age" "because it permeates society, changing the way we live, (and) work."

Has technology assisted in bringing about the Information Age? We can answer a resounding "Yes!" But how? The computer has been a significant factor in advancing the Information Age. It stores and organizes information, providing us with speedy access to the information that has been stored. In addition, when the computer is connected to the Internet, all users have access to information stored on millions of computers worldwide. A second answer, closely tied to the first, is globalization. Business and education, as well as leisure (travel) and entertainment, connect all cultures of the world. The issue of globalization, while an essential ingredient in the definition of the Information Age, is far greater than the scope of this chapter and therefore the author will not explore it in depth.

How has the Information Age affected higher education and in turn faculty members? A plethora of resources are available to assist in answering this question. The author will begin by looking at how the business community began reorganizing due to the Information Age, and then how that reorganization affected higher education and faculty members.

A major transition in the corporation world took place during the 1980s (Frand, 2000). Companies not only had to access information, but also needed to be able to manage it (knowledge management), and to change how they were doing business. The concepts of knowledge management, mass customization, and new markets were difficult but essential elements in a paradigm shift for businesses to make if they were to be successful. Demarie (2000) states, "Technologies...are changing the way that organization members work and interact" (p. 419). He believes that the restructuring in business organizations is being driven, in part, by the "application and evolution of information and communication technologies" (p. 419).

Higher education is now facing a similar reorganization (Frand, 2000). The paradox higher education is now experiencing, according to Frand, concerns the application of technology in teaching. He states, "If teachers continue to teach in the same way that they have always taught, there will be little value added from classroom and campus networks" (p.7). He continues by addressing changes also needed by students. He insists that those of us in education must "think in terms of transforming the educational experience so that it is meaningful to the information-age learner" (p.7). Lewis, Alexander, and Farris (1997) assert, "technology-based ... education is emerging as an increasingly important component of higher education" (p. 1). In 1999 Boettcher and Conrad (1999) wrote:

> The technology of education is the body of materials and methods used to extend or enhance the ability to learn, collect data, solve problems, and promote communication between and among faculty and students. (p. 7)

Higher education will be shaped by the technological abilities developed in the future (Connick, 1997), just as the economic forces in society shape the educational system. Duderstadt (1999) tells us that the first decade of this new millennium will "represent a period of significant transformation for colleges and universities as we respond to the challenges of serving a changing world" (p. 1). Because colleges and universities are knowledge-driven organizations, they are affected greatly by the changes that have taken place. These institutions have been designed to provide information, education, and the training that is necessary for future leaders in our world. Duderstadt points out that "most significant here is the way in which emerging information technology has removed the constraints of space and time." (p. 5)

Frequently it is observed that when institutions of higher education integrate technology into the classroom, they immediately step into distance education. However, e-learning is not equivalent to distance learning. Distance learning is a subset of e-learning. When technology helps to create a rich learning environment, distance learning is a viable solution to reach learners who would not otherwise be served by the educational institution. E-learning includes the appropriate use of technology within the face-to-face classroom as well as the use of technology to deliver an online course. Wiegel (2000) supports this concept as he discusses the difference between richness and reach: "Richness refers to the overall quality of information (for example, currency, accuracy, interactivity, relevance), and reach refers to the number of people involved in the exchange of information" (p. 12). The Information Age has provided the ability to create a rich, robust e-learning environment both in the traditional face-to-face classroom and in the distance-learning classroom as well as the ability to reach the previously underserved learner.

## Changing Demographics and Life-Long Learning

How does the Information Age affect those of us involved with higher education? Reflecting on what the literature is telling us, the educational system of the Information Age will be required to provide an educational environment that is rich, robust, interactive, communicative, and relevant, and also provide the learner with:

- Lifelong learning—the need and the desire to continue to learn throughout life in order to be a valuable asset to the community and culture in which s/he lives.
- Interactive and collaborative learning—requires the learner to become actively involved in the learning process and to collaborate with others.
- Asynchronous learning—learning that is without time and space boundaries, available whenever and wherever the learner needs it to be.

### Life-long Learning

Learning is considered to be a dynamic activity in which a person participates in order to advance his/her knowledge and information. The process of learning, therefore, can easily take a person a lifetime to complete. However, rapid changes in the needs of industry and business today require learners to acquire new skills and knowledge in order to remain an integral part of society. Due to the Information Age and globalization, the concept of life-long learning is now an essential element in higher education.

Institutions that provide educational experiences are increasingly faced with a growing number of students who have previously entered the workforce and are now in need of additional or totally new knowledge and skills. And the demands of these learners are (as stated above) that learning be asynchronous and interactive. Duderstadt (1999) refers to these societal changes, stating:

> We are beginning to see a shift in demand from the current style of "just-in-case" education, in which we expect students to complete degree programs at the undergraduate or professional level long before they actually need the knowledge, to "just-in-time" education, ... to "just-for-you" education, in which educational programs are carefully tailored to meet the specific lifelong learning requirements of particular students (p. 4).

Moore and Kearsley (1996) confirm that "most distance learning students are adults between the ages of 25 and 50" (p. 153). Understanding how adults learn (andragogy) is an essential ingredient in effective instruction in a distance format for higher education. To address the needs of adults, educators need to know who their students are and how they learn in order to plan an effective educational course (Merriam & Bracket, 1997).

A debate continues over whether a difference exists between pedagogy and andragogy, yet the author feels strongly that an understanding of the principles of both pedagogy and andragogy is intrinsic to effective distance education. Pedagogy is defined as "the art or science of teaching" (Boettcher, 1998, p. 2), and includes the collection of instructional methods used by the teacher. Andragogy has been defined as the study of how adults learn (Noren, 1997), and focuses on the student rather than the teacher (Wilson, 1997). Malcom Knowles has written extensively in this area, expanding and modifying his ideas over the years. In 1989, he described his assumptions about andragogy:

1. Let learners know why something is important to learn:
   * creating courses or training that applies to the learner's life situation is essential.
2. Showing learners how to direct themselves through information:
   * creating a template for learners, or an advance organizer, provides adult learners with a navigation system that permits them to immerse themselves into the information, yet prevents them from feeling overwhelmed.
3. Relating the topic to the learners' experiences:
   * asking questions, requesting that learners share their life situations, creating assignments that can be applied to their situation encourages and motivates them.
4. People will not learn until they are ready and motivated to learn:
   * creating a learning environment that is accessible and available when the learner is ready is an essential element.

5. creating a learning environment that is characterized by the four items above enables the adult learner to overcome inhibitions about education and learning.

Selecting and using learning strategies based on an understanding of pedagogy and andragogy provide guidance for the distance-learning instructor. By moving away from a focus on the teacher and centering the process on the learner, the designer of a distance course integrates the philosophies of Knowles, Dewey, Vygotsky, and others (Boettcher, 1998; Bourne, McMaster, Rieger, & Campbell, 1997). Strategies that are successful with adult learners enable them to be more responsible for their own learning, assist them in achieving a goal, and help them immediately to apply their learning to their life situations. Examples of appropriate strategies are:

a.   the use of advance organizers in the course syllabus,
b.   omitting inclusive information about a topic,
c.   the use of the reflection process,
d.   inclusion of case studies or other real-world applications for learning,
e.   encouragement to share life experiences that apply to the instruction, and
f.   career-applied assignments.

The demographics of learners in higher education are changing, resulting in the need for institutions of higher education to address a changed audience in a new era, the Information Age.

### Interactive and Collaborative Learning

Learners who actively engage in the learning process are more likely to meet stated objectives and have greater satisfaction with school (learning) experiences. Designing a course that requires students to become involved in the learning process and to collaborate with one another and/or the instructor is not an easy task. Heinich, Molenda, Russell, and Smaldino (2002) provide an instructional model, ASSURE, which is an excellent model for designing instruction. This model requires the educator to:

1. Analyze the learner
2. State Objectives
3. Select Methods, Media and Materials
4. Utilize Media and Materials
5. Require Learner Participation
6. Evaluate and Revise

Using a model like ASSURE allows the designer to carefully plan the learning environment to ensure that interaction and collaboration take place, enabling the learner to participate fully in his/her own learning.

In a study completed by Petrides (2002), one of her conclusions was that her graduate level course, created with an LMS, was viewed by students as "more learning-centered than teaching-centered, that it increased engagement with others" (p. 75). The conclusion also states that it "helped to create conditions for learning so that students learned on their own and in collaborative settings" (p. 75).

In addition, access to asynchronous learning opportunities through mechanisms such as LMS is essential for learners to be able to continually adjust and adapt to societal changes. The technology available to educators today enables them to remove the barriers of time and space from the learning environment. Paloff and Pratt (2001) maintain that the asynchronous learning community "allows students the luxury of time for thought and reflection on material, which we believe enhances the learning process" (p. 25). These discussions can easily take place in the discussion board area of the LMS. By guiding the discussion with thought-provoking questions, the instructor is able to create a learning community that will provide the same, if not better communication of ideas and thoughts among the learners.

## E-learning and Distance Education

Moore and Kearsey (1996) state:

The fundamental concept of distance education is simple enough: Students and teachers are separated by distance and sometimes by time. This contrasts with the ancient tutorial, in which a teacher and an individual learner met at the same time and place...and the more familiar contemporary model of instruction in a classroom, where a teacher talks to a group of learners, all together at the same time in the same place (p. 1).

Distance education has been used by most societies for years to be able to distribute educational materials to learners in remote areas not served by educational institutions. Distance education has included (but has not been limited to):

- Printed material sent through surface mail.
- Audiotapes sent through surface mail.
- Radio and television programs.
- Videotapes sent through surface mail.

All of these formats are asynchronous. So, why would the Information Age cause learners to require something different from distance education?

The literature suggests that one impetus for developing distance education using Information Age technology is the increasing demand from learners that the boundaries of time and place be removed (Duderstadt, 1999; Edwards, 1997; Murphy, 1996; Porter, 1997). As the technologies develop, students will be able to choose programs of study and institutions without leaving home, thus shifting the control to the student and away from the universities (Connick, 1997). Murphy states that society expects educational opportunities to be delivered to them without the need to attend class on a campus. These include students who are working full- or part-time, have family commitments, desire a convenient location, and/or may live at a distance from an institution that provides the instruction they want (Porter, 1997).

At this point let us return to two characteristics of the Information Age—the computer with an Internet connection, and globalization. As a result of the changes in our society, we are now faced with a major paradigm shift with the need for, and in the delivery of, educational experiences. The technology is available that permits the educator to create an e-learning environment that can be rich, robust, interactive, communicative, and relevant, as well as to reach the learner who would otherwise not be served by the educational institution because of distance, time, or life situations that prevent the learner from participating in a traditional face-to-face educational experience.

Because of the Information Age, members of our society are required to be life-long learners. These learners are numerous and located everywhere in the world. Many of these learners want to have their educational experience in an asynchronous format. But because they are members of the Information Age, they also want it to be interactive and collaborative. This changes the appearance of distance learning from the formats in which it was previously delivered. Learners own or have access to computers that are connected to the Internet and provide them with information from around the world. They are no longer satisfied with an educational experience that is passive and isolated. Instead, they want to interact with other learners, with the content, with information sources, with leaders in the field. They also want immediate (or pretty close to it!) feedback from all of these interactions. A computer connected to the Internet provides a platform for the delivery of distance education that can meet the needs and demands of these learners. Designers of effective distance courses delivered through the Internet must consider the interactivity of the medium and employ it to enhance the instruction of the distance learner (Hazari, 1998; Hirumi & Bemudez, 1996; Starr, 1997a). The online classroom must use technology appropriately in order to make it rich, robust, interactive, communicative and relevant. Conducting an effective distance course requires using higher-level instruction such as critical thinking or problem solving, employing communication and collaboration among students, and providing timely feedback from instructors (Starr, 1997b). Appropriate design of a distance course delivered through suitable media and using befitting strategies enhances learning. This is the type of educational experience that the learner in the Information Age is seeking.

## THE ISSUES

When faculty members who have been teaching in a traditional face-to-face format move into the arena of distance education, it is fundamental to prepare them for the new paradigm, strategies, technologies, and skills required. The paradigm that traditional higher education faculty members have about teaching and learning is based on a behaviorist model that maintains that the instructor is in control of what the student learns and how the student learns that information. As discussed previously in this chapter, learners in the Information Age require a learning environment that will provide them with life-long learning opportunities, and interactive and collaborative learning environments that are delivered in an asynchronous manner. This model demands that the learning environment be based on a cognitive-constructivist foundation. Leading faculty members into this teaching format will require professional development opportunities.

Omoregie (1997) holds that a successful distance education program requires faculty development. A host of authors support this tenet (Benas & Emory, 1998; Edmonds, 1999; Eisenberg, 1998; Grant, 1996; Hitch & Hirsch, 2001; Omoregie, 1997; Pitt & Stuckman, 1997; Steinert, 2000) and stress that the environment of distance education can only be optimized when the faculty members have been provided with faculty development. There are many advocates for faculty development programs (Benavides & Benavides, 1993; Bender, 1997; Cravener, 1998; Knapczyk, 1993; Robbins, 1997; Truman & Sorg, 1998) who acknowledge the importance of preparing faculty members for their new role in the distance education environment. The belief that faculty development is an essential ingredient in successful distance education courses is strongly advocated by Robbins (1997): "When [faculty] are given time and support necessary to develop distance learning courses properly, [they] will create an instructional program that is innovative, comprehensive, and rigorous" (p. 1).

Faculty members must realize how distance education delivered on the Internet is a systemic change for higher education. This systemic change includes the vision, the mission statement, and the organizational policies of a university. By understanding how a university views the roles of teaching and learning and how faculty members will fit into this new paradigm of education, teaching will become more effective. Often a faculty development program will include the new technology skills needed and, perhaps, an acknowledgement of the cognitive theories for learning, but rarely do such programs involve the entire structure of the university. Building a professional community with an understanding that the faculty member is part of a collaborative team is an essential component (Grant, 1996).

Banas and Emory (1998) maintain that distance teaching is "radically different" (p. 372) and requires that faculty change their understanding of how the teaching and learning process takes place. Facing this change in paradigm, faculty members may easily be overwhelmed or feel threatened. A comprehensive support system must be in place to assist faculty members during the transition from a traditional classroom to distance learning (Banas & Emory, 1998). Because faculty members may no longer feel in control of the course (Banas & Emory, 1998; Ewing, Dowling, & Coutts, 1999), focusing on how this new role is significant to successfully fulfill this initiative will motivate them to participate. Often, faculty members focus on the challenges that arise during the development and teaching of distance education courses. Eisenberg (1998) states that this attitude is shortsighted and that faculty development must encourage faculty members to look beyond the format and see the opportunities for the student. Encouraging faculty members to look at how the student benefits from an effective course delivered in a distance format will assist them during this transition period. Seeing their new role in education as one of facilitating new learners and creating a professional community both within and beyond the university, as well as understanding how they fit within the new structure, are basic components of faculty development.

In higher education, faculty members are concerned with the quality and integrity of a distance education program (Daugherty & Funke, 1998). Strategies and skills used in traditional teaching are insufficient when designing courses that are to be delivered in a distance format, and faculty are unsure about what strategies should be included in distance courses. Selecting new strategies based on the way students learn and not just on the technologies that are most convenient (Pitt & Stuckman, 1997) is fundamental for effective distance education. Grant (1996) emphasizes that new resources and content must be included in a distance course. Anderson and Kanuka (1997) acknowledge the importance of modeling collaboration during faculty development so that the participants will perceive it as a useful strategy in distance education and, consequently, employ the strategy in their courses. Truman and Sorg (1997) assert that instructors who successfully teach in a distance format must be familiar with a number of new concepts. These include: "[the] philosophy of distance learning, dealing with copyright, adapting teaching strategies, designing interactive courseware, identifying learner characteristics, organizing instructional resources for independent study, using telecommunications systems, collaborative planning and decision making, and evaluating student achievement and perceptions" (p. 342).

Faculty members then, must become comfortable with new technology skills (Morgan, 1991; Morton & Mojkowski, 1991). Creating a learning environment that encourages the learner to participate fully requires knowledge of technology skills and how to use them to support the learning process. Grant (1996) maintains that even after learning new technology skills, these will not be effectively used unless the faculty development program encourages their use and explains when and why to use them. With so many new factors involved, a professional entering the arena of distance education can be quickly overwhelmed; therefore, continued support following faculty development is crucial.

Creating faculty development for e-learning requires a unique design. Faculty must be immersed in the technology. This immersion does not just include how to use the computer or an LMS platform, but how to communicate effectively at a distance. The faculty member must be aware of the feelings that a distance learner has when a problem arises or communication is vague. Faculty development must include instruction about appropriate strategies for a Web-based distance learning course. Steinert (2000) states that: "Faculty development programs will need to broaden their focus, consider diverse training methods and formats, conduct more rigorous program evaluations, and foster new partnerships and collaborations" (p. 44).

In typical distance education correspondence-style courses, student retention is known to be poor. In order to improve student retention and reduce attrition rates, Web-based courses must be developed using appropriate design techniques that enhance student involvement in the learning process as well as in the learning community. In an article published by the 1998 Teaching in the Community College Online Conference, the following statement solidifies the importance of preparing faculty to teach in the online environment: "Online classroom design and software tools do have an impact on student performance and satisfaction, but in the end, it is faculty vision and creativity that matter most and that will ultimately determine whether students want to take an online course from one institution as opposed to another" (Ko & Rossen, 1998, ¶ 23). Hitch & Hirsch (2001) insist that student retention is the primary goal of all education, and therefore they focus on this when developing faculty training. They include in their faculty training of online teaching the following five factors:

- modeling the expected outcomes and delivery of the course through the training, totally online and asynchronously;
- exposing the instructor to the multiple ways to develop a facilitation style in a virtual environment;
- enabling the technology to become ubiquitous to solidify the facilitation and delivery;
- preparing access to articles and other materials evoking and reinforcing pedagogical discussion; and
- establishing an ongoing network of just-in-time ideas and updates on both teaching and changes to the technology.

The article written by Hitch and Hirsch concludes with an interesting reflection about these factors: "There is one more factor that stands out. That is the connection between exemplary online teaching and exemplary teaching in general and the need to develop individuals who can thrive in a knowledge-centered world" (p. 20). Keeping in mind that we, as educators, are teaching students who must compete in the Information Age, we must develop courses that will meet the instructional needs of these students. Therefore, faculty members must be able to communicate with these students in an educational environment in which they learn best. To do so, faculty members who have previously taught in a traditional face-to-face environment must be immersed in a faculty development program that will enable them to acquire the skills and strategies needed in this new learning community.

Providing faculty development opportunities, then, is essential to the success of e-learning. Based on the plethora of research that has been done and is currently under way, faculty members moving from the traditional face-to-face format of teaching in higher education must be given access to professional development as well as to continued support from the institution. Following these suggestions, the institution of higher education will be able to provide the type of education today's learners expect.

## AN ANALYSIS

Deciding on an LMS platform for an educational institution is a complex and often convoluted experience. Several online tools have made the process easier by providing a database of information about various LMS platforms.

### Deciding on a Platform

While employed at the Connected Learning Network in Louisville, KY, the author was responsible for the evaluation of the company's LMS platform and how it compared to other platforms. Determining the functions and features that were essential to create a rich, robust, interactive, communicative, relevant learning experience was done by performing a thorough literature review as well as exploring the LMS platforms that are available. During the platform review it became evident that there were functions and features that were consistently available in many of the LMSs, even if they were presented in a variety of formats. For example, every LMS available at that time included the ability to present course content to the student. All platforms also provided an asynchronous discussion forum (discussion board, bulletin board, discussion forum, etc.). Nearly all provided a synchronous chat area as well, enabling the instructor to employ real-time strategies throughout the course. It immediately became evident that most instructors desired a common list of features in an LMS.

A table that would include a listing of features and functions that were desirable in an LMS was developed after reviewing the literature, exploring other LMSs, and evaluating Websites devoted to comparing and contrasting LMSs. A team led by Bruce Landon of Douglas College has produced a highly respected site on the World Wide Web (WWW) available from http://www.c2t2.ca/landonline/ March 26, 2002. This site permits the user to compare and contrast LMS platforms that are included in the database created by this team. SiteTrainer (n.d.) (http://www.sitetrainer.com/platformcomparison.htm available March 26, 2002) also provides an online comparison of LMS platforms. Then, in collaboration with Connected Learning's Information Systems Manager, Robb Allen (robballen@connectedlearning.net), a recommendation to develop the Connected Learning Network on the foundational platform of the IntraLearn LMS was made. The software was adopted in the Fall of 1999, and the Connected Learning Network has been using, modifying, and building their business on this platform ever since.

Once a decision was made about the software, the Connected Learning Network needed to determine the services that would be provided in conjunction with the LMS. Based on experience in the field of distance education as well as a review of the literature, the author concluded that institutions of higher education that were entering the field of e-learning through a Web-based distance format, were looking for more direction than what was offered from a typical LMS provider. Appendix A lists not only the features of the software, but also the services provided by the Connected Learning Network for their clients. In the company profile the following statement describes the goals of the company: "Connected Learning.Network, Inc. (CL.N) (www.connectedlearning.net) is an industry leader in Web-based distance learning that offers a world-class Web platform (IntraLearn) and highly customized e-learning portal design. We are an education-based company empowering the e-learning community" (retrieved from http://128.121.207.177/ie/aboutus/profile.html, March 26, 2002).

When deciding on an LMS for an institution's e-learning courses, the features and functions listed in Appendix A were the items that this author reviewed.

### *From the Student's Viewpoint*

As discussed previously in this chapter, the learner in the Information Age has specific needs that must be addressed by the educational institution:

- Interactive and collaborative learning—requires the learner to become actively involved in the learning process and to collaborate with others.

- Asynchronous learning—learning that is without time and space boundaries, available whenever and wherever the learner needs it.

The LMS must provide a suitable environment for interactive and collaborative learning as well as be able to offer the course asynchronously. The items listed in the *Student* section of Appendix A state that this LMS does provide the technology necessary to meet these needs. The following list describes in more detail, items in the Appendix:

- It is *student-oriented*, i.e. a) the student is able to work in a linear or non-linear fashion; b) personal note-taking is encouraged and saved; c) interactive elements can easily be placed into the content of the course to provide a rich, robust learning environment; d) discussion boards and chat areas are integrated to encourage a communicative learning environment; and e) FAQ, Link List, Glossary, and Search functions are available and integrated to provide access to relevant content.
- Building on the functions of the LMS, Connected Learning Network provides a *24/7 manned help desk* (with e-mail access, an 800 number, and/or a live chat) for all students enrolled in any course provided by any client.
- If the course developer (usually the instructor of the course) chooses to have this learning environment be rich and robust, the LMS supports the inclusion of *multimedia* such as Flash, animations, Power-Point presentations, Java applets, Java scripts, executable files, and audio and video clips.
- For a robust learning environment, there is a *search* function that will search through the content that has been placed in the course content areas, glossary, discussion boards, and FAQ files. Since the LMS is built on a SQL database, the search function scans the database for any instances of a word or phrase for which the learner is searching, and then provides a list of hotlinks to that word or phrase.
- The *glossary* can be integrated into the content of the course if the course developer so chooses.
- There is an *e-mail function* that permits the student to send e-mail to classmates and/or the instructor, as well as to read e-mail while in the course. This feature is an interface only, using the students' own e-mail address and server. This allows the student access to his/her e-mail without the inconvenience of having to remember a new e-mail address/username/password.
- The *threaded discussion* area can be organized either by date, author, or thread. There is a threaded discussion area for each lesson in the course.

- There is a *chat* area available for each lesson within the course. If the course developer wishes to use the *whiteboard* function, it can be enabled.
- The student can access his/her grades for any course in which he/she is enrolled. All objective exams are automatically graded and the grades are instantaneously placed in the *Gradebook* area. Subjective (essay) type questions can also be included but must be graded by the instructor.

### From the Instructor's Viewpoint

When deciding on an LMS the instructor wants, most of all, an LMS that will provide an appropriate learning environment for the learner. Secondly, the instructor wants to be able to create a learning environment that is appropriate for his/her audience. Thirdly, the instructor wants and needs to be supported. The LMS described in Appendix A meets the needs of the instructor in the following ways:

- The Connected Learning Network provides *support* through professional development and/or training to the course developer/instructor. This training includes instruction about the software—its features and functions—but, more importantly, it includes information on instructional design for a Web-based, distance learning environment. Each institution is assigned a project director who remains in communication following the training. This project director provides additional support and instructional design guidance throughout the development of the course. The instructor also has access to the 24/7 technical help desk through e-mail, an 800 number, or live chat.
- The instructor must be able to *communicate* with the students enrolled in the course. The communication functions provide the ability to use e-mail, threaded discussion, chat or whiteboard.
- Instructors must be concerned with *security*. This LMS meets that need by encrypting content, exams and the *Gradebook* during delivery. The student must have a username and password to enter the course. Each username is unique. The data are regularly backed up and stored securely.
- Evaluation is supported within the LMS through online exams. The exams can be used as a self-assessment (no grade) or as a graded assessment tool. All objective exams are automatically scored, but essay questions remain the responsibility of the instructor. At all times the instructor manages the *Gradebook* feature.

### From the Administrator's Viewpoint

Overseeing the entire distance learning program is, of course, the administrator of the institution. The administrator has unique access to the LMS:

- A portal is assigned to each institution. The portal can be crafted so that it is *uniquely* the home of the institution.
- *Student tracking* is available through the report feature available to the administrator at each institution.
- The administrator can access the portal and retrieve records *through the WWW.*
- *Security and data backup* are essential concerns of the administrator.
- The administrator has the ability to *review the content.*

### From the Technical Viewpoint

Often the IT department of an institution does not readily accept the decision to deliver courses on the Internet. Since the IT group is responsible for servers, networks, etc., it is understandable that they do not wish to add new issues to the mix. The LMS reviewed above does not reside on the campus server, but on the server provided by Connected Learning Network—thus relieving the campus IT department of the responsibility of maintaining another server. Connected Learning Network and IntraLearn provide technical support for the LMS. While a campus network will need to meet the minimum requirements for easy use by instructors and/or course developers, most institutions already meet or exceed these minimum requirements. Concerns of the IT department are often relieved when they see the following standards built in to this LMS:

- AICC certified—the IntraLearn WWW site states: "The AICC standard allows Computer-Managed Instruction applications to launch interactive lessons that will pass performance data back and forth. This standard is based on the HTTP protocol, thereby, enabling student interaction through a standard Web browser. IntraLearn's support of this standard includes the ability to import AICC certified content, present the content and track the learner's usage data" (IntraLearn, 2002).
- SCORM compatible—SCORM (Shareable Courseware Object Reference Model) is an initiative of the Department of Defense and is "aimed at improving online education by enabling the reuse of teaching materials" (Bethoney, 2000). SCORM provides the e-learning community with guidelines that permit instructional components to be reused. An interesting article by Connelly about LMS platforms and the e-learning community was published in *InfoWorld* on October

15, 2001. In this article Connolly carefully explains SCORM and AICC and what they mean to the e-learning community.

- Level 1 IMS compliant—the IntraLearn Website explains: "As a member of the Developers Network, which consists of developers from academic, government and commercial organizations, IntraLearn is committed to continually supporting IMS specifications. Current support exists for the Meta Data and Content Packaging Specifications" (IntraLearn, 2002).
- LRN compatible—IntraLearn's Website states: "Learning Resource iNterchange is the first commercial application by Microsoft of the industry initiative known as the IMS Content Packaging Specification version 1.0" (IntraLearn, 2002).
- Built on a SQL Server database—the IntraLearn Website provides this information about the database: "(IntraLearn) has been designed to leverage the scalability of Microsoft SQL Server" (IntraLearn, 2002).

## Scalability and Reliability

Webopedia, available at http://www.pcwebopaedia.com/ on September 1, 2002, defines scalability as:

...a popular buzzword that refers to how well a hardware or software system can adapt to increased demands. For example, a scalable network system would be one that can start with just a few nodes but can easily expand to thousands of nodes. Scalability can be a very important feature because it means that you can invest in a system with confidence you won't outgrow it (retrieved from http://www.pcwebopaedia.com/TERM/s/scalable.html, September 1, 2002).

In a glossary provided by Learning Circuits, (http://www.learningcircuits.org/ September 1, 2002), scalability is defined as: "The degree to which a computer application or component can be expanded in size, volume, or number of users served and continue to function properly" (http://www.learningcircuits.org/glossary.html#S/ September 1, 2002). Scalability is essential in an LMS so that it will continue to serve an institution of higher education not only today, but also in the future.

When a college or university makes the decision to provide courses on the Internet, and has the philosophy to provide these courses to students anytime and anywhere, it must be prepared to increase its audience many-fold. The IntraLearn LMS is built on a powerful relational database management system and has been "designed to leverage the scalability of Microsoft SQL Server 7.0" (IntraLearn LSP, 2002). There is no limit to the number of courses, instructors, students, or connections to a course when using the IntraLearn platform.

The IntraLearn LMS has been successful for the Connected Learning Network. Statistics kept by the Information Systems Manager indicate that "the server has been up approximately 99.7% of the time" (Robb Allen, personal communication, April 2, 2002). Knowing that the server of the LMS is reliable is indispensable information for the institution that will be providing an instructional environment to students around the world.

## TRAINING FACULTY

This author, as the Project Director for Connected Learning Network, created the training workshop for faculty members of client institutions. Components of the workshop were created based on a review of the literature about professional development, training, andragogical principles, and learning theory. The workshop was created in response to a discrepancy between the potential of the software for e-learning and the courses being created by many faculty members using the software. Even though the software was robust and encouraged an interactive learning experience, many faculty members were creating text-based courses. Also, this author perceived that many of the faculty members of most of the client institutions of Connected Learning Network were unaware of appropriate strategies for an e-learning environment.

In this section we will examine a case study regarding the training of faculty members for an institution of higher education. This institution selected the Connected Learning Network as the provider of services, and the LMS platform for its e-learning courses offered at a distance.

The institution was founded in 1965 as a computer programming school in a mid-sized city in the Midwestern region of the United States. It currently has multiple locations throughout the United States and Canada. The institution awards "bachelor of science degrees and/or associate of science degrees in such areas as network technology, electronics, programming and business administration" (2002, History of the College). The college focuses on providing work-oriented courses and programs, assisting students in job placement in their respective fields.

In early 2001, the Connected Learning Network was selected by the college to assist in its expansion of offerings of online courses. Prior to this decision, the college had selected a different LMS that was not scalable and did not offer the features and functions of the IntraLearn platform. Reasons for selecting Connected Learning Network included scalability, reliability, security, functionality, instructional design assistance, training of faculty, and the 24/7 help desk.

## Designing the Training

When developing training for faculty members in higher education, issues beyond the technical skills needed to use the LMS must be addressed. Faculty members have already been recognized as leaders in their field, and are often reluctant to move into areas unfamiliar to them. Anxiety and resistance to change are both critical concerns to contend with when developing training for this audience. Based on the literature, low attendance and infrequent implementation of the skills taught are common results of such professional development workshops. Descriptions of the resistance of faculty members to training about technology skills is a pervasive concern in the literature (Cravener, 1998; Dillon & Walsh, 1992; Padgett & Conceao-Runlee, 2000; Siegel, 1995). Frequently, these training sessions deal with only technical skills, resulting in little interest by faculty members who seek to extend their knowledge-base about their discipline. In order to create a faculty-training workshop that would both engage the faculty and enhance their application of the new knowledge to the creation of online courses, the author designed the faculty training to go beyond the introduction of technical skills by including andragogical concepts that would involve the faculty members as learners. Taking this into consideration, the faculty training needed to address the issues of motivation on the part of the faculty members, content of the training, format of the workshop, and assessment (Padgett & Conceao-Runlee, 2000).

### *Motivation*

In addressing faculty members' resistance to professional development in areas beyond their comfort zone, four principles described by Knowles (1989) were considered during the development of the training. The first andragogical principle of Knowles was to inform the learners why the content of this workshop was important for them. It needed to be connected to their life situations (i.e., the fact that they were going to be developing an online course, and then teaching it). To facilitate this, an e-mail was sent to participants approximately two weeks prior to the training, informing them of what would take place, where, when and why. The second principle was to show learners how to navigate through the information being presented. To accomplish this, a document was sent to each participant to be used as an advance organizer. The document included pertinent information about accessing the online course created for this workshop, their username and password, and information about e-learning. The third andragogical principle considered during the development of the workshop was to relate the topic to the learner's experiences. This was achieved through interactive activities at the beginning of the workshop (described below) using Legos and Tinker Toys. Applying the fourth principle, that adults will not learn until they are ready and motivated to learn, required the creation of a learning environment that was accessible and available when the learner was ready. Consequently the entire workshop was duplicated in an online environment so that the participants could access it anytime and anywhere. By considering each of these principles, a learning environment was created that enabled the faculty members to overcome their inhibitions about learning technical skills.

### Content

Taking into consideration the volume of literature about what faculty members should know prior to creating an online course, the author decided that this training needed to include the following:

- technical skills that will be needed to use the LMS,
- strategies for teaching online,
- attributes of the online learner, and
- philosophy of e-learning.

### Format

The first faculty training session for this institution was scheduled as a two-day face-to-face seminar in May 2001 in a large metropolitan city in the southern region of the United States. This location was easily reachable for faculty members from the campuses throughout the United States. The workshop was followed up with online instruction. The online instruction lasted for about three months, providing reinforcement as well as practice using the LMS as a distance student. In addition, each participant received a training manual in print form. The manual included all the PowerPoint presentation printouts, handouts, discussion questions, and suggestions for building an online course.

## Face-to-face Workshop

The training session included introducing the faculty members to the software as students enrolled in a course entitled, *Training Workshop*. This course was created by the Project Director to assist the faculty members throughout the training session. It was this course that the faculty members used during the months following workshop. The course enabled them to interact with the content, the instructor (the Project Director), one another, and then apply the newly learned information to their own teaching situations. The content included text, graphics, animations, charts, PowerPoint presentations, video, and audio. Assignments were created and placed in the assignment area, requesting that the faculty members interact using the chat, the discussion board, and e-mail. Teams were created so that collaboration could take place. Exams and self-assessment tools were incorporated. Links to appropriate sources on the Internet were included. A glossary of frequently used terms in e-learning was developed. The outline of the course can be found in Appendix B.

### Technical Skills Needed

The training session included several hours of instruction on how to use the LMS platform, and the skills needed to access course content and to create a course (Appendix B-Lesson 3: Focus on the Technology and Lesson 4: Focus on Your Course). Demonstrations included using the e-mail interface, the discussion board, the chat area and the whiteboard. Faculty members were asked to discuss such issues as bandwidth and downloading files. Following demonstrations and discussions, the faculty members were instructed to simulate the online classroom by completing the assignments included in the sample lesson in Lesson 2 in which they were required to open files, download files, send files through e-mail, and participate in discussions and chats.

### Strategies for Teaching Online

Lesson 1 included information about Web-connected learning based on the research done by the author/instructor. The PowerPoint presentation included content about the learning phases (based on Bernice McCarthy's 4MAT system) and the integration of e-learning using these principles. Following the presentation, the faculty members became immersed in a new learning experience using Legos and Tinker Toys. This led to discussion about how students learn and how that knowledge of learning can be implemented in an e-learning environment.

### Attributes of the online learner

Lesson 1 continued with a discussion about the attributes of the online learner. The Project Director presented information about why Web-connected teaching/learning is important to students in the Information Age. These attributes have been discussed previously in this chapter in the section entitled, *Changing Demographics and On-Line Learning*.

### Philosophy of e-learning

Based on learning theory, pedagogical and andragogical principles, a philosophy of e-learning was developed. With input from the faculty members, several administrators who also attended the training, and the Project Director, the group created a philosophy of e-learning that emphasized the importance of a rich, robust, interactive, communicative, and relevant learning experience. Basic tenets of instructional design were also included in the presentation by the Project Director.

## Online Course

Following the face-to-face workshop, all participants had access to the online course for approximately three months. The purpose of this online follow-up was to enhance communication, reinforce learning that had taken place during the face-to-face training, and to provide the faculty members with a place to collaborate.

### Communication

The Project Director encouraged faculty members to use the communication tools within the online course to communicate with the members of the training workshop. Many of the participants communicated with the Project Director, but very few communicated with other participants through the venue of the course. The author does not have any data that would suggest that personal e-mails were being exchanged among participants, but this is a possibility.

### Reinforce Learning

Since all of the PowerPoint presentations, discussion questions, handouts, and questionnaires were made available to the participants, several took advantage of this opportunity to review the content of the training session.

### Collaboration

The author feels that there was little or no collaboration following the workshop within the venue of the course. This is based on the number of times the participants used the chat and/or discussion board. It is unknown if the participants collaborated outside of the course.

### Assessment

In order to determine the success of the training, the author used as an assessment tool a Likert scale-based questionnaire (Appendix C). At the close of the workshop, each faculty member was asked to complete the survey. Responses were positive, indicating that the face-to-face and print components were appropriate and beneficial. The survey did not ask participants to evaluate the online segment since it was ongoing. The survey was made available to the participants in the online course *Training Workshop,* but there were no surveys from the online course returned to the author.

### Other

The Project Director also made available to every participant a print version of most of the information shared in the training session and in the online course. Based on anecdotal information following the training workshop, it is believed that the print content was exceptionally beneficial to the participants as reinforcement to the learning that took place during the faculty-training workshop.

## CONCLUSIONS

Based on the information gleaned from the evaluation forms, personal communication, and anecdotal incidents following the faculty training, a combination of face-to-face, online and print resources provide the best solution for training faculty. The literature has and continues to support the need to train faculty members and to support them during the process of developing courses for e-learning as well as teaching these courses once they have been developed (Benas & Emory, 1998; Edmonds, 1999; Eisenberg, 1998; Grant, 1996; Hitch & Hirsch, 2001; Omoregie, 1997; Pitt & Stuckman, 1997; Steinert, 2000).

The instructors who participated in the training workshop provided by the Connected Learning Network created courses that were interactive, communicative, and included relevant learning experiences. When informally compared to courses created by those who did not participate, the courses created by the training participants demonstrated more of the attributes expected by successful online learners. Another variable noticed by the author several months after the workshop was that those who did not participate in the training had a higher level of frustration as well as more frequent phone calls to the 24/7 technical help desk. During the 8-month period in which data were collected, there were 52 calls made by the instructors included in this dataset to the help desk. The untrained instructors called the help desk 33 times or 63%, and the trained instructors called 19 times, or 37% (Shelpman, personal communication, April 10, 2002). It is suggested that this issue be explored in more depth at a future time.

Faculty training is a critical element in the development of rich, robust, interactive, communicative, and relevant e-learning courses. Faculty members have a need to be immersed in the technology needed for effective online instruction as well as the pedagogical and andragogical principles on which it must be designed. An LMS that provides the functions and features that support a rich, robust, interactive, communicative, relevant, e-learning course should be selected to assist those who are developing online instruction. The instruction delivered during such training must include the modeling of and instruction in effective teaching strategies (Kember et al., 1992; McClintock, 1992; Truman, 1995; Willis, 1993). In addition, when creating the training workshops andragogical principles must be applied. These elements will provide the training instructors need for creating courses and teaching in an e-learning environment.

## REFERENCES

Banas, E.J., Emory, W.F. (1998). History and issues of distance learning. *Public Administration Quarterly*, 22(3), 365-384.

Benavides, O., & Benavides, A. (1993). Internet and curriculum delivery: Training of teachers and administrators. *Second international symposium on educational telecommunications*, (pp. 15-23). Dallas, TX: Southwest Educational Development Laboratory.

Boettcher, J. (1998). Nuggets about the shift to Web-based teaching and learning. Retrieved March 26, 2002 from http://www.csus.edu/pedtech/nuggets.htm.

Boettcher, J. V. & Conrad, R. (1999). *Faculty guide for moving teaching and learning to the Web.* Mission Viejo, CA: League for Innovation in the Community College.

Bourne, J. R., McMaster, E., Rieger, J., & Campbell, J.O. (1997). Paradigms for on-line learning: A case study in the design and implementation of asynchronous learning networks (ALN) course. *Journal of Asynchronous Learning Networks*, 1(2). 38-56.

Connick, G. P. (1997). Issues and trends to take us into the twenty-first century. In T. Cyrs (Ed.), *Teaching and learning at a distance: What it takes to effectively design, deliver, and evaluate programs*, (pp. 7-12). San Francisco: Jossey-Bass.

Connected Learning.Network (n.d.). Company profile. Retrieved March 26, 2002 from http://128.121.207.177/ie/aboutus/profile.html.

Connolly, P.J. (2001). A standard for success. InfoWorld, 23(42), 57, 2p.

Cravener, P. (1998). *Faculty development programs: Teaching professional educators to drink from the fire hose.* Retrieved March 26, 2002 from http://cravener.net/articles/pioneers.htm.

Demarie, S. M. (2000). Strategic implications of the Information Age. *Journal of Labor Research*, Summer 2000, 21(3), 419–430.

Duderstadt, J. J. (1999). Can colleges and universities survive in the Information Age? In Richard N. Katz (Ed.), *Dancing with the devil: Information technology and the new competition in higher education* (pp. 1-25). San Francisco: Jossey-Bass Publishers.

Edmonds, G. S. (1999). Making change happen: Planning for success. Retrieved March 26, 2002 from http://horizon.unc.edu/TS/development/1999-03.asp

Edwards, R. (1997). *Changing places: Flexibility, lifelong learning, and a learning society.* New York, NY: Routledge.

Eisenberg, D. (1998). College faculty and distance education. *Virtual University Journal* 1(2), (pp.1-3).

Frand, J. L. (2000).The information-age mindset. *Educause Review*, 35, 14-21.

Grant, C. M. (1996). *Professional development in a technological age: New definitions, old challenges, new resources.* Retrieved March 26, 2002 from http://ra.terc.edu/publications/TERC_pubs/tech-infusion/prof_dev/prof_ dev_frame.html.

Hazari, S. (1998). *Evaluation and selection of Web course management tools.* Retrieved March 26, 2002 from http://sunil.umd.edu/Webct.

Hitch, L. P. & Hirsch, D. (2001). Model training. *Journal of Academic Librarianship*, 27(1), 15, 5p.

Hirumi, A. & Bermudez, A. (1996). Interactivity, distance education, and instructional systems design converge on the information superhighway. *Journal of Research on Computing in Education*, 29 (1), (pp.1-16).

Internet.com (2002). *Webopedia.* Retrieved April 2, 2002, from http://www.pcWebo-paedia.com/.

IntraLearn (n.d.). *IntraLearn e-learning product review.* Retrieved March 26, 2002 from http://www.intralearn.com/1000_Products.asp.

Knapczyk, D. (1993). A distance-learning approach to in-service training. *Educational Media International,* 30, (pp. 98-100).

Knowles, M. S. (1989). *The making of an adult educator: An autobiographical journey.* San Francisco, CA: Jossey-Bass.

Ko, S. S. & Rossen, S. (1998). *Faculty development for online instruction: Two models for effective training.* Paper presented at Teaching in the Community Colleges Online Conference.

Landon, B. (2002). *Online educational delivery applications: A Web tool for comparative analysis.* Retrieved March 26, 2002 from Centre for Curriculum, Transfer and Technology Web site: http://www.c2t2.ca/landonline/.

Learning Circuits (2002). *E-learning glossary.* Retrieved April 2, 2002 http://www.learningcircuits.com/glossary.html.

Lewis, L., Alexander D., & Farris, E. (1997). *Distance education in higher education institutions* (NCES Publication No. NCES 98-062). Washington, D.C.: U. S. Department of Education, National Center for Education Statistics.

Merriam, S. B., & Brockett, R. G. (1997). *The profession and practice of adult education: An introduction.* San Francisco, CA: Jossey-Bass.

Moore, M. G., & Kearsley, G. (1996). *Distance education: A systems view.* Belmont, CA: Wadsworth Publishing Company.

Murphy, T. (1996). Agricultural education and distance education: The time is now. *The Agricultural Education Magazine* 68, (11), 3,22-23.

Noren, J. (1997). *Andragogy: The teaching and learning of adults.* Retrieved March 26, 2002 from http://www.park.edu/fac/facdev/noren.htm.

Omoregie, M. (1997). *Distance learning: An effective educational delivery system.* Eighth international conference of the society for information technology and teacher education (SITE), (pp. 73-74). Orlando, FL: Association for the Advancement of Computing in Education.

Padgett, D. L. & Conceao-Runlee, S. (2000). Designing a faculty development program on technology: If you build it, will they come? *Journal of Social Work Education,* Spring/Summer 2000, 36(2), 325, 10p.

Palloff, R. M., & Pratt, K. (2001). *Lessons from the cyberspace classroom: The realities of online teaching.* San Francisco: Jossey-Bass.

Pitt, T. J. & Stuckman, R. E. (1997). *The transfer of traditional curriculum to online learning opportunities.* Eighth international conference of the society for information technology and teacher education (SITE) (pp. 140-145). Orlando, FL: Association for the Advancement of Computing in Education.

Porter, L. R. (1997). *Creating the virtual classroom: Distance learning with the Internet.* New York, NY: John Wiley & Sons, Inc.

Roueche, J. E. & Roueche, S. D. (2001). Pursuing the best thinking in the Information Age. *Community College Week,* Fall 2001 Supplement on Technology, 3-5.

Robbins, C. (1997). Training faculty to teach at a distance. *Distance Education Report,* 1(8): 1,3.

Site Trainer (n.d.). *Online course management platform comparison.* Retrieved March 26, 2002 from http://www.sitetrainer.com/platformcomparison.htm.

Starr, R. H. (1997). Asynchronous learning networks as a virtual classroom. Association for Computing Machinery. *Communications of the ACM*, 40 (9), 44-49.

Starr, R.H. (1997, May-June). Delivering instruction on the World Wide Web: Overview and basic design principles. *Educational Technology*, 7-13.

Steinert, Y. (2000). Faculty development in the new millennium: Key challenges and future directions. *Medical Teacher*, 22(1), 44, 7p.

Truman, B. & Sorg, S. (1997). Institutionalizing systematic faculty development for interactive distance learning. *Proceeding of the Eighth International Conference of the Society for Information Technology and Teacher Education (SITE)* (pp. 339-343). Orlando, FL: Association for the Advancement of Computing in Education.

Weigel, V. (2000). *E-learning and the tradeoff between richness and reach in higher education.* Sept/Oct 2000, 33(5) (pp.10–16).

## APPENDIX A: FEATURES AVAILABLE IN THE INTRALEARN SOFTWARE PROVIDED BY THE CONNECTED LEARNING NETWORK™

| Features | Connected Learning Network™ |
| --- | :---: |
| **STUDENT** | |
| Student-oriented instruction is encouraged | X |
| 24/7 manned help desk for technical questions (#800, e-mail or live chat) | X |
| Runs on PC running Windows 95/98/NT or Mac with OS 7.5 or greater | X/X |
| Students can view all current courses when they log on | X |
| Easy access to all courses | X |
| Integrated Search function | X |
| Multimedia supported | X |
| Integrated glossary | X |
| Security: | |
| Password protected | X |
| Data encrypted during delivery | X |
| Redundant, secure server insures highest security and backup | X |
| Communication tools: | |
| E-mail (integrated) | X |
| Threaded discussion | X |
| chatroom | X |
| File submissions | X |
| Whiteboard | X |

| Features | Connected Learning Network™ |
|---|:---:|
| Course management | |
|   Search tool for course content | X |
|   Student files/presentations can be uploaded | X |
|   Designated team area | X |
|   Bookmark management | X |
|   Study skill building—study notes | X |
|   Access to grades | X |
|   Un-timed quizzes | X |
|   Ability to pull content from a CD on the student's computer | X |

**INSTRUCTOR**

| | |
|---|:---:|
| Support: | |
|   Training | X |
|   Instructional Design | X |
|   24/7 manned help desk (#800, e-mail and live chat) | X |
| Communication: | |
|   Asynchronous communication | X |
|   e-mail | X |
|   threaded discussion board | X |
| | |
| Communications | |
|   Synchronous communication | X |
|   chatroom | X |
|   whiteboard | X |
| Security: | |
|   Password protected | X |
|   Data encrypted during delivery | X |
|   Regularly scheduled data backup | X |
| Grade management: | |
|   On-line testing | X |
|   Automated grading | X |
|   Instructor can manage student records | X |
|   Student tracking | X |

**ADMINISTRATOR (of an institution)**

| | |
|---|:---:|
| Student tracking through Reports feature | X |
| Remote access | X |
| Security/Data Backup | X/X |
| Content review | X |

**AUTHOR (of a course)**

| | |
|---|:---:|
| Support: | |
|   Training of authors supplied by company | X |
|   24/7 manned technical help desk (#800, e-mail or live chat) | X |
|   Instructional design assistance | X |

| Features | Connected Learning Network™ |
|---|---|
| Authoring tools: | |
| Content can be authored on PCs running Windows 95/98/NT or | X |
| Macs running OS 7.5 or higher | X |
| The author does NOT need to know HTML | X |
| Courses "debugged" before making them live to students | X |
| Allows author to view course as a student | X |
| Allows author to import test questions | X |
| Simple transfer from another vendor's platform | X |
| Encourages course planning | X |
| Course revising is quick and simple | X |
| Author can create specific course material for individuals or teams | X |
| Instructional design features for Web-based courses | X |
| Exams: | |
| Tutorials can be created | X |
| True/false, Multiple Choice | X |
| Customized feedback for all above | X |
| Essay questions (graded or non-graded) | X |
| **TECHNICAL/ DEVELOPMENTAL FEATURES** | |
| 24/7 manned technical help desk for students, instructors, authors | X |
| Courses are hosted on secure servers | X |
| Client maintains sole ownership of course content | X |
| Marketing guide provided | X |
| Multimedia products | |
| Video | X |
| Audio | X |
| Animations | X |
| Charts/ graphs | X |
| Mathcad/ Autocad | X |
| Can be integrated with Microsoft Netmeetingä | X |
| Simple transfer from another vendor's platform | X |
| Communication with existing university database applications | X |
| AICC certified | X |
| SCORM compatible | X |
| Level 1 IMS compliant | X |
| LRN compatible | X |
| SQL server | X |
| University library services access supported | X |
| Guest account registration | X |

*Notes:*   Information for this comparison was gleaned from a review of the courseware IntraLearn used by the Connected Learning Network. It is not meant to be a conclusive document of all features for the software reviewed.

## APPENDIX B: TRAINING COURSE OUTLINE

The outline of the training course was as follows:

***Getting Started***
Pre-workshop Preparation
Agenda
Presenter's Goals
Participant's Goals
Instructor Questionnaire
Tech Questionnaire

***Lesson 1: Focus on Teaching and Learning***
What is Web-connected learning?
Playing with the toys
What is Web-connected teaching?
Your course
Strategies

***Lesson 2: Sample lesson: Responsible Ecology***
Setting the Stage
Instructor's Insights
Reactions and Responses
Creations and Contributions

***Lesson 3: Focus on the Technology***
The Software
Hands on the Computer
New Course Wizard

***Lesson 4: Focus on Your Course***
Structure
Course Attributes
Topic Content
Assignments
Exams
Gradebook
Uploads
Announcements
FAQs
Glossary

*Evaluation*
  Self-assessment of your course
  Assessment of the workshop

*Communicating with the Instructor*
  Posting homework assignments
  Asking Questions about Assignments or Content
  Sending e-mail to the Instructor
  Instructor Office Hours

*"Students Only" Lounge*
  Chatting

*Updates*
  New Ideas

*Keeping in Touch*
  Posting Questions and Comments on the Discussion Board
  Using the Chat to...chat!

## APPENDIX C: EVALUATION OF WORKSHOP

1. Did the workshop meet the stated outcomes?
2. Did the content of the workshop assist you in achieving the outcomes?
3. Was the interaction between you and the workshop leader helpful?
4. Do you feel as though the workshop leader created an enjoyable learning environment?
5. Was the interaction between you and your peers helpful?
6. Did the leader of the workshop answer your questions and guide you through the learning process appropriately?
7. Do you feel as though you know the features of the CLEGA software?
8. Will you be able to apply the information you gained today to your personal situation (do you feel comfortable with the CLEGA software)?
9. Do you feel comfortable using the communication technologies?
10. Do you feel as though you know when to use the different communication technologies?
11. Are you able to define the purpose for Web-connected instruction for your institution?

12. What assistance do you feel that you will need in order to complete your course?
13. Do you feel comfortable contacting your Project Director for assistance?
14. List any ways that you feel this workshop could be improved upon:
15. List the ways in which this workshop was beneficial:

Thank you. I appreciate your comments!

Barbara Fennema

## CHAPTER 7

# GROW YOUR OWN COURSE MANAGEMENT THE WAY YOU WANT IT

**Matthew E. Mooney**

The current emphasis on Web-enabled or Web-enhanced courses in many cases has placed technology before learning. The selection of out-of-the-box course management systems available today requires instructors to design courses that fit predefined molds. This chapter discusses the movement away from preconfigured course management systems (CMS). The department of Agricultural Economics at Purdue University serves as the example for this chapter. With the use of tools like Macromedia Dreamweaver MX and Microsoft SQL Server, one can create a course management system to replace preconfigured tools such as WebCT or Blackboard. The new system can provide all the essential functionality of WebCT or Blackboard, but with far fewer resources. There are two key advantages to such a system. First, the system would be scalable to the needs of an individual course. Second, course administration can be greatly simplified to allow for a much shorter development time for individual instructors as well as provide improved ease of use for students.

**KEYWORDS:** course management system, Web-enabled, Web-enhanced, Macromedia Dreamweaver, SQL, WebCT, BlackBoard

Electronic Learning Communities—Issues and Practices, pages 271–299.
ISBN: 1-931576-96-3 (pbk.), 1-931576-97-1 (hardcover)

"Don't forget to download the assignment checklist from the course Website," and phrases like this are commonly heard in college and university classrooms around the nation. Where a few years ago it would have been new and cutting edge for a class to have a Website, today it is expected.

The rapid increase in the use of the Web to support courses has resulted in many institutions' electing to license course management systems such as WebCT and BlackBoard. Such systems were designed to help faculty develop and maintain course Websites for their students. The goal of these systems was to speed up the course development process through preconfigured layouts, tools, graphics, and templates. The use of these tools meant, in theory, that instructors did not need to possess or learn Web development skills, only how to use the system.

The idea behind these systems is wonderful. Most faculty members do not have the technical skills needed to meet the increasing technical demands of today's classrooms. Course management systems would allow an instructor to focus on teaching without worrying about how to make a hyperlink on their home page or add an assignment to their Website. Additionally, course management systems provide structure to course Websites. Navigation, color schemes, and page layout are all aspects of a Website maintained by course management systems.

However, these tools come with a price. As with any preconfigured system, options are limited. Some critics have referred to this as a "cookie cutter" approach to education, meaning simply for example, that a biology class has the same options as an English or geometry class. One size is intended to fit all.

Instructors have also found the so-called ease-of-use to be far more difficult than suggested by the CMS vendors. Many faculty find the user interfaces confusing (see Figure 1) and have difficulty remembering all the steps necessary to accomplish simple tasks.

This chapter describes the course of action taken to deal with these issues by one university department. A brief description of the department is followed by a discussion of the "home grown" course management system options available to faculty for integrating the World Wide Web into their classes.

## AGRICULTURAL ECONOMICS

The department of Agricultural Economics at Purdue University was faced with a difficult situation. The department teaches approximately 2,500 undergraduate students each semester with 20 faculty teaching between 32 and 35 courses per semester. The faculty have a wide variety of technical skills, ranging from those comfortable writing HTML or using tools such as

Macromedia Dreamweaver or Microsoft FrontPage, to those who feel anxious at the thought of checking their e-mail.

Until the Fall 2001 semester, faculty had four choices when it came to using the Web in their classes:

1. They could learn to create and maintain their course Website on their own.
2. They could hire a graduate or undergraduate student to handle their course Website.
3. They could use WebCT, which is provided by the university.
4. They could elect not to have a course Website.

The typical Agricultural Economics course was taught in a traditional instructional lecture environment. Students would meet at specific times during the week and receive lectures, assignments, demonstrations, and presentations. Classes did not fall into the typical distance education setting where asynchronous learning is typical and where online assessments are a normal practice. However, using the Web to enhance or supplement

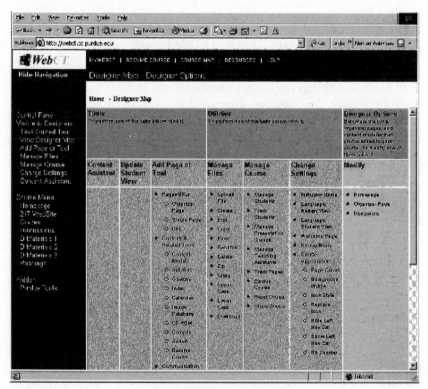

FIGURE 1
Designer Options of WebCT

course content was something the department wished to do. This left instructors with only three options:

1. learn to create a course site on their own;
2. hire someone to create a site for them; and/or
3. use WebCT.

Purdue University has used WebCT for many years. The university provides numerous resources for faculty to assist them in the use of this tool. However, most of the faculty in Agricultural Economics did not feel confident using WebCT. The system required them to constantly refer to tutorials and support materials to accomplish the simplest of tasks. It often was left to support personnel, either clerical staff or graduate assistants, to learn how to manage the course Website.

In response to this situation, the department hired a full-time Web specialist (the author of this chapter) to train the clerical staff and faculty to use Microsoft FrontPage and WebCT, to maintain their class Websites, and to help guide the department towards expanding the use of the Web.

## THE NEEDS ASSESSMENT

One of the first things the author did was to start looking at the way faculty used the Web in their courses. This was done through a needs assessment where each instructor was surveyed to determine what they were doing and what they wanted to be able to do with a course Website. Faculty were also asked to indicate their skill levels for specific software applications or procedures. For example, they were asked if they knew Microsoft PowerPoint or could create a PDF document. In addition, students were surveyed to see what they wanted to have on a course Website. The following section provides a brief description of the results of those surveys.

### Faculty Views

Most of the faculty saw maintaining a course Website in any fashion as more work than it was worth. They wanted a simple way to provide information to their students through the Web; they wanted to use the Web as a communication tool in their classes; and they wanted to be able to provide reminders and announcements to their students. Many felt it was important to provide course lecture material and additional resources such as reading lists, links to useful information, and grades to their students.

Some saw the Web as a way to really interact with their students. They wanted to maintain student profiles, the ability to e-mail individual students, or the entire class. They envisioned ways of tracking student progress and eliminating simple paper work. In addition, many faculty members frequently travel during the semester. They expressed a need for a course site that not only loaded quickly when using dial-up access from remote areas of the world, but also provided them full access to their class through the Web. This is particularly crucial for e-mail access and the ability to manage their site remotely. They frequently only have Web access from cyber cafés which do not provide access to standard e-mail or FTP applications.

More than anything, they wanted something simple that required as little additional work as possible. They didn't want to drastically alter their teaching style or have to learn new technologies; they wanted to use the Web as a tool without having to learn how to build the tool.

All of the faculty members were using Microsoft PowerPoint to deliver lecture material. They also had strong skills using Microsoft Excel or Microsoft Word. However, it was later discovered that most of them did not use features such as tables and styles in Microsoft Word. They mostly typed information, and used tabs to set up columns of data. Many did not have any experience creating PDF documents.

## Student Views

Students viewed the Web as a resource for their classes. They wanted access to anything that was handed out in class in case they missed class or lost the materials. They wanted the information to be accurate and timely, for example lecture notes to be available before the lecture or immediately following it. One of the most common requests from students was to have their grades accessible and up-to-date on the Web.

They also reported a desire for consistency. "Keep things simple and consistent. I don't want to spend time surfing a course site to find something. I have other things to do," was the statement reported by one student.

## THE SOLUTIONS

The information gathered from students and faculty provided a foundation from which to work. Some key ideas came from the needs assessment. First, both students and faculty wanted something simple and easy to use. Second, the Website needed to supplement the information presented in class. Additionally, when asked what they most frequently did with the information provided on a course Website, most students reported that they printed it out. This was a very important point. Since HTML was never really designed to print, students were most likely wasting reams of paper in the university computer labs. This was especially true if a faculty member used Microsoft Word to create a document, saved it as HTML or Microsoft FrontPage to create the Webpage, and the student later printed it with a browser other than Microsoft Internet Explorer.

These needs seemed to imply to the author that there was a need 1) to address simple methods for making documents available online, and 2) for a simple-to-use course management system.

The first requirement was more easily met. The use of Adobe PDF documents seemed to be the obvious choice for creating, storing, retrieving, and printing Web-based documents. The department maintained a PDF server, so faculty could create PDF documents from any personal computer in their office. A simple step-by-step tutorial for creating PDF documents was created and distributed to all the clerical staff, graduate assistants, and faculty members. Included with the tutorial was a simple rationale describing why PDF documents should be used rather than HTML pages, or posting the original document.

The second requirement, for an easy-to-use CMS was somewhat more complex to address. Since the author would be responsible for managing any new Web-based instructional processes, he wanted to create a system that had flexibility and was efficient. He did not want to spend days or hours setting up each class. He needed something simple to manage. The following section explains the components of the basic course management system, how it was created and the rationale for its features, as derived from the needs assessment.

## THE TECHNICAL ENVIRONMENT

When the need for a new CMS was first conceived, the university MIS department suggested a budget of $30,000-$50,000 for hardware and software. As it turned out, this was far in excess of what was eventually spent. In fact, most of the work was done with extant computing resources. Agriculture Economics runs its basic departmental Website on a Microsoft NT 4.0-based server, with two 20 GB hard drives for storage and 1 GB of RAM, running Microsoft SQL Server 2000. This turned out to be sufficient for the department's needs.

All the pages for the new system were created with Macromedia Dreamweaver UltraDev, now known as Macromedia Dreamweaver MX. This application allows someone to construct complex Webpages visually using standard HTML code. In addition, one can create dynamic (or data-driven) Websites using ASP, .NET, JSP, PHP, or ColdFusion to connect to databases through the Web. Since Dreamweaver MX can work with so many different types of languages, it will work with nearly any Web server on the market, from Microsoft Windows NT and 2000 Server, UNIX and Linux, to Macintosh OS X Server. Dreamweaver will connect to a variety of different databases including Microsoft Access or SQL Server, MySQL, and Oracle. Dreamweaver will let one create dynamic Websites in virtually any computing environment.

## Databases and Portals

With careful planning and the use of relational databases tables, it is rather simple to create an efficient and reliable data structure that can be used within a course management system.

The first thing that was required was to determine how to address user (student, staff, and faculty) system access and authentication needs. The department had previously struggled with how to maintain contact with students, faculty, and staff; a departmental Web portal seemed like a solution. A portal would provide a centralized means of login authentication, and help the department manage information better.

The portal that was developed, named *My Ag Econ*, consists of two parts. The first is for the actual account login information. Faculty, staff, and graduate assistants already had usernames and passwords for departmental network access. So accounts were created for each of them in *My Ag Econ*. For the portal, other users were allowed to pick their own username and password on a simple user registration page (see Figure 2). Purdue University utilizes a centralized login for all employees and students; future versions of this system will likely use centralized university logins to authenticate users.

Each user account stores the user's name, e-mail address, username, password, mother's maiden name and user access level. The username is the primary key for this system. Everything is referenced by username. Once a user logs in, the system validates him/her and compares the password with the one stored in the database. If everything is correct, the user is taken to their *My Ag Econ* Webpage (see Figure 3). This page is personalized for each user. My *Ag Econ* has five sections:

1. My Courses,
2. My Links,
3. My Profile,
4. Announcements, and
5. Events.

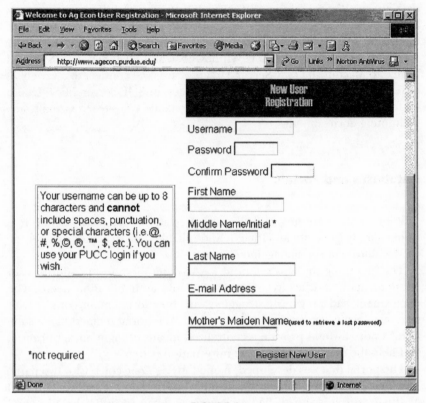

FIGURE 2
New User Registration Page

1. *My Courses* lists any of the Agricultural Economics courses in which the user is enrolled or teaches. *My Courses* requires users to manage course lists themselves. Users can add or delete courses from their list through a simple Web interface. All Agricultural Economics courses are listed for the user; they select the course(s) that want to appear in their *My Courses* section. The system then provides them with a link to the appropriate course Website.

2. *My Links* allows the user to store personal links or links to other courses at the university. Since students frequently move from computer lab to computer lab and/or have a computer at home, it was important to give them a place to store their personal links so they could have access to them from anywhere on the Internet.

3. *My Profile* allows students to update personal information such as their e-mail address. Their mother's maiden name is used to help them retrieve a forgotten or lost password. If they supply the system with their username

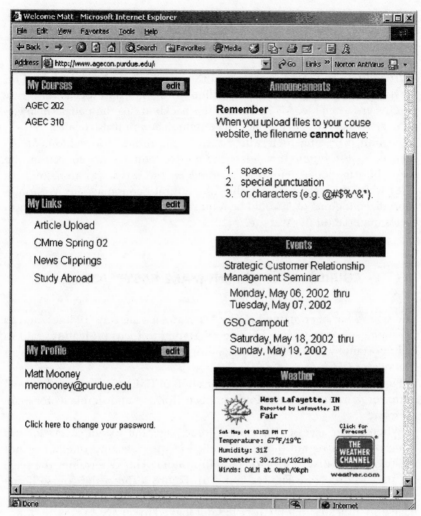

FIGURE 3
My Ag Econ

and their mother's maiden name, their password will be e-mailed to the e-mail address they have stored in their profile.

4. *Announcements* provides an essential departmental function. There are multiple announcements stored in the system. The user receives the announcement appropriate to his/her access level. Access levels are used to distinguish faculty and staff from undergraduate and graduate students. Select departmental staff maintain the announcements through a Web interface. There are specific announcements for undergraduate Agricultural Economics students, graduate students, departmental staff, and undergraduate students that are not Agricultural Economics majors.

5. *Events* highlights upcoming campus, school, and departmental events. Again, select departmental staff maintain the information in *Events*. A simple Web form is provided for them to manage the information.

In addition to these five sections, other university links are provided on *My Ag Econ*. Links to the libraries, online writing lab, and special university systems are available. *My Ag Econ* is the backbone of the course management system and the departmental communication infrastructure.

Beyond providing users with access to important information, *My Ag Econ* allows the system to validate the user's identity. Once logged in, the user's information is temporarily stored on the server (as a session variable) while the user is visiting the Agricultural Economics site. Without a centralized login, a user would be required to continually login in order to access material on the Website.

## COURSE MANAGEMENT MADE EASY™ (CMme)

The system has been named *Course Management made easy* (CMme), and as the name suggests, CMme has been designed to focus on features said to be important by the students and faculty. The following section provides an overview of CMme.

Figure 4 illustrates the basic organization of CMme Webpages. The goal of this organization was two-fold: simplicity for use, and simplicity for management.

When a user accesses the course home page, the system checks for two things; whether or not the user enrolled in the class, and whether or not the user is a course instructor (administrator). This determines the page the user will see (see Figures 5 and 6). Figure 5 shows the course home page if the user is not enrolled in the class and is not an instructor. This page also indicates that the user has not logged in on *My Ag Econ*.

Figure 6 shows the course home page if the user is the instructor for the course. If the user were an enrolled student, the page would be the same except the link to *Admin Option* would not be displayed. The course number, title, and the initial welcome message are retrieved from the database. The welcome message can be changed through the administrative options; these are discussed later in the chapter.

The two buttons on the page, *Course Materials* and *Contact Information*, provide the user with access to all the major portions of the site. *Contact Information* provides the instructor's contact information and any additional contacts such as teaching assistants, clerical staff, and so on. The *Course Materials* button links to the *Course Materials* page (see Figure 7).

Course instructors have full control over the buttons that appear on this page. The buttons can be added or removed via a simple administrative

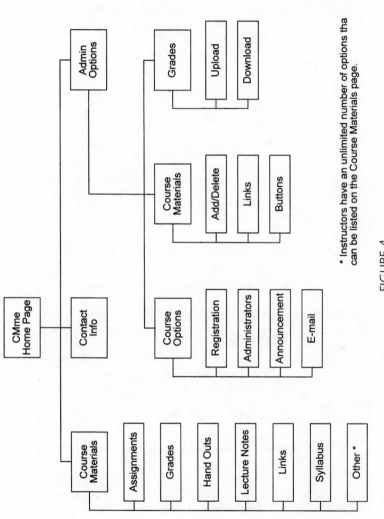

FIGURE 4
Organizational Chart of CMme webpages

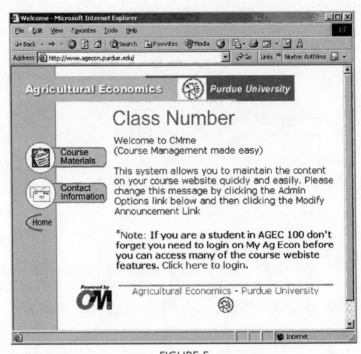

FIGURE 5
The User is Not Enrolled or an Administrator

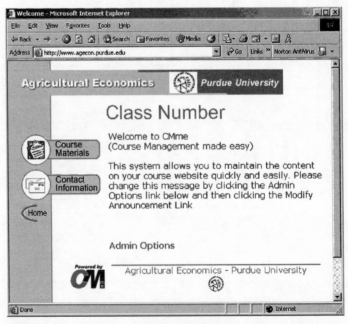

FIGURE 6
User is a Course Administrator

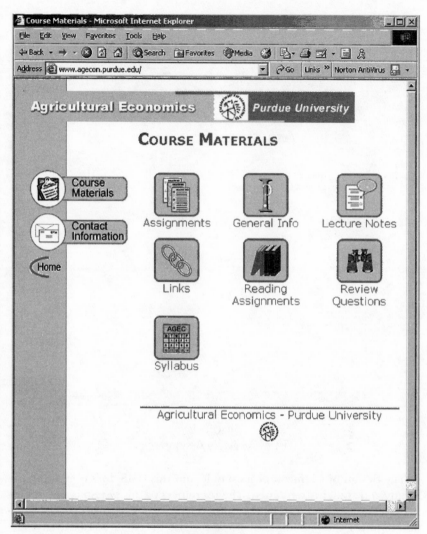

FIGURE 7
Course Materials Page

window. If a user were to click the *Assignments* button they would be taken to the page shown in Figure 8. This page lists all the assignments added to the course by an instructor.

The user can click on an assignment to download it from the Website. Course instructors have the ability to rank order the assignments as they please. In the example in Figure 8, the instructor has chosen to have the notes for an assignment (Homework 2 Notes) listed separately from the assignment (i.e., as the first assignment in the list).

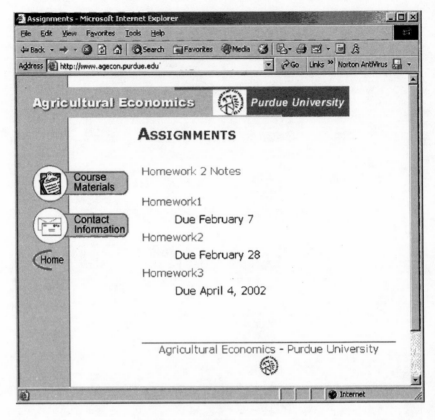

FIGURE 8
List of Available Assignments

The design of CMme appears simple, but this CMS does everything the faculty and students requested. The usefulness of this system is not only in its appearance which can be customized to anything an instructional situation requires, the real functionality of the system is in its administrative features.

## ADMINISTRATIVE OPTIONS

When instructors log on *My Ag Econ* and access their course Website, they can use the *Admin Options* link to manage their course Website (see Figure 9). There are three sections on this Webpage:

1. Course Options,
2. Course Materials, and
3. Grade Management.

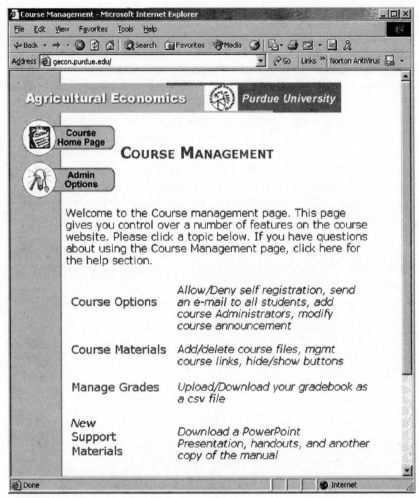

FIGURE 9
Administrative Options Page

Each offers a variety of function that will be discussed in the following sections.

## Course Options

This section offers the instructor four basic but important course management functions:

1. self registration management,
2. course administrator management,

3. announcement management, and
4. sending class e-mails.

### 1.   Self Registration Management—Allow/Deny Self Registration

Self registration allows students to add themselves to the course Website as enrolled students. This option is typically used at the beginning of a semester when students are first accessing the course Website.

If self registration is set to "allow," when a student visits the course Website after logging in on *My Ag Econ*, the system checks to see if the student is registered with the course Website. If not, they are presented with a simple confirmation page (see Figure 10). If the student clicks the "Yes" button, their user information is inserted into two SQL tables. Student self registration reduces the amount of work required by the instructor or other course administrator.

After the first few weeks of the semester, this option is turned off to control access to course material. Many faculty prefer to limit access to their course material to only registered students.

### 2.   Course Administrator Management

Many classes have teaching assistants or clerical support staff who need to have access to the course and to manage the content of the course. The Course Administrator's page provides four functions:

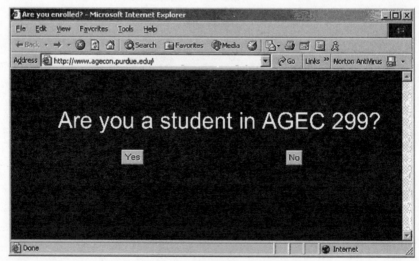

FIGURE 10
Self Registration Page Seen by Students

1. adding an instructor,
2. removing an administrator,
3. modifying contact information for an instructor, and
4. modifying the support staff label (see Figure 11).

Adding an instructor to a course is as simple as typing their username into the username text box and clicking the "Add Administrator" button. The system queries the SQL table that contains user information, and provides the user with a confirmation page detailing the information associated with the entered username. Removing an instructor is similar. After

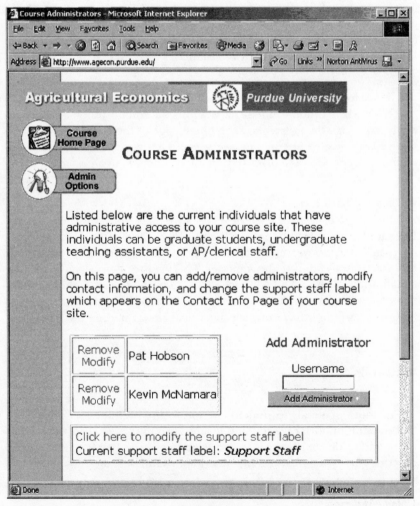

FIGURE 11
Course Administrators page

clicking the "Remove" link next to the instructor name to be removed, the system confirms the action before removing the instructor name.

If "Modify" is clicked, the contact information stored in the system is displayed so that it can be updated. For example, if an e-mail address or phone number were to be changed, the instructor could easily edit the information.

The "Support Staff" function is used in conjunction with the *Contact Information* page. The primary instructor is listed first on the *Contact Information* page. All other instructors are listed below the primary instructor. Many instructors in Agricultural Economics prefer that students send questions to the teaching assistants or clerical staff associated with the course. The support staff label appears between the primary instructor and the other instructors. This provides more flexibility for the primary instructor and other instructors by giving instructors a simple mechanism to provide instructions about how to receive assistance.

### 3. *Announcement Management*

The Modify Announcement page allows an administrator quickly and easily to change the message on the home page of the course Website (see Figure 12). This feature has been very useful for faculty when a class needs to change rooms, or as a place to post a reminder about an assignment.

### 4. *Sending Class E-mails*

The ability to send the entire class an e-mail from anywhere on the Internet has proven to be one of the most used and appreciated features. As mentioned above, many of the Agricultural Economics faculty are required to travel during the semester. This feature allows them to send an e-mail, with or without a file attached, to their entire class from any Internet-attached workstation (see Figure 13). (For additional technical information regarding this feature, see Technical Note 1 in the Appendix.)

## Materials

Providing materials to students is vital to the usefulness of any course Website. It is important that a simple administrative page allow the instructor to add or delete materials to and from the course Website. This section describes the system features that provide this functionality.

### *Upload Materials*

To upload materials the user needs to complete an online form and select a local file to be sent to the server (see Figure 14). All materials are stored in a predefined directory on the server. While the file is uploaded to the server, the system checks to confirm that the file name is unique. If it is not, the file is renamed and the database is updated with the new file name.

The information the user enters or selects on this *Materials Upload* page is stored in an SQL table. Each form element on the page tells the system something. For example, when the user selects the type of material from the first drop down list, the system uses the data to determine which page

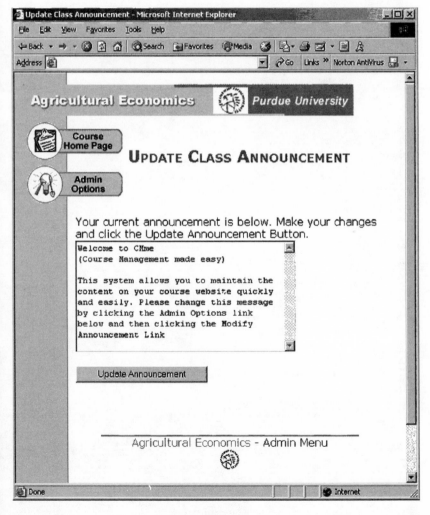

FIGURE 12
Modify Announcement page

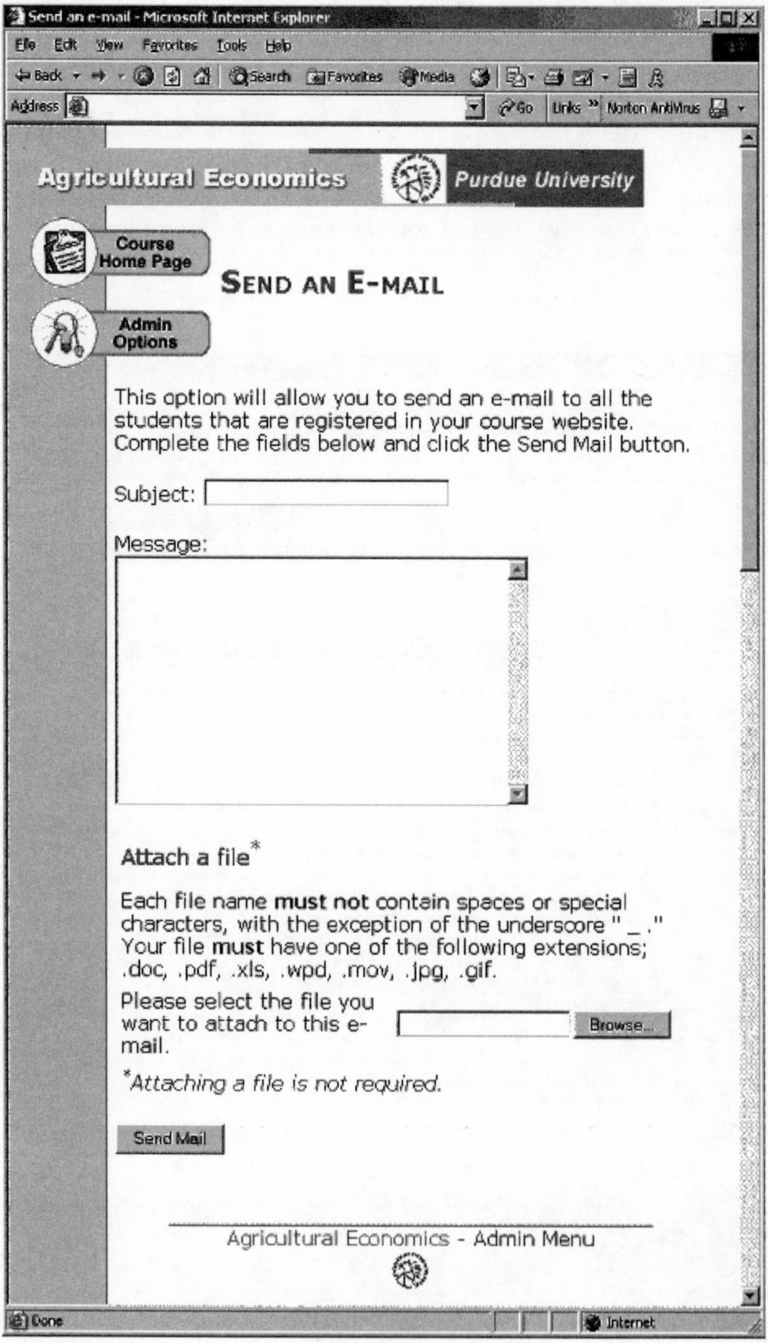


FIGURE 13
Send E-mail Page

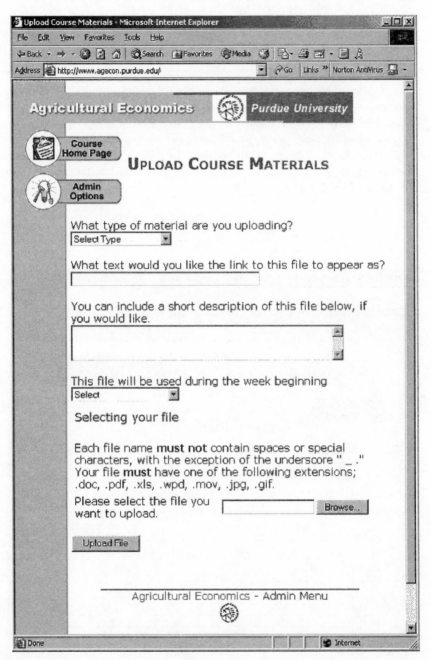

FIGURE 14
Upload Materials Page

to display the file on. If a file is an assignment, the system will display it on the *Assignments* page and on no others.

### Deleting Materials

This allows the instructor to remove file information from the database and remove the actual file from the server (see Figure 15). The system provides the instructor with a list of all the materials that have been uploaded to the course Website. Users can delete materials by clicking on the "Delete File" link. They will be asked to confirm their choice; the system removes the record from the database and deletes the file from the server. (See Technical Note 2 in the Appendix.)

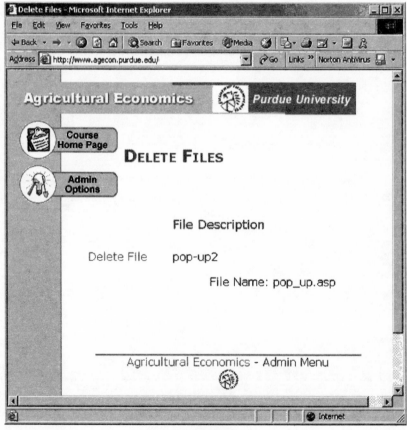

FIGURE 15
Delete Materials Page

### Hide/Show Buttons

The ability for an instructor to control the options a student can access is very important. An instructor can decide which buttons to hide or show on the *Course Materials* page. The example in Figure 16 shows a simple "Hide/Show" scenario. (See Technical Note 3 in the Appendix.) However, it would be very easy to add additional features to this page. For example, if an instructor wanted to limit access to assignments to currently enrolled students, the button could be set to Private, while buttons that were set to Public could be accessible to all visitors. Adding this feature would require adding just one field to the database table.

### Links

Many courses must have a site that lists useful links for students. This option is provided by a database table that contains the text that will be hyperlinked to the included URL. An instructor can easily copy and paste a URL into a text field and add the text they want to use as the title of the link. In addition there is a text box for a description of the link where the instructor can enter a short description of the link.

## Grades

A course management system is incomplete without the ability to manage student grades. Unfortunately, this can also be the most difficult function for CMS developers to provide due to the complexity of the coding required. The level of difficulty depends on the level of function needed. It is easy to provide a list of all the students in the class and allow an instructor to update the grades of each student, one at a time. However, with a large class or multiple classes, this procedure is very time consuming.

The difficulty comes in two areas: setting up the grade book, and providing descriptive statistics related to student grades. Allowing an instructor to customize the grade book through the Web, for example adding or deleting columns for assignments, is possible, but requires more sophisticated coding than the average developer can handle. Also, providing statistical information about assignments and grades (means, standard deviations, and frequencies) is possible through the use of SQL. However, this would require instructors to follow some specific and difficult semantic rules. For example, grades can only be numeric for the statistical features to work. So if an instructor adds an "L" to a grade to indicate that an assignment were turned in late, the statistical functions, like calculating the mean or standard deviation would stop working.

In the department of Agricultural Economics it was very difficult to get faculty members to agree on what a grade book should look like. To

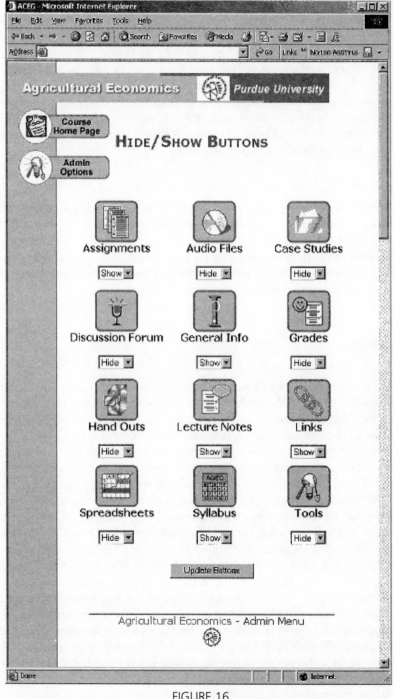

FIGURE 16
Hide/Show Buttons Page

address this, each faculty member was required to provide their grade book structure as a Microsoft Excel file. (All the faculty were already using Excel to manage their grades.) This meant that faculty had to have a good idea of the assignments and assessments before the course was taught. To some this was a very difficult process, but to most it was acceptable.

From each Excel file, an SQL table that incorporated the assessment/assignment columns was created. Students' usernames were also included allowing students to see their grades after logging in. Each faculty member was then able to use Excel to create any statistics they wanted. Each row of statistics was given a username such as "class_mean" in the grade book. These records were also displayed to students when they saw their grades online.

The really complex part of dealing with grades was determining how faculty could easily get their information from the Excel file into the SQL table. Through some customized conversion coding the only thing faculty members had to do was save their Excel table(s) as a .csv file and use the Web-based upload feature. For security reasons, once the information from the .csv file is imported, the file is automatically deleted.

(Technical Note 4 in the Appendix provides a more detailed description of the SQL tables used in this system.)

## THE RESULTS

CMme has been in use since Fall 2001 and has been a huge success. During the Fall semester there was some reluctance on the part of instructors to try the new system. By the end of the semester all but two undergraduate and many of the graduate course instructors had requested the use of CMme for the following semester.

The transition was not without some problems. The biggest problem experienced in the Fall semester was the inability of students to follow basic directions. The original system had a notice on the home page of each class telling students that they needed to login, or asking if they were enrolled in the class. Even with printed, step-by-step documentation, many students were unable to register for the courses. This problem obviously limited access to course materials and grades. The version shown in this chapter takes a more "aggressive" approach to student registration than the original, forcing students to answer the question, "Are you enrolled in [for example] course AGEC XYZ" before they can continue. This feature has greatly reduced the number of problems reported by faculty and students.

Another problem was getting students and faculty accustomed to using *My Ag Econ* as a central place for information and access to classes. Traditionally, students had been given direct URLs to their courses at the beginning of each semester. Using CMme required that students and faculty access courses from CMme to validate their identity. By the Spring semester this had become common practice.

As both faculty and students used the system, its reputation and utility quickly spread. In fact, students were even telling faculty to use the system. One faculty member received lower marks on student evaluation forms for not using CMme!

At the time of this writing, survey data are being collected from students and faculty to evaluate the latest version of CMme. Initial data suggest that both students and faculty appreciate the ease of use and flexibility of the system.

## IMPLICATIONS FOR OTHERS

Institutions that have the development staff and/or the time to acquire some proficiency with databases and dynamic Web tools such as Macromedia Dreamweaver MX can readily create their own course management system. In all, the cost to the author's department for the development of this system was half the author's time for six months, the cost of Macromedia Dreamweaver MX (previously UltraDev), and about $100 for some additional programming utilities. When compared to the price of systems like WebCT or Blackboard, these costs are very small.

While some may argue that the time that was invested would balance against the cost of a preconfigured system, it clear from the experience described in this chapter, that even if a department used a preconfigured system, it would need at least one employee continually dedicated to instructor training as well as maintenance of the system.

The only real requirement for developing a local course management system is to think outside of the box. Preconfigured systems are useful, but most require far more overhead than a department or small college really needs. The ability to customize and grow as an organization changes can save money and frustration. As well, making a system that is easier to use means that instructors are more likely to use it and will have more time to focus on their instruction. Shouldn't that be the goal of a course management system?

## APPENDIX

### Technical Note #1 – Send an E-mail
The *E-mail Your Class Feature* utilizes two extensions that are available from the Macromedia Exchange Website (http://www.macromedia.com/

exchange). The first is a basic CDO Mail extension. CDO Mail is an optional service that can run on a Microsoft Server. There are similar services such as JMail that can run on other servers, and each has an extension available on the Macromedia Exchange Website. This extension lets one add dynamic and static information to an e-mail that is generated from the server though a Web interface.

Adding an attachment is made possible by using the PureASPUpload extension. This extension can be purchased for a nominal fee at http://www.udzone.com. The extension is very powerful and flexible. It takes a local file from the user's computer and uploads it to a previously specified directory on the server through a Web interface, without the need for additional COMs or Services. In addition, this extension allows the developer to limit the file types that are allowed to be uploaded, thus adding a level of security against some viruses being uploaded, and passed on to other users.

### *Technical Note #2 – Deleting Materials*

Deleting the information from the database is nothing more than the standard Delete Record behavior within Dreamweaver. Deleting the actual file from the server requires the use of a server object on the server. Each server is different, but this can typically be accomplished with a few lines of code that are readily available on the Web. Websites like http://www.ASP100.com, http://www.jspin.com, and http://www.cfdev.com offer many code examples and resources.

### *Technical Note #3 – Hide/Show Buttons*

Each button is a record in the database, and each contains the graphic file name for the button graphic, the term associated with the button, and the visibility of the button.

Updating multiple records in a database requires some customized coding, but there are many examples on the Web for doing this with multiple languages and server models.

### *Technical Note #4 – How it All Works: SQL Tables*

The real beauty of this system is its simplicity. The entire base system is run from nine SQL tables for each class, and the SQL table for user information which is separate from the classes. The following discusses each table and its use:

Each course has the following tables in its database. I've included the actual table names to demonstrate my naming convention. I found it much easier to work with the tables using this convention rather than others I had tried. All the tables also have an auto-numbering ID field.

***ADMIN_Email_Sent.*** This table has five fields: subject, body, filename, sent_on, and sent_by. The author made the decision to store all the information sent in e-mails so if there were ever questions about an e-mail that was sent, he could recover the information and the file.

**ADMIN_Material_Types.** There are five fields in this table: value_displayed, value_sent, icon_file, hide_show, and upload_list. There are many situations when the value displayed in a dropdown menu is not the actual value one wishes to send. The author used value_displayed and value_sent for this purpose. The value_sent is sent when a user clicks on a button on the Course Materials page to provide sorting criteria for the database.

The icon_file is the image file name, and hide_show stores if the button should be displayed or not. The upload_list field is used to exclude some of the records from the "Materials Type" dropdown menu on the *Upload Materials* page (Figure 14). There are some materials that are not upload-able such as discussion forums and links.

This is also the table that could control the Private/Public access. Adding a field to this table to hold that information would work well.

**ADMIN_Options.** The ADMIN_options table has become a catch-all for information. The table currently has six fields: self_reg, support_staff, course_num, course_title, path_name, semester. The self_reg field controls if students can self register in the course. Course_num and course_title are used to dynamically provide this information on a variety of pages such as the home page and self registration page. The two most interesting fields are path_name and semester. The server has been configured to store CMme courses in a specific location. The path_name and semester fields are used to dynamically locate uploaded file directories and materials; adding this information to the database drastically reduced the amount of hand coding required when setting up a course.

**ADMIN_Users.** This table has 11 fields: username, access_level, f_name, l_name, email_, office, building, city, state_abbrev, zip_code, and phone_num. Many of the fields provide basic contact information. Originally, this information was retrieved from the departmental users database. However, when they started to be added to the system, there were instructors and graduate assistant that were not technically part of the department. It was easier to manage this information in a separate table than to establish user accounts for them. While there will be some data duplication initially, the ease of use outweighed the small amount of redundant data.

The use of access_levels was to allow for a true administrative account to be added to each course and not be displayed on the *Contact Information* page. The *Contact Information* page was set to show all records in this table that did not have an access_level equal to Webmaster.

**COURSE_Announcement.** This is a simple one field table that should be added to the ADMIN_Options table. This table holds the announcement being displayed. The original plan was to add a new record for each announcement and to display the most recent announcement to the students. However, the faculty did not want to have their announcements archived, so this feature was changed.

***COURSE_Grades.*** This table could have any number of fields. The only required field is username. Since each class has a different grade book structure, this table is variable. As a helpful hint, care should be taken to put the username as the last column of the grade book. The author discovered that in Microsoft Excel, when saving as a .csv file, after 15 rows, empty cells at the end of a row are dropped. This meant a grade book with 12 columns saved as a .csv file may only have 5 columns at the beginning of the semester when there are no grades in the last columns. This caused many errors when trying to upload the .csv file into an SQL table. If the username is the last column, it will make Excel include all the cells of the table when saving as a .csv file.

***COURSE_Links.*** There are four fields in this table: link_text, the_url, the_desc, week_num. Each of these holds the information needed on the *Links* page. The week_num field is used for sorting purposes and the_desc holds the description of the link

***COURSE_Materials.*** This table is very much like the COURSE_links table. It has five fields: title_text, material_type, the_desc, file_name, and week_num. The material_type field allows the system to properly sort the materials that are displayed on any given course materials page. The file_name field holds only the file name. The actual location of the file is written dynamically in the link using path_name, and semester from the ADMIN_options table.

***COURSE_Student_List.*** This table is a backup table for the course. On more than one occasion an instructor would delete all the student names in the grade book by uploading a bad .csv file, then throw everything away. This would, in essence, lock the students out of the course Website if they had private access files. This meant students had to re-register on the course Website. This table stores students' name, username, and e-mail address. Student access to the course Website is determined from this table rather than from COURSE_grades. The information can be exported in the event an instructor loses the class list. The grades are not duplicated in this table.

CHAPTER 8

# STRATEGIES FOR TEACHING THINKING AND PROMOTING INTELLECTUAL DEVELOPMENT IN ONLINE CLASSES

**William Peirce**

The chapter summarizes the research demonstrating that higher order thinking can be taught effectively in online classes; it presents 15 strategies for teaching critical thinking and disciplinary reasoning, and promoting intellectual development. The strategies include conducting opinion polls/ surveys before assigned readings, designing quizzes and tutorials to prepare students for well-grounded discussions, conducting interactive asynchronous discussions, asking well-designed questions, creating cognitive dissonance, assigning writing-to learn tasks, considering opposing views, assigning a mediatory argument promoting a resolution acceptable to both sides, using collaborative and cooperative learning techniques, evaluating Internet resources, assigning self-reflective metacognitive journals, engaging critical thinking dispositions, promoting critical consciousness, moving students to higher stages of intellectual development, and understanding students' levels of self-directedness. The chapter also provides essential references relevant to teaching thinking in online classes.

Electronic Learning Communities—Issues and Practices, pages 301–347.
Copyright © 2003 by Information Age Publishing, Inc.
All rights of reproduction in any form reserved.
ISBN: 1-931576-96-3 (pbk.), 1-931576-97-1 (hardcover)

**KEYWORDS:**   critical thinking, disciplinary thinking, intellectual development, distance learning, online learning, online pedagogy.

## INTRODUCTION AND OBJECTIVES

Can analytical and critical thinking be taught well online?

Can the reasoning and problem solving required to be a disciplinary practitioner be taught well asynchronously?

Can students in online classes grow intellectually?

My answer to these questions is a definite "yes, very well—if professors employ active learning strategies in their online classes."

Depending on the context, "critical thinking" has been defined in many ways. In this chapter "thinking" and "critical thinking" simply mean good thinking in its various applications as higher-order cognitive skills in college courses: analyzing, synthesizing, interpreting, evaluating, reaching conclusions, solving problems, making decisions, supporting arguments, and performing the disciplinary reasoning required by the course. The researchers cited here might have other definitions, and in their articles they make clear what they mean by critical thinking, higher order thinking, or reasoning. By "online courses" I mean courses taught completely over the Internet, with face-to-face meetings occurring very rarely or not at all. This definition excludes distance learning in correspondence, television, and audio courses and in Web-enhanced and e-mail discussions incorporated into traditional classroom courses. Research studies about critical thinking in such courses are not discussed in this chapter.

The objectives of this chapter are to:

- summarize the research demonstrating that higher order thinking can be taught effectively in online classes,
- assemble essential references relevant to teaching thinking in online classes and indicate their availability through the Internet,
- present strategies that engage students thoughtfully in course content, teach disciplinary thinking, promote critical consciousness, and promote intellectual development, and
- suggest future research.

Professors who are good at getting students to think in their face-to-face classrooms wonder if they can be as good online. Yes, they can. In an online class instructors can employ many of the same active learning strategies they use in their face-to-face classrooms to promote good thinking about the course content. After discussing strategies that work well in online classes, I deal with another issue bothering many instructors: Can online students be transformed intellectually? That is, can students move to higher stages of intellectual development without the physical presence of a talented classroom instructor directing spontaneous Socratic discussions and seizing on serendipitous teachable moments? My answer is that intellectual transformations can also occur in online students if their instructors use strategies that promote intellectual development.

The chapter closes with my speculations about future trends and research opportunities in teaching thinking online.

## DISCUSSION OF THE PROBLEM: CAN THINKING BE TAUGHT WELL IN ONLINE CLASSES?

### Research Findings

Some critics of online courses are concerned that distance education courses are simply another place for passively learning information, but not environments where students improve their thinking. A common concern is that an online course merely transfers lectures, readings, and tests from the classroom to the Web, with an added discussion forum or e-mail discussion list to answer students' questions (Weigel, 2000). Without interaction and participation, online students are merely receivers of knowledge (Henri & Kaye, 1993; Lauzon, 1992; Doherty, 1998). On our campuses, faculty who resist teaching online courses often have misgivings about how well critical thinking can be taught online. Some are suspicious that computer technology perpetuates mental laziness and undermines critical thinking. A frequent objection is that because an online class lacks direct personal contact between professor and fellow students, it is not as good as the face-to-face environment for developing critical thinking (Groothius, 1999). Kimberly S. Dozier, a writing instructor dissatisfied with her online students not doing the assigned task because they misunderstood it, attributes their misconceptions to their lack of face-to-face contact, where their misconceptions could be clarified—as they are clarified for her face-to-face students (2001). A recent issue on teaching in the online classroom in the *New Directions for Teaching and Learning* series concludes with the cautions of R. W. Carstens and Victor L. Worsfold (2000) who write, "Simply put, the technology of the online classroom does not allow for the personal transformation that is a necessary part of learning" (p. 83). Their chief concerns are centered on the implications of the physical removal of the professor and fellow students from the online class:

- Without this interpersonal connection, students will not challenge the authority of the instructor nor learn to argue a position as part of a classroom dialogue.
- Most of the discourse is not "writing in the liberal arts sense" because most e-mail messages are "neither composed nor structured" (p. 85).
- Without the spurring Socratic presence of the professor, the students will not engage in necessary self-examination.
- Students' inabilities in abstract and critical thinking caused by their growing up in a television culture will continue because a similar computer technology perpetuates these inabilities.

My reply to such worries is that in a poorly designed and minimally conducted online class, all these examples can indeed occur—as they can in a face-to-face class. There are online classes in need of improvement, just as there are face-to-face lecture classes where the learning is only fact-based and testing is limited to factual recall. In fact, a grim review of the research for the last three decades shows that most face-to-face classes are characterized by passive learning of factual material (Gardiner, 1998). Unfortunately, tell-them-and-test-them pedagogy can be found online as it can on campus. But it doesn't have to be this way.

Instructors can teach critical and analytical thinking well in an online class. As many distance educators are pointing out, computer-mediated communication need not be an impediment, but can be an asset to an instructor using collaborative and interactive learning strategies adapted to the medium (Althauser & Matuga, 1998; Bernard, de Rubalcava, & St.-Pierre, 2000; Anderson & Boud, 2001; see also Seaton, 1993; Willis, 1993). Courses conducted by computer-mediated communication require active learning strategies and interaction (Harasim, et al., 1995; Knowlton, 2000). Online pedagogy tends to be more learning-centered than the traditional face-to-face classroom (Berge, 1997; Bonk & Dennen, 1999). One of the major lessons learned by the authors of *Lessons from the Cyberspace Classroom* is that faculty should "move away from the lecture mode of teaching and toward the use of more active-learning approaches" (Palloff & Pratt, 2001, p. 153). Face-to-face instructors who use whole-class discussions know that sometimes they don't go very well. Sometimes only a small number of students participate, sometimes a few students dominate the discussion, sometimes students are not prepared; some students lack communication and reasoning skills, some are not interested, some come from cultures that discourage classroom participation; and some believe discussions are a waste of time (King, 1994). Online discussions can sometimes go better than face-to-face whole-class discussions.

At least 16 different articles describe successful experiences teaching higher order thinking in online courses. In their case studies, the authors of those articles directly assessed students' thinking before reaching the conclusion that their courses were successful in teaching thinking. All of them emphasized that interaction among students and with their professor was crucial to their seeing evidence of student thinking. Only with designed interaction among students can one expect to find evidence that online courses facilitate thinking.

Experience and discourse analysis have convinced several practitioners of the value of asynchronous discussion for promoting critical thinking. Newman, Johnson, Cochrane, and Webb (1996) found that students' critical thinking showed more depth in the online discussions than in parallel face-to-face seminars discussing information technology and society. A study by Martunnen and Laurinen (1997) found e-mail discussions to be better structured and better grounded than face-to-face discussions among students in an argument course. Likewise, in comparing the patterns of interaction in discussions in four face-to-face classes and two online classes of the same courses, Hillman (1999) found that the online, weekly asynchronous patterns "resembled discussions, whereas the patterns in the FTF [face-to-face] courses resembled recitation" (p. 37). Similar testimony comes from Redding and Rotzien (2001) who found that an online community college insurance class showed greater cognitive learning on the final exam when compared with parallel face-to-face private, commercial, and community college classes. Students in an online chemistry class outperformed their face-to-face counterparts on examinations requiring complex reasoning—chiefly because of the active learning strategies employed in the online class (Shapely, 2000). Although initially skeptical about being able to conduct an online history course using the dialectical strategies he used in his face-to-face classes, Zukas (1999) enthusiastically describes thoughtful, reflective, and well-developed discussions in his first online class. Student evaluations of the course showed a high degree of satisfaction that it had improved their critical thinking.

Holt, Kreiber, and Jill (1998) found that students discussing national issues in a Web-based conference showed deliberative discussion and reflective thinking. Their demonstration of critical thinking is attributed to the communities of inquiry created by the course and to the students' ability to review all the postings to a discussion thread before replying. Bullen (1998) designed a study to determine, among other things, whether computer conferencing elicited critical thinking when students responded to legal, ethical, and privacy issues in a course on information systems in organizations and society. According to a content analysis of their messages, he concluded that "all students appeared to be thinking critically at some level about the issues raised for discussion" (p. 9). Ryan, Carlton, and Ali (1999) found no significant difference between perceptions of critical thinking displayed in online and face-to-face nursing classes, as measured by a student questionnaire. Marttunen and Laurinen (2001) found that in an argument course studying academic debate, the e-mail students learned to choose relevant grounds better than the face-to-face students who were better at learning counterargument skills than the e-mail students; both e-mail and face-to-face students attended the same lectures in an argument course.

A problem-based learning course for teaching energy issues to laymen was taught successfully online using the group collaborative learning techniques associated with problem-based learning. Participants were working adults taking the course as part-time students. The course was evaluated using written inquiries, in-person interviews, and an analysis of the conference messages posted by the students. Instructors and students agreed that the course accomplished its goals, including increased competency in critical thinking—one of the major objectives of a problem-based learning course (Adelskold, Axelsson, & Blomgren, 1999).

By adding required writing to collaborative pedagogy, online instructors have found that both critical thinking and writing improved in online literature courses. A content analysis showed that students in the online classes exhibited a greater range of discussion, a more reflective discussion, and a more polished discussion than did students in parallel face-to-face literature classes. An analysis of the writing at the beginning and end of the online and face-to-face classes showed greater improvement in the online classes in both writing style and critical thought (Mulligan & Geary, 1999).

### Why Do Asynchronous Discussions Promote Thinking Better than Face-to-Face Classroom Discussions?

Four related articles by Judith Lapadat provide the explanation. Using her own observations of four graduate classes and a discourse analysis of the online contributions, Lapadat found that asynchronous posts in online conferences were more thoughtful than discussions in her parallel face-to-face classes (2000a). Discourse analysis of online discussions provided evidence that conceptual change occurred during the course and that students were using the online discussions for deep learning (2000b). She attributes the thoughtful nature of asynchronous discussion to features missing from face-to-face discussions (2001a, 2001b):

1. Asynchronous discussion is written and therefore promotes thinking:
   - Writing requires thinking about how to phrase ideas precisely and clearly.
   - Writing clarifies one's thinking during the act of writing.
2. Asynchronous discussion is permanent and therefore can be revisited:
   - Students need not rely on their possibly faulty memory of a previous post.
   - Students can carefully read and re-read a previous post.
   - Revisiting a previous post promotes reflection rather than a spontaneous outburst.

- Students can plan their own paths through previous posts, and paste sections into their responses.
3. Asynchronous discussion is not time limited:
    - Students can take time to consider their response to instructor-posed questions and to responses from other students.
    - Students can polish and edit their writing.
4. Asynchronous discussion is interactive, not instructor-dominated, and provides several discussions at once:
    - Students establish a contextual situation in which to respond.
    - Students have a real audience with which to communicate purposefully.
    - Students are motivated to provide responses that are well thought out.
    - Students need to support their opinions, argue against other opinions, and offer new perspectives.

## Is the Physical Presence of the Teacher Needed to Teach Thinking?

In his article in *Inquiry: Critical Thinking Across the Disciplines,* John Miller (1999) disputes claims made by proponents of computer-mediated communication that asynchronous discussion promotes critical thinking by its very nature. The proponents' basic claim is that asynchronous discussion "combines the dialogic form of discussion with the greater precision and thoughtfulness allowed by writing" (Miller's words, citing Harasim, 1989, p. 18). Miller notes three advantages claimed by proponents of asynchronous discussion:

1. Its relative anonymity promotes participation by the socially inhibited.
2. Participation can be required and monitored by the instructor.
3. The discussion is more thoughtful than spontaneous face-to-face responses.

But Miller argues that the thoughtful, reflective, composed nature of responses in asynchronous discussion is its chief *disadvantage* for the instructor of critical thinking. The basic liability of thoughtful asynchronous discussion is that it does not model the messy quality of face-to-face spontaneous oral discussion as the instructor coaches the critical thinking process of bringing evidence and sound reasoning into the discussion.

Miller explains four reasons why asynchronous discussion undermines the efforts of the instructor of critical thinking:

1. In asynchronous discussions students cannot observe uncritical thought as it is being formed, clarified, and refined by critical thinking processes brought into the ongoing discussion. The first comments made in an oral face-to-face discussion tend to be emotional and prejudiced. Miller explains, "Such unedited, unconsidered reactions are valuable in revealing the emotions, prejudices, ignorance, and simplifications that underlie unexamined opinions on issues. A well-managed discussion can demonstrate how to move from these initial reactions to a more thoughtful assessment of an issue" (p. 23).

2. Likewise, asynchronous discussion does not model the process of clarifying a thought as a student or group struggles with the task of finding exactly the precise words to articulate ideas.

3. The advantage claimed by requiring a response in asynchronous discussion is actually a disadvantage in that many required asynchronous responses are redundant and motivated by the need to fulfill a course requirement, not to further the group's understanding of an issue. Often asynchronous discussion responders do not "listen" to each other, and many students' comments go unacknowledged—a rude silence that does not occur in the face-to-face classroom.

4. The inefficiency of threaded discussions (especially when they are "open-mike sessions for airing thoughts on the subject") makes them very hard to manage in a way that teaches the process of critical thinking. Too often online discussion managers do not take the time or lack the talent to weave disorganized threads together. (Miller acknowledges that this is a talent an online instructor can acquire.)

I understand Miller's reservations from personal experience. Miller identifies some of the benefits I derive from teaching in face-to-face classrooms, which I do not get online. Certainly there are plenty of opportunities in my face-to-face classes for students to reveal their prejudices and oversimplifications and for me to intervene with Socratic questioning that coaches students in using the critical thinking process. But such responses also turn up in asynchronous discussions (although not as often) where some online students do indeed spontaneously type their unedited, emotional, and prejudiced comments. Impulsive emotional comments tend to diminish as the course progresses. Late in the semester I ask students in my online classes to consider in their journals when their earlier asynchronous responses show them applying impulsive emotional thinking and when their responses show evidence and sound reasoning. The advantage in my online class is that the students can review exactly what they wrote and in what context, whereas the face-to-face students have no record of their earlier class discussions. The reflective self-examination that promotes intellectual growth might be even more likely to occur in the online course because students can track their responses over the entire 15 weeks.

Rather than being a problem, an online class might be an even better environment than the traditional face-to-face classroom for teaching critical thinking and disciplinary reasoning. Online professors have in their toolboxes many of the strategies that work effectively in face-to-face classes. Indeed, employing active and interactive methods in online classes has transformed some professors' subsequent face-to-face practice (Palloff & Pratt, 2001).

## DISCUSSION OF SOLUTIONS: STRATEGIES FOR TEACHING THINKING IN ONLINE CLASSES

Many face-to-face classroom strategies for teaching students to think about course content can be used just as effectively online. Some are best suited for student responses as public postings in conference threads and bulletin board forums; some are more effective as private homework or formal writing assignments. Here are the recommended strategies:

1. Conduct opinion polls/surveys before assigned readings to arouse interest in topics and to assess and employ students' prior knowledge.
2. Design self-testing quizzes and tutorials to prepare students for well-grounded discussions.
3. Conduct interactive asynchronous discussions.
4. Pose well-designed questions for asynchronous discussion.
5. Create cognitive dissonance: provoke discomfort, unsettle confirmed notions, uncover misconceptions, inspire curiosity, pose problems.
6. Assign writing-to learn tasks as homework and/or discussion.
7. Present activities that require considering opposing views.
8. Assign a mediatory argument promoting a resolution acceptable to both sides.
9. Adopt collaborative and cooperative learning techniques, simulations, and role-plays to online uses.
10. Ask students to evaluate Internet resources.
11. Ask students to reflect on their responses to the course content and on their learning processes in private journals.
12. Develop critical thinking dispositions.
13. Promote critical consciousness.
14. Move students to higher intellectual stages.
15. Understand students' levels of self-directedness.

## 1.   Conduct Opinion Polls/Surveys Before Assigned Readings to Arouse Interest in Topics and to Assess and Employ Students' Prior Knowledge

Students, like everyone else, seem to have opinions on any issue whether they are well informed or not. A way to generate interest in assigned readings is before they are ready to take a survey of their opinions on the issue, or to pre-test their knowledge of the information presented in the readings. For example, one of my assignments in an argument and per-suasion class is to analyze and evaluate opposing views; students choose from a list of paired arguments in the textbook. Before their choice, stu-dents respond to a poll listing all the options and asking them with which of the two paired arguments they agree. For example, for the two environ-mental arguments, they are asked whether they agree with A or B, which restate the main claims of the two articles:

A.   The real environmental issue is not saving a few forests but adopting a philosophy of living in nature that contradicts the rationale of industrial capitalism.
B.   Radical environmentalists strangle innovation that could improve our economy.

A pre-reading variation of the poll-taking strategy is to list information and ideas from the assigned readings mixed with wrong information and ideas invented by the instructor. Ask students which information and ideas seem true/sensible and which seem not to be.

This strategy is useful for interesting students in issues and assigned readings but doesn't improve their thinking unless the next step is to ana-lyze and evaluate the evidence and reasons provided in the readings.

## 2. Design Self-Testing Quizzes and Tutorials to Prepare Students for Well-Grounded Discussions

In a Web course the usual sources of course content are a textbook and an instructor-written text, so it is important for students to test their under-standing of their reading. Some textbook publishers provide self-testing quizzes and tutorials at their companion Websites or provide software car-tridges for Web course delivery systems such as WebCT and Blackboard. Some Web course delivery packages include test-authoring software for professors to write their own quizzes, and provide secure procedures for students to take them. Free test-authoring software called *Hot Potatoes* is available at http://web.uvic.ca/hrd/halfbaked/. In addition to designating wrong answers, most test-authoring software allows the author to write comments about why the answers are wrong and what kind of erroneous thinking might have led students to choose them. Shapely (2000) designed online quizzes for her organic chemistry students, and this helped them to get better grades than her face-to-face students. Naidu and Bernard (1992) report that inserting questions and corrective feedback into textual materials improved learning among distance education nursing students. The University of Glasgow assesses knowledge of baseline philosophy concepts through its Web-based "assessment engine" (Stuart, 1999). An online tutorial for critical thinking (chiefly informal logic) is *Mission: Critical* at San Jose State University (http://www.sjsu.edu/depts/itl/). More and more universities are developing computer-based tutorials and intelligent agents to teach basic course material; for example, Andes at the U. S. Naval Academy to teach Newtonian physics (Schulze, Shelby, Treacy, & Wintersgill, 2000). A CD-ROM-based tutorial for nursing students improved their critical thinking skills (Oliver, Naidu, & Koronios, 2000).

How does a factual-recall quiz improve thinking? It doesn't, but a professor can make passing a quiz on an assigned reading the gateway to discussing it in the conference. Discussions are richer when students are prepared.

Tutorials and quizzes can also be used to teach concepts. The easiest way to provide self-testing quizzes to students is to ask questions in one file and provide sample good and poor answers in another. The students read the questions, write their answers privately, and then compare their answers with the models of good and poor answers provided online by the professor (with commentary). I use this approach in my argument and persuasion classes to model strong and weak explanations of logical fallacies.

## 3. Conduct Interactive Asynchronous Discussions

The active-learning strategies for teaching thinking described in this chapter can be used with individual students learning alone. However, situations in which students interact with other students have benefits that should not be passed up. A sense of being in a safe community helps some students take intellectual risks, helps people-oriented learners acquire the course content, exposes students to other perspectives, and provides additional student-generated ideas and information to think about. *All* the researchers who claim success at teaching critical thinking online attribute it to their use of discussion forums. One researcher who did observe more critical thinking in online discussions than in face-to-face classes believes he would have gotten even more with greater participation in the asynchronous discussions; well-managed online discussions are needed to improve student thinking (Bullen, 1998). Many other practitioners agree that interaction in discussions is crucial to promoting critical thinking in online classes (Zhu, 1998; see also Klemm, 1998; Klinger, 1992). Chong (1998) describes four basic models of asynchronous conference discussions in large classes:

1. ongoing discussion of topics,
2. case studies,
3. collaborative preparation for tests, and
4. discussions and projects in small groups, separate from the whole-class discussions.

Dennen (2001) provides useful strategies for creating and moderating online discussions.

A study by Marland et al., of what goes on in the heads of college-level distance learners when they read texts is not encouraging. Most of the time they were skimming, focusing only on information they knew were assessment items. They failed to employ strategies for deep learning even when they were aware of them; what thinking they did was of low quality (Marland, Patching, Putt, & Putt, 1990; Marland, Patching, & Putt, 1992). Active learning strategies are needed in distance learning courses to replace students' time-efficient strategies of skim-reading for tests. Asking students to discuss their reading with others sends them back to their reading.

Most of the strategies presented in this chapter for teaching thinking also promote student-student and student-teacher interaction in asynchronous discussions. The following list of common strategies for maintaining online discussions is gleaned from faculty training sessions and many articles about conducting asynchronous discussions—see, for example, Rossman (1999):

1. Create instructor- or student-initiated public discussion topics and make responding part of the course grade.
2. Begin by socializing. Ask for introductions and responses to introductions, reasons for taking the course, concerns about online courses, previous experiences with the course material or with online learning.
3. Require that students respond to each other's responses by asking questions, agreeing or disagreeing and elaborating, providing additional examples, etc.
4. Model appropriate responses without dominating the discussion; weave (integrate, summarize) several responses together and take the discussion a different direction every few days.
5. Make clear very early on that an online course takes as much time as a classroom course.
6. Establish guidelines for responses: civility (netiquette), length, depth, frequency.

7. Create a virtual lounge/cyber café for discussing topics that are peripheral to course-related topics or simply for socializing (discuss local sports teams, exchange interesting Websites, give away kittens).
8. Send a weekly e-mail message to the class telling them where they should be in the syllabus, announcing new discussion topics, and reminding them of looming deadlines.
9. Remind non-participants to get active.
10. Use chat sessions and study groups, with and without the instructor.

Bauer and Anderson (2000) suggest using rubrics to assess content, expression, and participation in online discussions. Based on their model, here is a sample rubric for assessing participation at the end of the semester. Each criterion, plus its value in points is shown:

• Contributions are timely, responsive to the instructions, thoroughly supported, relevant, refer to other students' posts, and display courtesy. (9-10)
• Contributions appear in all discussions but are not always thorough; participation is uneven throughout the semester. (7-8)
• Responses are usually brief; participation is occasional. (5-6)
• Responses are usually brief, sometimes irrelevant; participation is rare. (1-4)

Many of the other strategies discussed later in this chapter can be employed in asynchronous discussions. A longer list than these 10 tips may be found in *147 Practical Tips for Teaching Online: Essentials for Web-Based Education* by Donald E. Hanna, Michelle Glowacki-Dudka, and Simone Conceição-Runlee (2000). Two additional fine sources are by Rena M. Palloff and Keith Pratt: *Building Learning Communities in Cyberspace: Effective Strategies for the Online Classroom* (1999), and *Lessons from the Cyberspace Classroom: The Realities of Online Teaching* (2001). An article in the June 2000 issue of *Syllabus* magazine offers 12 tips for the new online instructor (Knowlton, Knowlton, & Davis, 2000).

## 4. Pose Well-Designed Questions for Asynchronous Discussion

Asynchronous discussions can take place in threaded conferences, study groups, chat sessions, or e-mail discussion lists. A survey of online instructors showed that the top technique for keeping online discussions on topic was to ask well-designed questions (Beaudlin, 1999). There are several approaches to asking good questions. Appendix A contains typical questions derived from the ubiquitous Bloom higher order thinking taxonomy.

Richard Paul (1993b, pp. 297-298) suggests an equally helpful list of questions. His questions (Appendix B) are useful in probing and extending student thinking in Socratic fashion (see also Paul, 1993c).

Browne and Keeley (2001) structure the chapters in their critical thinking textbook *Asking The Right Questions* around these broad questions (suitable for asking at the right moment in an asynchronous discussion):

- What is the issue and the conclusion?
- What are the reasons?
- What words or phrases are ambiguous?
- What are the value conflicts and assumptions?
- What are the descriptive assumptions?
- Are there any fallacies in the reasoning?
- How good is the evidence?
- Are there rival causes?
- Are the statistics deceptive?
- What significant information is omitted?
- What reasonable conclusions are possible?

Thoms and Juniad (1997) compile a similar list of questions that promote critical thinking.

## 5. Create Cognitive Dissonance: Provoke Discomfort, Unsettle Confirmed Notions, Uncover Misconceptions, Inspire Curiosity, Pose Problems

A major misgiving of critics of online learning is that without the physical presence of a Socratic teacher asking provocative questions, students will not learn to think critically (Groothius, 1999; Carstens & Worsford, 2000). The online professor, however, can pose questions that create cognitive dissonance. The point here is not to befuddle students but to dispel complacency. A student's reflective critical thinking process is started by a triggering question or event (Brookfield, 1987). Accompanying a disorienting intellectual situation is a wish to resolve it. Students who experience a gap in their knowledge will seek to fill it. Students who see that an incorrect or misapplied procedure won't solve a problem will want to learn a procedure that will. To create cognitive dissonance, the online instructor can design a task that uses students' prior learning but also requires factual information or procedures that the students do not know. Students become aware of a gap between the task's goal and what they need to know or to do to meet it (Beyer, 1987). Creating in students the need to know is a basic strategy underlying inquiry learning and problem-based learning; the strategy works in online classes as well as it does in face-to-face classrooms.

The questions suggested by Richard Paul in Section 4, above, are especially useful to push online discussions into areas that challenge students' unconfirmed assumptions. Socratic questioning is a variation on this theme. The basic structure of Socratic questioning begins with inquiry, leads to perplexity, and ends with enlightenment (Morse, 1998). Socratic questioning as Socrates practiced it was oral, spontaneous, and one-on-one; a professor cannot replicate Socrates' method asynchronously. But online variations of true Socratic dialogue can confront students with new contradictory evidence in mid-discussion, challenge old beliefs and prejudices, and lead to intellectual growth and enlightenment.

Other ways of creating cognitive dissonance are first to present a theory, concept, or principle and the examples that confirm it; then follow by presenting discrepant examples that do not match the theory. Ask for an explanation of why the new example does not fit the old knowledge. Because the students' engagement in the question was initially inspired by cognitive dissonance, their investigation and resolution of anomalies is more likely to lead to deep learning. On an historical scale, according to Thomas Kuhn (1970), this is the process that leads to paradigm shifts within disciplines.

Providing students with unsettled issues to explore is a very useful triggering event that can start the critical thinking process on a particular case and can also promote movement to higher intellectual stages. According to Nist (1993), students enter college with many misconceptions. Their high school experience has provided a mistaken schema of what learning is (acquiring and memorizing teacher-told facts) and of what research is (acquiring and reporting information on a topic). Students sometimes enter disciplinary studies with misconceptions of the research methods of that field (for example, believing that the scientific method is the enemy of faith or that the purpose of critical thinking is to attack opponents). It sometimes takes a disorienting experience to change their inaccurate schemata.

One of my own strategies to create cognitive dissonance is to ask my online students to identify a list of statements as fact or interpretation. Students arrive in college with a good many misconceptions, including the following:

- Questions have right or wrong answers.
- Facts are statements that are true (the right answers).
- Knowledge is out there somewhere for them to discover.

Being asked to identify a "fact" and "interpretation" is a step towards dispelling these misconceptions and to moving them to higher stages of intellectual development. For example, students could decide which of the following statements are facts and which are interpretations:

1. Timothy McVeigh bombed the federal building in Oklahoma City.
2. Smoking cigarettes causes lung cancer, heart disease, and emphysema, and may complicate pregnancy.
3. The population of the United States in 2000, according to the Census Bureau, was between 281-284 million people (depending on whether the actual count or adjusted count is used).
4. In the beginning God created the heaven and the earth.
5. The speed of light is 186,282 miles per second.
6. The sun revolves around the earth.
7. The earth revolves around the sun.
8. Women, African Americans, and Native Americans have been treated unfairly by white men in America during previous centuries.
9. George W. Bush won the 2000 Presidential election.
10. A "fact" is anything I believe is true.

Most students regard a fact as anything they believe to be "objectively proved" and therefore true. My intention, however, is to convince students that a fact is an interpretation that has been accepted. It might not be true. In my first-year classes, students disagree about these items, so they expect me to provide the correct answer. My reply is to tell them that there are problems with their notion of a fact: they believe that a fact is a statement that is "true" or that can be "objectively verified." Truth and fact are not always the same. This discussion is about fact, not truth. For some students, this discussion about fact and interpretation can be intellectually transforming—the first step towards the disorienting realization that certain truth is not out there to discover by learning from the authorities. Most students then begin to move beyond Perry's first stage of intellectual development, dualism (authorities know all the correct answers). Most now start their move beyond Perry's second stage, multiplicity (people have a right to their own opinion; who is to say who is right?), because they see the importance of considering an interpretation carefully before accepting it. They accept the responsibility of being a critical thinker, of evaluating evidence and reasons (Peirce, 2001).

Stewart (2001) describes a writing assignment using primary documents about the Conestoga Massacre of 1763 that challenges students' notions that knowledge is simple and absolute and produces the "excitement inherent in higher order thinking" (p. 165) in their struggle to make sense of differing perspectives on a troubling event in American history.

## 6.   Assign Writing-to-Learn Tasks as Homework and/or Discussion

Assigning formal and informal writing tasks in online classes is essential to improving student thinking. That writing shapes thinking has both a theoretical and a research base (Vygotsky, 1962; Langer & Applebee, 1987). The following list of potential writing-to-learn tasks comes from several fine books on teaching disciplinary thinking in face-to-face classes and are easily adapted to the online environment: John C. Bean, *Engaging Ideas: The Professor's Guide to Integrating Writing, Critical Thinking, and Active Learning in the Classroom* (1996); Chet Meyers and Thomas B. Jones, *Promoting Active Learning: Strategies for the Classroom* (1993); and Tracey E. Sutherland and Charles C. Bonwell (eds.) *Using Active Learning in College Classes: A Range of Options for Faculty* (1996).

### Formal Writing Assignments

In formal writing assignments, students fully develop their ideas, use topic sentences, and pay attention to sentence structure and grammar. These tasks can range from one-paragraph micro themes to semester-long research papers. Have students support a thesis that responds to an instructor-posed problem, or ask them to select their own thesis.

### Informal Exploratory Writing

Exploratory writing is unedited and rapid informal writing that resembles inner speech. Informal writing tasks on course-based topics are an especially good device for promoting course-based thinking. Tasks can range from simple ones that ask for 10 minutes of instant speculation, application of chapter concepts to simple or complex cases, complex problem solving, summaries or responses to assigned readings, analytical evaluations of assigned readings, and introspective connections of the course concepts to personal life and experience. Students can place private, personal applications in their assignment folders; less personal topics can be posted in a public conference (discussion group). For example, I ask students in my argument course to respond in the public conference to a question about whether the government should ban liquor ads on television; then a week later I ask them how their response demonstrated the characteristics of a good thinker as described in the textbook. This potentially embarrassing self-disclosure is posted in their assignment folder that only I can read. An example of a public personal response is one where I ask my online business-writing students to explain in a public conference whether their assignments in college courses have prepared them well for workplace writing. Some say yes, some say no; but the varied personal responses provoke an analysis of context and audience and the generalizability of writing experiences. Asking for personal responses and applications is especially useful when developing students' attitudes, and values is an important goal of the course.

### Apply the Concepts of the Textbook Chapters to Cases or Issues Every Week

Asking students to apply course concepts in informal writing tasks such as homework assignments is probably the most obvious and frequently used approach. These tasks can be posted on a conference or electronic bulletin board, stored in the student's assignment portfolio, or e-mailed to the instructor. Responses can be written by groups or by individuals, depending on what the instructor has in mind.

Asking 25 students to respond individually to one scenario or topic in a conference will result in thoughtful responses from the first three responders and "I think so too" from the remaining 22. To avoid boring repetition, a professor can pose variations of a generic scenario to a smaller population of 3-4 students. For example, assign scenario #1 to names beginning A-C, scenario #2 to D-G, etc.

Grading each student's homework every week is probably more work than most instructors have time for. One way to lighten the workload is to store the students' work in an assignment folder in the course Website and read it every four-six weeks, grading the accumulated collection holistically (one grade for the total accumulation) according to criteria such as timeliness, thoroughness, and responsiveness to the instructions. Another way to shorten the assessment time is to grade only a representative sample of a semester's homework assignments (after informing students of the sampling procedure). The use of rubrics similar to those devised by Bauer and Anderson (2000) will speed grading and feedback (see item 3, above).

### Tasks for Small-Group Problem Solving and Inquiry-Based Discussions

When small groups collaborate to prepare a single written response to an instructor-posed problem, students' thinking is clarified as they consider, negotiate, and evaluate several perspectives. Open-ended questions with no single right answer work especially well. Some examples of short, one-to-two week small-group projects are:

- Compare the usefulness/reliability of course-related Websites (instructor provides the URLs).
- Prepare both sides of a debatable issue.
- Predict what will happen if . . .
- Recommend two alternatives to solving problem X.
- List 10 significant questions NOT addressed by the assigned reading and select the top three, explaining their importance.
- Apply the principles relevant to case X in the textbook to this new situation (case Y); explain how the two cases are similar and different.

Some problems can prompt students to explore the full complexity of an issue. Examples are:

- How would you establish the reliability of procedure X?
- On what grounds could you oppose the theory that . . .?

- If we didn't believe that this theory explains X behavior, how else could you explain it?
- A problem in our society is X; what are some good ways to investigate its causes?
- How do we establish certainty/truth/validity/probability in the investigation of X?

Lynch and Wolcott (2001) describe four increasingly complex steps that produce critical thinking in solving open-ended problems:

Step 1.   Identify the problem to be addressed, identify needed relevant information, and identify any uncertainties that are part of the problem or issue.

Step 2.   Investigate various interpretations and the supporting evidence, including one's own biases and assumptions; organize the information.

Step 3.   List alternatives in priority order using appropriate criteria for audience and context.

Step 4.   Synthesize various solutions; consider limitations; consider strategies to re-examine the issue.

### Questions for Socratic Dialogue
Useful for systematic, follow-up probing to lead students to an increasingly complex discussion. See item 4, above for sample questions.

### Practice Exam Questions
Practice and feedback on representative essay questions.

### Other Sources of Activities and Writing Tasks
Instructors at universities with writing across the curriculum programs may be familiar with writing-to-learn tasks that can be assigned as weekly homework, exchanged among students, or collected in a course portfolio. The Clearinghouse for Resources on Academic Writing at Colorado State (http://aw.colostate.edu/resource_list.htm) lists resources, including Web links, bibliographies, articles, and programs at other colleges and universities. Instructors at colleges without teaching and learning centers can find many resources at Online Resources for Higher Education: University of Kansas Center for Teaching Excellence at http://eagle.cc.ukans.edu/~cte/OtherSites.html). Another useful source is the Web resources for teaching online and other uses of electronic communication across the curriculum maintained by Donna Reiss at http://www.tc.cc.va.us/faculty/tcreisd/projects/ecac/ecacsite.htm . The Center for Critical Thinking at Sonoma State University (http://www.criticalthinking.org) publishes

excellent resources for teaching thinking, as does the Maryland Community College Consortium for Teaching Reasoning (http://academic.pg.cc.md.us/~wpeirce/MCCCTR).

Several publishers have issued guides to writing that contain sample assignments as well as advice to students about how to do them. Allyn and Bacon publishes *Writing for Psychology* (Thaiss & Sanford, 2000), *Writing in Political Science* (Schmidt, 2000), *How to Write Psychology Papers* (Parrott, 1999), and the *Short Guide to Writing* series: art (Barnet, 2001), film (Corrigan, 2001), music, (Bellman, 2000), literature (Barnet & Cain, 2000), chemistry (Beal & Trimbur, 2001), social science (Cuba, 2002), history (Marius & Page, 2002), biology (Pechenik, 2001), science (Porush, 1995), Houghton Mifflin publishes the *Writer's Guide* series: history (Steffens & Dickerson, 1987), life sciences (Biddle & Bean, 1987), political science (Biddle & Holland, 1987), psychology (Bond & Magistrale, 1987). St. Martin's Press publishes *A Guide to Writing Sociology Papers* (Richlin-Klonsky & Strenski, E., 1994). Bedford/St. Martin's publishes *Thinking and Writing about Philosophy* (Bedau, 2002) and *Thinking and Writing about Literature* (Meyer, 2001).

Another well-known source of activities that apply course concepts and strategies for informally assessing students' work on them is Thomas D. Angelo and K. Patricia Cross, *Classroom Assessment Techniques* (1993). A few instructors have described their experience with these informal assessment techniques in computer-mediated classes: Gandolfo and Carver (1995); Creed (1998).

## 7.  Present Activities That Require Considering Opposing Views

Online students, like face-to-face students, tend to regard asynchronous discussions as a place to talk, not listen. In a study of reasons why college students wanted to have discussions, Trosset (1998) discovered that the chief reason was that the students wanted to convince others of their own strongly held views—not to understand other perspectives! To move students away from this self-centered and close-minded approach to discussion, online professors can ask students to consider opposing views, methods, data, principles, concepts, definitions, interpretations, and conclusions. Dialectical thinking (sometimes called dialogical thinking) is one of the best ways to engage students' minds, challenge their previously held beliefs, promote open-mindedness, defer the rush to judgment, and move them to higher intellectual stages. Discussing opposing points of view requires knowledge, reasoned judgment, and intellectual criteria to adopt a position and explain why it's better than the alternative (Paul, 1993b). Richard Paul (1994) writes that considering opposing views is crucial to developing critical thinking "in the strong sense." Critical thinking in the strong sense goes beyond merely applying technical thinking skills and becomes a path that "frees one from dominance by the views, the frames of reference, the worldviews" that one is exploring (p. 182).

*Academic Controversy* by David W. Johnson, Roger T. Johnson, and Karl A. Smith (1997) outlines a five-step procedure for structured four-student group projects that engage students in exploring opposing views on an issue. Although they used their method in face-to-face classes, it can work just as well online. Two pairs of students in each group are assigned the pro or con position; each pair begins by exploring the assigned position:

Step 1.   Each pair researches its assigned position and plans how to develop an argument presenting the evidence and reasons that support its assigned position.

Step 2.   Each pair presents its well-developed argument to the other pair. Each side listens attentively, taking notes and seeking to understand the other's position.

Step 3.   Students engage in free discussion, persuasively supporting their position and refuting the opposing position by criticizing its weaknesses.

Step 4.   Each pair reverses its positions and sincerely presents the best case possible for the opposite side, using notes from their Step 3 discussion and additional information. Both sides try to understand both positions equally well.

Step 5.   Students abandon advocacy of their assigned position to formulate a position all four students can support. This requires a synthesis of both perspectives into a new position that incorporates the best evidence and reasoning of both sides. The students finish by writing a single group report supporting the new consensus position.

The five-step group procedure encourages a group to look honestly at both sides of a controversy, although individual students often have trouble overcoming their prejudices and misconceptions. When thinking about controversial issues, students can delude themselves by cultural and ego-serving barriers that block a clear and honest consideration. Rooney (2000) describes an application of the academic controversy strategy to a business writing assignment that confronts students with ambiguity and multiple perspectives.

Individual students writing in their online journals (discussed in item 11, below) can use a different method of considering opposing views with an open mind. Peter Elbow (1973, 1986) recommends a method that students can use when they want to deal in a ruthlessly honest way with a difficult emotional and intellectual issue. Elbow calls his method playing the believing game and the doubting game; it asks the student to consider both sides of an issue with full sympathy for both sides, to take a dialectical approach to opposing views. To play the believing game, students must imagine that they genuinely believe everything they read in a text and fully sympathize with the values that support it. They need to identify with people such as the text's author whose experience has taught them that this point of view is right, honorable, and logically consistent. This deliberate, empathetic identification is easy with views students already hold, but it is difficult with viewpoints with which they disagree. The benefits for students in playing the believing game with ideas they already agree with are:

1.  They can write a better, more accurate summary of the text.
2.  They can identify connections with other values and ideas that are not in the text and therefore expand their understanding.
3.  With this fuller understanding they can explain their positions more clearly and forcefully.

But what about the benefits of imagining that they identify with viewpoints that they disagree with? Answer: They get the same benefits. In addition, the effort of understanding a position that they disagree with develops students' reasoning processes and maybe even their compassion and ability to empathize with their fellow human beings.

The doubting game has similar benefits. The doubting game is a search for the errors and limitations of the thinking and values that support a position. Discovering logical fallacies, identifying invalid or weak evidence, and uncovering shallow or self-serving values in an argument can result from playing the doubting game—whether it is the students' own position they are pretending to doubt, or opposing views to which they genuinely object. By discovering the limitations of the other side, students can have more confidence in the validity of their views. By discovering by ruthless examination the weaknesses of their own position, they can find better evidence, better reasoning, and more significant values to support it.

In actual practice, the believing and doubting games take written form in three ways: margin annotations, notes, and nonstop free writing. Here are the instructions to give students:

*   *Margin Annotations and Notes: Reading as a Believer*
    Write page annotations and notes, reading the text as a believer, agreeing with everything you read. Understand the line of reasoning, seek out the evidence, and appreciate the values that support the position. Underline them, identify them in the margins, and transfer the annotations to your notebook.
*   *Margin Annotations and Notes: Reading as a Doubter*
    Then read as a doubter, challenging the reasoning and evidence. Look for weaknesses and gaps; reject the values that support the position; come up with problems that the author does not deal with well;

think of examples from your experience or reading that counter what the author is saying. Note these objections in the margins; transfer them to your notebook.

- *Nonstop Free-writing in the Roles of Believer and Doubter*
  As a final step, do two nonstop free-writings of 10-30 minutes each: once as a believer, then for the same length of time as a doubter. Play the roles well; identify with people who hold those beliefs and doubts. Respond to the text and your notes. Use the fast, free-associating, non-censoring process of nonstop, controlled, focused free-writing to promote an emotional and intellectual connection with both sides of the issue.

Many textbook publishers offer anthologies containing opposing views. At least two publishers, Greenhaven Press and Dushkin of McGraw Hill, offer a rich series of paperback anthologies of opposing views.

## 8. Assign a Mediatory Argument Promoting a Resolution Acceptable to Both Sides

Whether in an online class or face-to-face, one unfortunate effect of teaching argumentative writing is that it encourages students to interest themselves only in supporting their position convincingly (winning), not in understanding the enculturation that underpins their opinions, nor in genuinely understanding other perspectives. Whether groups employ the academic controversy approach (Johnson, Johnson, & Smith, 1997, 2000) or individuals play the believing-doubting game (Elbow, 1973, 1986), students can be asked rather than to support a position on an issue, to instead propose a solution acceptable to both sides of an issue. The *Aims of Argument* by Timothy W. Crusius and Carolyn E. Channell (2000) teaches how to write an argument to mediate or negotiate. The purpose of the argument to negotiate, according to Crusius and Channell, is to seek consensus within an audience polarized by differences in a context where there is a need to cooperate and preserve relations. Such an argument requires students to understand the implications of their position and to understand how their proposal may affect others. Like other forms of argument, the mediatory argument requires reasons and evidence and a clear understanding of opposing views. But unlike the argument to support a position or to persuade, the mediatory argument seeks to persuade opposing sides to resolve the matter in a way that satisfies both sides. Writing an argument to mediate or negotiate approach can extend students' thinking beyond their simply supporting one side of a dichotomy.

A variation of this is the one already described by Johnson, Johnson, and Smith (2000) in *Academic Controversy*, who report evidence that students who use their approach in cooperative contexts are better at understanding perspectives other than their own initial position on an issue. Lynch, George, and Cooper (1997) describe an argument-writing course that combines features of both agonistic rhetoric and cooperative communication in a way that moves students to inquire deeply into an issue in order to understand the roots of their beliefs, to understand all perspectives on a social policy issue, to understand the history and circumstances surrounding an issue, and to understand how proposed solutions will affect those involved.

## 9.   Adopt Collaborative and Cooperative Learning Techniques, Simulations, and Role-Plays to Online Uses

Collaborative and cooperative learning techniques go beyond simply having students talk about the course content in asynchronous discussions. Professors can ask teams to collaborate on formal or informal writing-to-learn tasks these can range from formal reports to the professor, or informal briefings to the rest of the class. Constructivist pedagogy provides the theoretical base for collaborative learning in online courses (Mayes, 2001).

A shared component of both online and collaborative and cooperative learning is that students must learn the course material out of class—a feature that makes online and collaborative and cooperative learning especially compatible. The effectiveness of collaborative and cooperative learning is well established (Bruffee, 1999; Johnson, Johnson, & Smith, 1998; Millis, 2001). Also well established is the effectiveness of collaborative and cooperative learning in developing critical thinking and intellectual development (Nelson, 1994). By "collaborative and cooperative learning," some practitioners simply mean group tasks (or tasks done by pairs) using active learning strategies to apply course content. But other practitioners make a clear distinction between "collaborative" and "cooperative" learning, using "collaborative" as the broader term for work done by groups of two or more, and "cooperative" as the more specific term to refer to well-structured, outcome-focused tasks done by two or more students working together in ways that require group interdependence and individual accountability (Millis & Cottell, 1998; see Bruffee, 1995 for a different distinction). Most of the successful case studies and examples found in the literature about collaborative and cooperative learning are from face-to-face classrooms where this strategy is effective because of the immediate physical presence of the participants. However, many collaborative and cooperative learning activities can be adapted to synchronous discussions (instant messenger exchanges, chatrooms and MOOs where convenient), to asynchronous discussion, and to group projects. *[Editor's note:*

*MOOs are text-based, virtual reality sites that allow people to connect to the same place at the same time. They are completely unlike conventional chatrooms in that they allow the manipulation and interaction with cyber-objects in addition to live communication.]*

Group projects online need to be managed even more carefully than face-to-face groups. When graded cooperative group projects are set up, it is most important to give very clear instructions for the task and for how the group should function (roles and social processes), how they will be graded, and how they can get help from the instructor (Bailey, 1998; Felder & Brent, 2001; Millis, 2000a; 2000b).

Envisioning online classes as the ideal environment for learning centered teaching, Duffy, Dueber, and Hawley (1998) have designed a Web-hosted, text-based conferencing system supporting collaborative inquiry and critical thinking. Based on problem-based-learning strategies, it also employs many of the strategies described in this chapter. The Duffy, Dueber, and Hawley model (called ACT: Asynchronous Collaboration Tool) incorporates five goals of critical thinking and inquiry:

1. Acknowledge the common beliefs and goals that define the scientific community: seek a solution that satisfies the scientific community, use evidence to support claims, allowing results to be criticized.
2. Follow a structured method of inquiry: define the problem, develop and test alternate solutions, seek a resolution, develop an action plan, reflectively assess the process.
3. Use strong arguments at each stage of the problem-solving process: testing hypotheses, evaluating counterarguments, and examining evidence.
4. Establish a high quality of relevant reasons and evidence.
5. Conduct two forms of collaborative discussion: first employ conversational inquiry, followed by issue-based inquiry and systematic analysis where students use the elements of structured inquiry and argument.

Professors can adapt many features of their model even if the ACT conference software is not available to them.

Simulations on the Web are another opportunity for collaborative learning. Software especially designed for Web-based simulations (Fablusi) is described by Ip, Linser, and Naidu (2001); see also Linser and Naidu (1999). Casto and Bulcroft (2000) describe an election project using the Web; Holt, Kleiber, and Jill (1998) describe a collaborative project based on the National Issues Forum. Collis (1997) describes a collaborative project using the Web in an educational technology and instruction class.

Many of the activities already described in this chapter work well for pairs and small groups rather than as whole-class activities. Working in collaborative and cooperative groups online is worth a separate chapter, so this chapter will only provide a few resources. In addition to the sources already cited in this section, course-specific examples of collaborative and cooperative learning activities can be found in many places; for example, the *Journal of Cooperation and Collaboration in College Teaching* (http://63.77.23.108/news_jccpage.htm), and several collections published by the National Center on Postsecondary Teaching, Learning, and Assessment (http://www.ed.psu.edu/cshe/htdocs/pubs/nctla_pubs.htm). Many high school examples in *Enhancing Thinking Through Cooperative Learning* (Davidson & Worsham, 1992) can be adapted to college online courses. Several Websites serve as resources for cooperative learning: a list of sites recommended by Barbara Millis (2000c) can be found at the TLT Group (http://www.tlt-group.org/gilbert/cooplearning.htm); another very comprehensive site is maintained by Ted Panitz (http://home.capecod.net/~tpanitz/).

## 10.   Ask Students to Evaluate Internet Resources

One single task—evaluating Internet resources—requires critical thinking appropriate for any online course. Realizing that the Information Highway was quickly becoming the Information Landfill, librarians during the last several years have published many articles on why and how college professors should design research assignments that exercise students' critical thinking skills in using the Internet. The following general strategies for students to use are compiled from several articles encouraging critical thinking in evaluating Internet sources (Fitzgerald, 1997; see also Brem & Boyes, 2000; Browne, Freeman, & Williamson, 2000; Jones, 1996; Lederer, 2000; Lynch, Vernon, & Smith, 2001; Shively & Van Fossen, 1999):

- Adopt a skeptical attitude towards all Internet sources.
- Ground yourself thoroughly by wide reading on your topic.
- Discover the dates and authorship of information on Websites.
- Establish the reliability of sources.
- Distinguish fact from opinion.
- Examine the stated and unstated assumptions.
- Compare information from several sources.
- Discover bias: does the host Website support a point of view on the issue?

The online research tutorial at the University of California at Berkeley includes detailed evaluation criteria for Internet information, and strategies for applying the criteria to a variety of reliable and unreliable Websites on such topics as gun control, stem cell research and cloning humans, and aspartame (University of California, 1995, revised 2001). Among the most frequently cited guides to evaluating Internet information is Elizabeth E.

Kirk's detailed list of criteria (1996; revised 2001) at the Milton S. Eisenhower Library at the Johns Hopkins University. A comprehensive list of resources, including bibliographies, on evaluating Web information is maintained by Alistair Smith for the World Wide Web Virtual Library (Smith, 2001).

## 11. Ask Students to Reflect on Their Responses to the Course Content and on Their Learning Processes in Private Journals

Writing self-reflective responses improves students' metacognitive abilities, promotes personal holistic engagement in learning, and promotes intellectual development. The effectiveness of using journals and logs has been established for many years, and they are standard writing assignments in schools and colleges with writing across the curriculum programs (see Fulwiler, 1987; Kerka, 1996). Recently, the effective use of reflective journals in online classes has been enthusiastically described (Andrusynszyn, 1997; Kang, 1998).

Metacognition is thinking about thinking. "Metacognition is being aware of our thinking as we perform specific tasks and then using this awareness to control what we are doing" (Marzano et al., 1988, p. 9). Metacognition helps students transfer knowledge, skills, and abilities acquired in one context to other contexts. To increase their metacognitive abilities, students need to possess three kinds of knowledge: declarative, procedural, and conditional. Declarative knowledge is the factual information that students know; it can be declared—spoken or written. Procedural knowledge is their knowledge of how to do something, of how to perform the steps in a process. Conditional knowledge is knowledge about when to use a procedure, skill, or strategy (and when not to use it); why a procedure works and under what conditions; and why one procedure is better than another.

Metacognitive knowledge requires awareness of all three kinds of knowledge, and it is best developed by having students reflect on their thinking processes. Cognitive scientists believe that improving students' metacognitive abilities is crucial to improving their thinking. And educators believe that reflecting on one's learning processes is crucial to becoming a better learner. Students can move towards both goals by writing self-reflective commentary on the course content and on their learning processes in private journals. Most Web course delivery systems have private assignment areas accessible only by the student and the instructor; they serve as useful depositories for such tasks. I grade course journals holistically at the end of the semester on the criteria of thoroughness and responsiveness to my questions.

Self-reflective responses can also accompany formal writing assignments. In my online analytical reading and writing course, each student's graded formal writing assignment is accompanied by informal writing tasks in which students reflect on their thinking and learning processes. For example, accompanying their long researched persuasive argument are three separate informal writing tasks that ask students to reflect on their learning and to write self-assessments:

1.  Write a self-assessment of how well you employed the course guide's recommended strategies for writing in a personal voice.
2.  Write a self-assessment of how well you followed the textbook's advice about responding to a rough draft review by a classmate.
3.  To improve your performance on future research tasks, write a reflective, self-assessment of your research process for this assignment, responding to the specific items on the checklist in the course guide.

A similar example from a business writing class is provided by McEachern (1999) who has students write two papers in response to a case: one following the instructions for the case study, the other describing how they dealt with each component of the textbook's advice for analyzing the case. The metacognitive reflection helps students increase much-needed abilities and helps the professor give students useful feedback on their thinking process as well as their written product.

An essential component of metacognition is self-assessing one's learning process and then self-regulating in response to the self-assessment. Experts internalize their declarative, procedural, and conditional knowledge by frequently applying it. Beginners should be consciously aware at first of their metacognitive knowledge as they apply each piece of information at each step, consciously making decisions and knowing the reasons for their decisions. Automatic application soon follows.

In addition to its cognitive benefits, self-reflection promotes deep learning by engaging students in their learning and is a key component in holistic learning (Lee, 1999; Grauerholz, 2001). Reflection is especially helpful in moving students to higher stages of intellectual development (Baxter Magolda, 2000).

A free online assessment instrument can also be used by professors to obtain periodic anonymous information from students about difficulties they are having with any aspect of the course. The Student Assessment of Learning Gains (SALG) survey is available from the National Institute for Science Education at the Wisconsin Center for Education Research at http://www.wcer.wisc.edu/nise/Related_Links. After registering their courses, instructors can customize the SALG to suit their courses and ask students at intervals throughout the course to fill out the SALG. Instructors then access the site to read the tabulated results and anonymous student comments.

## 12. Develop Critical Thinking Dispositions

There is more to teaching critical thinking than showing online students how to analyze an argument, support a hypothesis, or solve the problems presented in online courses. It is not enough to require students to perform thinking operations and tasks. They should also be disposed to carrying them out on their own, unasked. Robert Ennis's (1987, p. 12) list of critical thinking dispositions has guided instructors of critical thinking for many years:

- Seek a clear statement of the thesis or question.
- Seek reasons.
- Try to be well informed.
- Use and mention believable sources.
- Take into account the total situation.
- Try to remain relevant to the main point.
- Keep in mind the original and/or basic concern.
- Look for alternatives.
- Be open-minded.
- Take a position (and change a position) when the evidence and reasons are sufficient to do so.
- Seek as much precision as the subject permits.
- Deal in an orderly manner with the parts of a complex whole.
- Use one's critical thinking abilities.
- Be sensitive to the feelings, level of knowledge, and degree of sophistication of others.

Beyer (pp. 211-213, 1987) recommends four teaching strategies for teaching these dispositions. All four can be employed online:

1. Model behaviors that demonstrate the desired dispositions.
2. Insist on student behavior that reflects the dispositions sought.
3. Engage students in repeated activities that require use of these dispositions.
4. Reinforce behaviors that demonstrate the appropriate disposition.

In a later book Beyer (1997) amplifies these recommendations and adds additional strategies such as acknowledging ambiguity and the impossibility or difficulty of achieving certainty on most problems or topics. Dealing with uncertainty is difficult for students at early stages of intellectual development.

Arthur Costa (2001) has developed a list of 16 habits of mind that are roughly similar to Ennis's list of 14 dispositions and includes such habits as persisting, thinking about thinking, and thinking interdependently.

Richard Paul, one of the leaders in promoting critical thinking in education, introduces one more dimension to critical thinking: fair-mindedness. Paul's (1993a) experience as a college professor showed him three kinds of thinkers:

1.  The uncritical thinker who sees or searches for one correct answer and whose views are acquired from the thinking of others (parents, teachers, peers).
2.  The self-serving critical thinker who finds confirmation of egocentric prejudices, is good at finding fallacies in others' arguments, and is primarily concerned with winning arguments—not with accuracy, fairness, and understanding other views.
3.  The fair-minded critical thinker who values reason as the path to belief, genuinely considers the other side, and genuinely wrestles with dilemmas.

In both the asynchronous and face-to-face class, the professor can exhort students to be fair-minded and can probably find in student discussions examples of all three kinds of thinkers.

## 13.   Promote Critical Consciousness

Professors can do more than teach thinking. Educators in the critical pedagogy movement are concerned that teaching the accepted patterns and formulas of disciplinary logic is a limited approach because it merely produces in students the technical competencies they need to function in their disciplines. Students are often taught disciplinary facts, theories, and methods as if these disciplinary concepts were value-free, producing in students an uncritical acceptance of the status quo (Giroux, 1994), promoting conformity rather than independent critical examination of the political perspectives that support the concepts (Kaplan, 1994). The theory of conscientization in Paulo Freire's *The Pedagogy of the Oppressed* (1970) presents a process of transformation ending in critical consciousness. Freire and those he has inspired see this transformation happening because of classroom dialogue (Stage, Muller, Kinzie, & Simmons, 1998). The democratic, authority-undermining student-teacher dialogue and student-student interaction that promotes critical consciousness might be even more successful asynchronously than face to face because of the absence of traditional symbols such as podiums and desks facing reverently forward. Lapadat (2001a) and Zukas (1999) note that asynchronous discussion can be more student-centered than the instructor-dominated discussion typical of the face-to-face classroom (Cooper & Selfe, 1990)

Courses that cross disciplinary boundaries are especially useful for promoting critical consciousness. In every discipline, knowledge is established by employing the standard methods and gathering the reliable data accepted by the experts in that field. It is almost inevitable that the values inherent in one discipline's epistemological assumptions will conflict with another discipline's. Two sources of dialogic learning can be exploited: the tension between established knowledge and newly acquired knowledge, and the tensions between different perspectives in different disciplines (Cooper, 1994). Borg and Borg (2001) describe the critical thinking that resulted when conflicts in methodology and world view were explored when an economics and literature course and an economics and biology course were combined in two interdisciplinary honors seminars,

Professors' questions can lead students to consider whether the methods of investigation in their field promote one approach over another. In psychology, for example, does the reigning methodology favor behavioral or pharmacological therapy over analytical therapy? Do research funding sources or procedures privilege some methods or goals over others? Do racial, ethnic, gender, political, economic groups, or corporations gain by some methods of investigation more than others?

Even critical thinking has its challenges: Is the argumentative paper a western, male-dominated, authoritarian, adversarial genre that puts women at a disadvantage, as Huber (1989) has argued? Academic discourse emphasizes a disguise of objectivity that separates the inquirer from the object of knowing, and it emphasizes that the arguer's goal is dominance over skeptics or rival claims (Ong, 1981). Does the adversarial argument encourage premature closure in student thinking? Do critical thinking courses undermine religious belief? Do critical thinking courses serve liberal or conservative agendas on their campuses? Is it time to reexamine our current notions of critical thinking, as recommended in a recent issue of *Inquiry* (Thayer-Bacon, 2000a)? Should we acknowledge that critical thinking is a culture- and gender-limited tool that needs to be enhanced by imagination, intuition, and emotion (Thayer-Bacon, 2000b).

## 14. Move Students to Higher Stages of Intellectual Development

One of the legitimate concerns about online learning is that online students are isolated from the potentially intellectual conversations that occur spontaneously in college dorm rooms, hallways, lounges, and lawns, and will therefore miss the intellectual growth that often comes from dealing with opposing views and the need to support one's opinion. Indeed, students often begin college at an intellectual stage of development where they uncritically believe anything that authorities tell them, or they regard all points of view as having equal validity. These are the first stages in three different models of intellectual development widely used to describe the stages of intellectual growth college students evolve through. Two older models of intellectual development are described by William G. Perry, Jr. (1970) in *Forms of Intellectual and Ethical Development in the College Years: A Scheme* and Mary Field Belenky, Blythe McVicker Clinchy, Nancy Rule Goldberger, and Jill Mattuck Tarule (1986) in *Women's Ways of Knowing: The Development of Self, Voice, and Mind.* Both books chart intellectual development from a beginning position of accepting factual knowledge from authorities without questioning either the facts or the authorities. The highest stage is commitment to a position arrived at through genuinely considering opposing views, examining personal experience, and engaging in personal reflection, without relying on the assurance of external authorities. A more recent model of intellectual growth is described by Patricia M. King and Karen Strohm Kitchener (1994) in *Developing Reflective Judgment: Understanding and Promoting Intellectual Growth and Critical Thinking in Adolescents and Adults.* They differ in details but all three models describe paths that start with the belief that knowledge is certain and knowable and end with the belief that knowledge is uncertain but validated by one's own assessment of the supporting reasons and evidence.

All three models of intellectual growth present as a final position the mature thinker who seeks to understand the full context of an issue in order to make up his or her own mind. Combining critical thinking and self-directed learning produces an intellectually mature adult (Garrison, 1992). In all three models, students reach a higher stage when they rely on reasoned judgment to construct their own beliefs and adopt attitudes about the uncertainty of knowledge and how best to deal with that uncertainty.

Beliefs about knowledge affect students' motivation and self-efficacy (Paulsen & Feldman, 1999). The more simple their epistemological beliefs, the lower their motivation and belief that they can succeed in learning tasks by their own efforts. If students start their online course motivated by obtaining three credits, they can acquire critical thinking competencies and skill with disciplinary methodologies—but intellectual transformation does not follow automatically. In the online classroom, students can be inspired to reach higher intellectual stages by the instructor's and the textbook's persuasive exhortations and by tasks employing active learning strategies—even if the students don't start the course motivated by a wish to grow intellectually but just want the three credits.

### Strategies to Move Students to Higher Intellectual Stages

As noted previously in this chapter, exploring opposing views in collaborative tasks is especially useful in presenting students with the uncertainty of knowledge. For moving students past the multiplicity stage (in Perry's scheme), Hopkins and Richardson (1989) recommend investigating issues where a decision has consequences for the community.

King and Kitchener (1994) end their book with 10 suggestions for moving students to higher stages of reflective thinking:

1. Respect students no matter what stage they seem to be at. Even when the reflective thinking seems to be at a low level in the instructor's appraisal, to the student it has an internal logic that makes good sense. Students' assumptions at one stage can form the basis of moving to the next stage.

2. Understand that students make different assumptions about knowledge and how to acquire it; respond in ways that move them to higher levels. When students seem dogmatic, introduce doubt. When they seem to avoid making a judgment, encourage making one. When they make unsupported judgments, ask for the support.

3. Provide students with ill-structured problems from your field. In the sciences, some previously held facts and theories are now errors; some current cause-effect issues are still not completely settled (for example, acid rain); some ethical issues are still unsettled.

4. Provide many opportunities for students to consider different points of view. There are debatable issues and multiple perspectives in every field; ask students to consider all views (for example, perspectives on food-labeling from the health field and from industry). Present conflicting views by experts and other authorities.

5. Design tasks where students make judgments and explain why. Debates, role-plays, and other simulations provide excellent opportunities.

6. Make your own informal assessment of where students seem to be. By assigning and reading students' reflective journals, and by discussing what makes a fact a fact, what constitutes valid evidence, and whether a conclusion is well or poorly supported, an instructor can discover the assumptions about knowledge that students seem to have.

7. Because students work within a range of stages, design assignments that target the optimal level of that stage. Students reason at different levels across stages. Assign tasks that require reasoning skills appropriate to the stage, but also provide opportunities for moving to higher reasoning skills. Provide feedback about students' reasoning skills that shows how to move beyond continuing to employ prior skills.

8. In interactions with students, offer challenges appropriate to the reflective judgment stage and also provide support by providing a safe environment. What students consider challenging and supportive varies, depending on their developmental level—which explains

why an instructor's favorite strategy will work with some students but not others.

9. Be aware that challenges and supports have emotional dimensions as well as cognitive. Challenges can be difficult emotionally for students. (For example, a religious student may be challenged by studying evolution.) Changes in reflective thinking can be very uncomfortable to students.

10. Recognize which reasoning skills are needed for particular tasks. Use active learning strategies that teach students to do the kinds of thinking needed.

## 15.   Understand Students' Levels of Self-Directedness

The ideal online students are highly self-directed and will reach any intellectual transformation the textbook and online instructor persuade them to attain if their textbook and instructor provide strategies for attaining it. But what about less self-directed learners who need lectures and face-to-face contact? Gerald O. Grow's (1991) model describes four stages of learners, according to their degree of self-direction:

Stage 1. Dependent learners with low self-direction: These students regard their instructor as the expert authority; they respond well to informative lectures and prefer clear instructions and specific tasks. Drill-and-practice exercises often work well. Providing immediate feedback is especially helpful. Being a Stage 1 learner is not necessarily a bad state; they can be very disciplined and productive as students, and can learn a subject well.

Stage 2. Interested learners with moderate self-direction: These students respond well to inspirational lectures and other motivational techniques. Applying course content to stimulating situations is an effective learning task. They learn from interaction with the instructor and are easily inspired by enthusiastic and charismatic instructors.

Stage 3. Involved learners with intermediate self-direction: Students at this stage see their instructor as a facilitator and themselves as participants in the educational process. They can learn a great deal from open-ended structured group projects. An online course is an ideal environment for them unless they have difficulty with new ways of disciplinary thinking.

Stage 4. Self-directed learners: These students set their own goals and standards; they are autonomous and independent learners. They can capably direct their own discussions. An online course is an ideal environment for them.

Although online classes could be a mismatch for them, Stage 1 and 2 learners can benefit from online classes and asynchronous discussions. While fact-filled lectures might be their preference, Stage 1 and 2 learners can become better critical thinkers by responding thoughtfully and thoroughly to instructor-posed questions, become more deeply engaged in the course content because of their own and their classmates' thorough and thoughtful responses, and move to higher stages of intellectual development by their instructor's use of active learning strategies.

Van B. Weigel, in *Deep Learning for a Digital Age* (2002), enthusiastically describes the potential of the Internet and computer technology for transforming higher education. His vision combines almost all of the strategies discussed in this chapter—especially collaborative learning and problem-based learning. The key ingredients in his recipe are knowledge applied by teams of learners in various disciplinary and interdisciplinary contexts, the development of metacognition, and communities of inquiry—enhanced by technology and the Internet.

## FUTURE TRENDS AND OPPORTUNITIES OF EMERGING TECHNOLOGIES

Asynchronous discussion capabilities will improve as Web-based course delivery systems such as Blackboard and WebCT and workplace conferencing systems such as QuickPlace continue to improve students' ability to work in teams. Improvements in Web simulation software can provide better opportunities for collaborative learning. Improved multimedia authoring programs and faculty training in these programs will surely result in better CD-ROMs and Webpages for presenting course content. Intelligent agents (bots) can improve the presentation of course content by customizing it for learners. But I doubt that improved multimedia presentations will result in improved thinking unless they are highly interactive. Better student thinking might result from instructors' providing coaching in response to wrong answers, by tracing the student's misconceptions or mistaken approaches that produced wrong answers, and by guiding the student's mental paths to better answers. For real-time discussions, improvements to current voice and videoconferencing technologies will surely assist practitioners of Socratic questioning, although asynchronous discussion will probably continue to be text-based. Paradoxically, technological improvements in rapid and accurate voice-to-text transcription might degrade thoughtful asynchronous discussion if students can simply talk into a microphone and instantly produce transcribed text. They will lose the benefits of writing unless they first review and edit their speech-transcribed text; otherwise they might fire off to the online discussion the spontaneous, impulsive, ill-considered speech typical of some face-to-face class discussions. Weigel (2002) predicts improvements in residential broadband access, voice over Internet protocol, voice recognition, videoconferencing, and electronic books.

## FURTHER RESEARCH

Assessing gains in critical thinking and the transfer of critical thinking from one discipline to another is difficult but ongoing; online classes can be added to the investigation. Several of the researchers cited in this chapter have suggested directions for future research in their areas of interest. Andrusyszyn and Davie (1997) encourage studying the reflective process and methods for encouraging deep learning in the online environment. Berge (1997) suggests studying barriers to online teaching, whether some subject matter is less suited to online teaching styles, and what is actually occurring when students perform online activities such as discussions. Bernard, de Rubalcava, and St.-Pierre (2000) would like to see more research into the transactions that occur during online collaborative learning. Bullen (1998) suggests studying the effects on student participation of different styles of instructor participation, the participation of students taking online courses fulltime compared with students taking only one online course while their other classes are face-to-face, and the effects of participation and critical thinking in online courses compared with other forms of distance education. Holt, Kleiber, and Swenson (1998) encourage more study of methods of structuring and facilitating online discussions, modeling critical thinking in online environments, and how best to combine face-to-face and online activities. Analyses of methods for teaching critical thinking can be conducted using the information-processing model described by Nordink and Naidu (1994). Hara, Bonk, and Angeli (2000) encourage research on the cognitive processes and products of computer-mediated communication. This need can be met by textual analyses in the manner of Lapadat (2000a, 2000b, 2001a, 2001b) and Newman, Johnson, Cochrane, and Webb (1996), which shed much light on the nature of thinking during asynchronous discussion.

## CONCLUSION

Analytical and critical thinking can be taught effectively using online methodologies. The reasoning and problem solving required to be a disciplinary practitioner can be taught very well online. Furthermore, online professors can aim higher than merely teaching competent thinking. They can promote intellectual growth and encourage students to question the favored approaches and methodologies that dominate our disciplines. Professors who use face-to-face classroom active-learning strategies to engage students and promote their intellectual growth will find they work just as well online.

## REFERENCES

Adelskold, G., Axelsson, R., & Blomgren, J. (1999). Problem-based learning of energy issues via computer network. Distance Education, 20(1), 129-143.

Althauser, R., & Matuga, J. M. (1998). On the pedagogy of electronic instruction. In C. J. Bonk & K. S. King (Eds.), *Electronic collaborators: Learner-centered technologies for literacy, apprenticeship, and discourse* (pp. 183-208). Mahwah, NJ: Erlbaum.

Anderson, S., & Boud, D. (2001). Learners still learn from experience. In J. Stephenson (Ed.) *Teaching and learning online: Pedagogies for new technologies* (pp. 3-15). London: Kogan Page.

Andrusyszyn, M. (1997). Facilitating reflection through interactive journal writing in an online graduate course: A qualitative study. *Journal of Distance Education, 12*(1/2), 103-26.

Angelo, T. D., & Cross, K. P. (1993). *Classroom assessment techniques: A handbook for college teachers* (2nd ed.). San Francisco: Jossey-Bass.

Bailey, M. (1998). Ten great tips for facilitating virtual learning teams. *Distance Learning '98: Proceedings of the Annual Conference on Distance Teaching and Learning.* (ERIC Document Reproduction Service No. ED422838)

Barnet, S. (2001). *A short guide to writing about art* (6th ed.). New York: Allyn and Bacon/Longman.

Barnet, S., & Cain, W. (2000). *A short guide to writing about literature* (8th ed.). New York: Allyn and Bacon/Longman.

Bauer, J. F., & Anderson, R. S. (2000). Evaluating student's written performance in the online classroom. In R. Weiss, D. S. Knowlton, & B. W. Speck (Eds.) *Principles of effective teaching in the online classroom.* (pp. 65-71). New Directions for Teaching and Learning No. 84. San Francisco: Jossey-Bass.

Baxter Magolda, M. B. (Ed.) (2000). *Teaching to promote intellectual and personal maturity: Incorporating students' worldviews and identities into the learning process.* New Directions for Teaching and Learning, no. 82. San Francisco: Jossey-Bass.

Beal, H., and Trimbur, J. (2001). *A short guide to writing about chemistry* (2nd ed.). New York: Allyn and Bacon/Longman.

Bean, J. C. (1996). *Engaging ideas: The professor's guide to integrating writing, critical thinking, and active learning in the classroom.* San Francisco: Jossey-Bass.

Beaudin, B. P. (1999). Keeping asynchronous discussions on topic. *ALN Journal, 3*(2). Retrieved November 26, 2001, from http://www.aln.org/alnweb/journal/Vol3_issue2/beaudin.htm

Bellman, J. (2000). *A short guide to writing about music.* New York: Allyn and Bacon/Longman.

Berge, Z. (1997). Characteristics of online teaching in post-secondary, formal education. *Educational Technology, 37*(3), 35-47.

Bernard, R. M., de Rubalcava, B. R., & St.-Pierre, D. (2000). Collaborative online distance learning: Issues for future practice and research. *Distance Education, 21*, 260-277.

Beyer, B. K. (1987). *Practical strategies for the teaching of thinking.* Boston: Allyn and Bacon.

Beyer, B. K. (1997). *Improving student thinking: A comprehensive approach.* Boston: Allyn and Bacon.

Biddle, A. W., & Bean, D. J. (1987). *Writer's guide: Life sciences.* Boston: Houghton Mifflin.

Biddle, A. W., & Holland, K. M. (1987). *Writer's guide: Political science.* Boston: Houghton Mifflin.

Bond, L. A., & Magistrale, A. S. (1987). *Writer's guide: Psychology.* Boston: Houghton Mifflin.

Bonk, C. J., & Dennen, V. (1999) Teaching on the Web: With a little help from my pedagogical friends. *Journal of Computing in Higher Education, 11*(1), 3-28.

Borg, J. R., & Borg, M. O. (2001). Teaching critical thinking in interdisciplinary economics courses. *College Teaching, 49*(1), 20-25.

Brem, S. K., & Boyes, A. J. (2000). Using critical thinking to conduct effective searches of online sources. *Practical Assessment, Research, and Evaluation, 7*(7). Retrieved October 5, 2001, from http://ericae.net/pare/getvn.asp?v=7&n=7

Brookfield, S. D. (1987). *Developing critical thinkers: Challenging adults to explore alternative ways of thinking and acting.* San Francisco: Jossey-Bass.

Browne, M. N., Freeman, K. E., & Williamson, C. L. (2000). The importance of critical thinking for student use of the Internet. *College Student Journal, 34*, 391-398.

Browne, M. N., & Keeley, S. M. (2001). *Asking the right questions: A guide to critical thinking* (6th ed.). Englewood Cliffs, NJ: Prentice Hall.

Bruffee, K. A. (1995). Sharing our toys: Cooperative learning versus collaborative learning, *Change: The Magazine of Higher Learning, 27*(1), 12-18.

Bruffee, K. A. (1999). *Collaborative learning: Higher education, interdependence, and the authority of knowledge* (2nd ed.). Baltimore: Johns Hopkins Press.

Bullen, M. (1998). Participation and critical thinking in online university distance education. *Journal of Distance Education, 13*(2), 1-32.

Carskadon, T. G. (1994). Student personality factors: Psychological type and the Myers-Briggs type indicator. In K. W. Prichard & R. M. Sawyer (Eds.) *Handbook of college teaching: Theory and applications* (pp. 69-81). Westport, CN: Greenwood Press.

Carstens, R. W. & Worsfold, V. L. (2000). Epilogue: A cautionary note about online classrooms. In R. E. Weiss, D. S. Knowlton, & B. W. Speck (Eds.), *Principles of effective teaching in the online classroom.* New Directions for Teaching and Learning, 84, (pp. 83-87). San Francisco: Jossey-Bass.

Casto, K., & Bulcroft, K. (2000). Play it again, Sam: Creating reusable projects that integrate instructional technology, critical thought and active, collaborative learning into the curriculum. In J. Chambers (Ed.), *Selected Papers from the 11th International Conference on College Teaching and Learning* (pp. 51-59). Gainesville, FL: Florida Community College at Jacksonville.

Chong, S. (1998). Models of asynchronous computer conferencing for collaborative learning in large college classes. In C. J. Bonk & K. S. King (Eds.), *Electronic collaborators: Learner-centered technologies for literacy, apprenticeship, and discourse* (pp. 157-182). Mahwah, NJ: Erlbaum.

Collis, B. (1997). Cooperative learning on the world wide Web. In J. Chambers (Ed.), *Selected Papers from the 8th International Conference on College Teaching and Learning* (pp. 47-55). Gainesville, FL: Florida Community College at Jacksonville.

Cooper, M. M. (1994). Dialogic learning across disciplines. *Journal of Advanced Composition, 14*(2), 531-545.

Cooper, M. M., & Selfe, C. L. (1990). Computer conferences and learning: Authority, resistance, and internally persuasive discourse. *College English, 52*, 847-869.

Corrigan, T. (2001). *A short guide to writing about film* (4th ed.). New York: Allyn and Bacon/Longman.

Costa, A. L. (2001). Habits of mind. In A. L. Costa (Ed), *Developing minds: A resource book for teaching thinking* (3rd ed., pp. 80-86). Alexandria, VA: Association for Supervision and Curriculum Development.

Creed, T. (1998). TechnoCATs. *National Teaching and Learning Forum, 7*(5), 6-8. Retrieved January 22, 2000, from http://www.ntlf.com/html/sf/vc75.htm

Crusius, T. W. & Channell, C. E. (2000). *The aims of argument: A rhetoric and reader* (3rd. ed.). Mountain View, CA: Mayfield.

Cuba, L. J. (2002). *A short guide to writing about social science* (4th ed.). New York: Allyn and Bacon/Longman.

Davidson, N., & Worsham, T. (Eds.) (1992) *Enhancing thinking through cooperative learning.* New York: Teachers College Press.

Dennen, V. (2001). The art and science of developing an asynchronous discussion topic. *Proceedings of the 17th Annual Conference on Distance Teaching and Learning. Madison, WI.* August 10, 2001, 121-126. Retrieved December 16, 2001, from http://edweb.sdsu.edu/people/vdennen/discussion_prompt.pdf

Doherty, A. (1998). The Internet: Destined to become a passive surfing technology? *Educational Technology, 38*(5), 61-63.

Dozier, K. S. (2001). Affecting education in the online "classroom": The good, the bad, and the ugly. *Journal of Interactive Instruction Development, 13*(4), 17-20.

Duffy, T. M, Dueber, B, and Hawley, C. L. (1998). Critical thinking in a distributed environment: A pedagogical base for the design of conferencing systems. In C. J. Bonk & K. S. King (Eds.), *Electronic collaborators: Learner-centered technologies for literacy, apprenticeship, and discourse* (pp. 51-78). Mahwah, NJ: Erlbaum.

Elbow, P. (1973). *Writing without teachers.* New York: Oxford University Press.

Elbow, P. (1986). *Embracing contraries: Explorations in learning and teaching.* New York: Oxford University Press.

Electronic Communication across the Curriculum. http://www.tc.cc.va.us/faculty/tcreisd/projects/ecac/ecacsite.htm

Ennis, R. H. (1987). A taxonomy of critical thinking dispositions and abilities. In J. B. Baron and R. J. Sternberg (Eds.), *Teaching thinking skills: Theory and practice* (pp. 9-26). New York: Freeman.

Felder, R. M., & Brent, R. (2001). Groupwork in distance learning. *Chemical Engineering Education, 35*(2), 102-103.

Fitzgerald, M. A. (1997). Misinformation on the Internet: Applying evaluation skills to online information. *Emergency Information, 24*(3), 9-14.

Fulwiler, T. (Ed.) (1987). *The journal book.* Portsmouth, NH: Boynton/Cook.

Gandolfo, A. & Carver, C. A. (November-December1995). Electronic classroom assessment: Assessment beyond the classroom in a networked environment. *Assessment Update, 7*, 3.

Gardiner, L. F. (1998). Why we must change: The research evidence. *NEA Higher Education Journal 14*(1), 71-88.

Garrison, D. R. (1992). Critical thinking and self-directed learning in adult education: An analysis of responsibility and control issues. *Adult Education Quarterly, 42*(3), 136-148.

Giroux, H. A. (1994). Towards a pedagogy of critical thinking. In K. S. Walters (Ed.), *Re-thinking reason: New perspectives in critical thinking* (pp.199-204). Albany: State University of New York Press.

Grauerholz, L. (2001). Teaching holistically to achieve deep learning. *College Teaching, 49,* 44-50.

Groothius, D. (1999). Cyberspace, critical thinking, and the return to eloquent realities. *Inquiry: Critical Thinking Across the Disciplines, 18,* 6-26.

Grow, G. O. (1991). Teaching learners to be self-directed. *Adult Education Quarterly, 3*(3), 125-149.

Hanna, D. E., Glowacki-Dudka, M., & Conceição-Runlee, S. (2000). *147 practical tips for teaching online: Essentials for Web-based education.* Madison, WI: Atwood.

Harasim, L. (1989). Online education: A new domain. In R. Mason & A. R. Kaye (Eds.), *Mindweave: Communication, computers, and distance education* (pp. 50-62). New York: Pergamon.

Harasim, L., Hiltz, S. T., Teles, L, & Turoff, M. (1995). *Learning networks: A field guide to teaching and learning online.* Cambridge: MIT Press.

Henri, F. & Kaye, A., (1993). Problems of distance education. In K. Harry, J. Magnus, & D. Keegan (Eds.) *Distance education: New perspectives* (pp. 25-32). New York: Routledge.

Hillman, D. C. A. (1999). A new method for analyzing patterns of interaction. *American Journal of Distance Education, 13*(2), 37-47.

Holt, M., Kleiber, P. B., & Swenson, J. D. (1998). Facilitating group Learning on the Internet. *New Directions for Adult and Continuing Education, 78,* 43-51.

Hopkins, M., & Richardson, M. (1989). Teaching critical thinking at a distance. *Distance Education, 10,* 135-147.

Ip, A., Linser, R., & Naidu, S. (2001). Simulated worlds: Rapid generation of Web-based role play. In Proceedings of the Seventh Australian World Wide Web Conference, Coffs Harbour. Retriived November 14, 2001, from http://ausweb.scu.edu.au/aw01/papers/refereed/ip/paper.html

Jones, D. (1996). Critical thinking in an online world. Retrieved October 10, 2001, from http://www.library.ucsb.edu/untangle/jones.html

Johnson, D. W., Johnson, R. T., & Smith, K. A. (1997). *Academic controversy: Enriching college instruction through intellectual conflict.* ASHE-ERIC Higher Education Report, vol. 25, no. 3. Washington, DC: George Washington University, Graduate School of Education and Human Development.

Johnson, D. W., Johnson, R. T., & Smith, K. A. (1998). Cooperative learning returns to college: What evidence is there that it works? *Change: The Magazine of Higher Learning, 30*(1), 27-35.

Johnson, D. W., Johnson, R. T., & Smith, K. A. (2000). Constructive controversy: The educative power of intellectual conflict. *Change: The Magazine of Higher Learning, 32*(1), 28-37.

Kang, I. (1998). The use of computer-mediated communication: Electronic collaboration and interactivity. In C. J. Bonk & K. S. King (Eds.), *Electronic collabora-*

*tors: Learner-centered technologies for literacy, apprenticeship, and discourse* (pp. 313-337). Mahwah, NJ: Erlbaum.

Kaplan, L. D. (1994). Teaching intellectual autonomy. In K. S. Walters (Ed.). *Re-thinking reason: New perspectives in critical thinking* (pp. 205-219). Albany: State University of New York Press.

Kerka, S. (1996). *Journal writing and adult learning,* ERIC Digest No.174. Columbus, OH: ERIC Clearinghouse on Adult, Career, and Vocational Education.

King, K. M. (1994). Leading classroom discussions: Using computers for a new approach. *Teaching Sociology, 22,* 174-182.

King, P. M., & Kitchener, K. S. (1994). *Developing reflective judgment: Understanding and promoting intellectual growth and critical thinking in adolescents and adults.* San Francisco: Jossey-Bass.

Kirk, E. E. (1996, revised 2001). Evaluating information found on the Internet. Retrieved January 20, 2002, from http://milton.mse.jhu.edu/research/education/net.html

Klemm, W. R. (1998). Eight ways to get students more engaged in online conferences. *Technological Horizons in Education Journal, 26*(1), 62-64.

Klinger, T. H., & Connet, M. R. (1992). Designing distance learning courses for critical thinking. *Technological Horizons in Education Journal, 20*(3), 87-90.

Knowlton, D. S. (2000). A theoretical framework for the online classroom: A defense and delineation of a student-centered pedagogy. In R. Weiss, D. S. Knowlton, & B. W. Speck (Eds.) *Principles of effective teaching in the online classroom.* (pp. 45-58). New Directions for Teaching and Learning No. 84. San Francisco: Jossey-Bass.

Knowlton, D. S., Knowlton, H. M., & Davis, C. (2000). The whys and hows of online discussion. *Syllabus: New Directions in Educational Technology, 13*(10), 54-58.

Kuhn, T. S. (1970). *The structure of scientific revolutions* (2nd ed., enlarged). Chicago: University of Chicago Press.

Langer, J. A., & Applebee, A. N. (1987). *How writing shapes thinking: A study of teaching and learning.* Urbana, IL: National Council of Teachers of English.

Lapadat, J. C. (2000a). Teaching Online: Breaking New Ground in Collaborative Thinking. Paper presented at the annual meeting of the Canadian Society for the Study of Education: Congress of the Social Sciences and Humanities, Edmonton, Alberta, Canada.

Lapadat, J. C. (2000b). Tracking conceptual change: An indicator of learning online. Paper presented at the 2000 International Online Conference on teaching Online in Higher Education.

Lapadat, J. C. (2001a). Online Interaction: A discourse analysis of a graduate level Webcourse. Paper presented at the eleventh annual meeting of the Society for text and Discourse, University of California, Santa Barbara.

Lapadat, J. C. (2001b). Qualities of writing in an interactive Webcourse: Implications for designing online classes. Paper presented at the BC Ministry of Education Sponsored Education Research Symposium, Vancouver, BC.

Lauzon, A. C. (1992). Integrating computer-based instruction with computer conferencing: An evaluation of a model for designing online education. *American Journal of Distance Education, 6*(2), 32-46.

Lederer, N. (2000). New form(at): Using the Web to teach research and critical thinking skills. *Reference Services Review, 28,* 130-153.

Lee, V. S. (1999). Educating the whole person: Heart, body, and mind. *National Teaching and Learning Forum, 8*(5). 1-5.

Linser, R., & Naidu, S. (1999). Web-based simulations as teaching and learning media in political science. In Proceedings of the Fifth Australian World Wide Web Conference, Lismore. Accessed November 14, 2001, from http://ausweb.scu.edu.au/aw99/papers/naidu/paper.html

Lynch, C. L., & Wolcott, S. K. (2001). Helping your students develop critical thinking skills. IDEA paper no. 37. Retrieved January 27, 2002, from http://www.idea.ksu.edu/products/Papers.html

Lynch, D., Vernon, R. F., & Smith, M. L. (2001). Critical thinking and the Web. *Journal of Social Work Education, 37*, 381-386.

Lynch, D. A., George, D., and Cooper, M. (1997). Moments of argument: Agonistic inquiry and confrontational cooperation. *College English, 48*(1), 61-85.

Marius, R., & Page, M. (2002). *A short guide to writing about history* (2nd ed.). New York: Allyn and Bacon/Longman.

Marland, P., Patching, W., & Putt, I. (1992). Thinking while studying: A process tracing study of distance learners. *Distance Education, 13*, 193-217.

Marland, P., Patching, W., Putt, I., & Putt, R. (1990). Distance learners' interactions with text while studying. *Distance Education, 11*, 71-91.

Marttunen, M., & Laurinen, L. (1999). Learning of argumentation in face-to-face and e-mail environments. In F. H. Van Eemeren, R. Grootendorst, J. A. Blair, & C. A. Willard (Eds.) *Proceedings of the Fourth International Conference of the International Society for the Study of Argumentation* (pp. 552-558). Amsterdam: International Centre for the Study of Argumentation.

Marttunen, M., & Laurinen, L. (2001). Learning of argumentation in networked and face-to-face environments. *Instructional Science, 29*, 127-153.

Maryland State Department of Education. [nd]. Questioning for quality thinking. [card]. Annapolis, MD: author.

Marzano, R. J., Brandt, R. S., Hughes, C. S., Jones, B. F., Presseisen, B. Z., Rankin, S. C., et al. (1988). *Dimensions of thinking: A framework for curriculum and instruction.* Alexandria, VA: Association for Supervision and Curriculum Development.

Mayes, T. (2001). Learning technology and learning relationships. In J. Stephenson (Ed.) *Teaching and learning online: Pedagogies for new technologies* (pp. 16-26). London: Kogan Page.

McEachern, R. W. (1999). A metacognitive approach to business communication. *Business Communication Quarterly, 62*(4), 80-83.

Meyers, C., & Jones, T. B. (1993) *Promoting active learning: Strategies for the classroom.* San Francisco: Jossey-Bass.

Miller, J. (1999). Critical thinking and asynchronous discussion. *Inquiry: Critical Thinking Across the Disciplines, 19*(1), 18-27.

Millis, B. J. (2001). Cooperative learning: It's here to stay. *Teaching Excellence, 12*(8), 1-2.

Millis, B. J. (2000a). Managing—and motivating!—distance learning group activities. Available: http://www.tltgroup.org/resources/millis.html

Millis, B. J. (2000b). Using new technologies to support cooperative learning, collaborative, services, and unique resources. Available: http://www.tltgroup.org/resources/millis3.html

Millis, B. J. (2000c). URLs pertinent to cooperative leaning activities. Available: http://www.tltgroup.org/gilbert/cooplearning.htm

Millis, B. J., & Cottell, P. G. (1998). *Cooperative learning for higher education faculty.* Phoenix, AZ: American Council on Education/Oryx Press.

Mission: Critical [interactive tutorial]. Retrieved January 22, 2000, from http://www.sjsu.edu/depts/itl/

Morse, J. M. (1998), Socratic questioning for the twenty-first century. *Inquiry: Critical Thinking Across the Disciplines, 18*(2), 9-23.

Mulligan, R, & Geary, S. (1999). Requiring writing, ensuring distance-learning outcomes. *International Journal of Instructional Media, 26,* 387-395.

Naidu, S. & Bernard, R. (1992). Enhancing academic performance in distance education with concept mapping and inserted questions. *Distance Education, 13,* 218-233.

Nelson, C. (1994). Critical thinking and collaborative learning. In K. Bosworth and Sharon J. Hamilton (Eds.) *Collaborative Learning: Underlying processes and effective techniques* (pp. 45-58). New Directions for Teaching and Learning No. 59. San Francisco: Jossey-Bass.

Newman, D. R., Johnson, C., Cochrane, C., & Webb, B. (1996). An experiment in group learning technology: Evaluating critical thinking in face-to-face and computer-supported seminars. *Interpersonal Computing and Technology, 4*(1), 57-74.

Nist, S. (1993). What the literature says about academic literacy. *Georgia Journal of Reading,* (Fall-Winter), 11-18.

Noordink, P. J., & Naidu, S. (1994). Analysis of instruction for critical thinking in distance learning materials. *Distance Education, 15,* 42-69.

Oliver, M., Naidu, S., & Koronios, A. (2000). Utilizing case-based reasoning and multimedia to enhance clinical decision making of novice practitioners: Product implementation and evaluation. Paper presented at ASCILTE 2000 conference at Coffs Harbour, Australia. Retrieved September 23, 2001, from http://www.ascilite.org.au/conferences/coffs00/papers/mary_oliver.pdf

Palloff, R. M. & Pratt, K. (1999). *Building learning communities in cyberspace: Effective strategies for the online classroom.* San Francisco: Jossey-Bass.

Palloff, R. M. & Pratt, K. (2001). *Lessons from the cyberspace classroom: The realities of online teaching.* San Francisco: Jossey-Bass.

Parrott, L., III. (1999). *How to write psychology papers.* New York: Allyn and Bacon/Longman.

Paul, R. W. (1993a). Critical thinking, moral integrity, and citizenship: Teaching for the intellectual values. In *Critical thinking: How to prepare students for a rapidly changing world* (pp. 255-268). Santa Rosa, CA: Foundation for Critical Thinking.

Paul, R. W. (1993b). Dialogical and dialectical thinking. In *Critical thinking: How to prepare students for a rapidly changing world* (pp. 291-301). Santa Rosa, CA: Foundation for Critical Thinking.

Paul, R. W. (1993c). Socratic questioning. In *Critical thinking: How to prepare students for a rapidly changing world* (pp. 335-365). Santa Rosa, CA: Foundation for Critical Thinking.

Paul, R. W. (1994). Teaching critical thinking in the strong sense: A focus on self-deception, world views, and a dialectical mode of analysis. In K. S. Walters

(Ed.), *Re-thinking reason: New perspectives in critical thinking* (pp. 181-198). Albany: State University of New York Press.

Paulsen, M. B., & Feldman, K. A. (1999). Student motivation and epistemological beliefs. *New Directions for Teaching and Learning, 78,* 17-25.

Pechenik, J. A. (2001). *A short guide to writing about biology* (4th ed.). New York: Allyn and Bacon/Longman.

Peirce, W. (2001). Using the distinction between fact and interpretation to promote intellectual development. *The Successful Professor, 1*(sample issue). Retrieved November 21, 2001, from http://www.thesuccessfulprofessor.com

Perry, W. G., Jr., (1970). *Forms of intellectual and ethical development in the college years: A scheme.* New York: Holt, Rinehart, Winston.

Perry, W. G., Jr., (1981). Cognitive and ethical growth: The making of meaning. In A. Chickering (Ed.), *The modern American college: Responding to the new realities of diverse students and a changing society* (pp. 76-116). San Francisco: Jossey-Bass.

Porush, D. (1995). *A short guide to writing about science.* New York: Allyn and Bacon/Longman.

Redding, T. R., & Rotzien, J. (2001). Comparative analysis of online learning versus classroom learning. *Journal of Interactive Instruction Development, 10,* 3-12.

Richlin-Klonsky, J., & Strenski, E. (1994). *A guide to writing sociology papers.* New York: St. Martin's.

Rooney, P. S. (2000). Constructive controversy: A new approach to designing team projects. *Business Communication Quarterly, 63*(1), 53-61.

Rossman, M. H. (1999). Successful online teaching using an asynchronous learner discussion forum. *ALN Journal, 3*(2). Retrieved November 26, 2001, from http://www.aln.org/alnweb/journal/Vol3_issue2/Rossman.htm

Ryan, M. E., Carlton, K. H., & Ali, N. G. (1999). Evaluation of traditional classroom teaching methods versus course delivery via the world wide Web. *Journal of Nursing Education, 38*(6), 272-277.

Schmidt, D. E. (2000). *Writing in political science: A practical guide* (2nd ed.). New York: Allyn and Bacon/Longman.

Schroeder, C. C. (1993). New students—New learning styles. *Change: The Magazine of Higher Learning, 25*(4). 21-26. Retrieved November 15, 2000, from http://virtualschool.edu/mon/Academia/KierseyLearningStyles.html

Schulze, K. G., Shelby, R. N., Treacy, D. J., & Wintersgill, M. C. (2000). Andes: A coached learning environment for classical Newtonian physics. In J. Chambers (Ed.), *Selected Papers from the 11th International Conference on College Teaching and Learning* (pp. 151-162). Gainesville, FL: Florida Community College at Jacksonville.

Seaton, W. J. (1993). Computer-mediated communication and student self-directed learning. *Open Learning, 8*(2), 49-54.

Shapely, P. (2000). On-line education to develop complex reasoning skills in organic chemistry [Special issue on learning effectiveness]. *ALN Journal, 4*(2). Retrieved November 26, 2001, from http://www.aln.org/alnweb/journal/jaln-vol4issue2.htm

Shively, J. M., & Van Fossen, P. J. (1999). Critical thinking and the Internet: Opportunities for the social science classroom. *The Social Studies, 90*(1), 42-46.

Smith, A. (2001). Evaluation of information sources. Retrieved January 20, 2002, from http://www.vuw.ac.nz/~agsmith/evaln/evaln.htm.

Stage, F. K., Muller, P. A., Kinzie, J., & Simmons, A. (1998). *Creating learning-centered classrooms: What does learning theory have to say?* ASHE-ERIC Higher Education Report, vol. 26, no. 4. Washington, DC: George Washington University, Graduate School of Education and Human Development.

Steffens, H. J., & Dickerson, M. J. (1987). *Writer's guide: History.* Boston: Houghton Mifflin.

Stewart, R. (2001). Teaching critical thinking in first-year composition: Sometimes more is more. *Teaching English in the Two-Year College, 29,* 162-171.

Stuart, S. (1999.) Teaching philosophy in cyberspace. *Inquiry: Critical Thinking Across the Disciplines, 18*(4), 55-63.

Sutherland, T. E. & Bonwell, C. C. (1996). *Using active learning in college classes: A range of options for faculty.* New Directions for Teaching and Learning No. 67. San Francisco: Jossey-Bass.

Thaiss, C., & Sanford, J. F. (2000). *Writing for psychology.* Boston, Allyn and Bacon.

Thayer-Bacon, B. J. (Ed.) (2000a). Transforming and redescribing critical thinking [special issue]. *Inquiry: Critical Thinking Across the Disciplines, 19*(4).

Thayer-Bacon, B. J. (2000b). *Transforming critical thinking: Thinking constructively.* New York: Teachers College Press.

Thoms, K. J., & Juniad, N. (1997). Developing critical thinking skills in a technology-related class. Proceedings of the Mid-South Instructional Technology Conference. Accessed October 30, 2001, from http://www.mtsu.edu/~itconf/proceed97/thinking.html

Trosset, C. (1998). Obstacles to open discussion and critical thinking. *Change: The Magazine of Higher Learning, 30*(5). 45-49.

University of California, Berkeley, Library. (1995, revised 2001). Evaluating Web pages: Experience why it's important. Retrieved January 20, 2002, from http://lib.berkeley.edu/TeachingLib/Guides/Internet/Evaluate.html

Vygotsky, L. S. (1962). *Thought and language.* Cambridge, MA: Harvard University Press.

Weigel, V. B. (2000). E-learning: The trade-off between richness and reach in higher education. *Change: The Magazine of Higher Learning, 33*(5). 10-15.

Weigel, V. B. (2002). *Deep learning for a digital age: Technology's untapped potential to enrich higher education.* San Francisco: Jossey-Bass.

Zhu, E. (1998). Learning and mentoring: Electronic discussion in a distance-learning course. In C. J. Bonk & K. S. King (Eds.), *Electronic collaborators: Learner-centered technologies for literacy, apprenticeship, and discourse* (pp. 233-258). Mahwah, NJ: Erlbaum.

Zukas, A. (1999). Cyberworld: Teaching world history on the world wide Web. *The History Teacher, 32*(4), 495-516.

## APPENDIX A: QUESTIONS DERIVED FROM BLOOM'S TAXONOMY

### Knowledge—Identification and recall of information

Who, what, when, where, how_____?

Describe_____.

## Comprehension—Organization and selection of facts and ideas

Retell_____in your own words.
What is the main idea of_____?

## Application—Use of facts, rules, principles

How is_____an example of_____?
How is_____related to_____?
Why is_____significant?

## Analysis—Separation of a whole into component parts

What are the parts or features of _____?
Classify _____ according to_____.
Outline/diagram/web _____.
How does _____ compare/contrast with _____?
What evidence can you present for _____?

## Synthesis—Combination of ideas to form a new whole

What would you predict/infer from _____?
What ideas can you add to _____?
How would you create/design a new _____?
What might happen if you combined _____ with ___?
What solutions would you suggest for _____?

## Evaluation—Development of opinions, judgments, or decisions

Do you agree _____?
What do you think about _____?
What is the most important _____?
Prioritize _____according to _____.
How would you decide about _____?
What criteria would you use to assess _____?

*Source:* Maryland State Department of Education flyer [no date]

## APPENDIX B:
## RICHARD PAUL'S FOUR KINDS OF
## QUESTIONS FOR ANY POSITION

## Origins

- How did you come to think this?
- Can you remember the circumstances in which you formed this belief?

## Support

- Why do you believe this?
- Do you have any evidence for this?
- What are some of the reasons why people believe this?
- In believing this, aren't you assuming that such and such is true?
- Is that a sound assumption do you think?

## Conflict with Other Thoughts

- Some people might object to your position by saying . . . How would you answer them?
- What do you think of this contrasting view?
- How would you answer the objection that . . . ?

## Implications and Consequences

- What are the practical consequences of believing this?
- What would we have to do to put it into action?
- What follows from the view that . . . ?
- Wouldn't we also have to believe that . . . in order to be consistent?
- Are you implying that . . . ?

CHAPTER 9

# ONLINE LEARNING AS AN IMPROVEMENT?
## The Case of Economic Principles

**Chiara Gratton-Lavoie and Denise Stanley**

How do students enrolled in online courses perform when compared to students who choose a more traditional classroom environment? Are there any student characteristics that can help to explain differences in student academic achievement in the two modes of instruction? This study addresses these important questions in relation to the teaching of introductory economics courses. We find that students in the 'live' section of the course perform significantly better than students enrolled in the virtual class, according to standard performance measures.

**KEYWORDS:** economics, education, distance learning, online teaching, online learning, assessment, performance.

Electronic Learning Communities—Issues and Practices, pages 349–365.
Copyright © 2003 by Information Age Publishing, Inc.
All rights of reproduction in any form reserved.
ISBN: 1-931576-96-3 (pbk.), 1-931576-97-1 (hardcover)

## INTRODUCTION

### Online Learning in the 21st Century

Online learning has been described as a solution to many of the educational challenges emerging in the 21st Century. As the children of the Baby Boomers enter college, both public and private universities face greater student enrollments and reduced budgets. This surge in enrollment statistics, predicted in the 1980s and labeled Tidal Wave II, has posed financial strains on many colleges across the nation. At Cal State Fullerton (CSUF), for example, total enrollment for Fall 2001 was 20,701 full-time-equivalent students (FTES), and the number increased to 21,003 FTES in Spring 2002 (Cal State Fullerton, 2001). One full-time-equivalent corresponds to 15 units of course work, and it is the measure used by the State of California to allocate financial resources across campuses. Because one FTES can be the sum of units taken by part-time students, the actual students headcount is always higher than the reported FTES.

As institutions of higher education become more crowded and financially strained, students reside at greater distances from universities, and they face increasing work and family demands on their time (Bonca, 1998). Because of these changes in student demographics and in general economic conditions, colleges and universities have implemented numerous innovations to the traditional classroom-based experience, ranging from classes incorporating the Web-based delivery of material to completely online instruction.

Online education could provide a cost-effective solution to these challenges. It is often argued that online students can master concepts as well, or better, than those in a traditional setting, and that information technology can help to reduce the costs of education. The delivery costs per student and per-concept taught could be lowered, with online delivery mode at least as effective as the classroom-based delivery. (See Twigg, 2001, for in-depth analysis of the issue of cost in distance learning environments.)

A widespread debate has begun to emerge among academics undertaking online activities. In a survey of instructors teaching economics online, Navarro (2000) found that the majority of respondents believed students would do as well or better in an online class, and that most pedagogical aspects of learning could be met in the online environment. But there are pros and cons.

On the positive side, an online class provides faster information access, it can be structured to accommodate different learning styles and student types (i.e. more motivated, self-directed and independent students, or older students with families), and it encourages students to take a more responsible, constructive role in the learning process, fostering independence of thought and critical thinking, rather than passive learning (Zhang, 1998; see also Brewer & Erickson, 1997; McCollum, 1997). And, of course, student time is used more efficiently when long travel times to a distant campus are eliminated. In one study, it was clear that more time-constrained students (not just long-distance commuters) are attracted to online classes (Vachris, 1999). Students can gain computer skills useful for future career paths (Agarwal & Day, 1998). Finally, student-professor interaction may be enhanced by online instruction. On the one hand, some students might prefer the relative anonymity of online communication to a face-to-face discussion. On the other hand, the distance learning format allows the instructor to rely on asynchronous communication for content delivery while dedicating the time spent (synchronously) online with the students, to class discussion and student-instructor interaction (Navarro & Shoemaker, 2000b).

However, critics say that students taking classes online do not learn as well as they do in a traditional setting, since realtime student-to-student interaction is missing. Furthermore, if the instructor structures the online course as a replica of the traditional course, simply transferring existing course material online, then the potential advantages of online learning (individualized instruction to accommodate different learning styles, interactive, hands-on learning material, etc.) would not be realized, and students might tend to stress memorization more than they would in the traditional setting (Twigg, 2001). Technical problems related to Web infrastructure and incompatible systems are common, and higher withdrawal rates occur in online teaching (Navarro, 2000). Finally, as Navarro (2000) points out, poorer students with limited computer access may be excluded, and small colleges with tighter budgets will lag behind.

There are relatively few studies to document the specific performance of students in online classes. Most studies discuss perceptions of the benefits of the online mode rather than assessing in a rigorous manner, student performance. Even fewer studies attempt to explore and compare the factors underlying student performance in traditional versus online environments. This study investigates the variables impacting performance of students in the online setting, and compares outcomes between two different modes of instruction for the case of teaching economics principles.

## Some Lessons from the Social Sciences and Previous Studies of Economics Online

Online learning methods have been implemented across nearly all academic disciplines. A noted expert in the field, Thomas Russell of North Carolina State University, has synthesized the findings of many studies comparing online and traditional courses. Nearly half the studies cited find that learning outcomes are comparable in the two teaching modes (Cahill & Catanzaro, 1997; Ridley, 1997, cited in Vachris, 1999). The "no

significant difference" outcome occurred in English, accounting, economics, philosophy, and nursing classes (Green & Gentemann, 2001; Gagne &
Shepherd, 2001; Navarro & Shoemaker, 1999; Virginia Tech, 1998; Blackley & Curran-Smith, 1998). Another group of studies suggests that student
performance in engineering, psychology, English, management, and
accounting did improve in the online setting (Kashy, et al., 2001; Maki, et
al., 2000; Stinson & Claus, 2000; Morrissey, 1998; Vasarhelyi & Graham,
1997). These studies represent only those incorporating Web-based materials in the online teaching mode and excluded studies concerning the use
of video learning techniques.

Regarding the discipline of economics, Navarro (2000) cites more than
50 institutions offering at least 100 online economics courses. The online
component varies from simple use of e-mail after lectures, to full online
delivery, testing, and teleconferencing, to provide content and to evaluate
students. Most offerings and related analyses focus on introductory economics. But, as Navarro and Shoemaker (2000b) emphasize, this body of
literature consists typically of case studies rather than rigorous, controlled
comparison of outcomes between live lecture-based economics and economics online. A common trend is to integrate Web-based news or active
games (e.g. the Iowa Electronic Markets) into class work (Simkins, 1999),
but the effectiveness of these techniques has not been fully assessed. Gregor and Cuskelly (1994, cited in Agarwal & Day, 1998) just note greater student participation through bulletin boards rather than focusing on
student performance evaluation.

Agarwal and Day (1998) offer one of the first attempts to measure the
value-added of a "partial" online learning experience that used supplemental e-mail, Web exercises, and class discussion groups. They focused on
student learning and retention of concepts as well as on students' perception of instructor effectiveness and possible changes in students' attitude
toward economics. They examined undergraduate principles classes and
graduate courses across two semesters, with each course mode taught by
both instructors across periods. They found that the "partially online" students performed significantly better on economic concept questions
added to the final exam. The Internet students also received higher final
grades in the course, after controlling for a variety of students' background
characteristics. Interestingly, they suggested that the Internet enhancements worked better for students with higher initial GPAs.

Navarro and Shoemaker (2000) found that online learners perform better than traditional students in a macroeconomics principles class. In their
case, a more costly innovation, multimedia CD-ROMs containing video,
audio and text lectures, were the principal online delivery mode. Their
study examined the results on a final exam of a short-essay graded by a single person. The statistical significance of the difference in performance
was consistent across various subgroups of students.

A contradictory result was reported by Brown and Liedholm (2002). Their study compared performance across three teaching modes: traditional lecture, online video lecture, and a hybrid course consisting of traditional lectures supplemented with online assignments. While online students had higher GPAs and ACT scores, they scored significantly lower on a common set of multiple-choice questions. However, women students did perform a bit better in the online setting, suggesting that the traditional gender gap in economics learning might be reduced by the use of information technology.

One should note that not all educational institutions have sufficient financial means to obtain, maintain, and support the technology required by the online video lectures referenced in these studies. The simple posting online of lecture notes, and the use of e-mail, discussion board, chatrooms and Web-based interactive exercises, may be more suitable for some colleges and universities than for others.

For our experiment we chose to adopt easy-to-use, and relatively simple, Internet tools, rather than more expensive and sophisticated multimedia technologies.

## A NEW EXPERIMENT AT CSUF

In this study we analyzed academic performance of students enrolled in two sections of Principles of Microeconomics at California State University Fullerton in Fall 2001.

Specifically, we attempted to address some of the questions raised, among others, by Navarro and Shoemaker (2000a, 2000b), and by Brown and Liedholm (in press), on whether students in introductory economics classes perform better online, and whether student background characteristics have an impact on performance, as well as on the choice of the mode of learning.

### The Research Design

We taught two sections of Introductory Microeconomics using two alternative modes of instruction, hereafter referred to as the online mode and the hybrid mode. As detailed below, while the instructional methods used for the control and the test groups had many features in common, they differed by design in *the degree* to which they used the online technology.

The two groups were similar in size (22 and 29 students respectively); we adopted the same textbook (Case & Fair, 2001), and the same exam format and exam content for both groups. Additionally, the same online support and instructional technology (Blackboard CourseInfo 4.0) were used to create course Websites for communication through posting of class information and material, class announcements, and e-mail.

The main differences between the two courses were: (1) the instructor teaching the course, and (2) the extent to which the classes relied on online instructional technology for student-to-instructor and student-to-student interactions. The online class was taught by Gratton-Lavoie, and it met in person only three times, for scheduled in-class examinations. Stanley taught the hybrid format of the course, and her class met face-to-face for two and a half hours per week.

Two potential sources of bias had to be addressed by our research design: instructor bias, and student self-selection bias. To minimize instructor bias we controlled for factors affecting teaching methodology and course information content. We selected the same textbook and we jointly prepared syllabi, reading and homework assignments, exams, lecture notes, and any other material used in the course. Additionally, during the semester of instruction we carefully coordinated the sequence in which topics were covered, as well as the timing of exams, assignments, etc.

We administered a confidential entry survey to all students in the first week of instruction. We used the survey to collect data on students' personal characteristics as well as information on their academic background and computer knowledge at the beginning of the experiment. These data, together with additional information from official university records, allowed us to control for selection bias and to isolate the effect of the instructional technology on students' performance.

### Class Composition, Course Design and Evaluation Instruments

Students' personal characteristics, and their academic background and computer knowledge at the beginning of the experiment for both the online class and the hybrid class are shown in Table 1 and Table 2.

The raw data show that the online students were on average older than the students in the hybrid group, and they lived farther from campus. The online group had more female students, had stronger mathematics background and economics class experience, and admitted studying fewer hours. They also reported working fewer hours per week than the hybrid group. Students were asked to rate their computer, e-mail and Internet skills using a scale from 1 = poor to 5 = expert. Levels of expertise were very similar across groups. Wary of the reliability of self-reported data, particularly with respect to computer skills, we decided to include in the survey a set of multiple-choice questions, testing the students on their Internet and computer knowledge as well as on their math background.

TABLE 1
Summary Statistics of Student Personal Characteristics

| Variable | Online GroupN=22 | | Hybrid Group N=29 | | Test Statistics |
|---|---|---|---|---|---|
| Age* | 23 (5.78) | | 21.62 (3.19) | | t test = 1.07 df=47, p=0.29 |
| Gender | | | | | |
| Male | 8 | 36.36% | 17 | 58.62% | Chi square = 2.48 |
| Female | 14 | 63.64% | 12 | 41.38% | df =1, p = 0.12 |
| Ethnicity | | | | | |
| Caucasian | 3 | 13.645 | 7 | 24.145 | Chi square = 2.01 |
| Hispanic | 4 | 18.18% | 6 | 20.69% | df = 4, p = 0.73 |
| African Am. | 1 | 4.55% | 1 | 3.54% | |
| Asian | 9 | 40.90% | 13 | 44.83% | |
| Other | 2 | 9.09% | 1 | 3.45% | |
| Primary Language | | | | | |
| English | 16 | 72.73% | 21 | 72.41% | Chi square = 0.88 |
| English + Other | 4 | 18.18% | 7 | 24.14% | df = 2, p = 0.64 |
| Other | 2 | 9.09% | 1 | 3.45% | |
| Marital Status | | | | | |
| Single | 18 | 81.82% | 27 | 93.10% | Chi square = 1.70 |
| Married | 4 | 18.18% | 2 | 6.90% | df = 1, p = 0.19 |
| Children | | | | | |
| Yes | 5 | 22.73% | 1 | 3.45% | Chi square = 4.48 |
| No | 17 | 77.27% | 28 | 96.55% | df = 1, p = 0.03 |
| Distance to Campus | | | | | |
| On campus | 0 | 0.0% | 1 | 3.45% | Chi square = 5.64 |
| Very Close | 2 | 0.90% | 1 | 3.45% | df = 4, p = 0.23 |
| 2-5 Miles | 0 | 0.0% | 4 | 13.79% | |
| 6-10 Miles | 6 | 27.27% | 4 | 13.79% | |
| 10+ Miles | 14 | 63.64% | 19 | 65.52% | |

*Note:*     * Mean, with standard deviation in parentheses.

Table 2 reports the average scores on the two sets of questions, as Computer Knowledge and Math Knowledge respectively. With regard to the technology-related questions, the two groups scored virtually the same.

To test for the statistical significance of differences in background characteristics, we performed Chi-square tests of independence for the categorical, non-numerical variables, and we computed t-test statistics to capture possible differences between mean values of non-categorical, numerical variables. Our tests indicate that statistically significant differences did not exist between the online students and the more traditional group, with two notable exceptions. The online students had more children, and official

TABLE 2
Summary Statistics of Student Academic and Computer Background
Characteristics

| Variable | Online Group N = 22 | | Hybrid Group N = 29 | | Test Statistics |
|---|---|---|---|---|---|
| Major | | | | | |
| Bus/Fin/Econ | 15 | 68.18% | 20 | 68.97% | Chi square=0.00 |
| Other | 7 | 31.82% | 9 | 31.03% | df=1, p=0.95 |
| College Algebra | | | | | |
| Yes | 19 | 86.36% | 24 | 82.76% | Chi square=0.12 |
| No | 3 | 13.64% | 5 | 17.24% | df=1, p=0.73 |
| College Calculus | | | | | |
| Yes | 10 | 45.45% | 15 | 51.72% | Chi square=0.20 |
| No | 12 | 54.55% | 14 | 48.28% | df=1, p=0.66 |
| Previous Econ Class | | | | | |
| Yes | 17 | 77.27% | 19 | 65.52% | Chi square=0.83 |
| No | 5 | 22.73% | 10 | 34.48% | df=1, p=0.36 |
| Previous Online Class | | | | | |
| Yes | 5 | 22.73% | 3 | 10.35% | Chi square=1.45 |
| No | 17 | 77.27% | 26 | 89.65% | df=1, p=0.23 |
| Student Status | | | | | |
| Full Time | 19 | 86.36% | 24 | 82.76% | Chi square=1 .65 |
| Part Time | 0 | 0.0% | 2 | 6.90% | df=2, p=0.44 |
| Evening Only | 3 | 13.64% | 3 | 10.34% | |
| Hours/wk. Work* | | 19.80 (13.54) | | 24.19 (13.50) | t test= 1.15 |
| | | | | | df=49, p=0.26 |
| Hours/wk. Study* | | 13.43 (7.93) | | 14.87 (14.05) | t test= 0.42 |
| | | | | | df = 45, p = 0.68 |
| Access to PC | | | | | |
| Yes | 22 | 100% | 26 | 89.66% | Chi square=2.42 |
| No | 0 | 0.0% | 3 | 10.34% | df=1,p=0.12 |
| Access to Internet | | | | | |
| Yes | 22 | 100% | 26 | 89.66% | Chi square=2.42 |
| No | 0 | 0.0% | 3 | 10.34% | df=1,p=0.12 |
| Computer Skills* | 3.36 | (0.95) | 3.28 | (0.75) | t test=0.37 |
| (1= Poor to 5=Expert) | | | | | df=49, p=0.71 |
| E-mail Skills* | | 4.41 (0.80) | | 4.59 (0.78) | t test=0.80 |
| (1=Poor to 5=Expert) | | | | | df=49, p=0.43 |
| Web Skills* | | 4.23 (0.92) | | 4.48 (0.83) | t test=1 .04 |
| (1=Poor to 5=Expert) | | | | | df=49, p=0.30 |

TABLE 2
Summary Statistics of Student Academic and Computer Background
Characteristics  (continued)

| Variable | Online Group N = 22 | Hybrid Group N = 29 | Test Statistics |
|---|---|---|---|
| Computer Knowledge (Score: 0~4)* | 3.77 (0.43) | 3.76 (0.51) | ttest=0.10 df=49, p=0.92 |
| Math Knowledge* (Score: 0-5) | 2.45 (1.06) | 2.41 (1.21) | t test=0.1 3 df=49, p=0.90 |
| Cumulative GPA* | 2.17 (1.16) | 2.53 (0.89) | ttest=1.26 df=48, p=0.21 |
| CSUF GPA* | 1.96 (1.22) | 1.69 (1.33) | t test=0.70 df=46, p=0.48 |
| SAT Scores* | | | t test=0.12, p=0.90 df=22 |
| Verbal | 482.5 (93.16) | 475.63 (81.89) | ttest=0.19, p=0.85 |
| Math | 520 (77.83) | 529.38 (69.71) | t test=0.02, p=0.98 |
| Enrollment Date* (w/r to ₁st day of class) | -7.86 (22.19) | -19.39 (17.99) | ttest=2.03 df=48, p=0.048 |
| Credits Enrolled* | 11.38 (3.94) | 12.28 (3.43) | t test=0.85 df=48, p=0.40 |
| Credits Earned* | 10.58 (3.47) | 11.25 (3.71) | t test=0.62 df=45, p=0.54 |

*Notes:*    * Means, with standard deviations in parentheses.

records indicated that the students enrolled in the class much later than the students in the hybrid course did. In fact, virtual learners enrolled only slightly more than a week before the beginning of the term, while the average student in the hybrid group enrolled almost 20 days in advance. For both variables, the differences are statistically significant at the 5% level.

Overall, we can conclude that the two groups were rather homogeneous in their entering characteristics, with the exception of number of children and date of enrollment. The higher number of children coupled with the fact that the online class had more women enrolled than the traditional course suggests the possibility that convenience and schedule flexibility were both important factors affecting students' enrollment decision. For women who work outside the house and have family responsibilities, a distance learning class might fit a tight and busy schedule when other options might not.

On the other hand, the fact that students enrolled in the virtual course quite late indicates the possibility of another source of selection bias in the sample. It raises the question of whether many students who chose the virtual environment were actually forced to do so by lack of viable alternatives due to a combination of personal constraints in their schedule and closed enrollment in other sections of Introductory Microeconomics.

In short, the background data suggest the possibility that students selected the online option because it was the most convenient and flexible alternative and/or because they did not have an alternative at all.

The key aspects of the two course designs are presented in Table 3, with differences highlighted. The hybrid course involved face-to-face weekly lectures for about one hour and 45 minutes and hands-on computer lab assignments for roughly another 45 to 50 minutes per week. The instructor maintained a Website for class announcements and to post grades, review exams, assignments, etc. Students used the Internet to access online study guide problems as well as various other Internet resources to complete the lab assignments. E-mail was used to communicate with the entire class and with individual students.

The online group met in person only for an introductory, orientation session, and three other times for two in-class midterm examinations and the final comprehensive exam. Delivery of the course content took place entirely in the virtual environment.

For synchronous interaction, students and instructor met weekly in a virtual chatroom for one hour and a half. Attendance at the weekly chat was

TABLE 3
Course Designs

| Online Course (N=22) | Hybrid Course (N=29) |
|---|---|
| • Standard Textbook | • Standard Textbook |
| • **Instructor's Lecture Supplements Online** | • Textbook Companion Website with Online Study Guide |
| • Instructor Website for Announcements, Posting of Relevant Material, Grades, etc. | • Instructor Website for Announcements, Posting of Relevant Material, Grades, etc. |
| • **Weekly Online Chats, Synchronous** | • **Face to Face Lectures** |
| • **Discussion Board, Asynchronous** | • E-mail |
| • E-mail | • **Weekly Computer Lab Assignments** |
| • **Mandatory Online Participation/ Online Attendance** | |
| • **Electronic Testing: Online quizzes** | • **In-class quizzes** |
| • In-class Midterm Examinations and Final Exam | • In-class Midterm Examinations and Final Exam |

mandatory. Asynchronous interaction took place via e-mail and a threaded discussion board. The online students supplemented their standard text-book readings with lecture modules that we prepared and posted in advance. The modules were Microsoft Word documents that provided additional analysis and discussion of the most important and/or difficult topics of the week. The main purpose of the lecture modules was to pro-vide the online students with a close substitute for the more traditional face-to-face lecture in the sense that the information content delivered to the online students through the modules reflected the information con-tent provided to the hybrid group in the live lectures.

Table 4 lists the evaluation instruments used in this experiment. Two in-class examinations and a comprehensive in-class final exam were admin-istered to both groups, and they contained the same set of questions for both the online and the hybrid course. In all three cases students had to work on a combination of basic definition and true/false questions, short worked problems, and multiple-choice questions. All answers were graded from common keys, and we used the same point allocation across ques-tions. Three short quizzes (multiple-choice questions only) were also administered. The online students took the quizzes on the Internet while the traditional group was presented with the same questions in class and was allowed to consult books and lecture notes.

TABLE 4
Performance Evaluation Instruments

| *Common Instruments* |
| --- |
| 3 Quizzes (online for Online Students Only) |
| • Common Multiple Choice Questions |
| • Open Books/Notes |
| 2 In-Person Exams |
| • Common Format & Content |
| • Multiple Choice, True/False, and Essay Questions |
| In-Person Final Examination |
| • Common Format & Content |
| • Multiple Choice, True/False, and Essay Questions |
| *Online Course Only* |
| Weekly Online Chat/Online Participation |
| *Hybrid Course Only* |
| Weekly Computer Lab Assignments |
| (Students had to attend class to be allowed to work on the lab assign-ments) |

Finally, the online learners were evaluated on their online class participation, particularly in the weekly chat, while the hybrid group was evaluated on weekly lab assignments. Since only those students who came to
class in person received the lab assignments, lab work counted as class par-
ticipation/attendance for the students in the hybrid course.

## Does Online Learning Improve Performance?

The summary statistics for the performance measures are presented in
Table 5. The most startling outcome we observed was the lower performance of the online learners in their total exam results; this score represented the weighted sum of points earned in the quizzes and in the three
exams, with a maximum possible score of 325. The measure that includes
class participation (maximum total score in this case was 400) is also significantly different between the two groups, with online students again performing worse than the hybrid group. The final grade distribution also
mirrored this trend. The differences are statistically significant at the 5%
level; the performance gap on the second midterm and on the overall
exam score was statistically significant at the 1% level.

Although the online students began the semester with indications of
stronger math background, higher Cal State Fullerton GPA, more academic experience with economics, and lower job-related demand on their
time, they performed significantly worse than the students enrolled in the

TABLE 5
Summary Statistics of Assessment Outcomes

| Variable | Online Group* N=22 | Hybrid Group* N=29 | Test Statistics t-test (p value) df=49 |
|---|---|---|---|
| Quiz 1 | 16.36 (4.61) | 17.84 (4.32) | 1.18 (0.24) |
| Quiz 2 | 17.73 (5.40) | 17.59 (6.66) | 0.08 (0.94) |
| Quiz 3 | 17.84 (4.10) | 14.40 (7.55) | 1.93 (0.06) |
| Midterm 1 | 68.34 (23.95) | 78.97 (10.99) | 2.12 (0.04) |
| Midterm 2 | 52.68 (28.52) | 74.21 (13.19) | 3.60 (0.00) |
| Final Exami- nation | 60.93 (19.51) | 70.81 (12.39) | 2.21 (0.03) |
| All Exams Score | 203.63 (48.86) | 235.52 (36.60) | 2.66 (0.01) |
| Participation | 62.27 (12.98) | 58.63 (14.21) | 0.94 (0.35) |
| Exams + Par- ticipation | 265.90 (52.24) | 294.15 (47.21) | 2.02 (0.049) |

*Note:*     * Means, with standard deviations in parentheses.

live section of the course. These results contradict those of Navarro and Shoemaker (2000a, 2000b) regarding student performance in economic principles, but they lend support to the outcome observed in Brown and Liedholm (2002).

Our finding of poorer performance of the online students was most polarized for midterms and comprehensive final exam results. All three exams included written, essay-type questions that required deeper understanding of the material, and the ability to apply economic concepts and methods to real-world situations. The second midterm, which incorporates analysis of consumer theory and production costs, is usually the most conceptually difficult exam of the semester, and here the online learners performed the worst. On the other hand, the virtual class did not score as poorly on simple multiple-choice quiz questions. This trend in performance outcomes seems to parallel that observed by Brown and Liedholm (2002), with the performance gap between online and traditional learners increasing with the growing sophistication of the test questions.

A review of the summary statistics presented in Table 1 and Table 2 might help to shed some light on to why the online learners performed so poorly.

As previously discussed, students enrolled in the virtual class about a week before instruction began, while students in the hybrid course enrolled almost 20 days before the beginning of instruction. This difference in enrollment dates may be important and indicative of selection bias in the online sample. Both instructors noted that some of the students enrolled in the online class stated that they could not "get into" other closed sections of Economics Principles. Thus, the online method of delivery may not have been their first, preferred choice. In statistical terms, these students may not have been correctly sorted into the teaching and delivery modes best suited to their learning styles, and a form of negative selection bias may have occurred.

Other important differences in student background characteristics were the higher female ratio and the higher percentage of students with children in the online group. In fact, unlike Brown and Liedholm, we found that online female students did worse than their male counterpart, and they performed much worse than the female population in the face-to-face lecture group. We also found that female students in the more traditional setting performed better than their male counterparts.

Table 6 summarizes these findings. Although the t-test statistics indicate that the differences in scores were not statistically significant, the raw data clearly suggest the possibility of the distance-learning environment being especially unfavorable to female students.

Female students, especially working mothers, have traditionally more pressing family needs to attend to. They might have initially thought that the online learning mode would be more flexible and adaptable to their busy schedules. Our results suggest that ultimately the heavy demands on

TABLE 6
Scores by Gender and Instruction Mode

| Variable | Men* | Women* | Test Statistics t-test (p value) |
|---|---|---|---|
| All Exams Score/Online | 204.80 | 202.96 | 0.08 (0.94) |
| | | | df=20 |
| All Exams Score/Hybrid | 231.27 | 241.53 | 0.74 (0.47) |
| | | | df=27 |

Note:    * Means, with standard deviations in parentheses.

working mothers' time did not allow them to dedicate the effort needed for a successful online experience. On the other hand, for the hybrid section of the class the data show better female performance.

To conclude, our results concerning gender-performance relationship in economics courses contradict the usual findings that women do worse than men in economics, and that the performance gap could be reduced with more intensive and comprehensive use of information technology in the course.

## CONCLUDING REMARKS AND SUGGESTIONS FOR FUTURE RESEARCH

This study finds that the virtual classroom environment, when compared to a more traditional setting, has a negative impact on the performance of students taking introductory economics classes. We believe that the use of information technology—beyond the now-pervasive supporting role that such technology has acquired in higher education—has negative effects on student academic performance as measured by traditional evaluation instruments. Furthermore, our data show that female students are potentially at greater disadvantage than their male counterpart when choosing the online option. This result is at odds with previous research that indicates how online delivery of course content might facilitate female learning and retention of economic concepts.

In designing our study, we chose to limit ourselves to easy-to-use, accessible, and relatively simple Internet tools, while other studies included multimedia presentations that used video, digital sound, animated photo images, and interactive graphs, for highly sophisticated content delivery. We think that the development of such multimedia and interactive tools still requires more professional expertise and support than what many small colleges and universities might be able to provide to their faculty and their students.

Our experimental design suffers from two limitations, both of which might have affected our findings. On one hand, because different instructors taught the two courses, there is the possibility of significant instructor bias. We feel quite confident that we addressed this problem as much as possible under the circumstances, controlling for about everything (related to course content and teaching style) that could reasonably be controlled for. Nevertheless, to eliminate any possibility of instructor bias, in future research we will collect data on two groups of students for each delivery mode, and we will have the same instructor teach both a test and a control section of the course each semester.

The second potential source of bias in the data comes from students' self-selecting the type of course. It is not clear to us whether in the future it will be possible to randomly assign students to each class without violating university rules and without artificially restricting the students' enrollment options. The second-best approach to addressing the self-selection problem is the one we took in our experiment. It involves collecting as much information as possible on student background characteristics in order to be able to control for factors different from the specifics of the course design, which might influence performance.

Finally, the authors are fully aware of a more general pedagogical issue concerning whether the traditional performance evaluation tools are all together obsolete and inadequate to evaluate teaching and learning in the virtual environment.

## REFERENCES

Agarwal, R., & Day, A.E. (1998). The Impact of the Internet on Economic Education. *Journal of Economic Education, 1998*(Spring), 99-110.

Blackley, J. A., & Curran-Smith, J. (1998). Teaching Community Health Nursing by Distance Methods: Devlopment, Process, and Evaluation. *Journal of Continuing Education for Nurses, 29*, 148-153,

Bonca, C. (September 4-10, 1998). Welcome to Virtual U. *OC Weekly.*

Brewer, S., & Erickson, D. (1997). A Tale of Two Classrooms. *Journal of Computing in Teacher Education, 13*, 20-22.

Brown, B. W., & Liedholm, C. E. (in press). Can Web Courses Replace the Classroom in Principles of Microeconomics? *American Economic Review.*

California State University Fullerton. (2001). Springtime Blossom With Record Crop of Students. *Public Affairs, March 12, 2001.* Retrieved July 5, 2002 from the Cal State Fullerton Web site: http://www.fullerton.edu

Carnevale, C. (2001). What Matters in Judging Distance Teaching? Not How Much It's Like a Classroom Course. *The Chronicle of Higher Education.*

Case, K. E., & Fair, R. C. (2001). *Principles of Microeconomics*, Sixth Ed., Prentice Hall.

Gagne, M., & Shepherd, M. (2001). Distance Learning in Accounting: A Comparison Between a Distance and Traditional Graduate Accounting Class. *T.H.E. Journal 28*, 58-65.

Green, R., & Gentemann, K. (2001). Technology in the Curriculum: An Assessment of the Impact of On-Line Courses. *George Mason University.*

Goldberg, D. (1998). Teaching Online-Education Review. *The Washington Post*, April 5.

Johnson, S. D., Aragon, S. R., Shaik, N., & Palma-Rivas, N. (2000). Comparative Analysis of Learner Satisfaction and Learning Outcomes in Online and Face-to-Face Learning Environments. *Journal of Interactive Learning Research, 11*, 29-49, 2000.

Kane, J., & Spizman, L. (1999). Determinants of Student Retention of Microeconomics Principles Concepts. *Working Paper,* SUNY-Oswego, 1999-01.

Kashy, D. A., Albertelli, G., Kashy, E., & Thoennessen, M. (2001). Teaching with ALN Technology: Benefits and Costs. *Journal of Engineering Education*, (October).

Maki, R. H., Maki, W. S., Patterson, M., & Whittaker, P. D. (2000). Evaluation of a Web-based Introductory Psychology Course: Learning and Satisfaction in On-line versus Lecture Courses. *Behavior Research Methods, Instruments, & Computers, 32*, 230-239.

McCollum, K. (1997). In Test, Students Taught on Line Outdo Those Taught in Class. *The Chronicle of Higher Education*, (February 21).

Morrissey, C. A. (1998). The Impact of the Internet on Management Education: What the Research Shows. *Pepperdine University.*

Navarro, P. (2000). Economics in the Cyberclassroom. *Journal of Economic Perspectives, 14*(Spring), 119-132.

Navarro, P., & Shoemaker, J. (DATE?). Economics in Cyberspace: A Comparison Study. *Mimeo*, University of California-Irvine.

Navarro, P., & Shoemaker, J. (1999). The Power of Cyberlearning: An empirical test. *Journal of Computing in Higher Education, 11*(Fall), 29-54.

Navarro, P., & Shoemaker, J. (2000a). Policy Issues in the Teaching of Economics in Cyberspace: Research Design, Course Design, and Research Results. *Contemporary Economic Policy 18*(July), 359-366.

Navarro, P., & Shoemaker, J. (2000b). Performance and Perceptions of Distance Learners in Cyberspace. *The American Journal of Distance Education, 14*, 15-35.

Sherry, A. C., Fulford C. P., & Zhang, S. (1998). Assessing Distance Learners' Satisfaction with Instruction: A Quantitative and a Qualitative Measure. *The American Journal of Distance Education 12*, 4-28.

Simkins, S. (1999). Promoting Active-Student Learning Using the World Wide Web in Economics Courses. *Journal of Economic Education, 1999*(Summer), 278-291.

Smeaton, A., & Keogh, G. (1999). An Analysis of the Use of Virtual Delivery of Undergraduate Lectures. *Computers and Education, 32*, 83-94.

Stinson, B. M., & Claus, K. (2000). The Effects of Electronic Classrooms on Learning English Composition. *The Journal, 27*(7).

Twigg, C. A. (2001). Innovation in Online Learning: Moving Beyond No Significant Difference. *Center for Academic Transformation*, The Pew Learning and Technology Program, Rensselaer Polytechnic Institute.

Vachris, M.A. (1997). Teaching Economics in a Virtual Classroom. *Virginia Economic Journal, 1997*(September).

Vachris, M.A. (1999). Teaching Principles of Economics without 'Chalk and Talk': The Experience of CNU Online. *Journal of Economic Education, 30,* 292-303.

Vasarhelyi, M., & Graham, L. (1997). Cybersmart: Education and the Internet. *Management Accounting, 1997*(August), 32-36.

Virginia Tech. (1998). Course Restructuring and the Instructional Development Initiative at Virginia Polytechnic Institute: A Benefit Cost Study. Virginia Tech.

Zhang, P. (1998). A Case Study on Technology Use in Distance Learning. *Journal of Research on Computing in Education, 30,* 398-416.

CHAPTER 10

# DEVELOPING AN EFFECTIVE ONLINE ORIENTATION COURSE TO PREPARE STUDENTS FOR SUCCESS IN A WEB-BASED LEARNING ENVIRONMENT

Maggie McVay Lynch

This chapter describes a study designed to provide tools for independent, self-directed learning in a Web-based distance learning environment. Previously, student drop-out rates during the term ranged from 35% to 50%. Faculty often complained that the majority of the first weeks of online classes were spent troubleshooting the problems students encountered with the technology. Students reported feeling isolated from peers and frequently had difficulty receiving timely feedback to questions and homework assignments from their instructors.

A Web-based student orientation course was created, implemented, and evaluated with regard to its impact in enhancing student success. During implementation, 392 students entered the orientation course and 376 completed it. An analysis of the data revealed that 89% of students showed an

Electronic Learning Communities—Issues and Practices, pages 367–411.
Copyright © 2003 by Information Age Publishing, Inc.
All rights of reproduction in any form reserved.
ISBN: 1-931576-96-3 (pbk.), 1-931576-97-1 (hardcover)

increase in computer skills; 74% indicated increased feelings of connected-ness, independence, and self-direction. The student attrition rate over nine months was reduced to 15% following this orientation course.

**KEYWORDS:** orientation, online, attrition, Web-based, drop-out, course

## INTRODUCTION

Much anecdotal information abounds in listservs and in interviews regarding high dropout rates in online courses and the lack of student re-enrollment following participation in an online course. During 1999 and 2000 this phenomena was studied in a small, private, urban university composed of roughly 5,000 students. This chapter presents research findings and provides one perspective on how effective creation and implementation of a required online student orientation course made a significant difference in student success and re-enrollment in Web-based learning.

The goal of the research was to afford students a satisfying experience in self-directed learning in a Web-based distance learning environment where they might develop and demonstrate technological competence and gain confidence in their ability to be successful, independent learners.

### Expected Outcomes

The following outcomes were projected for the study:

1. Eighty percent of students entering the university's Web-based distance learning program would demonstrate an increase in their technology skills within one trimester.
2. Seventy percent of students entering the university's Web-based distance learning program would experience an increase in independent, self-directed learning within two trimesters.
3. Ninety percent of students entering the university's Web-based distance learning program would discern their preferred learning styles and be able to adjust them as needed, to accommodate differences in the distance environment, within one trimester.
4. Ninety percent of students entering the university's Web-based distance learning program would demonstrate an ability to communicate effectively in a Web-based learning community by clarifying

course expectations and describing their learning needs within one trimester.

5. The attrition rate of entering online students would be reduced to 10% or less over a two-trimester period.

## DISCUSSION OF ISSUES

### Problem Description

As the university began offering some online courses, several difficulties soon surfaced:

- Student drop-out rates during the term ranged from 35% to 50%.
- Faculty complained that much of their time during the first three weeks of class was spent troubleshooting problems the students voice concerning the technology, i.e., their personal computer's hardware and software.
- Students reported some negative feelings toward the program. They cited feeling isolated from peers and also related they had difficulty receiving timely feedback on homework assignments and to questions they posed to their instructors.

The faculty's initial response to these difficulties was to withdraw from offering the online courses and to return primarily to classroom-based training. The faculty felt strongly that the online delivery model was not effective and that it, in fact, diminished the quality of education for which the university was renowned. Subsequently, the faculty senate recommended to the administration that the university no longer pursue an online delivery model.

The administration faced the following dilemma: faculty perceived that the Web-based course delivery method was a failure, but a Board-mandated five-year strategic initiative for online delivery remained in place. After further study, the university elected to hire up to three educators whose experience specifically related to distance education and online training. Because of the lack of faculty support within the existing divisional structure, a new division was formed that was comprised of distance education and technology services. This division would serve as the center of any development, training, and dissemination of online courses. Though campus-based faculty were offered the opportunity to participate in the new division, only one faculty member elected to do so. Faculty members for the division, then, were recruited from outside the university.

One of the mandates of this hiring process was to find staff who would resolve the identified problems of student attrition, faculty time spent on technology support, and students' feelings of isolation. The mandates included the charge to develop a course or curriculum that would reinforce positive online interaction and good learning theory throughout the online delivery experience.

Upon the hiring of two faculty in the distance education department, the author of this chapter began to document the difficulties anecdotally described by faculty and students. The following six methods were used to document the problem:

1. An informal interview was conducted with faculty members who had taught online courses.
2. A review of online student registration records was performed to determine attrition in online courses versus campus-based courses.
3. A survey of students' entering technology skills was conducted.
4. Following their first course, students' reflection papers regarding their learning process were collected.
5. Bulletin board questions were posted asking students to comment on their preferred learning style and its impact on their success in the online environment.
6. A literature review of difficulties students had with Web-based distance education was undertaken.

## Faculty Interviews

The following questions were asked of each faculty member in phone or in-person interviews:

1. What did you find most difficult or frustrating about teaching online?
2. Did you feel that teaching online was as effective as your classroom-based course? Why?
3. What did you find most rewarding about teaching online?

Eight of the 12 online teaching faculty members were interviewed. Two trends consistently appeared in the majority of responses: students were unprepared to use the Web-based technology; and faculty and students were unprepared to communicate effectively in an electronic environment. Appendix A provides the transcript of faculty responses.

## Review of Student Registration Records

A review of online students' registration records revealed a higher attrition rate in online courses than in classroom-based courses. During the academic year, the average attrition rate in classroom-based courses was approximately 10%, whereas the average attrition rate in online courses was almost three times higher at 28%, with the upper limit of attrition as much as 60% in some classes.

## Results of Student Technology Skills Survey

Beginning in the Fall, 323 students entering online courses were surveyed and requested to rate their current technology skills. The survey, administered via an Internet Webpage, asked 38 questions (see Appendix B). The students were asked to answer either "yes" or "no" as to whether they were able to perform the stated skill. Twelve of these questions were considered primary items. These were designated as the minimum technology skills required for successful participation in a fully online course (Table 1). Forty-two percent of entering students were unable to answer "yes" to all of the primary (bolded) items. Only 14% of entering students

TABLE 1
Survey Items Representing Minimum Required Technology Skills.

| Survey Item # | Statement |
|---|---|
| 2 | I use a computer every day. |
| 4 | When I have a problem with my computer I have someone I can call to fix it within 24 hours. |
| 6 | I know how to print a document from my word processing program. |
| 8 | I know how to set margins in my word processing program. |
| 9 | I know how to paginate (set page numbering) and set headers and footers in my word processing program. |
| 12 | I use an Internet e-mail program every day. |
| 15 | I have sent an attached document with e-mail. |
| 18 | I know how to use a search engine (e.g., Yahoo or AltaVista) to find information on the Internet. |
| 22 | I easily follow "hot links" from one Webpage to another. |
| 23 | I am able to navigate backward and forward among many Webpages. |
| 24 | I know how to print Webpages from the Internet. |
| 25 | I know how to navigate and print within frames. |

were able to perform all the technology skills required for successful participation in the university's online learning model.

## Student Reflections on Class Bulletin Board

In a Summer pilot program, 15 students were asked to respond to the following statement posted on the class bulletin board: "Analyze your learning style and determine what you need to do to be successful in an online learning environment." Ten of the students were not able to identify their learning style at all. Of the five students who could identify a learning style, not one was able to articulate how it impacted their online learning or what they might need to do to be successful in an online online learning environment.

At the end of their first online course the following Fall, 25 students were asked to reflect on their learning, and their perceived readiness for distance education at the beginning of the course compared to the end of the course. Students recorded their reflections in an essay of 500 to 1,000 words. Twenty-two of 25 students reported that they had perceived themselves as good independent, self-directed learners at the beginning of the course. However, by the end of the course, all 25 students reported discovering their independent and self-directed learning skills were lacking when they entered the online program. The experience of the course had clarified those realizations.

## Literature Review of Online Student Difficulties

A literature review was conducted to identify difficulties that students encountered at other institutions. Three areas of difficulty matched those found at the author's institution: student feelings of isolation, miscommunication of expectations regarding the online learning environment, and students' lack of confidence in their ability to learn the subject matter effectively. This literature review also provided a match with several of the problems already identified and documented by the faculty interviews, attrition analysis, student technology surveys, bulletin board responses, and the student reflection papers.

When analyzing student difficulties in completing online courses, myriad causes were considered. The causes most frequently documented in the literature included student lack of independence or self-directedness, interpersonal dynamics between students and teachers, unprepared or untrained faculty, lack of clarity of specific processes and procedures required in online learning, difficulties with hardware and software technologies, lack of support services, and feelings of isolation. In order to limit the initial analysis of causes, the investigation was confined to those causes that directly related to student preparedness for online learning.

The literature review was organized around the central concept of student preparedness for online learning. Five questions were investigated:

1. What effect does knowledge of technology have on student success?
2. When do online students perceive themselves as independent, self-directed learners?
3. How do online students generalize their mental models from a face-to-face learning experience to a primarily asynchronous online experience?
4. What impact does online course design have on student success?
5. What impact do teacher-student and student-student online communications have on student success?

### Technology

Students' frustration with technology in their distance education courses has been documented by several researchers (Burge, 1994; Gregor & Cuskelly, 1994; Hara & Kling, 2000; Kang, 1988; Wiesenberg & Hutton, 1995; Yakimovicz & Murphy, 1995). Hara and Kling (2000) specifically cited student frustration concerning access to technical support. Furthermore, they indicated that many students reported spending as much time trying to resolve technical problems as they did learning the content of the course. McMahon (1999) reported that students view their lack of training in computers as the strongest inhibitor to computer use.

### Experience

A few researchers cited students' experience in the distance learning environment as the primary causative agent in measurements of success or failure. Moore and Kearsley (1996) stated, "Since most students have little experience learning at a distance, they are unfamiliar with it and may be anxious about taking distance education courses ... this unfamiliarity is translated into resistance . . . ." (p.166). Charp (1994) noted that with greater autonomy, student characteristics such as active listing and the ability to work independently become crucial for success. Solloway and Harris (1999) found that students expressed discomfort at not having the instructor's input to guide them.

### Isolation and Self-direction

The problem of students' isolation in distance education courses has been the topic of many research papers (Abrahamson, 1998; Besser & Donahue, 1996; Brown, 1996; Rahm & Reed, 1998; Twigg, 1997). Certainly a part of this is directly related to not seeing the instructor or class peers. Not having the face-to-face questioning of professors was also cited by Young (1998) as a possible factor leading to the perceived lessening of self-discipline in online students. Harrell (1999) reported that students experience negative feelings about the lack of face-to-face social contact, and that those who have tried working at home report feelings of isolation and loneliness. Hara and Kling (2000) disagreed with the findings of student isolation as a primary difficulty in online learning. Instead they found two related difficulties provided the most frustration—promptness of instructor response, and ambiguity of instructor-to-student communication.

> Students' concerns about receiving prompt, unambiguous feedback continued throughout the term ... many of the students worked on the course during the late evenings and weekends ... What is needed is for the students and instructors to learn how to manage their expectations about when they should be able to have reliable, fast communicative responses." (p. 21)

Reid (1997) further elaborated on the interpersonal contact dilemma and traditional delivery design, concluding that some students will simply find that self-learning is too difficult or frustrating.

### Mental Models

An important part of student preparedness is described within the conceptual framework of students' ability to generalize their mental models to the new environment. Jonassen (1995) suggests that learners will generalize existing models to new phenomena through a process known as structure mapping—linking the old structural relations to new ones. However, frequently within the online environment students have not been given analogies to use for this structure mapping process. Carly and Palmquist (1992) examined this further by elaborating on five specific characteristics of successful mental models:

1. Mental models are internal representations.
2. Language is the key to understanding mental models.
3. Mental models can be represented as networks of concepts.
4. The meanings for the concepts are embedded in their relationships to other concepts.
5. The social meaning of concepts is derived from the intersection of different individuals' mental models.

These characteristics all presuppose a language and relationship among concepts that allow students to derive meaning. It would then follow that if students are not provided instruction or assistance in formulating the relationships, they may not be successful in generating the necessary new mental models. Harasim (1997) supported this analysis by suggesting that many online course problems can be traced to a lack of customized tools to support instructional activities, learning activities, and design and integration of multimedia.

Young (1998) argued that the "human element in the student-professor relationship is crucial for developing the skills needed to interpolate data gathered" (p. 570). This may then suggest that without the "human element," online students may not be able to generalize their mental models effectively. Solloway and Harris (1999) posed an interesting question that related to the generalization of mental models. Their question encapsulated the difficulty of developing online courses or dialogues that facilitate learning. They asked, "Does 'learner-centered' mean supporting the student in whatever way he or she interprets the instructor's role?" (p. 9). The answer to this question may well impact solutions for both traditional and online instruction.

### Online Course Design

Following the logic that effective course design is the primary component in online student success, Harasim (1997) concluded that most course design does not exploit the tools of the Internet to present information and increase interactivity. Specifically, she suggested that course design must include the following to be successful:

- high rates of student participation,
- group interaction among students,
- high quality of intellectual exchange, and
- spatial metaphors used as mental models to help students adjust to online structured courses.

Lefrere (1997) particularly agreed with concepts of interaction among students. He suggested a teaching/learning model called "conversation theory" that becomes an adaptive and reflective discourse between student and teacher. However, like Moore and Kearsley (1996), Lefrere questioned whether students are prepared to use primary materials meaningfully. Relating to interactivity, a more specific reason for student difficulty was offered by researchers who indicated that students are primarily in a passive role when interacting online (Charp, 1994; Duffy & Jonassen, 1992; Lefrere, 1997).

Holloway and Ohler (1991) spoke to the issues of learner motivation by suggesting that distance learning technology design or use does not make the performance of learning tasks rewarding. Other researchers (Carly & Palmquist, 1992; Duffy & Jonassen, 1992; Moore & Kearsely, 1996; Sponder, 1990) clarified these issues of motivation by specifying the relationship of course relevancy to the student's real-world experiences. These researchers suggested that a situated cognition model is necessary to ensure learning success.

### Online Communication

Several researchers (Lefrere, 1997; McVay, 2000; Moore & Kearsley, 1996; Sponder, 1990; Winn, 1997) expanded on the concepts of interaction and conversation between students and teachers by further indicating that miscommunication can obscure learning expectations. Furthermore, they agreed that better guidance toward learning in the new online environment is required. Insight regarding online miscommunication was given by Berge and Collins (1995) and Wegerif (1998), who found that students desire immediate feedback from instructors and express a need for more synchronous activities in the online environment. Porter's (1994) work also supported the need for timely feedback. Specifically, he found that students wanted tools to help them monitor their progress. He also concluded that teacher mediation during courses needed to be increased.

### Online Support Structures

Several researchers (Kimball, 1995; Moore & Kearsley, 1996; Porter, 1994; Sponder, 1990) found that many support structures and processes that might assist students' transition to Web-based learning were not in place. Specific structures mentioned included:

- student orientation to technology and learning,
- tutoring services,
- consistent methodologies for completing and submitting assignments,
- library or research services,
- registration and tracking, and
- bookstore access.

McCormack and Jones (1998) discovered that even the most basic of services—access to the Internet—was not consistent in many online classes. Their research stated: "The most cited problem with using Web-based classrooms is with providing access. Students struggle to gain access to electricity, computers, ISPs . . . ." (p. 22).

## Conclusion of Literature Review

In conclusion, the research upheld that distance students are faced with a lack of experience in the new online environment, and that this lack of experience impacts their ability to generalize mental models to the new environment. Students are faced with the need to integrate technology with the human element in order to communicate effectively. This communication influences feelings of connectedness, motivation, and self-direction in the online environment. Though researchers suggested many possible causes for student difficulties, it seems that this union of technology and human communication has frequently failed due to reliance on single solution methodologies. This union may ultimately only be accomplished through the implementation of a combined resource methodology that includes good support structures, clear learning guidance, effective tools for monitoring and feedback, and relevancy to students' real-world experiences.

## DISCUSSION OF SOLUTION STRATEGY

## Potential Solutions from the Literature

The literature review did not find any specific solutions to the problem of independence or self-directed learning in a Web-based environment. The majority of Web-based education research has centered on course development, faculty training, and generalized learning theory, rather than on the perspective of student success. Another substantial amount of research addresses access to technology and the effective use of technology specific to the online learning environment. Therefore the author derived potential solutions by extrapolating from these environments and re-interpreting findings to place them within the student perspective.

### *Course Development*

Because Web-based learning is a new field, the preponderance of research has focused on the development of effective courses. In the past four years, the recurring theme of interactivity has been paramount. Several researchers (Harasim, 1997; Lefrere, 1997; McVay, 2000; Moore & Kearsley, 1996; Sponder, 1990) indicated a need to increase interactivity and communication between students and teachers. They stated that this increase in interactivity would help to clarify learning expectations, increase group interaction, and provide more opportunities for high quality intellectual exchange. Harasim et al. (1997) further expanded on interactivity by focusing on the need to extensively develop the importance of learning communities. They insisted that active learning requires participation and that "participation is based on making input, responding to peers, and sharing ideas" (p.29). Sponder (1990) found that the increase in interactivity between students and teachers, in particular, would lessen the attrition rate of online students.

Specific to course content, many researchers suggested a curriculum that provides students an opportunity to practice skills needed in the distance learning environment (Solloway & Harris, 1999; Lefrere, 1997; McVay, 2000; Winn, 1997). These researchers advanced five principal suggestions to put into practice online:

1. Provide students time to familiarize themselves with the online environment.
2. Provide guidance to help students construct knowledge from information.
3. Provide opportunities for situated learning.
4. Provide support for social learning.
5. Provide instruction or tutorials in the use of all technology needed in the online environment.

Additional researchers contributed further studies on the specifics of these five elements. The use of a situated cognition approach to course design and assignment implementation is promoted by several researchers (Ackerman, 1996; Carly & Palmquist, 1992; Duffy & Jonassen, 1993; Harasim, 1997; Moore & Kearsley, 1996; Sponder, 1990). Providing support for social learning is specifically addressed by researchers who suggested increasing opportunities for synchronous activities (Ackerman, 1996; Berge & Collins, 1995; Wegerif, 1998; Winn, 1997).

Porter (1994) was one of the first to suggest that students would accept distance learning technology if they were presented with demonstrations on how to use the technology to increase their learning. Solloway and Harris (1999) suggested combining all of the course development attributes listed above and Porter's (1994) demonstration theory into a comprehensive student orientation course. Young (1998) agreed that "completion of such a course would be one way to ensure that students' computer knowledge would be adequate to proceed to the next step in developing cyberclasses" (p. 569). He went on to suggest that this orientation course include social science research and that it be worth one-credit hour.

### Faculty Training

Given the traditional model of teacher-centered education, it is not surprising that the issue of preparing faculty for online teaching has been a significant part of the research. A primary focus of faculty training research is in providing opportunities for active learning (Charp, 1994; Harasim, 1997; Jonassen, 1995; Lefrere, 1997; McVay, 2000; Moore & Kearsley, 1996). These researchers further suggested that active learning opportunities need to lead students toward taking responsibility for their own learning. Charp (1994) specifically noted that with greater autonomy, student characteristics such as active listening and the ability to work independently become crucial for success.

McVay (2000) addressed the issue of active learning by providing students with specifics on setting learning expectations. She suggested that students be self-aware of the need for independence, self-direction, and the synthesis of personal, professional, and study experiences in their learning process primarily through the use of reflective techniques. Moore and Kearsley (1996) also addressed the importance of setting expectations, but from an instructor's viewpoint. They related three typical mistaken assumptions about distance education that lead to student attrition:

1. Web-based courses are easier than conventional classes and require less work.
2. Distance education will be of lesser quality than traditional delivery methods.
3. Students don't understand the need to take responsibility for learning. Instead, they wait for instructor prompting.

Moore and Kearsley further suggested that instructors need to give "reassurance that mistakes and failures are a natural part of learning; that risk-taking is approved; and that there is no such thing as a dumb question" (p. 155).

Several researchers recommended that an effective way for online instructors to set student expectations and encourage active learning is by increasing teacher mediation during the course (Berge & Collins, 1995; Porter, 1994; Sponder, 1990). Specifically, the frequent use of e-mails, responsiveness to bulletin board postings, and increased opportunities for synchronous interaction are cited as good techniques. Porter (1994) extended the instructor mediation concept to also include opportunities for students to self-monitor. He suggested that instructors provide tools to help students monitor their progress and to obtain timely feedback on their activities.

### Learning Theory

The focus of learning theory in the online environment is found in the field of situated cognition or in the generalization of mental models, from traditional education to online education. In terms of the study problem, the theories around the generalization of mental models seemed the most applicable. Several researchers argued that for students to be successful online, instructors must assist them in recognizing their mental models and generalizing them to the new environment (Carly & Palmquist, 1992; Harasim, 1997; Jonassen, 1995). Jonassen (1995) offered criteria for evalu-

TABLE 2
Criteria for Evaluating Mental Models—Jonassen (1995), Section 3.3

| Characteristic | Measure |
|---|---|
| Coherence | Structural knowledge, think-aloud |
| Purpose/personal relevance | Self-report, cognitive interview |
| Integration | Cognitive simulation |
| Fidelity with real world | Comparison to expert |
| Imagery | Generating metaphors, analogies |
| Complexity | Structural knowledge |
| Applicability/transferability | Teach back, think-aloud |
| Inferential/implicational ability | Running the model |

ating mental models (see Table 2). These criteria may strengthen the course development process as well as the teacher-student interaction.

### Technology Access and Support

The final area of research centered on technology access issues and providing a variety of technological support structures for students. McCormack and Jones (1998) indicated that increasing Internet access points for students would lessen attrition. They argued that many students still struggle to gain simple access to clean phone lines, computers, and Internet Service Providers (ISPs). Several researchers expanded access issues to include specific online support structures such as tutoring, library services, guidance counseling, and student mentoring to help decrease attrition (Moore & Kearsley, 1996; Porter, 1994; Sponder, 1990).

## Description of Selected Solutions

The research upheld that distance students are faced with a lack of experience in the new online environment, and that this lack of experience impacts their ability to generalize mental models to the new setting. Students are faced with the need to integrate technology with the human element in order to communicate effectively. This clear communication enhances feelings of connectedness, motivation, and self-direction in the online milieu.

As suggested by several researchers (Porter, 1994; Solloway & Harris, 1999; Young, 1998), the creation and implementation of a student orientation course could provide a significant impact on the problem. The key to the production of this orientation course was to include those elements that would provide students with a robust experience that would familiarize them with the technology, the communication tools, and the learning process necessary to be successful. The course also needed to prepare students for future online courses by presenting expectations of the students' participation and conduct, and by introducing typical assignments they will encounter.

## DISCUSSION OF STUDY RESULTS

### Research Sample Description

A total of 483 students participated in the course during the eight-month implementation. However, 19% of the participants were students auditing the class. These consisted of community college faculty, various university advisers and support staff, and marketing personnel. These faculty and support staff did not intend to pursue additional distance education, therefore their participation data were not included in the analysis of outcomes and follow-up.

Four months into the implementation, the orientation course became institutionalized. It was the first required course for all Web-based distance students. In June 1999, the first version of the orientation course was offered to 213 students. The formative evaluation was undertaken in July and changes were made in August. In September 1999, the revised course was offered to 270 students. Excluding the audit student data, a total of 392 students were enrolled in the orientation course over the two-trimester period, with 376 students completing the course.

### Implementation

In developing the course content, close attention was paid to the research recommendations regarding course development, interaction, and learning theory. Specifically, the course included familiarization and practice with:

- setting expectations,
- interactivity,
- skill practice,
- situated learning,
- knowledge construction,
- socialization, and
- recognition and generalization of mental models.

During the implementation phase of the study, following a formative evaluation based on student and instructor feedback, the course was revised.

Instructors provided feedback via informal interviews based on their journal comments during the conduct of the course. Students provided formative feedback via the reflection paper required at the end of the orientation course. The combination of these tools provided information for making changes to the course.

In the second trimester, outcome data were gathered for each iteration of the course, and pre- and post-formative evaluation data were compared to determine if any of the course changes had impacted student success in this course and in subsequent classes. The findings were then compiled for recommending any future course changes.

The orientation course became institutionalized in two phases. First, it was made the first required course for all Web-based distance students registering at the university through the community college partnership program. Secondly, following the formative evaluation and subsequent course changes, the orientation course became required for all students (campus-based and distance) prior to undertaking any Web-based course offered by the university.

### Course Content Changes

During the first three months, the orientation course was offered in seven-week increments. After the formative evaluation of the pilot course in months two and three, the university began developing a new primary course delivery model. This model, called the "balanced learning format," required the bachelor's completion degree program courses be offered in a compressed format (six-week courses for four-credit hours, and three-week courses for two-credit hours) for both classroom-based and Web-based delivery. The orientation course had to be redesigned to reflect: content changes determined by the formative evaluation process; and a three-week format that could be adapted to six weeks as needed. Additionally, the administration wanted the orientation course to serve the needs of both compressed formats—classroom-based and Web-based compressed format. Finally, the redesigned orientation course took on a name change and increased significance in the university's curriculum. The name was changed from "Online Learning Orientation" to "Advanced Learning Strategies." The course number was also reassigned from PF100 to PF280, reflecting the faculty and administration view that the content was more significant than a 100 level course. In addition, the course credit allocation was changed from one credit-hour to two credit-hours to reflect the amount of work required of the students during the course.

### Instructional Changes

During the first four months of the implementation, faculty who indicated a desire to teach online were enrolled in a required 12-week Faculty Development Course. When the university adopted the compressed format model, it also impacted the faculty development course, changing it to a six-week course, incorporating content to meet the needs of both Web-based and classroom-based formats. The faculty had already demonstrated resistance to teaching in an online format. The added change to a compressed course model resulted in most faculty either refusing to teach online or choosing to leave the university. During this time the university experienced a 28% turn-over in full-time faculty, and thus a sudden increased need for additional adjunct recruitment and training.

In conclusion, the two largest impacts to the implementation plan were the unexpected influx of online students resulting in a need for more sections of the course, and the new university policy directive for implementing a compressed format delivery model. Both situations were addressed by compressing the course change and updates timeline, by creating additional course sections, and by mentoring additional faculty. Any influence these changes had on the students in the orientation course and the data collected and analyzed during this study then became an uncontrolled variable.

## Outcome Results

Five outcomes were identified and measured in this study. Four of five outcomes were met and exceeded expectations. This indicates that the orientation course made a significant difference in student success within the Web-based learning environment. The result of each outcome and its derivation is presented below.

> **Outcome 1:** Eighty percent (80%) of the students entering the university's Web-based distance learning program would report an increase in their technology skills within one trimester.

A self-report Computer Skills Survey (see Appendix B) was administered at both the onset and the conclusion of the orientation course. Students were asked to answer "yes" or "no" as to whether they possessed a particular computer skill. The data from the pre- and post-treatment were compared to measure the change. Eighty-nine percent of students displayed an increase in skill level in one or more computer skills. The Computer Skills Survey data (see Table 3 for summary) were analyzed according to three skill categories:

1. Minimum prerequisite skills for successful participation in Web-based courses (represented by survey: items 6, 8, 9, 12, 15, 18, 22, 23, 24, and 25).

TABLE 3
Summary Computer Skills Survey Data

| Item No. | PRE (n=392) | | | POST (n=376) | | | % Improved |
|---|---|---|---|---|---|---|---|
| | Yes | No | % Yes | Yes | No | % Yes | |
| 1 | 326 | 66 | 83.2% | 342 | 50 | 91.0% | 7.8% |
| 2 | 361 | 31 | 92.1% | 376 | 0 | 100.0 % | 7.9% |
| 3 | 224 | 168 | 57.1% | 283 | 93 | 50.5% | -6.6% |
| 4 | 321 | 71 | 81.9% | 371 | 5 | 97.3% | 15.5% |
| 5 | 285 | 107 | 72.7% | 373 | 3 | 98.4% | 25.7% |
| 6 | 392 | 0 | 100.0 % | 376 | 0 | 100.0 % | 0.0% |
| 7 | 311 | 81 | 79.3% | 341 | 51 | 77.1% | -2.2% |
| 8 | 377 | 15 | 96.2% | 376 | 0 | 100.0 % | 3.8% |
| 9 | 236 | 156 | 60.2% | 376 | 0 | 100.0 % | 39.8% |
| 10 | 153 | 239 | 39.0% | 376 | 0 | 100.0 % | 61.0% |
| 11 | 153 | 239 | 39.0% | 376 | 0 | 100.0 % | 61.0% |
| 12 | 361 | 31 | 92.1% | 376 | 0 | 100.0 % | 7.9% |
| 13 | 326 | 66 | 83.2% | 368 | 8 | 95.7% | 12.6% |
| 14 | 288 | 104 | 73.5% | 376 | 0 | 100.0 % | 26.5% |
| 15 | 336 | 56 | 85.7% | 376 | 0 | 100.0 % | 14.3% |
| 16 | 255 | 137 | 65.1% | 368 | 8 | 95.7% | 30.7% |
| 17 | 336 | 56 | 85.7% | 376 | 0 | 100.0 % | 14.3% |
| 18 | 300 | 92 | 76.5% | 376 | 0 | 100.0 % | 23.5% |
| 19 | 274 | 118 | 69.9% | 376 | 0 | 100.0 % | 30.1% |
| 20 | 143 | 249 | 36.5% | 371 | 5 | 97.3% | 60.9% |
| 21 | 123 | 269 | 31.4% | 372 | 4 | 97.9% | 66.5% |
| 22 | 340 | 52 | 86.7% | 376 | 0 | 100.0 % | 13.3% |
| 23 | 275 | 117 | 70.2% | 376 | 0 | 100.0 % | 29.8% |
| 24 | 340 | 52 | 86.7% | 376 | 0 | 100.0 % | 13.3% |
| 25 | 255 | 137 | 65.1% | 376 | 0 | 100.0 % | 34.9% |
| 26 | 265 | 127 | 67.6% | 376 | 0 | 100.0 % | 32.4% |
| 27 | 229 | 163 | 58.4% | 332 | 44 | 76.6% | 18.2% |
| 28 | 214 | 178 | 54.6% | 242 | 134 | 28.7% | -25.9% |
| 29 | 66 | 326 | 16.8% | 372 | 4 | 97.9% | 81.0% |
| 30 | 76 | 316 | 19.4% | 376 | 0 | 100.0 % | 80.6% |
| 31 | 66 | 326 | 16.8% | 372 | 4 | 97.9% | 81.0% |
| 32 | 183 | 209 | 46.7% | 374 | 2 | 98.9% | 52.3% |
| 33 | 92 | 300 | 23.5% | 355 | 21 | 88.8% | 65.4% |
| 34 | 173 | 219 | 44.1% | 376 | 0 | 100.0 % | 55.9% |
| 35 | 41 | 351 | 10.5% | 376 | 0 | 100.0 % | 89.5% |
| 36 | 189 | 203 | 48.2% | 376 | 0 | 100.0 % | 51.8% |
| 37 | 143 | 249 | 36.5% | 376 | 0 | 100.0 % | 63.5% |
| 38 | 158 | 234 | 40.3% | 376 | 0 | 100.0 % | 59.7% |

2.  Intermediate skills used in Web-based courses (items 7, 10, 11, 13, 16, 20, 21, 26, 34 and 35).
3.  Advanced skills used in Web-based courses (items 27-33 and 36-38).

Prior to implementation of the study, most student advisers and deans assumed that students who registered for online courses possessed the minimum prerequisite skills. This assumption proved to be inaccurate. Analysis of the data revealed that prior to the orientation course, students entering the program rarely reflected mastery in even the minimal computer skills. The highest percentages of positive responses were grouped around basic skills in word processing, e-mail usage, and Webpage navigation. These skills were: printing from a word processor (100%), setting margins in the word processor (96%) using an e-mail program (92%), sending an attachment with an e-mail (86%), following hot-links on Webpages (86%), and printing pages from the Web (87%). It is worth noting that only 3 of the 10 prerequisite skill items received a response of 90% or above.

The percentage of positive responses in the remainder of the prerequisite skills ranged from 60% to 77%. The lowest percentages of positive responses in the prerequisite skills centered around intermediate prerequisite skills in word processing, navigating Webpages, and printing Webpages. These skills included pagination in word processing (60%), navigation backward and forward among Webpages (70%), and navigating and printing Webpages within frames (65%).

In contrast, the non-prerequisite skills fared far worse. Five items scored below 20% for students' possessing the skill; nine items scored between 30% and 50%; 6 items scored between 50% and 75%; and the remaining three items scored over 80%. The only non-prerequisite items scoring over 80% were: using a computer for more than a year, accessing Webpages via their Webpage address (85%), and setting up and using an address list in e-mail (83%).

Analysis of the post-orientation data for prerequisite skills showed significant improvement in most skill items. For the 10 prerequisite skills, 31% of students showed an increase in at least 3 items and 8% of students showed a skill increase in at least 7 items.

The skill increase for non-prerequisite skills was significantly greater following the orientation course. In the intermediate skills category, 14% of students showed a skill increase in all 10 items, and 60% of students showed a skill increase in at least 4 items. The largest increase for intermediate skills related to those items requiring saving files in different formats, and using electronic library resources. One intermediate skill (item 7) showed a decrease in skill level. This item stated, "I have created several documents which exceed ten pages in my word processor."

Advanced skill items exhibited the largest increase between pre- and post-orientation. Fifty-one percent of students showed a skill increase in 8 out of 10 items; and 80% of students displayed an increase in at least 3 items. Those three items concerned the use of HTML for Webpage development and posting. One advanced item (item 28) exhibited a decrease in skill level. This item stated, "I use Microsoft PowerPoint (or an equivalent program) on a regular basis."

**Outcome 2:** Seventy percent (70%) of students entering the university's Web-based distance learning program would report an increase in independent, self-directed learning within two trimesters.

Quantitative data were analyzed with simple descriptive statistics (means, standard deviations, percentages). Qualitative data was acquired through analyses of reflective essays. An analysis of the survey data indicated that 74% of students perceived increased feelings of connectedness, independence, and self-direction. Students participated in an online suitability survey (Appendix C) at the beginning of their first trimester in online education to establish baseline data. The suitability survey asked students to rate their level of independent and self-directed learning, among other factors, using a four-point Likert scale. Responses were rated "rarely," "sometimes," "most of the time," or "all of the time." The same survey was repeated at the end of their second trimester of online classes. The data from the pre- and post-treatment were compared to measure any changes.

Summary data (see Table 4) from the suitability survey revealed that the mean response between pre- and post-treatment increased on every item.

Two items increased by more than a full point: items 5 "online education is equal to traditional," and item 6, "student background and experience is beneficial." The lowest increases were for items 4 and 12. These were "willingness to dedicate 8-12 hours per week," and "enjoyment of working independently." Table 5 displays the percentage of students moving from responding on the lower end of the scale (1, 2) to the higher end of the scale (3, 4), as well as the percentage of students who moved from selecting "most of the time" (response 3) to "all of the time" (response 4).

The writer was initially concerned about measuring student responses in the affective domain. Popham (1993) points out that in self-report surveys, "students' responses will tend to be distorted to the extent they can discern socially desirable responses" (p.158). As the statements reflected socially desirable behavior of self-direction, time management, goal setting, independence, and initiative, it is likely that students rated themselves higher (i.e., 3 and 4) than might be determined by some other type of measurement. In addition, some students may have felt that rating themselves too low on the survey would prevent their enrollment in online classes. Because of this possible distortion, the reflection papers were used as a second analysis tool to help determine the validity of student responses.

TABLE 4
Comparison of Pre- and Post-Test Mean Responses

| Item No. | Statement Paraphrase | Pre-test Mean (n = 392) | Std. Dev. | Post-test Mean (n = 347) | Std. Dev. | Mean Difference |
|---|---|---|---|---|---|---|
| 1 | Easy access to Internet | 2.58 | 0.57 | 3.40 | 0.67 | 0.82 |
| 2 | Communicate electronically | 2.76 | 0.62 | 3.54 | 0.53 | 0.78 |
| 3 | Communicate with class-mates | 2.63 | 0.58 | 3.35 | 0.51 | 0.72 |
| 4 | Dedicate 8-12 hours | 2.76 | 0.54 | 2.93 | 0.53 | 0.17 |
| 5 | Online equal to traditional | 2.29 | 0.53 | 3.56 | 0.61 | 1.27 |
| 6 | Background/experience bene-fits | 2.34 | 0.66 | 3.75 | 0.44 | 1.41 |
| 7 | Written communication com-fort | 2.27 | 0.59 | 2.75 | 0.58 | 0.48 |
| 8 | Self-directed in learning/studying | 2.69 | 0.66 | 3.24 | 0.50 | 0.54 |
| 9 | Reflection will help memory | 2.51 | 0.77 | 3.03 | 0.71 | 0.52 |
| 10 | Self-disciplined in studying | 2.63 | 0.76 | 3.05 | 0.68 | 0.42 |
| 11 | Manage study time | 2.51 | 0.61 | 3.11 | 0.71 | 0.60 |
| 12 | Enjoy working independently | 2.84 | 0.56 | 3.05 | 0.66 | 0.21 |
| 13 | Set goals/high initiative | 2.56 | 0.58 | 3.10 | 0.70 | 0.54 |
| 14 | Own responsibility for learn-ing | 2.78 | 0.74 | 3.27 | 0.55 | 0.50 |

Even with the probability of distorted higher survey scores, the survey results indicated that students perceived learning improvement in all 14 items (see Table 5). Additionally, student reflection papers verified feelings of growth in self-discipline, independence, time management, managing expectations, and taking responsibility for learning (see Table 6).

Finally, at the end of the first trimester of classes, students were encouraged to write a reflection paper in the form of an essay. The students were asked to contemplate what they had learned during the term, and to specify what improvements, if any, they experienced as a result of the course. Both quantitative and qualitative content analysis techniques were used to evaluate the student reflection papers.

The quantitative content analysis consisted of coding the reflected essays into content categories: self-discipline, independence, time management, managing expectations, and taking responsibility for learning. A frequency count of the occurrence of each coding category in each document was recorded, and the data across all documents were compiled.

In order to provide an in-depth interpretation of the content analysis and to determine the category designation, the author employed a qualita-

TABLE 5

Summary of Pre- to Post-Test Student Movement on Likert Scale Survey
Responses

| Item | Statement Paraphrase | % Move: 1,2 to 3,4 | % Move: Most (3) to all (4) | % Total Move 1 pt or More |
|------|---------------------|--------------------|-----------------------------|---------------------------|
| 1 | Easy access to Internet | 32% | 48% | 81% |
| 2 | Communicate electronically | 24% | 48% | 75% |
| 3 | Communicate with classmates | 41% | 31% | 72% |
| 4 | Dedicate 8-12 hours | 6% | 7% | 15% |
| 5 | Online equal to traditional | 63% | 33% | 98% |
| 6 | Background/experience benefits | 66% | 21% | 90% |
| 7 | Written communication comfort | 37% | 4% | 45% |
| 8 | Self-directed in learning/studying | 38% | 40% | 78% |
| 9 | Reflection will help memory | 38% | 12% | 51% |
| 10 | Self-disciplined in studying | 31% | 9% | 42% |
| 11 | Manage study time | 32% | 27% | 70% |
| 12 | Enjoy working independently | 8% | 15% | 24% |
| 13 | Set goals/high initiative | 25% | 27% | 53% |
| 14 | Own responsibility for learning | 36% | 13% | 49% |

tive approach to content analysis as suggested by Manning and Cul-lum-Swan (1994). The meaning of the content was analyzed within the context of the student, the class environment, and the specific assignment (Table 6). The combination of the reflective essay content analysis and the suitability survey was used for triangulation of data around the change in self-discipline and independence.

A positive change in self-discipline was reported by 92% of the student population in their reflective essays, and 100% of the essayists acknowl-

TABLE 6

Frequency Count of Student Reflection Papers Content Analysis

| Coding Category | Frequency Count (n=376) | | | |
|-----------------|-----|-----|------|-----|
| | 0 | 1-5 | 6-10 | >10 |
| Self-Discipline | 28 | 348 | | |
| Independence | | 142 | 234 | |
| Time Management | | 199 | 177 | |
| Managing Expectations | 107 | 269 | | |
| Taking Responsibility for Learning | 44 | 320 | 12 | |

edged an increase in independent learning skills. Combining the percentage of students increasing their Likert scale response on items 8 (self-directed learning) and 12 (enjoy working independently) with the responses in the reflection essays, 74% of students reported an increase in independent and self-directed learning within two trimesters.

In the reflection papers, many students also provided other feedback about their growth in the course (see Appendix F). Specifically, students reported increased self-esteem, self-knowledge, study skills, and overall confidence. Some students also shared anecdotal evidence of perceived life-changing or career-enhancing development based on what they learned in the orientation course.

**Outcome 3.** Ninety percent (90%) of students entering the university's Web-based distance learning program would discern their preferred learning styles and be able to adjust them, as needed, to accommodate differences in the distance environment, within one trimester.

One hundred percent of students enrolled in the orientation course participated in the learning style survey, and 94% participated in the bulletin board postings concerned with accommodations. This outcome was evaluated by a learning style survey (see Table 7) that categorized styles into Auditory, Visual, and Kinesthetic types. If students' scores were within 3 points of more than one type, those students were categorized into one of the split types (e.g., A-V, for auditory and visual). Table 7 presents a summary of the learning style categories captured from the survey.

During class bulletin board discussions, students were asked to describe their preferred learning style and any accommodations in learning style they made to work in the online environment. The bulletin board questions were:

1. Describe some of the challenges you anticipate in making the transition from a face-to-face classroom to online learning.
2. Describe your learning style at work and in the classroom.
3. What adaptations will you be making to ensure your success in online learning?

TABLE 7
Summarized Learning Style Data.

| (n=376) | | | | | | |
|---|---|---|---|---|---|---|
| *Strong Preferred Learning Style* | | | | *Split Learning Style* | | |
| Auditory | Visual | Kinesthetic | A-V | K-A | K-V | A-V-K |
| 51 | 210 | 15 | 65 | 16 | 11 | 8 |

Bulletin board content was analyzed using both qualitative and quantitative techniques. Again, the writer used the qualitative techniques of content analysis suggested by Manning and Cullum-Swan (1994) to derive the meaning of the content. The meaning was then coded into specific categories. A frequency count of the occurrence of each coding category in each bulletin board response was recorded, and the data across all responses were compiled (Table 8).

Given the 94% student participation in both the survey and the bulletin board postings, it is clear that 94% of students met Outcome 3.

Another comment in student reflection papers was on the usefulness of the learning style survey and discussions. Many students remarked that becoming aware of their learning style was important to increasing their self-esteem and to gaining confidence in their ability to become successful online students. Additionally, instructors reported that one of the most active bulletin board exercises was one asking students to describe their learning styles and the adjustments they made for the Web-based environment.

**Outcome 4.**   Within one trimester 90% of students entering the university's Web-based distance learning program would demonstrate an ability to communicate effectively in a Web-based learning community by clarifying course expectations and describing their learning needs.

Following completion of the orientation course, 95% of students entering the university Web-based distance learning program demonstrated an ability to communicate effectively in a Web-based learning community.

TABLE 8
Frequency Count of Learning Styles BB Content Analysis

| Accommodation Coding | 1 | 2+ | pop. % |
|---|---|---|---|
| Draw charts/maps for text | 116 | 28 | 38.3% |
| Read text aloud | 47 | | 12.5% |
| Print out Webpages | 302 | | 80.3% |
| Use voice recognition software | 12 | | 3.2% |
| Point to words/objects | 9 | 1 | 2.7% |
| Write/type notes | 217 | 12 | 60.9% |
| Prepare advanced organizers | 24 | | 6.4% |
| Focus attention | 16 | 22 | 10.1% |
| Self-monitor | 184 | 5 | 50.3% |
| Self-testing | 35 | | 9.3% |
| Work with a team | 129 | 42 | 45.5% |

This outcome was evaluated by an analysis of student participation in a variety of online communication methods including e-mail, bulletin board discussions, chatrooms, audio-conference, and whiteboard. Through open-ended questions, students were encouraged to use these communication methods to clarify expectations and describe their needs. A summary of the bulletin board responses to each question is displayed in Table 9. The questions posted to the course bulletin boards were:

1. Describe what electronic communication methods you might use to get to know your classmates better.
2. What are some of the communication methods you can use for questions to your professor?
3. What communication methods can you use for real-time discussions?
4. What is your favorite way to communicate online? Why?
5. What is your least favorite way to communicate online? Why?

On questions 1, 2, and 3, multiple responses were expected. On questions 4 and 5, single responses were expected. However, 3 students posted multiple methods on those questions, as well. When asked about the students' favorite form of online communication, the top three contenders captured 82% of the student population: e-mail (33.5%), bulletin board (26%), and chatroom (23%).

The course instructors also reported, via a pass/fail grade for each activity, their observations of student capabilities in each of these areas. Table 10 summarizes the pass/fail data for all sections of the orientation course.

TABLE 9
BB Posting Summary for Online Communications

| Communication Method | Question Numbers (n=376) | | | | |
|---|---|---|---|---|---|
| | 1 | 2 | 3 | 4 | 5 |
| E-mail (incl. attachments) | 325 | 376 | 4 | 126 | 5 |
| Bulletin board | 290 | 355 | 12 | 98 | 11 |
| Chatroom | 374 | 80 | 333 | 86 | 92 |
| Audiobridge | 28 | 2 | 309 | 51 | 119 |
| Whiteboard * (n=270) | 102 | 6 | 264 | 15 | 149 |
| Webpage development | 14 | 0 | 0 | 0 | 0 |

*Note:*　*The whiteboard was introduced in the revised course during month 4 of the implementation, thus the smaller sample size.

TABLE 10
Pass/Fail Summary of Online Communications

| (n=376) | | | |
|---|---|---|---|
| *Communication Method* | *Pass* | *Fail* | *% Pass* |
| E-mail (incl. Attachment) | 374 | 2 | 99.5% |
| Bulletin board | 373 | 3 | 99.2% |
| Chatroom | 361 | 15 | 96.0% |
| Audiobridge | 375 | 1 | 99.7% |
| Whiteboard * (n=270) | 232 | 38 | 85.9% |
| Webpage development | 345 | 31 | 91.8% |

*Note:*    * The whiteboard was introduced in the revised course during month 4 of the implementation, thus the smaller sample size.

Given the combination of pass/fail instructor observations and the bulletin board responses, it is likely that that following the orientation course, 95% of students met Outcome 4.

The need for effective Web-based communication between students and their instructors, and between students and their peers has been cited by many researchers (Abrahamson, 1998; Berge & Collins, 1995; Besser & Donahue, 1996; Brown, 1996; McVay, 2000; Porter, 1994; Rahm & Reed, 1998; Sponder, 1990; Twigg, 1997). In the orientation course, the use of effective communication via e-mail, bulletin boards, chats, whiteboards, and audiobridges was continually reinforced through practice in each learning module.

Analysis of student responses to the bulletin board questions on Web-based communication revealed that students used a variety of electronic tools to clarify course expectations and to describe their learning needs within the online course community. Though e-mail remained the primary communication tool, the use of bulletin boards and chats gained popularity as the course progressed. This is particularly interesting, given that the pre-treatment computer skills survey indicated that the majority of students reported not having previously posted to a bulletin board (89%) or used a chatroom (60%).

**Outcome 5.** The attrition rate of entering online students would be reduced to 10% or less over a two-trimester period.

Student attrition in the orientation course was only 4%. However, the student attrition rate over the two-trimester period was 15%. This outcome was measured by using registration records that indicated the number of students registering for the orientation course and the number who withdrew prior to course completion. Those who completed the orientation course were then tracked for a second trimester in subsequent courses. An attrition comparison was made on a course-by-course basis, in addition to the attrition rate of these students over the two-trimester period.

Table 11 provides a summary of the attrition data. The first item represents the attrition rate in the orientation course (PF282) over a two-trimester period. The second item represents those students who completed the orientation course who then registered for one course in the next trimester. Items 3, 4, and 5 represent those students who completed the orientation course who then registered for two, three, or more than three courses, respectively. Items 7-12 display the rates of attrition by specific course for those students who completed the orientation course and registered for one or more courses in the next trimester.

The attrition rate in the orientation course was only 4.1%. Following completion of the course however, 7.8% of the students did not register for a course in the next trimester. Of those who did register for one or more courses, their attrition rate varied significantly based on the number of online courses they took at one time. Students' attrition rates ranged from 7.5% for one course to 34.3% for those who attempted more than three courses.

Student attrition rates have been a concern of universities for some time. At the study university, attrition rates ranged between 15% and 20% for traditional classes. However, prior to the implementation of the orientation course, online course attrition ranged between 35% and 50%. Reducing attrition to an average of 15% earned the online delivery model a more favorable reputation among faculty and administrators.

TABLE 11
Attrition Summary

| Item Reference Numbers | Course | Enter | Complete | Attrition% |
|:---:|:---:|:---:|:---:|:---:|
| 1 | PF282 | 392 | 376 | 4.1% |
| 2 | 1 course | 107 | 99 | 7.5% |
| 3 | 2 courses | 124 | 108 | 12.9% |
| 4 | 3 courses | 81 | 63 | 22.2% |
| 5 | >3 courses | 35 | 23 | 34.3% |
| 6 | | | | |
| 7 | PF300 | 270 | 247 | 8.5% |
| 8 | PF302 | 26 | 20 | 23.1% |
| 9 | PF303 | 212 | 193 | 9.0% |
| 10 | PF304 | 226 | 209 | 7.5% |
| 11 | BA320 | 23 | 20 | 13.0% |
| 12 | BA403 | 17 | 12 | 29.4% |

Though the results of the attrition data were favorable, the outcome was not met. Several factors may have influenced the lower than expected results. In the literature on the subject, attrition is often equated with student withdrawal from the institution in which they are enrolled. In the statistics provided by the registrar's office, there is no differentiation between withdrawal from the course and withdrawal from the institution, nor is there any account of reasons for withdrawal. Furthermore, there is no built-in course-by-course tracking system that accounts for students who withdraw due to time or family difficulties, but later register for and complete the same course successfully.

Price, Harte and Cole (1991) argued that there are three main categories of withdrawal:

1. Internal Attrition: students who transfer between courses within the same institution. These students are not lost to a particular institution, but still contribute to course attrition in institutional and national statistics.
2. Institutional Attrition: students who leave the institution in which they commenced their university studies, but then continue at another university. These students are not lost to the university system, but appear as course attrition in institutional and national statistics.
3. Systemic Attrition: students who withdraw from a university and do not re-enroll in that or another university. These students are lost to the university system and are recorded as course attrition in university and national statistics.

As described in the university data above, students who interrupt their studies by taking leave from their course, particularly for an entire calendar year or longer, are also likely to be counted in the attrition statistics. Since attrition calculations do not differentiate between those on leave and those who withdraw, these students can contribute to increased attrition rates. If and when they return from leave has a statistical counter-effect, by decreasing attrition (or increasing retention rates) through adding to the size of the continuing student population.

Likewise, the usual statistical means of calculating attrition do not take into account any of the reasons students withdraw. Killen (1994) reviewed the literature on teaching and learning in higher education and concluded that there were a number of factors that could influence student success as measured by pass rates. The main factors identified were the motivation of students, their approach to studying, and their cultural expectations. These are all student characteristics rather than characteristics of the institution or of the higher education system itself.

Finally, Bernard and Amundsen (1989) also found that traditional attrition statistical models do not fit all needs. They found that the focus of attrition models included little consideration of differing course characteristics such as content and intended learning outcomes. Such characteristics may contribute to the student's decision to drop courses.

In the case of the author's attrition data, the course characteristics may have had a significant impact on the attrition rates. For example, the author had direct control over the PF282 (orientation) course. It was a prerequisite course for all online learning, and students were generally very interested in taking it. The attrition rate for that course was only 4.1%. However, the author had no control over several subsequent Web-based courses, wherein course content was often more difficult than students had anticipated. For example, PF302 was a quantitative methods course that students consistently reported as being very difficult. Many students stated they dropped the course in order to take a math refresher prior to re-enrolling. The attrition rate for the PF302 course was among the highest, at 23.1%. BA403 is a senior-level course, but has few prerequisites. Students may enroll in the course because of an interest in the topic (Ethical Issues in Business), only to find that the expected level of writing and analysis is beyond their capabilities. The attrition rate in BA403 was the highest, at 29.4%.

In addition to the differing course characteristics, the attrition data also showed significant growth based on the number of online courses students attempted during any one term. Attrition ranged from as low as 7.5% for those taking one online course to over 34% for those enrolled in three or more courses. Given that most Web-based students are older (average age 33), workings full-time jobs, and usually have family commitments, it is possible that taking more than two courses per term creates a significant burden. Perhaps students should be advised of these statistics and counseled to limit their enrollment to two courses per term. This would keep the attrition rate lower, helping more students experience success in online course completion.

## DISCUSSION OF RESEARCH OPPORTUNITIES AND FUTURE TRENDS

Though the work presented in this chapter concentrated on the impact of an online orientation course for student success, the research undertaken to develop that orientation course covered a significant portion of the field in determining what is important in course design and delivery. Furthermore, as with any project of this type, there are many additional variables that may or may not affect student learning, satisfaction, and attrition. Researchers continue to investigate many of these.

Muilenburg and Berge (2001) found 10 barriers that must be dealt with when delivering distance programs; administrative structure, organizational change, technical expertise, social interaction and quality, faculty compensation and time, threat of technology, legal issues, evaluations/ effectiveness, access, and student-support services. Specifics in any one of these areas would provide for rich research. In the study discussed in this chapter, several of these barriers were dealt with in advance of the online program being offered. Two barriers in Muilenburg and Berge's list were of particular interest to this study: social interaction and quality; and student support services.

## Social Interaction and Quality

In the area of social interaction, Tobin (2001) noted that distance education students and faculty must have good relationship skills. Poor relationship skills often manifest into conflict, problems, frustration and failure for both students and faculty. Tobin further noted that students in a distance education course or program who fail to engage and build relationships with peers and faculty are more likely to fail than those who do engage and build relationships. Moore (2001) also commented on the importance of relationships, in terms of interactions, between faculty and students. He noted that to be successful in delivering online courses, faculty must: allow student to student interaction with minimal faculty intervention; engage students in regular assignments in order to monitor progress and intervene when needed; provide specialized attention to students with low levels of self-directedness; and help students become more self-directed.

As a part of the orientation course, an emphasis on building community in order to lessen isolation was important. Further study regarding relationship building in online environments is warranted. With the advent of more online courses serving multiple sections or very large single sections, research into the importance of relationship-building and with whom (instructor, student, outside assistants) could be meaningful.

## Student Support Services

Moore and Kearsley (1996) and Lynch (2002) both emphasize the importance of providing good support systems for online learners. These support systems might include registration, bookstore ordering, technical support as in an electronic and telephone-based help desk, advising, and tutoring. The advanced selection of these support systems is necessary in order for them to be included in any orientation course. Additionally, further study of the importance of these support systems could be valuable. As well, the question of how much hands-on experience would be most effective for students during the orientation process should be investigated.

## Future Trends

Though the Web has now been in place for more than a decade, Web-based learning is relatively new and in flux, and online learning research and its application struggles to keep up. An online course that was considered state-of-the-art and selected as a best-practices example this year will be considered out of date within 12 months. Technology widely accepted by instructional designers and early adopter faculty this past Fall will likely be obsolete within two years. The task of keeping up with technological opportunities and yet providing stabilization of learning is a difficult one. Yet, it is necessary to identify some trends and to consider their potential impact as one evaluates research and application into the future.

Downes (1998) put it very succinctly when he said, "Technology ... should not drive content. However, when technology is the bottleneck through which instruction must be delivered, then technology, if it does not drive content, most certainly limits content."

Changes that are already evident and that need continued research include:

### *Movement from a Single Class Model to a Community Class Model*

The majority of online learning courses are designed and delivered by an individual instructor and thus remain within the control of only one instructor. Is there more or less efficacy in moving to a community course design that is fixed, yet open to accommodate a variety of instructors and their teaching styles? Some colleges have changed to this group course design model. How is it working? Is it as effective as or more effective than multiple individualized course models? Would a community model allow for more or less personalized education for the student? If resources are devoted to a community model, can it be designed to meet a variety of student levels and needs within a course?

### *Bandwidth Expansion*

Much of course design and technology instruction today is affected by limitations in telecommunications bandwidth. If bandwidth becomes essentially unlimited, or at least not an issue, what opportunities will that present for better instruction?

### Learning Style Accommodation

Currently much research, including the research described in this chapter, focuses on learning styles as an important piece of student success. Will changes in technology allow for faster creation of materials thus making learning style accommodation automatic with all courses? Furthermore, is learning style accommodation good? In the study described in this chapter, an integral part of the course was student awareness of learning style and selection of how to cope with learning in a non-preferred style.

### Computer Interface Changes

Downes (1998) predicted that operating systems that are task-based will become function-based. This means that instead of the user having to select and launch specific programs, the operating system will launch all programs needed for a specific function. Would this allow for less technically savvy users to become online learners and teachers? Could it change the pedagogical approach to teaching in the online environment?

### Ubiquitous Communication

Already we see a great upsurge in communication devices that are connected to the Web—PDAs (personal digital assistant), cell phones, PADs (personal access devices). If these become the norm, it is possible that they will replace notepads, laptops, and audio recording. Will this communication increase or decrease relationships online and how might that impact course design and development? Furthermore, electronic conferencing may become the norm. This could provide an opportunity for significant change in the design of distance courses.

### Convergence

Given the technology changes cited above, it is likely that an increasing convergence of methodologies and technologies will be employed by both online and classroom instructors. What is the best way to capitalize on this convergence? Will it increase community? Will it and/or should it allow for severing the distinction between campus-based and non-campus based instruction? Might one regularly offer a class that is both online and on-campus allowing for daily student selection in the need for physical presence?

It seems reasonable to conclude that changes in educational technology will continue to have a significant impact on instruction and learning. As researchers and practitioners it is important to try to anticipate change and to do ongoing action-research on its meaning and use for instructors, students, and institutions. Though some courses will always be more sophisticated in their use of technology than others, it is equally necessary to evaluate what results in better learning outcomes. Finally, as we embrace change we want to make sure that online education continues to provide a new overall paradigm for learning and teaching that embodies high levels of student interaction and participation.

## CONCLUSIONS

This chapter has discussed and presented several recommendations for online course design. Foremost is that since online learning is still new to most students and educators, organizations using Web-based education would benefit from implementing both a faculty development/orientation course and a student orientation to online studies. Both courses should be taught entirely online in order to simulate the actual environment that students and faculty face in Web-based course delivery.

The student orientation course should be required prior to their undertaking a program of online study. According to student feedback, it is not enough for online course designers to focus on the technology of the Web. They must also:

- Assist students to become aware of adult learning theory that they can apply to their context.
- Elicit self-awareness of personal suitability for the Web-based learning environment.
- Design courses to enhance the generalization of mental models.
- Analyze and discuss adjustments students might make to increase success in their studies.
- Provide students many opportunities to engage in extensive Web-based interaction and communication with their instructors and their peers.
- Allow significant time for student reflection regarding this new environment.

To effectively reach and teach these "beginner" students, administrators and educators must consider the human element when designing the electronic classroom. Hara and Kling (2000) stressed that the timing of instructor feedback and ambiguity of instructor-to-student communication caused the most frustration for students. To prevent these difficulties, potential online faculty should be immersed in the environment and given an opportunity to practice their delivery of coursework.

Many institutions have offered faculty orientations for Web-based learning. Unfortunately, these orientations are primarily implemented in a face-to-face environment with a lab. Though this is comfortable for traditional instructors, it does not effectively simulate the online teaching environment. Instead, the entire faculty development course should be experienced over the Web. And, though it may be met with resistance, the optimal way to train faculty may be to put them in the same situation that their students face: alone at home, preferably logging on in the evenings or on weekends, and without immediate personal support available.

The faculty course should include many of the same concepts and practice opportunities that the student orientation course will offer. In addition, faculty should have the opportunity to observe students working in the orientation course while being mentored in the problem-solving of course difficulties and the trouble-shooting of technical problems.

The student orientation course described in this chapter was adapted to this faculty development model with great success. One of the faculty course assignments was to "lurk" in a student orientation course by reading student bulletin board postings, reviewing chat transcripts, and attending audio-conferences. Faculty were also provided with a sample of typical student problems and asked to discuss how they might resolve them. Faculty could also observe the closure to the students' online experience by reading final bulletin board postings and reviewing sample student reflective essays. This helped faculty appreciate the student growth that occurred during the course. Ongoing emphasis on both faculty and student preparation for the online environment will be a significant factor in success of online programs and the inclusion of new technologies. These online courses provide one important venue for assisting in the paradigm shift that is necessary when teaching with technology.

## REFERENCES

Abrahamson, C.E. (1998). Issues in interactive communication in distance education. *College Student Journal, 32*(1), 33-43.

Ackerman, E. (1996). Perspective-taking and object construction: Two keys to learning. In Y. Kafai and M. Resnick (ed.), *Constructionism in Practice: Designing Thinking and Learning in a Digital World.* (pp. 25-32). Mahwah, NJ: Lawrence Erlbaum Associates.

Berge, Z., & Collins, M. (1995). *Computer mediated communication and the online classroom: Overview and perspectives (Vol. 1).* Creskill, NJ: Hampton Press.

Bernard, R. & Amundsen, C. (1989, Fall). Antecedents to Dropout in Distance Education. *Journal of Distance Education. 4 (2)*

Besser, H. & Donahue, S. (1996). Introduction and overview. *Journal of the American Society for Information Science: Perspectives on distance independent education, 47 (11),* 801-804.

Brown, K.M. (1996). The role of internal and external factors in the discontinuation of off-campus students. *Distance Education, 17(1),* 44-71.

Burge, E.J. (1994). Learning in computer conferenced contexts: The learners' perspective. *Journal of Distance Education. 9(1),* 19-43

Carley, K. & Palmquist, M. (1992). Extracting, representing, and analyzing mental models. *Social Forces, 70 (3),* 601-636.

Charp, S. (1994, April). Viewpoint. *The On-line Chronicle of Distance Education and Communication, 7(2).* Available Usenet Newsgroup alt.education.distance

Downes, S. (1998, Fall). The future of online learning. *Online Journal of Distance Education Administration.* [online] Available: http://www.westga.edu/~distance/downes13.html

Duffy, T.M., & Jonassen, D.H. (1992). Constructivism: New implications for instructional technology. In T. Duffy and D. Jonassen (Eds.), *Constructivism and the technology of instruction: A conversation* (pp.1-17). Hillsdale, NJ: Lawrence Erlbaum Associates.

Dyrli, O.E. & Kinnaman, D. (1996, February). Gaining the online edge part 3: Teaching effectively with telecommunications. *Technology & Learning, 16,* 57-62.

Killen, R. (1994). Differences between students' and lecturers' perceptions of factors influencing success at university, *Higher Education Research and Development, 13,* 199–211.

Gall, M., Borg, W., & Gall, J. (1996). *Educational Research: An Introduction, Sixth Edition.* White Plains, NY: Longman

Gregor, S.D. & Cuskelly, E.F. (1994). Computer mediated communication in distance education. *Journal of Computer Assisted Learning, 10,* 58-71.

Hara, N. & Kling, R. (2000, January). Students' distress with a Web-based distance education course. CSI Working Paper. [online] Available: http://www.slis.indiana.edu/CSI/wp00-01.html

Harasim (May 1997). Interacting in hyperspace. *University of Maryland System Institute for Distance Education and the International University Consortium Conference on Learning, Teachining, Interacting in Hyperspace: The Potential of the Web.* [online] Available: http://www2.ncsu.edu/ncsu/cc/pub/teachtools/ConfReport.htm

Harasim, L., Hiltz, S., Teles, L., & Turoff, M. (1997). *Learning networks: A field guide to teaching and learning online.* Cambridge, MA: MIT Press.

Harrell, William, Jr. (1999). Language Learning at a Distance via Computer. *International Journal of Instructional Media.* New York. 267.

Holloway, R.E., & Ohler, J. (1991). Distance education in the next decade. In G.J. Anglin, (ed.), *Instructional technology, past, present, and future.* Englewood, CO: Libraries Unlimited. 259-266

Jonassen, D. (1995). Operationalizing mental models: Strategies for assessing mental models to support meaningful learning- and design- supportive learning environments. [online] Available:
http://www-cscI95.indiana.edu/cscI95/jonassen.html

Kang, I. (1988). The use of computer-mediated communications: Electronic collaboration and interactivity. In C.J. Bonk and K. Kling (Eds.) *Electronic collaborators: Learner-centered technologies for literacy, apprenticeship, and discourse.* Mahwah, NJ: Erlbaum, 315-337.

Kimball, L. (1995, October). Ten ways to make online learning groups work. *Educational Leadership, 53,* 54-55.

Lefrere, P. (May 1997). Teaching in hyperspace. *University of Maryland System Institute for Distance Education and the International University Consortium Conference on Learning, Teaching, Interacting in Hyperspace: The Potential of the Web.* [On-line]. Available: http://www2.ncsu.edu/ncsu/cc/pub/teachtools/ConfReport.htm

Lynch, M. (2002). *The Online Educator: A Guide to Creating the Virtual Classroom.* London: Routledge, 50-52.

Manning, P. & Cullum-Swan, B. (1994). Narrative, content, and semiotic analysis. In N.K. Denzin & Y.S. Lincoln (Eds.), *Handbook of Qualitative Research.* Thousand Oaks, CA: Sage. 463-477.

McConnell, D. (1997, September). Interaction patterns of mixed sex groups in educational computer conferences. Part I—empirical findings. *Gender and Education, 9, 345-363.*

McMahon, J. et al. (1999, December). Barriers to computer usage: Staff and student perceptions. *Journal of Computer Assisted Learning, 15.* Oxford. 302.

McVay, M. (2000). *How to be a Successful Distance Student: Learning on the Internet. (2nd Ed.).* Needham Heights, MA: Pearson.

Moore, M. & Kearsley, G. (1996). Distance Education: A Systems View. Belmont, CA: Wadsworth Publishing Company.

Moore, M. G. (2001). Surviving as a distance teacher. *The American Journal of Distance Education, 15(2),* 1-5.

Muilenburg, L., & Berge, Z. L. (2001). Barriers to distance education: A factor-analytic study. *The American Journal of Distance Education, 15(2),* 7-22.

Price, D., Harte, J. & Cole, M. (1991). Student Progression in Higher Education: A Study of Attrition at Northern Territory University, Canberra: AGPS.

Popham, J. (1993). *Educational Evaluation.* Needham Heights, MA: Allyn and Bacon.

Porter, D. (Ed.). (1994, March). *New directions in distance learning: Interim report.* Available: David Porter, Manager, Schools Curriculum Programs, 4355 Mathissi Place, Burnaby, BC., Canada V5G 4S8

Rahm, D. & Reed, B.J. (1998). Tangled Webs in public administration: Organizational issues in distance learning. *Public Administration and Management: An Interactive Journal, 3(1).* [online] Available: http://www.pamij.com/rahm.html

Reid, J. (1997). Preparing students for the task of online learning. *Syllabus, 10,* 38-39.

Sheppard, R. (1998, November 23). Reinventing the classroom. *Maclean's, 111, 64-67.* Toronto.

Solloway, S., & Harris, E. (1999, March/April). Creating community online: Negotiating students' desires & needs in cyberspace. *Educom Review, 34,* 8. Atlanta, GA.

Sponder, B. (1990). *Distance education in rural Alaska: An overview of teaching and learning practices in audioconference courses.* (University of Alaska Monograph Series in Distance Education

No. 1) Fairbanks, Alaska: Alaska University, Center for Cross-Cultural Studies.

Stephenson, S. (2000). Using A Mentor Program To Reduce Course Attrition. Southwest Texas State University. [online] Available: http://www.ijoa.org/imta96/paper79.html

Stroud, B. (1998, October 6). Degrees of separation. *The Village Voice.* New York, p. 31.

Tobin, T. J. (2001, Fall). Dealing with problem students and faculty. *Online Journal of Distance Learning Administration.* [online] Available: http://www.westga.edu/~distance/ojdla/fall43/tobin43.html

Turnbell, L. (1999, April 16). Haves and have-nots. *The Columbus Dispatch, Columbus, OH, p. 1A.*

Twigg, C.A. (1997, March/April). Is technology a silver bullet? *Educom Review,* 28-29.

Wegerif, R. (1998). The social dimension of asynchronous learning networks. [Online]. *Journal of Asynchronous Learning Networks, 2(1),* 1-16. [online] Available: http://www.aln.org/

Weisenberg, F. & Hutton, S. (1995, November). Teaching a graduate program using computer mediated conferencing software. Paper presented at the Annual Meeting of the American Association for Adult and Continuing Education, Kansas City, MO.

Winn, W. (1997, May). Learning in hyperspace. *University of Maryland System Institute for Distance Education and the International University Consortium Conference on Learning, Teaching, Interacting in Hyperspace: The Potential of the Web.* [online] Available: http://www2.ncsu.edu/ncsu/cc/pub/teachtools/ConfReport.htm

Yakimovicz, A.D. & Murphy, K.L. (1995). Constructivism and collaboration on the Internet: Case study of a graduate class experience. *Computers and Education, 24(3),* 203-209.

Young, J. (1998, September). Computers and teaching: Evolution of a cyberclass. *PS, Political Science & Politics, 31,* 568-572.

## APPENDIX A: FACULTY INTERVIEW RESPONSES

| Faculty ID | What did you find most difficult or frustrating about teaching online? | Did you feel that teaching online was as effective as your classroom-based course? Why? | What did you find most rewarding about teaching online? |
|---|---|---|---|
| 1 | The students weren't truthful about how much they knew in how to do online stuff. It seemed I was always having to help them figure out even simple things, like how to login in to the course or how to pay attention to the instructions on the Webpages. I spent more time answering those questions than questions about the topic of the course. | No, because I couldn't see my students so I couldn't tell if they were getting it or not. There were a few students who did well—but I think they are the kind of studious loner types anyway. | The only rewarding part was not having to prepare lectures and not having to be here on campus for night classes or weekend classes. But there was still a lot of work—sometimes it seemed like more work. |
| 2 | The students e-mail way too much. Most of their questions are technical stuff—a lot of that stuff I don't know how to answer either. Also they expect immediate feedback from me. I could spend all day just answering e-mail. It isn't worth it. | I don't know if it's better or worse. For some it's better, for others "its worse. Of course, we never know about all those who drop out so early. I don't like the drop outs, it screws up everything in the plan—especially group stuff. | It was nice not having to be here on the weekends. A few students said they liked not having to talk in class in person—you know, the shyer students. |
| 3 | All the technical stuff drove me crazy. I don't have time to be answering those questions, and the help desk wasn't very helpful when students called. It seems they were just as lost as everyone else. I had some technical problems too and that made it really frustrating. Also, I really didn't feel comfortable not being able to see them and not being able to change my courses on-the-fly. | For me this is too hard. Maybe if we had some training or something it would help. I don't know though—they've kind of decided this is the way [the university] is going whether we like it or not. | Nothing. I can't really think of anything I liked about it. |

| 4 | I guess the most frustrating part was that I had no idea what I was doing, and that probably made it hard on my students. I'm not a techie type and I just felt out of my league all the time. I have good stuff to teach them, but I didn't know how to do it. If it wasn't on the Webpage I wasn't sure how to get it to them. Geez, I didn't even know how to send an attachment until you showed me the other day. Maybe if we had training or something it would help—but I don't know—it would take a lot of training to help me. | Maybe it could be effective. I don't know. I don't think this was a good test. | Some of my students said this was the only way they could take classes, so they were happy. I had one student who works two jobs and has four kids. She wants to see more online classes so she can finish her degree. So, I guess that's rewarding—that I could be a part of helping her. |
| 5 | Students just aren't used to learning this way. My students are Computer Science students, so they don't have a problem with the technology, but they also don't know how to learn using online Webpages. They are consistently late with homework—procrastinate even worse than in face-to-face classes. Then they get so far behind they have to drop out so they don't fail. And, you know, Computer Science types aren't good socially anyway, so you can't expect them to be very communicative online either. I don't know the answer to this problem, but when you figure it out let me know. I think chatrooms are a complete bust, and using the bulletin board is only marginally effective. | Doesn't seem to be, but all the students want online courses—even though they keep dropping out. So it's going to happen. | For me, I like the flexibility of not having to be in a lecture or a lab all the time. Not having to be here at night or on the weekend. I guess the students like that flexibility too—because they are all asking for more online courses. |

| Faculty ID | What did you find most difficult or frustrating about teaching online? | Did you feel that teaching online was as effective as your classroom-based course? Why? | What did you find most rewarding about teaching online? |
|---|---|---|---|
| 6 | I'm not convinced that this online course stuff is good. I'm really concerned about the quality of the teaching. This college has a reputation for quality teaching and just putting text up on Webpages with a few questions doesn't do it in my mind. Also, all the beginning technical stuff gets in the way of teaching. I don't have time to be playing help desk with my students. Even if I refer them to the help desk, they still come to me first. Also, I didn't feel comfortable with our level of communication. I found myself on the phone with students all the time, when I could have easily taken care of those questions in the classroom. | No. It's not as effective. It can't be. | It is flexible. I don't mind being able to work from home more often and not have to come here. But I love teaching, so I don't mind being here either. |
| 7 | I feel kind of powerless in the teaching process. The course is up on Webpages, including all the home-work assignments. So, what am I supposed to do? Answer e-mail? How do I know if they are getting it? How do I know they aren't cheating? If they have a question, how can I respond without having to send the same e-mail to the other 10 students who also ask the question? | I don't like it. I miss that face-to-face contact. Nothing can replace being able to see and touch students. I don't mind having some Web stuff available for classroom students—like the syl-labus or assignments—but putting it all on the Web just doesn't work. | I can't think of anything rewarding. Oh, I guess there is an occasional stu-dent who just can't make it to class and so it helps them. But that is rare. I don't think it's worth doing more online classes to meet that minority of student needs. |

| 8 | Too many technical questions I don't have time to deal with. Also, the students just don't know how to be responsible for reading the pages. I can't tell you how many times I get an e-mail saying something like, "I can't find the assignment for learning Unit 4," and I write back to point out exactly where it is under "graded assignments"—the same place it is in every online course. I don't know why they can't seem to read the pages. Also, there is way too much e-mail—each one asking the same general questions. It takes too much time to send them each a response. | I don't know if one is better than the other. Maybe if we could figure out how to make it work better this would work. But right now it's just too time consuming and not very rewarding. I don't think it's worth it. | Some of my online students wouldn't take any courses if this weren't an option. Their lives are just too busy to come to class—so I guess for them it's rewarding. For me, I don't know. |

## APPENDIX B. COMPUTER SKILLS SURVEY
## (MCVAY, 1998 AND 2000)

| No. | Statement | Response |
|---|---|---|
| 1. | I have used a computer for more than one year. | ◯ Yes<br>◯ No |
| **2.** | **I use a computer every day.** | ◯ Yes<br>◯ No |
| 3. | When I have a problem with my computer I can usually fix it. | ◯ Yes<br>◯ No |
| **4.** | **When I have a problem with my computer I have someone I can call to fix it within 24 hours.** | ◯ Yes<br>◯ No |
| 5. | I use a word processing program daily. | ◯ Yes<br>◯ No |
| **6.** | **I know how to print a document from my word processing program.** | ◯ Yes<br>◯ No |
| 7. | I have created several documents which exceed ten pages in my word processing program. | ◯ Yes<br>◯ No |
| **8.** | **I know how to set margins in my word processing program.** | ◯ Yes<br>◯ No |
| **9.** | **I know how to paginate (set page numbering) and set headers and footers in my word processing program.** | ◯ Yes<br>◯ No |
| 10 | I know how to save my word processing file as an RTF file. | ◯ Yes<br>◯ No |
| 11. | I know how to save my word processing file as an HTML file. | ◯ Yes<br>◯ No |
| **12.** | **I use an Internet e-mail program every day.** | ◯ Yes<br>◯ No |
| 13. | I know how to set up and use an address list or address book in my e-mail program. | ◯ Yes<br>◯ No |
| 14. | I correspond, via e-mail, with more than 5 people on a regular basis. | ◯ Yes<br>◯ No |
| **15.** | **I have sent an attached document with e-mail.** | ◯ Yes<br>◯ No |
| 16. | I have sent an attached picture or graphic with e-mail. | ◯ Yes<br>◯ No |
| 17. | I know how to access Webpages via their Webpage address (URL). | ◯ Yes<br>◯ No |
| **18.** | **I know how to use a search engine (e.g.,Yahoo or AltaVista) to find information on the Internet.** | ◯ Yes<br>◯ No |
| 19. | On several occasions I have used the Internet to research important information. | ◯ Yes<br>◯ No |
| 20. | I am familiar with electronic library databases. | ◯ Yes<br>◯ No |

| No. | Statement | Response |
|---|---|---|
| 21. | I have used electronic library resources (e.g., FirstSearch, InfoTrac, NTDB, etc.) to research a paper. | ○ Yes<br>○ No |
| **22.** | **I easily follow "hot links" from one Webpage to another.** | ○ Yes<br>○ No |
| **23.** | **I am able to navigate backward and forward among many Webpages.** | ○ Yes<br>○ No |
| **24.** | **I know how to print Webpages from the Internet.** | ○ Yes<br>○ No |
| **25.** | **I know how to navigate and print within frames.** | ○ Yes<br>○ No |
| 26. | I have taken surveys or answered questionnaires on the Internet. | ○ Yes<br>○ No |
| 27. | I have created more than three presentations using a graphical presentation program. | ○ Yes<br>○ No |
| 28. | I use Microsoft PowerPoint (or an equivalent program) on a regular basis. | ○ Yes<br>○ No |
| 29. | I have saved a presentation in HTML format. | ○ Yes<br>○ No |
| 30. | I have created Webpages using an HTML editor (e.g., Netscape Composer, Microsoft FrontPage, Dreamweaver, etc.). | ○ Yes<br>○ No |
| 31. | I have posted pages on the World Wide Web and made them accessible to others. | ○ Yes<br>○ No |
| 32. | I know how to subscribe to a list-serve or newsgroup. | ○ Yes<br>○ No |
| 33. | I participate in list-serves or newsgroups. | ○ Yes<br>○ No |
| 34. | I know how to access a bulletin board. | ○ Yes<br>○ No |
| 35. | I frequently post comments to bulletin boards. | ○ Yes<br>○ No |
| 36. | I know how to access different chatrooms on the Web. | ○ Yes<br>○ No |
| 37. | I know how to speak privately to an individual while in a community chat. | ○ Yes<br>○ No |
| 38. | I have actively participated in one or more chatrooms. | ○ Yes<br>○ No |

The above survey embodies the variety of levels of technological expertise expected of students in distance education programs. Depending on the selected school and program, the student may not be required to use all of these skills. However, those items in bold print represent the minimal skill levels required for most distance education studies. If you answered NO to any of the bolded items, you may want to concentrate on enhancing those skills during this course. Work with your instructor on a plan for learning those skills.

> Submit Answers for Feedback

> Clear Answers

## APPENDIX C. SUITABILITY SURVEY (MCVAY, 1998 AND 2000)

This survey is designed to assist you in rating your current readiness to pursue distance education courses. Please answer honestly by rating your agreement with each statement by clicking the button that best matches your feelings. The feedback from this survey may assist you in the areas where you need to focus during this course.

| No. | Question | Response |
|-----|----------|----------|
| 1. | I am able to easily access the Internet as needed for my studies. | ○ Rarely<br>○ Sometimes<br>○ Most of the Time<br>○ All of the Time |
| 2. | I am comfortable communicating electronically. | ○ Rarely<br>○ Sometimes<br>○ Most of the Time<br>○ All of the Time |
| 3. | I am willing to communicate actively with my classmates and instructors electronically. | ○ Rarely<br>○ Sometimes<br>○ Most of the Time<br>○ All of the Time |
| 4. | I am willing to dedicate a minimum of 8 to 12 hours per week for my studies. | ○ Rarely<br>○ Sometimes<br>○ Most of the Time<br>○ All of the Time |
| 5. | I feel that online learning is of at least equal quality to traditional classroom learning. | ○ Rarely<br>○ Sometimes<br>○ Most of the Time<br>○ All of the Time |
| 6. | I feel that bringing in my background and experience will be beneficial to my studies. | ○ Rarely<br>○ Sometimes<br>○ Most of the Time |

| No. | Question | Response |
|-----|----------|----------|
| 7. | I am comfortable with written communication. | ○ All of the Time<br>○ Rarely<br>○ Sometimes<br>○ Most of the Time |
| 8. | When it comes to learning and studying, I am a self-directed person. | ○ All of the Time<br>○ Rarely<br>○ Sometimes<br>○ Most of the time |
| 9. | I believe that looking back on what I've learned in a course will help me to remember it better. | ○ All of the Time<br>○ Rarely<br>○ Sometimes<br>○ Most of the Time |
| 10. | In my studies, I am self-disciplined and find it easy to set aside reading and homework time. | ○ All of the Time<br>○ Rarely<br>○ Sometimes<br>○ Most of the Time |
| 11. | I am able to manage my study time effectively and easily complete assignments on time. | ○ All of the Time<br>○ Rarely<br>○ Sometimes<br>○ Most of the Time |
| 12. | As a student, I enjoy working independently. | ○ All of the Time<br>○ Rarely<br>○ Sometimes<br>○ Most of the Time |
| 13. | In my studies, I set goals and have a high degree of initiative. | ○ All of the Time<br>○ Rarely<br>○ Sometimes<br>○ Most of the Time |
| 14. | I believe I am the only one responsible for my learning. | ○ All of the Time<br>○ Rarely<br>○ Sometimes<br>○ Most of the Time |

Submit Answers for Feedback

Clear Answers

# CHAPTER 11

# COURSE MANAGEMENT AS A PEDAGOGICAL IMPERATIVE

**Xiaoxing Han, Sally Dresdow, Robert Gail, and Don Plunkett**

Course management, a distinct aspect of instruction in active and collaborative learning in a structured and paced learning environment, is critical to the success of any asynchronous online program or course. Yet, course management is a significantly under-researched and under-developed area. At the course level, there are four specific instructional areas under the rubric of course management: 1) course structure, 2) class organization, 3) learning facilitation, and 4) student-instructor interactions. A competent instructor needs to be well grounded in all four areas. Program level issues are also critical to the success of virtual learning undertakings. Program policy, program structure, and resource allocation determine across-the-board, consistent, and enduring pedagogical success. In order to assure effective and efficient learning outcomes, course management must be elevated to the height of a pedagogical imperative.

**KEYWORDS:** attendance policy, course management, faculty evaluation, instructor availability, interactivity, learning facilitation, program level, relevance

Course management is a relatively weak area of distance education planning, development, and operation. Although intertwined with course

Electronic Learning Communities—Issues and Practices, pages 413–456.
Copyright © 2003 by Information Age Publishing, Inc.
All rights of reproduction in any form reserved.
ISBN: 1-931576-96-3 (pbk.), 1-931576-97-1 (hardcover)

design, student services, technical support, and academic assessment, course management is distinct from them all. The concern of this chapter is not about the technical functions of courseware that have garnered much attention in the literature; instead, this chapter focuses on the pedagogical perspective.

Course management has two dimensions: the course level and the program level; each concerns a different player and different issues. At the course level course management is about an instructor's pedagogical orientation and instructional preparedness. At the program level it is about issues that transcend a single course—issues that concern policies that are directly or indirectly related to all of the institution's distance education courses. This chapter focuses on course level factors but also discusses issues that relate to an integrated perspective of both courses and programs.

Elevating course management to the height of a pedagogical imperative, the premise of this chapter, is that attention to course management is critical. How it is handled by an academic administration and its faculty can explain the success or failure of a single distance education course or an entire distance education program.

The chapter starts by making a case for changing the common technological definition of course management. After introducing a pedagogically grounded course management model, the chapter discusses the critical relationship of sound course management with active and collaborative learning as a foundation for quality learning. Under the premise that the nature of a learning environment has substantial bearings on pedagogy, the chapter surveys the characteristics of the virtual environment. Next, a review of the criteria for a quality online education program is presented in light of what has been proposed by authoritative bodies, examined by empirical research, and adopted by various institutions. In preparation for proposing solutions, the chapter critically examines major challenges to course management principles guided by an active and collaborative learning model. Drawing from both the literature review and tested practices, the chapter advances proven strategies for effective and efficient course management. Recognizing the importance of institutional administrations' role at the program level, an entire section is devoted to its current state. With the conviction that faculty motivation and preparedness are key to successful course management, the chapter concludes with an examination of the state of faculty development and assessment in the area of course management.

## FACTORING COURSE MANAGEMENT INTO THE PEDAGOGICAL FRAMEWORK OF ONLINE LEARNING

In current academic parlance, course management is rarely used as a pedagogical term or is referred to separately as a distinct pedagogical competency. If used, it tends to be used purely in a technical sense, i.e., referring to courseware programs (Higher Learning Commission, 2002b). While attention has been given to improving various technical aspects or media selection as potential solutions for improving learning in virtual asynchronous learning environments (Usrey, 1999; Gilbert & Han, 1999; Hara & Kling, 2000), pedagogical strategies are not emphasized or are even overlooked. The oversight is substantially due to the lack of extensive and conclusive empirical research concerning pedagogical strategies.

In a case from Indiana University, an asynchronous class yielded a considerably higher degree of student dissatisfaction than its face-to-face counterpart. The researchers concluded that the instructor was "sufficiently experienced" in the asynchronous learning environment and that the causes of the dissatisfaction were due mostly to technical problems, lack of sufficient and timely feedback from the instructor, and ambiguous instructions to the students (Hara & Kling, 2000). Yet, many symptoms presented in the case point to another aspect of the situation which was overlooked or perhaps dismissed—the crucial issues of the level to which the instructor understood the environment and the instructor's proficiency in strategies suitable to the asynchronous environment.

There is "an issue of [the faculty member's] craft: an instructor with a strong sense of responsibility but a weak grasp of online course management strategies and techniques may not be as effective, and certainly not as efficient" (Han, 1999). Even though there have been many attempts to theorize effective course management principles, the noticeably neglected area is "the [instructor's] inability to translate the supposed understanding into professional practice" (R. Kling, personal communication, December 27, 1999). This sorely inadequate professional competency has more to do with course management than instructional design or technical skills.

Michael Moore downplayed course management's pedagogical impact by explicitly claiming that pedagogy is not so much a barrier for the development of distance education as are "organizational change, change of faculty roles, and change in administrative structures" (Moore, 1994). Moore's claim has been challenged. The US Department of Education conducted a nationwide survey of higher education faculty and staff who had a direct instructional role in distance education during the Fall of 1998. The survey demonstrated that workloads were heavier when teaching distance education courses compared to traditional teaching workloads (Bradburn & Zimbler, 2002). Berge and Lin (2001) reported that faculty compensation and time, "especially the lack of time, is the most consistently reported of all the barrier factors." Other surveys have produced similar findings. It is time to realize that workload and time factors have a significant bearing on pedagogy. Other than course design, course management remains the most vexing aspect in the struggle to achieve optimum and integrated outcomes of instructional effectiveness and efficiency.

The literature is still sparse regarding pedagogical discussions of course management. Some researchers have advocated "directive interaction" as opposed to simply infusing or imbuing content when teaching a course. They consider it as a key instructor function to implement a constructivist approach (Sherry, et al., 2001). Anderson and his colleagues are among the very few who have systematically addressed the issue of the nature and scope that the authors of this chapter advocate (Anderson, et al., 2001). Instead of calling it course management, they introduced the concept of "teaching presence" that is "constitutively defined as having three categories–design and organization, facilitating discourse, and direct instruction" (Anderson, et al., 2001, p. 1). Their definition of "design and organization" has most to do with class operation, teaching related rule making, and instructional design. "Facilitation discourse" is an activity "usually integrated within direct instruction and in-site design of instructional activity." The last "category" of their "teaching presence" is about content-specific engagement by the instructor (Anderson, et al., 2001, p. 7).

Even though the authors of this chapter do not necessarily share the view of Anderson et al., that "teaching presence" can be separate from "cognitive presence and social presence," the authors see merit in organizing key issues of course management at the course level along the general thread of the Anderson model. A somewhat modified and more elaborate course management definition may include:

1. Discipline enforcement
   a. Rule making (dynamically in consultation with students)
   b. Communication (conveying and clarifying class rules)
2. Discussion facilitation
   a. Promoting class-wide participation
   b. Assuring consistent engagement
   c. Stirring "cognitive conflict" and a higher level of learning
   d. Setting direction and gearing the discussion flow
3. Direct instruction
   a. Contextualization.
   b. Grading and feedback

What is missing in this model is the program level aspect of course management. In disputing Moore's claim regarding barriers to distance education, Berge and Lin (2001) argued that organizational change in terms of "administrative structure" is not important. In contrast, Rogers (2000) has come to a better understanding of the program level issues by pointing out that "a set of established institutional norms" related to pedagogy, faculty autonomy, faculty reward, teaching load, faculty development and support is the foremost barrier to the full adoption of information technology in the classroom. In spite of recognizing the value of instructor preparedness and attitude, program level characteristics should not be downplayed in achieving quality distance learning. Virtual learning demands substantially more involvement of a third party—the program level player—than does traditional learning. Other than the instructor and student, those involved in program management need to be active and accountable in the instructional process. Program management must be more involved in planning, organization, coordination, instructional support, orientation, evaluation, and faculty development.

Regional accreditation commissions have underscored the importance of program level factors in their statement on *Best Practices for Electronically Offered Degree and Certificate Programs* (Higher Learning Commission, 2002b). Of all the best practices, the Commissions first stress the "Institutional Context and Commitment," which includes not only the consistency of the online degree with the institution's role and mission, but also the corresponding budget, effective policies, proper resource provision and allocation, and sound "internal organizational structure." The other best practices concern curriculum, faculty and student support, and assessment. (These will be discussed more thoroughly later in this chapter.)

In order to assure quality learning outcomes, course management must be a key component of any distance education model. There has been a growing recognition that apart from an instructor's discipline expertise, the pedagogical competency of the instructor and his/her attitude toward virtual learning can make a critical difference in learning outcomes and learner satisfaction (Barab, Thomas, & Merrill, 2001; Chorodow, 2000; Arbaugh, 2000; Frankola, 2001). Successful course management methodology must be consistent with course content, student profiles, delivery media, course design, and instructional assessment.

## LEARNING OUTCOME, STUDENT SATISFACTION, AND COURSE MANAGEMENT

Learning is not just about knowledge acquisition. According to social learning theory, learning is ultimately about change—relatively permanent change in the learner's behavior. Successful learning, it follows, occurs when such change takes place as planned by an instructional model as well as when change is expected by the learners. This is not to argue that learners can predict and anticipate learning outcomes. On the contrary, learners normally do not have a specific and systemically clear idea about what may transpire in their learning at the outset of that process. If they can anticipate or comprehend specific and systemic academic and behavioral outcomes from a learning endeavor, they probably do not need to take the course. However, learners without expectations are those most likely to fail.

It is less likely for learners who are dissatisfied with an instructional model to pursue any permanent behavioral change called for by that model. Learners' expectations form the very basis of their satisfaction. Learners themselves use such expectations, consciously or otherwise, as the criteria and measurement for determining their own satisfaction. However, there most likely exists some discrepancy between learner expectations and expectations by faculty and their academic program based on some instructional model. It is incumbent on an academic program and the faculty responsible for instructional offerings, to be highly cognizant of critical learner expectations and also to be able to design and conduct courses that can produce optimal academic and behavioral changes.

The student body of postsecondary distance education is most often composed of working adults. Successful pedagogical strategies in distance education must take into full consideration this population's expectations—particularly its emphasis on relevance. While there are multiple factors that adult learners consider crucial to the success of their learning, *relevance* (defined here as applicability to career) is one that most adult educators cite as important to adult learners. For adult learners, relevance is rated the highest when assessing instructional quality (Spigner-Littles & Anderson, 1999; Pena-Shaff, et al., 2001; Viechnicki, et al., 1990; Oblinger & Verville, 1998; Zemke, 1984). Other factors such as higher-order thinking are also critical, but if they cannot be integrated with relevance, even traditional students will not wish to sign on (Brown, D.G., 2000; Richter, 2000).

The theory for teaching adults is in contrast to theories concerning teaching younger learners. Traditional principles of learning and instructional methods have been developed with and for children; teaching adults requires using a different set of techniques. For adult education, a balance must be maintained between the open and flexible styles that adults prefer and the requirements for conceptual integrity, specificity, and structure that a well-designed course demands.

At the course level, relevance is the key to successful learning, and relevance can be "most effectively accomplished when new information is connected to and built upon a student's prior knowledge and real-life experiences" (Spigner-Littles & Anderson, 1999, p. 203). At this level, relevance is manifested in the following four aspects of instructional design:

1. content,
2. material,
3. cases, and
4. activity.

The relevant *content* should combine education with training (Oblinger & Verville, 1998). Any successful instructional model will have to promote the acquisition of a healthy dose of theory that emphasizes application. *Material* selection is also important and should conform to appropriate theoretical demands. Material should be selected from both academic and practitioner perspectives. It should include prior experience of the adult learner to take advantage of the accumulation of their unique experiences related to the learning.

The authors believe that asynchronous virtual learning is highly suited to the active and collaborative learning model. Active in this context refers to intensive participation by the learners in the learning process and their contributions to the learning process with substantive, critical, and real-life oriented inputs. Collaborative refers to learners' participation that is across-the-board, not hindered by a dominant uniformity of opinion, and is consistently interactive with peers as well as between learners and instructor. The selection of *cases* and construction of activities that promote active and collaborative learning should be critical tasks in virtual learning design.

Cases and activities are closely related. The constructivist paradigm calls for a role-based and context-simulated learning process in which learners experiment and interact with initiative. Cases are helpful for role identification and context definition whether in class discussion or in individual assignments. The right kind of cases should be realistic, properly complex, closely related to the learning objectives, and with readily available references.

Learner *activity* is highly valued in the constructivist model and is considered a focal area of concern of instructional design (Fishman, 2001; Spigner-Littles & Anderson, 1999). Relevant activities should incorporate material and cases that engage learners both individually and collectively. Adult learners are more apt to learn those things they need to know and are able to do in order to cope effectively with real-life situations. They learn new knowledge, understandings, skills, values, and attitudes most effectively through cases and activities in a context of application to real-life situations.

While not excluding the legitimacy of other instructional paradigms, this discussion is limited to active and collaborative learning. Usually, for subjects that demand higher order learning, a class thoroughly grounded in active and collaborative learning pedagogy satisfies adult learners more than other styles of pedagogy. A major task of this chapter is to illustrate how such a learning paradigm may be employed via effective and efficient course management.

## CHARACTERISTICS OF ASYNCHRONOUS LEARNING ENVIRONMENTS

Learning, consequently pedagogy, is dependent upon the learning environment. A large lecture hall is different from a cozy seminar room. A lab that allows hands-on by all learners is different from a setting where only the instructor has control over media equipment. A survey of Course Management Systems (CMS) found that a large number of faculty adjusted their instructional approaches due to the CMS systems installed on their campuses (AAHESGIT, 2001). In its current state, virtual asynchronous learning is relatively well-established and several of its major characteristics have been exploited.

A virtual learning environment has to be defined on the basis of the prevailing Internet infrastructure and commercially available Internet technologies. The typical virtual asynchronous learning environment is based on a commercial CMS with learner dial-up access. This chapter is concerned solely with the group-paced/structured mode that requires well-defined class scheduling. Such classes are usually Web-based, created as small self-contained Websites easily linked to other material available on the Web, enabled with threaded discussion, and capable of handling audio and video files.

From the perspective of instructional design, digital technologies and the Web have ushered into the learning environment the following basic advantages:

- Component integration of core instructional material, auxiliary material, class activities, evaluation, class schedules, and class discussion.
- Current, instantaneous, and customized references from vast sources. With hyperlinks the learner has an almost limitless supply of material to use in any kind of activity or discussion that a particular learning endeavor requires.
- Breaking out of time or space constraints: learning can be carried out in active and constant multi-directional exchanges—many-to-one, one-to-many, one-to-one. With asynchronous courses, learners can structure their experiences to meet their requirements. There are fewer excuses or problems regarding time and space issues. It is also easier for instructors to structure the course so that learners interact with small groups, large groups, and one-on-one. This flexibility offers an exciting opportunity for learners to work with a diverse group of individuals, including the instructor.

Learner activity can be better facilitated in virtual asynchronous environment where the following characteristics have been shown to enhance learner engagement:

### Centrality of Writing
One area that learners can always improve is the ability to put thoughts into writing, clearly and concisely. Because the only contact in an asynchronous virtual environment that learners have with each other and the

instructor is by writing, it is vital to be able to write clearly and in an organized manner.

### More Focused on Comprehension as Opposed to Note Taking

Structuring the course to focus on comprehension challenges learners and encourages them to stay engaged and to be more actively involved in the learning process. Students will become active learners when they are held accountable for their comprehension of material as opposed to memorization from simple note-taking.

### Accommodation to Multiple Learning Styles and Preparedness

To engage learners in an asynchronous virtual course is both an opportunity and a challenge. Accommodating multiple learning styles and varying degrees of preparedness helps assure that students will be engaged in learning and that they will be motivated to stay with the course. McCarthy (2000a) specifically addresses what the instructor needs to do to have all students engaged in the process. To manage the course effectively, the instructor should ascertain that each segment or module of the course addresses the following four issues:

1. Why students are studying/learning the material?
2. What specifically the students are studying, defining the content, explaining the theories or frameworks?
3. How students should use or apply the material?
4. What if? Challenge and discover the relevance and how the learning can be applied to more complex situations?

In developing and managing the course, the instructor needs to understand the limits and strengths of each style of learning and assure that everything that students need is present. Both Meier (2000) and McCarthy, (2000b) advocate that each module of the course integrate the whole cycle of learning to maximize student involvement. The student's journey in the learning process moves from the role of preceptor to connector to reflector, to imaginer, to analyzer, to comprehender, to tinkerer, to adaptor, to performer, to critic and back to preceptor to start the process again.

### Receiving Timely Feedback Throughout the Course

In virtual environments instructors have the opportunity to respond quickly and regularly throughout the course. If the course is based on comprehension, and learners must consistently contribute to the class, the instructor can start the feedback early in the process. When feedback is more relevant and timely, learners have a greater opportunity to develop their skills. The instructor has the opportunity to provide feedback to the learner by commenting on and addressing a variety of comprehension issues. These include: clarity, accuracy, precision, relevance, depth, breadth, logic, and significance (Center for Critical Thinking, 1997).

### Collaborative Learning Among Peers

In face-to-face classes, there are challenges to encouraging students to work collaboratively. Those challenges include artificial barriers such as where learners sit and whom the learners know in the class. Asynchronous virtual learning can break down some of those barriers. There are no scheduling conflicts, and it does not matter where learners are located. The instructor can structure multiple collaborative learning experiences for the learners and the learners can learn from each other.

### Easy Linking to the Real World

Course Management Systems allow the instructor/designer to integrate an extensive body of online material and links to any kind of instructor-generated class activities. Proper incorporation of digital resources can both enhance the subject rigor and improve and enhance content. The ease of adding links can encourage learners to apply material to various situations. Learners can also be required to find their own links to places where they can apply or even analyze course concepts, theories, or frameworks.

There are also six significant potential *disadvantages* concerning virtual asynchronous learning environments:

1. Uni-dimensional interaction deprived of non-verbal, spontaneous, and extemporaneous communication: Since instructors cannot use enthusiastic mannerisms and body language to pique the interest of the students, alternative communication methods must be used. Stories and illustrations that bring the subject material alive (Arle, 2002) may be difficult to include.
2. Lack of prompt feedback: With the potential for a high volume of messages, the instructor can be overwhelmed and unable to respond to all messages in a timely manner.
3. Lack of concurrent exchanges of ideas to aid in synergistically building knowledge: The characteristics of the asynchronous environment can inhibit spontaneous ideas that can more easily occur in the traditional environment.
4. Difficulty in weaving the context of a series of dynamic and multi-party involved exchanges (Xin & Feenberg, 2002): Discussion postings may be disjointed and overwhelming, leaving learners confused. Instructors are challenged to follow a multitude of postings and to respond to them coherently. Sometimes the instructor is the only one who can weave the communication into a discussion thread that is a coherent, understandable set of exchanges.

5. Difficulty in discerning classroom conflicts at an early stage: In small discussion groups in a face-to-face setting, the instructor can watch the groups and diagnose interpersonal interactions. The asynchronous learning environment does not allow the instructor to see conflicts easily as they develop.
6. Challenges in team coordination: The very strength of asynchronous learning that helps bring people together creates challenges when trying to coordinate team activities. For a team to be productive, there are development stages that all groups go through including forming, storming, norming, performing, and adjourning (Tuckman & Jensen, 1977). Having an environment in which there is no face-to-face contact can create barriers to developing a high performing team. It takes time to become a high performing team and there may not even be enough time for a team in the asynchronous virtual learning to make it to the stage where they set norms as to what behavior is acceptable and what is not acceptable.

The state of asynchronous environments is bound to change, particularly with the continued development of interactive multimedia and this will likely mitigate some of the potential problem areas described above. It is also likely that the differences between asynchronous and synchronous models will blur over time, and that asynchronous components will be built into all of these learning environments. Similarly, a hybrid of virtual and face-to-face courses will also likely become more prevalent.

Recognizing distinct characteristics and advantages of virtual asynchronous learning environments is only the start for developing sound pedagogical strategies. Most of the advantages are not automatically present without special efforts on the part of an instructor as well as the support of the administration. On the other hand, the disadvantages are not insurmountable; asynchronous environments are by no means intrinsically less conducive to learning than synchronous environments, whether virtual or face-to-face. Both the advantages as well as the disadvantages can be managed to the benefit of the learning experience by enabling the instructor to focus on the key characteristics of the asynchronous virtual environment that are most directly associated with learner activity.

## QUALITY CRITERIA FOR ASYNCHRONOUS LEARNING COURSE MANAGEMENT

In 1987 the American Association for Higher Education endorsed, for traditional instruction, the following "Seven Principles for Good Practice in Undergraduate Education":

1. Good practice encourages contacts between students and faculty.
2. Good practice develops reciprocity and cooperation among students.
3. Good practice uses active learning techniques.
4. Good practice means prompt feedback.
5. Good practice emphasizes time on task.
6. Good practice communicates high expectations.
7. Good practice respects diverse talents and ways of learning.

Their principles have been widely embraced and have been extended to computer-mediated education (Chikering & Ehrman, 1997).

One could argue that all the seven principles have to be upheld via sound course management in the virtual environment. Integrating each of the seven good practices will help create a positive learning experience that will maximize the advantages of the asynchronous environment and minimize its disadvantages. In an effective asynchronous learning environment, the instructor can control the level of interaction between the students and the instructor as well as among the students. Without face-to-face contacts, the challenge for the instructor is to incorporate activities that maximize the experience for students. Effective use of active learning techniques encourages contact between students and faculty and has the potential for building cooperation among students. Structuring activities so that students must use critical thinking sets high expectations for student performance. The principles can be incorporated by effectively using active learning strategies and structuring courses so that students with all learning styles find ways to utilize their strengths.

At the program level issues are more amorphous; the lines are often blurred regarding what should be considered course management, instructional design, instructional support, faculty development, or technology support. The authors consider course management to be an integral and critical part of sound virtual learning pedagogy. As discussed above, our holistic view of virtual learning pedagogy establishes distinct as well as intertwined links among all those aspects. To elaborate on the relationship of course management to other aspects of distance education, the following list indicates the degree of direct or indirect relevance of each of those aspects to course management:

1. *Faculty Development* (Direct Relevance): It can improve technological and pedagogical instructional preparedness of instructors.
2. *Faculty Assessment* (Direct Relevance): It is the strongest impetus to promoting sound course management.
3. *Instructor Availability* (Direct Relevance): Course management is impossible without regular availability of the instructor.

4. *Attendance Policy* (Direct Relevance): The lack of a consistent, explicit, and strong set of rules at the program level will;
   i.   demand more faculty time in rule making and rule communications, and
   ii.  tempt muddle-through type students to "bargain" with faculty.
5. *Student Orientation* (Indirect Relevance): Insufficient or improper orientation will likely increase instructor course management burden.
6. *Academic Advising* (Indirect Relevance): Students struggling with program procedures are less likely to succeed and faculty are more likely to be tasked with non-instructional issues.
7. *Faculty Technological Support* (Indirect Relevance): It helps faculty, particularly the less technology-savvy ones, to focus on pedagogy and content.
8. *Student Technological Support* (Indirect Relevance): Insufficient or improper support will likely increase instructor course management work.

In 1999, in a study sponsored by the Institute for Higher Education Policy and the LMS vendor Blackboard, 24 benchmarks of quality online teaching were identified (Institute for Higher Education Policy, 2000). The benchmarks were primarily related to program level issues, with the exception of "student interactions." Of the student interactions, four benchmarks focused on engaging students among themselves, between the instructor and students, and on informative and timely response by instructors. Among the program level benchmarks relevant to course management, the research devoted three to "Student Technical Support and Student Orientation." To help faculty concentrate on teaching, another benchmark was stated as having "a structured system" to address program procedural issues which should cover student attendance policy.

The study reported as one benchmark, faculty-student agreement on assignment deadlines and on faculty availability. This is, in essence, another side of the student attendance policy. On the surface, such agreement seems to concern course level issues, but it is really a program level issue. Not only is it generally distracting for faculty to negotiate such agreements with students, it is also impossible for students to make enlightened decisions on such matters before the start of a class. For example, students should have the right, prior to registration, to reject a course based on their perception of the quality of the instructor and/or inconvenient course schedules. Normally, processes and policies concerning such matters can be created only by administrative authority at a program level, not by individual faculty.

In the area of *Faculty Development*, the study defines three benchmarks calling for assistance to faculty "in the transition from classroom teaching to online instruction" as well as during "the progression of the online course." The benchmarks also emphasize *Faculty Assessment* during the process.

Many regional accreditation commissions have addressed policy-making related to online education. They have issued statements on the evaluation of asynchronous learning and on best practices for "electronically offered degree and certificate programs" in which special emphasis is given to the "dynamic and interactive" nature of effective and quality learning. Interactivity among students and between students and instructors is stated to be a key to basic quality learning practice (Higher Learning Commission, 2002a; Higher Learning Commission 2002b). According to them, best practices can be classified into five major areas:

1. institutional context and commitment,
2. curriculum and instructionl,
3. faculty support,
4. student support, and
5. evaluation and assessment.

Each one of these, except the first, specifically addresses interactivity. Under *Curriculum and Instruction* the Commissions highlight the importance of designing a program and its courses to allow "appropriate interaction" between the instructor and students and among students. To verify the existence of such interaction, they suggest asking whether instructor-student and student-student interactions are articulated in program policies and course syllabi as well as what measures are taken to assure the interactions.

Regarding *Faculty Support*, the Commissions advise that faculty support services be available to ensure proper and direct interaction between faculty and students. *Student Support* likewise addresses the nature of interactions with faculty and students. The Commissions encourage the building of a "community of learning" to help ensure the success of the educational experience; they encourage the use of study groups; and they recommend that student directories be provided to assist with interactivity, particularly between and among students. Lastly, *Evaluation and Assessment* recommends the use of surveys to measure student satisfaction with online class discussion groups.

At this stage of distance education development, it is well-accepted that interactivity is the core of online learning. Agreement regarding how to assess it at both the course and program levels is quite another matter. Michael Moore (1989) may be the first to define interactivity as what happens between the learner and the subject matter, between the learner and the instructor, and among learners. At the course level, and based on auto associative neural networks ("special kinds of neural networks employed to simulate and explore associative processes"), a general schema is constructed that may be used to measure all three types of interactivity (Xin &

Feenberg, 2002). At the program level, the methodology is far less developed. Many online learning programs either ignore the emphasis by the regional accreditation commissions on academic community building, or poorly manage and assess this aspect of the program.

If the definition of course management is fluid, how it should be assessed at the course or program level is still open for debate. Authoritative bodies in higher education have not yet produced well-developed processes and procedures for assessing course management at both levels. Research has partially compensated for what has lagged in practice. Many survey studies have substantiated the quality criteria advanced by those authoritative bodies. Nonetheless, most surveys are limited to course level issues.

A survey, conducted among South Carolina online education administrators, faculty, and students, supported the notion that quality course management must serve the model of active, collaborative, structured, and guided learning while not being restricted by time, place, and, electronic communications bandwidth. Six or seven out of the top 10 critical success factors that the survey respondents identified can be classified as either solely or substantially related to course management. The respondents emphasized prompt and frequent interaction and feedback as well as active learning. The respondents also placed importance on the need for institutionally provided training in the practice of online education for both faculty and students (Hoskins, et al., 2001).

Judging by feedback from students in various institutions, nothing seems worse to students than an instructor who is perceived as unresponsive. Research shows a general correlation between student satisfaction and the quality of instructor-student interaction (Pena-Shaff, et al., 2001; Barab, et al., 2001; Frankola, 2001; Richard & Ridley, 2000). A survey conducted at the University of Wisconsin-Green Bay covering 10 courses and 100 students reported that "student overall satisfaction is not impacted by prior experience with technology. However ... [it] is greatly impacted by the quality of interaction[s] between the instructor and the students, and ... between students" (Lorenz, 2000, p. 11).

In recent years, various institutions have translated some of those criteria into practice at both the program level and course level. A leading online degree-granting institution has developed elaborate standards of behavioral norms for both faculty and students. One of the precepts of the development of such standards is an interactive and collaborative structure with a small student to faculty ratio. This institution currently maintains a 9.5:1 ratio with a goal of no more than 14 students in any class. The institution's experience indicates that when there are 10 students in a class, the instructor has to manage 100 "relationships." When the student headcount increases to 12, the number of relationships increases to 144. Clearly, the number of relationships grows in a non-linear fashion as the number of students increases. The concept of "relationship" is adopted because of the emphasis on the rapport built among the students and between the students and the instructor. There are typically hundreds, even thousands of postings during a five or six week class. Discussion threads generated by lectures, discussion questions, readings, and personal experiences of each student can go on for days. The instructor must be an astute navigator of these postings and an adept context weaver to keep the discussion on track and moving toward the required course objectives.

Small class size also promotes the building of student relationships which are often formed during the first course or two of a program and continue to develop through the two years of a graduate program, as students remain on the same learning teams. Some students continue to come to and go from these teams, but often there is an unchanging core.

The University of Maryland University College (UMUC) sponsors the virtual resource site for teaching with technology—"Systems Approach to Designing Online Learning Activities." Although UMUC provides general guidelines regarding online classroom education, it specifically includes pedagogical advice geared towards online teaching. UMUC's seven "steps" are presented as a roadmap for providing faculty with an opportunity to think through their courses, from start to finish:

- Steps 1-4—What the teacher wants students to learn:
  - specifying learning goals,
  - relating lesson learning performance objectives to the course learning goals,
  - designing valid assessment procedures, and
  - providing feedback.
- Steps 5-7—How technology helps achieve desired learning outcomes:
  - selecting appropriate teaching strategies,
  - constructing and/or selecting student involvement activities, and
  - selecting appropriate media for the learning activity.

In spite of the development of best practices, there is no consensus on all quality criteria proposed by various policy making bodies and institutions, and there are even less well-developed specifics and mechanisms needed to achieve high quality. In a 1999 debate waged in the listserv, World Wide Web Courseware Developers' Listserv Website (http://www.unb.ca/web/wwwdev/), participants, who are faculty, instructional designers or online administrators, took sides on whether there should be mandatory requirements for a certain level of faculty presence in teaching online. The debate is typical and reflective of what is still ongoing at many institutions.

A professor at a community college in New Jersey, a self-described "early adopter" in online teaching, suggested that a minimum number of days should be set to require faculty availability in online courses (11/09/1999 6:09 PM CST):

We're formulating guidelines for our online courses, and would like to specify a minimum number of days a week that faculty are expected to log on to their courses.

We few early adopters log in several times a day—but when the second tier begins offering courses next fall, we'd like to have clear minimum expectations. The dean tells us that specifying a certain number of days (assuming it's more than two or three, that is) will probably not fly either with the faculty or the faculty union.

Does anyone have a written rule about this? If not, what are the unstated expectations and how are they conveyed?

Another instructor in Texas rejected that suggestion rather strongly (11/09/1999 4:08 PM CST):

Perhaps it would be better to specify that professors should be expected to take care of all correspondence and course management in a timely and efficient manner and give a suggestion like within two working days rather than specify a "minimum" number of days, which to me assumes that you are not dealing with professionals. The old saying, treat people as if they were already where you want them to be, applies here.

Still another message, posted by an instructional specialist from Oregon, represented a supporting view of the initial suggestion, but from a somewhat different perspective (11/10/1999 2:52 PM CST):

I've also watched as fledgling online instructors who misunderstand the nature of online courses assume they can load course materials online and then never pay attention to the materials, or the students trying to make use of them, again. I like to think that most of this is due to innocent ignorance of online learning realities, but some of it is due to the sad fact that teaching is too often a low priority for many faculty ... who only chose to put their materials online because they thought they could then interact less with the students in the first place—a mistaken assumption! ... I'm afraid I can't agree that we can assume all instructors will behave as "professionals" and show up regularly in their online courses. We're dealing with a fairly new mode of instruction. If we truly want online learning to succeed, I think it's important to talk plainly about expectations.

At an institution with a nationally leading online degree program, the Dean's Council drafted a policy requiring instructors to log on to the course at least five days out of seven and to respond to questions and to student work in a timely manner. Yet, even though the spirit of the statement is factored into the formal policy, the explicit requirement of five days has never been adopted due to disagreements among those involved.

## COMMON CHALLENGES TO ASYNCHRONOUS COURSE MANAGEMENT

Fundamentally, learning is learning, and pedagogy is pedagogy, regardless of whether the environment is virtual or physical. Yet, differences do exist between the two, and not just in terms of instructional design, technology management, and faculty/student support. Challenges posed to course management by the virtual environment are substantial, and these need to be recognized at both the program and course levels.

At the program level, Donna Rogers (2000) argued that pedagogy integrated with instructional technology is dependent on a number of faculty-specific "institutional norms," and that pedagogy is often critically retarded by the conditions of those norms. To rephrase her observation in the context of this discussion, the state of course level factors is dependent on the state of program level factors. In turn, to develop effective course management policies at the program level requires a sound relationship between faculty and administration. This critical relationship always constitutes the basis for the orientation of program level factors and also affects course level factors.

At the course level, Stanley Chodorow's debate with detractors of online education can serve as an interesting reference. Chodorow (2001) sharply questioned, in response to those who assert that face-to-face interaction is essential for education, the actual quality of that interaction, and by extension, the quality of traditional education that has been built on that premise. Undoubtedly quality of instruction will inevitably come under question in virtual environments if the nature of participant interaction is weak due to intrinsic limitations of the asynchronous learning environment, haphazard course design, a poorly prepared and/or half-committed instructor, or combinations of these.

The fact that asynchronous virtual learning is completely distinct from "simple discursive interactions" based on serialized taking turns (Sherry, et al., 2001) requires faculty to develop better instructional competencies. The challenges of effective and efficient course management are increasingly being recognized. Harasim et al. (1995) were among the first to point out that the instructor's responsibility in creating a collaborative learning environment is a major challenge in virtual learning and that to address it requires substantial communication and technological skills. Bonk and Cunningham (1998) also noted the critical significance of "pedagogical guidance" in using tools to promote collaboration and communication in the virtual learning environment and the problematic state that occurs when these are not present. Anderson and his collaborators (2000) concluded that synchronizing class activities "so that learners feel 'in synch' with the rest of the class" is a well-documented challenge. Desperate to deal with such challenges, some faculty and program administrators have even resorted to using indiscriminate mechanical solutions such as count-ing words in student messages to measure a student's engagement (The WWWDEV listserv, August 2001).

The difficulties experienced by California State University, Monterey Bay (CSUMB) in assembling its founding teaching faculty in accordance with its computer-mediated curriculum requirements serve as a testimony to the still relatively impoverished state of pedagogical competency among higher education faculty. Even though CSUMB required only basic-to-medium levels of information literacy, it took CSUMB's screening of "over 6,000 resumes" to appoint 30 teaching faculty—and CSUMB still had to be content with the fact that most of those hired could not meet all the curriculum requirements (Baldwin, 1999). If this case is indicative, virtual pedagogical strategies that demand a higher level of competency from instructors in order to "influence the student's total course of study" (Ehr-mann, 1997) are very likely to be absent from most instructors' skill portfo-lios.

In a more recent case, the administration at Grand Valley State Univer-sity was compelled to limit the enrollment of online classes because faculty were overwhelmed by course management issues (Mangan, 2001). Others too have scrambled to adopt strategies to address instructor preparedness (see *Course for Instructors Helps Keep Students*, 1999). However, to acquire a preliminary level of understanding and a general set of competencies is one thing, but to become versed in active and collaborative pedagogy in virtual asynchronous learning is quite another. For the majority of faculty who are only newly acquainted with online learning, the real challenge is yet to come.

Virtual environments based on a heavily text-based learning mechanism are a major source of difficulty. Xin and Feenberg (2002) have systemati-cally examined the difficulty of "text weaving" in virtual learning. They pointed out that composing and reading at the same time is difficult; developing a set of keywords shared by a class is difficult; and typing and organizing a large amount of text are also difficult. Active and collabora-tive learning demands the contextualizing of a series of dynamic and multi-party-involved exchanges. Yet, it is very difficult to perform this vital function in the virtual environment, given underdeveloped tools as well as ill-prepared faculty.

At this time consensus has yet to emerge among practitioners in online education regarding the criticality of many course management issues such as instructor availability and faculty assessment. It should be noted that fac-ulty assessment too is a controversial issue, and the Higher Learning Com-mission, for example, objects to the term "faculty assessment." Other issues have only been addressed in a marginal way. For example, to be compliant with the Family Educational Right to Privacy Act while still performing course management may still be an issue of controversy. In the listserv of the National Association of College and University Attorneys an example was introduced in a posting in 2001. It is interesting that the posting was made anonymously. The questioner stated that in order to help with class interactions, an instructor asked students to post to the bulletin board the following:

- personal or professional background,
- special interests,
- description of the student's workplace,
- description of the student's community,
- description of the student's goals, and
- two ways the student plans to apply the course in their professional life.

Would such a request be a violation of Family Educational Right to Privacy Act? Some would see no problem with requesting such information; some might have doubts; and some, particularly those working in an office of student registration would object to an instructor's requiring such information. This example is representative of the dilemma and lack of consensus regarding such issues.

The particular nature and some characteristics of the typical asynchronous virtual learning environment constitute major challenges to quality learning and student satisfaction. So too does the relative lack of pedagogical preparedness of faculty and administrators/staff. The ever-evolving technology concerning the design of course management systems, and the improving functionality of digital learning tools can help ameliorate such challenges. From a pedagogical perspective nonetheless, the challenges are more immense, complex, and enduring. As has been argued in this chapter, faculty, staff, and administrators need to understand better the technological and pedagogical challenges. Only by doing so, can they address the challenges in virtual classes, and also better cooperate on developing policies, processes, and procedures that can effectively and efficiently manage issues underlying the challenges.

## EFFECTIVE COURSE MANAGEMENT METHODOLOGY AT THE COURSE LEVEL

Pioneer distance educators have started to offer faculty "checklists for action" at the course level. The following are some that are more relevant to course management, in accordance with our definition of the term. Feenberg and Harasim et al., for example, have proposed three major areas, which are in turn translated into three sets of instructional functions. These are adapted from University of Illinois Faculty Seminar, Table 6:

1. Contextualizing Functions:
   - Opening discussion: announce theme
   - Setting norms: give type of conference
   - Setting agenda: control flow of discussion
2. Monitoring Functions:
   - Recognition: welcome students, correct context
   - Prompting: solicit comments, assign work
3. Meta Functions:
   - Meta-commenting: remedy problems in context
   - Weaving: summarize state of discussion

Rogers (2000) summarized seven points for facilitating interactive learning communities which are not necessarily fully online:

1. more frequent and timely interactions,
2. creating "learning groups,"
3. well-planned online teaching environments supporting active learning techniques,
4. immediate instructional feedback,
5. immediate online access to important learning resources,
6. convenient, accessible, flexible forums for self and peer evaluation, and
7. allowing for self-paced study and using multimedia to support various learning styles.

Sherry et al. (2001) offer a practical menu of advice specific to virtual learning engagement:

- have a clear goal,
- state your intent,
- publish and follow guidelines,
- communicate using a cycle of request/respond/reply,
- respect multiple perspectives,
- articulate thought processes, and
- use the conferencing system appropriately.

While agreeing with those educators' conceptual understanding and practical insights, the authors offer a different approach that categorizes course management into four interrelated yet distinct aspects, along the line of virtual instructional activities:

1. course structure,
2. class organization,
3. learning facilitation, and
4. instructor-learner interaction.

This approach can closely match the instructional life cycle from design to delivery, and can help instructors systematically examine the process, development stage by development stage, and pedagogical aspect by pedagogical aspect.

### 1. Course Structure

This aspect is about the basic set up of instructional material and the orientation of evaluation strategies. It sets the tone of the whole course. Course structure is relevant to course management since strategies for conducting a course cannot be selected outside the context of the course design. The establishment of a certain structure and the deployment of a certain set of evaluation criteria will gear a course towards a certain course management approach.

The authors argue that instructional material should be modularized; the course structure and evaluation should facilitate a variety of learning styles; learning outcomes should be articulated; and evaluation strategies should match stated learning outcomes and all major components of the course structure.

Effective course structure is critical for successful course management. Course management challenges to instructors are pervasive throughout the instructional process: when designing learning outcomes, when structuring content, when creating assignments and activities, and when managing discussion and assessment activities.

A learner-centered environment that is directed by an active and collaborative learning philosophy calls for effective modularization of instructional material and learning activities. Not only is modularization conducive to the cognitive process, it is also easy to accomplish in a virtual asynchronous learning environment. It should be reflected in the way textual information is organized since it is not easy to read lengthy text on a screen. Keeping this in mind, key principles should be spelled out in the course syllabus, but detailed instruction should branch out into a number of auxiliary modules such as those for grading, case studies, team projects and discussion. Such a structure clarifies the course content in a compact and easy-to-browse format while providing ample specific instructions. In the same vein, instead of one large lecture for each unit, content material is better presented in segments.

Modularization also affects the timing of releasing instructional material. To accommodate different learning styles, different states of learner preparedness, and different degrees of student content familiarity, a balance should be struck in the release of instructional material to students. Modularization draws a distinction between material released at the outset of a class and other material released at various points during the class. This way, learners may obtain a certain amount of flexibility to control their own pace of progress. For example, a course focused on the utilization of certain computer application programs primarily addresses lower-order thinking subjects with myriad rote learning objectives. Many higher-order courses also involve familiarity of definitions and/or application of certain terms. In such cases, self-tests that allow students free and unlimited access and provide immediate feedback are beneficial. Other material may be released at different points of time to help draw the attention of a whole class to a certain topic within a well-defined and limited timeframe. Timed-release can enhance students' comprehension. When done properly, timed-release material can also create collective attention and foster collaborative engagement. Higher-order subjects are also better served with periodic releases of thought-provoking comments.

Clear, concise, and explicit expectations and assignments are necessary to manage the non-verbal and non-visual nature of asynchronous learning. There are no visual or audio opportunities to see if students understand a theory, framework, assignment, or test questions, so the instructor's communication must be explicit. While designing an assignment, writing a test question, or asking discussion questions, instructors must always go back to see if they have:

- clearly explained what is to be done in step-by-step instructions,
- included a deadline and appropriate length guidelines, and
- communicated grading criteria.

In constructivist learning, cases play a critical role in helping learners move to the center stage. Cases can be selected from both public sources and student postings. Public sources have the advantage of more available references while student postings tend to be relevant to course-specific discussion subjects. The best cases often involve student exchanges from previous classes where those exchanges contain well-argued views of contrasting positions buttressed by real world experience. An active and interactively engaged instructor can and should collect and classify examples from student discussions, paper assignments, or e-mail exchanges, as cases. The instructor can also have the students develop comprehensive cases as assignments. Instructors should obtain students' permission to use their comments in future courses. The advantage to this approach is that students immediately see the relevance of the cases to their situations.

Little has been published about how to conduct student evaluation in the asynchronous virtual learning environment, especially how to distribute grade points among various course requirements. In spite of various attempts to improve testing capabilities, closed-book testing is still problematic in this environment. Using activities that focus on writing and comprehension can often offset the drawbacks to closed-book testing. Discussion and teamwork have been shown to be major components of effective evaluation in the asynchronous learning environment.

There is still ongoing debate on the weighting of grades in such courses. One for-profit leading online degree granting institution's guideline is 60% for assignments, 30% for group projects, and 10% for discussion. Another bases 20-50% of its final grade on class participation. One of the authors assigns 35% to assignments, 40% for group project, and 25% for discussion. Coming from a former online student perspective, another author found that classes that emphasized discussion kept his classmates more motivated and satisfied overall. Furthermore, discussion fueled group project work, and the resulting group dynamics also provided impetus to complete individual assignments more thoroughly.

## 2.   *Class Organization*

The second aspect of the authors' approach to course management focuses on the organization of learning activities that require students to take actions which will be registered by the courseware for evaluation purposes. The authors believe that there are usually four issues related to managing class activities:

1. participation,
2. assignment submission,
3. class pacing, and
4. project collaboration.

Instructors must be able to integrate all the activities into a coherent whole. They must also be able to reconcile individual initiative and flexibility with collective endeavor and "learning community"-based pacing. Toward that end, the authors believe that a proper understanding and use of the dialectics of two pairs of dynamics in class activities is critical. They are 1) collectivity versus individuality, and 2) reflectivity versus interactivity. The two sides of each are complementary to one another, but also often at odds with one another.

Collaborative class discussion is a critical part of a constructivist model. It demands student participation with both reflectivity and interactivity. Interactivity in this context refers to the frequency of dialog-based postings. Reflectivity refers to the depth and substance of those postings. Several surveys referenced in this chapter indicate that the majority of students feel that discussion and interaction are highly beneficial. A prime challenge is how to encourage the entire class to engage in consistent participation. Many new practitioners feel vexed with off-topic discussions that can overshadow the "serious discussion," or with many "me too" postings that serve no purpose other than meeting participation obligations (Hardless & Nulden, 1999).

Bruffee (1999) theorizes that there are two major modes of activity in virtual communication: "referential" and "relational." The former is meant to "transit" or convey information and the latter to connect or to establish collaborative understanding. But even in the relational mode, frequency and substance are not necessarily congruent. Whereas interactivity is a common problem for classes conducted by new faculty and/or attended by students who have no asynchronous experience, reflectivity is actually harder to address. To reconcile both is even more a challenge. Ironically, when reflective postings become the norm, interactivity tends to decline (Pena-Shaff, et al., 2001).

Students do not always come to the course with skills or abilities to communicate at a high interactivity level. It is incumbent upon the instructor to develop a proper class organization so that all students understand the expectations to "fit" into the course structure. If there are requirements regarding the quantity and quality of discussions and group output, these should be clearly articulated.

Criteria for grading must also be communicated. If students do not understand the basis upon which the instructor is grading material, they are less likely to be involved in discussions. Class size is a key to organizing discussion and participation. It may be necessary to divide the class into discussion groups that carry on their own deliberations, and then post each group's consolidated contributions to the entire class.

One of the authors has experimented with a variety of formats to address the dichotomy between interactivity and reflectivity. As the discussion format evolved, the depth of the discussion significantly increased while interactivity was maintained at the same level or even increased.

Of the three formats, one required every student to answer the same discussion questions. The second divided the class into two groups, one answering questions, and the other following up with comments or observations. The two groups alternated roles weekly. Through experiments in 40 classes for five years, the most successful format proved to be an elaborate role-play where the class was divided into Readers, Commentators, Devils, and Sages. Readers summarized the readings of the week and were asked not to answer assigned questions. Commentators provided answers while commenting on the relevance or significance of concepts included in the Readers' summaries. Devils punched holes in Commentators' arguments. Sages concluded with the best of both Commentators and Devils. Each role, other than the Readers', has a built in interactivity requirement. Roles rotated weekly, and for flexibility, students were allowed to make postings outside assigned roles.

This role-play model helped produce thoughtful discussions. Even students who normally just "go with the flow" will provide original comments when they play the role of Commentator or Devil.

One possible problem with this model is that weekly role changes can cause confusion among students, and some may lose track of the role to play in a particular week. The instructor must provide a role assignment sheet that all students can follow easily.

Another pair of dynamics in structured and cohort-based online learning is made up of collectivity and individuality. Even though both are fundamental to such learning, they are also often at odds, not unlike the dichotomy of reflectivity and interactivity. For example, team projects, often adopted for upper or graduate level courses, are a popular pedagogical vehicle for promoting collectivity or class/group-based collaborative learning. On the other hand, a defining characteristic of asynchronous learning is individuality-based flexibility in learning time management, pace control, and learning approach selection. To reconcile these is a major challenge, and one that sound course management strategies must rise to.

Constructivist proponents highly value team projects as a learning vehicle. A leading online degree-granting institution adopts learning teams as an integral part of its adult learning model, and dictates its adoption with an elaborate set of procedures and even agenda for each course. However, students' opinions on the benefits of team projects are disparate. One group of students hails their teamwork as the most valuable part of class activities while others dismiss the project as a burden unfairly placed on the truly motivated.

Instructors should provide clear guidance about team formation, but avoid dictating it. One author found that in almost every class there was at least one person who did not contribute to the group effort. He recommends a mandatory peer evaluation form to help discourage team members from not participating. Another author found a similar useful practice of building into the grade a "team dynamic penalty" of about 10-15% of the total project grade. With such a deterrent, a "free rider" or anyone who materially and adversely affects a team's performance may lose a part or all of his/her team dynamic points. Such mechanisms help instructors grade students fairly. One author also recommends an allowance of 10% of extra credit to help more active students from being adversely affected by "free riders."

While modularization is accepted as a guiding principle in course construction, how to modularize is still a wide open question. The norm, as seen from publishers' electronic course packages, is to chunk content into equivalently weighted units—each requiring coverage in an equivalent timeframe. But the logical framework of learning objectives may not fit neatly into such fixed units. Furthermore, all students may not be prepared at the same level for the same subject, and their time availability can vary greatly depending on their professional and family situations. A major challenge is to address the dilemma of carrying out a collaborative venture while sanctioning individual endeavors in light of each student's learning style, personal schedules, and familiarity with the subject matter.

The condensed and intensive six-week course structure at a for-profit degree granting institution demands a fast-paced and rigorously maintained schedule. For 14-15 week courses in traditional academic programs, the resistance to such highly structured scheduling is strong, and for good reason. At public institutions that only offer undergraduate degrees, a leading cause of student attrition in online programs is their dissatisfaction with or inability to keep up with the fast week-based pace.

To address this problem, one author divided a course into six stages—each ranging from seven to 42 days. Each stage had a distinct content focus, and its length was determined by weighting its content in relation to the overall course objectives as well as by the perceived degree of subject difficulty. Larger stages were broken into phases, for discussion purposes. Students were given flexibility to complete readings and assignments within the timeframe of that stage rather than by a set of fixed deadlines. Students more familiar with the subject of a certain stage or with more leisure time early on in a stage could move faster than the rest of the class. Conversely, those who were struggling were entitled to more time in the stage. Nonetheless, all students were asked to follow the class discussion "in sync." Such scheduling allowed flexibility for students who had diverse levels of preparedness or time conflict issues, while maintaining a basic collectivity for class discourse.

How to make instructional material available to students also has a bearing on the issue of collectivity versus individuality. As discussed earlier, the authors recommend that instructional material be divided into two groups according to the ways by which the material is to be released. In this way, faster readers are accommodated while all students can manage to meet the course schedule and follow the class-wide discussion.

Requirements for submitting assignments are subject to the same considerations. Students are often required to submit their assignments electronically. As soon as the submission deadline passes, they also need to post their assignments to the discussion area to foster collaborative learning.

### 3.  *Learning Facilitation*

This aspect of the course management paradigm concerns how to invigorate the class and to accomplish broad and persistent student participation. Consequently this aspect focuses on class discussion. The following tasks are particularly important in this regard:

- directing the class in one general direction and within a certain time,
- enforcing discipline, and
- encouraging broad participation in thoughtful discourses.

Even with optimal set-up of a course and thorough rule-making regarding class organization, the participation of students in a class may still fall short being of consistent and across-the-board. A successful instructor achieves the class participation objectives through communication. Conceptually, half of instruction activity concerns communication between the instructor and the students. What really counts, argued Chodorow (2000) is "joint performance of teacher and students" (p. 16).

To engage students throughout the whole class, the authors believe that certain positions need to be established and strategies adopted regarding instructor facilitation. These are:

- encouraging independent thinking, initiative, thematic focus, and integration of theory and practice,
- providing substantial and timely instructions or comments,
- recognizing every student individually as well as a part of the class, and
- offering practical models to follow, and negative examples to illustrate common problems.

Instructors should refrain from interjecting themselves into student discussions too often unless there are questions directed at the instructor or there is procedural confusion. Alternatively, instructors can synthesize student postings periodically and use a distinct subject line for such postings instead of just replying to student postings. This approach is more in line with previous research calling for contextualization. In this approach, instructors can succinctly cite well-stated views and/or good examples given by students in threads, and conceptualize the discussion to a higher level. This approach also involves a delicate balance between not preempting students' reflective deliberations and standing by as a neutral observer. This point is explored in the section, "Student-Instructor Interaction."

The authors have found the following techniques to be effective:

- not revealing your opinion(s) all at once by:
  - posing provocative questions in the context of the ongoing discussion to redirect the discussion to an angle more relevant to the learning objectives, and/or
  - summing up relevant material at the end of each unit;
- commenting substantively on content, when appropriate;
- encouraging independent thinking by citing in positive terms, examples of student disagreement with you;
- explaining rules and expectations with positive and negative examples; and
- relating discussions to real-world cases.

Constructing questions as a facilitator is a critical task. It is tempting to focus on questions that require factual responses since they are the easiest to grade and state whether the answer is correct. The factual question tends to be used by an instructor who focuses on knowledge acquisition rather than comprehension. When a course focuses on comprehension and application issues, a different type of question is required. Instructors must construct questions that require students to develop well-reasoned answers.

Facilitating discussion also requires the encouragement of the participation of all students. Silberman and Lawson (1995) suggest additional ways to encourage participation. Some include:

- *Open discussion questions.* For maximum effect, the question should require some mix of facts, feelings, and reasoned responses.
- *Learning partners.* Instead of using groups of four or more, try pairs for some issues and activities.
- *Polling.* Conduct a short poll about a topic. Report the results and have the students respond to the results.
- *Using "whips."* Ask for a very short response to a question from the students. One of the authors uses this strategy to start discussion for certain subjects. Two examples of this type of strategy are: "What is one characteristic of the best boss you have ever had?" and, "What one thing motivates you to do your best work?"
- *Using "panels."* Ask a group of students to present their views on a subject. Ask the "observers" to respond with questions and evaluation. This can work particularly well for areas that require a pro and con response.

### 4. Instructor-Learner Interaction

The authors' experiences and the surveys referenced in this chapter point to the crucial significance of strategies that efficiently create a strong and practical sense of instructor connection with students. Therefore, the fourth aspect of the proposed paradigm in course management focuses on instructor-learner interactions.

Effective interaction requires certain attitudinal traits and "crafts." In light of the authors' experience and many institutions' adopted training guidelines, the following appear to be the most in demand:

- responsiveness,
- effectiveness,
- courteousness,
- honesty,
- efficiency, and
- motivational

The significance of instructor-learner interaction cannot be overestimated. Students need to feel that they are heard, appreciated, and respected. Given the rules established for facilitation, the instructor does not need to reply to most postings individually, but must reply to all the students in public at some point, or recognize in their postings, every student by name for his/her contributions. Instructors should be careful with students who have voiced disagreement with them in public, and should go out of their way to acknowledge their distinct contributions.

Even though instructor responsiveness is important, substantiality of instructor comments should not be overlooked. Students require both. Students want substance in addition to timeliness. An extensive study of 3000 students found that learners may view unsubstantial comments that lack specificity as being indicative of "a disinterested or lazy faculty member" (Rossman, 1999). In the authors' experience in both a monitoring role demanded by academic management or a feedback receiving role from students, a frequent student complaint is that some faculty are not substantive enough in their responses to students.

"Timeliness and quality," argued Han, "are not necessarily related: the former is more of an indicator of responsiveness while the latter is of competency. Given the former, and in absence of the latter, students will be more tolerant of instructor blunders, but will not have an overall satisfactory experience" (X. Han, personal communications with R. Kling and N. Hara and comments on their draft "Our Publishing Trajectory and the Literatures of Distance Education," December 29, 1999). Other studies have found that both the substance and timeliness of instructor responses matter, and neither alone suffices (Collis, et al., 2000). This is a point that some who subscribe to the facilitator school, which limits the role of instructor to creating an interactive environment, have failed to fully understand.

Regarding techniques to develop instructional substance, Anderson et al. (2001) present some categories, including providing explanatory feedback, misconception diagnosis, and direction of reference resources. To help gauge the appropriate level of faculty engagement from the perspective of frequency, one of the authors has experimented with a tool called Faculty Posting Index (FPI) which represents total instructor postings as a percentage of total postings of a class. In a graduate program of a leading online degree granting institution, FPI usually stands at 15-25%. In an undergraduate program for the same instructor that combines a face-to-face and virtual asynchronous learning, FPI increased by a factor of 2-3. One reason for such high FPI may be the independent study tradition to which such students are accustomed. Given the frame of reference of independent study, students feel that online discussion is too "intensive." This is an interesting area for further research: online students may not be satisfied, even when the learning outcome is better, due to the heavier load of work (Sarah, 2000; Vachris, 1999). In a public university's online program, 38% of the students who dropped courses cited workload as a reason.

Honesty in interacting with students is also critical. Instructors must be honest when they make a mistake, whether content-, procedure-, or communication-related. Students must believe that the instructor cares about them as people as well as learners. Students tend to be perceptive about instructors' motivations.

Instructors should keep students posted about any challenges that they are facing as instructors. If the instructor will be unable to access the course for two or three days, students should be informed. Students might have an important issue to discuss and if there is no instructor response, students might misunderstand the silence. Being direct and honest about schedules and conflicts will minimize student frustration. Just as the instructor expects to be contacted by students regarding their problems, students also want to know what kind of performance is expected by the instructor. Problems should not be left to escalate. Student progress must be monitored.

The demands on instructors seem to be onerous. They must be responsive, affective, substantive, reflective, and attentive to all the students in the class. This borders on the impossible for many faculty who struggle to live up to students' expectations while wondering how they can teach a large class or multiple classes online compared to their experience with face-to-face settings (McCollum, 1998, 1999; Mangan, 2001). The solution can be found only in improved efficiency.

Efficiency, defined as spending relatively less faculty time per student per class while achieving similar learning efficacy, is not a commonly embraced concept in academe. But efficiency in course management, particularly in interaction, is a competency that should not be dismissed (Han, 1999). As with the familiar rule governing the use of the emergency oxygen mask in flight, the faculty must be able to help themselves first. They must be able to meet instructional demands satisfactorily with equal amount of time if not less than what they spend on teaching a similarly sized face-to-face class. Without a reasonable measure of efficiency, faculty teaching online cannot assure sustaining power throughout a program and throughout their teaching career. Without sustaining power by faculty, no substantial help can be consistently provided to students.

In conjunction with the aforementioned strategies for faculty engagement, three more suggestions can be offered to boost efficiency of online instruction:

1. Exploit the advantages enabled by electronic copying, forwarding, and easy editing and modification. Whenever the instructor states something substantive in a message, unless confidentiality is involved, he/she should consider making the content available to the entire class. Often, the substantive content—be it subject-related or a class procedural matter—is relevant to most students.

2. Focus on patterns of the discourse. Instructors should recognize the common issues in one and even multiple discussion threads, and provide substantive statements at appropriate intervals. In one

author's observation, each of such intervals is marked by a wave of student postings. Depending on the class size and participation intensity, a wave of postings may contain 5-10 postings by different students (in a class of 12 students). When the wave ebbs, it is usually the right time for the instructor to step in to synthesize. According to this strategy, it is not worthwhile for the instructor to follow the discussion "play by play," but rather to perform a movie director's role while partially acting as a movie reviewer. In this dual role, the instructor is not only obligated to provide direction and instructions when necessary, but is also no less valued for his/her contributions to contextualization.

3. Build a library of short essays, cases, and Q&A. The essays and cases the instructor collects should be scenario- and context-specific to a particular course. Given the structure and content of that course, those scenarios or topics will have a high probability of recurring in subsequent classes. In such cases, instructors can formulate quick responses by tailoring those library elements to similar situations in the future.

## CURRENT STATE OF PROGRAM LEVEL COURSE MANAGEMENT

If course level issues for course management are still under-researched, there is even less research at the program level. In order to obtain a composite picture of mature online programs across a spectrum of institutions, systematic information has been collected and compiled from five institutions, with assistance from faculty and staff at these institutions. These are:

1. Institution A—a leading online degree institution and for-profit entity.
2. Institution B—a public institution with a leading online program offering more than 200 courses and more than six degrees programs.
3. Institution C—a for-profit, primarily online-based institution.
4. Institution D—a public institution with a three year old online program.
5. Institution E—a well-known institution dedicated to serving adult learners via distance learning. The information described here for Institution E is limited to graduate programs.

For the purpose of this discussion, the practices of the online programs at the institutions are grouped according to six program level issues related to course management:

### Student Orientation

This issue concerns the manner in which the institutions assist students in becoming familiar with course management systems, program policies, course structures, and rules for student interactions as well as student-instructor interactions.

Institution A has designed a communications management course and requires all new online students to take it. The course covers a number of issues including introduction to the platform it uses for its online courses.

Institution B sends out an orientation CD-ROM for online students with information regarding how to get started, how the tools work, and what software is needed. It sends out a letter to each student, in addition to posting "getting started" information on the Web.

Institution C requires all new students to take a for-credit course of the same duration as regular courses in the program. The course exposes students to the institution's educational philosophy, policy, and standard course structure. There is also one optional unit built into each course, about courseware functionality.

Institution D has created a Web-based, self-conducted online orientation and requires all students to complete it. Students receive an advising session, by phone or face-to-face, about the program's procedural and process matters. The session also covers other academic advising issues. An "initiation letter" is sent to each student containing the instructor's personal greeting, instruction on how to login to the course, and requirements to be met in the first few days of class.

Institution E has adopted a multi-faceted approach to orientation. A student starts orientation with a CD-ROM, and this is followed by a practice course on the Web. The practice course is mostly self-conducted although staff assistance is available. There is an optional unit of "Getting Started" in every course. For program policy and procedures, a handbook is distributed.

### Instructor Availability

This issue concerns policies regarding faculty presence in the virtual classroom.

Institution A demands that its instructors make themselves available to students five days for each week of the course, even though it does not stringently define "availability." Instructors can simply post at least one message to the class at any time, to provide instruction, or to respond to discussion-postings or questions. Institution A does not specify how long or at what time an instructor should login. It maintains a team of instructional specialists as an integral part of its academic management model. Their responsibilities include monitoring classrooms and handling instructor issues. For example, if they discover that an instructor is not available for the number of days specified in the instructor contract, or if the instructor is not involved in discussions to the degree required, they coach the instructor to improve his/her facilitation skills.

Institution B requires online instructors follow a traditional instructional model such as providing "office hour" information in the course Web syllabus. But Institution B refrains from dictating specific regulations in this regard.

Institution C does not have a standardized policy, even though it demands that its faculty "participate." Its best practice guideline advises faculty to check in on a daily basis.

Institution D demands its faculty be responsive, but adopts an overall hands-off approach akin to that of Institution B. It has issued a guideline document with suggested good practices concerning instructor availability and other course management issues. It requires faculty to incorporate the key elements of the guideline into syllabi. Faculty can modify or tailor suggested practices in their own courses.

Institution E spells out in the contract, basic expectations for its "facilitators." A facilitator should post at least three times a week. Facilitators are also encouraged to hold virtual office hours via chat. Over the duration of a course, a facilitator usually conducts two to three chat sessions, while some may do so weekly.

### Student Attendance

This issue concerns policies related to students' participation in virtual classrooms and their adherence to deadlines.

Institution A deploys electronically enabled class attendance procedures, and very rigorously enforces them. It uses the number of student postings as the basis for recording attendance. Each student must post at least once on two different days each week. If these postings are not made, the student loses access to the classroom. The only grade that can be given is a "Withdrawal" or a "Withdrawal/Fail," which even the instructor cannot change.

Institution B allows individual faculty to determine guidelines on student attendance. Instructors' standards vary. For example, some require students to be online and submit items daily while others require students to be online weekly.

Institution C has explicit requirements of students' involvement in classes. Students must complete reading assignments, and they must make at least one "major posting" each week as well as respond to two postings by other students. When a student is behind in meeting such requirements for more than two weeks, he/she will be asked to withdraw. Faculty are responsible for enforcing the rule.

Institution D has a two-part attendance policy. One is a uniform policy across the program and is made available to all students when they sign up for online courses. As an example, students must log into their courses within seven days after the course begins. The second part, required as a component of each syllabus, covers the rest of the attendance policy. Even though the key points of the second part, such as participation requirements and deadline observation must be explicitly stated in each syllabus, specific requirements are left to individual faculty to determine.

Institution E dictates that students must participate at least twice a week. If a student is missing from class participation for three weeks, the student will receive a failing grade for participation, even though he/she may still be able to pass the course. For gauging student participation, Institution E also has produced a rubric containing three components:

1. *Dialog with Curriculum* which measures content comprehension,
2. *Dialog with Others* which encourages interactions and "cognitive conflict" among students, and
3. *Meeting Course Requirements* which speaks specifically to requirements related to online participation such as serving as group facilitator, posting assignments on time, and completing peer evaluations of team members.

### Academic Advising

This issue concerns student counseling and advising. Advisers/counselors are responsible for advising students on procedural issues such as dropping courses, disputing grades, or requesting an incomplete grade.

Institution A employs a large number of "academic counselors" whom students may contact. Institution A even urges faculty not to provide administrative advice to students. Instead, it asks them to suggest that students discuss these kinds of issues with their enrollment advisers or academic counselors.

Institution B provides advising via the Internet. Students have online access to catalogs and departmental information. A scheduled live online advising center exists for students to access and converse with real people.

Even though Institution C has advisers assigned to each student, its overall approach to advising is to build up the most efficient menu of multiple channels, but not to force students to use any particular one. It prefers and expects students to use the Internet. Other than their advisers, students send messages to a support address, and the messages are routed, depending on their nature, to particular people best able to handle them.

Institution D makes its advising available throughout the program, but does not have advisers dedicated to the online program. For online students, contact is maintained primarily via e-mail and a toll free phone number.

Institution E has staffed academic advisers in every program. Advisers use e-mail to assist students with academic difficulties. The advisers are responsible for following a student's academic progress. When a student takes fewer than two courses a year, he/she is contacted by an adviser.

### Faculty Development

This issue focuses on whether a systemic process is in place to assist faculty to prepare pedagogically for teaching in virtual environments.

Institution A is strict and systematic about virtual course management related-training. Its four to six-week long new instructor training program is intense and hands-on. Training covers a wide scope of issues such as facilitation strategies, plagiarism, grade complaints, dealing with code of conduct problems, copyright issues, and using American Psychological Association (APA) format. Instructional specialists create and facilitate faculty training classes. Institution A also periodically convenes fully online "content area meetings" to examine certain pedagogical issues.

Institution B organizes a team of instructional designers to assist faculty in converting course content into appropriate designs for online courses. A faculty mentoring project is also planned where faculty mentor each other within academic disciplines.

Institution C mandates a 12-week course for all new faculty who play the role of online students in simulated learning environments. A "how-to-mentor" course is also required of doctoral program faculty. On a quarterly basis, each school conducts telephone conference calls with about 25 faculty, to review instructional issues and program policy.

Institution D emphasizes individual consultation with all online faculty, from the design stage to course management, for the first few classes they teach.

Institution E conducts a facilitator orientation by bringing candidates to the institution, or by phone. Online orientation is currently being developed. A staff member is always in close contact with faculty. There is also a Web portal that contains announcements and material useful for facilitator development.

### Faculty Assessment

This issue concerns the use of systemic mechanisms and policies to assess faculty effectiveness in course management.

Institution A ends each course with an online student survey and makes the results available to faculty. An instructional specialist periodically reviews the surveys, and there is an annual peer review process. If class-specific instructional issues arise, an instructional specialist reviews classroom proceedings, counsels the instructor involved, or suggests additional training. Faculty also complete end-of-course surveys.

Institution B stipulates that each online course go through an evaluation process in which the department chair or the dean approves the course. At the end of each course, an online assessment survey is conducted.

Institution C relies primarily on anonymous student course evaluations which are read by the dean. These are later shared with faculty. Faculty are also told that unannounced, random, spot-checks of their courses may take place.

Institution D conducts survey evaluations for every course. An annual consolidated survey is also conducted. Individual follow-up meetings are held with faculty whose evaluations fall below average.

Institution E has a student evaluation for each course. The instructor is also asked to evaluate him/herself at that time. A staff member monitors ongoing courses and contacts facilitators if a problem is discerned. An annual evaluation of each facilitator is conducted based on those evaluations and on staff observations.

### Other

At almost all institutions that offer online courses, there exists the controversial issue of "academic freedom" and faculty control of online teaching. The American Federation of Teachers has passed a resolution demanding higher education institutions adopt a set of "standards" for online programs. The first standard states that "academic teaching faculty must maintain control of shaping, approving and evaluating distance education courses" (American Federation of Teachers, 2000a). This standard is indicative of two thorny issues: 1) how much academic management should be involved in course management; and 2) whether academic management should codify any course management rules that conventionally fall in the domain of individual faculty.

Undoubtedly, virtual learning demands a great deal of program level planning. The authors contend that program management is an absolutely necessary component of course management, but optimization of its elements is still a subject of debate. Academic participation in developing practices related to program management is essential, and administrative participation must not be perceived as heavy handed or intrusive into faculty's traditional domains. The essence of the dilemma is where to draw the lines and how to reconcile institutional responsibilities toward students versus the academic freedom of faculty.

Shared governance is a fundamental consideration towards addressing the problem, but it is not the only one. Institution A, because it is a for-profit entity, has adopted and is able to maintain a high degree of management (administrative) influence and control. Most other institutions run into much more resistance that often seems uncompromising. But sound academic management is far more than assessing and monitoring faculty performance. There is a need to focus on coordination and faculty assistance which Institution A also seems to have resolved better than many other institutions.

In course management, the authors consider instructor availability and student attendance to be inextricably intertwined. At Institution D these are addressed within the same policy. Institution A's policies also interrelate the two issues. For example, its policy states that if the instructor does not make any postings to the class for a number of days, policies governing student attendance will not be enforced.

## FACULTY DEVLOPMENT AND ASSESSMENT IN PEDAGOGY-DRIVEN ONLINE COURSE MANAGEMENT

Faculty development, in terms of instructional technology and pedagogical methodology related to computer-mediated learning is problematic (Rogers, 2000). As Xin and Feenberg (2002) assert, "Trainers focus on helping teachers use [presentation] techniques and rarely emphasize the management of online discussion" (p. 2). Instructors' training needs, as we have discussed, extend beyond managing online discussion.

Faculty development is an issue about program level management and one that requires serious attention. Training instructors to be effective and efficient regarding their activities related to course structure, class organization, learning facilitation, and instructor-learner interaction is a fundamental capital investment that institutions need to address. This requires a long-term plan and systematic implementation mechanisms.

Current faculty incentive structures that most institutions employ are also problematic and constitute a serious hindrance to individual competency enhancement and program building. It is essential for administrations to reconsider their incentive programs, both from a monetary and non-monetary standpoint, to reflect the true value of their online programs. The American Federation of Teachers' appeal should be heeded: "Institutional reward systems for faculty—including policies regarding promotion, tenure and special funding for faculty projects—should accord positive recognition for the creative work of formulating distance programs" (American Federation of Teachers, 2000b, p. 6).

Faculty assessment is a very sensitive issue when it comes to the review of faculty for the purposes of any kind of incentive, whether monetary or for purposes of retention and promotion. In traditional academic environments, the assessment of teaching is a weak area of academic management. Administration, faculty, staff, and students often do not pay adequate attention to assessment even when they are aware of its purposes, standards, and processes. It is not uncommon for faculty to demonstrate a substantial degree of suspicion or apathy towards assessment requirements that go beyond student course evaluations. For many reasons, institutional

administrations also tend to be negligent in conducting systemic and continuous assessment of faculty.

Faculty assessment faces additional challenges in online programs when
compared to traditional programs. The current reliance by virtually all the
programs on student opinion surveys is not all that reliable. And even
when such assessment methodologies are utilized, student response rates
tend to be lower than in traditional classroom settings. In fully online programs, faculty participation in these kinds of evaluations is also lower than
in traditional classroom settings.

Still, the most challenging of all issues is to incorporate assessment findings in "teaching methods, curriculum, course content, instructional
resources, and in academic support services ... into regular departmental
and/or institutional planning and budgeting processes and ... into the
determination of the priorities for funding and implementation" (Higher
Learning Commission, 2002c, p. 28). The vast majority of programs are
still far from that "promised land." Faculty and staff need to see the
organic and persistent as well as reasonable connection between assessment and all the critical practical decisions. Such connection is absolutely
necessary for the best practices at the course level to take hold.

## CONCLUSION

The basic premise of this chapter is that course management should be an
essential concern for institutions offering courses that demand active and
collaborative learning. Challenges to successful course management are
substantial and are often at the core of the failure to provide effective and
efficient online education. Quality course management is the lever for a
course to succeed; without it, even a well-designed virtual course may be little more than a showpiece. Course management needs to be approached
holistically—at both the program and course levels. A pedagogically-driven
course management model calls for active and interactive instructor
engagement within a supportive program level environment.

The most critical success factor in course management is instructor preparedness in terms of 1) competency and 2) attitude. A practitioner-ori-
ented model breaks course management at the course level into four
distinct but related components: course structure, class organization,
learning facilitation, and instructor-learner interaction. A truly pedagogically prepared instructor needs to be well grounded in each of these.

Even though course level issues directly affect learning outcomes and
student satisfaction, it is program level factors that have strategic importance. These factors include institutional program policies and program
incentives that cover faculty assessment, faculty development, and faculty
and student interaction and collaboration. Overall, norms for faculty

assessment and faculty availability for students are issues currently not well defined across institutions and are the least addressed issues in most teaching environments. When well resolved, these program level issues become the best and strongest guarantees for quality course management.

**Acknowledgments:** The authors would like to acknowledge the generosity of the following individuals who shared information and/or spared time in response to requests for help: Cindy Knott and Russ Paden of University of Phoenix Online, Bruce Francis and Jerome Halverson of Capella University, Debbie Sopczyk and David Brigham of Excelsior College, Peg Wherry and Rene Eborn of Weber State University, Barbra Hoskins of Clemson University, Trudy Jacobson of University of Wisconsin-Green Bay, and Elizabeth Larson.

# REFERENCES

AAHESGIT. (2001, Mar.16). Electronic mailing list.

American Federation of Teachers. (2000a). *Resolution on Ensuring High Quality in Distance Education for College Credit.* Retrieved from http://www.aft.org/about/resolutions/2000/distanceed.html

American Federation of Teachers (The Higher Education Program and Policy Council of the American Federation of Teachers). (2000b). *Distance Education: Guidelines for Good Practice.* Retrieved from http://www.aft.org/higher ed/downloadable/distance.pdf

Anderson, T., Rourke, L., Garrison, D. R., & Archer, W. (2001). Assessing Teaching Presence in a Computer Conferencing Context [Electronic version]. *Journal of Asynchronous Learning Networks*, Vol. 5, No. 2.

Andres, Y.M. (1995). "Collaboration in the Classroom and Over the Internet." Retrieved from http://www.globalschoolhouse.com/teach/articles/collaboration.htm l.

Arbaugh, J.B., (2000). Virtual classroom characteristics and student satisfaction with Internet-based MBA courses. *Journal of Management Education*, 24 (1).

Arle, J. (2002). "What Makes Students Stay? *eLearn Magazine: Education and Technology in Perspective.* Retrieved from http://www.elearnmag.org/subpage/sub page.cfm?article_pk=1301&pag_e_number_nb=1&title=FEATURE%20STORY

Baldwin, G. (1999). The Evolution of electronic pedagogy in an outcome based learning environment: learning, teaching, and the culture of technology at California's newest university—CSU Monterey Bay. In P. de Bra, & J. Leggett (Eds.), *Proceedings of WebNet 1999: World Conference on the World Wide Web and Internet* (pp. 87-93). Charlottesville, VA: Association for the Advancement of Computing in Education (AACE).

Barab, S. A., Thomas, M. K., & Merrill H. (2001). Online learning: From information dissemination to fostering collaboration. *Journal of Interactive Learning Research*, 12 (1), 105-143.

Berge, Z. L., & Lin, M. (2001). *Obstacles Faced at Various Stages Of Capability Regarding Distance Education In Institutions Of Higher Education: Survey Results.* Retrieved from http://www.emoderators.com/barriers/hghred_stgs.shtml

Bloom, B.S., Englehart, M.D., Furst, E. Hill, W. H., & Dratwohl, D.R. (1956). *Taxonomy of Educational Objectives, Handbook 1: Cognitive Domain.* New York: David McKay Company, Inc.

Bonk, C.J., & Cunningham, D.J. (1998). Searching for Learner-Centered, Constructivist, and Sociocultural Components of Collaborative Educational Learning Tools. In Bonk, C.J., and King, K.S. (Eds), *Electronic Collaborators: Learner-Centered Technologies for Literacy, Apprenticeship, and Discourse.* Mahwah, NJ: Lawrence Erlbaum Associates.

Bradburn, E. M. & Zimbler, L. (2002). *Distance Education Instruction by Postsecondary Faculty and Staff: Fall 1998.* US Department of Education, National Center for Education Statistics. Washington, D.C.

Brown, G. (2000). The Venn of assessment: Transforming instructional design. *Syllabus, 14*(4), 36-39.

Brown, D. G. (2000). The Low-hanging fruit. *Syllabus.*

Bruffee, K. A. (1999). *Collaborative Learning: Higher Education, Interdependence, and the Authority of Knowledge.* Baltimore, MD: John Hopkins University Press.

Center for Critical Thinking. (1997). *Critical Thinking: Basic Theory and Instructional Structures.* Dillon Beach, CA: Foundation for Critical Thinking.

Course for instructors helps keep students. (1999, November 5). *Chronicle of Higher Education.* p. A 59.

Daily, N. (1984). Adult Learning and organizations. *Training and Development Journal, 38,* 66-68.

Chickering, A. W., & Ehrman, S. C. (1997). Implementing the Seven Principles: Technology as Lever [Electronic version]. *American Association for Higher Education.* Retrieved from http://www.aahe.org/technology/ehrmann.htm.

Chodorow, S. (2000) Faculty, intellectual property, and online education. *Continuing Education Review, 64,* 12-22.

Collis, B., Winnips, K., & Moonen, J. (2000). Structured support versus learner choice via the WWW: Where is the payoff? *Journal of Interactive Learning Research,* 11 (2).

Coppola N., Hiltz, S.R. & Rotter, N. (2001). Becoming a virtual professor: Pedagogical roles and ALN. *Proceedings of the 34th Hawaii International Conference on Systems Sciences.* Los Alamitos, CA: IEEE Computer Society Press.

Ehrmann, S. C. (1997). *Asking the right question.* Annenberg/CPB. Retrieved April 01, 2001 from http://www.learner.org/edtech/rscheval/rightquestion.html

Fishman, B. J. (2001) How Activity Fosters CMC Tool Use in Classrooms: Reinventing Innovations in Local Contexts. *Journal of Interactive Learning Research,* 11 (1).

Frankola, K. (2001). The e-Learning taboo: High dropout rates in online courses. Syllabus.

French, W. L., & Bell, C. H. (1999). *Organization development: Behavioral science interventions for organization improvement* (6th ed). Upper Saddle River, NJ: Prentice Hall.

Gilbert, J., & Han, C. Y. (1999). Arthur: Adapting instruction to accommodate learning style. In P. de Bra, & J. Leggett (Eds.), *Proceedings of WebNet 1999: World*

*Conference on the World Wide Web and Internet* (pp. 433-438). Charlottesville, VA: Association for the Advancement of Computing in Education (AACE).

Han, X. (1999). *Exploring an effective and efficient online course management model. Teaching with Technology Today* . Madison, WI: University Wisconsin System. Retrieved Feb 15, 2001, from http://www.uwsa.edu/olit/ttt/han.htm.

Han, X. (2001). *Report on the Distance Learning Staff Survey Result: Conducted for the Distance Learning Community of Practice, UCEA.* Unpublished report.

Hara, N., & Kling, R. (2000). Students' distress with a Web-based distance education course: An ethnographic study of participants' experience. *Information, Communication & Society.* Retrieved May 20, 2001 from http://www.slisindiana.edu/CSI/wp00-01.html.

Harasim, L., Hiltz, S. R., Teles, L., & Turoff, M. (1995). *Learning Networks: A Field Guide to Teaching and Learning Online.* Cambridge, MA: MIT Press.

Hardless, C., & Nulden U. (1999). Mandatory participation as examination. In P. de Bra, & J. Leggett (Eds.), *Proceedings of WebNet 1999: World Conference on the World Wide Web and Internet (pp. 481-486).* Charlottesville, VA: Association for the Advancement of Computing in Education (AACE).

Higher Learning Commission (A Commission of North Central Association of Colleges and Schools). (2002a).*Statement of Commitment by Regional Accreditation Associations for the Evaluation of Electronically Offered Degree and Certificate Programs.* Addendum to the Handbook of Accreditation ($2^{nd}$ edition). Chicago, IL: Author.

Higher Learning Commission. (A Commission of North Central Association of Colleges and Schools). (2002b). *Best Practices For Electronically Offered Degree and Certificate.* Addendum to the Handbook of Accreditation($2^{nd}$ edition). Chicago, IL: Author.

Higher Learning Commission. (2002c; revised March 1, 2002). *Assessment of Student Academic Achievement: Levels of Implementation.* Addendum to the Handbook of Accreditation ($2^{nd}$ edition). Chicago, IL: Author.

Hodgins, W. H. (2000). *Into the future: A Vision Paper. Report for Commission on Technology and Adult Learning.* Retrieved May 23, 2001 from the World Wide Web: http://www.learnativity.com/into_the_future2000.html.

Hoskins, B. J., Reardon, L. B., & Walter, S. B. (2001). *Guidelines for On-Line Course Development and Evaluation.* Retrieved from http://www.sc-partnership.org/grants/SCPDE%20Grant%20Final%20Repo rt.Clemson.htm

Knowles, M. S. (1998). *The adult learner: The definitive classic in adult education and human resource development* ($5^{th}$ ed). Woburn, MASS: Butterworth-Heinemann.

Lorenz, J. (2000). *University of Wisconsin-Green Bay Online Student Satisfaction Study.* Unpublished paper

Institute for Higher Education Policy. (2000). *Quality on the Line: Benchmarks for Success in Internet-Based Distance Education.* Retrieve from http://www.ihep.com/Pubs/PDF/Quality.pdf

Mangan, K. S. (2001). Internet remains an important tool for business education, speakers assert. *Chronicle of Higher Education.* Retrieved May 4, 2001 from http://chronicle.com/free/2001/04/2001042501u.htm

McCarthy, B. (2000a). *About Learning.* Wauconda, IL: About Learning, Inc.

McCarthy, B. (2000b). *About Teaching: 4MAT in the Classroom.* Wauconda, IL: About Learning, Inc

McCollum, K. (1998). Computer requirement for students changes professors' duties as well. *Chronicle of Higher Education.* Retrieved October 4, 1999 from http://chronicle.com/free/v44/i42/42a02201.htm

McCollum, K. (1999). Online ways to misbehave can outpace college rules. *Chronicle of Higher Education.* Retrieved October 4, 1999 from http://chronicle.com/free/v46/i04/04a03501.htm

Meier, D. (2000). *The Accelerated Learning Handbook.* New York: McGraw Hill.

Moore, M. G. (1989). Editorial: Three Types of Interaction. *American Journal of Distance Education,* 3 (2).

Moore, M.G. (1994). Administrative barriers to adoption of distance education. *The American Journal of Distance Education,* 8 (3).

Oblinger, D. & Verville, A. (1998). *What business wants from higher education.* Phoenix, AZ: Oryx Press.

Odin, J. (1999). Effective online teaching/learning: A case study. In P. de Bra, & J. Leggett (Eds.), *Proceedings of WebNet 1999: World Conference on the World Wide Web and Internet* (pp. 1381-1382). Charlottesville, VA: Association for the Advancement of Computing in Education (AACE).

Pena-Shaff, J., Martin, W., & Gay. G. (2001). An epistemological framework for analyzing student interactions in computer-mediated communication environments. *Journal of Interactive Learning Research, 12*(1), 41-68.

Richter, S. (2000). *Help from the devil in boosting course enrollments.* Chronicle of Higher Education. Retrieved May 4, 2001 from http://www.pkal.org/pipermail/si-psychology-tf/2000-July/000090.h tml

Rogers. D. (2000) A Paradigm Shift: Technology Integration for Higher Education in the New Millennium. *Educational Technology Review, 13*(Spring/Summer), 19-27

Rossman, M. (1999). Successful online teaching using an asynchronous learner discussion Forum [Electronic version]. *Journal of Asynchronous Learning Networks,* 3(2).

Sarah, C. (2000). Online psychology instruction is effective, but not satisfying, study finds. *Chronicle of higher Education.* Retrieved May 4, 2001 from http://chronicle.com/free/v46/i27/27a04801.htm

Sherry, L., Billing, S. H., & Tavalin, F. (2001). Good Online Conversation: Building on Research to Inform Practice. *Journal of Interactive Learning Research,* 11 (1).

Silberman, Mel. (1995). *101 Ways to Make Training Active.* San Francisco, CA. Pfeiffer.

Spigner-Littles, D. & Anderson, C. E. (1999). Constructivism: A Paradigm for Older Learners. *Educational Gerontology,* 25 (3).

Sternberg, R. J. (1996). *Successful intelligence.* New York: Simon and Schuster.

Tuckman, B.W., & Jensen, M.C. (1977). Stages of small-group development revisited. *Group and Organizational Studies.* December, 419-427.

University of Maryland University College. *Systems approach to designing online learning activities. Web Site for University of Maryland University College for best practices in online learning.* Retrieved February 21, 2002 from http://www.umuc.edu/virtualteaching/module1/systems.html

University of Illinois Faculty Seminar. (1999). *Teaching at an Internet distance: The pedagogy of online teaching and learning. Report of 1998-1999.* Retrieved Jan 20, 2000 from http://www.vpaa.uillinois.edu/tid/report/tid_report.html.

Usrey, M. W. (1999). Preferences of asynchronous adult distance learners. In P. de Bra, & J. Leggett (Eds.), *Proceedings of WebNet 1999: World Conference on the World Wide Web and Internet* (pp. 1105-1110). Charlottesville, VA: Association for the Advancement of Computing in Education (AACE).

Vachris, M.A. (1999). Teaching principles of economics without "chalk and talk": The experience of CNU online. *Journal of Economic Education.* 30 (3).

Viechnicki, K.J., Bohlin, R.M., & Milheim, W.D. (1990). Instructional motivation of adult learners: Analysis of student perceptions in continuing education. *Journal of Continuing Higher Education,* 38, 3, 10-14.

Xin, C., & Feenberg, A. (2002). Designing for Pedagogical Effectiveness: the TextWeaver™. *Presentation to the 35ᵗʰ Annual Hawaii International Conference on System Sciences.* Retrieved from http://www-rohan.sdsu.edu/faculty/feenberg/textweaver/HICSS_textw eaver_dec21.pdf

Zemke, R., & Zemke, S. (1984). 30 Things we know for sure about adult learning. *Innovation Abstracts,* 6 (8).

CHAPTER 12

# EXCLUSION IN INTERNATIONAL ONLINE LEARNING COMMUNITIES

**S. Mavor and B. Trayner**

Advances in communications technology have meant that some higher education institutions are now able to offer online courses to a wider audience of students from different parts of the world. However, the process of internationalizing online courses is more complex and more problematic than it may seem. In this chapter the authors question some of the assumptions underpinning teaching, learning, and the building of learning communities in international online courses. They suggest that considerable care in course design and teaching is needed to avoid participant feelings of exclusion from these communities and the consequent risk of students giving up or failing to benefit fully from the course. Writing from the context of Portuguese higher education, they discuss the related issues of socio-discursive practices of online learning, pedagogies for online learning communities, cultures and policies in higher education, and the choice of software for supporting online learning and international learning communities. The chapter concludes with recommendations for designing and teaching online courses and for creating international online learning communities. The authors suggest that as international online courses grow in number, further research will be needed into international communication in online environ-

Electronic Learning Communities—Issues and Practices, pages 457–488.
Copyright © 2003 by Information Age Publishing, Inc.
All rights of reproduction in any form reserved.
ISBN: 1-931576-96-3 (pbk.), 1-931576-97-1 (hardcover)

ments and the discoursal, socio-political / cultural and technological issues involved in building international learning communities.

**KEYWORDS:**  exclusion; international learning communities; socio-political discourses; cultures of learning.

## INTRODUCTION

With the widening range of teaching and learning opportunities offered by new technologies in higher education, there are a number of challenges facing educators working in an increasingly international online learning environment. The apparent ease with which a student can join an international learning community often masks discoursal, socio-political and cultural barriers to effective participation and learning. In the context of this chapter we take discourse to mean language as social practice with its conventions, implicit hierarchies and relations of power within and upon social institutions (Fairclough, 1989, p. 16). That is, in the same way that we can easily recognize the conventions and intended persuasions of a political speech or an advertising campaign, we consider how current discourses, in the form of educational, economic or technological rhetoric, can affect perceptions of learning and community building, especially in international contexts. In identifying some of these barriers to becoming active, participating members of international learning communities, we aim to raise questions for online course designers and teachers and suggest that the different discourses and histories of students coming from different "cultures of learning" (Cortazzi & Jin, 1996) need to be accounted for in both course design and teaching practices.

In this chapter we address some of the multiple, interrelated issues of teaching, learning, and course design for international online learning communities. Our objective is to explore these issues and to offer some suggestions for the design of a culturally sensitive, international online course. Our position has been that the pedagogical, socio-political, intercultural, and even ethical responsibilities of higher education in an international context are more complex than is often realized. In which case, we have considered our task to be primarily one of trying to expose these complexities rather than writing simple recipes for success.

The chapter was written as a reflective response to our participation, in 1999, as students in an online, post-graduate certificate course for teachers and trainers, which we will refer to as TTO.[1] The 20 week course, run by a prestigious British University, was aimed at both British and international students. Ten weeks of the course were conducted in English in an international group and 10 weeks in local groups, in local languages, with local tutors.

After successfully completing the course we were invited to be local tutors for the Portuguese group. While welcoming the invitation, we were concerned about unquestioningly importing a course with its taken-for-granted, British university perspectives of teaching and learning, and applying it in a country with a different socio-cultural history and a different context of learning. We felt that inviting potential Portuguese participants to join a Portuguese group that would make up part of an international learning community was more complex than the view put forward in the course guide "that it would be most useful for people from (other countries) to discuss their own conditions of education with fellow academics in their own language, and also focus on Internet sites in those languages." On another level, our concern extended to our experience of misunderstandings apparently caused by lack of clarity and coherence in course presentation and design. We feared that such misunderstandings were likely to be more frequent among students who were working in a second or foreign language and who came from different learning cultures.

Undertaking to be tutors in this project, therefore, raised two questions that we wanted to address. First, on a general level, in what ways would we be acting as agents of a learning project which was promoting (exporting?) values and ideologies in the name of online learning which we did not feel were sufficiently taking into account the dialectic of international and local contexts? With our Portuguese students in mind, the words of a leading Portuguese sociologist on the influence of internationalization echoed our concern that "to be ours, our future cannot be reduced to the future of others" (Boaventura Sousa Santos, 1993, p. 66).

Second, this time on an ethical level, we were worried about being involved in a learning project where the rhetoric did not always seem to match its practice. Although we were clearly interested in teaching an international online course for a prestigious British University, would any misalignment between discourse and practice cause unnecessary misunderstandings and obstacles in learning and communicating in international online communities? An example which we take up later, is that although the course is described as "experiential" and that it values "participation" in online discussions, course assessment is in the form of a traditional "essay" about an aspect of online learning. In other words, online participation and experience is said to be crucial but is given no value in the system of student assessment.

These questions led us to carry out an analysis of the TTO course in relation to the Portuguese context in order to be able to articulate more precisely the roles and responsibilities of critical educators and course designers involved in international online learning and community building in higher education. This analysis included questioning some of the underlying assumptions about socio-political and socio-cultural factors in the design and implementation of such courses.

Our methodological approach involves a small-scale case study of a Portuguese student in the course, Roberto, who became one of the early dropouts after only six weeks of active participation. The case study involves two semi-structured interviews (one face-to-face and one e-mail) with Roberto, discourse analysis of (1) some of his online contributions, and (2) the course title, rationale and assessment as provided in the course manual. We also include data from semi-structured, e-mail interviews carried out with other international participants, including a German participant, Gertrude, who was considered to be one of the best students in the course. The interviews took place both in English (transcribed directly) and Portuguese. All Portuguese contributions or citations are our translation and are shown in italics.[2]

In summary, this chapter discusses, from the Portuguese higher educational perspective, the three related issues of:

- socio-political discursive practices—both the discourse used in the official course presentation and the local and international discourses of change in higher education,
- cultures of learning as they influence the interactions and interpretations of a British based course in a Portuguese context, and
- pedagogies for international online learning communities.

Throughout our study we illustrate our findings with contributions from and descriptions of Roberto, building a portrait of a Portuguese post-graduate student who could be seen as representative of many potential Portuguese students in post-graduate online courses such as TTO. We conclude by making recommendations both for practice and for future research regarding the international context of online learning communities.

## SOCIO-POLITICAL DISCURSIVE PRACTICES

According to Barnett "the professional through her critical thinking and her action, is a discursive creator" (1997, p. 142), and the role of critical higher education is "exposure to multiple discourses (both practical and intellectual)," and "purposive and positive engagement" in them (Barnett, 1997, p. 168). Being critical practitioners means understanding the inherently ideological nature of seemingly apolitical, pedagogical choices concerning curriculum decisions, course design and implementation. Rather than playing the role of "neutral" professionals uncritically using and applying discursive practices, we have chosen to examine the values and ideologies embedded in such discursive practices in an attempt to provide honest accounts of teaching and learning practices of online learning and community building in international contexts and to explore possibilities for change and growth through ongoing critique.

The current discourse of online learning is often an integral part of the discursive practices used in Information and Communication Technologies (ICT) and higher education; these are increasingly influenced by managerial discourse, with terms such as cost efficiency, quality service, just-in-time (course) delivery, marketable commodities and business solutions. This type of managerial discourse is influencing the structure, strategies, and decision-making processes of higher education institutions that were traditionally considered as having non-profit objectives. In this way and through their policies of "internationalization," higher education institutions are now playing a significant role in spreading the discourses and practices associated with that of new workplace values on an increasingly global scale. However, the danger in treating these discourses as inherently neutral and not serving the purposes of an increasingly global business agenda "serves the important ideological function of legitimating certain forms of knowledge and educational practice over others" (Pennycook, cited in Tollefson, 1995, p.11).

With this in mind, we decided to analyze critically some of the discourse used in the presentation of the TTO course in order to help understand its implicit positioning.

## Course Presentation and Representation: A Critical Analysis

In this section, we analyze a short piece of representative discourse from the front page of the course guide:

1. to show how seemingly neutral discourse is not as neutral as it presents itself, and
2. to illustrate a contradiction between the course title and the course aims, which could help explain how someone might misinterpret those objectives.

In fact, Roberto described his disappointment regarding the course as being due to the fact that:

> ...the expectations that the course created in people was not what the course was about... and immediately I felt cheated. Completely. Why? Perhaps it was my interpretation. I thought that they were going to teach or at least direct us to the problems involved in putting courses online. (Tr.)

And in a later interview:

I think that the expectations which the course brochure created did not actually represent what the course was. And that's where I felt cheated. Completely." (Direct Quote, DQ)

So, how did this misunderstanding come about? In answer to this question, let us analyse the discourse of the sub-title of the course, as presented to the students:

PROBLEMS AND PRINCIPLES
In the use of
COMPUTER NETWORKS FOR COURSE DELIVERY

In this sub-title, the phrase "the use" is significant. It uses the definite article "the," instead of "a use" or "uses," and employs nominalization (i.e., the transformation of a verb "to use," into a noun form "the use"). Employment of the definite article implies only *one* possible "use" and the nominalization of the phrase implies a "thing" or a concrete, material phenomenon rather than an ongoing and changing process involving people negotiating multiple possibilities of "using" for their different contexts and learning objectives. Put in such a way, it precludes any consideration of our *choices* regarding different uses and ways of using computer networks, as well as the social, moral and political responsibility for such choices.

Furthermore, we are also presented with "the use of COMPUTER NETWORKS" as something without human or social agents, as if there are no social agents promoting computer networks (e.g. business interests); somehow computer networks are themselves the agents. They appear to be inevitable, inviting neither exploration about whether different learning communities need different interfaces, nor different underlying system metaphors or different hardware architectures, nor whether those different learning communities are peopled by learners and tutors with vastly different roles, skills, expectations, and learning histories.

The phrase "COURSE DELIVERY" (a commonly used term in the marketing of learning management software) is presented as a finished given product rather than a consequence of social practice and human values. The collocation of *course* and *delivery* reflects a dominant managerial discourse of strategy, efficiency, and performance, constructing online learning as a value-neutral rational instrument devoid of the rich human tapestry it actually represents. The "organizing metaphor (...of such a discourse...) defines education as a 'thing' which can be produced and consumed in standardized units." (Agre, 1999, p. 3). In no way does this collocation suggest a teaching approach that offers to create supportive and appropriate learning conditions based on different student and teacher needs and contexts.

Use of this managerial style of discourse hides the realities of the many different kinds of teachers and students involved in all kinds of educational contexts with different values, beliefs and practices, working within different structures and systems, using different discourses, genres and voices. However, it is *this* type of discourse that is shaping institutional and individual perceptions of the goals and methods by which online education should proceed. Its appearance as a *fait accompli* artificially closes off debate about the goals that technology should be supporting and enabling. All this has clear implications regarding who can speak, who and what is valued, and who and what counts.

At this point, let us pencil in the first lines of our portrait of Roberto:

---

### Roberto: Educational Qualifications

Roberto teaches undergraduate students in a business degree course in the business school of a university in Lisbon. He has a first degree and a master's degree in different areas of management from a reputable Portuguese university. At the time the TTO course was running, he was 36 years old and preparing to start his doctoral studies at the same university. He was doing this TTO course because he would like to run his own course online within the university. With his educational background, Roberto would clearly be most familiar with (and possibly uncritical of) managerial discourse. It is also quite possible that his reading of the sub-title alone would have confirmed his expectations of a course that would *efficiently present problems* and *provide solutions* for *online course delivery*.

---

On the other hand, in the course manual's section on "course rationale," the course director purports to be "sceptical about many of the hasty or financially motivated initiatives." However, by uncritically participating in the current, business-led discursive practices of online learning, how far are we supporting the layers of unreflective usage that have characterized technological and business discourse and which is permeating our approaches to education and critical approaches to learning? To what extent are we uncritically propelling a dynamic whereby learning and knowledge are becoming commodities, subject to processes of economic calculation and intervention? This is not to suggest that education does not have much to learn from technological and business discourse, nor that it cannot benefit from economic calculation and intervention. Rather, it is to acknowledge that there is an inherent contradiction in uncritically using the prevailing managerial, discursive practices of online learning, while at the same time claiming principles that "put educational goals ahead of commercial ones" (Course Manual).

The course rationale also puts forward a further principle: "We believe that we should be less concerned with how and where learners gain access to knowledge, and more concerned with how we can establish frameworks for mutual processes of co-operation among the learning community." In fact, while we can fully sympathize with the latter part of this statement, we think that we *must* be equally concerned with how, where, and the ways in which we and our students approach knowledge and its production and reproduction, and to understand the vested interests involved in the process. "The learning community" is not, as could be understood in such a sentence, homogeneous, especially if we are referring to people from different cultures. Learning communities represent a host of different voices with different interests, values, histories, and possibilities of access. What exactly does co-operation among these different players mean? And in particular, what does co-operation among these different players mean when the locale of learning is spreading outside the borders in which its frameworks were created? As Lian states, "It is the task of pedagogues to ensure honesty as the founding principle of the processes thus put in place. Ultimately, the question about learning appears to be a question about the sources of interest that our educational environments serve" (2000, p. 12). Unquestioningly giving voice to the most prevailing interests is to accept an agenda for a political project that reaches beyond our micro-world of course design and implementation. As critical educators who are involved in some way in the increasing globalization of education, it is important to be continuously checking that our multiple and conflicting interests are honest and active trajectories in the shaping of international discourses and genres, and not merely allowing ourselves to be shaped by them.

Having concluded that we need to account for different discourses representing different interests of individuals from different learning communities, we now move on to a brief overview of local and international discourses in higher education.

## Local and International Discourses in Higher Education

On both national and international levels, political, educational, and managerial discourses proclaim the need for educational change, for educational integration of Information and Communication Technologies (ICT), for lifelong learning and for the education and training of a highly qualified workforce. These discourses echo each other and build the pressure on higher education institutions to respond to these current economic, social and technological shifts and influences. *The World Declaration on Higher Education for the 21st. Century: Vision and Action* (1998, sponsored by UNESCO) warns of the implications arising from the dramatic increase in the student population worldwide. In fact, according to the Declaration, between 1960 and 1995, global student enrolments increased six times (p. 1). An example of the European response to widening participation in higher education was the 1997 *Dearing Report* in Britain which outlined a review of institutional policies regarding quality teaching and learning systems; the need to accredit programs of training for higher education teachers; to commission research and development in learning and teaching practices; to stimulate innovation and "to exploit the potential of communications and information technology for learning and teaching" (Dearing Report, Recommendation, p. 14).

Also, at a European level, it has become almost commonplace to hear of the prospective drop in the number of "traditional" 18 year old students. Almost in the same breath, the importance of "lifelong learning" is stressed, not only in educational terms, but also in terms of economics. Globalization of the economy and increasing international competition have required countries to invest in new technologies, with the corresponding pressure on higher education to mirror the investment and lead the way in adapting Information and Communication Technologies (ICT) to current educational needs. Accordingly, European policy initiatives and funding are articulated in the discourse of innovation, lifelong learning, European mobility, and the international transparency of qualifications and credit transfer systems.

In the increasingly prevalent managerial discourse of higher education in Portugal we also see a convergence between national educational policies and international trends and guidelines put forward by the World Bank and the OECD (Seixas, 2001, p. 229). According to the *Direção-Geral do Ensino Superior (DGESup)* paper on higher education in Portugal (*Ensino Superior em Portugal, Dezembro* 1999), the four major challenges facing Portugal are organization, quality, widening participation, and internationalization. All of these challenges impact on and are interlinked with each other.

Firstly, the challenges are located in the context of massive expansion in higher education in Portugal where we find that the situation is quite different from the global average. The number of students enrolled in Portuguese higher education institutions rose by 243% between 1987 and 1998 (Seixas, 2001, p. 230) reflecting government policy changes towards a democratization of the education system. This explains the current perceived need to move from quantitative improvement towards a solid, organizational and qualitative "*consolidation*" (*DGESup,* Dec. 1999) of a higher education system that experienced relatively uncontrolled expansion for over a decade.

Secondly, the requirement of quality upgrading is revealed in the persistent call for improved higher education "teacher qualification." Over the last 20 years in Portugal, this term has exclusively been interpreted as the need for post-graduate qualifications. However, reflecting the European scene, the relatively new national discourse now points to teacher qualification in terms of the "necessity to rethink the contents and curricular organization of teaching" as well as "valuing the pedagogical component of the methodologies for teaching and learning" (*DGESup,* Dec.1999).

As for the changes in the student population, the Portuguese situation further mirrors international discourse. The *DGESup* paper warns of the imminent decrease in the number of "traditional" students, and argues for the importance of reaching out to new segments of the population, such as "degree-holders, who should be encouraged to continue their professional development, with an individualized, flexible offer of a diversity of study options." The paper goes on to highlight "once again, the importance of the organization of teaching, the valuing of the pedagogical dimension and respective methodologies, particularly Distance Learning."

Lastly, the fourth challenge which the DGESup paper addresses is that of internationalization, saying that "it is not possible to defend the quality of an education system which is disconnected from the international, especially European, reference system."

We will look at this fourth challenge in more detail in the following section.

## INTERACTING CULTURES OF LEARNING

Influenced by the pressure of these resonating national and international interpretations of the challenges facing higher education, there are growing demands for international benchmarking and quality standards in this sector. However, is it wise to make assumptions that there is an automatic fit between these discourses and their application in different contexts? Stoer, writing from within the Portuguese education world, warns against uncritical acceptance of "concepts and theories almost always designed and realized in the so-called 'central' countries" (cited in Correia and Stoer, 1995, p. 58). Stoer and Araújo point out how "in the formulation of (Portuguese) educational policy, the appeal to international organizations (OECD, the World Bank, and the European community) to justify political decision-making, has traditionally been unwavering" (1991, p. 206), while at the same time Stoer warns against the danger of being caught in a "kind of conceptual imperialism" (cited in Correia and Stoer, 1995, p. 58).

Caution in introducing (or effectively, 'importing') programs and methodologies from the socio-educational cultures of northern developed countries to other learning cultures also comes from the years of international experience of Teaching English as a Foreign Language (TEFL) where the authors find that this importation process has not been entirely free of problems. There is now a general consensus (Holliday, 1994; Coleman, 1996) concerning the uncritical importation of methodologies and language teaching technologies to other cultures. Uncritical importation often leads to what Holliday describes as "tissue rejection," as something that happens when a curriculum innovation fails to "become an effectively functioning part of the system" (Hoyle, cited in Holliday, 1994, p. 134). This tissue rejection arises from the failure to be aware of and account for the interactions among different "cultures of learning," that is, those "taken for granted frameworks of expectations, attitudes, values and beliefs about what constitutes good learning (and) how to teach and learn" (Cortazzi & Jin, 1996, p. 169). In the case of TEFL, Holliday specifies the origins of the imported, "communicative" methodologies as coming from the countries of Britain, North America and Australasia. Not altogether surprisingly, by far the largest body of research and experience in flexible learning approaches and the use of technology in higher education stem from those same countries and their socio-educational roots. It follows that international online courses and their learning communities could benefit from the same reflective consideration of curriculum innovation, methodological importation, and interacting cultures of learning.

Furthermore, drawing from this TEFL experience, Holliday suggests that, in order to avoid tissue rejection, educational innovations need to take into account "the cultural, socio-political, logistical, administrative, psycho pedagogic, and methodological features of the host environment as it changes in time before and during the process of innovation" (1994, p. 199). He argues that only an informed appreciation of the culture of the host educational environment can contribute to the avoidance of problems of "technology transfer" when, "the recipients of the technology are seen as 'periphery' to a technology producing 'centre'" (Phillipson, cited in Holliday, 1994, p. 13).

Let us look at an example of a socio-cultural factor to be considered in the Portuguese case. A large percentage of potential (post-graduate) distance learning students in Portugal were either educated during the longest surviving right-wing dictatorship of the 20th Century, the *Estado Novo* (New State) of António Salazar (1933-1974), or were educated and brought up by people who received their socio-educational acculturation during that time. Education during the *Estado Novo* was strictly elitist, using "an authoritative and repressive pedagogy, which was repetitive and moralizing" in which school was a "tool for indoctrination" (Benavente, 1990, pp. 51-52). Whilst those under 30 may seem to have benefited from educational values introduced after the Portuguese revolution of 1974, it should not be forgotten that their own educators would, consciously or not, still have been influenced by years of educational practice and inherent values of a dictatorial regime. It may, therefore, be unwise to make a simple assumption that Portuguese post-graduate students are accustomed to more than "being taught" or to managing the kind of independent learning which full distance learning and online courses often require. A socio-educationally sensitive, "flexible" approach in this context should ideally include the design of specific structures and methodologies to support students in their independent learning processes.

### Roberto: Culture of Learning

We begin to see an emerging picture of Roberto's culture of learning that is influenced both by managerial discourses and possibly by the remnants of education policies established and developed by the *Estado Novo* (in which academic authority was held solely in the hands of the teacher). In fact, his description of the ideal teacher was:

> Someone who maybe can have easy way to sources of knowledge or information and can be like a gatekeeper of information and translate what is relevant to students and what is not relevant to students and in that kind of way disseminate knowledge to them. (DQ)

Let us now move on from cultures of learning to look more closely at pedagogies for creating international online learning communities.

## PEDAGOGIES FOR INTERNATIONAL ONLINE LEARNING COMMUNITIES

In order to build a pedagogical framework for the design of international online communities we would like to draw on the work of Wenger (1998, developing the work of Lave & Wenger, 1991) on communities of practice as sites for learning, meaning, and identity. In creating an online learning environment, we reflect on our conceptions of learning and their effect(s) on the ways in which we design our courses, heeding Wenger's words that "our designs are hostage to our understanding, perspectives, and theories" (1998, p. 10).

As part of a social constructivist approach to learning, Lave and Wenger (1991) consider learning to be socially situated, with social participation as its primary focus. Participation not only refers to engaging in certain activities with certain people, but to "a more encompassing process of being *active participants* in the *practices of social communities* and *constructing identities* in relation to those communities" (Wenger, 1998, p. 4, our italics). Wenger goes on to identify the importance of learning and participation as a process of "*the negotiation of meaning* rather than on the mechanics of information transmission and acquisition" (Wenger, 1998, p. 265, our italics). It is through the negotiation of meanings that we are learning and investing ourselves. Learning and being part of a learning community, therefore, require *social interaction, processes of identity formation,* and *negotiation of meaning.*

In this following section we now consider these aspects of learning communities in our international online context, extending them to include *collaborative learning, the 'threshold experience'* (Wegeriff, 1998) and *learning through discussion.* We then briefly examine, in terms of choice of software and the implications of these considerations for designing for an international online learning community.

## Social Interaction and Collaborative Learning

In their work on the creation of online learning communities, Palloff and Pratt also emphasize the importance of an interactive approach to learning. They state that "key to the learning process are the *interactions* among students themselves, the *interactions* between faculty and students, the *collaboration in learning* that results from these interactions" (1999 p. 5, italics in the original). In fact, collaborative learning is seen to play a central role "in facilitating the development of a learning community and in achieving the desired learning outcomes of the course. The collaborative effort among learners helps them achieve a deeper level of knowledge generation while moving from independence to interdependence" (Palloff & Pratt, 1995, p. 110).

The TTO course guidelines also indicate that it supports the notions of social interaction and collaborative learning approaches:

> (The course offers) "opportunities for collaborative experience"; (the course) "depends heavily on participation" *and* "It is the ongoing experience of communicating with fellow-students and tutors (...) that lies at the heart of what we have to offer."

As both learning and the building of a learning community depend on active participation, interaction, and collaboration, we may be concerned that, despite the apparent importance given to participation in the presentation of the course, there was, in fact, a very low level of participation in the online discussions. Also, as we have suggested earlier, it concerned us that Roberto's disappointed expectations and frustration in the course may well reflect a socio-culturally and educationally influenced digital divide which we would have to account for with future cohorts of Portuguese students.

> In the case of Roberto, the chances of benefiting from collaborative interactions in the course dwindled quickly from the beginning of the course, until he stopped posting any contributions to the course, after only six weeks of participation.

We could lay responsibility for this lack of participation on the participants for being "good" or "bad" learners, or we can analyse "the very categories, or values, on which we build our assumptions that our environments do indeed encourage thinking, exploration, discussions, exchange, collaboration, and hence learning" (Lian, 2000, p. 6).

So, given that different perceptions and discourses of learning do exist, we are led to some initial conclusions. First, it is imperative that course guidelines be very specific in their description of the course aims and objectives as well as the teaching and learning philosophies behind them.

And second, an important element of the description should include the recognition of different discourses, different realities, and different expectations from the participants who come from diverse cultures of learning, attempting to build bridges among them.

Indeed, Wenger suggests that learning communities incorporate both the past and the future experiences and learning histories of its participants through what he refers to as "a learning trajectory" which values the *identity* of participants and their participation as an integral and dynamic part of the learning process" (1998, p. 215). He continues by affirming that learning communities "will become places of identity to the extent that they make trajectories possible—that is, to the extent they offer a past and a future that can be experienced as personal trajectory." Wenger says that we "strengthen the identity of participation" in two connected ways: first by incorporating the history of its members, "by letting what they have been, what they have done, and what they know contribute to the constitution of its practice," and second, by "opening trajectories of participation that place engagement in its practice in the context of a valued future."

By incorporating the participants' history (of learning) into the course activities and by making engagement a valued part of its practice, we would hope to avoid participants' dropping out of the course as a result of feelings as expressed by Roberto:

> ...the discussions for me had nothing to do either with online courses, nor with the reality of online courses that I know, and much less with what the expectations created by the course." (Tr)

## Identity Formation and the "Threshold Experience"

According to Wenger, collective interactive learning results in practices that reflect both the pursuit of our own enterprises and attendant social relations in communities of learning. "Because learning transforms who we are and what we can do, it is an experience of identity. It is not just an accumulation of skills and information, but a process of becoming—to become a certain person or conversely, to avoid becoming a certain person"(1998, p. 215).

In our view, this concept of learning and identity is related to Wegeriff's description of the "threshold experience," which is essentially a social experience of belonging: "It is the line between feeling part of a community and feeling that one is outside that community looking in" (1998). Wegeriff continues by suggesting that active successful participation in an online course depends on the extent to which participants are able to cross a threshold from feeling like an outsider to feeling like an insider. Similarly, Wenger proposes that "to support learning is not only to support the process of acquiring knowledge, but also to offer a place where new ways of knowing can be realized in the forming of an identity" as part of the learning community (1998, p. 215). He states that if someone fails to learn as expected, it could be because of the lack of a place to form an identity as part of the process of belonging to a learning community. And indeed, we can see that Roberto found no place to form an identity when he says:

> I didn't identify much with the subjects we covered ... It was more a course for people in the area of education, not someone from management. Education doesn't have anything to do with reality. (Tr.)

It is also useful to reflect on the comments by other participants (British and international,[3] responding to the e-mail questionnaire, about their feelings in crossing (or not) the threshold from outsider to insider, observing that it may not be such a one-time experience as suggested by the words, "threshold experience."

> Hope: The discussions were a powerful vehicle, drawing you in and making you feel like a course participant.
>
> Janet: I tried very hard to make myself an insider through constant participation. Sometimes I did feel like an outsider, though, because it seemed that most people were involved with higher education and I was the only one in lower education. The other participants' feedback went a long way in making me feel like an insider. The lack of feedback from the teacher made me feel like I was not an important participant.
>
> Haines: I felt both an insider and an outsider at different times .... Factors which tended to make me feel like an insider:
> * people responding to my contribution
> * people referring to me in an inclusive way ("... as X, Y and Haines have remarked ...")
>
> Factors which tended to make me feel like an outsider:
> * people not responding to my contributions
> * the impression, sometimes that discussion is dominated by a group of insiders (who respond to each other, and refer to each other in an inclusive way)
> * the topic being outside my field of experience or concerns.
>
> Anya: At the beginning I felt a bit like an outsider, mainly because of the language gap: I felt I didn't say all I wished (DQ)

What made her change was:

> ...reply messages and feedback, both from peers and tutor(s), some private messaging and chat."(DQ)

And Gertrude, one of the most active members of the course described her feeling that:

> I felt like an insider from the very beginning. (DQ)

However, as indicated by Roberto in the interview, these views contrast starkly with his experience of the course:

> I didn't feel like a student in that course. If it was a traditional course I would have failed for my lack of attendance. Because that course didn't do anything for me ..." (Tr.)

Here we remind ourselves of the need for both the course designer to construct bridges from the "outside" to the "inside," and for the online tutor to facilitate the process of participants' moving from "outsider" to "insider." Furthermore, this process should be viewed as an ongoing formation of identity as members of an *international* learning community where participants come from different cultures of learning and from different areas of discourse. It is worth noting that the notion of "threshold experience" does not necessarily result from any one activity, but is more of an emerging process of identification and confidence building.

## Learning through Discussion and the Negotiation of Meaning

If, as Wenger suggests, negotiation of meaning represents the kind of interaction that supports learning, identity formation, and the feeling of community in a learning environment, then it follows that we need to identify interaction types that reflect negotiation of meaning rather than mere information transmission and acquisition. We suggest that activities such as reading and the factual answering of questions are more related to information transmission and acquisition whereas activities that are related to the negotiation of meaning include:

- weaving (an online discursive skill required "to summarize the state of the discussion and to find unifying threads in participants´ comments (which) encourages these participants and implicitly prompts them to pursue their ideas" (Feenberg, 1989, p. 4),
- articulating and negotiating arguments or ideas through extended discussion and dialogue, and
- summarizing the threads of the discussions.

Interestingly, if we look at some of the ways that the participants viewed their participation, we see that Gertrude's description of her interactions implies a negotiation of meaning rather than information transmission. Gertrude viewed her online participation as:

> ...helping others, listening what was being said, taking up pros and cons/ Weaving in other people's opinion/summarizing ideas or concepts or group work a couple of times. (DQ)

As for questions, Gertrude claimed to ask:

> ...clarifying questions, probing questions, questions about content. (DQ)

On the other hand, Roberto's description of his interactions suggests a view of learning which echoes his previous discourse of the ideal teacher. He claimed that his participation was:

> Mostly reading, listing and participating with arguments whenever I could add some "value." (DQ)

This makes sense when participation is seen as transmitting and acquiring information. It is reflected in his observation that:

> If someone poses a question or if someone presents a doubt, they want replies that are going to resolve the problem. So replies have to give an added value or, if not, it's not worth replying ... (DQ)

While Roberto perceives himself as participating in a discussion, the discussion, in his view, exists to present a solution to a problem and is not, per se, part of a collaborative learning process. In fact, participation in a discussion for Roberto appears to be in the form of posting a reply (with "added value") to a question, and not one that views discussion as a vehicle for negotiating meaning.

This perception of *how* learning takes place probably influences *what* learning takes place or does not take place. There is a different type of learning experienced by Gertrude who felt that she had learned through discussion, and Roberto who, as noted earlier, did not feel that the discussions were of any relevance to him. These different perspectives are further reflected in their replies to the following question asked in the e-mail questionnaire:

> Question: How useful (or not) did you find the online discussions in helping your learning? In what ways?
> Gertrude: On reflection I only noticed recently how useful certain discussions were, and how much they meant to me - like the discussions on the role of the tutor, inhibitions, feedback, learner

> friendly atmosphere. They helped me to structure my thoughts and express myself more clearly (I hope). *(DQ)*
>
> Roberto: It brought to me some relevant issues concerning diffusion knowledge/learning through the Web, like meaningful objectives, structure, means of diffuse, technology, people on the other side, language way of "talking"/English (best known in all the world). (DQ)

The answers given to this question are pertinent because, in our view, they suggest two different attitudes to learning, which consequently shaped the kind of learning that took place, or failed to take place. Whereas Gertrude is aware of the benefits of a level of participation which requires engagement with the learning community and the articulation of her "thoughts," Roberto perceived the online discussions as something which "brought to me some issues." Recalling his description of an ideal teacher as someone who is a "gatekeeper of information" who can "translate what is relevant to students and what is not relevant," and who should "disseminate knowledge to them," we begin to sketch in a picture of a participant who views teaching as information or knowledge dissemination, and learning as the acquisition of that information. A participant with this perspective on learning and teaching may have difficulty experiencing learning in a course whose framework is based on the principles of dialogue and negotiation of meaning rather than the simple transmission of content. Unless we assume that all who come to international courses have similar views of learning, then only those who are already at least partially familiar with the view of learning through discussion (and those who are ready to play with the unfamiliar) will be ready to participate and learn in this type of course. This clearly holds implications for course design and pedagogies that effectively address these issues of students who come from different cultures of learning.

In raising the importance of such concepts as social interaction, collaborative learning, identity formation, the "threshold experience" of belonging (as an insider) to a learning community, and discussion and negotiation of meaning, we must inevitably turn to the increased complexity of the dynamics of these concepts when talking about *international* learning communities. If "identity is the vehicle that carries our experiences from context to context" (Wenger, 1998, p. 268), then how much more complex is the formation of identities in an international environment? In such an environment there are participants with different first languages coming from numerous different contexts, and with different historic, socio-cultural and professional identities, who meet for moments of a learning experience where they will be negotiating meaning that will become further material for creating their ongoing identity. All this complex process of interaction and learning is forming and directing an ongoing interactive process of identity formation. If an international learning project is to include all types of students from different academic and cultural learning backgrounds, and is to allow space for the creation of new relations of identification and new forms of membership and changing positions within communities, then it is clear that this will need careful consideration and planning. Moreover, if we believe that, "our learning models should create conditions flexible enough for all to want to play rather than for those who would play no matter what game would be played" (Lian 2000, p. 7), we would benefit from considering what needs to be done to enable more people to play.

## RECOMMENDATIONS FOR SUPPORTING INTERNATIONAL ONLINE COMMUNITIES

In our view, the international online course in which we participated is an example of the third of Mason's (1998) models of online courses, - the integrated model where "the heart of the course takes place online through discussion, accessing and processing information and carrying out tasks." Mason suggests that online courses are "leading the development of new learning environments ... particularly at postgraduate and professional development level," and that the integrated model, in particular, "provides the greatest opportunity for multiple teaching and learning roles." She further defines the integrated model as course design that offers contents that "are fluid and dynamic, as they are largely determined by the individual and group activity. In a sense, the integrated model dissolves the distinction between content and support, and is *dependent on the creation of a learning community*" (our italics). It is this last critical point which is a relatively new concept in higher education teaching and which, as we have seen, is considerably more complex in an international context.

Furthermore, with the growing understanding that learning is socially situated, it becomes clear, as stated earlier, that the "key factors in supporting learning are those which make a community open to its newcomers, allowing them to participate in its practices and move from peripheral to central status as rapidly and smoothly as possible" (Wegeriff, 1998). The ability to participate fully in the community of learning "depends upon a high degree of interactivity" as well as collaborative teaching and learning (Wegeriff, 1998, p. 1). In his description of the threshold experience of the students who "failed to cross a threshold into full participation into the collaborative learning of the course," Wegeriff examines the implications for course design and teaching which supports the movement from peripheral to central status, and makes the following six recommendations for course design:

1.  overcoming differential access,

2. overcoming conflicts of discourse,
3. staging exercises to move from more structured to more open,
4. providing teaching opportunities,
5. allowing time for reflection at the end, and
6. creating opportunities for discussion.

We will adopt and extend these recommendations, integrating our considerations for international learning communities. Then, we will examine the importance of choice of software to support the kind of learning and interactions that foster the creation of an online learning community.

## 1.  Overcoming Differential Access

Wegeriff refers to the students' difficulties in access to the learning in the course in terms of the availability of technology and of having the time to enable "shared conversation" (1998). Therefore, if online interactivity is seen as a pre-requisite for learning from and for participating in the community of learning, then it must be clear at the outset that students need to be able to use the computer more than just during their working hours.

Extending this view of the importance of access to our international context, this notion of access can also be understood in terms of language.

Although Roberto (a Portuguese participant) reads English fluently and communicates effectively orally, his written English is often quite difficult to understand. This creates a communication barrier of which he is apparently unaware. As there was no prerequisite language test to ascertain the linguistic ability of students, he may have entered the course with at least two possible disadvantages. Firstly, although Roberto does participate in several international discussion lists, his description of the interactions suggests question and answer interactions rather than the extended argumentation and negotiation of meaning of the online learning discussions; and secondly, in early online discussions, it was impossible to reply to at least two of Roberto's contributions which were unintelligible even to the authors who are both very familiar with the kind of communication difficulties experienced by Portuguese speakers and writers.

In an online course that is based on interactions among participants, not receiving any response to a message can be very demoralizing, and easily gives rise to feeling excluded. In the absence of other cues or feedback, it is easy to feel marginal to the discussion, an onlooker whose contribution, and therefore presence is being ignored.

This raises questions about setting language entry requirements, and even requiring language entrance tests for such courses, or at least for providing language support. We suggest that language support should not be provided merely as an add-on, but rather as an integral part of the course design. This is especially critical early on when participants are being introduced to different modes of interaction and to new and different cultures of learning. Such support would include activities for all participants (regardless of mother tongue) which encourage reflection on international and online communication and which would be integrated early in the course (in small groups) with the aim of raising awareness of the online skills and strategies needed for interacting online in English.

## 2. Overcoming Conflicts of Discourse

Beyond the issues of technology and language, Wegeriff (1998) identifies differences in "educational learning styles, background and confidence levels" related to the discourses of participants' educational and professional communities of practice. In the course described in his study, Wegeriff discusses how these differences led to the participation of a dominant group, and to the alienation of those who felt they did not belong. He explains that this was exacerbated by the fact that the most abstract and unstructured tasks occurred in the initial stages of the course, highlighting differences rather than fostering a sense of community. Wegeriff suggests that if exercises that focused on the social aspects of the course had been carefully structured earlier in the course, this would have helped students to cross the barrier from feeling an outsider to feeling an insider.

Within the context of our international course we are reminded of this need for structuring and reflecting on the social interactions early in the course. In Roberto's fifth online message to the whole group he says that:

> In Portugal, we have a very big problem, that is when we talk about courses or learning we mean something presential. So it is very important to design a course that put people in connection and in communication (DQ)

Also criticizing the lack of structure in the course, Roberto described it as:

> ...more confusing than educational." (DQ)

This reflects our earlier concern regarding the often-underestimated influence of socio-political discursive practices and interacting cultures of learning on international learning communities. Based on these concerns, we would support Wenger's suggestion of "incorporating its members' pasts into its history" (1998, p. 215) by letting what they have done and what they know contribute to the building of an online community. For example, this could mean that an international course might have as its starting point the locally situated experience where participants from the same country discuss their own personal experiences of learning, and consequent attitudes to learning in their own language. This discussion could then be presented as a group summary to the international group, in English, for comparison and reflection. Not only could this serve to sensitize the participants to the diversity of learning contexts and discourses, but it could also encourage them to articulate parts of their personal learning identities (in their own language) as the first step in the process of engaging and developing newly forming identities in the international group, and in English.

Secondly, we would reiterate the importance of rigorously explicit, coherent, and theoretically grounded course descriptions and instructions which accurately describe the actual learning activities, interactions, assessment practices, and expected outcomes. Given the diversity of learning backgrounds and discourses in an international course, it is imperative that considerable care be taken to avoid misrepresentation of the values and practices of the course. This does not preclude sensitive and facilitative response to the unfolding process of the course and to individual learners, but allows for a transparent and principled foundation for course design and teaching.

## 3. Staging Exercises to Move from More Structured to More Open

According to Wegeriff, "scaffolding," where learners are provided with structures and models to support their learning, and which are gradually reduced as they become more able and confident to work independently, should be "applied to the complex skill of collaboratively learning online" (1998).

Part of the staging of exercises could involve starting with small groups of students and, if necessary, increasing to slightly larger groups. Only once was there a grouping of three participants in the TTO course after the tenth week when the students had already been divided into national groups. By then few of the set tasks on the course were being carried out because a pattern of majority non- or partial-participation had already been established. The first weeks of the course, which are critical in terms of the threshold experience, involved activities of groups of 25 or 50 students. If someone missed only a few days, they were faced with seemingly endless screens of red flags beside messages, heralding unread messages and flourishing discussions that required intensive reading in order to catch up.

Roberto writes in only his third online message, saying:

This [sic] guys don't play. I'm completely lost in so many messages. *(DQ)*

The sense of being an outsider is all too easily reached when everyone is "talking" at once and you cannot find a conversation that you can enter.

This emphasis on staged structuring is echoed by Roberto's observations that for the course:

> An easily understandable structure would be great. Define that and maintain it until the end of the course. (DQ: online message 12)

This is a point that Roberto repeated frequently in personal communications and in the interview. One of his main difficulties regarding the course was his perception of the lack of structure.

This also reflects our earlier point that care must be taken to avoid assumptions that international students have similar views and prior learning experiences. Staged structuring would seem to offer students from different learning backgrounds an opportunity to "acclimatize," not only to the online environment, but also to the pedagogical and interactional expectations implicit in a collaborative learning environment. At the same time, staged structuring can also provide students with opportunities to establish their online identity.

Moreover, if we take the view that the course design framework should provide a staged structuring to enable people to cross from structured to more open, from being reactive to proactive, from being either the transmitter or receiver of knowledge to a partner in the construction of knowledge, then we also need explicitly to value this process through the course system of assessment strategies.

## 4. Providing Teaching Opportunities

Wegeriff's recommendation that an online course designed to prepare post-graduate students to teach online should provide opportunities for participants to practice teaching online. This further reinforces the notion of joining the community of learning by crossing the threshold through participating in the discourse and practices of the target community. Future online teachers must master a complex set of skills which are clearly important to practice, rather than merely theorize about their importance. Related to this, Mason puts forward the view that one of the key aspects of online learning is the learning potential of the "breakdown between the teacher and the taught," thereby providing opportunities to "realize the potential of the student to the advantage of all participants" (1998).

In an online environment, effective teaching depends on online communication skills. According to Feenberg, "the moderator's most basic task is to choose at the outset a 'communication model' for the group" (1989,

p. 33). Feenberg goes on to identify the key communicative functions of a moderator to be:

- Contextualizing Functions: opening discussions, setting norms and agendas.
- Monitoring Functions: prompting and recognition (referring explicitly to participants, reassuring and valuing contributions).
- Meta Functions: meta commenting—using the communication skills of summarizing and weaving to solve problems in context, such as misunderstandings of norms and agenda, lack of clarity or relevance, information overload.

Tutor modelling is clearly an important initial step in acquiring moderator skills. And as models of these functions, the TTO tutors were clearly skilled, especially in contextualizing, and monitoring.

> For example, Roberto commented (personal communication) that a private e-mail exchange with one of the tutors had helped him carry on longer, at a point when he was about to give up.

However, the moderating role clearly encompasses more than engaging in private exchange and monitoring. It also involves skills such as weaving, which helps to unify a discussion and to push the ideas forward, and summarizing. But as Feenberg observes, "Many conferences lack weaving because no-one has the time or the talent to perform the function for the group" (p. 35). While it is important to avoid giving too much work to the moderator, it would seem to be equally important in a course for future online teachers or course designers for them to benefit from consistent tutor modelling and student practice of the communication skills required of moderators. The meta function—weaving—which most supports "the content of the discussion" (p. 34) is perhaps one of the most important of these skills to practice. In fact, Feenberg asserts that discussions "are most absorbing and successful when members of the group share these functions with the moderator" (p. 35). Therefore, the design of tasks where students share the role of weaving and summarizing with the moderator would seem an apt solution to avoid overloading teachers while at the same time valuing students' practice of key moderating skills.

## 5.   Allowing Time for Reflection at the End

"The process of taking charge of the process of learning is aided by reflection on the process itself" (Wegeriff, 1998). One of the much-touted benefits of asynchronous communication is the support it can provide for reflection both by providing a transcript of the discussions and by allowing time for the thoughtful formulation of a contribution. However, the technology itself does not enable reflection without appropriate task design. One of the most basic requirements for reflection is time. The design of a task which values reflection on the process of carrying out that task and on the learning that it has involved should, naturally, include the time needed for that reflection. For example, after allocating one student per workgroup to be the summarizer after a week's activity, time could then be usefully spent in reflecting and discussing the advantages, difficulties and different styles of summarizing. This kind of reflective participation is especially important if the cohort of students comes from different cultures of learning, speaks different languages, and belongs to different communities of practice and discourse communities. Although Wegeriff recommends both a specific time and facilitated discussion for this reflection, we would reinforce this recommendation with the reminder that, according to Brockbank and McGill, "for students used to transmission, their expectations of process are hierarchical, they may not be ready, experiencing the new way as harder, they may not like it to begin with, and therefore we recommend that facilitators attend to expectations and negotiation as part of their move to cooperative mode" as early and as often as possible in the course (1998, p. 160). As we have seen in our Portuguese perspective of studying on an international course, this change in approach to learning was particularly disorienting, therefore further emphasizing the need for time for reflection on learning to be integrated with the earlier recommendations for structuring and staging in the course design.

## 6.   Creating Opportunities for Discussion

Wegeriff argues that forming a sense of belonging to a learning community where people feel comfortable enough to "take the risks involved in learning" depends largely on engaging effectively in collaborative learning online through active, reflective discussion and participation. The way to belong to an online learning community, therefore, lies in engaging in collaborative learning online which is "best supported by a particular style of communicating [that is] democratic, respectful, open to challenges, prepared to give grounds for statements and seeking critically grounded consensus" (1998).

As mentioned earlier, the TTO course appears to hold a similar view regarding the importance of discussion as expressed in these excerpts from the Course Rationale (November 1999):

> **Principles behind this course ...**
>
> At the heart of the educational process, for us, is not the passing of information from teacher to pupil, but the encouragement of attitudes of critical discovery and enquiry through both individual and collaborative learning modes. [We are] concerned with how we can establish frameworks for mutual processes of co-operation among the learning community.

However, in what seems to us to be stark contrast, the *assessment requirements* for the final essay included the statement:

> Participation in the course is not assessed.

Recalling Roberto's misinterpretation of the course objectives and methodological approach (due to the lack of coherence of the course program) and his subsequent lack of participation in the online discussions and his feeling of being cheated, it is clearly not sufficient simply to say that participation in online discussion and collaborative learning is important. These online activities have to be valued in the assessment process to be seen to be worthwhile for someone coming from a culture of learning which values transmission rather than interactive learning. This is clearly reflected in his response concerning the viability of this course in Portugal:

> ...this course is not viable in Portugal .... The reaction of a typical Portuguese student would be ... zero. Not evaluated during the six months? He wouldn't even show up. What are they doing? Only in the last week for people to remember that I was there? (Tr.)

If we look at the literature on teaching and course design in higher education, we find that there is considerable guidance on how to engage students in graduate level learning. According to Toohey, "Research into students' learning has shown that one of the strongest factors in determining what and how students learn is the form of assessment they expect" (1999, p. 131). If we can also agree that "learning is the result of the constructive activity of the student," . . . [then] . . . "a good teaching system aligns teaching method and assessment to the learning activities stated in the objectives, so that all aspects of the system are in accord in supporting appropriate student learning. This system is called constructive alignment, based as it is on the twin principles of constructivism in learning and alignment in teaching" (Biggs 1999, p. 11).

Biggs continues by pointing out:

> It is easy to see why alignment should work. In aligned teaching, there is maximum consistency throughout the system. The curriculum is stated in the form of clear objectives, which state the level of understanding required, rather than a list of topics to be covered. All components of the system address the same agenda and support each other."

Moreover, especially given the post-graduate context where learners often have work and/or family commitments, adult, professional learners need a "structure provided by the course requirements [to] give them the impetus they need to make learning a priority" (Toohey, 1999, p. 127).

In the world of international online learning and teaching, where the distinctions between the teacher and the taught are blurring, such a "web of consistency" is strongly advisable. In constructive alignment the focus is not merely on teaching techniques or student differences and abilities, but rather on what students actively do in engaging in appropriate learning activities. The design of the assessment processes influences the students' understanding of what is valued in the course. Aligned assessment, therefore, causes positive backwash in both the teaching and learning processes.

In our "experiential" online course, there are a number of student and tutor-friendly procedures that could appropriately assess (and encourage) students' participation and collaborative learning. According to Toohey, experiential courses usually encourage students to present evidence of achievement and to be able to reflect on and assess their own work, "often in collaboration with teachers or peers" (1999, p. 61). Project work, learning journals, and portfolio assessment, which could be worked on progressively throughout the course, could also be considered to be appropriate methods for evaluating students' participation and understanding.

## Learning Communities and CMC software

We would now like to examine the implications of selecting software to support collaborative learning, negotiation of meaning, identity formation, and the sense of belonging to a learning community. If activities such as collaborative participation, expression of identity, and discussion as part of an inclusive learning environment are guiding principles in course design, then can we say that collaborative conferencing software such as FirstClass which was used for this course, is appropriate? Our overall conclusion would be that it is. There is an important collection of features of FirstClass, not seen at the time of this TTO course, in other well-known software packages. These facilitate the dynamics of weaving and collaborating needed for the negotiation of meaning and participation.

Features facilitating collaborative participation and discussion include:

- The "reply" function that highlights, as a quotation, the part of the message to which you want to reply to in your reply message.
- The ability to open several messages at once allowing one to refer to other messages, or to copy and paste more freely.
- The ability to save a message if the computer loses the connection. If we view participation and engagement (which is expressed in our written contributions) as part of our identity formation, we can

understand that losing a message in which we have invested part of ourselves can be a personal, de-motivating loss.

- The facility for synchronous chat.

Features facilitating the expression of online identity include:

- Easy access to different fonts and different colors (which were used freely by participants in the course).
- The space for writing messages on an independent page (similar to Microsoft Word) with its own user-friendly, tool bar (rather than in a small box with only one font and CAPITAL letters as the only visual variation, as is common in many conferencing systems).
- The ability to create a personalized workspace—by having a location on the screen to place the icons (conferences) that one chooses.
- Being able to choose from a selection of icons for folders in a personal mailbox or for sent messages.

Features facilitating the sense of belonging to a learning community include:

- Accessing the system through a different channel other than e-mails or Web. (According to one student, this gives the course a "sense of occasion," helping to create the feeling of a learning community with boundaries.)
- Being able to see the "history" of a message in order to see the people who have opened a message (helping to establish the perception of a listening audience and contributing to a sense of inclusion in a listening community). Even if no one replies to a message, there is confirmation that it has been read, and by whom).
- The "find" function for locating messages that contain specific words, or for messages to or from particular people (helping to create a sense of management and ownership of the content and interactions).
- The presence indicator which lets one see "Who's Online" (promoting social interaction and helping in the feeling of belonging).

We believe that the choice of a collaborative, conferencing system such as FirstClass for a course such as the TTO certificate is an appropriate one, given that a wide range of its facilities support collaborative communication. This leads us to suggest that becoming a competent user of collaborative conferencing software, not only in terms of system management but also in terms of supporting certain discourses of learning, would seem to be an integral part of the course's potential, and deserving of a central place in the design of course tasks, activities, and assessment. In addition, the informed choice of software can be a critical factor in determining the quality of the learning environment for a course that intends to establish an online learning community with collaborative learning, identity, and negotiation of meaning as central to its design.

## CONCLUDING COMMENTS

In order to support students in crossing the threshold from outsider to insider and from being passive receiver to active constructor of knowledge in an international learning community, we would like to make the following suggestions for course design in international contexts:

- Consider pre-course language tests to alert students to possible difficulties in participating in the extended discourse of online learning discussions.
- Address the need for ongoing language support throughout the course.
- Provide integrated, small group tasks, which will raise awareness of the importance and challenges of international online communication and collaboration at the outset of the course.
- Account for and stimulate discussion about different discourses coming from the worlds of online learning and from different communities of practice.
- Be explicit, in pre-course documents and in meta-discussions throughout the course, about the philosophy behind the course design.
- Ensure that the learning activities, methodology, and assessment tasks and criteria are in alignment and reflect those philosophies.
- Design activities that will value and encourage discussion about participants' learning histories.
- Structure activities to allow students with time for ongoing critical reflection and discussion regarding the learning process and the process of identification with the learning community.
- Stage exercises, interactions, and learning activities progressively— from structured to more open ones.
- Stage group sizing from smaller to larger.
- Explicitly value the importance of summarizing and weaving for online communication and teaching, and create opportunities for students to practice these discursive skills.
- Value the place of collaborative learning and online discussion by aligning collaborative learning activities and discussion tasks with the course assessment (such as in project work, learning journals and portfolio assessment).
- Choose course software that facilitates the sense of belonging to a learning community and supports collaborative participation, discussion, and the expression of identity.

Implicit in all these suggestions is the novel situation that the online environment is much more transparent than the traditional face-to-face classroom. In the latter situation, a higher education instructor goes into the classroom and usually only the students and the instructor know what has taken place. The stated objectives of the course may or may not have been supported by the chosen methodology. There is usually no record of the classroom activities or discourse. The online classroom however, is made of transparent film. Everything can be seen and the record of inter-actions is available to all. This makes it all the more necessary to be meticu-lously explicit about course presentation, objectives, and structure which must be visibly consistent with the chosen methodology, learning activities, assessment tasks, and assessment criteria.

Such an environment requires an approach which both supports collab-orative learning and the expression and formation of identity as well as the active negotiation of meaning through staged teaching activities which value interactivity, reflection, and the diverse learning cultures of its inter-national students. In this way all the components of the course explicitly signal to the students the value attributed to the building of an interna-tional learning community through online participation, and critical reflection on that participation.

Finally, it is clear that a small-scale study such as this can only offer tenta-tive insights regarding the experience of international online learning and community building. At this stage, our conclusions can only be seen as serving to question that which can too easily be taken for granted in inter-national contexts, and as providing an impetus for further debate and research in this area. Our hope is that this chapter serves to alert online course designers, teachers and managers to the need to account for the diversity of perspectives, experiences, expectations and learning cultures of their international students. We have no doubt that as such courses grow in number, considerable research will be needed into international com-munication in online environments and the complex discoursal, socio-political/cultural and technological issues involved in building interna-tional learning communities.

## NOTES

1. The names of the course and it participants have been changed in our chap-ter. It is also important to add that the course has undergone significant changes since 1999.

2. Note that Roberto's written contributions were in both English and Portu-guese. The English has been kept in the original, uncorrected form (Direct Quota-tion – DQ) and the Portuguese has been translated (Translation – Tr.)

3. Native English speaker participant responses are not recorded in italics.

**Acknowledgments:** We would like to thank David Hardisty, *Universidade Nova de Lisboa,* Lisbon, Portugal for his support and helpful review of our article.

## REFERENCES

Agre, P. (1999) Reinventing Technology, Rediscovering Community, http://dlis.gseis.ucla.edu/pagre, last retrieved on 31st. March 2002.

Barnett, R. (1997) *Higher education: A Critical Business,* Buckingham, SRHE and Open University Press

Benavente, A. (1990) *Escola, Professoras e Processos de Mudança,* Biblioteca do Educador

Biggs, J. (1999) *Teaching for Quality Learning at University,* SRHE and Open University Press

Brockbank, A. and McGill, I. (1998) *Facilitating Reflective Learning in Higher Education,* SRHE and Open University Press

Coleman, H. (1996) Autonomy and Ideology in the English Language Classroom in *Society and the Language Classroom,* edited by Coleman, H., Cambridge, Cambridge University Press

Correia, J. and Stoer, S. (1995) Investigação em Educação em Portugal in *A Investigação Educacional em Portugal,* ed. Campos, B., Instituto de Inovação Educacional

Cortazzi, M. and Jin, L. (1996) Cultures of Learning: Language Classrooms, in China in *Society and the Language Classroom,* edited by Coleman,H., Cambridge, Cambridge University Press

The Dearing Report, http://www.ncl.ac.uk/ncihe/index.htm, last retrieved on the 31st. March 2002.

Direcção-Geral Do Ensino Superior (1999) *Ensino Superior em Portugal,* editorial do Ministério da Educação.

Fairclough, N. (1989) *Language and Power,* New York, Longman Group ltd.

Feenberg, A. (1989) The Written World: On the Theory and Practice of Computer Conferencing in *Mindweave: Communication, Computers and Distance Education* (eds.) MASON, R: KAYE, A:, Oxford, Pergamon Press and at http://www-icdl.open.ac.uk/literaturestore/mindweave/mindweave. html, last retrieved 31st. March 2002.

Holliday, A. (1994) *Appropriate Methodology and Social Context,* Cambridge, Cambridge University Press

Lave, J. and Wenger, E. (1991) *Situated Learning: legitimate peripheral participation.* Cambridge, Cambridge University Press

Lian, A. (2000) knowledge transfer and technology in education: towards a complete learning environment, in *Educational Technology & Society 3(3),* last retrieved 31st. March 2002. http://ifets.ieee.org/periodical/vol_3_2000/lian.html

Mason, R. (1998) *Globalising education: trends and applications,* London /New York, Routledge

Mason, R. (1998) *Models of Online Courses* in Asynchronous Learning Networks Magazine, Volume 2, Issue 2, http://www.aln.org/alnweb/magazine/maga_v2_i2.htm, last retrieved 31st. March 2002.

Palloff, R. and Pratt, K. (1999) *Building Learning Communities in Cyberspace: effective strategies for the online classroom*, San Francisco, Jossey-Bass Publishers

Pennycook, A. (1994) *The Cultural Politics of English as an International Language*, London, Longman

Seixas, A.M. (2001) Políticas educativas para o ensino superior: A globalização neoliberal e a emergência de novas formas de regulação estatal in *Transnacionalização da educação: da crise da educação a "educação" da crise*, ed. Sousa Santos, B., Porto, Edições Afrontamento

Sousa Santos, B. (1993) O Estado, as Relações Salariais e o Bem Estar Social na Periferia, in *Portugal: Um Retrato Singular*, edited by Sousa Santos, B., Porto, Edições Afrontamento

Stoer, S. and Araújo, H. (1991) Educação e democracia num pais semiperiférico (no contexto europeu) in *Educação, Ciências Sociais e Realidade Portuguesa: uma abordagem pluridisciplinar*, edStoer, S., Porto, edições Afrontamento

Tait, A. and Mills, R. (1999) The convergence of distance and conventional education in *The Convergence of Distance and Conventional Education: patterns of flexibility for the individual learner*, eds. Tait, A. and Mills, R., London and New York, Routledge

Toohey, S. (1999) *Designing Courses for Higher Education*, SRHE and Open University Press

Tollefson, J. (1995) *Power and Inequality in Language Education*, Cambridge University Press

UNESCO (1998) *World Declaration on Higher Education for the 21st. Century: vision and action*, last retrieved on the 31st. March 2002. http://www.unesco.org/education/educprog/wche/declaration_eng.htm

Urry, J. (1998) *Locating HE in the Global Landscape*, last retrieved on 31st. March 2002. http://www.comp.lancs.ac.uk/sociology/soc010ju.html

Wegeriff, R. (1998) *The Social Dimension of Asynchronous Learning Networks* in the Journal of Asynchronous Learning Networks, Volume 2, Issue 1, last retrieved on 31st. March2002: http://www.aln.org/alnweb/journal/jaln_vol2issue1.htm

Wenger, E. (1998) *Communities of Practice: Learning, Meaning and Identity*, Cambridge University Press, Cambridge

CHAPTER 13

# YOURS, THEIRS, MINE
# Just Who Owns Those
# Distance Courses?

**John G. Bryan**

This chapter discusses the origins and concepts of intellectual property in general and as they pertain to distance learning. American universities have two prevalent traditions for assigning intellectual property ownership, largely based on whether such property is perceived to be fungible. Distance learning has confounded those traditions by making fungible some types of intellectual property that previously were not thought to be so. Complicating the issues are the high start-up costs of distance learning curricula, the multiple media that may be employed, the number of people involved in the creation of course products, and the difficulty of substituting replacement course products for products that may be withdrawn by their owners. The chapter also describes the considerations given and decisions made by the University of Cincinnati in settling intellectual property issues for its Early Childhood Learning Community, a distance version of an associate degree program in early childhood education.

**KEYWORDS:** copyright, early childhood learning community (ECLC), intellectual property, moral rights, patent, royalty, trade secret, work for hire

Electronic Learning Communities—Issues and Practices, pages 489–500.
Copyright © 2003 by Information Age Publishing, Inc.
All rights of reproduction in any form reserved.
ISBN: 1-931576-96-3 (pbk.), 1-931576-97-1 (hardcover)

## INTELLECTUAL PROPERTY AND HIGHER EDUCATION

Few distance learning issues hold as much potential for conflict and programmatic failure as the issue of intellectual property (IP). University lawyers attend conferences entirely devoted to the topic. Faculty cite it as a battle at the heart of the ongoing debate over academic freedom, and eventually Web designers and others who support the creation and delivery of distance courses may enter the fray to claim their own property rights. Even institutions that have already launched and run distance courses or entire programs should carefully attend to this issue.

The term *intellectual property* includes both legal and moral concepts of property derived from intellectual labor. The legal concept applies to original art works, compositions, documents, designs, formulas, inventions, machines, manufactures, performances, processes, and other products protected by patent, copyright, and trade-secret laws. In most respects, the legal concept is driven by economic and commercial interests. The moral concept, in addition to applying to virtually everything encompassed by the legal concept, applies in ways that the legal concept often does not. It is driven not so much by economic and commercial interests as it is by traditional beliefs about the association between a worker and his or her work products, between a creator and his or her creations (Anawalt, 1988).

### Two Models of Intellectual Property in Higher Education

American universities thought they had settled most of their intellectual property issues decades ago. And though practices tended to vary widely from one discipline to another, they reflected a pair of premises:

- A faculty member who receives time and pay to develop intellectual property that generates significant income owes at least something to his or her employer—though not necessarily in the form of money.
- A university that wishes to recruit faculty capable of developing intellectual property and wishes to encourage current faculty to develop intellectual property must provide incentives for the faculty to do so.

In common practice, those premises have led to two models. One model includes highly formalized arrangements and accommodations for faculty in those disciplines that typically require significant facilities, equipment, and overhead support, but that also generate significant patent, royalty, and contract income. The natural sciences, the health sciences, engineering, and some other disciplines adhere to this first model. The income-sharing agreements may vary widely by discipline and institution, but most will split income, with both faculty and institution taking significant shares. This tradition recognizes the potential for intellectual property's income generation.

The other model includes those disciplines that require little more than an office, a networked computer, and libraries for faculty to do their research and scholarship: typically the arts, humanities, social sciences, and business disciplines, in which arrangements tend to be informal and ad hoc because little or no income generation is likely. Even when research in these fields requires extensive travel, such as in the case of archaeology, universities may provide little or no special funding and may require no share of any income generated by such work. Artists, scholars, business and information technology (IT) consultants, social scientists, and textbook authors do not usually share their "outside" income with their employers. Even an English department's novelist who hits the jackpot and receives advances, royalties, and movie and paperback rights would be shocked and outraged if asked to share such income. He or she may well be expected to write and publish novels and may receive a reduced teaching load so that time can be spent writing, but the university expects in return only institutional prestige, improved student recruitment, and presumably stronger classroom performance. While that may seem strange to people outside higher education, that's the tradition within those disciplines, and it probably acknowledges the slender odds of a humanist or social scientist earning much from scholarly, creative, or consulting pursuits.

In practical and admittedly simplistic terms, the distinction between the two models often echoes the distinction between patents and copyrights—though not always, especially as genomic and similar researchers seek to use copyrights to protect the products of their research: The individual faculty member and the employer usually divide patent income but do not usually divide a faculty member's copyright income.

## THE FOUNDATION OF INTELLECTUAL PROPERTY

### Historical Origins

Unfortunately, the beneficiaries of the second model just described often know neither that the first model exists nor that they are largely out of sync with the historical origins of patents and copyrights. Western culture of the pre-industrial ages seems always to have had some sense of intellectual products as property. For example, much of what passed from master to apprentice in the European guild system would qualify as intellectual property: techniques, styles, and processes that identified a worker as having come from the tutelage of a particular master. Guilds jealously guarded their craft secrets and maintained monopolies on some products.

Nonetheless, "authorship" was collective, not individual, and while the fraudulent use of another artisan's mark was illegal, the making of a competitive imitation required skill—even if not imagination—that rivaled the skill of the original's maker. Indeed, authorial recognition itself was elusive since an author could never rely on the accurate replication or attribution of his or her works. The "terms plagiarism and copyright did not exist for the minstrel. It was only after [the invention of mechanical] printing that they began to hold significance for the author" (Eisenstein, 1979, p. 121). Without easy means of replicating tangible products, the would-be thieves of intellectual property had limited opportunity, and threats to intellectual property seemed less significant than threats to real or personal properties.

What finally transformed the concept of intellectual property was the development of technologies that enabled even unskilled, unimaginative workers to replicate the products of talented visionaries and that enabled the visionaries themselves to establish themselves as individual authors. Such technologies include the printing press and, much later, cameras and film, magnetic tape, the photocopier, magnetic and optical data storage disks, and the digital scanner, among others. All have brought forms of mass reproduction to masses of novices, thereby threatening the commercial value of the originals and both the eminence and marketability of the originals' creators. As Eisenstein (1979) notes,

> The wish to see one's work in print (fixed forever with one's name in card files and anthologies) is different from the desire to pen lines that could never get fixed in a permanent form, might be lost forever, altered by copying, or–if truly memorable–be carried by oral transmission and assigned ultimately to 'anon.' [Printing and patent laws] transformed the anonymous artisan into the eponymous inventor, released individual initiative from the secretive cocoon of the guild, and rewarded ingenuity with the luster of fame as well as the chance to make a fortune (p. 121).

We see the natural extension of this issue in the current controversy over the "sharing" of digital music and video among Internet users. The technologies of reproduction now enable people who can create neither music nor movies to create exact copies of commercial music and movies. If left unchecked, rampant copyright violations will lead producers of copyright-protected works either to find technologies that thwart the making of copies or to abandon commercial production. Without effective copyright protection, two powerful incentives will be lost: the ability to benefit financially from the creation of commercially desirable works and the ego-fulfilling ability to be recognized as a work's individual creator. We will have returned to the Middle Ages, not technologically but creatively (p. 121).

### Origins of Patents

Patent laws had their earliest form in monopolies granted in ancient Greece and Rome (Foster & Shook, 1989). In England, monarchs began to confer monopolies, franchises, and other grants of exclusivity and protection in the Middle Ages in order to encourage the development of certain trades. "The first privilege granted to a printer and the first law pertaining to patenting both appeared in ... Venice between 1469 and 1474" (Eisenstein, 1979, p. 240). Not until the reign of Elizabeth I (17th Century) did the practice of granting patents to inventors gain regularity; the principal purpose of the patents was to generate revenues for the monarch's treasury. The Statute of Monopolies, enacted under England's James I in 1624, did not end some of the abusive practices of Elizabeth, but it did begin to regulate the patent process and became the basis of all succeeding patent law in both England and the United States (Foster & Shook, 1989). The US Constitution (Art. I, Sec. 8) became the world's first constitution to recognize individuals' intellectual property rights, stating that Congress shall have the power "to promote the Progress of Science and useful Arts, by securing for limited Times to Authors and Inventors the exclusive Right to their respective Writings and Discoveries" (Foster & Shook, 1989, p. 9).

### Origins of Copyrights

Copyright law originated in England, first (in the 16th Century) in the form of royal restrictions intended to control the dissemination of political ideas, and later (1709) in the form of the Statute of Queen Anne, to protect authors and publishers from losing revenues to pirate reprinters of published works. In the United States, copyright law evolved from the English system and over the years has moved to protect what are seen as individual property rights as well as economic and commercial interests (Foster & Shook, 1979).

Copyrights in the United States extend for the life of the author plus 50 years; the copyright begins with the moment the work is first fixed in a tangible expression. Ordinarily, copyrights belong to the individual authors of the work, but copyrights of works made for hire may belong to the author's employer, depending upon the terms of employment. The copyright of "a work for hire extends for 75 years from the date of first publication or 100 years from the date of creation, whichever is the shorter period" (Strong, 1993, p. 55).

### Moral Rights

Some countries, not including the United States, do recognize "moral rights" of authors and artists.

> The moral rights ... most commonly recognized are the right to prevent the distortion or truncation of his work, the right to prevent false attribution of his name to works not written by him, ... the right to prevent others from using his work or name so as to injure or reflect on his professional reputation or standing ... [and the right] to be known as the author of his work" (Kinter & Lahr, 1982, p. 383).

Common among these so-called moral rights is an implication of the existence of another form of intangible property—the reputation associated with one's name. Although moral rights associated with intellectual property do not have a legal tradition in the United States, IP lawyers often attempt to craft copyright agreements that preclude any prospect of a claimant's succeeding in getting a court to recognize moral rights.

## THE FUNDAMENTAL DILEMMA

### Competing Interests

The issue of who owns on-campus course instruction and instructor-developed course materials did not often arise in the past because, for the most part, those materials were not generally considered fungible—unlike the patents that result from scientific and technological research. Even the scholarly work of a faculty member, documented through publication, has not been valued primarily as fungible, though theft through plagiarism would be considered a grievous affront to the integrity and values of academic life.

The fundamental dilemma for higher education as it moves into an era of "distributed" education is this: Which of the two models described above should apply to video-taped lectures, Web-based documents, assignments, examinations, syllabi, and similar materials recorded for distance courses, especially when those materials may be used numerous times over several years? As higher education assesses this issue, we should recall the origins and traditions of intellectual property—as very briefly summarized above—and realize that the long-term feasibility and forms of distance education may well depend on how we settle the IP issue today.

### The Faculty's Interests

Faculty naturally wish to control the products of their intellectual work. They want to ensure that the ongoing demand for their services is not made obsolete by the recording and repeated distribution of that work. They want to protect their reputations by preventing others from continuing to use their work when it is no longer current. (This follows one of the precepts of putative moral law. For example, a biology instructor recorded in January 1997 as saying that the cloning of mammals is likely not to occur for another 20 years, would be embarrassed to have that recording played for students who in late February 1997 were reading in their newspapers about Dolly the sheep.) And they want to protect their academic freedom by ensuring that others do not distort or edit their recorded materials. (For example, the biology instructor would probably object to an editing of his online writing that added the qualifier "theory of" to every occurrence of the word "evolution"; or, worse, that entirely replaced his online writing with tracts about creationism.)

## The Institution's Interests

Significant as the faculty interests may be, institutions also have significant interests in the creation, control, distribution, and ownership of course-related intellectual property. Perhaps the most dangerous prospect of surrendering control of course ownership is the potential for losing control over course development: deciding which courses will be developed, on what schedule they will be developed, and when they will be revised or redeveloped. Without that control, an institution may not be able to put together a coherent distance program that includes everything a student requires to complete a credential. Institutions without a commitment to distance education have often approached the enterprise as they would never approach on-campus course offerings. Instead of recruiting all the faculty necessary to put together a distance version of an academic program, based on faculty members' content mastery, they have recruited the faculty whose inclinations toward technology or pedagogical innovation identify them as early adopters. The institution then pays them to develop distance courses simply in order to create a presence in that market. Without a coherent program that meets student needs, though, that presence will be negligible, will attract few students, and will engender in other faculty cynicism about the feasibility of distance education.

If faculty own course content and have not licensed it to the institution, they may well choose at some point to withdraw a course if they are unhappy with their own performance in the course, if they decide in retrospect that they were paid too little for the course, if they leave that institution's employment, if they decide that the distance version is threatening their on-campus job security, if they simply decide they don't believe in distance education, or for virtually any other reason. Similarly, the sudden death of the faculty member could put all such decisions into the hands of the heirs or executor of the estate.

A faculty member may hold a course hostage in negotiating for completely unrelated terms of employment. Or a group of faculty could withhold their courses—as they do their on-campus services—in instances of strikes and labor disputes.

Some of these scenarios may seem simple enough to address. After all, universities already deal with faculty who refuse to teach a course, who decide to rework their courses, who die. Distance programs differ, though, from on-campus courses. In many cases, a substitute may be quickly found for an ill or deceased or otherwise absent faculty member. And the systems of discipline for addressing faculty who simply fail to show up to teach are well established. An instructor who simply withdraws the right of an institution to use copyrighted course content may be replaced, but the course content may not—especially in courses that incur lengthy and expensive front-end production. A faculty member's withdrawal of a course does not merely shut the course down for a day or two, but may shut it down for a year or more while costing the institution lost revenues and thousands of dollars in new production costs.

Some of these scenarios may seem far-fetched or paranoid. Would faculty, after all, use distance courses as part of a labor action? We almost found out last year when the university's faculty union voted to strike after contract negotiations stalemated. The negotiations finally succeeded and a strike was averted, but in weeks leading up to the strike date, faculty did question whether we intended to continue to broadcast their courses during the strike. We said that we did, and we could do so because of our position from the beginning that the university owned the courses, which had been produced as "work for hire."

### Producers' Interests

Others engaged in the production of distance courses may also seek some control of content and some ownership of copyright. The placement of online course materials into a template, such as that provided in a Blackboard course management system, isn't likely to elicit any claim from the template designer that the copyright should be shared, but an institution's use of either consultants or its own employees to design custom Webpages using instructors' content could elicit such a claim if ownership issues have not been explicitly defined and agreed to in advance.

The ownership issue grows murkier as the media involved multiply. A professional course-related video may well include 10 or more people in its production: producer, director, camera operators, sound and lighting technicians, editors, encoders, graphics specialists, and so on. Each person has a part in the creative activity that results in the video recording. When we created a program with some 500 hours of recorded video for the University of Cincinnati, we were entirely unaware of the potential for a production crew's claiming copyright ownership. Fortunately, during contract negotiations, the production company's representative told us that he would get all the company employees to sign releases that surrendered any copyright claim.

Interestingly though, the same representative in the negotiations did ask to preserve some right to control course elements, largely to preserve the production company's own reputation since their name would also appear in the video credits. The request baffled us. What aspect of the course content could they presume to control? His answer surprised us and illustrates the extent to which distance courses on video are true collaborations involving people well beyond the faculty. "Suppose," he said, "you put before our cameras a faculty member who just isn't well-prepared and who doesn't do a good job? Or suppose the faculty member shows up with long, greasy hair and disheveled clothes?" (They may have been remembering some of their own classroom experiences as they worried about these issues.) While the company was not wishing to control academic content or to share in copyright ownership, they—understandably—wished to ensure that the *performance* of the academic content met their standards and reflected well on them. Ultimately, we were able to incorporate appropriate reassurances into the video production contract without inappropriately encroaching on faculty rights.

## A COMPROMISE AT UNIVERSITY OF CINCINNATI

### Spending $2M in Three Years

The Early Childhood Learning Community (ECLC) is an associate degree program in early childhood care and education. University College, which operates ECLC, is a two-year college on the main campus of the University of Cincinnati (UC). In 1999 and 2000, UC began creating a complete degree program, relying on integrated satellite-broadcast video and Internet-based interactivity. [Editor's Note: See Chapter 5—A Different Practice: Spanning the Digitial Divide Through Distance Learning.] By Spring 2002, we had created and deployed 23 of the program's 27 courses. ECLC now enrolls some 300 students from Virginia to California, in Singapore and Venezuela. The program includes course work for a complete associate's degree. Each course consists of about 20 hours of pre-recorded coursework on video, which may resemble traditional lectures or may more closely resemble a television talk show, depending on the instructor's intentions.

The videos are produced by a professional video production company. Unlike many pre-recorded video courses, ECLC's productions use commercial-quality equipment, multiple cameras, professional technical crews (even a make-up artist), and a professional production studio and editing facilities.

Students' regular interactions with each other and with instructors occur through the Internet and the Blackboard course management system licensed by the university. Existing university faculty taped the lectures and often served as the instructors for the online portions of the course.

The cost of all this course development for the complete program—exclusive of continuing operating costs—approached $2M. Clearly, UC has a large investment and a strong interest in ensuring that their investment—that *intellectual property*—is protected.

### Serving Competing Interests

Recognizing the legitimate interests of both faculty and the university, and after extensive guidance from the university's Office of General Counsel, we arrived at a standard faculty contract that has been accepted by faculty while still protecting the ownership rights of the university. The university retains the copyright for all ECLC courses but extends a license to faculty and pays a royalty. The terms of our agreements with course developers now provide for a royalty payment of $500 for each academic term in which a course developed by that faculty member is offered, regardless of the number of students enrolled or the number of sections offered. (Our actual cost is about $650 because we must pay 30% of the royalty into the university benefits pool.) The royalty will continue indefinitely, even if the recipient leaves the university's employment. Faculty have found these terms satisfactory, and other distance programs on campus are considering adoption of the model for their own programs.

The following excerpt from the contract template contains the principal protections:

Works Made For Hire: ECLC and other courses created under this Memorandum are Works Made For Hire and are the intellectual property of UC. Faculty who provide services under this Memorandum may receive incentive compensation, as described below, in addition to their regular compensation as UC employees.

Copyrights: UC shall own all right, title, and interest in and to the work, including the entire copyright in the work. With respect to any Audiovisual Work, Faculty expressly waives any and all rights of attribution and integrity with respect to any and all uses of the work. Faculty further agree that to the extent the work is not a "Work Made For Hire," Faculty will assign to UC ownership of all right, title, and interest in and to work, including ownership of the entire copyright of the work. Faculty also agrees to execute all papers necessary for UC to perfect its ownership of the entire copyright in the work.

Derivative Works: UC reserves the right to use any part of the Course in promotional or other derivative works without additionally compensating Faculty. If the Faculty has left the employment of UC, UC may continue to use portions of the Course in Redevelopment.

Faculty License: Faculty will be granted a nonexclusive, royalty-free license to use Course materials, including Audiovisual Works created by Faculty, in uncompensated conferences and other professional circumstances during but not beyond the term of Faculty's employment by UC. Such use must be approved in advance by_____ and may not be used in a manner that competes, directly or indirectly with any actual or intended use of the Course materials by UC.

Moral Rights to Redevelopment: Faculty retain the right to update, edit, or otherwise revise materials produced under this Memorandum, provided such changes shall not occur more frequently than once in three years, provided the Course is not being Redeveloped by another faculty member, and provided UC intends to continue to use the Course. Faculty may or may not receive additional compensation for such Redevelopment, at UC's sole discretion, based on UC's determination of whether Redevelopment was necessary.

Permissions of Third Parties: Faculty are responsible for the timely identification to UC of all non-original material intended to be used in the Course and are responsible for securing necessary permissions or licenses for the use of those materials. UC agrees to assist Faculty in securing such permissions or licenses by providing reasonable clerical services. Faculty agree not to use such materials (1) if permissions or licenses have not been secured; and (2) if UC deems the associated royalties or licenses fees to be too expensive and is unwilling to pay such royalties or fees.

At about the time we concluded development of this standard contract, we learned that an office of the university had created a committee to develop a policy on intellectual property in distance learning. The committee consisted mostly of faculty, and its initial drafts almost exclusively reflected faculty interests. That may have resulted in part from the desire of faculty and administration to position themselves for the latest round of collective bargaining. The draft vested ownership of almost all distance materials in the faculty, but provided nothing like a royalty payment to facilitate the mutual interests of faculty and institution. For more than a year we have heard nothing from that committee—not too surprising, given the draft's apparent failure to recognize the tradition and purposes of intellectual property.

## Already Seeing What Could Have Happened

In late Spring 2002, we faced the first instance of potential conflict over our faculty agreement. A faculty member who had taped a course in 2001, receiving the standard compensation after signing the standard faculty contract, contacted me to ask to retape some or all of the course because the textbook he used in the video had been superceded by a new edition. He also cited a recent US Supreme Court ruling that affected the content of his course. I explained that our budget could not afford redevelopment of the course after just one year. He persisted, noting that he would be happy to retape just portions of the course, not all 20 hours. He clearly did not understand the economics of video production. And he may well argue that he has a moral right not to be made to look foolish by discussing on videotape issues that shift and change in public discourse. I didn't dismiss the faculty member's concerns, and I urged him to use the ever-changeable online portion of the course to alert students to changes in course content.

An intellectual property agreement that vested ownership of the video course in faculty would have given this eager faculty member the right to withdraw the course if we failed to meet his request. Unable to afford to replace the course, the students in our program would be unable to complete the program and receive their degrees.

## CONCLUSION

The per-course production costs of ECLC exceed those of most distance programs because of the heavy use of video. Those high costs put unusually high pressure on the up-front disposition of the intellectual property issues. However, even less expensive production programs deserve early consideration of IP issues. Otherwise, the potential for disruption or failure of entire programs is great.

## REFERENCES

Anawalt, H.C. (1988). *Ideas in the workplace: planning for protection.* Carolina Academic Press.

Eisenstein, Elizabeth L. The Printing Press as an Agent of Change. 2 vols. Cambridge: Cambridge University Press, 1979.

Foster, F.H., & Shook, R.. *Patents, Copyrights, & Trademarks.* New York: John Wiley & Sons, 1989.

Kintner, E.W., & Lahr, J. *An Intellectual Property Law Primer.* 2nd ed. New York: Clark Boardman Co., Ltd., 1982.

Strong, W.S. *The Copyright Book: A Practical Guide.* 4th ed. Cambridge: MIT Press, 1993.

CHAPTER 14

# WRITING WINNING DISTANCE EDUCATION TEACHING AND LEARNING GRANTS

## Catherine S. Bolek and Ronald G. Forsythe

In the past, locating funding sources was a difficult task. Competing demands made by our increasingly complex lives left little time for the task of proposal writing. Fortunately, the introduction of the World Wide Web has made the process easier and less demanding. Funding sources have taken full advantage of the Internet to post funding information, provide electronic applications forms, guidelines and review criteria, and offer other resources and tools.

By developing some specialized search skills and taking advantage of Websites designed for the grants seeker, one can quickly locate organizations that are interested in supporting their ideas or projects, complete applications (in many cases, using online forms), and obtain information from online databases on who is currently funded.

This chapter will provide several types of information on grant seeking and proposal writing, from where to look for funding sources, through preparing a competitive application, to submission and award. Included in the chapter are sample proposals, budget forms and preparation information, and lists of resources and tools for the grant seeker wanting to support distance education projects.

Electronic Learning Communities—Issues and Practices, pages 501–548.
Copyright © 2003 by Information Age Publishing, Inc.
All rights of reproduction in any form reserved.
ISBN: 1-931576-96-3 (pbk.), 1-931576-97-1 (hardcover)

**KEYWORDS:**   assurances, budget preparation, evaluation, federal, foundations, grants management, indirect costs, internet searching, cost sharing, private sector

## OVERVIEW

Obtaining research, program, or development funding is an increasingly complicated task even for the most sophisticated academic. Faculty often find the task of seeking external support to be an overwhelming obstacle because of the competing demands made on their time. Given the job requirements of teaching, advising, and providing service, faculty view the prospect of preparing a highly competitive grant application with little enthusiasm.

Fortunately, a little practice with the Internet and some good advice from grantwriters can help to overcome many barriers and obstacles. To be competitive, potential grantees and applicant organizations will have to develop new strategies to improve the probability that research, projects, program and development proposals are approved and awarded. To be successful, applicants must match strong technical and academic skills with grantsmanship techniques.

The purpose of this chapter is to:

- identify strategies for locating funding sources,
- discuss the role of the Internet in grantsmanship,
- provide strategies for improving proposals,
- review common errors and fatal flaws, and
- provide a compendium of Internet and print resources including:
    - references,
    - funding sources,
    - grantwriters and consultants,
    - information sources in print,
    - information sources and the internet,
    - libraries,
    - tutorial and other grantwriting resources,
    - application forms and templates,
    - grant and contract policy, and
    - other tools and resources.

## FUNDING SOURCES AND THE INTERNET

According to Susan Peterson (2001), foundations award an estimated $20B annually. Estimates of annual federal awards may be as high as 10 times that amount and growing. There are several strategies for locating potential funding sources (e.g., grant directories, newsletters, printed announcements, etc.). These resources are found in most libraries. While the information contained in these publications can be useful, it can also be out of date or incomplete.

The best strategy for finding funding sources is to use the Internet. All federal agencies and most other funding sources (e.g., foundations, businesses, other private sector sources) are moving their method of interaction with the public to the Internet. The Webpages of these organizations contain program announcements (grants) and requests for proposals (contracts), application forms, searchable indexes of awards, grant and contract administration guidelines, library databases, and other important resources and tools for the grantwriter.

Unfortunately, some funding sources have created elaborate and frequently difficult to navigate sites. To ensure that time is well spent, one must develop funding-specific searching skills.

### *Locating a Federal Funding Source*

One-stop-shopping is provided at the *Federal Acquisition Jumpstation* which includes departments, independent agencies of the Executive Branch, and other acquisition information. Other agency information can be located from the following sources listed in the *Information Sources on the Internet* and the *Distance Education Funding* Sources sections at the end of this chapter.

While funding opportunities are not static, the following funding sources have maintained a longstanding interest in technology and serve as prime examples of the types of projects that can be found on the Internet.

- **Department of Education**—offers a broad range of funding opportunities for the grantwriter seeking support for distance education and distance learning projects. The Fund for the Improvement of Education–Learning Anytime Anywhere Partnerships (LAAP) Grants are designed to support distance learning opportunities for college students, adult learners, welfare recipients, individuals with disabilities, workers seeking additional skills training, and other populations that have been underserved by traditional postsecondary education programs.

  The Fund for the Improvement of Postsecondary Education (FIPSE) was designed by the US Department of Education (DoED) "… to support innovative reform projects that hold promise as models for the resolution of important issues and problems in postsecondary education." The Learning Anytime Anywhere Partnerships (LAAP) program "… supports partnerships among colleges and universities, employers, technology companies, and other relevant organizations to create postsecondary programs that deliver distance education." In addition to these grant opportunities, the DoED Website offers many other funding opportunities.

- **Department of Health and Human Services (DHHS)**—offers a large number of programs that support technology, distance education and learning, telemedicine, and related activities. Each agency within the Department of Health and Human Services has a searchable index of available grant and contract opportunities and databases containing lists of recent awards. Moreover, DHHS supports a large number of electronic clearinghouses that contain valuable information that can be easily used for building a proposal.
- **Department of Commerce**—This department has "… interest in providing access to technology to rural and underserved areas as a means for business and economic development. Included in this effort are a number of programs that fund training, welfare-to-work initiatives, and provide support services through videoconferencing and distance education infrastructure. The Technology Opportunities Program (TOP) and the Public Telecommunications Facilities Program (PTFP) are administered through the National Telecommunications and Information Administration. TOP provides matching funds for projects that help develop information infrastructures that promote the widespread use of advanced telecommunications and information technologies for all citizens. The goal of PTFP is to provide funding for equipment that helps to disseminate noncommercial educational and cultural programs to the American public."
- **Department of Defense**—The Department of Defense is a promoter of distance education resources and supports both grants and contracts. *Broad Agency Announcements* (BAA) are published regularly by DOD and can be found on the Internet.
- **National Science Foundation**—"The Directorate for Computer and Information Sciences and Engineering promotes basic research and education in the computer and information sciences and engineering, and helps maintain the nation's preeminence in these fields"; other directorates also offer distance education funding opportunities.
- **US Department of Agriculture**—The Distance Learning and Telemedicine Loan and Grant Program solicits applications that propose to use telemedicine, telecommunications, computer networks, and related advanced technologies to provide educational and medical benefits.

These are but a few samples of federal funding sources for distance education and distance learning projects. These and other funding sources frequently change contents, so applicants should check back if they do not find a funding source on their first try.

## Finding State Funding Sources

State and local government agencies and offices are sources of grants and contracts; generally these applications are not burdensome and can result in rapid turnaround time from application to award.

- **Block Grants to States**—federal dollars are redistributed within each state.
- **National Association of State Procurement Offices**—provides insight into how states go about selecting contractors, proposal-writing tips, and other useful advice.
- **Federal Market Place's Listing of State and Local Government Procurement Sites**—state and/or city contract opportunities.

## Finding Non-Federal Funding Sources

Several sources provide access to a wide variety of government and private sector funding sources. Other sites provide keyword searchable sites where one can search for funding sources in their area of interest.

- **National Network of Grant Makers** offers *"A Resource for Social Change Funders & Grant Seekers"* available for a fee of $60. The resource focuses on democracy-related projects.
- **The Charity Channel**, an online community of non-profit sector professionals with a reported membership of 50,000, provides forums for grant seekers and grant providers. The GuestShare System provides access to samples and examples of proposals.
- **The Chronicle of Higher Education** is a weekly publication offering print copy and daily e-mail alerts including grant opportunities and a searchable index of past articles and news.
- **The Chronicle of Philanthropy** is a monthly publication covering the entire range of philanthropy issues, organizations, and news. This searchable site covers seven days of ever-changing content. Some services are free (such as an alerting service, and specialized online bookstore); others are restricted to paid subscribers.
- **The Foundation Center** is an independent nonprofit information clearinghouse established in 1956. "The Center's mission is to foster public understanding of the foundation field by collecting, organizing, analyzing, and disseminating information on foundations, corporate giving, and related subjects. The Foundation Center currently tracks 60,000 grantmakers and logs over 14,000 visits per day to their comprehensive Website. There is a virtual classroom that covers top-

ics ranging from Orientation to Grantseeking to Proposal Budgeting Basics to a Proposal Writing Short Course."

- **GrantSelect** is among a number of services that provide access to thousands of funding opportunities. Unlike other fee for service organizations, Grantselect provides a trial membership that opens up "... more than 10,000 funding opportunities." In addition, Grantselect offers e-mail alert services that notify a user when a funding opportunity is found that matches their keyword profile. There are specialty sections including: arts and humanities, children and youth, community development, biomedical and health care, K-12 and adult basic education, international programs, and operating grants.

- **GuideStar** is a free service with information on the programs and finances of more than 600,000 American charities and nonprofit organizations, up-to-date news stories on philanthropy, and resources for donors and volunteers.

- **GrantStation** provides search tools and funder profiles. Fees range from $299 to $499 (with local options) per year.

- **Illinois Research Information Service** (IRIS) "... is a part of the University of Illinois Library at Urbana-Champaign that offers three Web-based funding and research services. The IRIS database contains approximately 8,000 federal and private funding opportunities in a wide range of disciplines. The IRIS Alert Service is a subscription service that allows researchers to create unique profiles. The IRIS Expertise Service assists researchers with the development of electronic curricula vitae for posting on a Web-accessible database. IRIS also provides other services of value to the grant seeker." Fees are listed on their Website.

- **InfoEd International** provides a number of Web-based services that are in compliance with federal Electronic Research Administration (ERA) practices. In addition, to databases of funding sources, InfoEd provides Web-based pre- and post- award research administration services. There are free links to important sponsored programs sites, such as the *Federal Register, Commerce Business Daily, Catalog of Federal Domestic Assistance, FedWorld Information Network, Library of Congress, Fedbizops,* and selected federal agency sites.

- **MERLOT** provides "... free and open resources designed primarily for faculty and students of higher education. Links to online learning materials are collected there along with annotations such as peer reviews and assignments." Merlot offers information useful to the proposal writer.

- **Community of Science** (COS) Website reports that they can provide access to over 400,000 funding opportunities. COS provides a number of useful services. This is a membership organization; their policies and fees are listed on their Website.

- **ScienceWise** (FEDIX and MOLIS) provides access to resources including electronic grantwriting, access to federal, state and private funding sources, and a gateway to FEDIX, the federal information exchange, and to MOLIS, the minority online information exchange.
- **Miscellaneous** Professional journals and newsletters are another sources for locating funding sources for distance education projects and activities. Many of these offer electronic access to information from their Websites.

### Using an Internet-based Funding Site

While these organizations provide powerful search engines and a great deal of information on grants, GrantSelect appears to be the easiest and most straightforward of the funding opportunity sites. By conducting a search using the term "information technology," the Grantselect database identified 222 possible funding sources. Users have a number of options that allow for a more refined search. For example, items such as state, deadline, sponsor, title, etc. can be used to refine a search. Selecting a specific search result allows one to access a brief description, eligibility criteria, and contact information including direct access to the sponsored homepage, when available. This is a quick and easy system for identifying potential sources without the need to read lengthy and often cumbersome program descriptions. For an in-depth discussion on electronic grant submission see Council on Foundations located in the Information Sources on the Internet Section at the end of the chapter.

### Using Office of Sponsored Research Internet Sites

Universities involved in research and externally funded projects support business offices that are charged with a wide variety of responsibilities, including:

- Identification of funding sources.
- Preparation of budgets and forms.
- Internal review and processing.
- Consultation and editorial services.
- Coordination of Internal Review Boards (IRBs).
- Pre- and post- award administration services, from pre-proposal through award negotiation to extensions and close-outs.
- Coordination of federal and institutional reporting requirements.
- Compliance with federal and institutional policies and regulations.

If the applicant institution cannot provide these services, try the Websites of the "big" research institutions. Major institutions such as Harvard, Yale, Cornell, and Stanford maintain Websites that are of great value to the grant seeker. Their sites include funding sources, proposal guidelines, sample proposals, electronic forms and budget templates, and other helpful resources and tools. For example, the Office of Sponsored Programs at the University of Maryland Eastern Shore provides links to funding sources, a principal investigator's manual, and tips on proposal writing, including PowerPoint presentations on topics related to proposal development.

Offices of sponsored research generally subscribe to periodicals such as the *Chronicle of Higher Education* and to electronic database services that make finding funding sources relatively easy. Many institutions make these services available on their Websites.

## Using Federal Agency Documents

The federal government is not shy when it comes to publishing guidelines, regulations, and policies. Listed below are a number of resources related to grant and contract acquisition and award management. While most of this information is of interest to the grant accountant and the auditor, it is important to be familiar with some of the basics of grants management. Knowing something about how the funding agencies monitor awards can help reduce or avoid most problems. Since these sites contain searchable databases, it is easy to locate agency policies and regulations that may affect performance. For example, a principal investigator could quickly learn whether the purchase of food was permissible under their award.

- **Federal Register**—is published by the government every business day. The contents are limited to agency regulations, rulemaking and notices, procurement actions, and Executive Orders. With Web-assisted access and keyword searchable databases, a grantwriter can access an enormous volume of useful material.
- **Commerce Business Daily (CBD)**—is published each business day. It contains notices of proposed procurement actions, contract awards, sales of government property, and other procurement information related to the actions of the federal government.
- **National Archives**—is a major research source of national and international records of historical significance including presidential papers, Acts of Congress, Executive Orders, etc.
- **Catalog of Federal Domestic Assistance**—provides access to a database of all federal, state, and municipal governments.
- **Federal Acquisitions Regulations (FARs)**—the FARs outlines the uniform policies and procedures for doing business with the federal government.
- **Federal Market Place**—provides access to procurement opportunities, and other tools and resources.

- **Office of Management and Budget Circulars (OMB)**—does not award grants. "This office is responsible for working with federal grantmaking agencies and the grantee community to assure that grants are managed properly and according to applicable laws and regulations. Circulars outline the requirements for cost principles, administrative requirements and audit requirements for non-profit organizations, education institutions, state and local governments, and Indian tribes."
- **General Services Administration (GSA)**—"The GSA affects almost $66B in financial transactions throughout the federal government with an annual budget of approximately $16B. Getting on a GSA Schedule or partnering with a corporation that provides services through the GSA Schedule is one method for providing services to the federal government."

## PREPARING THE BODY OF PROPOSAL

An effective strategy is to use the Internet to conduct literature searches (e.g., ERIC) for the background and/or rationale sections. One can check their quotations and support their statements using Internet searches, and craft a reference section using the editing features on their browser (e.g., cut and paste, save to file).

### Phase I

One strategy for creating proposal content is to download the application instructions and save them as a word processing file. For example, funding sources provide many items that can be downloaded from their site (refer to Table 1):

### Phase II

In one sitting, use the "fill in the blank" approach maintaining the funding agency's headings. Even if it is possible to only add a sentence or two in some sections, try to complete a rough draft in one session. Add questions, notes, names and phone numbers of persons that must be contacted for letters of support, etc. Complete those sections that are the easiest. Return to the more complex sections later.

### Phase III

Continue the "fill in the blank exercise" until each section is complete. Have someone carefully edit the proposal including checking the budget and resumes for possible errors.

TABLE 1
Items Downloadable from the Internet.

| | |
|---|---|
| 1. | Title |
| 2. | Appicant Organization |
| 3. | Address |
| 4. | Contact Information |
| 5. | Abstract (200 words) |
| 6. | Project |
| | A. Significance |
| | B. Goal(s) |
| | C. Objectives |
| | D. Approach |
| | E. Timeline |
| | F. Evaluation |
| | G. Key personnel and Management Plan |
| | H. Sustainability |
| 7. | Budget |
| 8. | Budget Justification |
| 9. | Appendices |
| 10. | Letters of Support |
| 11. | Resumes |

### *Phase IV*

The completed proposal should be routed to the institution's business office for institutional sign-off, and arrangements should be made for shipping the proposal to the funder (e.g., Federal Express) before the deadline.

### *Using Graphics*

Expressing complex ideas in textual form is risky. There is always a chance that reviewers will become confused or miss important concepts. Another problem is the use of limited space when the funding agency has placed restrictions on the number of pages (e.g., 20 pages is a frequently used number of pages for the body of the proposal). Using common software such as Microsoft Office, one can create graphics that provide visual representations of complex concepts.

There are a number of ways to present this material. Many of the major consulting firms that receive millions of dollars in grant and contract awards use a matrix format. The method provides a lot of information in a relatively small space. The chart in Figure 1 was used in a proposal submitted to the Department of Defense. With three partners and 13 task areas it was important to be sure to identify each area that would require staff.

| NAME | 5.1: Program and TO Management | 5.2: Systems Engineering | 5.3: Telecommunication | 5.4: Acquisition Management | 5.5: Soft/Comp Sys/ Ntwk App Dev. And Sup. | 5.6: Systems Eval, Integration and Testing Service | 5.7: Program and Information Management | 5.8: Info. Systems Security and Info. Assurance | 5.9: Modeling and Simulation | 5.10: Electronic Commerce/Electronic Business | 5.11: Information Technology Training | 5.12: Studies in Advanced IT | 5.13: Business Process Re-Engineering |
|---|---|---|---|---|---|---|---|---|---|---|---|---|---|
| **University** | • | • | • | • | • | • | • | • | • | • | • | • | • |
| Barnes, Kathy | • | | | | | | • | | | • | • | | • |
| Bobwell, Bill | • | • | • | • | | | • | • | | • | • | • | • |
| Lewis, Erika | | | | • | • | • | • | | | • | • | | • |
| Moore, Ron | | • | • | • | • | • | • | • | • | • | • | | • |
| Stodson, Jill | | | | • | | • | • | | | | • | | • |
| Ward, Jack | | | | • | • | • | • | • | • | • | • | | • |
| **BCA Corporation** | • | • | • | | | | • | • | | | • | • | |
| Greene, Carla | • | • | | | | | • | | | | | | |
| Limon, Kevin | | • | • | | | | • | | | | • | • | |
| Maak, Jim | | • | | | | | • | | | | | | |
| Tanner, Brock | | • | | | | | • | | | | | | |
| Zorb, Elissa | | • | • | | | | • | • | | | • | | |
| **MORB, Inc.** | • | • | • | | • | • | • | | | | • | | • |
| Pearson, Nancy | • | • | • | | • | • | • | | | | • | | • |
| Potter, Betsy | • | • | | | • | • | • | | | | • | | • |
| **Sontec, Inc.** | • | • | | • | • | • | • | | | | | • | • |
| Dodge, Frank | • | • | | | • | • | | | | | | • | • |
| Keenan, Karen | • | | | • | | | | | | | | | |
| Simpson, Stan | | • | • | | | | • | | | | | | |

FIGURE 1
Staff Loading Chart for a Collaborative Project

### Past Performance

Most funding agencies want to know something about the past performance of the institution. This information provides evidence that the applicant institution is skilled at grants and contracts management and provides an external recommendation in support of the proposed effort. One way to provide this information is with a graphic depiction of information (see Figure 2).

## GRANTWRITING CHECKLIST

When first getting started, it is important to create a checklist of concepts or strategies that will improve the overall proposal. Many application guidelines have checklists included in the instructions; be sure to carefully read and follow the instructions.

### Writing Tips

- Capture the reviewer's attention—use simple, jargon free language.
- Use paragraph headings, charts and other graphics to help clarify complex concepts.
- Organize the proposal to facilitate the best understanding of the project.
- Make logical transitions as one moves from section to section.
- Be enthusiastic—create excitement for the reader.
- Avoid ambiguous language (e.g., could, may, ought, should).
- Support statements with appropriate citations.
- Have all forms and the proposal carefully edited by a professional editor.
- Consider involving a colleague as a co-writer or co-applicant.

| Program Management & Administrative Support | |
|---|---|
| **Client Name:** Department of Defense | **Contract Officer:** Jason Walston<br>DOD, Arlington, VA<br><br>**Project Officer:** Mary Jones<br>DISA HQ, Arlington, VA |
| **Contract Number:** DCA-123-45-67-8 | **Contract Type:** Time & Materials |
| **Total Contract Value:** $200,000 | **Period of Performance:** 9/1998 - 9/2001 |
| **Narrative:** UMES was tasked to provide logistical support services in the areas of internal program management. | |

FIGURE 2
Example of a Past Performance Form.

## Preparing the Proposal

- Carefully read the program announcement or request for proposal (RFP) and the application instructions.
- Define the proposed project by creating carefully articulated goals and objectives.
- Create a proposal writing timeline; allot a sufficient amount of time to prepare a quality application.
- Prepare a pre-proposal and submit it to the project officer and several colleagues for review.
- Provide an extensive literature search for research projects.
- Review grants funded over the past 12 months by checking federal databases.
- Contact principal investigators and ask for assistance—most principal investigators will provide assistance to a new investigator.

## CREATING A REALISTIC BUDGET

Most funding sources (e.g., government agencies, foundations, business sector sources) require a detailed budget, including justifications for the proposed expenditures. The federal government has established guidelines under the supervision of the White House's Office of Management and Budget (OMB) for allowable costs. Many non-federal government agencies and private sector funding sources use the OMB guidelines to determine allowable costs. *OMB Circular A-21* sets forth cost principles for educational institutions. Refer to the Information Sources on the Internet section of this chapter for detailed information.

Allowable costs can be determined by answering several commonsense questions. For example, are the costs reasonable, are the expenses associated with the proposed work, are the costs consistent with other proposals submitted by the applicant institution, are the costs allowable according the program announcement criteria and instructions, and are the costs justified?

Budget preparation can be time consuming and may require assistance from business offices or offices of sponsored research at the home institution. Since the budget is included in the review of grants (but not for contracts), it is worth the time and effort to identify all costs to be incurred in the conduct of the project, to accurately estimate total costs by category, and to provide ample justification.

Costs generally fall into three categories:

1. personnel,

2.   other direct costs, and
3.   indirect costs.

Personnel should include all persons who will be paid by the grant for work performed on the proposed project, including those who will be released from other duties (e.g., teaching, administration) and their fringe benefits. Other direct costs may include equipment, supplies, consultants, travel, and other costs related to the conduct of the project. Indirect costs (overhead) are those expenses that are incurred by the home institution (e.g., cost of facilities and services including general administration, physical plant operation, and research administration expenses). Indirect cost rates are established by a federal agency assigned to the applicant institution (e.g., DHHS) and are based on submission of indirect cost proposals (e.g., 42% of salaries, wages and fringe benefits for on-campus work and 23% of the same base for off-campus work).

In addition, the federal government requires the completion of budget forms (e.g., SF424, PHS 398). The most commonly used budget form is the Standard Form 424 used by such agencies as the Department of Education and the Department of Health and Human Services. These standard forms and related forms such as budget, assurances, financial status, disclosure statements, are available from most agency Websites and from other sources on the Internet. The Department of Health and Human Services provides a comprehensive site for government-wide support services. The forms can be completed electronically and require basic information related to the applicant organization. For example, Harvard has created Microsoft Excel versions of federal forms that allow the user to complete the budget without incurring costs for Adobe Acrobat software. Refer to the section in this chapter, on Information Sources on the Internet for access to these tools and to the Application Forms and Templates section for sites where these and other forms are available.

Key concepts in budget building are:

- The proposed budget must fall within the limits set by the funding agency.
- There must be a one-to-one correlation between the technical proposal and the costs being proposed.
- There must be a clear role for all personnel, consultants, and subcontractors.
- The forms must be accurate, complete, and contain no mathematical errors.

The proposed amount must be adequate to complete the proposed project.

Figure 3 illustrates a sample budget for a one-year information technology survey project. In addition, an overall budget *justification* is generally required as well as justifications for each item or category (e.g., travel, equipment) listed on the budget form. It is the responsibility of the principal investigator (PI) to determine the budget in collaboration with the business office or sponsored research office. The reason for the justification is to provide evidence for institutional support of the requested funds, and to eliminate any questions that may negatively affect the outcome of the peer review process.

Some common information that the grantseeker may want to have in their records as they prepare to complete the forms includes the following:

| Network Inventory Activity One Budget | |
|---|---|
| **Personnel** | **Year 1** |
| Project Manager | 58,500 |
| Webmaster | 12,500 |
| GIS Technician | 12,500 |
| Grad. Student Assistant | 14,000 |
| Salaries subtotal | 97,500 |
| Fringe & benefits @ 30% | 29250 |
| **Subtotal** | **126,750** |
| | |
| **Other Direct Costs** | |
| Consultants | 12,000 |
| Communications | 800 |
| GIS Map Reproductions | 18,500 |
| General and Misc. Supplies | 1,250 |
| **Subtotal** | **32,550** |
| | |
| **Travel** | |
| Local vehicle | 1800 |
| Tolls | 500 |
| Field work per diem | 700 |
| **Travel total** | **3000** |
| | |
| **Total Direct Costs** | **162,300** |
| | |
| **Indirect Costs (10%)** | **12675** |
| | |
| **Total** | **174,975** |

FIGURE 3
Sample Budget for a One-Year Information Technology Survey Project.

1. Face Page:
   - Type of applicant (e.g., state, county, independent school district, private university).
   - Congressional district.
   - Compliance with State Executive Order 12372 (the federal government may require that copies of proposals be sent to state agencies to keep them informed of applications submitted within their state).
   - Potential debt status.
2. Budget Page:
   - The home institution's indirect cost rate.
   - Matching and cost sharing policies.
   - Fringe benefit rates (e.g., academic year versus Summer).
   - Potential program income.

### Cost Sharing and Matching Funds

While most institutions of higher learning support the research efforts of their faculty, the need for cost sharing and matching raises financial concerns among most departmental administrators. To be competitive, institutions may be required by the funding source to commit funds to the proposed project. The applicant should become familiar with their institution's regulations regarding cost sharing and matching.

There are generally two types of cost sharing: mandatory or voluntary. The first type is generally required by a funding agency (e.g., National Science Foundation) as a condition for making an award. The funding agency will state the percent requirement or dollar value of the cost share in the Program Announcement. The second type, or voluntary cost sharing, is not required by the funding agency and is usually contributed by the principal investigators or their institution. Cost sharing must be verifiable, nonduplicative, and not come from other federal funds unless authorized by the agency. Matching is typically used when sponsors require institutional funds to cover specific costs such as equipment. The Program Announcement will provide guidelines for any matching requirements. Examples of sources for matching funds may include the following:

- State or private salary used as cash match for project.
- Private (non-federal) grants from third parties in support of the project.
- Departmental budgets.
- Community foundations.

Maintaining strong relationships with funding organizations and groups with interests aligned with the program efforts will help to secure matching grants. It is important to initiate these efforts early. For example, it is not uncommon to begin soliciting third party matching funds for annual program announcements several months in advance of the anticipated release date.

Both cost sharing and matching funds require documentation as a condition of an award. The Principal Investigator will be required to maintain careful records of expenditures (e.g., personnel time, travel, equipment). The home institution will maintain financial records that must be available for audit.

## TUTORIALS AND RESOURCES FOR THE GRANTWRITER

Federal agencies, business sector sources, foundations and other funding sources have developed very sophisticated grant writing tutorials. Many organizations have prepared these resources as self-protection. Well-written grant applications reduce administrative burdens and increase the probability that the funding sources will be able to award more projects. Refer to the section on Tutorials and Other Grantwriting Resources.

*Examples of Federally Supported Tutorial Services.*
SPIRIT was developed for the National Institute of Alcohol Abuse and Alcoholism (NIAAA) to accomplish the following:

- Improve the quality and sharpen the focus of alcohol research proposals by enhancing a user's understanding of the grant application process, from pre-proposal through application, to review and award.
- Facilitate grant development by providing software programs which guide the alcohol researcher through the mechanical procedures required in the PHS 398 grant application kit.
- Increase the accuracy of the budgets sections by incorporating specifically designed spreadsheet programs.
- Enhance research design skills and avoid common, often fatal errors through the use of a research-mentoring program.

The Environmental Protection Agency (EPA) maintains a Website on grant writing. The contents are of use to grantwriters from a wide variety of fields. Even if grants from the EPA are not of interest, this powerful resource created by Purdue University is worthy of review. Contained in the tutorial are examples of completed grant applications, links to useful sites, and a fine glossary of terms.

## RESEARCH PROTECTION AND ETHICAL ISSUES

Institutional Review Boards (IRBs) generally include the following committees:

- Human Subject Protection.
- Biohazard Safety.
- Hazardous Waste.
- Radiological Safety.
- Institutional Animal Care and Use Committee.
- Recombinant DNA.

In general, universities and research organizations follow guidelines that are in accordance with the basic requirements of the Department of Health and Human Services (45 CFR 46) and other federal agencies and offices. Typically, IRB committees are charged with the following responsibilities:

1. the protection of human and animal subjects of research,
2. educating faculty and administrators,
3. assisting with protocol development,
4. reviewing protocols, and
5. maintaining records in accordance with federal government and home institution regulations.

The National Institutes of Health (NIH) maintains an extensive Website containing information, guidance, educational materials, assurance documents, resources, and references related to the protection of human subjects of research. In addition, NIH maintains an equally comprehensive site on the protection of animals (Institutional Animal Use and Care Committee). Refer to IRB Resources and Standards Section at the end of this chapter.

Standards and Certifications by other federal agencies should be carefully followed. For example, the Americans with Disabilities Act published criteria to be used when designing Web-based and other distance learning projects.

## SURVIVING THE PEER REVIEW PROCESS

There are a few strategies that may help principle investigators and program managers from falling into traps that can otherwise doom a good project.

### Common Problems and Fatal Flaws

- Failure to address the mission of the funding source.
- Failing to address all the requirements.

- Being unrealistic.
- No prior knowledge of the funding source's priorities, eligibility criteria, and requirements.
- Responding to the general mission of a funding source and not to a specific Program Announcement (grant), cooperative agreement, or request for proposal (contract).
- Failing to meet the submission deadline. (If the funding agency says 3:00 PM on Tuesday, they don't mean 3:01 PM.)
- Failing to follow directions in the published programs announcement or request for proposal.
- Spelling and grammar errors.
- Sloppy presentation.
- Excuses.
- Assumptions.
- Jargon.

## Problems with Forms and Instructions

*Face page*
- No original signature page.
- Insufficient number of copies.
- Unacceptable font size.
- Incomplete entries.
- Mistakes.

*Abstract Page*
- Lacking in sufficient detail.
- Unclear language.
- Content does not relate to proposed work.

*Budget*
- Arithmetic errors.
- No justification.
- No clear role for proposed personnel or consultant(s).
- Request for equipment in the final year.
- Budget exceeds allowable amount.
- Budget was insufficient or excessive.
- Incomplete forms.

*Personnel (Bibliographic Sketch)*
- No prior experience.
- Unrelated training.

- Poorly presented material.
- Unrelated material.
- Resume not updated since 1978.
- Poor publication record.
- Everyone has better training and experience than the PI.
- Missing biographic sketches.

## Problems in the Body of the Proposal

### *Background*
- No pilot work.
- No basis for proposed work.
- Uncritical acceptance of referenced literature.
- Poor or out-of-date literature review.
- Reliance on non-peer reviewed work.
- Citation problems.
- Failing to reference critical work of peer reviewers.

### *Significance*
- Failure to discuss applied or theoretical significance of the problem.
- Failure to discuss potential contribution to the field of study.
- Failure to convince the committee that the approach to the problem was robust.

### *Rationale*
- Failure to support from the literature, the proposed effort.
- Lack of clarity.
- Failure to convince the committee of the originality of the proposed work.

### *Approach*
- Objectives unclear.
- Design is unclear (e.g., why was a quasi-experimental design selected?).
- Goals and measurable objectives that are unrealistic or do not relate to each other.
- Failure to determine sample size.
- Inadequate recruitment and retention plan (e.g., attrition, replacement).
- Failure to discuss alternative approaches.
- Inadequate discussion of threats to validity and reliability.
- Development of potentially un-testable models.

## Institutional Review Board Issues

### Resources and Environment
- Resources not related to proposed work.
- Resources in a location not discussed in the proposal.
- Old equipment.

### Human Subjects
- Risks to subjects are not adequately addressed.
- Missing or inadequate informed consent statements/forms.
- No IRB approval.

### Animal Use and Care
- No IRB approval.
- Risk not addressed adequately.
- Non-animal model available.
- Problems with rare or endangered species.

### Biohazard, Biosafety, Recombinant DNA
- Failure to provide assurances.

### Resumes
- Failure to update content.
- Failure to demonstrate directly related training and experience.

One of the best strategies for learning about the craft of proposal writing is to serve on grant review panel. Most federal agencies and many foundations ask for volunteer reviewers. For example, go to the Website of an agency or foundation that supports projects in an area where the future principal investigator or program manager has experience as demonstrated by publications and scholarly/technical presentations. Another strategy is to ask colleagues with grant review experience to circulate a resume or CV during the next review meeting.

## ADMINISTERING THE AWARD

Upon acceptance of the award by the home institution, one should carefully review all terms and conditions of the award. Contact the funding agency and discuss any concerns or questions that may have arisen as a consequence of the review process. Meet with the financial officers from the home institution and discuss the procedures related to the expenditure of funds, financial reporting policies, and other related regulations (e.g., human resources, use of state vehicles).

Contact all members of the project team and host a "kick-off meeting" to ensure that everyone involved in the project understands their roles and the principal investigator's expectations regarding their performance. Providing project members with clear written statements regarding project outcomes, deadlines, and other critical information makes the process of conducting the research or project easier to manage.

Although one may not have to be involved with financial reporting and the more administrative functions related to grants management, one should be aware that the federal government and many other funding sources have published numerous regulations regarding how grant and contract money can be expended. The major regulations are listed below.

Most institutions provide a monthly or quarterly report of expenditures on the award. Be sure to carefully review these report to avoid a surprise. Simple typographical errors or transpositions of numbers can create serious problems. Being proactive is the best insurance against over- or underexpenditure of awards.

## White House, Office of Management and Budget

- *A-21 Cost Principles for Educational Institutions*
  The *OMB Circular A-21* establishes principles for determining costs applicable to grants, contracts, and other agreements with educational institutions. The principles deal with the subject of cost determination. The principles are designed to provide that the federal government bears its fair share of total costs, determined in accordance with generally accepted accounting principles, except where restricted or prohibited by law.
- *A-110—Uniform Administrative Requirements for Grants and other Agreements with Institutions of Higher Education, Hospitals and Non-profit Organizations.*
  The purpose of this circular is to set standards for obtaining consistency and uniformity among federal agencies in the administration of grants and agreements with universities.
- *A-133 Audits of States, Local Governments, and Non-Profit Organizations*
  This circular sets standards for the audit of entities expending federal awards.
- *Federal Acquisition Regulations (FARs)*, govern how institutions administer contract awards. The FAR is the primary regulation for use by all federal agencies in their acquisition of supplies and services with appropriated funds (e.g., contracts).

In general, federal regulations govern the administration of awards, including the following in order of precedence:

- Award terms and conditions.
- Special conditions.
- Program rules.
- Agency rules.
- OMB Circulars.

It is a good idea to create a spreadsheet to monitor expenditures, chart progress, examine data, etc. In addition, it is important to contact the funding source if any changes in the proposed work are anticipated. This action may result in renegotiations of the budget. Generally, the overall budget will not be increased; rather individual line items may be changed (e.g., reducing the level of effort of the principal investigator in order to increase the level of effort for the evaluation specialist).

## SAMPLE GRANT PROPOSAL

To assist the reader in proposal preparation, we have provided in Appendix A, a copy of a grant awarded by the Verizon Foundation, Inc. to the University of Maryland Eastern Shore. The authors provide no guarantee that the contents will always result in an award; however, for the first time grantwriter it is usually helpful to have a copy of a funded project to refer to when preparing an initial application.

## WRITING CONTRACT PROPOSALS

While most university faculty receive grants, the authors of this chapter thought it would be useful to say a few words about contracts. Contract awards are performance-based. Work must be performed according to a schedule of deliverables. Unlike grant applications which are investigator driven, contracts are awarded to universities and businesses after the agency identifies a need for a service or a product and publishes a Request for Proposal (RFP). Contracts typically follow a "boilerplate" or predetermined format and may be 100 pages or more in length, unlike grant applications that may be restricted to 25 pages or less. Moreover, contracts generally require two proposals: a technical proposal and a business proposal.

## Technical Proposal Format

- Understanding of the Problem.

- Technical Approach.
- Key Personnel and Management Plan.
- Facilities and Resources.
- Appendices.
  - Resumes.
  - Letters of Commitment.
  - Memorandum of Understanding.

## Business Proposal Format

- Representations and Certifications.
- Budget.
- Justification.

The language used in a contract proposal can differ significantly from that used in a grant application. In Appendix B we have provided the Key Personnel section of a proposal submitted to the Department of Defense (DOD). The full application was reviewed by the DOD and resulted in the award of several task orders (TOs) valued at $1,800,000.

## CONCLUSION

The Internet has solved many problems for the new grantwriter. Funding sources ranging from federal and state government agencies to foundations and private sector sources host Websites that include program announcements, requests for proposals, forms, instructions, and databases full of funded projects. Publications offered by academic publishing houses and university Websites provide step-by-step instructions for creating competitive applications. Moreover, commercial Internet sites offer consultation, from identification of funding sources to proposal writing, through review and award management.

Grantwriters can combine grant writing resources with the ability to:

1. electronically search library holdings,
2. document the rationale for the proposed idea,
3. support the selection of data collection and data analysis strategies,
4. review currently support projects, and
5. locate potential consultants and partners.

Using these capabilities, new grantwriters should be able to develop sophisticated applications that will result in support for distance education projects.

## APPENDIX A: SAMPLE GRANT PROPOSAL

## Executive Summary

*Project Title*
  Digital Divide—Reducing Barriers to Equal Access on Maryland's Eastern Shore

*Amount of Grant Request*
  $24,776

*Description of Project*
  The Digital Divide creates an increasingly difficult problem for residents of the State of Maryland who lack access to computers and information technology. UMES proposes to deliver a certificate program for Eastern Shore teachers and school administrators aimed at increasing the use of information technology for the classroom. Forty participants will attend a series of workshops and hand-on activities conducted by UMES faculty and staff leading to a certificate of accomplishment in information technology for the classroom. Follow-up resources will include access to a password protected Website of tips, tools, and strategies.

  The requested amount of $24,776 will support a year long training program including the purchase and installation of software at participating schools and supporting documentation for participants. A rigorous evaluation plan has been designed to ensure that robust data collection and accompanying analysis plan will provide an accurate picture of project results. The media plan is designed to provide local, regional and national educational audiences and an opportunity to learn about the program and follow its progress. Based on the nature of the data, UMES project staff will submit a paper for presentation at a national conference.

## History and Mission of UMES

  The University of Maryland Eastern Shore (UMES) is a historically black university with an 1890 Land Grant mission. UMES serves primarily African American college students offering BA and BS degrees in 26 disciplines, 13 master level degree programs and two PhD degree programs. To meet the competitive demands of the academic market place, UMES provides a broad range of technical and research training for its faculty and students.

UMES serves constituencies that range from first generation college students to an international clientele including over 3,000 students from across the State of Maryland, around the nation, and from over 50 foreign countries. In keeping with the University's mission, other constituencies are served through inter-agency agreements and contracts with government agencies, business and industry, and the non-profit sector.

The University has dedicated information technology equipment and facilities including smart classrooms that support faculty use of technology in the delivery of instruction. These resources and facilities combined with experienced faculty and staff led to the successful development of instructional packages for K-16 teachers and academics. UMES has been named a Microsoft Mentor and we have taken the lead in delivering instructional technology on Maryland's Eastern Shore.

## Current Programs and Accomplishments

During FY 2000, the University received $11M in grant and contract awards from government agencies, private and business sector sources, and other universities. UMES received a prestigious Theodore M. Hesburg Award for a New Faculty Development Initiative in 1998. Building on this foundation, UMES has initiated a number of faculty, student and staff training programs in the area of technology including Microsoft Office Suite programs, Internet, Webpage development, distance education, and the use of multimedia technologies for the classroom. UMES has been the recipient of federal and private sector grants and contracts (estimated value of $3.5M) to support a wide variety of information technology programs including computer security, training and testing of new technologies, and instructional programs for teachers seeking to include information technology in the classroom. Moreover, UMES took the lead in winning a $333,000 multi-university grant awarded from the Maryland Higher Education Commission to create information technology faculty development training programs on Maryland's Eastern Shore.

## Project Description

### Problem—Background

Defined broadly, the Digital Divide describes the growing disparity between information technology "haves" and "have-nots". CitySkills, a grass roots organization working to improve workforce development in information technology, reports that the Digital Divide is "...most acute across the divisions of race, ethnicity, and socio-economic lines." This statement is supported by the US Department of Commerce 1999 report that states that households with incomes of over $75,000 were 20 times more likely to have Internet access and nine times more likely to have a home computer. Further, 40% of non-minorities were reported to have Internet access compared to approximately 19.5% of African Americans and Hispanics.

The theory that the Internet would become an equalizing force has been proven false. A Markle Foundation supported study noted that the "...same divergence found in society along cultural and racial lines is found online and offline."

### *Location and Target Audience*

The location for the intervention is counties on the Eastern Shore. These counties experience low educational attainment rates and high unemployment and underemployment rates when compared with other counties in the State of Maryland. While local schools have access to information technology, the resources tend to be on the low-end of technology with little access to programs for teacher training and certification. There exists no point of access to the high-speed network outside of the University of Maryland Eastern Shore.

Access to grant supported training through the use of UMES's capabilities can offer teachers and administrators an opportunity to experience the power of information technology and the knowledge to seek additional support to obtain the necessary resources including smart classrooms, high-speed connectivity, computers, and related resources.

UMES plans to train forty (40) teachers and school administrators during the initial year of the project.

## Funding Request

The University is requesting costs to cover release time for an Instructional Technologist, who will work 30% time on the project and costs to support two (2) graduate assistants, purchase for software (e.g., up grades to Microsoft Office Suite, Web authoring tools for participating local schools) and supporting materials (e.g., textbooks, references, and manuals) for these schools.

The Instructional Technologist and graduate assistants will design and deliver the courses listed in the Primary Purpose section of the proposal. The courses will be based on similar programs originally designed for university faculty. Modifications will ensure that the content and the products resulting from the training meet the needs of a K-12 audience. Purchase and installation software will ensure that the local school system has programs that are compatible with UMES and other USM schools. This strategy will allow the school system to operate on a common platform with its mentors and access Internet-based resources.

The University will contribute release time for a Project Administrator and a Project Evaluator. Moreover, the University will make available to counties on the Eastern Shore, Web-based resources and computer laboratories to ensure the continuation of the project after the initial period of support.

Software will be installed at participating sites and materials, books and supporting documentation will be given to each participant.

In addition, project staff will continue to work with current and new funding sources to enhance and sustain the project after the initial period of support. Refer to the section on Sustainability.

| Personnel: | Salary & Fringe |
|---|---|
| Principal Investigator | Contributed |
| Instructional Technologist | $10,476 |
| Graduate Assistants ($2,500 x 2) | $ 5,000 |
| Evaluator | Contributed |
| **Other Direct Costs**: | |
| Software | $ 7,900 |
| Duplication | 750 |
| Books and materials | 650 |
| Computer labs | Contributed |
| Website site support | Contributed |
| Templates and other online resources | Contributed |
| Total | $ 24,776 |

## Primary Purpose

UMES recognizes the need to address the effects of the digital divide among the residents of the Eastern Shore, particularly among African Americans and the economically disadvantaged. UMES plans to design and implement a program of activities including hands-on workshops for teachers and school administrators aimed at increasing their information technology knowledge and skill sets.

### Goals

The goals of the proposed effort are designed to:

a.   increase teacher and administrator understanding of the importance of information technology,

b.   increase the use of information technology in the classroom,

c.   provide a certificate program for teachers and administrators seeking continuing education credits, and

d.   provide strategies for identifying additional sources of funding to support the purchase of necessary resources and tools.

### Objectives

UMES will modify an existing set of workshops to meet the needs of a K-12 audience of teachers and administrators. In addition, existing materials will be redesigned to accompany the workshops and to provide references for later use.

**Workshops** will include the following topics:

- PC Basics And Introduction To The Internet (4 Hours).
- Using Classroom-Based Information Technology Tools (7 Hours).
- Using The WWW For Educators (3.5 Hours).
- Creating A Classroom Website (3.5 Hours).
- Concepts Of Instructional Design (1 Hours).
- Creating An Online Presentation (2 Hours).
- Collaborating Online (1.5 Hours).
- Using Scheduling And Time Management Tools (1.5 Hours).
- Identifying Funding Sources To Support IT Development (1 Hour).

Total hours—25 hours

### Follow-up Resources

Participants will have access to a password-protected Website of resources located on the UMES homepage. These Internet-based resources will contain electronic templates (e.g., syllabus, seating charts, grade book calculator), news (e.g., future training events), and access to a chatroom dedicated to using technology in the classroom.

### Certificate and Continuing Education Credits

Participants will receive a certificate of completion and access to follow-up resources that will are located on the UMES home page. Participants seeking continuing education credit can apply to the University's Office of Continuing Education for up to 25 hours of continuing education credits.

## Timeline—Month One

- Inform UMES and staff and partners.
- Conduct planning meeting with all involved staff and partners.
- Arrange for release time for UMES staff and hire graduate students.
- Dedicate resources and facilities.

- Notify teachers and administrators.
- Development media materials.
- Announce the award.
- Develop a pre- and post-test data collection instrument and a satisfaction survey.
- Test instruments for reliability.
- Initiate data collection.

## Month Two

- Purchase materials and software.
- Book conference and training facilities.
- Hold orientation meetings with teachers and administrators.
- Conduct registration.
- Redesign training content and materials based on input from teachers and administrators.
- Conduct pre-test assessment.

## Months Three through Twelve and Beyond

- Conduct training.
- Continue media and other reporting activities.
- Provide mentoring and consultation services.
- Continue data collection.
- Prepare and submit grant applications to external funding agencies.
- Provide certifications and CEUs.
- Analyze data and prepare a report on first year's activities.
- Continue to seek funding support to enhance teacher and administrator training.
- Make presentations and, if warranted, submit a paper to an academic journal.

### Recruitment of Participant

UMES staff will work with teachers and administrator to identify a pool of applicants. A registration process will be designed to ensure that the applicants have a common set of skills (e.g., basic computer and Internet skills), and the interest and the commitment to complete the certificate process. In addition, applicants must have the approval of their supervisors prior to completing the application progress. A pool of replacements will be developed and special "catch-up" mentoring will be provided to a small number of participants.

*Project Personnel—Key Personnel and Program Administration*

UMES is the applicant organization on behalf of the education community. (Refer to letter of collaboration and support in Appendix A. [Editor's Note: This Appendix is not included in this chapter.]) The grant will be administratively managed by UMES in compliance with the Verizon Foundation, Inc. regulations and policies.

Project staff include a Project Administrator, Instructional Technologist and two graduate students. The staff has been selected based on their expertise in technology training and good pedagogical techniques. The **Project Administrator**, Vice President for Information Technology, will be responsible for the oversight of the project and will interact with institutions to ensure compliance with the proposed effort and preparation of reports. Dr. Right's time will be contributed to the project. The **Instructional Technologist**, Mr. Smith, has an extensive background in the development and delivery of faculty training programs. Mr. Smith will be responsible for redesigning existing workshops and materials to meet the needs of a K-12 audience, scheduling and delivery of training, and follow-up. The **Evaluator**, Mrs. Black, has an extensive background in the evaluation of educational and psychosocial research. The Evaluator will be responsible for the development of the pre- and post- test assessment instrument and satisfaction survey, data collection, analysis of data, and preparation of a report of results. The **graduate students** will assist the Instructional Technologist in the delivery of the workshops, workshop scheduling, installation of software, and troubleshooting. Refer to Appendix B for resumes. [Editor's Note: This Appendix is not included in this chapter.]

*Duration of the Project and Period of Performance*

One Year—October 1, 2002 to September 30, 2003

## Sustainability

UMES will seek opportunities to continue the project as part of its commitment to community outreach and enhancement of instruction using new and emerging technologies. UMES will identify potential funding sources including local, state, federal government support, foundation and private sector support, and delivery of fee-for-service continuing education and certificate programs. Programs supported by the US Department of Education, US Department of Agriculture, National Science Foundation, State of Maryland, and Maryland foundations will be examined and applications submitted during the first six months of operation of the project.

Given the successful track record of securing external support, UMES anticipates continuation and likely enhancement of the proposed effort.

## Evaluation Plan

Two levels of evaluation will be used to assess the project's outcomes.

### Pre- and Post-Test Assessment

The evaluation will consist of a quasi-experimental design. A pre-test survey instrument will examine dependent measures (e.g., information technology knowledge, intention to use technology in the classroom) prior to implementation of the training. A post-test will be conducted in two waves: immediate post-intervention and three months (the second post-intervention test will measure the robustness of the intervention over time). The pre-test measures will serve as covariates and post-test measures will serve as dependent measures.

Dependent measures will consist of the following: knowledge acquisition, attendance, and reported behavioral intentions. Existing scales that have been validated and found reliable will be used for the purpose of evaluation.

### Satisfaction Survey

Using a Likert scale developed by the project evaluator, teachers and administrators will ask participants to rate the quality of the workshops and gains in knowledge.

### Analysis

Analysis of data will be conducted by the evaluator. The results will be included as part of the final reports.

## Media Plan

UMES will use the skills and resources of it's Community Outreach and Public Affairs staff to develop and disseminate information to the print and electronic media regarding the project including Verizon's involvement in the current effort and related resources. Our professional staff has extensive experience in the development and careful implementation of media campaigns. The media plan will include, but not be limited to, the following:

- A press conference/planned media event will be held with UMES's WESM 91.3 radio station and local print and TV media to announce the project.
- A Website dedicated to the project with links to Verizon's site and related sites will be linked to the UMES homepage.
- Press release/media advisories/press kits will be designed to highlight the program and its expected outcome.
- Press release/media advisories/press kits will be designed to highlight accomplishments of the program.
- Development of a project newsletter for dissemination locally, regionally and nationally to other educational communities outlining the objectives of the program and its successes.
- Quarterly and annual reports will be prepared and will contain sufficient detail to cover each aspect of the project including results of the evaluation.
- Based on the nature of the data, UMES project staff will submit a paper for presentation at a national conference. If warranted by the quality of the data and nature of he findings, a paper will be submitted to a peer-reviewed journal for publication.

Appendix—Letters of Support
Appendix—Resumes
[Editor's Note: These appendices are not included in this chapter.]

## APPENDIX B: EXCERPT FROM A DOD CONTRACT PROPOSAL

### Task Area 1: Program and Task Order Management.

This section represents the organizational and staffing structure, operating and control procedures, and scheduling and reporting functions, as well as key personnel for the University of Maryland Eastern Shore and its partner corporations. Our management approach is designed to ensure the high degree of efficiency, responsiveness, and quality required to provide DISA with the services described in DCA100-99-R-4030.

The personnel UMES and its partner corporations will assign to the project include:

- A UMES Project Manager who has a MS degree and over 20 years of experience in the management of technical, logistical and publications contracts and grants with the federal government and private sector clients;

- A UMES Project Leader who has a PhD in Engineering and over five years of high-end technical expertise in IT project management and training projects;
- Corporate partners, Cetech, Inc., Cinecom, Inc., Columbia Services Group, Inc., and Modern Technology Systems, Inc. that are experienced in the support services listed in the SOW Tasks Areas;
- A management structure that provides experienced UMES and partner organization staff in key positions that will ensure that the diverse requirements of this procurement will be effectively and efficiently met;
- A management and supervisory structure that provides ready access and integration of a wide range of staff expertise to meet the varied requirements of this procurement and will accommodate varying workloads;
- A diversity of expertise ranging from administrative management of large federal procurements through high-end information technology expertise to a broad range of technical and logistical skills;
- An effective quality control plan that includes a quality control group composed of senior UMES and corporate partners who will meet regularly to review progress/products and provide advice and guidance to the project team;

| | University of Maryland Eastern Shore | Cetech, Inc. | Cinecom, Inc. | Columbia Services Group, Inc. | Modern Technology Solutions, Inc. |
|---|---|---|---|---|---|
| TA 1: Program and Task Order Management | • | • | • | • | • |
| TA 2: Systems Engineering | • | • | • | • | • |
| TA 3: Telecommunication | • | • | • | • | |
| TA 4: Acquisition Management | • | • | • | • | • |
| TA 5: Software/Computer Systems/Ntwrk App Dev and Support | • | | • | • | • |
| TA 6: Systems Evaluation, Integration and Testing Services | • | | • | • | |
| TA 7: Program and Information Management | • | • | • | • | • |
| TA 8: Information Systems Security and Information Assurance | • | • | | | |
| TA 9: Modeling and Simulation | • | | | | |
| TA 10: Electronic Commerce/Electronic Business | • | | | • | |
| TA 11: Information Technology Training | • | • | • | | |
| TA 12: Studies in Advanced Information Technologies | • | • | | • | |
| TA 13: Business Process Re-Engineering | • | | • | • | • |

SAMPLE EXHIBIT 1
Corporate Skills Matrix

- University and corporate partners who are committed to this project, as evidenced by senior staff placed in key roles, our experience in federal contracting, information technology, computer science, training, and publishing;
- Procedures to ensure effective and efficient scheduling and management of Task Orders and sub-tasks, documents and materials preparation; and,
- Senior staff with training and experience in contract administration including financial management, accounting, and auditing services.

UMES and its corporate partners will form a management team responsible for the development and delivery of products required under each Task Order approved by DISA Contract Officer.

## Project Operation

UMES and its partner organizations have established the following guidelines for the management and administrative components of the project:

- *Efficiency and Effectiveness*—to coordinate and integrate all project tasks and sub-tasks and participants through appropriate staffing and clear reporting relationships;
- *Flexibility*—to provide both the specialized expertise and depth of personnel required to meet diverse support needs and peak-load periods;
- *Cost Control*—to deliver task products within planned person-hour and dollar budgets; and,
- *Quality Control*—to produce high-quality, innovative task products in a timely manner.

Our plan to achieve these objectives consists of an experienced project team, a full range of supporting facilities and resources, and sound project management and operating procedures. Using these components as the basis of our management plan will assure successful performance of the project.

## Task Staffing and Use of Resources and Facilities

The plans that UMES and its partner corporations implement for organizing and managing staff are designed to achieve maximum flexibility. Assignment of personnel to specific tasks and sub-tasks and use of resources and facilities will depend on DISA's specific needs and requirements.

Our task-oriented system entails the assignment of a Task Coordinator and, as warranted, specialists for each task and sub-task coordinators will be assigned according to the nature of the assignment, resources availability, and particular set of skills and areas of expertise required by the DISA Contract Officer.

The Project Manager and the Project Leader will work collaboratively with the partner corporations to select the most appropriate staff, the staffing level, and the resources and facilities to ensure an appropriate skill mix, level of effort, and ability to deliver required services and products on time and within budget. For each task and sub-task, specific needs requirements will be assessed and leadership assigned to the staff most qualified to meet those needs.

Each partner corporation will have a Co-Project Manager and a Co-Project Leader. Their roles and responsibilities will mirror those of UMES key personnel. The UMES Project Manager will assume responsibility to the total project. Refer to Appendix C for Memorandum of Understanding among the participating corporations. [Editor's Note: This Appendix is not included in this chapter.]

## Quality Assurance

In order to provide DISA with quality products delivered in a timely manner, UMES and its partner corporations believe there are three key elements to success:

1. highly competent and motivated staff of technical experts,
2. an organizational design capable of being responsive to the needs of DISA, and
3. development and implementation of an efficient quality assurance system.

This section describes the methodology that we will apply to ensure that both technical and contractual obligations are met effectively.

Our quality assurance plan comprises two components:

1. quality control and
2. technical services evaluation.

The first component of this effort, quality control, will encompass monitoring all aspects of each task and sub-task in order to anticipate potential problems and to assess our performance against its contractual obligations.

The second component will include the evaluation of the technical services provided by the staff to ensure that they are of consistently high quality and are tailored to the needs and requirements of DISA.

Procedures we plan to use in assuring the highest quality of DISA products and services include:

- Involvement of the Project Manager and the Project Leader in all aspects of the contract;
- Involvement of the partner corporations in the development, management and delivery of each Task Order based on their areas of expertise;
- Periodic project review, at least biweekly, by the Project Manger, Project Leader, Co-Project Mangers and Co-Project Leaders and key personnel (key personnel will change to meet the needs of the DISA Contracts Officer) to review all task in terms of method, approach, progress, plans, schedule, and costs;
- Reviews by A UMES Project Manager and Co-Project Managers from each corporate partner to include occasional attendance at project meetings and focused reviews of individual task and products;
- Day-to-day attention by the Project Managers and Co-Project Managers and Project Leader and corporate Co-Project Leaders to task performance, including accuracy, timeliness, completeness, precision, and appropriateness;
- Supervision of task and sub-task and attention deadlines by all staff; and,
- Maintenance of frequent communications with the DISA Contracts Officer to review progress and performance, identify or potential problems, and seek solutions.

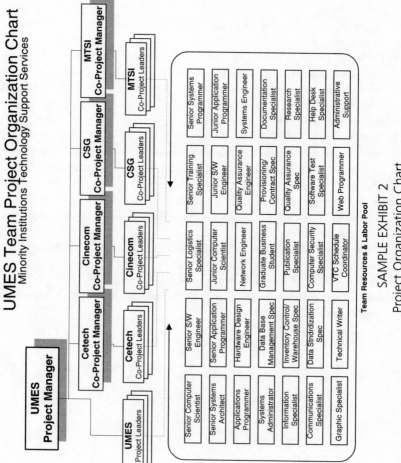

**UMES Team Project Organization Chart**
Minority Institutions Technology Support Services

SAMPLE EXHIBIT 2
Project Organization Chart

## REFERENCES

Bolek, Catherine, Bielawski, Larry, Niemcryk Steve, Needle, Richard, Baker, Steve, "Developing a Competitive Research Proposal, *Ethnic and Multicultural Drug Abuse, Perspectives on Current Research,* Haworth Press, New York, 1992.

Peterson, Susan, The Grantwriter's Internet Companion, Corwin Press, Inc., California, 2001.

## RESOURCES

### Search Engines

**Altavista**, www.altavista.digal.com
**AskJeeves**, www.askjeeves.com/
**Dogpile**, www.dogpile.com/
**FindWhat**, www.findwhat.com
**Go,** www.go.com
**Google**, www.google.com
**Hotbot**, www.hotbot.com
**Infoseek**, www, infoseek.com
**Lycos**, www.lycos.com
**Metacrawler**, www.metacrawler.com/index.html
**Teoma**, www.teoma.com
**Tracerlock**, www.tracerlock.com/
**Yahoo**, www.yahoo.com.

### Information Sources on the Internet

**ADEC,** homepage, http://www.adec.edu.
**ADEC,** Federal Programs and Grants, http://www.adec.edu/fed-pgms.html.
**Adobe Acrobat Reader,** http/adobe.com/products/acrobat/read-step.htm
**ARIS Student Funding,** http://www.arisnet.com/newstu.html.
**Athabascau University,** Distance Education, Resources. http://ccism.pc.athabascau.ca/html/ccism/deresrce/de.htm.
**Catalog of Federal Domestic Assistance**, http://www.cfds.gov/public/cat-writing.htm.
**The Charity Channel**, http://charitychannel.com.
**The Chronicle of Higher Education,** http://chronicle.com.
**The Chronicle of Philanthropy,** http://www.philanthropy.com.
**Council on Foundations,** Technology: Web-based Grant Applications:

Several Grantmakers are Trying Out New Online Proposal Systems, http://www.cof.org.

**Cybergrant Services**, http://cybergrants.com/.

**Department of Education**, http://www.ed.gov/funding.html.

**Department of Health and Human Services**, Support Services Center including access to grant application forms, http://forms.psc.gov/forms/SF/sf.html.

**Dell Foundation**, grant making restricted to Texas, http://www.dell.com/us/en/gen/default.htm.

**Distance Education Clearinghouse, Funding,** http://www.uwex.edu/disted/zfunding.html.

**Distance Educator,** http://www.distance-educator.com.

**Educause,** professional services for electronic education, http://www.educause.edu/.

**Federal Acquisition Jumpstation,** access to all federal agencies, http://nais.nasa.gov/fedproc/home.html.

**FEDIX,** federal funding opportunities, provides an e-mail alert services, http://content.sciencewise.com/fedix/aid/index.htm.

**Federal Business Opportunities (Fedbizops),** http://www.fedbizopps.gov/.

**Foundation Center,** http://fdncenter.org.

**Funding Sources for Water Quality**, http://www.nal.usda.gov/wqic/funding.html.

**Gates Learning Foundation,** http://www.gatesfoundation.org/.

**Georgetown University,** http://gulib.lausun.georgetown.edu/internet/effectiv.htm.

**Grant Search and Information,** http://www.silcom.com/~paladin/grants.html.

**GrantsNet** provides free membership, http://grantsnet.com.

**GrantsNet**, DHHS, http://www.hhs.gov/grantsnet.

**GrantSelect**, http://grantselect.com.

**Harvard Graduate School of Education,** federal forms and budget templates available in Excel, http://www.gse.harvard.edu/~hgseosr/proposals-templates.html.

**Instructional Technology Council**, http://www.itcnetwork.org/grants.htm.

**International Center for Distance Education,** http://www-icdl.open.ac.uk.

**International Funding Sources**, http://www.uiowa.edu/~vpr/research/sources/intfund.htm.

**MOLIS,** minority funding opportunities, http://content.sciencewise.com/molis.

**National Archives,** http://www.nara.gov.

**National Endowment for the Arts,** http://arts.endow.gov.

**National Endowment for the Humanities,** http://www.neh.fed.us.

**National Network for Child Care,** http://www.nncc.org/Funding/funding.page.html, provides access to sources of grant funds and related resources.

**National Network of Grantmakers,** http://www.nng.org.

**National Oceanographic and Atmospheric Administration,** http://www.rdc.noaa.gov/~grants.

**National Science Foundation,** https://www.fastlane.nsf.gov/a0/about/fastlane_history.htm, Fastlane, electronic proposal submission information.

**Northwest Educational Technology Consortium,** Grant and Funding Information, http://www.netc.org/grants.

**Novel,** donations of equipment and programs, http://www.novell.com.

**Packard Foundation,** wide variety of program grants, http://www.packard.org.

**Procurement Jumpstation,** http://www.opm.gov/procure/HTML/FEDERAl.HTM.

**The Office of Management and Budget,** Circular A-21, forth cost principles for educational institutions, http://www.whitehouse.gov/omb/circulars/a021/a021.html.

**Resources for Distance Education,** http://Webster.commnet.edu/HP/pages/darling/distance.htm.

**Resource Guide for Federal Funding of Technology in Education,** http://www.ed.gov/Technology/tec-guid.html.

**ScienceWise,** http://content.sciencewise.com/fedix/aid/index.htm.

**SBIR/STTR,** http://www.zyn.com/sbir/, small business innovative research grants.

**Small Business Administration,** federal Grants Resources, http://www.sba.gov/expanding/grants.html.

**Society of Research Administrators,** GrantWeb, http://www.srainternational.org/NewWeb/default.cfm.

**TGIC International Grants,** http://www.tgci.com/intl.

**Tracerlock,** http://www.tracerlock.com, create a customized Internet profile of resources.

**United States Department of Agriculture,** http://content.sciencewise.com/fedix/agr/index.htm?id=-1.

**Verizon,** technology in the classroom grants, http://foundation.verizon.com/index.shtml.

**WestEd,** grant writing resources and tools, http://www.wested.org/tie/grant.html.

**World Wide Web, Distance Education,** set-up problems, scroll down to locate resources, http://www.cisnet.com/~cattales/Deducation.html.

**Writing a Competitive Proposal,** http://www.umes.edu/osrp, a step by step PowerPoint presentation on contract writing prepared by Catherine Bolek and Ronald Forsythe for the Society for Information Technology Educators national conference, August 2001.

## DISTANCE EDUCATION FUNDING SOURCES

### Federal Funding Sources

**Department of Agriculture,** http://www.tgci.com/fedrgtxt/00-28388.txt.

**Department of Education** - http://www.tgci.com/fedrgtxt/01-1243.txt.

**Department of Defense,** National Security Education Program (NSEP) Institutional Grants Program, http://www.ndu.edu/nsep.

**Department of Health and Human Services,** Support Services Center including access to grant application forms, http://forms.psc.gov/forms/SF/sf.html.

**Federal Acquisition Jumpstation,** guide to federal grants and contracts accessible through the Internet, http://nais.nasa.gov/fedproc/home.html.

**Federal Market Place,** great source of federal information, http://www.proposalworks.com.

**FEDIX,** federal funding opportunities, http://content.science-wise.com/fedix/aid/index.htm.

**MOLIS,** minority funding opportunities, http://content.science-wise.com/molis.

**Environmental Protection Agency,** Grant Writing Tutorial, http://www.epa.gov/seahome/grants/src/msieopen.htm.

**National Science Foundation,** http://www.nsf.gov.

**National Space and Atmospheric Administration,** http://ideas.stsci.edu/.

**National Institutes of Health,** http://www.nih.gov.

### State Sources

**National Association of State Procurement Officers,** http://www.naspo.org.

**State and Local Government Listings on the Federal Market Place,** http://www.fedmarket.com/sales_resources/jumpstation/bids/state_local.html.

### Non-Federal Sources

**Adobe,** partners in education, http://www.adobe.com.

**Alfred P. Sloan Research Fellowships,** http://www.sloan.org/programs/fellowship_brochure.htm.

**Anheuser-Busch Foundation Grants,** http://www.anheuser-busch.com.

**AT&T Foundation,** http://www.att.com/foundation/index.html.

**Benton Foundation,** communication http://www.benton.org/ in the public interest.

**Chatlos Foundation,** http://www.chatlos.org.

**Compaq Computer Teaching with Technology Grants,** http:// www6.compaq.com/education/k12.

**John and Mary R. Markle Foundation,** grants, http://www.markle.org/ grants/index.html.

**Distance Education Clearinghouse, Funding,** http://www.uwex.edu/ disted/zfunding.html

**Hewlett Foundation,** http://www.hewlett.org.

**Paul G. Allen Foundation Virtual Education Grants,** http://www.paula-llen.com/foundations.

**SBA Foundation,** http://www.sbc.com/Community/SBC_Foundation.

**William Bingham Foundation,** http://www.pgafoundations.com.

**Verizon Foundation Grants,** http://foundation.verizon.com.


## GRANTWRITERS AND CONSULTANTS


**Association of Fund Raising Professionals** located at http:// www.nsfre.com.

**National Grantwriters Association** located at www.researchassoci-atesco.com/ngwa.htm.

**International Alliance of Grant and Nonprofit Management Consultants** located at http://www.iaogwanc.org/aboutus.asp.

INFORMATION SOURCES IN PRINT

**Annual Register of Grant Support,** National Register Publishing Co.

**Directory of Research Grants,** The Oryx Press.

**Foundation Grants to Individuals,** Foundation Center, Washington, DC.

**The Internet for Dummies,** 6th[h] Edition John R. Levine, Carol, Baroudi, Margaret Levine Young and Hy Beneder, IDG Books World Wide, 2000.

**Demystifying Grant Seeking: What You REALLY Need to Do to Get Grants,** Larissa Golden Brown, Martin John Brown, Judith E. Nichols.


## DATABASES OF FUNDED PROJECTS


**Canadian Database of Distance Education Activities,** http:// node.on.ca/courses.

**Community of Science**, funded research database, http://login.cos.com.

**CRISP**, National Institutes of Health, database on grant awards, https://www-commons.cit.nih.gov/crisp/.

**Department of Education**, grant award database, http://gcs.ed.gov/grntinfo/grntawd.htm.

**National Library of Medicine**, funded projects, http://www.nlm.nih.gov/ep/funded.html.

**National Science Foundation**, grant award database, http://www.nsf.gov/home/grants/grants_awards.htm.

## JOURNALS AND NEWSLETTERS

**Compendium of Electronic Resources for Distance Education**, http://www.oak-ridge.com/ierdrep1.html.

**Distance Education Journals**, http://seamonkey.ed.asu.edu/~mcisaac/disted/journals.html.

**Education Journals**, http://www.scre.ac.uk/is/Webjournals.html.

**Educational Journals**, http://www.columbia.edu/~sss31/Education/journals.html.

**Journals and Newsletters for Distance Education**, http://Webster.commnet.edu/HP/pages/darling/journals.htm.

**World Wide Web Virtual Library - Distance Education**, http://www.cis-net.com/~cattales/Deducation.html.

## LIBRARIES

**Association of Research Libraries**, http://www.arl.org.

**Berkeley's compendium of library resources**, http://sunsite.berkeley.edu/LibWeb.

**Choice, academic reviews**, http://www.ala.org/acrl/choice/home.html.

**ERIC**, the education database, http://www.askeric.org.

**Library of Congress**, http://www.loc.gov.

**National Library of Medicine**, http://www.nlm.nih.gov.

**Presidential Libraries**, http://www.nara.gov/nara/president/address.html.

**Special Libraries Association**, http://www.sla.org.

**Stanford**, library resources, http://www-sul.stanford.edu.

**The English Server**, http://eserver.org.
**Yahoo**, library resources, http://dir.yahoo.com/Reference/Libraries/
Academic_Libraries/.


## TUTORIALS AND OTHER GRANTWRITING RESOURCES

**AIResources, Inc.**, SPIRIT, http://www.airesources.net/spirit.
**California Department of Education,** tutorial on educational grant writing, http://www.cde.ca.gov/iasa/writing2.html.
**Catalog of Federal Domestic Assistance**, Developing and Writing Grant Proposals, http://aspe.hhs.gov/cfda/ia6.htm.
**Copyright information,** http://www.uwex.edu/disted/zintprop.html.
**Department of Energy,** Grant Application Guide, http://www.er.doe.gov/production/grants/guide.html.
**Department of Health and Human Services**, "Developing a Proposal", http://www.cfda.gov/public/cat-writing.htm.
**Environmental Protection Agency,** Grant-Writing Tutorial, http://www.epa.gov/seahome/grants.html.
**Evaluation of distance education programs,** http://www.uwex.edu/disted/evaluation.html.
**Foundation Center,** Proposal Writing Short Course, http://fdn-center.org/learn/shortcourse/prop1.html.
**Guide to Proposal Planning and Writing,** http://www.whitaker.org/sanders.html.
**National Institute of Health**, Hints for Writing Successful , NIH grants, http://chroma.med.miami.edu/research/Ellens_how_to.html.
**Oryx Press**, Guide to Proposal Planning and Writing, http://www.oryx-press.com/miner.htm.
**Proposal Writing & Research Development,** http://www.umass.edu/research/ora/dev.html.
**Public Broadcasting Corporation**, Basic Elements of Grant Writing, http://www.cpb.org/grants/grantwriting.html.
**University of Wisconsin Madison**, proposal writing, http://www.library.wisc.edu/libraries/Memorial/grants/proposal.htm.


## APPLICATION FORMS AND TEMPLATES

**Catalog of Federal Domestic Assistance,** Federal application forms, http://aspe.os.dhhs.gov/funding.htm.
**Centers for Disease Control and Prevention**, http://www.cdc.gov/od/pgo/forminfo.htm.

**Department of Education,** http://gcs.ed.gov/grntinfo/appforms.htm.

**Department of Energy Application Forms,** http://www.science.doe.gov/production/grants/forms.html.

**Department of Health and Human Services,** Program Support Center, http://forms.psc.gov/forms/SF/sf.html.

**Multi-agency forms,** Office of Management and Budget, http://www.whitehouse.gov/omb/grants/#forms.

- SF-424, Application for Federal Assistance.
- SF-424A, Budget Information - Nonconstruction Programs.
- SF-424B, Assurances - Nonconstruction Programs.
- SF-424C, Budget Information - Construction Programs.
- SF-424D, Assurances - Construction Programs.
- SF-269, Financial Status Report (Long Form).
- SF-269A, Financial Status Report (Short Form).
- SF-270, Request for Advance or Reimbursement.
- SF-271, Outlay Report and Request for Reimbursement for Construction Programs.
- SF-272, Federal Cash Transactions Report.
- SF-272A, Federal Cash Transactions Report.
- SF-LLL, Disclosure of Lobbying Activities – as codified in 1989.
- SF-LLL, Disclosure of Lobbying Activities – as revised in 1996
- SF-SAC, Data Collection Form for Single Audits.

**National Endowment for the Humanities,** http://www.neh.fed.us/grants.

**National Institutes of Health,** http://grants.nih.gov/grants/forms.htm.

**National Science Foundation,** http://www.nsf.gov/home/grants.htm.

**TRAM,** multiple agency forms site from Texas Research Administrators Group, http://tram.east.asu.edu/forms.

## GRANT AND CONTRACT POLICIES

**Catalog of Federal Domestic Assistance,** http://www.cfda.gov/

**Commerce Business Daily (CBD),** http://cbdnet.access.gpo.gov/

**Federal Acquisitions Regulations (FARs),** http://www.arnet.gov/far/

**Federal Market Place,** http://www.fedmarket.com/

**National Archives,** http://www.nara.gov

**Chief Financial Officer's Council Grants Management Committee,** grant policies, http://www.financenet.gov/financenet/fed/cfo/grants/grants.htm.

**Federal Assistance Award Data System,** Federal Assistance Award Data System, http://www.census.gov/govs/www/faads.html.

**Federal Audit Clearinghouse,** http://www.census.gov/govs/www/faads.html.

**Federal Register,** http://www.access.gpo.gov/su_docs/aces/aces140.html

**General Services Administration (GSA),** http://www.gsa.gov/Portal/home.jsp

**Office of Management and Budget, Circulars,** A-21, A-110, A133, http://www.georgetown.edu/finaff/budget/cost.htm.

## CLEARINGHOUSES AND RESEARCH INFORMATION

**Adult Education Data and Statistics,** http://www.ed.gov/offices/OVAE/datahome.html.

**Adult Education and Literacy Clearinghouse,** http://www.ed.gov/offices/OVAE/division.html.

**Argus Clearinghouse,** http://www.clearinghouse.net.

**Distance Education Clearinghouse,** http://www.uwex.edu/disted/home.html.

**ERIC Clearinghouse on Adult, Career, and Vocational Education,** http://erciacve.org.

**ERIC Clearinghouse for Community Colleges,** http://www.gseis.ucla.edu/ERIC/eric.html.

**National Center for Education Statistics** http://nces.ed.gov.

## DISTANCE LEARNING ASSOCIATIONS

**ADEC,** http://www.adec.edu.

**Commonwealth of Learning,** http://www.col.org/resources/Weblinks/associations.htm.

**Compendium of Distance Learning Associations**, http://dmoz.org/Reference/Education/Distance_Learning/Associations.

**Google compendium**, http://directory.google.com/Top/Reference/Education/Distance_Learning/As sociations.

**United States Distance Learning Association**, http://www.usdla.org.

## IRB AND STANDARDS RESOURCES

**American With Disabilities Act,** http://www.usdoj.gov/crt/ada/adahom1.htm

**Animal Welfare Information Center,** http://www.nal.usda.gov/awic.

**Code of Federal Regulations,** http://www.med.umich.edu/irbmed/ FederalDocuments/hhs/HHS45CFR46.html.

**Department of Education,** http://www.ed.gov/offices/OCFO/human-sub.html.

**International Fund for Animal Welfare,** http://www.ifaw.org.

**Office for Human Research Protections,** http://ohrp.osophs.dhhs.gov.

**Office of Laboratory Animal Welfare, National Institutes of Health,** http://grants.nih.gov/grants/olaw/olaw.htm.

# ABOUT THE AUTHORS

**James Benjamin**, PhD is Associate Director and Faculty Training Coordinator in the Division of Distance Learning at The University of Toledo. He is also a Professor in the Department of Communication. He taught at The University of Hawaii and at Southwest Texas State University before joining the faculty at The University of Toledo in 1986. He has developed and taught a variety of undergraduate and graduate communication courses in both traditional and distance learning formats. His distance learning courses have included both interactive television and Internet formats. He is the author of over two dozen research and instructional publications including articles in *Philosophy and Rhetoric, Presidential Studies Quarterly, Communication Quarterly,* and *The Southern Speech Communication Journal.* His most recent article appeared in *Distance Education Report.* He is also the author of several textbooks in the field of communication including *Principles, Elements, Techniques of Persuasion* published by Harcourt.

**Catherine S. Bolek,** Director for Sponsored Research and Programs, University of Maryland Eastern Shore, Princess Anne, Maryland. Directs a program of institutional oversight for approximately $13.5 million of externally funded projects, teaches information technology and proposal writing courses, and serves as the Principal Investigator for multiple government and private sector contracts and grants.

Electronic Learning Communities—Issues and Practices, pages 549–554.
Copyright © 2003 by Information Age Publishing, Inc.
All rights of reproduction in any form reserved.
ISBN: 1-931576-96-3 (pbk.), 1-931576-97-1 (hardcover)

**David Brigham**, Ph.D. is the Dean of Learning Services at Excelsior College where he oversees the development and maintenance of the College's student support services, including the Electronic Peer Network described in this chapter.

**John Bryan** is Dean of the University of Cincinnati's University College and is Associate Professor of English in the College of Arts and Sciences where he teaches professional writing, document design, and desktop publishing. He taught his first online course in 1992. Before returning to academic life in 1989, he worked for 10 years as a technical writer and marketing manager for engineering firms in Colorado and Missouri.

**Sally Dresdow**, Associate Professor in Business Administration at the University of Wisconsin Green Bay, brings to her teaching over 10 years of management experience in the private sector and 10 years of college level teaching. Her asynchronous courses incorporate many collaborative learning principles, and she has worked with numerous colleagues in helping them develop online courses.

**Dr. Denzil Edge**, Associate Editor, is the President and CEO of The Learning House, Inc., a comprehensive e-learning services company that develops and customizes content for online and offline use. Dr. Edge holds a Ph.D. from The Ohio State University in the areas of Learning and Behavioral Theory and Computer and Information Systems. Dr. Edge has developed more than 120 distance learning courses for television, compressed video and Internet systems. He pioneered the development of distance learning television and Internet programs in the field of disabilities and teacher education.

Dr. Edge served as Professor and Director of Distance Education Programs at the University of Louisville. He was a recipient of the University of Louisville's Board of Trustees Award for Outstanding Teaching and Support of Graduate and Undergraduate Education. Additional honors for his distance learning programs include three awards from the United States Distance Learning Association (USDLA) in the category of "Best Distance Learning Programs in Higher Education." He was a founding member of the Kentucky Distance Learning Association (KyDLA), and he is a Board Member of the United States Distance Learning Association (USDLA).

**Sharon M. Edge**, PhD is a Professor in the University Libraries Faculty at the University of Louisville where she administers the Office of Distance Learning Library Services (DLLS). Sharon's focus is on assisting teaching faculty with development and deployment of information-rich, scholarly online courses that result in learner acquisition of technological, media, and information fluency.

**Mark Evans** is Interim Dean, Extended University Division, and Professor of Economics at California State University, Bakersfield (CSUB). Dr. Evans received his Ph.D. in Economics from University of New Mexico and joined CSUB's faculty in 1978. Prior to joining the Extended University, he developed two of the online degree programs currently offered to remote students: the B.S. in Environmental Resource Management and the M.S. in Administration.

**Barbara Fennema**, Ed.D. was employed by the Connected Learning.Network as Project Manager from August 2000 through April 2002. She received her B.S. degree from the University of Indianapolis, M.Ed. from John Carroll University, and Ed.D. from Nova Southeastern University. Throughout her career she has been committed to the appropriate integration of technology (e-learning) into the curriculum of a learning environment. Currently she is employed by the Ohio SchoolNet Commission as a Program Manager.

**Dr. John G. Flores**, Associate Editor, is an authority in the field of education, technology and telecommunications. As Executive Director of the United States Distance Learning Association, Dr. Flores, leads a global association focused on the support, development and application of distance learning.

Throughout his career he has used his leadership and knowledge to promote high expectations and improve the overall quality of school programs, student achievement and public awareness. As a businessperson he has combined that same ability in the development and implementation of very successful business practices resulting in profitable companies and quality products.

He has been published in numerous journals and is a leading national spokesperson on educational technology and distance learning applications. Dr. Flores resides in Boston and Nantucket, Massachusetts with his wife, Donna Elle and four daughters.

**Ronald G. Forsythe**, Ph.D., is Vice President for Information Technology & Outreach, University of Maryland Eastern Shore, Princess Anne, Maryland. He provides institutional oversight for information and instructional technology initiatives and serves as the Project Manager for a number of technology training, broadband telecommunications, and distance education projects.

**Dr. Robert Gail** holds an M. Ed. from the University of Portland and a Doctor of International Business Administration from Nova Southeastern University. He is Director of Academic Affairs at University of Phoenix, Hawaii Campus and the past Chair of the College of Graduate Business and Management for the University of Phoenix Online.

**Chiara Gratton-Lavoie** is full-time Lecturer of Economics at California State University, Fullerton. She earned her Ph.D. in Economics from Virginia Polytechnic Institute and State University, VA. She teaches Principles of Microeconomics and Intermediate Microeconomics courses.

**Xiaoxing Han** is currently Dean of Business and Coordinator of Online Learning of Athens Technical College. Dr. Han has developed rich expertise in online learning in areas of instruction, curriculum development, faculty training, assessment, and academic management through his work at both the University of Wisconsin-Green Bay and University of Phoenix Online.

**Lisa Holstrom** is the director of the Early Childhood Learning Community, a complete AA degree, delivered via video and the Internet and offered through the University of Cincinnati. She is a member of the Advisory Board of the United States Distance Learning Association and an e-learning consultant to the Great Cities' Universities Urban Educator Corp.

**Sally Mavor**, MA in Education, teaches in the Escola Superior da Educação de Leiria. She has published *Socioculturally Appropriate Methodologies for Teaching and Learning in a Portuguese University* (2001) in Vol.6, No.2 in *Teaching in Higher Education*, Carfax Publishing Ltd. Mavor, who is an experienced, international online tutor, has published "Aligning genre and practice with learning in higher education: an interdisciplinary perspective for course design and teaching" with her coauthor Beverly Trayner in *English for Specific Purposes: an international journal*, Vol. 20, No. 4, Elsevier Science Ltd.

**Maggie McVay Lynch**'s career spans 25 years in education, with the past two decades devoted to distributed learning environments. Her background includes K-12, higher education, and private industry. She has developed over 40 online courses for colleges and universities and has taught online courses in Counseling, Education, Business Administration, Management Information Systems, and Computer Science. Dr. Lynch is currently a faculty member in Instruction and Research Services at Portland State University in Portland, Oregon, where she provides faculty instruction in the tools and pedagogy of developing Web-based curricula. She also teaches several courses in educational technology and distributed learning systems in the Graduate School of Education.

**Matthew E. Mooney** was the WWW Specialist for Agricultural Economics. He has recently become the Distance Education Specialist for the Arizona Area Health Education Centers at the University of Arizona. He has consulted Fortune 500 companies, co-authored a book on UltraDev, and is in the process of finishing his Ph.D. at Purdue University.

**William Peirce** has been teaching in the English department of Prince George's Community College in Maryland since 1965. He now serves as coordinator of reasoning across the curriculum and coordinator of academic outcomes assessment. He has taught part-time at University of Maryland University College since 1991.

**Don Plunkett** teaches graduate business as an adjunct professor at City University of New York and is presently working toward a doctorate at Fielding Graduate Institute. He has completed his MBA through University of Phoenix Online, and a MA, done partly online, through Landegg International University in Switzerland. He also helped facilitate online class forums as a student teacher at the Fielding.

**Sorel Reisman**, Senior Editor, is Professor of Information Systems in the College of Business at California State University, Fullerton (CSUF). He is also Academic Technology Coordinator at CSUF, and Director of System-wide Academic Technology Services at the California State University Office of the Chancellor. His industrial experience includes senior technical and management positions at IBM, Toshiba America, and Thorn EMI.

Dr. Reisman's teaching and research are concerned with multimedia, information systems development, the management of information technology, e-commerce, electronic communities, and Internet-based distance learning. He is a member of the Publications Board of the United States Distance Learning Association, has served as Chair of the Magazines Operations Committee of the IEEE Computer Society, is or has been a member of the editorial boards of *IEEE ITPro*, *IEEE Software*, *IEEE Multimedia*, the *Journal of Global Information Systems*, the *Journal of End User Computing*, the *Journal of Information Management*, and is Associate Editor of *Annals of Cases in Information Technology*. Dr. Reisman has published more than 50 papers and made more than 50 presentations and his previous book, "Multimedia Computing: Preparing for the 21$^{st}$ Century" was published in 1996.

**Denise Stanley** is Assistant Professor of Economics at California State University, Fullerton. She earned her Ph.D. in Economics from the University of Wisconsin-Madison. She teaches Principles of Microeconomics and Economics of Latin America.

**Penelope Walters Swenson** is an associate professor in Advanced Educational Studies at California State University, Bakersfield. She received her Ph.D. in Education from the Claremont Graduate University. Prior to coming to CSUB in 2000, Dr. Swenson was a school administrator in rural regions of California where she gained an interest in distance learning. At CSUB, Dr. Swenson has developed online and hybrid courses and an online M.A. program in conjunction with School of Education colleagues and Mark Evans.

**Beverly Trayner**, M.Sc. in Development Studies, teaches in a School of Business Sciences in Setúbal, Portugal. Her Ph.D. research at the University of Aveiro focuses on international communication, collaboration and learning online. Trayner, who is an experienced, international online tutor, has published "Aligning genre and practice with learning in higher education: an interdisciplinary perspective for course design and teaching" with her coauthor Sally Mavor in *English for Specific Purposes: an international journal*, Vol. 20, No. 4, Elsevier Science Ltd.

# SUBJECT INDEX

AACRAO (*see* American Association of Collegiate Registrars and Admissions Officers)

Academic honesty policy, 93

ACRL (*see* Association of College and Research Libraries)

Affect policy, 194

AICC certification, 254

ALN (*see* Asynchronous learning network)

American Association of Collegiate Registrars and Admissions Officers (AACRAO), 92, 111

Anderson model, 416

Andragogy, 243

  assumptions regarding, 243-244

  strategies, 244

ARMA (*see* Association of Records Managers and Administrators)

Association of College and Research Libraries (ACRL), 145

  guidelines, 163-164

  survey, 164

Association of Records Managers and Administrators (ARMA), 92, 111

ASSURE model, 244

Asynchronous Collaboration Tool model, 325

Asynchronous learning environments, 419-423

  accommodation of multiple learning styles, 421

  advantages, 420

  collaborative, 422

  comprehension vs. note taking, 421

  disadvantages, 422-423

  linking to real world, 422-423

  writing, 420-421

Asynchronous learning network (ALN), 56

Authority Finder, 163

Balanced learning format, 382

Best practices, 44

Blackboard, 29, 74, 229, 230, 272, 335, 425

Electronic Learning Communities—Issues and Practices, pages 555–565.
Copyright © 2003 by Information Age Publishing, Inc.
All rights of reproduction in any form reserved.
ISBN: 1-931576-96-3 (pbk.), 1-931576-97-1 (hardcover)